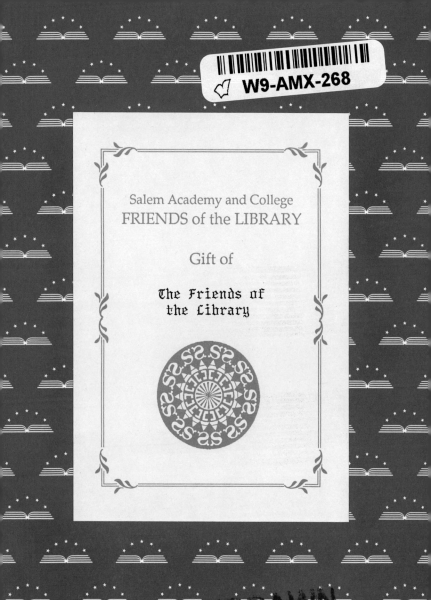

JOHN DOS PASSOS

John Dos Passos

TRAVEL BOOKS
AND OTHER WRITINGS
1916–1941

THE LIBRARY OF AMERICA

The paper used in this publication meets the
minimum requirements of the American National Standard for
Information Sciences—Permanence of Paper for Printed
Library Materials, ANSI Z39.48–1984.

Distributed to the trade in the United States
by Penguin Putnam Inc.
and in Canada by Penguin Books Canada Ltd.

Library of Congress Catalog Number: 2003040143
For cataloging information, see end of Index.
ISBN 1-931082-40-5

———

First Printing
The Library of America—143

Manufactured in the United States of America

TOWNSEND LUDINGTON
WROTE THE NOTES FOR THIS VOLUME

Contents

ROSINANTE TO
THE ROAD AGAIN

I: A Gesture and a Quest

TELEMACHUS had wandered so far in search of his father he had quite forgotten what he was looking for. He sat on a yellow plush bench in the café El Oro del Rhin, Plaza Santa Ana, Madrid, swabbing up with a bit of bread the last smudges of brown sauce off a plate of which the edges were piled with the dismembered skeleton of a pigeon. Opposite his plate was a similar plate his companion had already polished. Telemachus put the last piece of bread into his mouth, drank down a glass of beer at one spasmodic gulp, sighed, leaned across the table and said:

"I wonder why I'm here."

"Why anywhere else than here?" said Lyaeus, a young man with hollow cheeks and slow-moving hands, about whose mouth a faint pained smile was continually hovering, and he too drank down his beer.

At the end of a perspective of white marble tables, faces thrust forward over yellow plush cushions under twining veils of tobacco smoke, four German women on a little dais were playing *Tannhauser*. Smells of beer, sawdust, shrimps, roast pigeon.

"Do you know Jorge Manrique? That's one reason, Tel," the other man continued slowly. With one hand he gestured to the waiter for more beer, the other he waved across his face as if to brush away the music; then he recited, pronouncing the words haltingly:

> 'Recuerde el alma dormida,
> Avive el seso y despierte
> Contemplando
> Cómo se pasa la vida,
> Cómo se viene la muerte
> Tan callando:
> Cuán presto se va el placer,
> Cómo después de acordado
> Da dolor,
> Cómo a nuestro parecer
> Cualquier tiempo pasado
> Fué mejor.'

3

"It's always death," said Telemachus, "but we must go on."

It had been raining. Lights rippled red and orange and yellow and green on the clean paving-stones. A cold wind off the Sierra shrilled through clattering streets. As they walked, the other man was telling how this Castilian noble-man, courtier, man-at-arms, had shut himself up when his father, the Master of Santiago, died and had written this poem, created this tremendous rhythm of death sweeping like a wind over the world. He had never written anything else. They thought of him in the court of his great dust-colored mansion at Ocaña, where the broad eaves were full of a cooing of pigeons and the wide halls had dark rafters painted with arabesques in vermilion, in a suit of black vel-vet, writing at a table under a lemon tree. Down the sun-scarred street, in the cathedral that was building in those days, full of a smell of scaffolding and stone dust, there must have stood a tremendous catafalque where lay with his arms around him the Master of Santiago; in the carved seats of the choirs the stout canons intoned an endless growling litany; at the sacristy door, the flare of the candles flashing occasionally on the jewels of his mitre, the bishop fingered his crosier restlessly, asking his favorite choir-boy from time to time why Don Jorge had not arrived. And messengers must have come running to Don Jorge, telling him the ser-vice was on the point of beginning, and he must have waved them away with a grave gesture of a long white hand, while in his mind the distant sound of chanting, the jingle of the silver bit of his roan horse stamping nervously where he was tied to a twined Moorish column, memories of cavalcades filing with braying of trumpets and flutter of crimson damask into conquered towns, of court ladies dancing, and the noise of pigeons in the eaves, drew together like strings plucked in succession on a guitar into a great wave of rhythm in which his life was sucked away into this one poem in praise of death.

> Nuestras vidas son los ríos
> Que van a dar en la mar,
> Que es el morir. . . .

Telemachus was saying the words over softly to himself as they went into the theatre. The orchestra was playing a Sevillana; as they found their seats they caught glimpses beyond people's heads and shoulders of a huge woman with a comb that pushed the tip of her mantilla a foot and a half above her head, dancing with ponderous dignity. Her dress was pink flounced with lace; under it the bulge of breasts and belly and three chins quaked with every thump of her tiny heels on the stage. As they sat down she retreated bowing like a full-rigged ship in a squall. The curtain fell, the theatre became very still; next was Pastora.

Strumming of a guitar, whirring fast, dry like locusts in a hedge on a summer day. Pauses that catch your blood and freeze it suddenly still like the rustling of a branch in silent woods at night. A gipsy in a red sash is playing, slouched into a cheap cane chair, behind him a faded crimson curtain. Off stage heels beaten on the floor catch up the rhythm with tentative interest, drowsily; then suddenly added, sharp click of fingers snapped in time; the rhythm slows, hovers like a bee over a clover flower. A little taut sound of air sucked in suddenly goes down the rows of seats. With faintest tapping of heels, faintest snapping of the fingers of a brown hand held over her head, erect, wrapped tight in yellow shawl where the embroidered flowers make a splotch of maroon over one breast, a flecking of green and purple over shoulders and thighs, Pastora Imperio comes across the stage, quietly, unhurriedly.

In the mind of Telemachus the words return:

> Cómo se viene la muerte
> Tan callando.

Her face is brown, with a pointed chin; her eyebrows that nearly meet over her nose rise in a flattened "A" towards the fervid black gleam of her hair; her lips are pursed in a half-smile as if she were stifling a secret. She walks round the stage slowly, one hand at her waist, the shawl tight over her elbow, her thighs lithe and restless, a panther in a cage. At the back of the stage she turns suddenly, advances; the snapping of her fingers gets loud, insistent; a thrill whirrs through the guitar like a covey of partridges scared in a field. Red heels tap threateningly.

> Decidme: la hermosura,
> La gentil frescura y tez
> De la cara
> El color y la blancura,
> Cuando viene la viejez
> Cuál se para?

She is right at the footlights; her face, brows drawn together into a frown, has gone into shadow; the shawl flames, the maroon flower over her breast glows like a coal. The guitar is silent, her fingers go on snapping at intervals with dreadful foreboding. Then she draws herself up with a deep breath, the muscles of her belly go taut under the tight silk wrinkles of the shawl, and she is off again, light, joyful, turning indulgent glances towards the audience, as a nurse might look in the eyes of a child she has unintentionally frightened with a too dreadful fairy story.

The rhythm of the guitar has changed again; her shawl is loose about her, the long fringe flutters; she walks with slow steps, in pomp, a ship decked out for a festival, a queen in plumes and brocade. . . .

> ¿Qué se hicieron las damas,
> Sus tocados, sus vestidos,
> Sus olores?
> ¿Qué se hicieron las llamas
> De los fuegos encendidos
> De amadores?

And she has gone, and the gipsy guitar-player is scratching his neck with a hand the color of tobacco, while the guitar rests against his legs. He shows all his teeth in a world-engulfing yawn.

When they came out of the theatre, the streets were dry and the stars blinked in the cold wind above the houses. At the curb old women sold chestnuts and little ragged boys shouted the newspapers.

"And now do you wonder, Tel, why you are here?"

They went into a café and mechanically ordered beer. The seats were red plush this time and much worn. All about them groups of whiskered men leaning over tables, astride chairs, talking.

"It's the gesture that's so overpowering; don't you feel it in your arms? Something sudden and tremendously muscular."

"When Belmonte turned his back suddenly on the bull and walked away dragging the red cloak on the ground behind him I felt it," said Lyaeus.

"That gesture, a yellow flame against maroon and purple cadences . . . an instant swagger of defiance in the midst of a litany to death the all-powerful. That is Spain. . . . Castile at any rate."

"Is 'swagger' the right word?"

"Find a better."

"For the gesture a medieval knight made when he threw his mailed glove at his enemy's feet or a rose in his lady's window, that a mule-driver makes when he tosses off a glass of aguardiente, that Pastora Imperio makes dancing. . . . Word! Rubbish!" And Lyaeus burst out laughing. He laughed deep in his throat with his head thrown back.

Telemachus was inclined to be offended.

"Did you notice how extraordinarily near she kept to the rhythm of Jorge Manrique?" he asked coldly.

"Of course. Of course," shouted Lyaeus, still laughing.

The waiter came with two mugs of beer.

"Take it away," shouted Lyaeus. "Who ordered beer? Bring something strong, champagne. Drink the beer yourself."

The waiter was scrawny and yellow, with bilious eyes, but he could not resist the laughter of Lyaeus. He made a pretense of drinking the beer.

Telemachus was now very angry. Though he had forgotten his quest and the maxims of Penelope, there hovered in his mind a disquieting thought of an eventual accounting for his actions before a dimly imagined group of women with inquisitive eyes. This Lyaeus, he thought to himself, was too free and easy. Then there came suddenly to his mind the dancer standing tense as a caryatid before the footlights, her face in shadow, her shawl flaming yellow; the strong modulations of her torso seemed burned in his flesh. He drew a deep breath. His body tightened like a catapult.

"Oh to recapture that gesture," he muttered. The vague inquisitorial woman-figures had sunk fathoms deep in his mind.

Lyaeus handed him a shallow tinkling glass.

"There are all gestures," he said.

Outside the plate-glass window a countryman passed singing. His voice dwelt on a deep trembling note, rose high, faltered, skidded down the scale, then rose suddenly, frighteningly like a skyrocket, into a new burst of singing.

"There it is again," Telemachus cried. He jumped up and ran out on the street. The broad pavement was empty. A bitter wind shrilled among arc-lights white like dead eyes.

"Idiot," Lyaeus said between gusts of laughter when Telemachus sat down again. "Idiot Tel. Here you'll find it." And despite Telemachus's protestations he filled up the glasses. A great change had come over Lyaeus. His face looked fuller and flushed. His lips were moist and very red. There was an occasional crisp curl in the black hair about his temples.

And so they sat drinking a long while.

At last Telemachus got unsteadily to his feet.

"I can't help it. . . . I must catch that gesture, formulate it, do it. It is tremendously, inconceivably, unendingly important to me."

"Now you know why you're here," said Lyaeus quietly.

"Why are you here?"

"To drink," said Lyaeus.

"Let's go."

"Why?"

"To catch that gesture, Lyaeus," said Telemachus in an over-solemn voice.

"Like a comedy professor with a butterfly-net," roared Lyaeus. His laughter so filled the café that people at far-away tables smiled without knowing it.

"It's burned into my blood. It must be formulated, made permanent."

"Killed," said Lyaeus with sudden seriousness; "better drink it with your wine."

Silent they strode down an arcaded street. Cupolas, voluted baroque façades, a square tower, the bulge of a market building, tile roofs, chimneypots, ate into the star-dusted sky to the right and left of them, until in a great gust of wind they came out on an empty square, where were few gas-lamps; in front of them was a heavy arch full of stars, and Orion sprawling above it. Under the arch a pile of rags asked for alms whiningly. The jingle of money was crisp in the cold air.

"Where does this road go?"

"Toledo," said the beggar, and got to his feet. He was an old man, bearded, evil-smelling.

"Thank you. . . . We have just seen Pastora," said Lyaeus jauntily.

"Ah, Pastora! . . . The last of the great dancers," said the beggar, and for some reason he crossed himself.

The road was frosty and crunched silkily underfoot.

Lyaeus walked along shouting lines from the poem of Jorge Manrique.

> 'Cómo se pasa la vida
> Cómo se viene la muerte
> Tan callando:
> Cuán presto se va el placer
> Cómo después de acordado
> Da dolor,
> Cómo a nuestro parecer
> Cualquier tiempo pasado
> Fué mejor.'

"I bet you, Tel, they have good wine in Toledo."

The road hunched over a hill. They turned and saw Madrid cut out of darkness against the starlight. Before them sown plains, gulches full of mist, and the tremulous lights on many carts that jogged along, each behind three jingling slow mules. A cock crowed. All at once a voice burst suddenly in swaggering tremolo out of the darkness of the road beneath them, rising, rising, then fading off, then flaring up hotly like a red scarf waved on a windy day, like the swoop of a hawk, like a rocket intruding among the stars.

"Butterfly net, you old fool!" Lyaeus's laughter volleyed across the frozen fields.

Telemachus answered in a low voice:

"Let's walk faster."

He walked with his eyes on the road. He could see in the darkness, Pastora, wrapped in the yellow shawl with the splotch of maroon-colored embroidery moulding one breast, stand tremulous with foreboding before the footlights, suddenly draw in her breath, and turn with a great exultant gesture back into the rhythm of her dance. Only the victorious culminating instant of the gesture was blurred to him. He walked with long strides along the crackling road, his muscles aching for memory of it.

II: *The Donkey Boy*

Where the husbandman's toil and strife
Little varies to strife and toil:
But the milky kernel of life,
With her numbered: corn, wine, fruit, oil!

THE PATH zigzagged down through the olive trees between thin chortling glitter of irrigation ditches that occasionally widened into green pools, reed-fringed, froggy,
about which bristled scrub oleanders. Through the shimmer
of olive leaves all about I could see the great ruddy heave of
the mountains streaked with the emerald of millet-fields, and
above, snowy shoulders against a vault of indigo, patches of
wood cut out hard as metal in the streaming noon light. Tinkle of a donkey-bell below me, then at the turn of a path the
donkey's hindquarters, mauve-grey, neatly clipped in a pattern of diamonds and lozenges, and a tail meditatively swishing as he picked his way among the stones, the head as yet
hidden by the osier baskets of the pack. At the next turn I
skipped ahead of the donkey and walked with the *arriero*, a
dark boy in tight blue pants and short grey tunic cut to the
waist, who had the strong cheek-bones, hawk nose and slender hips of an Arab, who spoke an aspirated Andalusian that
sounded like Arabic.

We greeted each other cordially as travellers do in mountainous places where the paths are narrow. We talked about
the weather and the wind and the sugar mills at Motril and
women and travel and the vintage, struggling all the while
like drowning men to understand each other's lingo. When it
came out that I was an American and had been in the war,
he became suddenly interested; of course, I was a deserter, he
said, clever to get away. There'd been two deserters in his
town a year ago, *Alemanes*; perhaps friends of mine. It was
pointed out that I and the *Alemanes* had been at different
ends of the gunbarrel. He laughed. What did that matter?
Then he said several times, "Qué burro la guerra, qué burro
la guerra." I remonstrated, pointing to the donkey that was
following us with dainty steps, looking at us with a quizzical

air from under his long eyelashes. Could anything be wiser than a burro?

He laughed again, twitching back his full lips to show the brilliance of tightly serried teeth, stopped in his tracks, and turned to look at the mountains. He swept a long brown hand across them. "Look," he said, "up there is the Alpujarras, the last refuge of the kings of the Moors; there are bandits up there sometimes. You have come to the right place; here we are free men."

The donkey scuttled past us with a derisive glance out of the corner of an eye and started skipping from side to side of the path, cropping here and there a bit of dry grass. We followed, the *arriero* telling how his brother would have been conscripted if the family had not got together a thousand pesetas to buy him out. That was no life for a man. He spat on a red stone. They'd never catch him, he was sure of that. The army was no life for a man.

In the bottom of the valley was a wide stream, which we forded after some dispute as to who should ride the donkey, the donkey all the while wrinkling his nose with disgust at the coldness of the speeding water and the sliminess of the stones. When we came out on the broad moraine of pebbles the other side of the stream we met a lean blackish man with yellow horse-teeth, who was much excited when he heard I was an American.

"America is the world of the future," he cried and gave me such a slap on the back I nearly tumbled off the donkey on whose rump I was at that moment astride.

"En América no se divierte," muttered the *arriero*, kicking his feet that were cold from the ford into the burning saffron dust of the road.

The donkey ran ahead kicking at pebbles, bucking, trying to shake off the big pear-shaped baskets of osier he had either side of his pack saddle, delighted with smooth dryness after so much water and such tenuous stony roads. The three of us followed arguing, the sunlight beating wings of white flame about us.

"In America there is freedom," said the blackish man, "there are no rural guards; roadmenders work eight hours and wear silk shirts and earn . . . un dineral." The blackish man stopped, quite out of breath from his grappling with infinity. Then he went on: "Your children are educated free, no priests, and at forty every man-jack owns an automobile."

"*Ca,*" said the *arriero.*

"*Sí, hombre,*" said the blackish man.

For a long while the *arriero* walked along in silence, watching his toes bury themselves in dust at each step. Then he burst out, spacing his words with conviction: "*Ca, en América no se hase na'a que trabahar y de'cansar.* . . . Not on your life, in America they don't do anything except work and rest so's to get ready to work again. That's no life for a man. People don't enjoy themselves there. An old sailor from Malaga who used to fish for sponges told me, and he knew. It's not gold people need, but bread and wine and . . . life. They don't do anything there except work and rest so they'll be ready to work again. . . ."

Two thoughts jostled in my mind as he spoke; I seemed to see red-faced gentlemen in knee breeches, dog's-ear wigs askew over broad foreheads, reading out loud with unction the phrases, "inalienable rights . . . pursuit of happiness," and to hear the cadence out of Meredith's *The Day of the Daughter of Hades*:

> Where the husbandman's toil and strife
> Little varies to strife and toil:
> But the milky kernel of life,
> With her numbered: corn, wine, fruit, oil!

The donkey stopped in front of a little wineshop under a trellis where dusty gourd-leaves shut out the blue and gold dazzle of sun and sky.

"He wants to say, 'Have a little drink, gentlemen,'" said the blackish man.

In the greenish shadow of the wineshop a smell of anise and a sound of water dripping. When he had smacked his lips over a small cup of thick yellow wine he pointed at the *arriero*. "He says people don't enjoy life in America."

"But in America people are very rich," shouted the barkeeper, a beet-faced man whose huge girth was bound in a red cotton sash, and he made a gesture suggestive of coins, rubbing thumb and forefinger together.

Everybody roared derision at the *arriero*. But he persisted and went out shaking his head and muttering "That's no life for a man."

As we left the wineshop where the blackish man was painting with broad strokes the legend of the West, the *arriero* explained to me almost tearfully that he had not meant to speak ill of my country, but to explain why he did not want to emigrate. While he was speaking we passed a cartload of yellow grapes that drenched us in jingle of mulebells and in dizzying sweetness of bubbling ferment. A sombre man with beetling brows strode at the mule's head; in the cart, brown feet firmly planted in the steaming slush of grapes, flushed face tilted towards the ferocious white sun, a small child with a black curly pate rode in triumph, shouting, teeth flashing as if to bite into the sun.

"What you mean is," said I to the *arriero*, "that this is the life for a man."

He tossed his head back in a laugh of approval.

"Something that's neither work nor getting ready to work?"

"That's it," he answered, and cried, *"arrh he"* to the donkey.

We hastened our steps. My sweaty shirt bellied suddenly in the back as a cool wind frisked about us at the corner of the road.

"Ah, it smells of the sea," said the *arriero*. "We'll see the sea from the next hill."

That night as I stumbled out of the inn door in Motril, overfull of food and drink, the full moon bulged through the arches of the cupola of the pink and saffron church. Everywhere steel-green shadows striped with tangible moonlight. As I sat beside my knapsack in the plaza, groping for a thought in the bewildering dazzle of the night, three disconnected mules, egged on by a hoarse shouting, jingled out of the shadow. When they stopped with a jerk in the full moonglare beside the fountain, it became evident that they were attached to a coach, a spidery coach tilted forward as if it were perpetually going down hill; from inside smothered voices like the strangled clucking of fowls being shipped to market in a coop.

On the driver's seat one's feet were on the shafts and one had a view of every rag and shoelace the harness was patched with. Creaking, groaning, with wabbling of wheels, grumble of inside passengers, cracking of whip and long strings of oaths from the driver, the coach lurched out of town and across a fat plain full of gurgle of irrigation ditches, shrilling of toads, falsetto rustle of broad leaves of the sugar cane. Occasionally the gleam of the soaring moon on banana leaves and a broad silver path on the sea. Landwards the hills like piles of ash in the moonlight, and far away a cloudy inkling of mountains.

Beside me, mouth open, shouting rich pedigrees at the leading mule, Cordovan hat on the back of his head, from under which sprouted a lock of black hair that hung between his eyes over his nose and made him look like a goblin, the driver bounced and squirmed and kicked at the flanks of the mules that roamed drunkenly from side to side of the uneven road. Down into a gulch, across a shingle, up over a plank bridge, then down again into the bed of the river I had forded that morning with my friend the *arriero*, along a beach with fishing boats and little huts where the fishermen slept; then barking of dogs, another bridge and we roared and crackled up a steep village street to come to a stop suddenly, catastrophically, in front of a tavern in the main square.

"We are late," said the goblin driver, turning to me suddenly, "I have not slept for four nights, dancing, every night dancing."

He sucked the air in through his teeth and stretched out his arms and legs in the moonlight. "Ah, women . . . women," he added philosophically. "Have you a cigarette?"

"*Ah, la juventud,*" said the old man who had brought the mailbag. He looked up at us scratching his head. "It's to enjoy. A moment, a *momentito*, and it's gone! Old men work in the day time, but young men work at night. . . . *Ay de mí,*" and he burst into a peal of laughter.

And as if some one were whispering them, the words of Jorge Manrique sifted out of the night:

¿Qué se hizo el Rey Don Juan?
Los infantes de Aragón
¿Qué se hicieron?
Qué fué de tanto galán,
Qué fué de tanta invención,
Cómo truxeron?

Everybody went into the tavern, from which came a sound of singing and of clapping in time, and as hearty a tinkle of glasses and banging on tables as might have come out of the *Mermaid* in the days of the Virgin Queen. Outside the moon soared, soared brilliant, a greenish blotch on it like the time-stain on a chased silver bowl on an altar. The broken lion's head of the fountain dribbled one tinkling stream of quicksilver. On the seawind came smells of rotting garbage and thyme burning in hearths and jessamine flowers. Down the street geraniums in a window smouldered in the moonlight; in the dark above them the merest contour of a face, once the gleam of two eyes; opposite against the white wall standing very quiet a man looking up with dilated nostrils—*el amor.*

As the coach jangled its lumbering unsteady way out of town, our ears still throbbed with the rhythm of the tavern, of hard brown hands clapped in time, of heels thumping on oak floors. From the last house of the village a man hallooed. With its noise of cupboards of china overturned the coach crashed to stillness. A wiry, white-faced man with a little waxed moustache like the springs of a mousetrap climbed on the front seat, while burly people heaved quantities of corded trunks on behind.

"How late, two hours late," the man spluttered, jerking his checked cap from side to side. "Since this morning nothing to eat but two boiled eggs. . . . Think of that. *¡Qué incultura! ¡Qué pueblo indecente!* All day only two boiled eggs."

"I had business in Motril, Don Antonio," said the goblin driver grinning.

"Business!" cried Don Antonio, laughing squeakily, "and after all what a night!"

Something impelled me to tell Don Antonio the story of King Mycerinus of Egypt that Herodotus tells, how hearing from an oracle he would only live ten years, the king called for torches and would not sleep, so crammed twenty years' living into ten. The goblin driver listened in intervals between his hoarse investigations of the private life of the grandmother of the leading mule.

Don Antonio slapped his thigh and lit a cigarette and cried, "In Andalusia we all do that, don't we, Paco?"

"Yes, sir," said the goblin driver, nodding his head vigorously.

"That is *lo flamenco*," cried Don Antonio. "The life of Andalusia is *lo flamenco*."

The moon has begun to lose foothold in the black slippery zenith. We are hurtling along a road at the top of a cliff; below the sea full of unexpected glitters, lace-edged, swishing like the silk dress of a dancer. The goblin driver rolls from side to side asleep. The check cap is down over the little man's face so that not even his moustaches are to be seen. All at once the leading mule, taken with suicidal mania, makes a sidewise leap for the cliff-edge. Crumbling of gravel, snap of traces, shouts, uproar inside. Some one has managed to yank the mule back on her hind quarters. In the sea below the shadow of a coach totters at the edge of the cliff's shadow.

"*Hija de puta*," cries the goblin driver, jumping to the ground.

Don Antonio awakes with a grunt and begins to explain querulously that he has had nothing to eat all day but two boiled eggs. The teeth of the goblin driver flash white flame as he hangs wreath upon wreath of profanity about the trembling, tugging mules. With a terrific rattling jerk the coach sways to the safe side of the road. From inside angry heads are poked out like the heads of hens out of an overturned coop. Don Antonio turns to me and shouts in tones of triumph: "*¿Qué flamenco, eh?*"

When we got to Almuñecar Don Antonio, the goblin driver, and I sat at a little table outside the empty Casino. A waiter appeared from somewhere with wine and coffee and tough purple ham and stale bread and cigarettes. Over our heads dusty palm-fronds trembled in occasional faint gusts off the sea. The rings on Don Antonio's thin fingers glistened in the light of the one tired electric light bulb that shone among palpitating mottoes above us as he explained to me the significance of *lo flamenco*.

The tough swaggering gesture, the quavering song well sung, the couplet neatly capped, the back turned to the charging bull, the mantilla draped with exquisite provocativeness: all that was *lo flamenco*. "On this coast, *señor inglés*, we don't work much, we are dirty and uninstructed, but by God we live. Why the poor people of the towns, d'you know what they do in summer? They hire a fig-tree and go and live under it with their dogs and their cats and their babies, and they eat the figs as they ripen and drink the cold water from the mountains, and man-alive they are happy. They fear no one and they are dependent on no one; when they are young they make love and sing to the guitar, and when they are old they tell stories and bring up their children. You have travelled much; I have travelled little—Madrid, never further,—but I swear to you that nowhere in the world are the women lovelier or is the land richer or the cookery more perfect than in this vega of Almuñecar. . . . If only the wine weren't quite so heavy. . . ."

"Then you don't want to go to America?"

"¡*Hombre por dios!* Sing us a song, Paco. . . . He's a Galician, you see."

The goblin driver grinned and threw back his head.

"Go to the end of the world, you'll find a Gallego," he said. Then he drank down his wine, rubbed his mouth on the back of his hand, and started droningly:

> ' Si quieres qu'el carro cante
> mójale y dejel'en río
> que después de buen moja'o
> canta com'un silbi'o.'

(If you want a cart to sing, wet it and soak it in the river, for when it's well soaked it'll sing like a locust.)

"Hola," cried Don Antonio, "go on."

> ' A mí me gusta el blanco,
> ¡viva lo blanco! ¡muera lo negro!
> porque el negro es muy triste.
> Yo soy alegre. Yo no lo quiero.'

(I like white; hooray for white, death to black. Because black is very sad, and I am happy, I don't like it.)

"That's it," cried Don Antonio excitedly. "You people from the north, English, Americans, Germans, whatnot, you like black. You like to be sad. I don't."

" 'Yo soy alegre. Yo no lo quiero.' "

The moon had sunk into the west, flushed and swollen. The east was beginning to bleach before the oncoming sun. Birds started chirping above our heads. I left them, but as I lay in bed, I could hear the hoarse voice of the goblin driver roaring out:

'A mí me gusta el blanco,
¡viva lo blanco! ¡muera lo negro!'

At Nerja in an arbor of purple ipomoeas on a red jutting cliff over the beach where brown children were bathing, there was talk again of *lo flamenco*.

"In Spain," my friend Don Diego was saying, "we live from the belly and loins, or else from the head and heart: between Don Quixote the mystic and Sancho Panza the sensualist there is no middle ground. The lowest Panza is *lo flamenco*."

"But you do live."

"In dirt, disease, lack of education, bestiality. . . . Half of us are always dying of excess of food or the lack of it."

"What do you want?"

"Education, organization, energy, the modern world."

I told him what the donkey-boy had said of America on the road down from the Alpujarras, that in America they did nothing but work and rest so as to be able to work again. And America was the modern world.

And *lo flamenco* is neither work nor getting ready to work.

That evening San Miguel went out to fetch the Virgin of Sorrows from a roadside oratory and brought her back into town in procession with candles and skyrockets and much chanting, and as the swaying cone-shaped figure carried on the shoulders of six sweating men stood poised at the entrance to the plaza where all the girls wore jessamine flowers in the blackness of their hair, all waved their hats and cried, *"¡Viva la Virgen de las Angustias!"* And the Virgin and San Miguel both had to bow their heads to get in the church door, and the people followed them into the church crying *"¡Viva!"* so that the old vaults shivered in the tremulous candlelight and the shouting. Some people cried for water, as rain was about due and everything was very dry, and when they came out of the church they saw a thin cloud like a mantilla of white lace over the moon, so they went home happy.

Wherever they went through the narrow well-swept streets, lit by an occasional path of orange light from a window, the women left behind them long trails of fragrance from the jessamine flowers in their hair.

Don Diego and I walked a long while on the seashore talking of America and the Virgin and a certain soup called *ajo blanco* and Don Quixote and *lo flamenco*. We were trying to decide what was the peculiar quality of the life of the people in that rich plain (*vega* they call it) between the mountains of the sea. Walking about the country elevated on the small grass-grown levees of irrigation ditches, the owners of the fields we crossed used, simply because we were strangers, to offer us a glass of wine or a slice of watermelon. I had explained to my friend that in his modern world of America these same people would come out after us with shotguns loaded with rock salt. He answered that even so, the old order was changing, and that as there was nothing else but to follow the procession of industrialism it behooved Spaniards to see that their country forged ahead instead of being, as heretofore, dragged at the tail of the parade.

"And do you think it's leading anywhere, this endless complicating of life?"

"Of course," he answered.

"Where?"

"Where does anything lead? At least it leads further than *lo flamenco*."

"But couldn't the point be to make the way significant?"

He shrugged his shoulders. "Work," he said.

We had come to a little nook in the cliffs where fishing boats were drawn up with folded wings like ducks asleep. We climbed a winding path up the cliff. Pebbles scuttled underfoot; our hands were torn by thorny aromatic shrubs. Then we came out in a glen that cut far into the mountains, full of the laughter of falling water and the rustle of sappy foliage. Seven stilted arches of an aqueduct showed white through the canebrakes inland. Fragrances thronged about us; the smell of dry thyme-grown uplands, of rich wet fields, of goats, and jessamine and heliotrope, and of water cold from the snowfields running fast in ditches. Somewhere far off a donkey was braying. Then, as the last groan of the donkey faded, a man's voice rose suddenly out of the dark fields, soaring, yearning on taut throat-cords, then slipped down through notes, like a small boat sliding sideways down a wave, then unrolled a great slow scroll of rhythm on the night and ceased suddenly in an upward cadence as a guttering candle flares to extinction.

"Something that's neither work nor getting ready to work," and I thought of the *arriero* on whose donkey I had forded the stream on the way down from the Alpujarras, and his saying: *"Ca, en América no se hase na'a que trabahar y de'cansar."*

I had left him at his home village, a little cluster of red and yellow roofs about a fat tower the Moors had built and a gaunt church that hunched by itself in a square of trampled dust. We had rested awhile before going into town, under a fig tree, while he had put white canvas shoes on his lean brown feet. The broad leaves had rustled in the wind, and the smell of the fruit that hung purple bursting to crimson against the intense sky had been like warm stroking velvet all about us. And the *arriero* had discoursed on the merits of his donkey and the joys of going from town to town with merchandise, up into the mountains for chestnuts and firewood, down to the sea for fish, to Malaga for tinware, to Motril for sugar from the refineries. Nights of dancing and guitar-playing at vintage-time, *fiestas* of the Virgin, where older, realer gods were worshipped than Jehovah and the dolorous Mother of the pale Christ, the *toros*, blood and embroidered silks aflame in the sunlight, words whispered through barred windows at night, long days of travel on stony roads in the mountains. . . . And I had lain back with my eyes closed and the hum of little fig-bees in my ears, and wished that my life were his life. After a while we had jumped to our feet and I had shouldered my knapsack with its books and pencils and silly pads of paper and trudged off up an unshaded road, and had thought with a sort of bitter merriment of that prig Christian and his damned burden.

"Something that is neither work nor getting ready to work, to make the road so significant that one needs no destination, that is *lo flamenco*," said I to Don Diego, as we stood in the glen looking at the seven white arches of the aqueduct.

He nodded unconvinced.

III: The Baker of Almorox

THE *señores* were from Madrid? Indeed! The man's voice was full of an awe of great distances. He was the village baker of Almorox, where we had gone on a Sunday excursion from Madrid; and we were standing on the scrubbed tile floor of his house, ceremoniously receiving wine and figs from his wife. The father of the friend who accompanied me had once lived in the same village as the baker's father, and bought bread of him; hence the entertainment. This baker of Almorox was a tall man, with a soft moustache very black against his ash-pale face, who stood with his large head thrust far forward. He was smiling with pleasure at the presence of strangers in his house, while in a tone of shy deprecating courtesy he asked after my friend's family. Don Fernando and Doña Ana and the Señorita were well? And little Carlos? Carlos was no longer little, answered my friend, and Doña Ana was dead.

The baker's wife had stood in the shadow looking from one face to another with a sort of wondering pleasure as we talked, but at this she came forward suddenly into the pale greenish-gold light that streamed through the door, holding a dark wine-bottle before her. There were tears in her eyes. No; she had never known any of them, she explained hastily—she had never been away from Almorox—but she had heard so much of their kindness and was sorry. . . . It was terrible to lose a father or a mother. The tall baker shifted his feet uneasily, embarrassed by the sadness that seemed slipping over his guests, and suggested that we walk up the hill to the Hermitage; he would show the way.

"But your work?" we asked. Ah, it did not matter. Strangers did not come every day to Almorox. He strode out of the door, wrapping a woolen muffler about his bare strongly moulded throat, and we followed him up the devious street of whitewashed houses that gave us glimpses through wide doors of dark tiled rooms with great black rafters overhead and courtyards where chickens pecked at the manure lodged between smooth worn flagstones. Still between whitewashed walls we struck out of the village into the deep black mud of the high road, and at last burst suddenly into the open country, where patches of sprouting grass shone vivid green against the gray and russet of broad rolling lands. At the top of the first hill stood the Hermitage—a small whitewashed chapel with a square three-storied tower; over the door was a relief of the Virgin, crowned, in worn lichened stone. The interior was very plain with a single heavily gilt altar, over which was a painted statue, stiff but full of a certain erect disdainful grace—again of the Virgin. The figure was dressed in a long lace gown, full of frills and ruffles, grey with dust and age.

"*La Virgen de la Cima,*" said the baker, pointing reverently with his thumb, after he had bent his knee before the altar. And as I glanced at the image a sudden resemblance struck me: the gown gave the Virgin a curiously conical look that somehow made me think of that conical black stone, the Bona Dea, that the Romans brought from Asia Minor. Here again was a good goddess, a bountiful one, more mother than virgin, despite her prudish frills. . . . But the man was ushering us out.

"And there is no finer view than this in all Spain." With a broad sweep of his arm he took in the village below, with its waves of roofs that merged from green to maroon and deep crimson, broken suddenly by the open square in front of the church; and the gray towering church, scowling with strong lights and shadows on buttresses and pointed windows; and the brown fields faintly sheened with green, which gave place to the deep maroon of the turned earth of vineyards, and the shining silver where the wind ruffled the olive-orchards; and beyond, the rolling hills that grew gradually flatter until they sank into the yellowish plain of Castile. As he made the gesture his fingers were stretched wide as if to grasp all this land he was showing. His flaccid cheeks were flushed as he turned to us; but we should see it in May, he was saying, in May when the wheat was thick in the fields, and there were flowers on the hills. Then the lands were beautiful and rich, in May. And he went on to tell us of the local feast, and the great processions of the Virgin. This year there were to be four days of the *toros*. So many bullfights were unusual in such a small village, he assured us. But they were rich in

Almorox; the wine was the best in Castile. Four days of *toros*, he said again; and all the people of the country around would come to the *fiestas*, and there would be a great pilgrimage to this Hermitage of the Virgin. . . . As he talked in his slow deferential way, a little conscious of his volubility before strangers, there began to grow in my mind a picture of his view of the world.

First came his family, the wife whose body lay beside his at night, who bore him children, the old withered parents who sat in the sun at his door, his memories of them when they had had strong rounded limbs like his, and of their parents sitting old and withered in the sun. Then his work, the heat of his ovens, the smell of bread cooking, the faces of neighbors who came to buy; and, outside, in the dim penumbra of things half real, of travellers' tales, lay Madrid, where the king lived and where politicians wrote in the newspapers,—and *Francia* and all that was not Almorox . . . In him I seemed to see the generations wax and wane, like the years, strung on the thread of labor, of unending sweat and strain of muscles against the earth. It was all so mellow, so strangely aloof from the modern world of feverish change, this life of the peasants of Almorox. Everywhere roots striking into the infinite past. For before the Revolution, before the Moors, before the Romans, before the dark furtive traders, the Phoenicians, they were much the same, these Iberian village communities. Far away things changed, cities were founded, hard roads built, armies marched and fought and passed away; but in Almorox the foundations of life remained unchanged up to the present. New names and new languages had come. The Virgin had taken over the festivals and rituals of the old earth goddesses, and the deep mystical fervor of devotion. But always remained the love for the place, the strong anarchistic reliance on the individual man, the walking, consciously or not, of the way beaten by generations of men who had tilled and loved and lain in the cherishing sun with no feeling of a reality outside of themselves, outside of the bare encompassing hills of their commune, except the God which was the synthesis of their souls and of their lives.

Here lies the strength and the weakness of Spain. This intense individualism, born of a history whose fundamentals lie in isolated village communities—*pueblos*, as the Spaniards call them—over the changeless face of which, like grass over a field, events spring and mature and die, is the basic fact of Spanish life. No revolution has been strong enough to shake it. Invasion after invasion, of Goths, of Moors, of Christian ideas, of the fads and convictions of the Renaissance, have swept over the country, changing surface customs and modes of thought and speech, only to be metamorphosed into keeping with the changeless Iberian mind.

And predominant in the Iberian mind is the thought *La vida es sueño*: "Life is a dream." Only the individual, or that part of life which is in the firm grasp of the individual, is real. The supreme expression of this lies in the two great figures that typify Spain for all time: Don Quixote and Sancho Panza; Don Quixote, the individualist who believed in the power of man's soul over all things, whose desire included the whole world in himself; Sancho, the individualist to whom all the world was food for his belly. On the one hand we have the ecstatic figures for whom the power of the individual soul has no limits, in whose minds the universe is but one man standing before his reflection, God. These are the Loyolas, the Philip Seconds, the fervid ascetics like Juan de la Cruz, the originals of the glowing tortured faces in the portraits of El Greco. On the other hand are the jovial materialists like the Archpriest of Hita, culminating in the frantic, mystical sensuality of such an epic figure as Don Juan Tenorio. Through all Spanish history and art the threads of these two complementary characters can be traced, changing, combining, branching out, but ever in substance the same. Of this warp and woof have all the strange patterns of Spanish life been woven.

II

In trying to hammer some sort of unified impression out of the scattered pictures of Spain in my mind, one of the first things I realize is that there are many Spains. Indeed, every village hidden in the folds of the great barren hills, or shadowed by its massive church in the middle of one of the upland plains, every fertile *huerta* of the seacoast, is a Spain. Iberia exists, and the strong Iberian characteristics; but Spain as a modern centralized nation is an illusion, a very unfortunate one; for the present atrophy, the desolating resultlessness of a century of revolution, may very well be due in large measure to the artificial imposition of centralized government on a land essentially centrifugal.

In the first place, there is the matter of language. Roughly, four distinct languages are at present spoken in Spain: Castilian, the language of Madrid and the central uplands, the official language, spoken in the south in its Andalusian form; Gallego-Portuguese, spoken on the west coast; Basque, which does not even share the Latin descent of the others; and Catalan, a form of Provençal which, with its dialect, Valencian, is spoken on the upper Mediterranean coast and in the Balearic Isles. Of course, under the influence of rail communication and a conscious effort to spread Castilian, the other languages, with the exception of Portuguese and Catalan, have lost vitality and died out in the larger towns; but the problem remains far different from that of the Italian dialects, since the Spanish languages have all, except Basque, a strong literary tradition.

Added to the variety of language, there is an immense variety of topography in the different parts of Spain. The central plateaux, dominant in modern history (history being taken to mean the births and breedings of kings and queens and the doings of generals in armor) probably approximate the warmer Russian steppes in climate and vegetation. The west coast is in most respects a warmer and more fertile Wales. The southern *huertas* (arable river valleys) have rather the aspect of Egypt. The east coast from Valencia up is a continuation of the Mediterranean coast of France. It follows that, in this country where an hour's train ride will take you from Siberian snow into African desert, unity of population is hardly to be expected.

Here is probably the root of the tendency in Spanish art and thought to emphasize the differences between things. In painting, where the mind of a people is often more tangibly represented than anywhere else, we find one supreme example. El Greco, almost the caricature in his art of the Don Quixote type of mind, who, though a Greek by birth and a Venetian by training, became more Spanish than the Spaniards during his long life at Toledo, strove constantly to express the difference between the world of flesh and the world of spirit, between the body and the soul of man. More recently, the extreme characterization of Goya's sketches and portraits, the intensifying of national types found in Zuloaga and the other painters who have been exploiting with such success the peculiarities—the picturesqueness—of Spanish faces and landscapes, seem to spring from this powerful sense of the separateness of things.

In another way you can express this constant attempt to differentiate one individual from another as caricature. Spanish art is constantly on the edge of caricature. Given the ebullient fertility of the Spanish mind and its intense individualism, a constant slipping over into the grotesque is inevitable. And so it comes to be that the conscious or unconscious aim of their art is rather self-expression than beauty. Their image of reality is sharp and clear, but distorted. Burlesque and satire are never far away in their most serious moments. Not even the calmest and best ordered of Spanish minds can resist a tendency to excess of all sorts, to over-elaboration, to grotesquerie, to deadening mannerism. All that is greatest in their art, indeed, lies on the borderland of the extravagant, where sublime things skim the thin ice of absurdity. The great epic, *Don Quixote*, such plays as Calderon's *La Vida es Sueño*, such paintings as El Greco's *Resurrección* and Velasquez's dwarfs, such buildings as the Escorial and the Alhambra—all among the universal masterpieces—are far indeed from the middle term of reasonable beauty. Hence their supreme strength. And for our generation, to which excess is a synonym for beauty, is added argumentative significance to the long tradition of Spanish art.

Another characteristic, springing from the same fervid abundance, that links the Spanish tradition to ours of the present day is the strangely impromptu character of much Spanish art production. The slightly ridiculous proverb that genius consists of an infinite capacity for taking pains is well controverted. The creative flow of Spanish artists has always been so strong, so full of vitality, that there has been no time for taking pains. Lope de Vega, with his two thousand-odd plays—or was it twelve thousand?—is by no means an isolated instance. Perhaps the strong sense of individual validity, which makes Spain the most democratic country in Europe, sanctions the constant improvisation, and accounts for the confident planlessness as common in Spanish architecture as in Spanish political thought.

Here we meet the old stock characteristic, Spanish pride. This is a very real thing, and is merely the external shell of the fundamental trust in the individual and in nothing outside of him. Again El Greco is an example. As his painting progressed, grew more and more personal, he drew away from tangible reality, and, with all the dogmatic conviction of one whose faith in his own reality can sweep away the mountains of the visible world, expressed his own restless, almost sensual, spirituality in forms that flickered like white flames toward God. For the Spaniard, moreover, God is always, in essence, the proudest sublimation of man's soul. The same spirit runs through the preachers of the early church and the works of Santa Teresa, a disguise of the frantic desire to express the self, the self, changeless and eternal, at all costs. From this comes the hard cruelty that flares forth luridly at times. A recent book by Miguel de Unamuno, *Del Sentimiento Trágico de la Vida*, expresses this fierce clinging to separateness from the universe by the phrase *el hambre de inmortalidad*, the hunger of immortality. This is the core of the individualism that lurks in all Spanish ideas, the conviction that only the individual soul is real.

III

In the Spain of to-day these things are seen as through a glass, darkly. Since the famous and much gloated-over entrance of Ferdinand and Isabella into Granada, the history of Spain has been that of an attempt to fit a square peg in a round hole. In the great flare of the golden age, the age of ingots of Peru and of men of even greater worth, the disease worked beneath the surface. Since then the conflict has corroded into futility all the buoyant energies of the country. I mean the persistent attempt to centralize in thought, in art, in government, in religion, a nation whose every energy lies in the other direction. The result has been a deadlock, and the ensuing rust and numbing of all life and thought, so that a century of revolution seems to have brought Spain no nearer a solution of its problems. At the present day, when all is ripe for a new attempt to throw off the atrophy, a sort of despairing inaction causes the Spaniards to remain under a government of unbelievably corrupt and inefficient politicians. There seems no solution to the problem of a nation in which the centralized power and the separate communities work only to nullify each other.

Spaniards in face of their traditions are rather in the position of the archæologists before the problem of Iberian sculpture. For near the Cerro de los Santos, bare hill where from the ruins of a sanctuary has been dug an endless series of native sculptures of men and women, goddesses and gods, there lived a little watchmaker. The first statues to be dug up were thought by the pious country people to be saints, and saints they were, according to an earlier dispensation than that of Rome; with the result that much Kudos accompanied the discovery of those draped women with high head-dresses and fixed solemn eyes and those fragmentary bull-necked men hewn roughly out of grey stone; they were freed from the caked clay of two thousand years and reverently set up in the churches. So probably the motives that started the watchmaker on his career of sculpturing and falsifying were pious and reverential.

However it began, when it was discovered that the saints were mere horrid heathen he-gods and she-gods and that the foreign gentlemen with spectacles who appeared from all the ends of Europe to investigate, would pay money for them, the watchmaker began to thrive as a mighty man in his village and generation. He began to study archaeology and the style of his cumbersome forged divinities improved. For a number of years the statues from the Cerro de los Santos were swallowed whole by all learned Europe. But the watchmaker's imagination began to get the better of him; forms became more and more fantastic, Egyptian, Assyrian, *art-nouveau* influences began to be noted by the discerning, until at last someone whispered forgery and all the scientists scuttled to cover shouting that there had never been any native Iberian sculpture after all.

The little watchmaker succumbed before his imagining of heathen gods and died in a madhouse. To this day when you stand in the middle of the room devoted to the Cerro de los

Santos in the Madrid, and see the statues of Iberian goddesses clustered about you in their high head-dresses like those of dancers, you cannot tell which were made by the watchmaker in 1880, and which by the image-maker of the hill-sanctuary at a time when the first red-eyed ships of the Phoenician traders were founding trading posts among the barbarians of the coast of Valencia. And there they stand on their shelves, the real and the false inextricably muddled, and stare at the enigma with stone eyes.

So with the traditions: the tradition of Catholic Spain, the tradition of military grandeur, the tradition of fighting the Moors, of suspecting the foreigner, of hospitality, of truculence, of sobriety, of chivalry, of Don Quixote and Tenorio.

The Spanish-American war, to the United States merely an opportunity for a patriotic-capitalist demonstration of sanitary engineering, heroism and canned-meat scandals, was to Spain the first whispered word that many among the traditions were false. The young men of that time called themselves the generation of ninety-eight. According to temperament they rejected all or part of the museum of traditions they had been taught to believe was the real Spain; each took up a separate road in search of a Spain which should suit his yearnings for beauty, gentleness, humaneness, or else vigor, force, modernity.

The problem of our day is whether Spaniards evolving locally, anarchically, without centralization in anything but repression, will work out new ways of life for themselves, or whether they will be drawn into the festering tumult of a Europe where the system that is dying is only strong enough to kill in its death-throes all new growth in which there was hope for the future. The Pyrenees are high.

IV

It was after a lecture at an exhibition of Basque painters in Madrid, where we had heard Valle-Melan, with eyes that burned out from under shaggy grizzled eyebrows, denounce in bitter stinging irony what he called the Europeanization of Spain. What they called progress, he had said, was merely an aping of the stupid commercialism of modern Europe. Better no education for the masses than education that would turn healthy peasants into crafty putty-skinned merchants; better a Spain swooning in her age-old apathy than a Spain awakened to the brutal soulless trade-war of modern life. . . . I was walking with a young student of philosophy I had met by chance across the noisy board of a Spanish *pensión*, discussing the exhibition we had just seen as a strangely meek setting for the fiery reactionary speech. I had remarked on the very "primitive" look much of the work of these young Basque painters had, shown by some in the almost affectionate technique, in the dainty caressing brush-work, in others by that inadequacy of the means at the painter's disposal to express his idea, which made of so many of the pictures rather gloriously impressive failures. My friend was insisting, however, that the primitiveness, rather than the birth-pangs of a new view of the world, was nothing but "the last affectation of an over-civilized tradition."

"Spain," he said, "is the most civilized country in Europe. The growth of our civilization has never been interrupted by outside influence. The Phoenicians, the Romans—Spain's influence on Rome was, I imagine, fully as great as Rome's on Spain; think of the five Spanish emperors;—the Goths, the Moors;—all incidents, absorbed by the changeless Iberian spirit. . . . Even Spanish Christianity," he continued, smiling, "is far more Spanish than it is Christian. Our life is one vast ritual. Our religion is part of it, that is all. And so are the bull-fights that so shock the English and Americans,—are they any more brutal, though, than fox-hunting and prize-fights? And how full of tradition are they, our *fiestas de toros*; their ceremony reaches back to the hecatombs of the Homeric heroes, to the bull-worship of the Cretans and of so many of the Mediterranean cults, to the Roman games. Can civilization go farther than to ritualize death as we have done? But our culture is too perfect, too stable. Life is choked by it."

We stood still a moment in the shade of a yellowed lime tree. My friend had stopped talking and was looking with his usual bitter smile at a group of little boys with brown, bare dusty legs who were intently playing bull-fight with sticks for swords and a piece of newspaper for the toreador's scarlet cape.

"It is you in America," he went on suddenly, "to whom the future belongs; you are so vigorous and vulgar and uncul-

tured. Life has become once more the primal fight for bread.
Of course the dollar is a complicated form of the food the
cave man killed for and slunk after, and the means of combat
are different, but it is as brutal. From that crude animal brutality comes all the vigor of life. We have none of it; we are
too tired to have any thoughts; we have lived so much so long
ago that now we are content with the very simple things,
—the warmth of the sun and the colors of the hills and the
flavor of bread and wine. All the rest is automatic, ritual."

"But what about the strike?" I asked, referring to the one-
day's general strike that had just been carried out with fair
success throughout Spain, as a protest against the government's apathy regarding the dangerous rise in the prices of
food and fuel.

He shrugged his shoulders.

"That, and more," he said, "is new Spain, a prophecy,
rather than a fact. Old Spain is still all-powerful."

Later in the day I was walking through the main street of
one of the clustered adobe villages that lie in the folds of the
Castilian plain not far from Madrid. The lamps were just being lit in the little shops where the people lived and worked
and sold their goods, and women with beautifully shaped pottery jars on their heads were coming home with water from
the well. Suddenly I came out on an open *plaza* with trees
from which the last leaves were falling through the greenish
sunset light. The place was filled with the lilting music of a
grind-organ and with a crunch of steps on the gravel as
people danced. There were soldiers and servant-girls, and
red-cheeked apprentice-boys with their sweethearts, and respectable shop-keepers, and their wives with mantillas over
their gleaming black hair. All were dancing in and out among
the slim tree-trunks, and the air was noisy with laughter and
little cries of childlike unfeigned enjoyment. Here was the
gospel of Sancho Panza, I thought, the easy acceptance of life,
the unashamed joy in food and color and the softness of
women's hair. But as I walked out of the village across the
harsh plain of Castile, grey-green and violet under the deepening night, the memory came to me of the knight of the
sorrowful countenance, Don Quixote, blunderingly trying to
remould the world, pitifully sure of the power of his own

ideal. And in these two Spain seemed to be manifest. Far indeed were they from the restless industrial world of joyless enforced labor and incessant goading war. And I wondered to what purpose it would be, should Don Quixote again saddle Rosinante, and what the good baker of Almorox would say to his wife when he looked up from his kneading trough, holding out hands white with dough, to see the knight errant ride by on his lean steed upon a new quest.

IV: Talk by the Road

TELEMACHUS and Lyaeus had walked all night. The sky to the east of them was rosy when they came out of a village at the crest of a hill. Cocks crowed behind stucco walls. The road dropped from their feet through an avenue of pollarded poplars ghostly with frost. Far away into the brown west stretched reach upon reach of lake-like glimmer; here and there a few trees pushed jagged arms out of drowned lands. They stood still breathing hard.

"It's the Tagus overflowed its banks," said Telemachus.

Lyaeus shook his head.

"It's mist."

They stood with thumping hearts on the hilltop looking over inexplicable shimmering plains of mist hemmed by mountains jagged like coals that as they looked began to smoulder with dawn. The light all about was lemon yellow. The walls of the village behind them were fervid primrose color splotched with shadows of sheer cobalt. Above the houses uncurled green spirals of wood-smoke.

Lyaeus raised his hands above his head and shouted and ran like mad down the hill. A little voice was whispering in Telemachus's ear that he must save his strength, so he followed sedately.

When he caught up to Lyaeus they were walking among twining wraiths of mist rose-shot from a rim of the sun that poked up behind hills of bright madder purple. A sudden cold wind-gust whined across the plain, making the mist writhe in a delirium of crumbling shapes. Ahead of them casting gigantic blue shadows over the furrowed fields rode a man on a donkey and a man on a horse. It was a grey sway-backed horse that joggled in a little trot with much switching of a ragged tail; its rider wore a curious peaked cap and sat straight and lean in the saddle. Over one shoulder rested a long bamboo pole that in the exaggerating sunlight cast a shadow like the shadow of a lance. The man on the donkey was shaped like a dumpling and rode with his toes turned out.

34

Telemachus and Lyaeus walked behind them a long while without catching up, staring curiously after these two silent riders.

Eventually getting as far as the tails of the horse and the donkey, they called out: *"Buenos días."*

There turned to greet them a red, round face, full of little lines like an over-ripe tomato and a long bloodless face drawn into a point at the chin by a grizzled beard.

"How early you are, gentlemen," said the tall man on the grey horse. His voice was deep and sepulchral, with an occasional flutter of tenderness like a glint of light in a black river.

"Late," said Lyaeus. "We come from Madrid on foot."

The dumpling man crossed himself.

"They are mad," he said to his companion.

"That," said the man on the grey horse, "is always the answer of ignorance when confronted with the unusual. These gentlemen undoubtedly have very good reason for doing as they do; and besides the night is the time for long strides and deep thoughts, is it not, gentlemen? The habit of vigil is one we sorely need in this distracted modern world. If more men walked and thought the night through there would be less miseries under the sun."

"But, such a cold night!" exclaimed the dumpling man.

"On colder nights than this I have seen children asleep in doorways in the streets of Madrid."

"Is there much poverty in these parts?" asked Telemachus stiffly, wanting to show that he too had the social consciousness.

"There are people—thousands—who from the day they are born till the day they die never have enough to eat."

"They have wine," said Lyaeus.

"One little cup on Sundays, and they are so starved that it makes them as drunk as if it were a hogshead."

"I have heard," said Lyaeus, "that the sensations of starving are very interesting—people have visions more vivid than life."

"One needs very few sensations to lead life humbly and beautifully," said the man on the grey horse in a gentle tone of reproof.

Lyaeus frowned.

"Perhaps," said the man on the grey horse turning towards Telemachus his lean face, where under scraggly eyebrows glowered eyes of soft dark green, "it is that I have brooded too much on the injustice done in the world—all society one great wrong. Many years ago I should have set out to right wrong— for no one but a man, an individual alone, can right a wrong; organization merely substitutes one wrong for another—but now. . . . I am too old. You see, I go fishing instead."

"Why, it's a fishing pole," cried Lyaeus. "When I first saw it I thought it was a lance." And he let out his roaring laugh.

"And such trout," cried the dumpling man. "The trout there are in that little stream above Illescas! That's why we got up so early, to fish for trout."

"I like to see the dawn," said the man on the grey horse.

"Is that Illescas?" asked Telemachus, and pointed to a dun brown tower topped by a cap of blue slate that stood guard over a cluster of roofs ahead of them. Telemachus had a map torn from Baedecker in his pocket that he had been peeping at secretly.

"That, gentlemen, is Illescas," said the man on the grey horse. "And if you will allow me to offer you a cup of coffee, I shall be most pleased. You must excuse me, for I never take anything before midday. I am a recluse, have been for many years and rarely stir abroad. I do not intend to return to the world unless I can bring something with me worth having." A wistful smile twisted a little the corners of his mouth.

"I could guzzle a hogshead of coffee accompanied by vast processions of toasted rolls in columns of four," shouted Lyaeus.

"We are on our way to Toledo," Telemachus broke in, not wanting to give the impression that food was their only thought.

"You will see the paintings of Dominico Theocotopoulos, the only one who ever depicted the soul of Castile."

"This man," said Lyaeus, with a slap at Telemachus's shoulder, "is looking for a gesture."

"The gesture of Castile."

The man on the grey horse rode along silently for some time. The sun had already burnt up the hoar-frost along the sides of the road; only an occasional streak remained glistening in the shadow of a ditch. A few larks sang in the sky. Two men in brown corduroy with hoes on their shoulders passed on their way to the fields.

"Who shall say what is the gesture of Castile? . . . I am from La Mancha myself." The man on the grey horse started speaking gravely while with a bony hand, very white, he stroked his beard. "Something cold and haughty and aloof . . . men concentrated, converging breathlessly on the single flame of their spirit. . . . Torquemada, Loyola, Jorge Manrique, Cortés, Santa Teresa. . . . Rapacity, cruelty, straightforwardness. . . . Every man's life a lonely ruthless quest."

Lyaeus broke in:

"Remember the infinite gentleness of the saints lowering the Conde de Orgaz into the grave in the picture in San Tomás. . . ."

"Ah, that is what I was trying to think of. . . . These generations, my generation, my son's generation, are working to bury with infinite tenderness the gorgeously dressed corpse of the old Spain. . . . Gentlemen, it is a little ridiculous to say so, but we have set out once more with lance and helmet of knight-errantry to free the enslaved, to right the wrongs of the oppressed."

They had come into town. In the high square tower churchbells were ringing for morning mass. Down the broad main street scampered a flock of goats herded by a lean man with fangs like a dog who strode along in a snuff-colored cloak with a broad black felt hat on his head.

"How do you do, Don Alonso?" he cried; "Good luck to you, gentlemen." And he swept the hat off his head in a wide curving gesture as might a courtier of the Rey Don Juan.

The hot smell of the goats was all about them as they sat before the café in the sun under a bare acacia tree, looking at the tightly proportioned brick arcades of the mudéjar apse of the church opposite. Don Alonso was in the café ordering; the dumpling-man had disappeared. Telemachus got up on his numbed feet and stretched his legs. "Ouf," he said, "I'm tired." Then he walked over to the grey horse that stood with hanging head and drooping knees hitched to one of the acacias.

"I wonder what his name is." He stroked the horse's scrawny face. "Is it Rosinante?"

The horse twitched his ears, straightened his back and legs and pulled back black lips to show yellow teeth.

"Of course it's Rosinante!"

The horse's sides heaved. He threw back his head and whinnied shrilly, exultantly.

V: A Novelist of Revolution

MUCH as G.B.S. refuses to be called an Englishman, Pío Baroja refuses to be called a Spaniard. He is a Basque. Reluctantly he admits having been born in San Sebastián, outpost of Cosmopolis on the mountainous coast of Guipuzcoa, where a stern-featured race of mountaineers and fishermen, whose prominent noses, high ruddy cheek-bones and square jowls are gradually becoming known to the world through the paintings of the Zubiaurre, clings to its ancient un-Aryan language and its ancient song and customs with the hard-headedness of hill people the world over.

From the first Spanish discoveries in America till the time of our own New England clipper ships, the Basque coast was the backbone of Spanish trade. The three provinces were the only ones which kept their privileges and their municipal liberties all through the process of the centralizing of the Spanish monarchy with cross and faggot, which historians call the great period of Spain. The rocky inlets in the mountains were full of shipyards that turned out privateers and merchantmen manned by lanky broad-shouldered men with hard red-beaked faces and huge hands coarsened by generations of straining on heavy oars and halyards,—men who feared only God and the sea-spirits of their strange mythology and were a law unto themselves, adventurers and bigots.

It was not till the Nineteenth century that the Carlist wars and the passing of sailing ships broke the prosperous independence of the Basque provinces and threw them once for all into the main current of Spanish life. Now papermills take the place of shipyards, and instead of the great fleet that went off every year to fish the Newfoundland and Iceland banks, a few steam trawlers harry the sardines in the Bay of Biscay. The world war, too, did much to make Bilbao one of the industrial centers of Spain, even restoring in some measure the ancient prosperity of its shipping.

Pío Baroja spent his childhood on this rainy coast between green mountains and green sea. There were old aunts who filled his ears up with legends of former mercantile glory, with talk of sea captains and slavers and shipwrecks. Born in the late seventies, Baroja left the mist-filled inlets of Guipuzcoa to study medicine in Madrid, febrile capital full of the artificial scurry of government, on the dry upland plateau of New Castile. He even practiced, reluctantly enough, in a town near Valencia, where he must have acquired his distaste for the Mediterranean and the Latin genius, and, later, in his own province at Cestons, where he boarded with the woman who baked the sacramental wafers for the parish church, and, so he claims, felt the spirit of racial solidarity glow within him for the first time. But he was too timid in the face of pain and too sceptical of science as of everything else to acquire the cocksure brutality of a country doctor. He gave up medicine and returned to Madrid, where he became a baker. In *Juventud-Egolatria* ("Youth-Selfworship") a book of delightfully shameless self-revelations, he says that he ran a bakery for six years before starting to write. And he still runs a bakery.

You can see it any day, walking towards the Royal Theatre from the great focus of Madrid life, the Puerta del Sol. It has a most enticing window. On one side are hams and red sausages and purple sausages and white sausages, some plump to the bursting like Rubens's "Graces," others as weazened and smoked as saints by Ribera. In the middle are oblong plates with patés and sliced bologna and things in jelly; then come ranks of cakes, creamcakes and fruitcakes, everything from obscene jam-rolls to celestial cornucopias of white cream. Through the door you see a counter with round loaves of bread on it, and a basketful of brown rolls. If someone comes out a dense sweet smell of fresh bread and pastry swirls about the sidewalk.

So, by meeting commerce squarely in its own field, he has freed himself from any compromise with Mammon. While his bread remains sweet, his novels may be as bitter as he likes.

II

The moon shines coldly out of an intense blue sky where a few stars glisten faint as mica. Shadow fills half the street, etching a silhouette of roofs and chimneypots and cornices on the cobblestones, leaving the rest very white with moonlight.

The façades of the houses, with their blank windows, might be carved out of ice. In the dark of a doorway a woman sits hunched under a brown shawl. Her head nods, but still she jerks a tune that sways and dances through the silent street out of the accordion on her lap. A little saucer for pennies is on the step beside her. In the next doorway two guttersnipes are huddled together asleep. The moonlight points out with mocking interest their skinny dirt-crusted feet and legs stretched out over the icy pavement, and the filthy rags that barely cover their bodies. Two men stumble out of a wineshop arm in arm, poor men in corduroy, who walk along unsteadily in their worn canvas shoes, making grandiloquent gestures of pity, tearing down the cold hard façades with drunken generous phrases, buoyed up by the warmth of the wine in their veins.

That is Baroja's world: dismal, ironic, the streets of towns where industrial life sits heavy on the neck of a race as little adapted to it as any in Europe. No one has ever described better the shaggy badlands and cabbage-patches round the edges of a city, where the debris of civilization piles up ramshackle suburbs in which starve and scheme all manner of human detritus. Back lots where men and women live fantastically in shelters patched out of rotten boards, of old tin cans and bits of chairs and tables that have stood for years in bright pleasant rooms. Grassy patches behind crumbling walls where on sunny days starving children spread their fleshless limbs and run about in the sun. Miserable wineshops where the wind whines through broken panes to chill men with everempty stomachs who sit about gambling and finding furious drunkenness in a sip of *aguardiente*. Courtyards of barracks where painters who have not a cent in the world mix with beggars and guttersnipes to cajole a little hot food out of softhearted soldiers at mess-time. Convent doors where ragged lines shiver for hours in the shrill wind that blows across the bare Castilian plain waiting for the nuns to throw out bread for them to fight over like dogs. And through it all moves the great crowd of the outcast, sneak-thieves, burglars, beggars of every description,—rich beggars and poor devils who have given up the struggle to exist,—homeless children, prostitutes, people who live a half-honest existence selling knick-

nacks, penniless students, inventors who while away the time
they are dying of starvation telling all they meet of the riches
they might have had; all who have failed on the daily tread-
mill of bread-making, or who have never had a chance even
to enjoy the privilege of industrial slavery. Outside of Russia
there has never been a novelist so taken up with all that society and respectability reject.

Not that the interest in outcasts is anything new in Spanish
literature. Spain is the home of that type of novel which the
pigeonhole-makers have named picaresque. These loafers and
wanderers of Baroja's, like his artists and grotesque dreamers
and fanatics, all are the descendants of the people in the
Quijote and the *Novelas Ejemplares*, of the rogues and bandits
of the Lazarillo de Tormes, who through *Gil Blas* invaded
France and England, where they rollicked through the novel
until Mrs. Grundy and George Eliot packed them off to the
reform school. But the rogues of the seventeenth century
were jolly rogues. They always had their tongues in their
cheeks, and success rewarded their ingenious audacities. The
moulds of society had not hardened as they have now; there
was less pressure of hungry generations. Or, more probably,
pity had not come in to undermine the foundations.

The corrosive of pity, which had attacked the steel girders
of our civilization even before the work of building was completed, has brought about what Gilbert Murray in speaking of
Greek thought calls the failure of nerve. In the seventeenth
century men still had the courage of their egoism. The world
was a bad job to be made the best of, all hope lay in driving
a good bargain with the conductors of life everlasting. By the
end of the nineteenth century the life everlasting had grown
cobwebby, the French Revolution had filled men up with extravagant hopes of the perfectibility of this world, humanitar-
ianism had instilled an abnormal sensitiveness to pain,—to
one's own pain, and to the pain of one's neighbors. Baroja's
outcasts are no longer jolly knaves who will murder a man for
a nickel and go on their road singing "Over the hills and far
away"; they are men who have not had the will-power to continue in the fight for bread, they are men whose nerve has
failed, who live furtively on the outskirts, snatching a little joy
here and there, drugging their hunger with gorgeous mirages.

One often thinks of Gorki in reading Baroja, mainly because of the contrast. Instead of the tumultuous spring freshet of a new race that drones behind every page of the Russian, there is the cold despair of an old race, of a race that lived long under a formula of life to which it has sacrificed much, only to discover in the end that the formula does not hold.

These are the last paragraphs of *Mala Hierba* ("Wild Grass"), the middle volume of Baroja's trilogy on the life of the very poor in Madrid.

"They talked. Manuel felt irritation against the whole world, hatred, up to that moment pent up within him against society, against man. . . .

" 'Honestly,' he ended by saying, 'I wish it would rain dynamite for a week, and that the Eternal Father would come tumbling down in cinders.'

"He invoked crazily all the destructive powers to reduce to ashes this miserable society.

"Jesús listened with attention.

" 'You are an anarchist,' he told him.

" 'I?'

" 'Yes. So am I.'

" 'Since when?'

" 'Since I have seen the infamies committed in the world; since I have seen how coldly they give to death a bit of human flesh; since I have seen how men die abandoned in the streets and hospitals,' answered Jesús with a certain solemnity.

"Manuel was silent. The friends walked without speaking round the Ronda de Segovia, and sat down on a bench in the little gardens of the Vírgen del Puerto.

"The sky was superb, crowded with stars; the Milky Way crossed its immense blue concavity. The geometric figure of the Great Bear glittered very high. Arcturus and Vega shone softly in that ocean of stars.

"In the distance the dark fields, scratched with lines of lights, seemed the sea in a harbor and the strings of lights the illumination of a wharf.

"The damp warm air came laden with odors of woodland plants wilted by the heat.

" 'How many stars,' said Manuel. 'What can they be?'

" 'They are worlds, endless worlds.'

" 'I don't know why it doesn't make me feel better to see this sky so beautiful, Jesús. Do you think there are men in those worlds?' asked Manuel.

" 'Perhaps; why not?'

" 'And are there prisons too, and judges and gambling dens and police? . . . Do you think so?'

"Jesús did not answer. After a while he began talking with a calm voice of his dream of an idyllic humanity, a sweet pitiful dream, noble and childish.

"In his dream, man, led by a new idea, reached a higher state.

"No more hatreds, no more rancours. Neither judges, nor police, nor soldiers, nor authority. In the wide fields of the earth free men worked in the sunlight. The law of love had taken the place of the law of duty, and the horizons of humanity grew every moment wider, wider and more azure.

"And Jesús continued talking of a vague ideal of love and justice, of energy and pity; and those words of his, chaotic, incoherent, fell like balm on Manuel's ulcerated spirit. Then they were both silent, lost in their thoughts, looking at the night.

"An august joy shone in the sky, and the vague sensation of space, of the infinity of those imponderable worlds, filled their spirits with a delicious calm."

III

Spain is the classic home of the anarchist. A bleak upland country mostly, with a climate giving all varieties of temperature, from moist African heat to dry Siberian cold, where people have lived until very recently,—and do still,—in villages hidden away among the bare ribs of the mountains, or in the indented coast plains, where every region is cut off from every other by high passes and defiles of the mountains, flaming hot in summer and freezing cold in winter, where the Iberian race has grown up centerless. The pueblo, the village community, is the only form of social cohesion that really has roots in the past. On these free towns empires have time and again been imposed by force. In the sixteenth and seventeenth centuries the Catholic monarchy wielded the sword of the faith to such good effect that communal feeling was killed and the Spanish genius forced to ingrow into the mystical realm where every ego expanded itself into the solitude of God. The eighteenth century reduced God to an abstraction, and the nineteenth brought pity and the mad hope of righting the wrongs of society. The Spaniard, like his own Don Quixote, mounted the warhorse of his idealism and set out to free the oppressed, alone. As a logical conclusion we have the anarchist who threw a bomb into the Lyceum Theatre in Barcelona during a performance, wanting to make the ultimate heroic gesture and only succeeding in a senseless mangling of human lives.

But that was the reduction to an absurdity of an immensely valuable mental position. The anarchism of Pío Baroja is of another sort. He says in one of his books that the only part a man of the middle classes can play in the reorganization of society is destructive. He has not undergone the discipline, which can only come from common slavery in the industrial machine, necessary for a builder. His slavery has been an isolated slavery which has unfitted him forever from becoming truly part of a community. He can use the vast power of knowledge which training has given him only in one way. His great mission is to put the acid test to existing institutions, and to strip the veils off them. I don't want to imply that Baroja writes with his social conscience. He is too much of a novelist for that, too deeply interested in people as such. But it is certain that a profound sense of the evil of existing institutions lies behind every page he has written, and that occasionally, only occasionally, he allows himself to hope that something better may come out of the turmoil of our age of transition.

Only a man who had felt all this very deeply could be so sensitive to the new spirit—if the word were not threadbare one would call it religious—which is shaking the foundations of the world's social pyramid, perhaps only another example of the failure of nerve, perhaps the triumphant expression of a new will among mankind.

In *Aurora Roja* ("Red Dawn"), the last of the Madrid trilogy, about the same Manual who is the central figure of *Mala Hierba*, he writes:

"At first it bored him, but later, little by little, he felt himself carried away by what he was reading. First he was enthusiastic about Mirabeau; then about the Girondins; Vergniau,

Petion, Condorcet; then about Danton; then he began to
think that Robespierre was the true revolutionary; afterwards
Saint Just, but in the end it was the gigantic figure of Danton
that thrilled him most. . . .

"Manuel felt great satisfaction at having read that history.
Often he said to himself:

"'What does it matter now if I am a loafer, and good-for-
nothing? I've read the history of the French Revolution; I believe I shall know how to be worthy. . . .'

"After Michelet, he read a book about '48; then another on
the Commune, by Louise Michel, and all this produced in
him a great admiration for French Revolutionists. What men!
After the colossal figures of the Convention: Babeuf, Prou-
dhon, Blanqui, Bandin, Deleschize, Rochefort, Félix Pyat,
Vallu. . . . What people!

"'What does it matter now if I am a loafer? . . . I believe I
shall know how to be worthy.'"

In those two phrases lies all the power of revolutionary
faith. And how like phrases out of the gospels, those older ex-
pressions of the hope and misery of another society in decay.
That is the spirit that, for good or evil, is stirring throughout
Europe to-day, among the poor and the hungry and the oppressed and the outcast, a new affirmation of the rights and
duties of men. Baroja has felt this profoundly, and has presented it, but without abandoning the function of the novelist, which is to tell stories about people. He is never a
propagandist.

IV

"I have never hidden my admirations in literature. They
have been and are Dickens, Balzac, Poe, Dostoievski and,
now, Stendhal . . ." writes Baroja in the preface to the Nelson
edition of *La Dama Errante* ("The Wandering Lady"). He
follows particularly in the footprints of Balzac in that he is primarily a historian of morals, who has made a fairly consistent
attempt to cover the world he lived in. With Dostoievski there
is a kinship in the passionate hatred of cruelty and stupidity
that crops out everywhere in his work. I have never found any
trace of influence of the other three. To be sure there are a

few early sketches in the manner of Poe, but in respect to form he is much more in the purely chaotic tradition of the picaresque novel he despises than in that of the American theorist.

Baroja's most important work lies in the four series of novels of the Spanish life he lived, in Madrid, in the provincial towns where he practiced medicine, and in the Basque country where he had been brought up. The foundation of these was laid by *El Arbol de la Ciencia* ("The Tree of Knowledge"), a novel half autobiographical describing the life and death of a doctor, giving a picture of existence in Madrid and then in two Spanish provincial towns. Its tremendously vivid painting of inertia and the deadening under its weight of intellectual effort made a very profound impression in Spain. Two novels about the anarchist movement followed it, *La Dama Errante*, which describes the state of mind of forward-looking Spaniards at the time of the famous anarchist attempt on the lives of the king and queen the day of their marriage, and *La Ciudad de la Niebla*, about the Spanish colony in London. Then came the series called *La Busca* ("The Search"), which to me is Baroja's best work, and one of the most interesting things published in Europe in the last decade. It deals with the lowest and most miserable life in Madrid and is written with a cold acidity which Maupassant would have envied and is permeated by a human vividness that I do not think Maupassant could have achieved. All three novels, *La Busca*, *Mala Hierba*, and *Aurora Roja*, deal with the drifting of a typical uneducated Spanish boy, son of a maid of all work in a boarding house, through different strata of Madrid life. They give a sense of unadorned reality very rare in any literature, and besides their power as novels are immensely interesting as sheer natural history. The type of the *golfo* is a literary discovery comparable with that of Sancho Panza by Cervantes.

Nothing that Baroja has written since is quite on the same level. The series *El Pasado* ("The Past") gives interesting pictures of provincial life. *Las Inquietudes de Shanti Andia* ("The Anxieties of Shanti Andia"), a story of Basque seamen which contains a charming picture of a childhood in a seaside village in Guipuzcoa, delightful as it is to read, is too muddled in romantic claptrap to add much to his fame. *El Mundo es Así*

("The World is Like That") expresses, rather lamely it seems to me, the meditations of a disenchanted revolutionist. The latest series, *Memorias de un Hombre de Acción*, a series of yarns about the revolutionary period in Spain at the beginning of the nineteenth century, though entertaining, is more an attempt to escape in a jolly romantic past the realities of the morose present than anything else. *César o Nada*, translated into English under the title of "Aut Cæsar aut Nullus" is also less acid and less effective than his earlier novels. That is probably why it was chosen for translation into English. We know how anxious our publishers are to furnish food easily digestible by weak American stomachs.

It is silly to judge any Spanish novelist from the point of view of form. Improvisation is the very soul of Spanish writing. In thinking back over books of Baroja's one has read, one remembers more descriptions of places and people than anything else. In the end it is rather natural history than dramatic creation. But a natural history that gives you the pictures etched with vitriol of Spanish life in the end of the nineteenth and the beginning of the twentieth century which you get in these novels of Baroja's is very near the highest sort of creation. If we could inject some of the virus of his intense sense of reality into American writers it would be worth giving up all these stale conquests of form we inherited from Poe and O. Henry. The following, again from the preface of *La Dama Errante*, is Baroja's own statement of his aims. And certainly he has realized them.

"Probably a book like *La Dama Errante* is not of the sort that lives very long; it is not a painting with aspirations towards the museum but an impressionist canvas; perhaps as a work it has too much asperity, is too hard, not serene enough.

"This ephemeral character of my work does not displease me. We are men of the day, people in love with the passing moment, with all that is fugitive and transitory and the lasting quality of our work preoccupies us little, so little that it can hardly be said to preoccupy us at all."

VI: Talk by the Road

S PAIN," said Don Alonso, as he and Telemachus walked out
of Illescas, followed at a little distance by Lyaeus and the
dumpling-man, "has never been swept clean. There have been
the Romans and the Visigoths and the Moors and the French—
armed men jingling over mountain roads. Conquest has
warped and sterilised our Iberian mind without changing an
atom of it. An example: we missed the Revolution and suffered
from Napoleon. We virtually had no Reformation, yet the
Inquisition was stronger with us than anywhere."

"Do you think it will have to be swept clean?" asked
Telemachus.

"He does." Don Alonso pointed with a sweep of an arm towards a man working in the field beside the road. It was a
short man in a blouse; he broke the clods the plow had left
with a heavy triangular hoe. Sometimes he raised it only a foot
above the ground to poise for a blow, sometimes he swung it
from over his shoulder. Face, clothes, hands, hoe were brown
against the brown hillside where a purple shadow mocked each
heavy gesture with lank gesticulations. In the morning silence
the blows of the hoe beat upon the air with muffled insistence.

"And he is the man who will do the building," went on
Don Alonso; "It is only fair that we should clear the road."

"But you are the thinkers," said Telemachus; his mother
Penelope's maxims on the subject of constructive criticism
popped up suddenly in his mind like tickets from a cash
register.

"Thought is the acid that destroys," answered Don Alonso.

Telemachus turned to look once more at the man working
in the field. The hoe rose and fell, rose and fell. At a moment
on each stroke a flash of sunlight came from it. Telemachus
saw all at once the whole earth, plowed fields full of earth-
colored men, shoulders thrown back, bent forward, muscles
of arms swelling and slackening, hoes flashing at the same moment against the sky, at the same moment buried with a thud
in clods. And he felt reassured as a traveller feels, hearing the
continuous hiss and squudge of well oiled engines out at sea.

VII: Cordova no Longer of the Caliphs

WHEN we stepped out of the bookshop the narrow street steamed with the dust of many carriages. Above the swiftly whirling wheels gaudily dressed men and women sat motionless in attitudes. Over the backs of the carriages brilliant shawls trailed, triangles of red and purple and yellow.

"Bread and circuses," muttered the man who was with me, "but not enough bread."

It was fair-time in Cordova; the carriages were coming back from the *toros*. We turned into a narrow lane, where the dust was yellow between high green and lavender-washed walls. From the street we had left came a sound of cheers and handclapping. My friend stopped still and put his hand on my arm.

"There goes Belmonte," he said; "half the men who are cheering him have never had enough to eat in their lives. The old Romans knew better; to keep people quiet they filled their bellies. Those fools——" he jerked his head backwards with disgust; I thought, of the shawls and the high combs and the hair gleaming black under lace and the wasp-waists of the young men and the insolence of black eyes above the flashing wheels of the carriages, "—those fools give only circuses. Do you people in the outside world realize that we in Andalusia starve, that we have starved for generations, that those black bulls for the circuses may graze over good wheatland . . . to make Spain picturesque! The only time we see meat is in the bullring. Those people who argue all the time as to why Spain's backward and write books about it, I could tell them in one word: malnutrition." He laughed despairingly and started walking fast again. "We have solved the problem of the cost of living. We live on air and dust and bad smells."

I had gone into his bookshop a few minutes before to ask an address, and had been taken into the back room with the wonderful enthusiastic courtesy one finds so often in Spain. There the bookseller, a carpenter and the bookseller's errand-boy had all talked at once, explaining the last strike of farm-laborers, when the region had been for months under martial law, and they, and every one else of socialist or republican sympathies, had been packed for weeks into overcrowded prisons. They all regretted they could not take me to the Casa del Pueblo, but, they explained laughing, the Civil Guard was occupying it at that moment. It ended by the bookseller's coming out with me to show me the way to Azorín's.

Azorín was an architect who had supported the strikers; he had just come back to Cordova from the obscure village where he had been imprisoned through the care of the military governor who had paid him the compliment of thinking that even in prison he would be dangerous in Cordova. He had recently been elected municipal councillor, and when we reached his office was busy designing a schoolhouse. On the stairs the bookseller had whispered to me that every workman in Cordova would die for Azorín. He was a sallow little man with a vaguely sarcastic voice and an amused air as if he would burst out laughing at any moment. He put aside his plans and we all went on to see the editor of *Andalusia*, a regionalist pro-labor weekly.

In that dark little office, over three cups of coffee that appeared miraculously from somewhere, with the pungent smell of ink and fresh paper in our nostrils, we talked about the past and future of Cordova, and of all the wide region of northern Andalusia, fertile irrigated plains, dry olive-land stretching up to the rocky waterless mountains where the mines are. In Azorín's crisp phrases and in the long ornate periods of the editor, the serfdom and the squalor and the heroic hope of these peasants and miners and artisans became vivid to me for the first time. Occasionally the compositor, a boy of about fifteen with a brown ink-smudged face, would poke his head in the door and shout: "It's true what they say, but they don't say enough, they don't say enough."

The problem in the south of Spain is almost wholly agrarian. From the Tagus to the Mediterranean stretches a mountainous region of low rainfall, intersected by several series of broad river-valleys which, under irrigation, are enormously productive of rice, oranges, and, in the higher altitudes, of wheat. In the dry hills grow grapes, olives and almonds. A country on the whole much like southern California. Under the Moors this region was the richest and most civilized in Europe.

When the Christian nobles from the north reconquered it, the ecclesiastics laid hold of the towns and extinguished industry through the Inquisition, while the land was distributed in huge estates to the magnates of the court of the Catholic Kings. The agricultural workers became virtually serfs, and the communal village system of working the land gradually gave way. Now the province of Jaen, certainly as large as the State of Rhode Island, is virtually owned by six families. This process was helped by the fact that all through the sixteenth and seventeenth centuries the liveliest people in all Spain swarmed overseas to explore and plunder America or went into the church, so that the tilling of the land was left to the humblest and least vigorous. And immigration to America has continued the safety valve of the social order.

It is only comparatively recently that the consciousness has begun to form among the workers of the soil that it is possible for them to change their lot. As everywhere else, Russia has been the beacon-flare. Since 1918 an extraordinary tenseness has come over the lives of the frugal sinewy peasants who, through centuries of oppression and starvation, have kept, in spite of almost complete illiteracy, a curiously vivid sense of personal independence. In the backs of taverns revolutionary tracts are spelled out by some boy who has had a couple of years of school to a crowd of men who listen or repeat the words after him with the fervor of people going through a religious mystery. Unspeakable faith possesses them in what they call *"la nueva ley"* ("the new law"), by which the good things a man wrings by his sweat from the earth shall be his and not the property of a distant señor in Madrid.

It is this hopefulness that marks the difference between the present agrarian agitation and the violent and desperate peasant risings of the past. As early as October, 1918, a congress of agricultural workers was held to decide on strike methods, and, more important, to formulate a demand for the expropriation of the land. In two months the unions, (*"sociedades de resistencia"*) had been welded—at least in the province of Cordova—into a unified system with more or less central leadership. The strike which followed was so complete that in many cases even domestic servants went out. After savage repression and the military occupation of the whole province, the strike petered out into compromises which resulted in considerable betterment of working conditions but left the important issues untouched.

The rise in the cost of living and the growing unrest brought matters to a head again in the summer of 1919. The military was used with even more brutality than the previous year. Attempts at compromise, at parcelling out uncultivated land have proved as unavailing as the Mausers of the Civil Guard to quell the tumult. The peasants have kept their organizations and their demands intact. They are even willing to wait; but they are determined that the land upon which they have worn out generations and generations shall be theirs without question.

All this time the landlords brandish a redoubtable weapon: starvation. Already thousands of acres that might be richly fertile lie idle or are pasture for herds of wild bulls for the arena. The great land-owning families hold estates all over Spain; if in a given region the workers become too exigent, they decide to leave the land in fallow for a year or two. In the villages it becomes a question of starve or emigrate. To emigrate many certificates are needed. Many officials have to be placated. For all that money is needed. Men taking to the roads in search of work are persecuted as vagrants by the civil guards. Arson becomes the last retort of despair. At night the standing grain burns mysteriously or the country house of an absent landlord, and from the parched hills where gnarled almond-trees grow, groups of half starved men watch the flames with grim exultation.

Meanwhile the press in Madrid laments the *incultura* of the Andalusian peasants. The problem of civilization, after all, is often one of food calories. Fernando de los Ríos, socialist deputy for Granada, recently published the result of an investigation of the food of the agricultural populations of Spain in which he showed that only in the Balkans—out of all Europe—was the working man so under-nourished. The calories which the diet of the average Cordova workman represented was something like a fourth of those of the British workman's diet. Even so the foremen of the big estates complain that as a result of all this social agitation their workmen have taken to eating more than they did in the good old times.

How long it will be before the final explosion comes no one can conjecture. The spring of 1920, when great things were expected, was completely calm. On the other hand, in the last municipal elections when six hundred socialist councillors were elected in all Spain—in contrast to sixty-two in 1915—the vote polled in Andalusia was unprecedented. Up to this election many of the peasants had never dared vote, and those that had had been completely under the thumb of the *caciques*, the bosses that control Spanish local politics. However, in spite of socialist and syndicalist propaganda, the agrarian problem will always remain separate from anything else in the minds of the peasants. This does not mean that they are opposed to communism or cling as violently as most of the European peasantry to the habit of private property.

All over Spain one comes upon traces of the old communist village institutions, by which flocks and mills and bakeries and often land were held in common. As in all arid countries, where everything depends upon irrigation, ditches are everywhere built and repaired in common. And the idea of private property is of necessity feeble where there is no rain; for what good is land to a man without water? Still, until there grows up a much stronger community of interest than now exists between the peasants and the industrial workers, the struggle for the land and the struggle for the control of industry will be, in Spain, as I think everywhere, parallel rather than unified. One thing is certain, however long the fire smoulders before it flares high to make a clean sweep of Spanish capitalism and Spanish feudalism together, Cordova, hoary city of the caliphs, where ghosts of old grandeurs flit about the zigzag ochre-colored lanes, will, when the moment comes, be the center of organization of the agrarian revolution. When I was leaving Spain I rode with some young men who were emigrating to America, to make their fortunes, they said. When I told them I had been to Cordova, their faces became suddenly bright with admiration.

"Ah, Cordova," one of them cried; "they've got the guts in Cordova."

VIII: Talk by the Road

A T the first crossroads beyond Illescas the dumpling-man and Don Alonso turned off in quest of the trout stream. Don Alonso waved solemnly to Lyaeus and Telemachus.

"Perhaps we shall meet in Toledo," he said.

"Catch a lot of fish," shouted Lyaeus.

"And perhaps a thought," was the last word they heard from Don Alonso.

The sun already high in the sky poured tingling heat on their heads and shoulders. There was sand in their shoes, an occasional sharp pain in their shins, in their bellies bitter emptiness.

"At the next village, Tel, I'm going to bed. You can do what you like," said Lyaeus in a tearful voice.

"I'll like that all right."

"Buenos días, señores viajeros," came a cheerful voice. They found they were walking in the company of a man who wore a tight-waisted overcoat of a light blue color, a cream-colored felt hat from under which protruded long black moustaches with gimlet points, and shoes with lemon-yellow uppers. They passed the time of day with what cheerfulness they could muster.

"Ah, Toledo," said the man. "You are going to Toledo, my birthplace. There I was born in the shadow of the cathedral, there I shall die. I am a traveller of commerce." He produced two cards as large as postcards on which was written:

ANTONIO SILVA Y YEPES
UNIVERSAL AGENT
IMPORT EXPORT NATIONAL PRODUCTS

"At your service, gentlemen," he said and handed each of them a card. "I deal in tinware, ironware, pottery, lead pipes, enameled ware, kitchen utensils, American toilet articles, French perfumery, cutlery, linen, sewing machines, saddles, bridles, seeds, fancy poultry, fighting bantams and objects *de vertu.* . . . You are foreigners, are you not? How barbarous Spain, what people, what dirt, what lack of culture, what impoliteness, what lack of energy!"

The universal agent choked, coughed, spat, produced a handkerchief of crimson silk with which he wiped his eyes and mouth, twirled his moustaches and plunged again into a torrent of words, turning on Telemachus from time to time little red-rimmed eyes full of moist pathos like a dog's.

"Oh there are times, gentlemen, when it is too much to bear, when I rejoice to think that it's all up with my lungs and that I shan't live long anyway. . . . In America I should have been a Rockefeller, a Carnegie, a Morgan. I know it, for I am a man of genius. It is true. I am a man of genius. . . . And look at me here walking from one of these cursed tumbledown villages to another because I have not money enough to hire a cab. . . . And ill too, dying of consumption! O Spain, Spain, how do you crush your great men! What you must think of us, you who come from civilized countries, where life is organized, where commerce is a gentlemanly, even a noble occupation. . . ."

"But you savor life more . . ."

"*Ca, ca,*" interrupted the universal agent with a downward gesture of the hand. "To think that they call by the same name living here in a pen like a pig and living in Paris, London, New York, Biarritz, Trouville . . . luxurious beds, coiffures, toilettes, theatrical functions, sumptuous automobiles, elegant ladies glittering with diamonds . . . the world of light and enchantment! Oh to think of it! And Spain could be the richest country in Europe, if we had energy, organization, culture! Think of the exports: iron, coal, copper, silver, oranges, hides, mules, olives, food products, woolens, cotton cloth, sugarcane, raw cotton . . . couplets, dancers, gipsy girls. . . ."

The universal agent had quite lost his breath. He coughed for a long time into his crimson handkerchief, then looked about him over the rolling dun slopes to which the young grain sprouting gave a sheen of vivid green like the patina on a Pompeian bronze vase, and shrugged his shoulders.

"*¡Qué vida!* What a life!"

For some time a spire had been poking up into the sky at the road's end; now yellow-tiled roofs were just visible humped out of the wheatland, with the church standing guard over them, its buttresses as bowed as the legs of a bulldog. At the sight of the village a certain spring came back to Telemachus's fatigue-sodden legs. He noticed with envy that Lyaeus took little skips as he walked.

"If we properly exploited our exports we should be the richest people in Europe," the universal agent kept shouting with far-flung gestures of despair. And the last they heard from him as they left him to turn into the manure-littered, chicken-noisy courtyard of the Posada de la Luna was, "*¡Qué pueblo indecente!* . . . What a beastly town . . . yet if they exploited with energy, with modern energy, their exports. . . ."

IX: An Inverted Midas

EVERY AGE must have had choice spirits whose golden fingers turned everything they touched to commonplace. Since we know our own literature best it seems unreasonably well equipped with these inverted Midases—though the fact that all Anglo-American writing during the last century has been so exclusively of the middle classes, by the middle classes and for the middle classes must count for something. Still Rome had her Marcus Aurelius, and we may be sure that platitudes would have obscured the slanting sides of the pyramids had stone-cutting in the reign of Cheops been as disastrously easy as is printing to-day. The addition of the typewriter to the printing-press has given a new and horrible impetus to the spread of half-baked thought. The labor of graving on stone or of baking tablets of brick or even of scrawling letters on paper with a pen is no longer a curb on the dangerous fluency of the inverted Midas. He now lolls in a Morris chair, sipping iced tea, dictating to four blonde and two dark-haired stenographers; three novels, a couple of books of travel and a short story written at once are nothing to a really enterprising universal genius. Poor Julius Caesar with his letters!

We complain that we have no supermen nowadays, that we can't live as much or as widely or as fervently or get through so much work as could Pico della Mirandola or Erasmus or Politian, that the race drifts towards mental and physical anæmia. I deny it. With the typewriter all these things shall be added unto us. This age too has its great universal geniuses. They overrun the seven continents and their respective seas. Accompanied by mænadic bands of stenographers, and a music of typewriters deliriously clicking, they go about the world, catching all the butterflies, rubbing the bloom off all the plums, tunneling mountains, bridging seas, smoothing the facets off ideas so that they may be swallowed harmlessly like pills. With true Anglo-Saxon conceit we had thought that our own Mr. Wells was the most universal of these universal geniuses. He has so diligently brought science, ethics, sex, marriage, sociology, God, and everything else—properly de-

58

odorized, of course—to the desk of the ordinary man, that he may lean back in his swivel-chair and receive faint susurration from the sense of progress and the complexity of life, without even having to go to the window to look at the sparrows sitting in rows on the telephone-wires, so that really it seemed inconceivable that anyone should be more universal. It was rumored that there lay the ultimate proof of Anglo-Saxon ascendancy. What other race had produced a great universal genius?

But all that was before the discovery of Blasco Ibáñez.

On the backs of certain of Blasco Ibáñez's novels published by the Casa Prometeo in Valencia is this significant advertisement: *Obras de Vulgarización Popular* ("Works of Popular Vulgarization"). Under it is an astounding list of volumes, all either translated or edited or arranged, if not written from cover to cover, by one tireless pen,—I mean typewriter. Ten volumes of universal history, three volumes of the French Revolution translated from Michelet, a universal geography, a social history, works on science, cookery and house-cleaning, nine volumes of Blasco Ibáñez's own history of the European war, and a translation of the Arabian Nights, a thousand and one of them without an hour missing. "Works of Popular Vulgarization." I admit that in Spanish the word *vulgarización* has not yet sunk to its inevitable meaning, but can it long stand such a strain? Add to that list a round two dozen novels and some books of travel, and who can deny that Blasco Ibáñez is a great universal genius? Read his novels and you will find that he has looked at the stars and knows Lord Kelvin's theory of vortices and the nebular hypothesis and the direction of ocean currents and the qualities of kelp and the direction the codfish go in Iceland waters when the northeast wind blows; that he knows about Gothic architecture and Byzantine painting, the social movement in Jerez and the exports of Patagonia, the wall-paper of Paris apartment houses and the red paste with which countesses polish their fingernails in Monte Carlo.

The very pattern of a modern major-general.

And, like the great universal geniuses of the Renaissance, he has lived as well as thought and written. He is said to have been thirty times in prison, six times deputy; he has been a cowboy in the pampas of Argentina; he has founded a city in Patagonia with a bullring and a bust of Cervantes in the middle of it; he has rounded the Horn on a sailing-ship in a hurricane, and it is whispered that like Victor Hugo he eats lobsters with the shells on. He hobnobs with the universe.

One must admit, too, that Blasco Ibáñez's universe is a bulkier, burlier universe than Mr. Wells's. One is strangely certain that the axle of Mr. Wells's universe is fixed in some suburb of London, say Putney, where each house has a bit of garden where waddles an asthmatic pet dog, where people drink tea weak, with milk in it, before a gas-log, where every bookcase makes a futile effort to impinge on infinity through the encyclopedia, where life is a monotonous going and coming, swathed in clothes that must above all be respectable, to business and from business. But who can say where Blasco Ibáñez's universe centers? It is in constant progression.

Starting, as Walt Whitman from fish-shaped Paumonauk, from the fierce green fertility of Valencia, city of another great Spanish conqueror, the Cid, he had marched on the world in battle array. The whole history comes out in the series of novels at this moment being translated in such feverish haste for the edification of the American public. The beginnings are stories of the peasants of the fertile plain round about Valencia, of the fishermen and sailors of El Grao, the port, a sturdy violent people living amid a snappy fury of vegetation unexampled in Europe. His method is inspired to a certain extent by Zola, taking from him a little of the newspaper-horror mode of realism, with inevitable murder and sudden death in the last chapters. Yet he expresses that life vividly, although even then more given to grand vague ideas than to a careful scrutiny of men and things. He is at home in the strong communal feeling, in the individual anarchism, in the passionate worship of the water that runs through the fields to give life and of the blades of wheat that give bread and of the wine that gives joy, which is the moral make-up of the Valencian peasant. He is sincerely indignant about the agrarian system, about social inequality, and is full of the revolutionary bravado of his race.

A typical novel of this period is *La Barraca*, a story of a peasant family that takes up land which has lain vacant for years under the curse of the community, since the eviction of the tenants, who had held it for generations, by a landlord who was murdered as a result, on a lonely road by the father of the family he had turned out. The struggle of these peasants against their neighbours is told with a good deal of feeling, and the culmination in a rifle fight in an irrigation ditch is a splendid bit of blood and thunder. There are many descriptions of local customs, such as the Tribunal of Water that sits once a week under one of the portals of Valencia cathedral to settle conflicts of irrigation rights, a little dragged in by the heels, to be sure, but still worth reading. Yet even in these early novels one feels over and over again the force of that phrase "popular vulgarization." Valencia is being vulgarized for the benefit of the universe. The proletariat is being vulgarized for the benefit of the people who buy novels.

From Valencia raids seem to have been made on other parts of Spain. *Sonnica la Cortesana* gives you antique Saguntum and the usual "Aves," wreaths, flute-players and other claptrap of costume novels. In *La Catedral* you have Toledo, the church, socialism and the modern world in the shadow of Gothic spires. *La Bodega* takes you into the genial air of the wine vaults of Jerez-de-la-Frontera, with smugglers, processions blessing the vineyards and agrarian revolt in the background. Up to now they have been Spanish novels written for Spaniards; it is only with *Sangre y Arena* that the virus of a European reputation shows results.

In *Sangre y Arena*, to be sure, you learn that *toreros* use scent, have a home life, and are seduced by passionate Baudelairian ladies of the smart set who plant white teeth in their brown sinewy arms and teach them to smoke opium cigarettes. You see *toreros* taking the sacraments before going into the ring and you see them tossed by the bull while the crowd, which a moment before had been crying "hola" as if it didn't know that something was going wrong, gets very pale and chilly and begins to think what dreadful things *corridas* are anyway, until the arrival of the next bull makes them forget it. All of which is good fun when not obscured by grand, vague ideas, and incidentally sells like hot cakes. Thenceforward the Casa Prometeo becomes an exporting house dealing in the good Spanish products of violence and sunshine, blood, voluptuousness and death, as another vulgarizer put it.

Next comes the expedition to South America and *The Argonauts* appears. The Atlantic is bridged,—there open up rich veins of picturesqueness and new grand vague ideas, all in full swing when the war breaks out. Blasco Ibáñez meets the challenge nobly, and very soon, with *The Four Horsemen of the Apocalypse*, which captures the Allied world and proves again the *mot* about prophets. So without honor in its own country is the *Four Horsemen* that the English translation rights are sold for a paltry three thousand pesetas. But the great success in England and America soon shows that we can appreciate the acumen of a neutral who came in and rooted for our side; so early in the race too! While the iron is still hot another four hundred pages of well-sugared pro-Ally propaganda appears, *Mare Nostrum*, which mingles Ulysses and scientific information about ocean currents, Amphitrite and submarines, Circe and a vamping Theda Bara who was really a German Spy, in one grand chant of praise before the Mumbo-Jumbo of nationalism.

Los Enemigos de la Mujer, the latest production, abandons Spain entirely and plants itself in the midst of princes and countesses, all elaborately pro-Ally, at Monte Carlo. Forgotten the proletarian tastes of his youth, the local color he loved to lay on so thickly, the Habañera atmosphere; only the grand vague ideas subsist in the cosmopolite, and the fluency, that fatal Latin fluency.

And now the United States, the home of the blonde stenographer and the typewriter and the press agent. What are we to expect from the combination of Blasco Ibáñez and Broadway?

At any rate the movies will profit.

Yet one can't help wishing that Blasco Ibáñez had not learnt the typewriter trick so early. Print so easily spins a web of the commonplace over the fine outlines of life. And Blasco Ibáñez need not have been an inverted Midas. His is a superbly Mediterranean type, with something of Arretino, something of Garibaldi, something of Tartarin of Tarascon. Blustering, sensual, enthusiastic, living at bottom in a real world—which can hardly be said of Anglo-Saxon vulgarizers—even if it is a real world obscured by grand vague ideas, Blasco Ibáñez's mere energy would have produced interesting things if it had not found such easy and immediate vent in the typewriter. Bottle up a man like that for a lifetime without means of expression and he'll produce memoirs equal to Marco Polo and Casanova, but let his energies flow out evenly without resistance through a corps of clicking typewriters and all you have is one more popular novelist.

It is unfortunate too that Blasco Ibáñez and the United States should have discovered each other at this moment. They will do each other no good. We have an abundance both of vague grand ideas and of popular novelists, and we are the favorite breeding place of the inverted Midas. We need writing that shall be acid, with sharp edges on it, yeasty to leaven the lump of glucose that the combination of the ideals of the man in the swivel-chair with decayed puritanism has made of our national consciousness. Of course Blasco Ibáñez in America will only be a seven days' marvel. Nothing is ever more than that. But why need we pretend each time that our seven days' marvels are the great eternal things?

Then, too, if the American public is bound to take up Spain it might as well take up the worth-while things instead of the works of popular vulgarization. They have enough of those in their bookcases as it is. And in Spain there is a novelist like Baroja, essayists like Unamuno and Azorín, poets like Valle Inclán and Antonio Machado, . . . but I suppose they will shine with the reflected glory of the author of the *Four Horsemen of the Apocalypse*.

X: Talk by the Road

WHEN they woke up it was dark. They were cold. Their legs were stiff. They lay each along one edge of a tremendously wide bed, between them a tangle of narrow sheets and blankets. Telemachus raised himself to a sitting position and put his feet, that were still swollen, gingerly to the floor. He drew them up again with a jerk and sat with his teeth chattering hunched on the edge of the bed. Lyaeus burrowed into the blankets and went back to sleep. For a long while Telemachus could not thaw his frozen wits enough to discover what noise had waked him up. Then it came upon him suddenly that huge rhythms were pounding about him, sounds of shaken tambourines and castanettes and beaten dish-pans and roaring voices. Someone was singing in shrill tremolo above the din a song of which each verse seemed to end with the phrase, *"y mañana Carnaval."*

"To-morrow's Carnival. Wake up," he cried out to Lyaeus, and pulled on his trousers.

Lyaeus sat up and rubbed his eyes.

"I smell wine," he said.

Telemachus, through hunger and stiffness and aching feet and the thought of what his mother Penelope would say about these goings on, if they ever came to her ears, felt a tremendous elation flare through him.

"Come on, they're dancing," he cried dragging Lyaeus out on the gallery that overhung the end of the court.

"Don't forget the butterfly net, Tel."

"What for?"

"To catch your gesture, what do you think?"

Telemachus caught Lyaeus by the shoulders and shook him. As they wrestled they caught glimpses of the courtyard full of couples bobbing up and down in a *jota*. In the doorway stood two guitar players and beside them a table with pitchers and glasses and a glint of spilt wine. Feeble light came from an occasional little constellation of olive-oil lamps. When the two of them pitched down stairs together and shot out reeling among the dancers everybody cried out: *"Hola,"* and shouted that the foreigners must sing a song.

"After dinner," cried Lyaeus as he straightened his necktie. "We haven't eaten for a year and a half!"

The *padrón*, a red thick-necked individual with a week's white bristle on his face, came up to them holding out hands as big as hams.

"You are going to Toledo for Carnival? O how lucky the young are, travelling all over the world." He turned to the company with a gesture; "I was like that when I was young."

They followed him into the kitchen, where they ensconced themselves on either side of a cave of a fireplace in which burned a fire all too small. The hunchbacked woman with a face like tanned leather who was tending the numerous steaming pots that stood about the hearth, noticing that they were shivering, heaped dry twigs on it that crackled and burst into flame and gave out a warm spicy tang.

"To-morrow's Carnival," she said. "We mustn't stint ourselves." Then she handed them each a plate of soup full of bread in which poached eggs floated, and the *padrón* drew the table near the fire and sat down opposite them, peering with interest into their faces while they ate.

After a while he began talking. From outside the hand-clapping and the sound of castanettes continued interrupted by intervals of shouting and laughter and an occasional snatch from the song that ended every verse with *"y mañana Carnaval."*

"I travelled when I was your age," he said. "I have been to America . . . Nueva York, Montreal, Buenos Aires, Chicago, San Francisco . . . Selling those little nuts . . . Yes, peanuts. What a country! How many laws there are there, how many policemen. When I was young I did not like it, but now that I am old and own an inn and daughters and all that, *vamos*, I understand. You see in Spain we all do just as we like; then, if we are the sort that goes to church we repent afterwards and fix it up with God. In European, civilized, modern countries everybody learns what he's got to do and what he must not do . . . That's why they have so many laws . . . Here the police are just to help the government plunder and steal all it wants . . . But that's not so in America . . ."

"The difference is," broke in Telemachus, "as Butler put it, between living under the law and living under grace. I should rather live under gra . . ." But he thought of the maxims of Penelope and was silent.

"But after all we know how to sing," said the *Padrón*. "Will you have coffee with cognac? . . . And poets, man alive, what poets!"

The *padrón* stuck out his chest, put one hand in the black sash that held up his trousers and recited, emphasizing the rhythm with the cognac bottle:

> 'Aquí está Don Juan Tenorio;
> no hay hombre para él . . .
> Búsquenle los reñidores,
> cérquenle los jugadores,
> quien se précie que le ataje,
> a ver si hay quien le aventaje
> en juego, en lid o en amores.'

He finished with a flourish and poured more cognac into the coffee cups.

"*¡Qué bonito!* How pretty!" cried the old hunchbacked woman who sat on her heels in the fireplace.

"That's what we do," said the *padrón*. "We brawl and gamble and seduce women, and we sing and we dance, and then we repent and the priest fixes it up with God. In America they live according to law."

Feeling well-toasted by the fire and well-warmed with food and drink, Lyaeus and Telemachus went to the inn door and looked out on the broad main street of the village where everything was snowy white under the cold stare of the moon. The dancing had stopped in the courtyard. A group of men and boys was moving slowly up the street, each one with a musical instrument. There were the two guitars, frying pans, castanettes, cymbals, and a goatskin bottle of wine that kept being passed from hand to hand. Each time the bottle made a round a new song started. And so they moved slowly up the street in the moonlight.

"Let's join them," said Lyaeus.

"No, I want to get up early so as . . ."

"To see the gesture by daylight!" cried Lyaeus jeeringly. Then he went on: "Tel, you live under the law. Under the law there can be no gestures, only machine movements."

Then he ran off and joined the group of men and boys who were singing and drinking. Telemachus went back to bed. On his way upstairs he cursed the maxims of his mother Penelope. But at any rate to-morrow, in Carnival-time, he would feel the gesture.

XI: Antonio Machado: Poet of Castile

I SPENT fifty thousand pesetas in a year at the military school . . . *J'aime le chic*," said the young artillery officer of whom I had asked the way. He was leading me up the steep cobbled hill that led to the irregular main street of Segovia. A moment before we had passed under the aqueduct that had soared above us arch upon arch into the crimson sky. He had snapped tightly gloved fingers and said: "And what's that good for, I'd like to know. I'd give it all for a puff of gasoline from a Hispano-Suizo . . . D'you know the Hispano-Suizo? And look at this rotten town! There's not a street in it I can speed on in a motorcycle without running down some fool old woman or a squalling brat or other . . . Who's this gentleman you are going to see?"

"He's a poet," I said.

"I like poetry too. I write it . . . light, elegant, about light elegant women." He laughed and twirled the tiny waxed spike that stuck out from each side of his moustache.

He left me at the end of the street I was looking for, and after an elaborate salute walked off saying:

"To think that you should come here from New York to look for an address in such a shabby street, and I so want to go to New York. If I was a poet I wouldn't live here."

The name on the street corner was *Calle de los Desemparados* . . . "Street of Abandoned Children."

We sat a long while in the casino, twiddling spoons in coffee-glasses while a wax-pink fat man played billiards in front of us, being ponderously beaten by a lean brownish swallow-tail with yellow face and walrus whiskers that emitted a rasping *Bueno* after every play. There was talk of Paris and possible new volumes of verse, homage to Walt Whitman, Maragall, questioning about Emily Dickinson. About us was a smell of old horsehair sofas, a buzz of the poignant musty ennui of old towns left centuries ago high and dry on the beach of history. The group grew. Talk of painting: Zuloaga had not come yet, the Zubiaurre brothers had abandoned their Basque coast towns, seduced by the bronze-colored people and the saffron hills of the province of Segovia. Sorolla was dying, another had gone mad. At last someone said, "It's stifling here, let's walk. There is full moon to-night."

There was no sound in the streets but the irregular clatter of our footsteps. The slanting moonlight cut the street into two triangular sections, one enormously black, the other bright, engraved like a silver plate with the lines of doors, roofs, windows, ornaments. Overhead the sky was white and blue like buttermilk. Blackness cut across our path, then there was dazzling light through an arch beyond. Outside the gate we sat in a ring on square fresh-cut stones in which you could still feel a trace of the warmth of the sun. To one side was the lime-washed wall of a house, white fire, cut by a wide oaken door where the moon gave a restless glitter to the spiked nails and the knocker, and above the door red geraniums hanging out of a pot, their color insanely bright in the silver-white glare. The other side a deep glen, the shimmering tops of poplar trees and the sound of a stream. In the dark above the arch of the gate a trembling oil flame showed up the green feet of a painted Virgin. Everybody was talking about *El Buscón*, a story of Quevedo's that takes place mostly in Segovia, a wandering story of thieves and escapes by night through the back doors of brothels, of rope ladders dangling from the windows of great ladies, of secrets overhead in confessionals, and trysts under bridges, and fingers touching significantly in the holy-water fonts of tall cathedrals. A ghostlike wraith of dust blew through the gate. The man next me shivered.

"The dead are stronger than the living," he said. "How little we have; and they . . ."

In the quaver of his voice was a remembering of long mule-trains jingling through the gate, queens in litters hung with patchwork curtains from Samarcand, gold brocades splashed with the clay of deep roads, stained with the blood of ambuscades, bales of silks from Valencia, travelling gangs of Moorish artisans, heavy armed Templars on their way to the Sepulchre, wandering minstrels, sneakthieves, bawds, rowdy strings of knights and foot-soldiers setting out with wine-skins at their saddlebows to cross the passes towards the debatable lands of Extremadura, where there were infidels to kill and cattle to drive off and village girls to rape, all when the gate was as new and crisply cut out of clean stone as the blocks we were sitting on. Down in the valley a donkey brayed long and dismally.

"They too have their nostalgias," said someone sentimentally.

"What they of the old time did not have," came a deep voice from under a bowler hat, "was the leisure to be sad. The sweetness of putrefaction, the long remembering of palely colored moods; they had the sun, we have the colors of its setting. Who shall say which is worth more?"

The man next to me had got to his feet. "A night like this with a moon like this," he said, "we should go to the ancient quarter of the witches."

Gravel crunched under our feet down the road that led out of moonlight into the darkness of the glen—to *San Millán de las brujas*.

You cannot read any Spanish poet of to-day without thinking now and then of Rubén Darío, that prodigious Nicaraguan who collected into his verse all the tendencies of poetry in France and America and the Orient and poured them in a turgid cataract, full of mud and gold-dust, into the thought of the new generation in Spain. Overflowing with beauty and banality, patched out with images and ornaments from Greece and Egypt and France and Japan and his own Central America, symbolist and romantic and Parnassian all at once, Rubén Darío's verse is like those doorways of the Spanish Renaissance where French and Moorish and Italian motives jostle in headlong arabesques, where the vulgarest routine stone-chipping is interlocked with designs and forms of rare beauty and significance. Here and there among the turgid muddle, out of the impact of unassimilated things, comes a spark of real poetry. And that spark can be said—as truly as anything of the sort can be said—to be the motive force of the whole movement of renovation in Spanish poetry. Of course the poets have not been content to be influenced by the outside world only through Darío. Baudelaire and Verlaine had a very large direct influence, once the way was opened, and their influence succeeded in curbing the lush impromptu manner of romantic Spanish verse. In Antonio Machado's work—and he is beginning to be generally considered the central figure—there is a restraint and terseness of phrase rare in any poetry.

I do not mean to imply that Machado can be called in any real sense a pupil of either Darío or Verlaine; rather one would say that in a generation occupied largely in more or less unsuccessful imitation of these poets, Machado's poetry stands out as particularly original and personal. In fact, except for the verse of Juan Ramón Jiménez, it would be in America and England rather than in Spain, in Aldington and Amy Lowell, that one would find analogous aims and methods. The influence of the symbolists and the turbulent experimenting of the Nicaraguan broke down the bombastic romantic style current in Spain, as it was broken down everywhere else in the middle nineteenth century. In Machado's work a new method is being built up, that harks back more to early ballads and the verse of the first moments of the Renaissance than to anything foreign, but which shows the same enthusiasm for the rhythms of ordinary speech and for the simple pictorial expression of undoctored emotion that we find in the renovators of poetry the world over. *Campos de Castilla*, his first volume to be widely read, marks an epoch in Spanish poetry.

Antonio Machado's verse is taken up with places. It is obsessed with the old Spanish towns where he has lived, with the mellow sadness of tortuous streets and of old houses that have soaked up the lives of generations upon generations of men, crumbling in the flaming silence of summer noons or in the icy blast off the mountains in winter. Though born in Andalusia, the bitter strength of the Castilian plain, where half-deserted cities stand aloof from the world, shrunken into their walls, still dreaming of the ages of faith and conquest, has subjected his imagination, and the purity of Castilian speech has dominated his writing, until his poems seem as Castilian as Don Quixote.

> "My childhood: memories of a courtyard in Seville,
> and of a bright garden where lemons hung ripening.
> My youth: twenty years in the land of Castile.
> My history: a few events I do not care to remember."

So Machado writes of himself. He was born in the eighties, has been a teacher of French in government schools in Soria and Baeza and at present in Segovia—all old Spanish cities very mellow and very stately—and has made the migration to Paris customary with Spanish writers and artists. He says in the *Poema de un Día*:

> Here I am, already a teacher
> of modern languages, who yesterday
> was a master of the gai scavoir
> and the nightingale's apprentice.

He has published three volumes of verse, *Soledades* ("Solitudes"), *Campos de Castilla* ("Fields of Castile"), and *Soledades y Galerías* ("Solitudes and Galleries"), and recently a government institution, the Residencia de Estudiantes, has published his complete works up to date.

The following translations are necessarily inadequate, as the poems depend very much on modulations of rhythm and on the expressive fitting together of words impossible to render in a foreign language. He uses rhyme comparatively little, often substituting assonance in accordance with the peculiar traditions of Spanish prosody. I have made no attempt to imitate his form exactly.

I

Yes, come away with me—fields of Soria,
quiet evenings, violet mountains,
aspens of the river, green dreams
of the grey earth,
bitter melancholy
of the crumbling city—
perhaps it is that you have become
the background of my life.

Men of the high Numantine plain,
who keep God like old—Christians,
may the sun of Spain fill you
with joy and light and abundance!

II

A frail sound of a tunic trailing
across the infertile earth,
and the sonorous weeping
of the old bells.
The dying embers
of the horizon smoke.
White ancestral ghosts
go lighting the stars.

—Open the balcony-window. The hour
of illusion draws near . . .
The afternoon has gone to sleep
and the bells dream.

III

Figures in the fields against the sky!
Two slow oxen plough
on a hillside early in autumn,
and between the black heads bent down
under the weight of the yoke,
hangs and sways a basket of reeds,
a child's cradle;
And behind the yoke stride
a man who leans towards the earth
and a woman who, into the open furrows,
throws the seed.
Under a cloud of carmine and flame,
in the liquid green gold of the setting,
their shadows grow monstrous.

IV

Naked is the earth
and the soul howls to the wan horizon
like a hungry she-wolf.
                              What do you seek,
poet, in the sunset?

Bitter going, for the path
weighs one down, the frozen wind,
and the coming night and the bitterness
of distance . . . On the white path
the trunks of frustrate trees show black,
on the distant mountains
there is gold and blood. The sun dies . . .

                    What do you seek,
poet, in the sunset?

V

Silver hills and grey ploughed lands,
violet outcroppings of rock
through which the Duero traces
its curve like a cross-bow
about Soria,
dark oak-wood, wild cliffs,
bald peaks,
and the white roads and the aspens of the river.

Afternoons of Soria, mystic and warlike,
to-day I am very sad for you,
sadness of love,
Fields of Soria,
where it seems that the rocks dream,
come with me! Violet rocky outcroppings,
silver hills and grey ploughed lands.

VI

We think to create festivals
of love out of our love,
to burn new incense
on untrodden mountains;
and to keep the secret
of our pale faces,
and why in the bacchanals of life
we carry empty glasses,

while with tinkling echoes and laughing
foams the gold must of the grape. . . .
A hidden bird among the branches
of the solitary park
whistles mockery. . . . We feel
the shadow of a dream in our wine-glass,
and something that is earth in our flesh
feels the dampness of the garden like a caress.

VII

I have been back to see the golden aspens,
aspens of the road along the Duero
between San Polo and San Saturio,
beyond the old stiff walls
of Soria, barbican
towards Aragon of the Castilian lands.

These poplars of the river, that chime
when the wind blows their dry leaves
to the sound of the water,
have in their bark the names of lovers,
initials and dates.
Aspens of love where yesterday
the branches were full of nightingales,
aspens that to-morrow will sing
under the scented wind of the springtime,
aspens of love by the water
that speeds and goes by dreaming,
aspens of the bank of the Duero,
come away with me.

VIII

Cold Soria, clear Soria,
key of the outlands,
with the warrior castle
in ruins beside the Duero,
and the stiff old walls,
and the blackened houses.

Dead city of barons
and soldiers and huntsmen,
whose portals bear the shields
of a hundred hidalgos;
city of hungry greyhounds,
of lean greyhounds
that swarm
among the dirty lanes
and howl at midnight
when the crows caw.

Cold Soria! The clock
of the Lawcourts has struck one.
Soria, city of Castile,
so beautiful under the moon.

IX
AT A FRIEND'S BURIAL

They put him away in the earth
a horrible July afternoon
under a sun of fire.

A step from the open grave
grew roses with rotting petals
among geraniums of bitter fragrance,
red-flowered. The sky
a pale blue. A wind
hard and dry.

Hanging on the thick ropes,
the two gravediggers
let the coffin heavily
down into the grave.

It struck the bottom with a sharp sound,
solemnly, in the silence.

The sound of a coffin striking the earth
is something unutterably solemn.

The heavy clods broke into dust
over the black coffin.

A white mist of dust rose in the air
out of the deep grave.

And you, without a shadow now, sleep.
Long peace to your bones.
For all time
you sleep a tranquil and a real sleep.

X
THE IBERIAN GOD

Like the cross-bowman,
the gambler in the song,
the Iberian had an arrow for his god
when he shattered the grain with hail
and ruined the fruits of autumn;
and a gloria when he fattened
the barley and the oats
that were to make bread to-morrow.
"God of ruin,
I worship because I wait and because I fear.
I bend in prayer to the earth
a blasphemous heart.

"Lord, through whom I snatch my bread with pain,
I know your strength, I know my slavery.
Lord of the clouds in the east
that trample the country-side,
of dry autumns and late frosts
and of the blasts of heat that scorch the harvests!

"Lord of the iris in the green meadows
where the sheep graze,
Lord of the fruit the worms gnaw
and of the hut the whirlwind shatters,
your breath gives life to the fire in the hearth,

your warmth ripens the tawny grain,
and your holy hand, St. John's eve,
hardens the stone of the green olive.

"Lord of riches and poverty,
Of fortune and mishap,
who gives to the rich luck and idleness,
and pain and hope to the poor!

"Lord, Lord, in the inconstant wheel
of the year I have sown my sowing
that has an equal chance with the coins
of a gambler sown on the gambling-table!

"Lord, a father to-day, though stained with yesterday's blood,
two-faced of love and vengeance,
to you, dice cast into the wind,
goes my prayer, blasphemy and praise!"

This man who insults God in his altars,
without more care of the frown of fate,
also dreamed of paths across the seas
and said: "It is God who walks upon the waters."

Is it not he who put God above war,
beyond fate,
beyond the earth,
beyond the sea and death?

Did he not give the greenest bough
of the dark-green Iberian oak
for God's holy bonfire,
and for love flame one with God?

But to-day . . . What does a day matter?
for the new household gods
there are plains in forest shade
and green boughs in the old oak-woods.

Though long the land waits
for the curved plough to open the first furrow,
there is sowing for God's grain
under thistles and burdocks and nettles.

What does a day matter? Yesterday waits
for to-morrow, to-morrow for infinity;
men of Spain, neither is the past dead,
nor is to-morrow, nor yesterday, written.

Who has seen the face of the Iberian God?
I wait
for the Iberian man who with strong hands
will carve out of Castilian oak
The parched God of the grey land.

XII: A Catalan Poet

It is time for sailing; the swallow has come chattering and the mellow west wind; the meadows are already in bloom; the sea is silent and the waves the rough winds pummeled. Up anchors and loose the hawsers, sailor, set every stitch of canvas. This I, Priapos the harbor god, command you, man, that you may sail for all manner of ladings. (Leonidas in the Greek Anthology.)

CATALONIA like Greece is a country of mountains and harbors, where the farmers and herdsmen of the hills can hear in the morning the creak of oars and the crackling of cordage as the great booms of the wing-shaped sails are hoisted to the tops of the stumpy masts of the fishermen's boats. Barcelona with its fine harbor nestling under the towering slopes of Montjuic has been a trading city since most ancient times. In the middle ages the fleets of its stocky merchants were the economic scaffolding which underlay the pomp and heraldry of the great sea kingdom of the Aragonese. To this day you can find on old buildings the arms of the kings of Aragon and the counts of Barcelona in Mallorca and Manorca and Ibiza and Sardinia and Sicily and Naples. It follows that when Catalonia begins to reëmerge as a nucleus of national consciousness after nearly four centuries of subjection to Castile, poets speaking Catalan, writing Catalan, shall be poets of the mountains and of the sea.

Yet this time the motor force is not the sailing of white argosies towards the east. It is textile mills, stable, motionless, drawing about them muddled populations, raw towns, fattening to new arrogance the descendants of those stubborn burghers who gave the kings of Aragon and of Castile such vexing moments. (There's a story of one king who was so chagrined by the tight-pursed contrariness of the Cortes of Barcelona that he died of a broken heart in full parliament assembled.) This growth of industry during the last century, coupled with the reawakening of the whole Mediterranean, took form politically in the Catalan movement for secession from Spain, and in literature in the resurrection of Catalan thought and Catalan language.

Naturally the first generation was not interested in the manufactures that were the dynamo that generated the ferment of their lives. They had first to state the emotions of the mountains and the sea and of ancient heroic stories that had been bottled up in their race during centuries of inexpressiveness. For another generation perhaps the symbols will be the cluck of oiled cogs, the whirring of looms, the dragon forms of smoke spewed out of tall chimneys, and the substance will be the painful struggle for freedom, for sunnier, richer life of the huddled mobs of the slaves of the machines. For the first men conscious of their status as Catalans the striving was to make permanent their individual lives in terms of political liberty, of the mist-capped mountains and the changing sea.

Of this first generation was Juan Maragall who died in 1912, five years after the shooting of Ferrer, after a life spent almost entirely in Barcelona writing for newspapers,—as far as one can gather, a completely peaceful well-married existence, punctuated by a certain amount of political agitation in the cause of the independence of Catalonia, the life of a placid and recognized literary figure; *"un maître"* the French would have called him.

Perhaps six centuries before, in Palma de Mallorca, a young nobleman, a poet, a skilled player on the lute had stood tiptoe for attainment before the high-born and very stately lady he had courted through many moonlight nights, when her eye had chilled his quivering love suddenly and she had pulled open her bodice with both hands and shown him her breasts, one white and firm and the other swollen black and purple with cancer. The horror of the sight of such beauty rotting away before his eyes had turned all his passion inward and would have made him a saint had his ideas been more orthodox; as it was the Blessed Ramón Lull lived to write many mystical works in Catalan and Latin, in which he sought the love of God in the love of Earth after the manner of the sufi of Persia. Eventually he attained bloody martyrdom arguing with the sages in some North African town. Somehow the spirit of the tortured thirteenth-century mystic was born again in the calm Barcelona journalist, whose life was untroubled by the impact of events as could only be a life comprising the last half of the nineteenth century. In Maragall's

writings modulated in the lovely homely language of the
peasants and fishermen of Catalonia, there flames again the
passionate metaphor of Lull.

Here is a rough translation of one of his best known
poems:

> At sunset time
> drinking at the spring's edge
> I drank down the secrets
> of mysterious earth.
>
> Deep in the runnel
> I saw the stainless water
> born out of darkness
> for the delight of my mouth,
>
> and it poured into my throat
> and with its clear spurting
> there filled me entirely
> mellowness of wisdom.
>
> When I stood straight and looked,
> mountains and woods and meadows
> seemed to me otherwise,
> everything altered.
>
> Above the great sunset
> there already shone through the glowing
> carmine contours of the clouds
> the white sliver of the new moon.
>
> It was a world in flower
> and the soul of it was I.
>
> I the fragrant soul of the meadows
> that expands at flower-time and reaping-time.
>
> I the peaceful soul of the herds
> that tinkle half-hidden by the tall grass.
>
> I the soul of the forest that sways in waves
> like the sea, and has as far horizons.
>
> And also I was the soul of the willow tree
> that gives every spring its shade.

I the sheer soul of the cliffs
where the mist creeps up and scatters.

And the unquiet soul of the stream
that shrieks in shining waterfalls.

I was the blue soul of the pond
that looks with strange eyes on the wanderer.

I the soul of the all-moving wind
and the humble soul of opening flowers.

I was the height of the high peaks . . .

The clouds caressed me with great gestures
and the wide love of misty spaces
clove to me, placid.

I felt the delightfulness of springs
born in my flanks, gifts of the glaciers;
and in the ample quietude of horizons
I felt the reposeful sleep of storms.

And when the sky opened about me
and the sun laughed on my green planes
people, far off, stood still all day
staring at my sovereign beauty.

But I, full of the lust
that makes furious the sea and mountains
lifted myself up strongly through the sky
lifted the diversity of my flanks and entrails . . .

At sunset time
drinking at the spring's edge
I drank down the secrets
of mysterious earth.

The sea and mountains, mist and cattle and yellow broom-flowers, and fishing boats with lateen sails like dark wings against the sunrise towards Mallorca: delight of the nose and the eyes and the ears in all living perceptions until the poison of other-worldliness wells up suddenly in him and he is a Christian and a mystic full of echoes of old soul-torturing. In

Maragall's most expressive work, a sequence of poems called
El Comte Arnau, all this is synthesized. These are from the
climax.

> All the voices of the earth
> acclaim count Arnold
> because from the dark trial
> he has come back triumphant.

> "Son of the earth, son of the earth,
> count Arnold,
> now ask, now ask
> what cannot you do?"

> "Live, live, live forever,
> I would never die:
> to be like a wheel revolving;
> to live with wine and a sword."

> "Wheels roll, roll,
> but they count the years."

> "Then I would be a rock
> immobile to suns or storms."

> "Rock lives without life
> forever impenetrable."

> "Then the ever-moving sea
> that opens a path for all things."

> "The sea is alone, alone,
> you go accompanied."

> "Then be the air when it flames
> in the light of the deathless sun."

> "But air and sun are loveless,
> ignorant of eternity."

> "Then to be man more than man
> to be earth palpitant."

> "You shall be wheel and rock,
> you shall be the mist-veiled sea

you shall be the air in flame,
you shall be the whirling stars,
you shall be man more than man
for you have the will for it.
You shall run the plains and hills,
all the earth that is so wide,
mounted on a horse of flame
you shall be tireless, terrible
as the tramp of the storms.
All the voices of earth
will cry out whirling about you.
They will call you spirit in torment
call you forever damned."

Night. All the beauty of Adalaisa
asleep at the feet of naked Christ.
Arnold goes pacing a dark path;
there is silence among the mountains;
in front of him the rustling lisp of a river,
a pool . . . Then it is lost and soundless.
Arnold stands under the sheer portal.

He goes searching the cells for Adalaisa
and sees her sleeping, beautiful, prone
at the feet of the naked Christ, without veil
without kerchief, without cloak, gestureless,
without any defense, there, sleeping . . .

She had a great head of turbulent hair.

"How like fine silk your hair, Adalaisa,"
thinks Arnold. But he looks at her silently.
She sleeps, she sleeps and little by little
a flush spreads over all her face
as if a dream had crept through her gently
until she laughs aloud very softly
with a tremulous flutter of the lips.

"What amorous lips, Adalaisa,"
thinks Arnold. But he looks at her silently.

A great sigh swells through her, sleeping,
like a seawave, and fades to stillness.

"What sighs swell in your breast, Adalaisa,"
thinks Arnold. But he stares at her silently.

But when she opens her eyes he, awake,
tingling, carries her off in his arms.

When they burst out into the open fields
it is day.

But the fear of life gushes suddenly to muddy the clear wellspring of sensation, and the poet, beaten to his knees, writes:

And when the terror-haunted moment comes
to close these earthly eyes of mine,
open for me, Lord, other greater eyes
to look upon the immensity of your face.

But before that moment comes, through the medium of an extraordinarily terse and unspoiled language, a language that has not lost its earthy freshness by mauling and softening at the hands of literary generations, what a lilting crystal-bright vision of things. It is as if the air of the Mediterranean itself, thin, brilliant, had been hammered into cadences. The verse is leaping and free, full of echoes and refrains. The images are sudden and unlabored like the images in the Greek anthology: a hermit released from Nebuchadnezzar's spell gets to his feet "like a bear standing upright"; fishing boats being shoved off the beach slide into the sea one by one "like village girls joining a dance"; on a rough day the smacks with reefed sails "skip like goats at the harbor entrance." There are phrases like "the great asleepness of the mountains"; "a long sigh like a seawave through her sleep"; "my speech of her is like a flight of birds that lead your glance into intense blue sky"; "the disquieting unquiet sea." Perhaps it is that the eyes are sharpened by the yearning to stare through the brilliant changing forms of things into some intenser beyond. Perhaps it takes a hot intoxicating draught of divinity to melt into such white fire the various colors of the senses. Perhaps earthly joy is intenser for the beckoning flames of hell.

The daily life, too, to which Maragall aspires seems strangely out of another age. That came home to me most strongly once, talking to a Catalan after a mountain scramble in the eastern end of Mallorca. We sat looking at the sea that was violet with sunset, where the sails of the homecoming fishing boats were the wan yellow of primroses. Behind us the hills were sharp pyrites blue. From a window in the adobe hut at one side of us came a smell of sizzling olive oil and tomatoes and peppers and the muffled sound of eggs being beaten. We were footsore, hungry, and we talked about women and love. And after all it was marriage that counted, he told me at last, women's bodies and souls and the love of them were all very well, but it was the ordered life of a family, children, that counted; the family was the immortal chain on which lives were strung; and he recited this quatrain, saying, in that proud awefilled tone with which Latins speak of creative achievement, "By our greatest poet, Juan Maragall":

> Canta esposa, fila i canta
> que el patí em faras suau
> Quan l'esposa canta i fila
> el casal s'adorm en pau.

It was hard explaining how all our desires lay towards the completer and completer affirming of the individual, that we in Anglo-Saxon countries felt that the family was dead as a social unit, that new cohesions were in the making.

"I want my liberty," he broke in, "as much as—as Byron did, liberty of thought and action." He was silent a moment; then he said simply, "But I want a wife and children and a family, mine, mine."

Then the girl who was cooking leaned out of the window to tell us in soft Mallorquin that supper was ready. She had a full brown face flushed on the cheekbones and given triangular shape like an El Greco madonna's face by the bright blue handkerchief knotted under the chin. Her breasts hung out from her body, solid like a Victory's under the sleek grey shawl as she leaned from the window. In her eyes that were sea-grey there was an unimaginable calm. I thought of Pe-

nelope sitting beside her loom in a smoky-raftered hall, grey
eyes looking out on a sailless sea. And for a moment I understood the Catalan's phrase: the family was the chain on which
lives were strung, and all of Maragall's lyricizing of wifehood,

> When the wife sits singing as she spins
> all the house can sleep in peace.

From the fishermen's huts down the beach came an intense
blue smoke of fires; above the soft rustle of the swell among
the boats came the chatter of many sleepy voices, like the
sound of sparrows in a city park at dusk. The day dissolved
slowly in utter timelessness. And when the last fishing boat
came out of the dark sea, the tall slanting sail folding suddenly
as the wings of a sea-gull alighting, the red-brown face of the
man in the bow was the face of returning Odysseus. It was
not the continuity of men's lives I felt, but their oneness. On
that beach, beside that sea, there was no time.

When we were eating in the whitewashed room by the light
of three brass olive oil lamps, I found that my argument had
suddenly crumbled. What could I, who had come out of
ragged and barbarous outlands, tell of the art of living to a
man who had taught me both system and revolt? So am I, to
whom the connubial lyrics of Patmore and Ella Wheeler
Wilcox have always seemed inexpressible soiling of possible
loveliness, forced to bow before the rich cadences with which
Juan Maragall, Catalan, poet of the Mediterranean, celebrates
the *familia*.

And in Maragall's work it is always the Mediterranean that
one feels, the Mediterranean and the men who sailed on it in
black ships with bright pointed sails. Just as in Homer and
Euripides and Pindar and Theocritus and in that tantalizing
kaleidoscope, the Anthology, beyond the grammar and the
footnotes and the desolation of German texts there is always
the rhythm of sea waves and the smell of well-caulked ships
drawn up on dazzling beaches, so in Maragall, beyond the
graceful well-kept literary existence, beyond wife and children
and pompous demonstrations in the cause of abstract freedom, there is the sea lashing the rocky shins of the Pyrenees,—actual, dangerous, wet.

In this day when we Americans are plundering the earth far and near for flowers and seeds and ferments of literature in the hope, perhaps vain, of fallowing our thin soil with manure rich and diverse and promiscuous so that the somewhat sickly plants of our own culture may burst sappy and green through the steel and cement and inhibitions of our lives, we should not forget that northwest corner of the Mediterranean where the Langue d'Oc is as terse and salty as it was in the days of Pierre Vidal, whose rhythms of life, intrinsically Mediterranean, are finding new permanence—poetry richly ordered and lucid.

To the Catalans of the last fifty years has fallen the heritage of the oar which the cunning sailor Odysseus dedicated to the Sea, the earth-shaker, on his last voyage. And the first of them is Maragall.

XIII: Talk by the Road

O_{N THE} top step Telemachus found a man sitting with his head in his hands moaning *"¡Ay de mí!"* over and over again.

"I beg pardon," he said stiffly, trying to slip by.

"Did you see the function this evening, sir?" asked the man looking up at Telemachus with tears streaming from his eyes. He had a yellow face with lean blue chin and jowls shaven close and a little waxed moustache that had lost all its swagger for the moment as he had the ends of it in his mouth.

"What function?"

"In the theatre . . . I am an artist, an actor." He got to his feet and tried to twirl his ragged moustaches back into shape. Then he stuck out his chest, straightened his waistcoat so that the large watchchain clinked, and invited Telemachus to have a cup of coffee with him.

They sat at the black oak table in front of the fire. The actor told how there had been only twelve people at his show. How was he to be expected to make his living if only twelve people came to see him? And the night before Carnival, too, when they usually got such a crowd. He'd learned a new song especially for the occasion, too good, too artistic for these pigs of provincials.

"Here in Spain the stage is ruined, ruined!" he cried out finally.

"How ruined?" asked Telemachus.

"The *Zarzuela* is dead. The days of the great writers of *zarzuela* have gone never to return. O the music, the lightness, the jollity of the *zarzuelas* of my father's time! My father was a great singer, a tenor whose voice was an enchantment . . . I know the princely life of a great singer of *zarzuela* . . . When a small boy I lived it . . . And now look at me!"

Telemachus thought how strangely out of place was the actor's anæmic wasplike figure in this huge kitchen where everything was dark, strong-smelling, massive. Black beams with here and there a trace of red daub on them held up the ceiling and bristled with square iron spikes from which hung hams and sausages and white strands of garlic. The table at which they sat was an oak slab, black from smoke and generations of spillings, firmly straddled on thick trestles. Over the fire hung a copper pot, sooty, with a glitter of grease on it where the soup had boiled over. When one leaned to put a bundle of sticks on the fire one could see up the chimney an oblong patch of blackness spangled with stars. On the edge of the hearth was the great hunched figure of the *padrón*, half asleep, a silk handkerchief round his head, watching the coffee-pot.

"It was an elegant life, full of voyages," went on the actor. "South America, Naples, Sicily, and all over Spain. There were formal dinners, receptions, ceremonial dress . . . Ladies of high society came to congratulate us . . . I played all the child rôles . . . When I was fourteen a duchess fell in love with me. And now, look at me, ragged, dying of hunger—not even able to fill a theatre in this hog of a village. In Spain they have lost all love of the art. All they want is foreign importations, Viennese musical comedies, smutty farces from Paris . . ."

"With cognac or rum?" the *padrón* roared out suddenly in his deep voice, swinging the coffee pot up out of the fire.

"Cognac," said the actor. "What rotten coffee!" He gave little petulant sniffs as he poured sugar into his glass.

The wail of a baby rose up suddenly out of the dark end of the kitchen.

The actor took two handfuls of his hair and yanked at them.

"*Ay* my nerves!" he shrieked. The baby wailed louder in spasm after spasm of yelling. The actor jumped to his feet, "¡Dolóres, Dolóres, *ven acá*!"

After he had called several times a girl came into the room padding softly on bare feet and stood before him tottering sleepily in the firelight. Her heavy lids hung over her eyes. A strand of black hair curled round her full throat and spread raggedly over her breasts. She had pulled a blanket over her shoulders but through a rent in her coarse nightgown the fire threw a patch of red glow curved like a rose petal about one brown thigh.

"*¡Qué desvergonza'a!* . . . How shameless!" muttered the *padrón*.

The actor was scolding her in a shrill endless whine. The girl stood still without answering, her teeth clenched to keep them

from chattering. Then she turned without a word and brought
the baby from the packing box in which he lay at the end
of the room, and drawing the blanket about both her and the
child crouched on her heels very close to the flame with her
bare feet in the ashes. When the crying had ceased she turned
to the actor with a full-lipped smile and said, "There's nothing
the matter with him, Paco. He's not even hungry. You woke
him up, the poor little angel, talking so loud."

She got to her feet again, and with slow unspeakable dignity walked back and forth across the end of the room with
the child at her breast. Each time she turned she swung the
trailing blanket round with a sudden twist of her body
from the hips.

Telemachus watched her furtively, sniffing the hot aroma of
coffee and cognac from his glass, and whenever she turned
the muscles of his body drew into tight knots from joy.

"*Es buena chica*. . . . She's a nice kid, from Malaga. I
picked her up there. A little stupid . . . But these days . . ."
the actor was saying with much shrugging of the shoulders.
"She dances well, but the public doesn't like her. *No tiene
cara de parisiana*. She hasn't the Parisian air. . . . But these
days, *vamos*, one can't be too fastidious. This taste for French
plays, French women, French cuisine, it's ruined the Spanish
theatre."

The fire flared crackling. Telemachus sat sipping his coffee
waiting for the unbearable delight of the swing of the girl's
body as she turned to pace back towards him across the
room.

XIV: Benavente's Madrid

ALL the gravel paths of the Plaza Santa Ana were encumbered with wicker chairs. At one corner seven blind musicians all in a row, with violins, a cello, guitars and a mournful cornet, toodled and wheezed and twiddled through the "Blue Danube." At another a crumpled old man, with a monkey dressed in red silk drawers on his shoulder, ground out "*la Paloma*" from a hurdygurdy. In the middle of the green plot a fountain sparkled in the yellow light that streamed horizontally from the cafés fuming with tobacco smoke on two sides of the square, and ragged guttersnipes dipped their legs in the slimy basin round about it, splashing one another, rolling like little colts in the grass. From the cafés and the wicker chairs and tables, clink of glasses and dominoes, patter of voices, scuttle of waiters with laden trays, shouts of men selling shrimps, prawns, fried potatoes, watermelon, nuts in little cornucopias of red, green, or yellow paper. Light gleamed on the buff-colored disk of a table in front of me, on the rims of two beer-mugs, in the eyes of a bearded man with an aquiline nose very slender at the bridge who leaned towards me talking in a deep even voice, telling me in swift lisping Castilian stories of Madrid. First of the Madrid of Felipe Cuarto: *corridas* in the Plaza Mayor, *auto da fé*, pictures by Velasquez on view under the arcade where now there is a doughnut and coffee shop, pompous coaches painted vermilion, cobalt, gilded, stuffed with ladies in vast bulge of damask and brocade, plumed cavaliers, pert ogling pages, lurching and swaying through the foot-deep stinking mud of the streets; plays of Calderon and Lope presented in gardens tinkling with jewels and sword-chains where ladies of the court flirted behind ostrich fans with stiff lean-faced lovers. Then Goya's Madrid: riots in the Puerta del Sol, *majas* leaning from balconies, the fair of San Isidro by the river, scuttling of ragged guerrilla bands, brigands and patriots; tramp of the stiffnecked grenadiers of Napoleon; pompous little men in short-tailed wigs dying the *dos de Mayo* with phrases from Mirabeau on their lips under the brick arch of the arsenal; frantic carnivals of the Burial of the Sardine; naked backs of flagellants dripping blood, lovers hiding under the hoop-skirts of the queen. Then the romantic Madrid of the thirties, Larra, Becquer, Espronceda, Byronic gestures, vigils in grave-yards, duels, struttings among the box-alleys of the Retiro, pale young men in white stocks shooting themselves in attics along the Calle Mayor. "And now," the voice became sud-denly gruff with anger, "look at Madrid. They closed the Café Suizo, they are building a subway, the Castellana looks more like the Champs Elysées every day . . . It's only on the stage that you get any remnant of the real Madrid. Benavente is the last *madrileño. Tiene el sentido de lo castizo.* He has the sense of the . . ." all the end of the evening went to the dis-cussion of the meaning of the famous word *"castizo."*

The very existence of such a word in a language argues an acute sense of style, of the manner of doing things. Like all words of real import its meaning is a gamut, a section of a spectrum rather than something fixed and irrevocable. The first implication seems to be "according to Hoyle," following tradition: a neatly turned phrase, an essentially Castilian ca-dence, is *castizo*; a piece of pastry or a poem in the old tradi-tion are *castizo*, or a compliment daintily turned, or a cloak of the proper fullness with the proper red velvet-bordered lining gracefully flung about the ears outside of a café. *Lo castizo* is the essence of the local, of the regional, the last stronghold of Castilian arrogance, refers not to the empty shell of traditional observances but to the very core and gesture of them. Ulti-mately *lo castizo* means all that is salty, savourous of the red and yellow hills and the bare plains and the deep *arroyos* and the dust-colored towns full of palaces and belfries, and the beggars in snuff-colored cloaks and the mule-drivers with blankets over their shoulders, and the discursive leanfaced gentlemen grouped about tables at cafés and casinos, and the stout dowagers with mantillas over their gleaming black hair walking to church in the morning with missals clasped in fat hands, all that is acutely indigenous, Iberian, in the life of Castile.

In the flood of industrialism that for the last twenty years has swelled to obliterate landmarks, to bring all the world to the same level of nickel-plated dullness, the theatre in Madrid has been the refuge of *lo castizo*. It has been a theatre of manners and local types and customs, of observation and natural history, where a rather specialized well-trained audience accustomed to satire as the tone of daily conversation was tickled by any portrayal of its quips and cranks. A tradition of character-acting grew up nearer that of the Yiddish theatre than of any other stage we know in America. Benavente and the brothers Quintero have been the playwrights who most typified the school that has been in vogue since the going out of the *drame passionel* style of Echegaray. At present Benavente as director of the *Teatro Nacional* is unquestionably the leading figure. Therefore it is very fitting that Benavente should be in life and works of all *madrileños* the most *castizo*.

Later, as we sat drinking milk in la Granja after a couple of hours of a shabby third-generation Viennese musical show at the Apollo, my friend discoursed to me of the manner of life of the *madrileño* in general and of Don Jacinto Benavente in particular. Round eleven or twelve one got up, took a cup of thick chocolate, strolled on the Castellana under the chestnut trees or looked in at one's office in the theatre. At two one lunched. At three or so one sat a while drinking coffee or anis in the Gato Negro, where the waiters have the air of cabinet ministers and listen to every word of the rather languid discussions on art and letters that while away the afternoon hours. Then as it got towards five one drifted to a matinee, if there chanced to be a new play opening, or to tea somewhere out in the new Frenchified Barrio de Salamanca. Dinner came along round nine; from there one went straight to the theatre to see that all went well with the evening performance. At one the day culminated in a famous *tertulia* at the Café de Lisboa, where all the world met and argued and quarreled and listened to disquisitions and epigrams at tables stacked with coffee glasses amid spiral reek of cigarette smoke.

"But when were the plays written?" I asked.

My friend laughed. "Oh between semicolons," he said, "and *en route*, and in bed, and while being shaved. Here in Madrid you write a comedy between biscuits at breakfast . . . And now that the Metro's open, it's a great help. I know a young poet who tossed off a five-act tragedy, sex-psychology and all, between the Puerta del Sol and Cuatro Caminos!"

"But Madrid's being spoiled," he went on sadly, "at least from the point of view of *lo castizo*. In the last generation all one saw of daylight were sunset and dawn, people used to go out to fight duels where the Residencia de Estudiantes is now, and they had real *tertulias*, *tertulias* where conversation swaggered and parried and lunged, sparing nothing, laughing at everything, for all the world like our unique Spanish hero, Don Juan Tenorio.

> 'Yo a las cabañas baje,
> yo a los palacios subí,
> y los claustros escalé,
> y en todas partes dejé
> memorias amargas de mí.'

Talk ranged from peasant huts to the palaces of Carlist duchesses, and God knows the crows and the cloisters weren't let off scot free. And like good old absurd Tenorio they didn't care if laughter did leave bitter memories, and were willing to wait till their deathbeds to reconcile themselves with heaven and solemnity. But our generation, they all went solemn in their cradles . . . Except for the theatre people, always except for the theatre people! We of the theatres will be *castizo* to the death."

As we left the café, I to go home to bed, my friend to go on to another *tertulia*, he stood for a moment looking back among the tables and glasses.

"What the Agora was to the Athenians," he said, and finished the sentence with an expressive wave of the hand.

It's hard for Anglo-Saxons, anti-social, as suspicious of neighbors as if they still lived in the boggy forests of Finland, city-dwellers for a paltry thirty generations, to understand the publicity, the communal quality of life in the region of the Mediterranean. The first thought when one gets up is to go out of doors to see what people are talking of, the last thing before going to bed is to chat with the neighbors about the events of the day. The home, cloistered off, exclusive, can hardly be said to exist. Instead of the nordic hearth there is the courtyard about which the women sit while the men are away at the marketplace. In Spain this social life centers in the café and the casino. The modern theatre is as directly the offshoot of the café as the old theatre was of the marketplace where people gathered in front of the church porch to see an interlude or mystery acted by travelling players in a wagon. The people who write the plays, the people who act them and the people who see them spend their spare time smoking about marbletop tables, drinking coffee, discussing. Those too poor to buy a drink stand outside in groups on the sunny side of squares. Constant talk about everything that may happen or had happened or will happen manages to butter the bread of life pretty evenly with passion and thought and significance, but one loses the chunks of intensity. There is little chance for the burst dams that suddenly flood the dry watercourse of emotion among more inhibited, less civilized people. Generations upon generations of townsmen have made of life a well-dredged canal, easy-flowing, somewhat shallow.

It follows that the theatre under such conditions shall be talkative, witty, full of neat swift caricaturing, improvised, unselfconscious; at its worst, glib. Boisterous action often, passionate strain almost never. In Echegaray there are hecatombs, half the characters habitually go insane in the last act; tremendous barking but no bite of real intensity. Benavente has recaptured some of Lope de Vega's marvellous quality of adventurous progression. The Quinteros write domestic comedies full of whim and sparkle and tenderness. But expression always seems too easy; there is never the unbearable tension, the utter self-forgetfulness of the greatest drama. The Spanish theatre plays on the nerves and intellect rather than on the great harpstrings of emotion in which all of life is drawn taut.

At present in Madrid even café life is receding before the exigencies of business and the hardly excusable mania for imitating English and American manners. Spain is undergoing great changes in its relation to the rest of Europe, to Latin America, in its own internal structure. Notwithstanding Madrid's wartime growth and prosperity, the city is fast losing ground as the nucleus of the life and thought of Spanish-speaking people. The *madrileño*, lean, cynical, unscrupulous, nocturnal, explosive with a curious sort of febrile wit is becoming extinct. His theatre is beginning to pander to foreign tastes, to be ashamed of itself, to take on respectability and stodginess. Prices of seats, up to 1918 very low, rise continually; the artisans, apprentice boys, loafers, clerks, porters, who formed the back-bone of the audiences can no longer afford the theatre and have taken to the movies instead. Managers spend money on scenery and costumes as a way of attracting fashionables. It has become quite proper for women to go to the theatre. Benavente's plays thus acquire double significance as the summing up and the chief expression of a movement that has reached its hey-day, from which the sap has already been cut off. It is, indeed, the thing to disparage them for their very finest quality, the vividness with which they express the texture of Madrid, the animated humorous mordant conversation about café tables: *lo castizo.*

The first play of his I ever saw, *"Gente Conocida,"* impressed me, I remember, at a time when I understood about one word in ten and had to content myself with following the general modulation of things, as carrying on to the stage, the moment the curtain rose, the very people, intonations, phrases, that were stirring in the seats about me. After the first act a broad-bosomed lady in black silk leaned back in the seat beside me sighing comfortably *"Qué castizo es este Benavente,"* and then went into a volley of approving chirpings. The full import of her enthusiasm did not come to me until much later when I read the play in the comparative light of a surer knowledge of Castilian, and found that it was a most vitriolic dissecting of the manner of life of that very dowager's own circle, a showing up of the predatory spite of "people of consequence." Here was this society woman, who in any other country would have been indignant, enjoying the annihilation of her kind. On such willingness to play the game of wit, even of abuse, without too much rancor, which is the unction to ease of social intercourse, is founded all the popularity of Benavente's writing. Somewhere in Hugo's Spanish grammar (God save the mark!) is a proverb to the effect that the wind of Madrid is so subtle that it will kill a man without putting out a candle. The same, at their best, can be said of Benavente's satiric comedies:

> El viento de Madrid es tan sutil
> que mata a un hombre y no apaga un candil.

From the opposite bank of the Manzanares, a slimy shrunken stream usually that flows almost hidden under clothes lines where billow the undergarments of all Madrid, in certain lights you can recapture almost entire the silhouette of the city as Goya has drawn it again and again; clots of peeling stucco houses huddling up a flattened hill towards the dome of San Francisco El Grande, then an undulating skyline with cupolas and baroque belfries jutting among the sudden lights and darks of the clouds. Then perhaps the sun will light up with a spreading shaft of light the electric-light factory, the sign on a biscuit manufacturer's warehouse, a row of white blocks of apartments along the edge of town to the north, and instead of odd grimy aboriginal Madrid, it will be a type city in Europe in the industrial era that shines in the sun beyond the blue shadows and creamy flashes of the clothes on the lines. So will it be in a few years with modernized Madrid, with the life of cafés and *paseos* and theatres. There will be moments when in American automats, elegant smokeless tearooms, shiny restaurants built in copy of those of Buenos Aires, someone who has read his Benavente will be able to catch momentary glimpses of old intonations, of witty parries, of noisy bombastic harangues and feel for one pentecostal moment the full and by that time forgotten import of *lo castizo*.

XV: Talk by the Road

THE SUN next morning was tingling warm. Telemachus strode along with a taste of a milky bowl of coffee and crisp *churros* in his mouth and a fresh wind in his hair; his feet rasped pleasantly on the gravel of the road. Behind him the town sank into the dun emerald-striped plain, roofs clustering, huddling more and more under the shadow of the beetling church, and the tower becoming leaner and darker against the steamy clouds that oozed in billowing tiers over the mountains to the north. Crows flapped about the fields where here and there the dark figures of a man and a pair of mules moved up a long slope. On the telegraph wires at a bend in the road two magpies sat, the sunlight glinting, when they stirred, on the white patches on their wings. Telemachus felt well-rested and content with himself.

"After all mother knows best," he was thinking. "That foolish Lyaeus will come dragging himself into Toledo a week from now."

Before noon he came on the same Don Alonso he had seen the day before in Illescas. Don Alonso was stretched out under an olive tree, a long red sausage in his hand, a loaf of bread and a small leather bottle of wine on the sward in front of him. Hitched to the tree, at the bark of which he nibbled with long teeth, was the grey horse.

"*Hola*, my friend," cried Don Alonso, "still bent on Toledo?"

"How soon can I get there?"

"Soon enough to see the castle of San Servando against the sunset. We will go together. You travel as fast as my old nag. But do me the honor of eating something, you must be hungry." Thereupon Don Alonso handed Telemachus the sausage and a knife to peel and slice it with.

"How early you must have started."

They sat together munching bread and sausage to which the sweet pepper mashed into it gave a bright red color, and occasionally, head thrown back, let a little wine squirt into their mouths from the bottle.

Don Alonso waved discursively a bit of sausage held between bread by tips of long grey fingers.

"You are now, my friend, in the heart of Castile. Look, nothing but live-oaks along the gulches and wheat-lands rolling up under a tremendous sky. Have you ever seen more sky? In Madrid there is not so much sky, is there? In your country there is not so much sky? Look at the huge volutes of those clouds. This is a setting for thoughts as mighty in contour as the white cumulus over the Sierra, such as come into the minds of men lean, wind-tanned, long-striding . . ." Don Alonso put a finger to his high yellow forehead. "There is in Castile a potential beauty, my friend, something humane, tolerant, vivid, robust . . . I don't say it is in me. My only merit lies in recognizing it, formulating it, for I am no more than a thinker . . . But the day will come when in this gruff land we shall have flower and fruit."

Don Alonso was smiling with thin lips, head thrown back against the twisted trunk of the olive tree. Then all at once he got to his feet, and after rummaging a moment in the little knapsack that hung over his shoulder, produced absent-mindedly a handful of small white candies the shape of millstones which he stared at in a puzzled way for some seconds.

"After all," he went on, "they make famous sweets in these old Castilian towns. These are *melindres*. Have one . . . When people, d'you know, are kind to children, there are things to be expected."

"Certainly children are indulgently treated in Spain," said Telemachus, his mouth full of almond paste. "They actually seem to like children!"

A cart drawn by four mules tandem led by a very minute donkey with three strings of blue beads round his neck was jingling past along the road. As the canvas curtains of the cover were closed the only evidence of the driver was a sleepy song in monotone that trailed with the dust cloud after the cart. While they stood by the roadside watching the joggle of it away from them down the road, a flushed face was poked out from between the curtains and a voice cried "Hello, Tel!"

"It's Lyaeus," cried Telemachus and ran after the cart bubbling with curiosity to hear his companion's adventures.

With a jangle of mulebells and a hoarse shout from the driver the cart stopped, and Lyaeus tumbled out. His hair was
mussed and there were wisps of hay on his clothes. He immediately stuck his head back in through the curtains. By the
time Telemachus reached him the cart was tinkling its way
down the road again and Lyaeus stood grinning, blinking
sleepy eyes in the middle of the road, in one hand a skin of
wine, in the other a canvas bag.

"What ho!" cried Telemachus.

"Figs and wine," said Lyaeus. Then, as Don Alonso came
up leading his grey horse, he added in an explanatory tone, "I
was asleep in the cart."

"Well?" said Telemachus.

"O it's such a long story," said Lyaeus.

Walking beside them, Don Alonso was reciting into his
horse's ear:

> 'Sigue la vana sombra, el bien fingido.
> El hombre está entregado
> al sueño, de su suerte no cuidando,
> y con paso callado
> el cielo vueltas dando
> las horas del vivir le va hurtando.'

"Whose is that?" said Lyaeus.

"The revolving sky goes stealing his hours of life. . . . But
I don't know," said Don Alonso, "perhaps like you, this Spain
of ours makes ground sleeping as well as awake. What does a
day matter? The driver snores but the good mules jog on
down the appointed road."

Then without another word he jumped on his horse and
with a smile and a wave of the hand trotted off ahead of
them.

XVI: A Funeral in Madrid

Doce días son pasados
después que el Cid acabára
aderézanse las gentes
para salir a batalla
con Búcar ese rey moro
y contra la su canalla.
Cuando fuera media noche
el cuerpo así como estaba
le ponen sobre Babieca
y al caballo lo ataban.

AND when the army sailed out of Valencia the Moors of King Bucar fled before the dead body of the Cid and ten thousand of them were drowned trying to scramble into their ships, among them twenty kings, and the Christians got so much booty of gold and silver among the tents that the poorest of them became a rich man. Then the army continued, the dead Cid riding each day's journey on his horse, across the dry mountains to Sant Pedro de Cardeña in Castile where the king Don Alfonso had come from Toledo, and he seeing the Cid's face still so beautiful and his beard so long and his eyes so flaming ordered that instead of closing the body in a coffin with gold nails they should set it upright in a chair beside the altar, with the sword Tizona in its hand. And there the Cid stayed more than ten years.

Mandó que no se enterrase
sino que el cuerpo arreado
se ponga junto al altar
y a Tizona en la su mano;
así estuvo mucho tiempo
que fueron más de diez años.

In the pass above people were skiing. On the hard snow of the road there were orange-skins. A victoria had just driven by in which sat a bored inflated couple much swathed in furs.

"Where on earth are they going?"

"To the Puerta de Navecerrada," my friend answered.

"But they look as if they'd be happier having tea at Molinero's than paddling about up there in the snow."

"They would be, but it's the style . . . winter sports . . . and all because a lithe little brown man who died two years ago liked the mountains. Before him no *madrileño* ever knew the Sierra existed."

"Who was that?"

"Don Francisco Giner."

That afternoon when it was already getting dark we were scrambling wet, chilled, our faces lashed by the snow, down through drifts from a shoulder of Siete Picos with the mist all about us and nothing but the track of a flock of sheep for a guide. The light from a hut pushed a long gleaming orange finger up the mountainside. Once inside we pulled off our shoes and stockings and toasted our feet at a great fireplace round which were flushed faces, glint of teeth in laughter, schoolboys and people from the university shouting and declaiming, a smell of tea and wet woolens. Everybody was noisy with the rather hysterical excitement that warmth brings after exertion in cold mountain air. Cheeks were purple and tingling. A young man with fuzzy yellow hair told me a story in French about the Emperor of Morocco, and produced a tin of potted blackbirds which it came out were from the said personage's private stores. Unending fountains of tea seethed in two smoke-blackened pots on the hearth. In the back of the hut among leaping shadows were piles of skis and the door, which occasionally opened to let in a new wet snowy figure and shut again on skimming snow-gusts. Everyone was rocked with enormous jollity. Train time came suddenly and we ran and stumbled and slid the miles to the station through the dark, down the rocky path.

In the third-class carriage people sang songs as the train jounced its way towards the plain and Madrid. The man who sat next to me asked me if I knew it was Don Francisco who had had that hut built for the children of the Institución Libre de Inseñanza. Little by little he told me the history of the Krausistas and Francisco Giner de los Ríos and the revolution of 1873, a story like enough to many others in the annals of the nineteenth century movement for education, but in its overtones so intimately Spanish and individual that it came as the explanation of many things I had been wondering about and gave me an inkling of some of the origins of a rather special mentality I had noticed in people I knew about Madrid.

Somewhere in the forties a professor of the Universidad Central, Sanz del Río, was sent to Germany to study philosophy on a government scholarship. Spain was still in the intellectual coma that had followed the failure of the Cortes of Cadiz and the restoration of Fernando Septimo. A decade or more before, Larra, the last flame of romantic revolt, had shot himself for love in Madrid. In Germany, at Heidelberg, Sanz del Rio found dying Krause, the first arch-priest who stood interpreting between Kant and the world. When he returned to Spain he refused to take up his chair at the university saying he must have time to think out his problems, and retired to a tiny room—a room so dark that they say that to read he had to sit on a stepladder under the window in the town of Illescas, where was another student, Greco's San Ildefonso. There he lived several years in seclusion. When he did return to the university it was to refuse to make the profession of political and religious faith required by a certain prime minister named Orovio. He was dismissed and several of his disciples. At the same time Francisco Giner de los Ríos, then a young man who had just gained an appointment with great difficulty because of his liberal ideas, resigned out of solidarity with the rest. In 1868 came the liberal revolution which was the political expression of this whole movement, and all these professors were reinstated. Until the restoration of the Bourbons in '75 Spain was a hive of modernization, Europeanization.

Returned to power Orovio lost no time in republishing his decrees of a profession of faith. Giner, Ascárate, Salmerón and several others were arrested and exiled to distant fortresses when they protested; their friends declared themselves in sympathy and lost their jobs, and many other professors resigned, so that the university was at one blow denuded of its best men. From this came the idea of founding a free university which should be supported entirely by private subscription. From that moment the life of Giner de los Ríos was completely entwined with the growth of the Institución Libre de Inseñanza, which developed in the course of a few years into a coeducational primary school. And directly or indirectly there is not a single outstanding figure in Spanish life to-day whose development was not largely influenced by this dark slender baldheaded old man with a white beard whose picture one finds on people's writing desks.

> . . . Oh, sí, llevad, amigos,
> su cuerpo a la montaña
> a los azules montes
> del ancho Guadarrama,

wrote his pupil, Antonio Machado—and I rather think Machado is the pupil whose name will live the longest—after Don Francisco's death in 1915.

> . . . Yes, carry, friends
> his body to the hills
> to the blue peaks
> of the wide Guadarrama.
> There are deep gulches
> of green pines where the wind sings.
> There is rest for his spirit
> under a cold live oak
> in loam full of thyme, where play
> golden butterflies . . .
> There the master one day
> dreamed new flowerings for Spain.

These are fragments from an elegy by Juan Ramon Jiménez, another poet-pupil of Don Francisco:

"Don Francisco. . . . It seemed that he summed up all that is tender and keen in life: flowers, flames, birds, peaks, children. . . . Now, stretched on his bed, like a frozen river that perhaps still flows under the ice, he is the clear path for endless recurrence. . . . He was like a living statue of himself, a statue of earth, of wind, of water, of fire. He had so freed himself from the husk of every day that talking to him we might have thought we were talking to his image. Yes. One would have said he wasn't going to die: that he had already passed, without anybody's knowing it, beyond death; that he was with us forever, like a spirit.

.   .   .   .

"In the little door of the bedroom one already feels well-being. A trail of the smell of thyme and violets that comes and goes with the breeze from the open window leads like a delicate hand towards where he lies. . . . Peace. All death has done has been to infuse the color of his skin with a deep violet veiling of ashes.

"What a suave smell, and how excellent death is here! No rasping essences, none of the exterior of blackness and crêpe. All this is white and uncluttered, like a hut in the fields in Andalusia, like the white-washed portal of some garden in the south. All just as it was. Only he who was there has gone.

. . . . . .

"The day is fading, with a little wind that has a premonition of spring. In the window panes is a confused mirroring of rosy clouds. The blackbird, the blackbird that he must have heard for thirty years, that he'd have liked to have gone on hearing dead, has come to see if he's listening. Peace. The bedroom and the garden strive quietly light against light: the brightness of the bedroom is stronger and glows out into the afternoon. A sparrow flutters up into the sudden stain with which the sun splashes the top of a tree and sits there twittering. In the shadow below the blackbird whistles once more. Now and then one seems to hear the voice that is silenced forever.

"How pleasant to be here! It's like sitting beside a spring, reading under a tree, like letting the stream of a lyric river carry one away. . . . And one feels like never moving: like plucking to infinity, as one might tear roses to pieces, these white full hours; like clinging forever to this clear teacher in the eternal twilight of this last lesson of austerity and beauty.

. . . . . .

"'Municipal Cemetery' it says on the gate, so that one may know, opposite that other sign 'Catholic Cemetery,' so that one may also know.

"He didn't want to be buried in that cemetery, so opposed to the smiling savourous poetry of his spirit. But it had to be. He'll still hear the blackbirds of the familiar garden. 'After all,' says Cossio, 'I don't think he'll be sorry to spend a little while with Don Julián. . . .'

"Careful hands have taken the dampness out of the earth with thyme; on the coffin they have thrown roses, narcissus, violets. There comes, lost, an aroma of last evening, a bit of the bedroom from which they took so much away. . . .

"Silence. Faint sunlight. Great piles of cloud full of wind drag frozen shadows across us, and through them flying low, black grackles. In the distance Guadarrama, chaste beyond belief, lifts crystals of cubed white light. Some tiny bird trills for a second in the sown fields nearby that are already vaguely greenish, then lights on the creamy top of a tomb, then flies away. . . .

"Neither impatience nor cares; slowness and forgetfulness. . . . Silence. In the silence, the voice of a child walking through the fields, the sound of a sob hidden among the tombstones, the wind, the broad wind of these days. . . .

"I've seen occasionally a fire put out with earth. Innumerable little tongues spurted from every side. A pupil of his who was a mason made for this extinguished fire its palace of mud on a piece of earth two friends kept free. He has at the head a euonymus, young and strong, and at the foot, already full of sprouts with coming spring, an acacia. . . ."

Round El Pardo the evergreen oaks, encinas, are scattered sparsely, tight round heads of blue green, over hills that in summer are yellow like the haunches of lions. From Madrid to El Pardo was one of Don Francisco's favorite walks, out past the jail, where over the gate is written an echo of his teaching: "Abhor the crime but pity the criminal," past the palace of Moncloa with its stately abandoned gardens, and out along the Manzanares by a road through the royal domain where are gamekeepers with shotguns and signs of "Beware the mantraps," then up a low hill from which one sees the Sierra Guadarrama piled up against the sky to the north, greenish snow-peaks above long blue foothills and all the foreground rolling land full of clumps of encinas, and at last into the little village with its barracks and its dilapidated convent and its planetrees in front of the mansion Charles V built. It was under an encina that I sat all one long morning reading up in reviews and textbooks on the theory of law, the life and opinions of Don Francisco. In the moments when the sun shone the heat made the sticky cistus bushes with the glistening white flowers all about me reek with pungence. Then a cool whisp of wind would bring a chill of snow-slopes from the mountains and a passionless indefinite fragrance of distances. At intervals a church bell would toll in a peevish importunate manner from the boxlike convent on the hill opposite. I was reading an account of the philosophical concept of monism, cudgelling my brain with phrases. And his fervent love of nature made the master evoke occasionally in class this beautiful image of the great poet and philosopher Schelling: "Man is the eye with which the spirit of nature contemplates itself"; and then having qualified with a phrase Schelling's expression, he would turn on those who see in nature manifestation of the rough, the gross, the instinctive, and offer for meditation this saying of Michelet: "Cloth woven by a weaver is just as natural as that a spider weaves. All is in one Being, all is in the Idea and for the Idea, the latter being understood in the way Platonic substantialism has been interpreted . . ."

In the grass under my book were bright fronds of moss, among which very small red ants performed prodigies of mountaineering, while along tramped tunnels long black ants scuttled darkly, glinting when the light struck them. The smell of cistus was intense, hot, full of spices as the narrow streets of an oriental town at night. In the distance the mountains piled up in zones olive green, Prussian blue, ultramarine, white. A cold wind-gust turned the pages of the book. Thought and passion, reflection and instinct, affections, emotions, impulses collaborate in the rule of custom, which is revealed not in words declared and promulgated in view of future conduct, but in the act itself, tacit, taken for granted, or, according to the energetic expression of the Digest: *rebus et factis.* Over "factis," sat a little green and purple fly with the body curved under at the table. I wondered vaguely if it was a Mayfly. And then all of a sudden it was clear to me that these books, these dusty philosophical phrases, these mortuary articles by official personages were dimming the legend in my mind, taking the brilliance out of the indirect but extraordinarily personal impact of the man himself. They embalmed the Cid and set him up in the church with his sword in his hand, for all men to see. What sort of legend would a technical disquisition by the archbishop on his theory of the angle of machicolations have generated in men's minds? And what can a saint or a soldier or a founder of institutions leave behind him but a legend? Certainly it is not for the Franciscans that one remembers Francis of Assisi.

And the curious thing about the legend of a personality is that it may reach the highest fervor without being formulated. It is something by itself that stands behind anecdotes, death-notices, elegies.

In Madrid at the funeral of another of the great figures of nineteenth century Spain, Pérez Galdós, I stood on the curb beside a large-mouthed youth with a flattened toadlike face, who was balancing a great white-metal jar of milk on his shoulder. The plumed hearse and the carriages full of flowers had just passed. The street in front of us was a slow stream of people very silent, their feet shuffling, shuffling, feet in patent-leather shoes and spats, feet in square-toed shoes, pointed-toed shoes, *alpargatas*, canvas sandals; people along the sides seemed unable to resist the suction of it, joined in unostentatiously to follow if only a few moments the procession of the legend of Don Benito. The boy with the milk turned to me and said how lucky it was they were burying Galdós, he'd have an excuse for being late for the milk. Then suddenly he pulled his cap off and became enormously excited and began offering cigarettes to everyone round about. He scratched his head and said in the voice of a Saul stricken on the road to Damascus: "How many books he must have written, that gentleman! *¡Cáspita!* . . . It makes a fellow sorry when a gentleman like that dies," and shouldering his pail, his blue tunic fluttering in the wind, he joined the procession.

Like the milk boy I found myself joining the procession of the legend of Giner de los Ríos. That morning under the encina I closed up the volumes on the theory of law and the bulletins with their death-notices and got to my feet and looked over the tawny hills of El Pardo and thought of the little lithe bald-headed man with a white beard like the beard in El Greco's portrait of Covarrubias, who had taught a generation to love the tremendous contours of their country, to climb mountains and bathe in cold torrents, who was the first, it almost seems, to feel the tragic beauty of Toledo, who in a lifetime of coura-geous unobtrusive work managed to stamp all the men and women whose lives remotely touched his with the seal of his personality. Born in Ronda in the wildest part of Andalusia of a family that came from Vélez-Málaga, a white town near the sea in the rich fringes of the Sierra Nevada, he had the mental agility and the sceptical tolerance and the uproarious good na-ture of the people of that region, the sobriety and sinewiness of a mountaineer. His puritanism became a definite part of the creed of the hopeful discontented generations that are gradu-ally, for better or for worse, remoulding Spain. His nostalgia of the north, of fjords where fir trees hang over black tidal waters, of blonde people cheerfully orderly in rectangular blue-tiled towns, became the gospel of Europeanization, of wholesale destruction of all that was individual, savage, African in the Spanish tradition. *Rebus et factis.* And yet none of the things and acts do much to explain the peculiar radiance of his memory, the jovial tenderness with which people tell one about him. The immanence of the man is such that even an outsider, one who like the milk boy at the funeral of Galdós meets the procession accidentally with another errand in his head, is drawn in almost without knowing it. It's impossible to think of him buried in a box in unconsecrated ground in the Cementerio Civil. In Madrid, in the little garden of the Institución where he used to teach the children, in front of a certain open fire in a certain house at El Pardo where they say he loved to sit and talk, I used to half expect to meet him, that some friend would take me to see him as they took people to see Cid in San Pedro de Cardeña.

> Cara tiene de hermosura
> muy hermosa y colorada;
> los ojos igual abiertos
> muy apuesta la su barba
> Non parece que está muerto
> antes vivo semejaba.

II

Although Miguel de Unamuno was recently condemned to fifteen years' imprisonment for *lèse majesté* for some remark made in an article published in a Valencia paper, no attempt has been made either to make him serve the term or to remove him from the chair of Greek at the University of Salamanca. Which proves something about the efficiency of the stand Giner de los Ríos and his friends made fifty years before. Furthermore, at the time of the revolutionary attempt of August, 1917, the removal of Bestiero from his chair caused so many of the faculty to resign and such universal protest that he was reinstated although an actual member of the revolutionary committee and at that time under sentence for life. In 1875 after the fall of the republic it had been in the face of universal popular reaction that the Krausistas founded their free university. The lump is leavened.

But Unamuno. A Basque from the country of Loyola, living in Salamanca in the highest coldest part of the plateau of old Castile, in many senses the opposite of Giner de los Ríos, who was austere as a man on a long pleasant walk doesn't overeat or overdrink so that the walk may be longer and pleasanter, while Unamuno is austere religiously, mystically. Giner de los Ríos was the champion of life, Unamuno is the champion of death. Here is his creed, one of his creeds, from the preface of the *Vida de Don Quijote y Sancho*:

"There is no future: there is never a future. This thing they call the future is one of the greatest lies. To-day is the real future. What will we be to-morrow? There is no to-morrow. What about us to-day, now; that is the only question.

"And as for to-day, all these nincompoops are thoroughly satisfied because they exist to-day, mere existence is enough for them. Existence, ordinary naked existence fills their whole soul. They feel nothing beyond existence.

"But do they exist? Really exist? I think not, because if they did exist, if they really existed, existence would be suffering for them and they wouldn't content themselves with it. If they really and truly existed in time and space they would suffer not being of eternity and infinity. And this suffering, this passion, what is it but the passion of God in us? God who suffers in us from our temporariness and finitude, that divine suffering will burst all the puny bonds of logic with which they try to tie down their puny memories and their puny hopes, the illusion of their past and the illusion of their future.

.   .   .   .   .   .

"Your Quixotic madness has made you more than once speak to me of Quixotism as the new religion. And I tell you that this new religion you propose to me, if it hatched, would have two singular merits. One that its founder, its prophet, Don Quixote—not Cervantes—probably wasn't a real man of flesh and blood at all, indeed we suspect that he was pure fiction. And the other merit would be that this prophet was a ridiculous prophet, people's butt and laughing stock.

"What we need most is the valor to face ridicule. Ridicule is the arm of all the miserable barbers, bachelors, parish priests, canons and dukes who keep hidden the sepulchre of the Knight of Madness, Knight who made all the world laugh but never cracked a joke. He had too great a soul to bring forth jokes. They laughed at his seriousness.

"Begin then, friend, to do the Peter the Hermit and call people to join you, to join us, and let us all go win back the sepulchre even if we don't know where it is. The crusade itself will reveal to us the sacred place.

.   .   .   .   .   .

"Start marching! Where are you going? The star will tell you: to the sepulchre! What shall we do on the road while we march? What? Fight! Fight, and how?

"How? If you find a man lying? Shout in his face: 'lie!' and forward! If you find man stealing, shout: 'thief!' and forward! If you find a man babbling asininities, to whom the crowd listens open-mouthed, shout at them all: 'idiots!' and forward, always forward!

.   .   .   .   .   .

"To the march then! And throw out of the sacred squadron all those who begin to study the step and its length and its rhythm. Above everything, throw out all those who fuss about this business of rhythm. They'll turn the squadron into a quadrille and the march into a dance. Away with them! Let them go off somewhere else to sing the flesh.

"Those who try to turn the squadron on the march into a dancing quadrille call themselves and each other poets. But they're not. They're something else. They only go to the sepulchre out of curiosity, to see what it's like, looking for a new sensation, and to amuse themselves along the road. Away with them!

"It's these that with their indulgence of Bohemians contribute to maintain cowardice and lies and all the weaknesses that flood us. When they preach liberty they only think of one: that of disposing of their neighbor's wife. All is sensuality with them. They even fall in love sensually with ideas, with great ideas. They are incapable of marrying a great and pure idea and breeding a family with it; they only flirt with ideas. They want them as mistresses, sometimes just for the night. Away with them!

"If a man wants to pluck some flower or other along the path that smiles from the fringe of grass, let him pluck it, but without breaking ranks, without dropping out of the squadron of which the leader must always keep his eyes on the flaming sonorous star. But if he put the little flower in the strap above his cuirass, not to look at it himself, but for others to look at, away with him! Let him go with his flower in his buttonhole and dance somewhere else.

"Look, friend, if you want to accomplish your mission and serve your country you must make yourself unpleasant to the sensitive boys who only see the world through the eyes of their sweethearts.

Or through something worse. Let your words be strident and rasping in their ears.

"The squadron must only stop at night, near a wood or under the lee of a mountain. There they will pitch their tents and the crusaders will wash their feet, and sup off what their women have prepared, then they will beget a son on them and kiss them and go to sleep to begin the march again the following day. And when someone dies they will leave him on the edge of the road with his armor on him, at the mercy of the crows. Let the dead take the trouble to bury the dead."

Instead of the rationalists and humanists of the North, Unamuno's idols are the mystics and saints and sensualists of Castile, hard stalwart men who walked with God, Loyola, Torquemada, Pizarro, Narváez, who governed with whips and thumbscrews and drank death down greedily like heady wine. He is excited by the amorous madness of the mysticism of Santa Teresa and San Juan de la Cruz. His religion is paradoxical, unreasonable, of faith alone, full of furious yearning other-worldliness. His style, it follows perforce, is headlong, gruff, redundant, full of tremendous pounding phrases. There is a vigorous angry insistence about his dogmas that makes his essays unforgettable, even if one objects as violently as I do to his asceticism and death-worship. There is an anarchic fury about his crying in the wilderness that will win many a man from the fleshpots and chain gangs.

In the apse of the old cathedral of Salamanca is a fresco of the Last Judgment, perhaps by the Castilian painter Gallegos. Over the retablo on a black ground a tremendous figure of the avenging angel brandishes a sword while behind him unrolls the scroll of the *Dies Irae* and huddled clusters of plump little naked people fall away into space from under his feet. There are moments in *"Del Sentimiento Trágico de la Vida"* and in the *"Vida de Don Quijote y Sancho"* when in the rolling earthy Castilian phrases one can feel the brandishing of the sword of that very angel. Not for nothing does Unamuno live in the rust and saffron-colored town of Salamanca in the midst of bare red hills that bulge against an enormous flat sky in which the clouds look like piles of granite, like floating cathedrals, they are so solid, heavy, ominous. A country where barrenness and the sweep of cold wind and the lash

of strong wine have made people's minds ingrow into the
hereafter, where the clouds have been tramped by the angry
feet of the destroying angel. A Patmos for a new Apocalypse.
Unamuno is constantly attacking sturdily those who clamor
for the modernization, Europeanization of Spanish life and
Spanish thought: he is the counterpoise to the northward-
yearning apostles of Giner de los Ríos.

In an essay in one of the volumes published by the *Residencia de Estudiantes* he wrote:

"As can be seen I proceed by what they call arbitrary affirmations,
without documentation, without proof, outside of a modern European logic, disdainful of its methods.

"Perhaps. I want no other method than that of passion, and when
my breast swells with disgust, repugnance, sympathy or disdain, I let
the mouth speak the bitterness of the heart, and let the words come
as they come.

"We Spaniards are, they say, arbitrary charlatans, who fill up with
rhetoric the gaps in logic, who subtilize with more or less ingenuity,
but uselessly, who lack the sense of coherence, with scholastic souls,
casuists and all that.

"I've heard similar things said of Augustine, the great African,
soul of fire that spilt itself in leaping waves of rhetoric, twistings of
the phrase, antithesis, paradoxes and ingenuities. Saint Augustine
was a Gongorine and a conceptualist at the same time, which makes
me think that Gongorism and conceptualism are the most natural
forms of passion and vehemence.

"The great African, the great ancient African! Here is an expression—ancient African—that one can oppose to modern European,
and that's worth as much at least. African and ancient were Saint Augustine and Tertullian. And why shouldn't we say: 'We must make
ourselves ancient African-style' or else 'We must make ourselves
African ancient-style.'"

The typical tree of Castile is the encina, a kind of live-oak
that grows low with dense bluish foliage and a ribbed, knotted and contorted trunk; it always grows singly and on dry
hills. On the roads one meets lean men with knotted hands
and brown sun-wizened faces that seem brothers to the encinas of their country. The thought of Unamuno, emphatic,
lonely, contorted, hammered into homely violent phrases,

oak-tough, oak-twisted, is brother to the men on the roads and to the encinas on the hills of Castile.

This from the end of *"Del Sentimiento Trágico de la Vida"*:

"And in this critical century, Don Quixote has also contaminated himself with criticism, and he must charge against himself, victim of intellectualism and sentimentalism, who when he is most sincere appears most affected. The poor man wants to rationalize the irrational, and irrationalize the rational. And he falls victim of the inevitable despair of a rationalism century, of which the greatest victims were Tolstoy and Nietzsche. Out of despair he enters into the heroic fury of that Quixote of thought who broke out of the cloister, Giordano Bruno, and makes himself awakener of sleeping souls, '*dormitantium animorum excubitor*,' as the ex-Dominican says of himself, he who wrote: 'Heroic love is proper to superior natures called insane—*insane*, not because they do not know—*non sanno*—but because they know too much—*soprasanno*—.'

"But Bruno believed in the triumph of his doctrines, or at least at the foot of his statue on the Campo dei Fiori, opposite the Vatican, they have put that it is offered by the century he had divined—'*il secolo da lui divinato*.' But our Don Quixote, the resurrected, internal Don Quixote, does not believe that his doctrines will triumph in the world, because they are not his. And it is better that they should not triumph. If they wanted to make Don Quixote king he would retire alone to the hilltop, fleeing the crowds of king-makers and king-killers, as did Christ when, after the miracle of the loaves and fishes, they wanted to proclaim him king. He left the title of king to be put above the cross.

"What is, then, the new mission of Don Quixote in this world? To cry, to cry in the wilderness. For the wilderness hears although men do not hear, and one day will turn into a sonorous wood, and that solitary voice that spreads in the desert like seed will sprout into a gigantic cedar that will sing with a hundred thousand tongues an eternal hosanna to the Lord of life and death."

XVII: Toledo

"LYAEUS, you've found it."

"Her, you mean."

"No, the essence, the gesture."

"I carry no butterfly net."

The sun blazed in a halo of heat about their heads. Both sides of the straight road olive trees contorted gouty trunks as they walked past. On a bank beside a quietly grazing donkey a man was asleep wrapped in a brown blanket. Occasionally a little grey bird twittered encouragingly from the telegraph wires. When the wind came there was a chill of winter and wisps of cloud drifted across the sun and a shiver of silver ran along the olive groves.

"Tel," cried Lyaeus after a pause, "maybe I have found it. Maybe you are right. You should have been with me last night."

"What happened last night?" As a wave of bitter envy swept over him Telemachus saw for a moment the face of his mother Penelope, brows contracted with warning, white hand raised in admonition. For a fleeting second the memory of his quest brushed through the back of his mind. But Lyaeus was talking.

"Nothing much happened. There were a few things. . . . O this is wonderful." He waved a clenched fist about his head. "The finest people, Tel! You never saw such people, Tel. They gave me a tambourine. Here it is; wait a minute." He placed the bag he carried on his shoulder on top of a milestone and untied its mouth. When he pulled the tambourine out it was full of figs. "Look, pocket these. I taught her to write her name on the back; see, 'Pilar.' She didn't know how to write."

Telemachus involuntarily cleared his throat.

"It was the finest dive . . . Part house, part cave. We all roared in and there was the funniest little girl . . . Lot of other people, fat women, but my eyes were in a highly selective state. She was very skinny with enormous black eyes, doe's eyes, timid as a dog's. She had a fat pink puppy in her lap."

"But I meant something in line, movement, eternal, not that."

"There are very few gestures," said Lyaeus.

They walked along in silence.

"I am tired," said Lyaeus; "at least let's stop in here. I see a bush over the door."

"Why stop? We are nearly there."

"Why go on?"

"We want to get to Toledo, don't we?"

"Why?"

"Because we started for there."

"No reason at all," said Lyaeus with a laugh as he went in the door of the wineshop.

When they came out they found Don Alonso waiting for them, holding his horse by the bridle.

"The Spartans," he said with a smile, "never drank wine on the march."

"How far are we from Toledo?" asked Telemachus. "It was nice of you to wait for us."

"About a league, five kilometers, nothing. . . . I wanted to see your faces when you first saw the town. I think you will appreciate it."

"Let's walk fast," said Telemachus. "There are some things one doesn't want to wait for."

"It will be sunset and the whole town will be on the *paseo* in front of the hospital of San Juan Bautista. . . . This is Sunday of Carnival; people will be dressed up in masks and very noisy. It's a day on which they play tricks on strangers."

"Here's the trick they played me at the last town," said Lyaeus agitating his bag of figs. "Let's eat some. I'm sure the Spartans ate figs on the road. Will Rosinante,—I mean will your horse eat them?" He put his hand with some figs on it under the horse's mouth. The horse sniffed noisily out of black nostrils dappled with pink and then reached for the figs. Lyaeus wiped his hand on the seat of his pants and they proceeded.

"Toledo is symbolically the soul of Spain," began Don Alonso after a few moments of silent walking. "By that I mean that through the many Spains you have seen and will see is everywhere an undercurrent of fantastic tragedy, Greco on the one hand, Goya on the other, Moráles, Gallegos, a

great flame of despair amid dust, rags, ulcers, human life rising in a sudden pæan out of desolate abandoned dun-colored
spaces. To me, Toledo expresses the supreme beauty of that
tragic farce . . . And the apex, the victory, the deathlessness
of it is in El Greco. . . . How strange it is that it should be
that Cypriote who lived in such Venetian state in a great
house near the abandoned synagogue, scandalizing us austere
Spaniards by the sounds of revelry and unabashed music that
came from it at meal-times, making pert sayings under the
nose of humorless visitors like Pacheco, living solitary in a
country where he remained to his death misunderstood and
alien and where two centuries thought of him along with
Don Quixote as a madman,—how strange that it should be
he who should express most flamingly all that was imper-
turbable in Toledo . . . I have often wondered whether that
fiery vitality of spirit that we feel in El Greco, that we felt in
my generation when I was young, that I see occasionally in
the young men of your time, has become conscious only because it is about to be smothered in the great advancing
waves of European banality. I was thinking the other day that
perhaps states of life only became conscious once their intensity was waning."

"But most of the intellectuals I met in Madrid," put in
Telemachus, "seemed enormously anxious for subways and
mechanical progress, seemed to think that existence could be
made perfect by slot-machines."

"They are anxious to hold stock in the subway and slot-
machine enterprises that they may have more money to un-
Spanish themselves in Paris . . . but let us not talk of that.
From the next turn in the road, round that little hill, we shall
see Toledo."

Don Alonso jumped on his horse, and Lyaeus and
Telemachus doubled the speed of their stride.

First above the bulge of reddish saffron striped with dark of
a plowed field they saw a weathercock, then under it the slate
cap of a tower. "The Alcázar," said Don Alonso. The road
turned away and olive trees hid the weathercock. At the next
bend the towers were four, strongly buttressing a square
building where on the western windows glinted reflections of
sunset. As they walked more towers, dust colored, and domes

and the spire of a cathedral, greenish, spiky like the tail of a
pickerel, jutted to the right of the citadel. The road dipped
again, passed some white houses where children sat in the
doorways; from the inner rooms came a sound of frying oil
and a pungence of cistus-twigs burning. Starting up the next
rise that skirted a slope planted with almond trees they caught
sight of a castle, rounded towers, built of rough grey stone,
joined by crenellated walls that appeared occasionally behind
the erratic lacework of angular twigs on which here and there
a cluster of pink flowers had already come into bloom. At the
summit was a wineshop with mules tethered against the walls,
and below the Tagus and the great bridge, and Toledo.

Against the grey and ochre-streaked theatre of the Cigarrales were piled masses of buttressed wall that caught the
orange sunset light on many tall plane surfaces rising into
crenellations and square towers and domes and slate-capped
spires above a litter of yellowish tile roofs that fell away in terraces from the highest points and sloped outside the walls towards the river and the piers from which sprang the enormous
arch of the bridge. The shadows were blue-green and violet.
A pale cobalt haze of supperfires hung over the quarters near
the river. As they started down the hill towards the heavy pile
of San Juan Bautista, that stood under its broad tiled dome
outside the nearest gate, a great volley of bell-ringing swung
about their ears. A donkey brayed; there was a sound of
shouting from the town.

"Here we are, gentlemen, I'll look for you tomorrow at the
fonda," shouted Don Alonso. He took off his hat and gal-
loped towards the gate, leaving Telemachus and Lyaeus
standing by the roadside looking out over the city.

Beyond the zinc bar was an irregular room with Nile-
green walls into which light still filtered through three little
round arches high up on one side. In a corner were some
hogsheads of wine, in another small tables with three-legged
stools. From outside came the distant braying of a brass band
and racket of a street full of people, laughter, and the occasional shivering jangle of a tambourine. Lyaeus had dropped
onto a stool and spread his feet out before him on the tiled
floor.

"Never walked so far in my life," he said, "my toes are pulverized, pulverized!" He leaned over and pulled off his shoes. There were holes in his socks. He pulled them off in turn, and started wiggling his toes meditatively. His ankles were grimed with dust.

"Well . . ." began Telemachus.

The *padrón*, a lean man with moustaches and a fancy yellow vest which he wore unbuttoned over a lavender shirt, brought two glasses of dense black wine.

"You have walked a long way?" he asked, looking with interest at Lyaeus' feet.

"From Madrid."

"*¡Carai!*"

"Not all in one day."

"You are sailors going to rejoin your ship in Sevilla." The *padrón* looked from one to another with a knowing expression, twisting his mouth so that one of the points of his moustache slanted towards the ceiling and the other towards the floor.

"Not exactly . . ."

Another man drew up his chair to their table, first taking off his wide cap and saying gravely: "*Con permiso de ustedes.*" His broad, slightly flabby face was very pale; the eyes under his sparse blonde eyelashes were large and grey. He put his two hands on their shoulders so as to draw their heads together and said in a whisper:

"You aren't deserters, are you?"

"No."

"I hoped you were. I might have helped you. I escaped from prison in Barcelona a week ago. I am a syndicalist."

"Have a drink," cried Lyaeus. "Another glass . . . And we can let you have some money if you need it, too, if you want to get out of the country."

The *padrón* brought the wine and retired discreetly to a chair beside the bar from which he beamed at them with almost religious approbation.

"You are comrades?"

"Of those who break out," said Lyaeus flushing. "What about the progress of events? When do you think the pot will boil over?"

"Soon or never," said the syndicalist . . . "That is never in our lifetime. We are being buried under industrialism like the rest of Europe. Our people, our comrades even, are fast getting the bourgeois mentality. There is danger that we shall lose everything we have fought for . . . You see, if we could only have captured the means of production when the system was young and weak, we could have developed it slowly for our benefit, made the machine the slave of man. Every day we wait makes it more difficult. It is a race as to whether this peninsula will be captured by communism or capitalism. It is still neither one nor the other, in its soul." He thumped his clenched fist against his chest.

"How long were you in prison?"

"Only a month this time, but if they catch me it will be bad. They won't catch me."

He spoke quietly without gestures, occasionally rolling an unlit cigarette between his brown fingers.

"Hadn't we better go out before it gets quite dark?" said Telemachus.

"When shall I see you again?" said Lyaeus to the syndicalist.

"Oh, we'll meet if you stay in Toledo a few days. . . ."

Lyaeus got to his feet and took the man by the arm.

"Look, let me give you some money; won't you be wanting to go to Portugal?"

The man flushed and shook his head.

"If our opinions coincided. . . ."

"I agree with all those who break out," said Lyaeus.

"That's not the same, my friend."

They shook hands and Telemachus and Lyaeus went out of the tavern.

Two carriages hung with gaudily embroidered shawls, full of dominos and pierrots and harlequins who threw handfuls of confetti at people along the sidewalks, clattered into town through the dark arches of the gate. Telemachus got some confetti in his mouth. A crowd of little children danced about him jeering as he stood spluttering on the curbstone. Lyaeus took him by the arm and drew him along the street after the carriages, bent double with laughter. This irritated Telemachus who tore his arm away suddenly and made off with long strides up a dark street.

A half-waned moon shone through the perforations in a round terra-cotta chimney into the street's angular greenish shadow. From somewhere came the seethe of water over a dam. Telemachus was leaning against a damp wall, tired and exultant, looking vaguely at the oval of a woman's face half surmised behind the bars of an upper window, when he heard a clatter of unsteady feet on the cobbles and Lyaeus appeared, reeling a little, his lips moist, his eyebrows raised in an expression of drunken jollity.

"Lyaeus, I am very happy," cried Telemachus stepping forward to meet his friend. "Walking about here in these empty zigzag streets I have suddenly felt familiar with it all, as if it were a part of me, as if I had soaked up some essence out of it."

"Silly that about essences, gestures, Tel, silly. . . . Awake all you need." Lyaeus stood on a little worn stone that kept wheels off the corner of the house where the street turned and waved his arms. "Awake! *Dormitant animorum excubitor.* . . . That's not right. Latin's no good. Means a fellow who says: 'wake up, you son of a gun.'"

"Oh, you're drunk. It's much more important than that. It's like learning to swim. For a long time you flounder about, it's unpleasant and gets up your nose and you choke. Then all at once you are swimming like a duck. That's how I feel about all this. . . . The challenge was that woman in Madrid, dancing, dancing. . . ."

"Tel, there are things too good to talk about. . . . Look, I'm like St. Simeon Stylites." Lyaeus lifted one leg, then the other, waving his arms like a tight-rope walker.

"When I left you I walked out over the other bridge, the bridge of St. Martin and climbed. . . ."

"Shut up, I think I hear a girl giggling up in the window there."

Lyaeus stood up very straight on his column and threw a kiss up into the darkness. The giggling turned to a shrill laughter; a head craned out from a window opposite. Lyaeus beckoned with both hands.

"Never mind about them. . . . Look out, somebody threw something. . . . Oh, it's an orange. . . . I want to tell you how I felt the gesture. I had climbed up on one of the hills of the Cigarrales and was looking at the silhouette of the town so black against the stormy marbled sky. The moon hadn't risen yet. . . . Let's move away from here."

"*Ven, flor de mi corazón,*" shouted Lyaeus towards the upper window.

"A flock of goats was passing on the road below, and from somewhere came the tremendous lilt of. . . ."

"Heads!" cried Lyaeus throwing himself round an angle in the wall.

Telemachus looked up, his mind full of his mother Penelope's voice saying reproachfully: "You might have been murdered in that dark alley." A girl was leaning from the window, shaken with laughter, taking aim with a bucket she swung with both hands.

"Stop," cried Telemachus, "it's the other. . . ."

As he spoke a column of cold water struck his head, knocked his breath out, drenched him.

"Speaking of gestures. . . ." whispered Lyaeus breathlessly from the doorway where he was crouching, and the street was filled with uncontrollable shrieking laughter.

ORIENT EXPRESS

With Illustrations in Color from
Paintings by the Author

Contents

I. Eastward

1. Pico

Hoity-toity
Cha de noite
Sea's still high
An' sky's all doity

they sang as they propped themselves
against the bar and fought seasickness with madeira. On the
bench opposite the other passengers sat in a row with green
faces. Every long roll of the Mormugaō ended in a lurch
and a nasty rattling of busted clockwork from the direction
of the engineroom. Outside, the wind yelled and the spray
flew as the boat wallowed deeper and deeper in the trough
of the sea; inside, the madeira got lower and lower in the
dark amber bottle and the eastbound Americans sang louder
and louder into the twitching peagreen faces of the other
passengers propped in a row

Sea's still high
An' sky's all doity.

Later we are driving along over a huge easy gradual swell
with a moist west wind behind us. The madeira is all drunk
up. Sky and sea are blurred in a great sweeping scud, silver as
thistledown in the hidden moonlight. In that scud the shoving
wetnosed wind is carrying spring eastward to fall in rain on
Lisbon, San Vicente, Madrid, to beat against windows in
Marseilles and Rome, to quicken the thrusting sprouts in weedy
cemeteries in Stamboul. Now and then the scud breaks and a
tiny round moon shows through among whorls and spirals of
speeding mist that thickens into sagging clots and thins into
long spaces bright and crinkly as tinfoil.

The bow quivers as it nuzzles deep into each new lunging
hill. A squall hides the moon and spatters my head nervously
with rain and rushes on leaving some streaks of clear moonlight eastward where the islands are. Then we are driving
along muffled in thistledown mist again. I have fallen asleep
huddled in the V of the bow.

When I open my eyes the wind has stopped. Only a few patches of scud swirl eastward overhead. The huge swells are bright and heavy like mercury in the still moonlight. It isn't a sound coming across the water, it's a smell, a growing fragrance beating against my face on a burst of warm air out of the east, a smell of roses and dung burnt by the sun, a rankness like skunk-cabbage overlaid with hyacinth, pungence of musk, chilly sweetness of violets. Hours later, eastward we made out, wrapped in clouds, the dark cone of Pico.

2. Terminus Maritime

At Ostend the boat for the Continent lands alongside of a tall black hotel. After they have gone through the customs and had their passports stamped the passengers for Central Europe and the Orient file through the tall tragic black doorway into a vast restaurant thinly sprinkled with round tables. They sit at the tables and a sound of talk in various languages drifts up into the high coffered ceiling and out over the dark squares of the rainlashed harbor. People order food and eat it hurriedly with an occasional nervous glance at the clock. Having eaten they take their places, which they have previously reserved with pieces of baggage, in the various trains. The trains are rather empty, all the lean windows of the hotel are closed with dark grey shutters, the great squares of the harbor are empty. A conductor with gold braid on his cap paces back and forth on the platform, occasionally stroking the bristles of a rusty moustache.

At the other end of the platform beside a slot machine is a large thermometer constructed, so it announces in red letters, by Monsieur Guépratte, that gives you the chilliness in Centigrade, Fahrenheit, and Réaumur degrees and adds little informatory mottoes such as that 60° is the mean temperature of Pondichéry, that 35° is best for an ordinary bath, that silkworms are happiest at 25°, and also sickrooms.

It is not traintime yet. The eastbound American goes back through the portals of doom into the empty restaurant where in the arctic stillness a lone waiter stands beside a table teetering like a penguin. He sits down beside the waiter and orders a brandy and soda, telling himself with passionate melancholy that 60° is the mean temperature of Pondichéry. If it's sixty in the shade in Pondichéry how cold does it have to be to freeze vodka in Nijni Novgorod? Answer me that Michel Strogoff.

Through the doorway I can read the bronze letters on the west side of the sleeping car, *Compagnie Internationale des Wagons Lits et des Grands Expresses Européens.* A gust of wet air slaps me in the face from time to time, bringing a smell of varnish and axlegrease and couplings, a smell of departure and distance that evokes a very small boy being coaxed trembling onto a new huge shining train in a shed somewhere. A train fresh painted fresh varnished that smells like new rubber balls, like tin toys, like sewing machines, a train that is going to start but that never starts. We're going to move. The engine whistles long. We're off. No it's only the walls moving, towns and mountains and trees and rivers moving: Panorama of the Trans-Siberian.

En voiture messieurs, mesdames. . . . The eastbound American is yanked to his feet, spills money for his drink onto the table, runs out through the tall portal down the wet platform, boards the train that has begun very slowly to move.

3. Luna

Dinner alone beside a pink and yellow lampshade (categoria de lusso), out of the window the colored postcard of San Giorgio Maggiore. Venice the Coney Island of Coney Islands, the Midway of history built for goggle-eyed westerners out of the gaudy claptrap of the east, and through it all the smell of tidewater, rotting piles, mudflats, a gruff bodysmell under the lipstick and perfume and ricepowder, a smell desolately amorous like chestnut blooms, like datura, like trodden cabbages. Women passing on the quai wear their hair fluffed up the way the prostitutes in Carpaccio's pictures do, and long black silk shawls with fringes longer than the fringes of the shawls of the women of Seville; their skin is a firm yellowish color and they have straight ivory noses. An occasional flicker of lightning behind the dome and tapering tower of San Giorgio reveals the fact that it is merely a cutout, that the water is an excellently contrived effect, that the people on the quai are an opera chorus intermingled with a few supers, that the moon is a baby spot.

I hustle out of the restaurant for fear the act will be over, walk hastily along overhung streets, over humped bridges, down alleys where through tavern doorways you can see people drinking at long varnished tables. Redhaired girls behind bars, drunken men playing guitars in front of a cathouse by the waterside, clanging smells of wine and garlic; in every direction spaghetti-tenors singing in boats. In the piazza an orchestra playing William Tell for all it's worth, on the Grand Canal Santa Lucia carried high by a soprano above a croaking of fat basses. In the sky the electrician has killed the moon. I can make out the big and the little Dipper in a spangled black cyclorama. In the canals the ripple of water would be as excellently imitated as in the Nile scene from "Aida," if it weren't for the inexorable smell of the tide creeping up slime-covered steps, of mudflats and waterlogged barges, chilly hands of the Adriatic groping for your throat.

Florian's; broad shirtfronts of waiters, icecream-colored parasols, women in fluffy summer clothes, white flannels, under a grey sky that someone at the top of the Campanile has suddenly filled with fluttering green, pink, yellow papers that ultimately light among the tables announcing Lulli's toilet articles. Young men swagger in fours and fives through the crowds singing Giovanezza, giovanezza. Somewhere behind the ornate facades, in alleys hidden away so as not to scare the tourists, there is fighting going on. There is something in the air that makes you uncomfortable in the aviary twitter of Florian's. On every bare wall there are signs VV LENIN or M LENIN. I wander irresolutely about over the marble pavements through the dying light of a yellow sunset. A boat with an ochre sail that has a great crimson patch in the middle of it proceeds slowly across the daffodil water, a black barge with four men rowing in effortless unison crawls away towards the Lido. Under an archway behind me some people are looking at a pasquinade scrawled in black chalk. The words are in English in thick rounded letters:

THIS BUNDLE MUST DIE

Aha, says the stiffwhiskered gentleman in a straw hat addressing the crowd, That means in English, Death to the Socialisti.

4. Express

Joggling three times a day in a dining car. First through the Kingdom of the Serbs, Croats and Slovenes, then through Bulgaria and a slice of Greece. There's the lady from Wellesley who writes for the Atlantic Monthly; an eggshaped Armenian from New York who was brought up at the monastery of San Lazzaro in Venice, studied painting in Asolo, hates priests, clergymen and Balkan cookery and talks plaintively of Tiffany's and old Martin's restaurant on 28th Street; there's another Armenian whose mother, father and three sisters were cut up into little pieces before his eyes by the Turks in Trebizond; there's a tall irongrey Standard Oil man, very tall with a little pot belly the shape of half a football. He says he can size up people at a glance and he sits all day writing doggerel descriptive of his travels to his favorite niece. Then there's a man with many seals on his watch who looks like a 14th Street auctioneer, and two scrawny colonial Englishwomen; all these against a changing background of sallow Balkan people with big noses and dark rings under their eyes.

Between meals I sit in the privacy of my little green compartment full of nickel knobs and fixings reading Diehl, who is very dull, occasionally interrupted by passport men, customs agents, detectives, secret police or by the porter, an elderly Belgian who breathes heavily like a locomotive, a man irrevocably exhausted by too many miles of railroad, by too many telegraph poles counted, by too many cinders brushed off green plush seats. At stations I walk up and down with a brittle Frenchman smoking the local cigarettes; he talks knowingly about Bucharest, love, assassination, triangular marriage and diplomacy. He knows everything and his collars and cuffs are always spotless. His great phrase is Aller dans le luxe . . . Il faut toujours aller dans le luxe.

Day by day the hills get scrawnier and dryer and the train goes more and more slowly and the stationmasters have longer and longer moustaches and seedier and seedier uniforms until at last we are winding between a brightgreen sea and yellow sunburned capes. Suddenly the train is trapped between mustard-colored crumbling walls, the line runs among rubbish heaps and cypresses. The train is hardly moving at all, it stops imperceptibly as if on a siding. Is it? No, yes, it must be . . . Constantinople.

II. *Constant' July 1921*

1. Pera Palace

Under my window a dusty rutted road with here and there a solitary pavingstone over which carts jolt and jingle continually, climbing jerkily to Pera, rumbling down towards the old bridge, all day long from dawn to dusk; beyond, tall houses closer-packed than New York houses even, a flat roof where a barelegged girl hangs out laundry, and across red tiles the dusty cypresses of a cemetery, masts, and the Golden Horn, steel-colored, with steamers at anchor; and, further, against the cloudy sky, Stamboul, domes, brown-black houses, bright minarets set about everywhere like the little ivory men on a cribbage board. Up the road where it curves round the cemetery of the Petits Champs—more dusty cypresses, stone posts with turbans carved on them tilting this way and that—carts are dumping rubbish down the hill, ashes, rags, papers, things that glitter in the sunlight; as fast as they are dumped women with sacks on their backs, scrambling and elbowing each other, pick among the refuse with lean hands. A faint rasping of querulous voices drifts up from them amid the cries of vegetable-sellers and the indeterminate swarming rumor of many lives packed into narrow streets.

Thum-rum-tum: thum-rum-tum on an enormous tambourine and the conquering whine of a bagpipe. Two tall men with gaudy turbans round their fezzes come out of a lane leading a monkey. The thumping, wheezing tune is the very soul of the monkey's listless irregular walk. Carters stop their carts. Beggars jump up from where they had been crouching by the shady wall. The ragpickers try to straighten their bent backs and shade their eyes against the sun to see. Waiters in dress-suits hang out from the windows of the hotel. Taking advantage of the crowd, two men carrying a phonograph with a white enamelled horn on a sort of a table with handles, set it down and start it playing an amazing tune like a leaky water-faucet. The tall men with the monkey thump their tambourine in derision and swagger away.

Downstairs in the red plush lobby of the Pera Palace there is scuttling and confusion. They are carrying out a man in a frock coat who wears on his head a black astrakhan cap. There's blood in the red plush armchair; there's blood on the mosaic floor. The manager walks back and forth with sweat standing out on his brow; they can mop up the floor but the chair is ruined. French, Greek and Italian gendarmes swagger about talking all together each in his own language. The poor bloke's dead, sir, says the British M.P. to the colonel who doesn't know whether to finish his cocktail or not. Azerbaidjan. Azerbaidjan. He was the envoy from Azerbaidjan. An Armenian, a man with a beard, stood in the doorway and shot him. A man with glasses and a smooth chin, a Bolshevik spy, walked right up to him and shot him. The waiter who brings drinks from the bar is in despair. The drinkers have all left without paying.

2. Jardin de Taxim

A table under a striped umbrella at the edge of the terrace of the restaurant at Taxim Garden (Entrée 5 piastres, libre aux militaires). Dardenella from a Russian orchestra. On the slope below a fence made of hammered-out Standard Oil tins encloses a mud hut beside which a donkey grazes. Two men squat placidly on the slope at the gate and look out, across some tacky little villas, like villas at Nice, and a gas tank streaked red with fresh paint, at the Bosphorus and the Asian hills. It is nearly dark. The Bosphorus shines about the string of grey battleships at anchor. Between the brown hills in the foreground and the blue hills in the distance curls up a thick pillar of smoke. One thinks of villages burning, but this is too far to the north, and they have a habit at this season in the back country of burning off the hills to smoke out brigands. The orchestra is resting for a moment. From the yellow barracks to the left comes a tune on a hurdygurdy and a quavering voice singing.

Then the rim of an enormous bloodorange moon rolls up out of Asia.

Presently when one has eaten caviar and pilaf and swordfish from the Black Sea washed down by Nectar beer, made at the edge of town in the brewery of a certain gentleman of immeasurable wealth named Bomonti, the show begins on the stage among the trees. International vaudeville. First a Russian lady waves a green handkerchief in a peasant dance with a certain timid grace one feels sure was learned at some fashionable dancing academy in Moscow. Then two extraordinarily tough English girls in socks and jumpers, perhaps ex of the pony ballet at the Folies Bergères. One of them croons in a curious bored and jerky manner as they go through the steps and kicking that shocked country parsons at the Gaiety when Queen Victoria was a girl. Then come Greek acrobats, a comic Russian lady understood only by her compatriots, a Frenchwoman in black with operatic arms and a conservatoire manner who sings the mad scene from "Lucia" several times to huge applause, a pitiful little woman in pink tulle dancing the Moment Musicale with that peculiar inanity of gesture encouraged by dancing instructresses in American state capitals, and so on endlessly.

Meanwhile people move about the gardens among the locust-trees; jokes are passed, drinks poured. There are flirtations, pairings off. Three girls arm in arm dart into a side path followed by three Italian sailors, brown sinewy youngsters in white suits. A party of Greek officers are very gay. Their army has taken Eski Chehir. The Kemalists are about to leave Ismid. Tino is a great king after all. Opposite them two elderly Turkish gentlemen in frock coats and white vests pull impassively on their narghiles. Further back seven gobs are getting noisily drunk at a round table. Toward the gate stands an Italian gendarme, imported all complete from the buttons on his coattails to his shiny tricorne, and a British M.P. with A.P.C. (standing for Allied Police Commission) in handsome letters on his sleeve.

Why do you want to learn Turkish? a Greek girl asks me, a look of puzzled irritation on her face. You must side with the Greeks; you mustn't learn Turkish.

Flits through my head a memory of the little yellow tables and chairs under the great planetree beside the mosque of Bayazid over in Stamboul, the pigeons, and the old men with beards as white as their white cotton turbans who sat there gravely nodding their heads in endless slow discussions; and how a beggar inconceivably old, yellow like frayed damask, gnarled like a dying plumtree, had asked for a light from my cigarette and then smiling had pointed to the glass of water that stood beside my little coffeecup, and how when I had handed him the water, he had had to crouch low to the ground to drink it, his back was so bent; and the gesture full of sceptered kings with which he had put back the glass and thanked me with a wave of a skinny corded hand. There was something in that wave of the hand of the soaring of minarets and the cry of muezzins and the impassive eyes of the elderly Turkish gentlemen in white vests sitting so quiet beside rejoicing Greeks in the Jardin de Taxim. There are reasons for learning Turkish.

Then when one has seen all one can stand of international vaudeville, of Russian ladies trying to earn a few pennies for the hard bread of exile, of Levantine dancers and beached European singers, one walks home along the Grande Rue de Pera. Along the curbs are more Russian refugees, soldiers in varied worn uniforms that once were Wrangel's army, selling everything imaginable out of little trays slung about their necks—paper flowers and kewpie dolls, shoelaces and jumping jacks and little colored silhouettes under glass of mosques and cypresses, and cakes round and square and lifepreserver-shaped. They are men of all ages and conditions, mostly with dense white northern skins and fair close-cropped hair, all with a drawn hungry look about the cheekbones and a veiled shudder of pain in their eyes. In the restaurants one can see through the open windows pale girls with veils bound tight about their hair. On the arms of two stout Armenians two rouged and densely powdered ladies in twin dresses of flounced pink ride out of an alleyway on the jingling waves that spurt from a mechanical piano.

Further along a onelegged Russian soldier stands against a lamppost, big red hands covering his face, and sobs out loud.

3. Massacre

The red plush salon of the Pera Palace Hotel. The archbishop, a tall man in flowing black with a beautiful curly chestnut-colored beard and gimlet eyes, is pouring out an impetuous torrent of Greek. Listening to him a Greek lady elaborately dressed in rose satin, an American naval officer, a journalist, some miscellaneous frock-coated people. Clink of ice in high-balls being brought to two British majors across the room. The archbishop lifts a slender Byzantine hand and orders coffee. Then he changes to French, lisping a little his long balanced phrases, in which predominate the words *horreur, atrocité, œuvre humanitaire, civilisation mondiale*. The Turks in Samsoun, the Kemalists, who some weeks since deported the men of orthodox faith, have now posted an order to deport the women and children. Three days' notice. Of course that means . . . . Massacre, says someone hastily.

The archbishop's full lips are at the rim of his tiny coffeecup. He drinks quickly and meticulously. In one's mind beyond the red plush a vision of dark crowds crawling inland over sun-shrivelled hills. The women were crying and wailing in the streets of Samsoun, says the officer. The news must be sent out, continues the archbishop; the world must know the barbarity of the Turks; America must know. A telegram to the President of the United States must be sent off. Again in one's mind beyond red plush salons, and the polished phrases of official telegrams, the roads at night under the terrible bloodorange moon of Asia, and the wind of the defiles blowing dust among huddled women, stinging the dark attentive eyes of children, and far off on the heatbaked hills a sound of horsemen.

In a big armchair beside the window a Turk with grizzled eyebrows and with eyes as soft and as brown as the archbishop's beard looks unmovedly at nothing. One by one the oval amber beads of a conversation chaplet drop through his inscrutably slow white fingers.

4. Assassination

Extracts from a letter published under "Tribune Libre" in the *Presse du Soir* that comes out in Pera every evening with two pages of French and four of Russian:

The eighteenth of June my husband, Bekhboud Djevanchir Khan, was murdered.

I the undersigned, his wife, of Russian origin, trust to your kindness for the publication of certain facts which will put an end I hope to the false rumors that are attainting the dead man's good name.

I have never been separated from my husband and God has made me witness of all the horror of these last years.

March 1918. The wreck of the Russian army crawling back from the Turkish front. At Baku the power is in the hands of Armenians who have adopted the Bolshevist platform. By order of no one knows who, according to a prearranged plan, there is organized a massacre of the Muslim population.

Never till my last breath shall I forget those terrible days. They were tracking my husband; his name was on the list of the proscribed. By a miracle he escaped. We fled the town and after unbelievable privations, succeeded in getting to Elisabethpol.

Months passed. Power changed hands, and my husband was called to the post of Minister of the Interior in the first Azerbaidjan cabinet. Turkish detachments draw near to Baku and again, before they reach the town, the bloody happenings of September are unrolled. It was the terrible reply of the Muslims to the March massacres.

My husband hastens to Baku to put an end to these riots, but by the time he arrives the wave of national hatred has subsided. National hate gives way to class hate; the Bolsheviki aspire towards power and the local population, tired of national and religious strife, see in the Reds a neutral force.

In the beginning of 1920, the Bolsheviki have control and start settling their scores with the representatives of the national parties. We are driven out of our house; everything we have is taken from us. My husband is arrested by the extraordinary commission and sentenced to death. But the particular conditions in Baku and his great influence oblige the Soviet powers to free him. In spite of his reiterated solicitations they refuse to let him leave the country, knowing that he is a mining engineer and one of the best specialists on the naphtha industry. Fate itself reserves for him the rôle of "spec." He is offered a post in the commissariat of foreign affairs which offers possibilities of a foreign mission.

My husband accepts and some time afterwards we leave for Constantinople. Here death awaited him: an assassin's hand ended the life of my husband whose only crime was to love above all things his people and his country, to which he had consecrated his studies, his work and all his life.

Two words more on the subject of the rumors that my husband had betrayed his companions of the "Moussavat" party, and that for this they had condemned him to death. In the eyes of those who have even slightly known the defunct, these rumors are so absurd that they are not worth the trouble of denying. Such gossip will not be able to tarnish, in the hearts of those who intimately knew him, the glorious memory of the defunct.

I am, yours etc.

5. The Crescent

They sell amber beads and the notaries and scribes have their little tables and stools in the court of the mosque of Bayazid. Charitable people have left foundations for the feeding of the pigeons that circle among the dappled branches of its planes and perch, drinking, beaks tilted up, throats shimmering with each swallow, on the marble verge of its washing fountain. One flaring noon I stood against the cold granite of a column watching a Bedoueen in a stiff bournous of white wool dictate a letter to a scribe with the gestures of an emperor composing an edict to a conquered city, when I noticed that a constant string of people was going in under the high portal of the mosque. Adventuring inquisitively near, I was beckoned in by a young man who dangled a green silk tassel at the end of his string of amber beads. An old man obsequiously pushed big slippers over my shoes, and I stepped over the high threshold. The huge red-carpeted floor under the dome and the dais along the sides were full of men, beggars and porters and artisans in leather aprons and small boys with fezzes too large for their bullet heads and stately gentlemen in frock coats and white vests with festooned watch chains and gravebearded theological students in neatly wound white cotton turbans, all squatting close together with their shoes beside them. A yellowbright beam of sunlight striking across the pearly shimmer of the dome gave full on the bronze face and shining beard of the mollah who was reading the Koran and brought fierce magenta flame into the silk hanging that fell from the front of the pulpit platform. He read in a wooden staccato voice, swaying slightly with the rhythm, and in the pause at the end of each verse a soft Ameen growled through the crowd.

—It is for the fall of Adrianople, this day every year, the young man with the green tassel on his beads whispered in French in my ear.—Many of these people come from Adrianople, fled from the Greeks. . . . Commemoration.

The man who had been reading climbed down clumsily across the magenta silk hanging and a taller man with full lips and dark cheeks flushed under hollow eyes took his place. .

—Now he will pray for the army in Anatolia.

His body erect, his eyes staring straight into the sunlight, his hands raised level with his beard in the attitude of prayer, the new mollah shouted a prayer full of harsh ringing consonants and brazen upward cadences. His voice was like warhorns and kettledrums. And all through the mosque under the faintly blue dome men looked beyond the palms of their raised hands at the flaming magenta silk and the priest praying in the yellow shaft of sunlight, and the Ameen at every pause rose from a growl to a roar, grew fierce and breathless till the little glass lamps tinkled in the huge flat chandeliers above the turbans and the fezzes, rolled up the stucco walls, shook the great dome as the domes of the churches must have shaken with the shout of the fighting-men of Islam the day Constantine's city was carried by assault and the last Constantine killed in his purple boots.

At the door as they left everyone was presented with a card on which was a cut of the great mosque of Adrianople, and with a small tissuepaper bag of candies.

6. Douzico

A fragile savor comes from the tiny rounded leaves of the basil in a pot on the edge of the café table. Behind on a little platform fenced with red baize, musicians keep up a reiterant humming and twanging out of which a theme in minor climbs and skids in an endless arabesque. There is a kind of lute, a zither, a violin and a woman who sings. In the midst is a stool with coffeecups and a bottle of mastic. The zither is played by a grizzled man with a bottlenose and spectacles who occasionally throws his head back and opens his mouth wide and lets out happily a great Gregorian yodel which the other voices follow and lead back with difficulty into the web of sound. At the tables packed under the locusttree where they will get shade in the afternoon sit people with narghiles or cigarettes or German pipes or American cigars drinking mastic and beer and coffee and even vodka. There is a smell of tobacco and charcoal and anis from the mastic and douzico and grilled meat from the skewers of chiche kebab, and a discordance of many hostile languages and a shuffle of feet from the street under the terrace.

Leaning my chin on my hands and looking down at the strip of cracked and dusty pavement between the bare feet of the boys who sell cakes and pistachio nuts and flyspotted candy along the terrace wall, and the row of autos for hire, of which the drivers, mostly Russians in various patched uniforms, loll and sleep and chat, waiting for a fare through the long afternoon hours. . . . Across that space shoes, feet, shambling legs, crossed arms, arms swinging vacantly, stoop shoulders, strongly moulded backs under thin cotton, chests brown, sweatbeaded, shawls, black veils of women, yakmaks, faces. All life is sucked into the expressiveness of faces. A boy, skin the color of an earthen pot, eyes and lips of a drunken Bacchus, swaggers by jauntily, on his head a tray of roasted yellow corn. A girl patters along, mouselike, features droop white as a freesia behind a thin black veil. A whitebearded man in a blue gown, redrimmed eyes as bleared as moonstones, being led by a tiny brown boy. Two hammals, each strong enough to carry a piano alone, with deeplymarked mindless features, and the black beards of Assyrian bowmen. Three Russians, blond, thickchested of the same height, white canvas tunics pulled down tight under their belts, blue eyes, with a freshwashed look and their hair parted and slicked like children dressed for a party. A stout Greek businessman in a Palm Beach suit. Tommies very pink and stiff. Aggressive thickjawed gobs playing with small maggotlike beggar-children. Palefaced Levantines with slinking eyes and hooked noses. Armenians with querulous mouths and great gold brown eyes. In the bright sun and the violent shadows faces blur and merge as they pass. Faces are smooth and yellow like melons, steely like axes; faces are like winter squashes, like death's heads and jack o'lanterns and cocoanuts and sprouting potatoes. They merge slowly in the cruel white sunlight, brown faces under fezzes, yellow faces under strawhats, pale northern faces under khaki caps—into one face, brows sullen and contracted, eyes black with suffering, skin taut over the cheekbones, hungry lines about the corners of the mouth, lips restless, envious, angry, lustful. The face of a man not quite starved out.

They are the notes, these faces, twanged on the trembling strings of this skein of frustrate lives that is Pera. So many threads out of the labyrinth. If one could only follow back into the steep dilapidated streets where the black wooden houses overhang, and women with thick ankles look down with kohl-smeared eyes at the porters who stumble under their huge loads up the uneven steps, sweating so that the red out of their fezzes runs in streaks down their knobbed and shaggy cheeks; through the sudden plane-shaded lanes that snatch occasional unbelievable blue distances of sea or umber distances of hills seen through the tilting and delicately-carved tombposts of Turkish cemeteries, and lead out into the pathless heaps of masonry of burnt-over places, where gapes an occasional caving dome with beside it a gnawed minaret, where sneakthieves and homeless people live in the remnants of houses or in shattered cisterns; or down through the waterfront streets of Galata with their fruitstands and their Greek women jiggling in doorways and their sailors' cafés full of the jingle of mechanical pianos or the brassy trombone music of an orchestra, where the dancing of ill-assorted close-hugged couples has a sway of the sea to it; or through the cool bazaars of Stamboul where in the half darkness under the azure-decorated vault Persian and Greek and Jewish and Armenian merchants spread out print cloths and Manchester goods which an occasional beam of dusty sunlight sets into a flame of colors; or into the ruined palaces along the Bosphorus where refugees from one place or another live in dazed and closepacked squalor; or into the gorgeous tinsel-furnished apartments where Greek millionaires and Syrian war-profiteers give continual parties just off the Grande Rue de Pera; or to the yards and doorways where the Russians sleep huddled like sheep in a snowstorm: somewhere some day one might find the core, the key to decipher this intricate arabesque scrawled carelessly on a ground of sheer pain.

This afternoon I can only sit sipping douzico made opal white with water, ears drowsy with the strangely satisfying monotony of the Turkish orchestra's unending complaint. The cool north wind off the Black Sea has come up and is making dust and papers dance in whirlwinds across Taxim Square.

Along the line of taxis, abolishing them, abolishing the red trolleycars and the victorious puttees of Greek officers, his head in embroidered cap bowed against the wind, his almond eyes closed to black slits against the dust, taking little steps in his black embroidered slippers, the great sleeves of his flowing crimson silk gown flapping in the wind, walks a mandarin of China.

Cathay!

7. *Constantine and the Classics*

Little Mr. Moscoupoulos threw up pudgy hands.

—But the Turks have not studied the Greek classics. They are ignorant. They do not know Aristophanes or Homer or Demosthenes, not even the deputies. Et sans connaître les classiques grecs on ne peut être ni politicien, ni orateur, ni diplomate. Turkey does not exist. I assure you, sir, it is a mere question of brigandage. And this city—we peered out of the window of the Pera Palace at a passing Allied staffcar—you know the legend. A Constantine built it, a Constantine lost it, and a Constantine shall regain it. . . .

Overhead bunches of green grapes hang down from the dense thatch of vineleaves and twined stems. A café outside one of the gates in the great wall of Heraclius. The dusty road dips into a low gateway that seems too small for the heavy dust-raising carts that clatter through it. On either side grey square towers timecrumbled at the top. Endlessly in either direction, grey walls occasionally splotched with the bright green of a figtree, and grey square towers. Towards the east a patch of the luminous aquamarine blue of the Sea of Marmora; westward bare umber-colored hills. In the purplish shadow of the vine arbor little tables and stools of unpainted wood and on each table a pot of rosemary or basil or thyme or a geranium in flower. In a group in one corner old men with grave gestures discuss some problem with quietly modulated voices. Their white turbans are almost motionless; now and then there is a flash of white when a head nods in a patch of sun, or a hand, lean and brown, is lifted to a grey beard. Beside me three young men in fezzes of new bright red are exchanging witticisms. An old gentleman with a puffy red face, dressed in the eternal white vest and broadtailed frock coat, listens, looks across his narghile with eyes sparkling and occasionally throws his head back and roars with laughter. A yellow slender man with green carpet slippers beside him is looking into vacancy with large yellow-brown eyes, in his hand a long amber cigarette-holder that is bright gold when the sun strikes it.

Sans connaître les classiques on ne peut être ni diplomate, ni politicien, ni orateur. . . . But one can sit in the shade where the cool wind rustles the vineleaves, letting the days slip through the fingers smooth and decorously shaped as the lumps of amber of the conversation beads with which one hand or the other constantly plays.

Out of the gate snorting and grinding in low gear comes a staffcar full of Allied officers, glint of gold braid and a chattering of voices. A cloud of dust hides it as it crawls up the uneven road.

A flock of sheep forms bleating out of the dust, followed by two shepherds who shout and throw stones and beat with their sticks until the sheep begin to flow through the narrow gate like water through the outlet in a trough.

Sans connaître les classiques. . . . A party of the Inter-Allied policeforce has come up and they stare searchingly in the faces of the Turks in the café. There are two Italian gendarmes with shiny threecornered hats and buttons on their coattails, some British M.P.s with hard red necks, French flics with the whiskers familiar to Paris cartoonists. They are all redfaced and sweaty from their rounds and there is dust on their highly polished shoes. When they have stared their fill at the people in the café they turn and go through the gate into town. Under the vines no one has noticed them. The voices of the old men continue, and the slow movement of a hand stroking a beard. In the upper bowl of the narghiles there is a little red glow at long intervals when the smoker pulls deeply.

Above the grey towers and the wall, kites with black curved wings and hawk-beaks circle in the porcelain-blue sky.

8. Alexanders

Going down to Therapia they pointed out the place where two nights before a French truck with a regimental fanfare in it had gone over the khud. Ah, monsieur, nous avons vécu des journées atroces, said the tall Greek lady beside me with a dangerous roll of her black eyes. At the next curve the car gave a terrible lurch to avoid an old man with a mule.—Four of them were killed outright. They say they were dead drunk anyway. They never found the truck or the bodies . . . le Bosphore, vous comprenez. She smiled coyly with her large lips on which the rouge was restricted to a careful Cupid's bow.

At Therapia we sat on the terrace with the green swift Bosphorus in front of us and watched Englishmen in white flannels play tennis. A hot stagnant afternoon. Locusts whirred madly among the dusty cypresses. People in frock coats sat whispering round the little tables. Mr. Deinos who was starting a steamship line to run from Constantinople to New York, sat in a lavender grey linen suit between the two tall ladies with lurching eyes and Cupid's-bow mouths coyly puckered. . . . Greece, he began, is going to fulfil her historic mission. . . .

I slipped away and strayed into the bar. A British major with a face like the harvest moon was shaking up Alexanders. A man in a frock coat was trying to catch in his mouth olives that an American relief worker was tossing in the air. The talk in the bar was English, Oxford drawl, Chicago burr, Yankee twang, English and American as spoken by Greeks, Armenians, Frenchmen, Italians. Only the soberer people in the corners spoke French.

—Intelligence service cleaned up another Bolo plot . . . yessiree. Collected all the Bolos in town and towed them up into the Black Sea in a leaky scow and left 'em there.—Best place for them. Ungrateful beggars, these Russians. . . . Here we evacuate them from Odessa and Sebastopol and now they go turning red on us. The leader was a woman. . . . Picked her out of a room at the Tokatlian. When the A.P.C. knocked at the door she took off all her clothes and went to bed. Thought they'd be too gentlemanly to break in. Well they just wrapped her up in a blanket and carried her off the way she was.

—Well, sir, I was the last white man outa Sebastopol. . . . Agricultural machinery's my line.

—Turkish bandits carried off six Greeks last night from that village opposite. . . .

—Did you hear the one about young Stafford was walking with a Red Cross nurse out on the road near the Sweet Waters and bandits held them up? They didn't touch the girl but they stripped him down to the skin. . . . The girl made them give him back his drawers for decency.

—And the General said: There's not enough light, we want a flambeau in each of the windows. People tried to point out that the lace curtains might catch, but the General had had beaucoup champagne and kept calling for his flambeaux; well, they brought his flambeaux and the curtains did catch and now the Sultan has one less palace. . . . It was a great sight.

—This is extremely confidential, what I'm telling you now. This man we were talking about. His name begins with a Z. . . . You know the Vickers man. . . . You ask me some time about Vickers and the Ismid Roads. It seems that he's not a Jew at all but a Constantinople Greek. Everybody knew him around Pera, some little clothing business or other. Then one day he disappeared with the contents of a safe and turns up a couple of years later as a millionaire silk buyer in Lyon, and benefactor of the French Republic and all that sort of thing.

—No, this chap was a colonel on Wrangel's staff. They were starving and one day he found out that his wife and daughter had been . . . you know . . . for money and he shot 'em both dead and disappeared. Last night some charcoal burners found his body out in the hills. . . .

—Yessir I was the last white man outa Sebastopol . . . strange things you see in the Black Sea. . . . Agricultural machinery's my line. Last time I was out in Batum I seen upwards of six hundred women in swimmin' an' not one of 'em had a stitch on, in their birthday suits every one of 'em.

—Well, Major, how about another shakerful of Alexanders? They're mild and they hit the right spot.

—Kemal! He's finished. . . . Like hell he is. There's a lot of legendary stuff about him going round. How at Eski Chehir the Turkish army sank into the ground and came up behind the Greek lines. That's the kind of stuff that makes a hero in the east.

—They say that three divisions of Bolos are going in through Armenia and that he's promised 'em Constantinople in return for their help.

—Let 'em try and get it.

—They will get it some day.

—Nonsense the Greeks'll have it—The British—The French —The Bulgarians . . . —The League of Nations,—The Turks. —I suggest it be made neutral and presented to Switzerland, that's the only solution.

Outside on the terrace Mr. Deinos and the two tall Greek ladies with Cupid's-bow mouths were eating pistachio nuts and drinking douzico in the amethyst twilight.—Greece, continued Mr. Deinos, has always been the bulwark of civilization against the barbarians. Inspired by Marathon and Salamis and I hope by the help and sympathy of America, Greece is once more going to take up her historic mission. . . .

III. Trebizond

Between Ineboli and Samsoun. Lying on the empty boat-deck of the Italian steamer *Aventino*, a scrawny boat that used to be Austrian, empty this trip except for several hundred Russian soldiers crowded into the forward hold, prisoners being repatriated. I'm lying on my face; through my shirt the two o'clock sun claws my back already stinging from the burn of a day's swimming at Prinkipo. In the space between the deck and the lifeboat I can sleepily see a great expanse of waves grey and green like the breast of a pigeon, and beyond the khaki hills of Asia Minor rising in enormous folds up to bloated white clouds that float in slaty reaches of mist. The wind stirs my hair and whispers in my ears; under my face the deck trembles warmly to the throb of the engines. There's no past and no future, only the drowsy, inexplicable surge of moving towards the sunrise across the rolling world. There's no opium so sweet as the unguarded sunny sleep on the deck of a boat when it's after lunch in summer and you don't know when you are going to arrive nor what port you will land at, when you've forgotten east and west and your name and your address and how much money you have in your pocket.

And then awake again looking up into the shimmering blue sky, thinking of Constant' and the interallied police strutting about and the bedbugs at the Pera Palace and long lines of ragged people waiting for visas for their passports, and the blue eyes of Russians, blue as the sky in sagged tallow faces; Russians standing at every corner selling papers and kewpie dolls, cigarettes, sugar buns, postcards, paper flowers, jumping jacks and jewelry; and the longnosed Armenians sitting on squares of matting in the courtyards of falling down palaces, and the Turks from Macedonia sitting quiet under trees round the mosques in Stamboul, and the Greek refugees and the Jewish refugees and the charred streets of burnt-out bazaars; and late one night the onelegged man sobbing into his knotted hands.

Groggy with sleep and sun I got to my feet. Gulls were circling about the ship. Here the air was clean of misery and refugees and armies and police and passport officers. The Russian soldiers in the bow of the boat looked very happy. It was like looking down into a pit full of bear cubs. In their cramped quarters they played and wrestled and rolled each other about, big clumsy towheaded men in dirty tunics belted tight at the waist. They throw each other down with great bearlike swats, pick each other up laughing as if nothing could hurt them, kiss and start sparring again. They are restless like children kept in after school.

In a corner a bunch of Tatars squat gravely by themselves, broadfaced men with black slits for eyes. They sit motionless looking over the bright plain of the sea; a few of them play cards or cut up their bread in strips to dry it in the sun.

The captain, a tall man with white Umberto Primo whiskers, has come up gravely beside me and looks down into the hold, making a clucking noise with his tongue.—They smell bad, those Russians. They have no officers. What's the use of sending them back just to make more Bolsheviki? I Alleati son' pazzi . . . tutti. They're crazy, the Allies, all of them. Aren't there enough Bolsheviki?

2. Angora

It was a surprise to find six Turkish army doctors in uniform sitting on the bench in the companionway. They certainly had been nowhere visible when we left Constantinople. They were worried about the Greek cruiser *Chilkis* that was sinking fishing boats and taking potshots at villages along the coast. They had the set faces of men with their backs to the wall. They treated me with jerky and very cold politeness.

—You Europeans are all hypocrites. When Turkish soldiers get out of hand and kill a few Armenians who are spies and traitors, you roll your eyes and cry massacre, but when the Greeks burn defenseless villages and murder poor fishermen it's making the world safe for democracy.

—I'm not a European, I'm an American.

—We believed your Meester Veelson. . . . All we want is to be left alone and reorganize our country in peace. If you believed in the rights of small nations why did you let the

British set the Greeks on us? You think the Turk is an old man and sick, smoking a narghile. Perhaps we are old men and sick men, but originally we were nomads. We are sober and understand how to fight. If necessary we will become nomads again. If the Allies drive us out of Constantinople, very good. It is a city of misery and decay. We will make Angora our capital. We were not made to live in cities. Our life is in the fields and on the plains. If they drive us out of Angora we will go back to the great plains of central Asia, where we came from. Tell that to your high commissioners and your Meester Veelson. You have been to Stamboul. Did you see any Turks there? Only old people, beggars, Armenians and Jews, riffraff. The Turks are all in Angora with Mustapha Kemal.

—Are you going to Angora?

They nodded gravely.—We are going to Angora.

3. Inexplicable Staircases

We are at anchor in the bay in front of Trebizond. I wear out the upper deck walking up and down. The authorities won't let any one ashore, as the *Chilkis* shelled the town this morning. There's a rumor that they are carrying out reprisals on the remaining Greeks and Armenians, so I wear out the upper deck and stare at the town till my eyes are ready to pop out of my head.

A pink and white town built on arches, terracing up among cypresses, domes and minarets and weather-gnawed towers against a mother-of-pearl sky piling up over the shoulder of a bulky escarped hill. Further along, dull vermilion cliffs zigzagged with inexplicable white staircases climbing up from the sea and stopping suddenly in the face of the cliff.

Black luggers are coming out over the grassgreen water to unload the cargo.

Trebizond, one of the capitals of my childhood geography, a place of swords and nightingales and a purple-born princess in a garden where the trees grew rubies and diamonds instead of flowers, a lonely never-to-be-rescued princess bright and cold and slender as an icicle, guarded by gold lions and automaton knights and a spray of molten lead and roar and smoke of Greek fire.

And what is happening in this Trebizond under the white mask of walls and domes? There's no smoke from any of the houses, no sound comes across the water. I walk up and down wearing out the upper deck wondering at the white staircases that zigzag up from the sea and stop suddenly in the face of the cliff.

At sunset we hove anchor and started nudging down the coast into the gloom eastward.

a pigeon a huge sun swells red to bursting. Palm-fronds and broad leaves of planes sway against a darkening zenith. In the space of dust outside of their barracks Georgian soldiers are gathered lazily into a circle. They wear ragged greyish uniforms, some with round fur caps, some with the pointed felt helmets of the Red Army. Many of them are barefoot. Blows off them a sweaty discouraged underfed smell. One man, seated, starts thumping with his palms a double shuffle on a small kettledrum held between his legs. The rest beat time by clapping until one man breaks out into a frail melody. He stops at the end of a couple of phrases, and a young fellow, blond, rather sprucely dressed with a clean white fur cap on the back of his head, starts dancing. The rest keep time with their hands and sing Tra-la-la, Tra-la-la to the tune in a crooning undertone. The dance is elegant, mincing, with turkeylike struttings and swift hunting gestures, something in it of the elaborate slightly farded romance of eastern chivalry. One can imagine silver swords and spangled wallets and gaudy silk belts with encrusted buckles. Perhaps it is a memory that makes the men's eyes gleam so as they beat time, a memory of fine horses and long inlaid guns and toasts drunk endlessly out of drinking horns, and of other more rousing songs sung in the mountains at night of the doughty doings of the Knight of the Pantherskin.

3. *Proletcult*

On the walls some crude squares of painting in black and white, a man with a pick, a man with a shovel, a man with a gun. The shadows are so exaggerated they look like gingerbread men. Certainly the man who painted them had not done many figures before in his life. The theater is a long tin shed that used to be a cabaret show of some sort, the audience mostly workmen and soldiers in white tunics open at the neck, and women in white muslin dresses. Many of the men and all the children are barefoot and few of the women wear stockings. When the curtain goes up romping and chattering stop immediately; everyone is afraid of missing a word of what is said on the stage. It's a foolish enough play, an Early-Victorian sob-story, about a blind girl and a good brother and a wicked brother, and a bad marquis and a frequently fainting marquise, but the young people who play it—none of them ever acted before the Red Army entered Batum three months ago—put such conviction into it that one can't quite hold aloof from the very audible emotion of the audience during the ticklish moments of the dagger-fight between the frail good brother and the wicked and hearty elder brother who has carried off the little blind girl against her will. And when at last all wrongs are righted, and the final curtain falls on felicity, one can't help but feel that the lives of these people who crowd out through the dilapidated ex-beergarden in front of the theater have somehow been compensated for the bareness of the hungry livingrooms and barracks they go home to. In the stamping and the abandon with which the two heroes fought was perhaps an atom of some untrammelled expression, of some gaudy bloodcurdling ritual which might perhaps replace in people's hopes and lives the ruined dynasty of Things.

4. Bees

The secretary of the commission for schools recently set up in Batum was a blackhaired man, hawknosed, holloweyed, with a three-day growth of beard. Undernourishment and overwork had made his eyes a little bloodshot and given them a curious intense stare. He had a sheaf of papers in front of him among which he scribbled an occasional hasty word, as if pressed for time. He spoke French with difficulty, digging it up word by word from some long-forgotten layer of his mind. He talked about the new school-system the Bolsheviki were introducing in the new republic of Adjaria, of which Batum was the capital, explained how already children's summer colonies had been started in several villages, how every effort was being made to get equipment ready to open the primary and secondary schools at the end of September.

—All education is to be by work, nothing without actual touch; he spread his hands, that were angular tortured painful hands, wide, and closed them with a gesture of laying hold onto some slippery reality. The words he used, too, were concrete, dug out of the soil.—From the very first, work. . . . In summer in the fields, the children must cultivate gardens, raise rabbits, bees, chickens, learn how to take care of cattle.

They must go into the forests and learn about trees. Everything they must learn by touch. Then in the winter they must study their native languages and Esperanto. . . . Here there will be schools for Armenians, Greeks, Muslims, Georgians, Russians . . . and the rudiments of sociology, arithmetic, woodworking, cooking. For in our republic every man must be able to attend to his wants himself. That will be the primary education. You see, nothing by theory, everything by practice. Then the secondary education will be more specialized, preparation for trades and occupations. Then those who finish the high schools can go to the universities to do independent work in the directions they have chosen. You see, merit will be according to work, not by theories or examinations. And all through there will be instruction in music and gymnastics and the theater; the arts must be open to anyone who wants to work in them. But most important will be nature; the young children must be all the time in the fields and forests, among the orchards where there are bees. . . . It is in the little children that all our hope lies . . . among orchards where there are bees.

5. Bedbug Express

Ce n'est pas serios, the tall Swede had said when he and I and an extremely evil-looking Levantine with gimlet-pointed whiskers had not been allowed to go down the gangplank at Batum. Ce n'est pas serios, he had said, indicating the rotting harbor and the long roofs of the grey and black town set in dense pyrites-green trees and the blue and purple mountains in the distance and the Red Guards loafing on the wharf and the hammer and sickle of the Soviet Republic painted on the wharfhouse. The last I saw of him he was still standing at the end of the gangplank, the points of his standup collar making pink dents in his thick chin, shaking his head and muttering, Ce n'est pas serios.

I thought of him when, accompanied by a swaggering interpreter and by a cheerful man very worried about typhus from the N.E.R., I stood in front of the Tiflis express waving a sheaf of little papers in my hand, passes in Georgian and in Russian, transport orders, sleeping car tickets, a pass from the

Cheka and one from the Commissar for Foreign Affairs of the Republic of Adjaria. The Tiflis express consisted of an engine, three huge unpainted sleepers and a very gaudy suncracked caboose. One car was reserved for civil officials, one for the military and one for the general public. So far it was extremely serious, but the trouble was that long before the train had drawn into the station it had been stormed by upwards of seven thousand people, soldiers in white tunics, peasant women with bundles, men with long moustaches and astrakhan caps, speculators with peddlers' packs and honest proletarians with loaves of bread, so that clots of people all sweating and laughing and shoving and wriggling obliterated the cars, like flies on a lump of sugar. There were people on every speck of the roof, people hanging in clusters from all the doors, people on the coal in the coalcar, people on the engine; from every window protruded legs of people trying to wriggle in. Those already on board tried to barricade themselves in the compartments and with surprising gentleness tried to push the newcomers out of the windows again. Meanwhile the eastbound American ran up and down the platform dragging his hippopotamus suitcase, streaking sweat from every pore and trying to find a chink to hide himself in. At last recourse had to be had to authority. Authority gave him a great boost by the seat of the pants that shot him and his suitcase in by a window into a compartment full of very tall men in very large boots, six of the seven soldiers who occupied his seat were thrown out, all hands got settled and furbished up their foreign languages and sat quietly sweating waiting for the train to leave.

Eventually after considerable circulation of rumors that we were not going to leave that day, that the track was torn up, that a green army had captured Tiflis, that traffic was stopped on account of the cholera, we started off without the formality of a whistle. The train wound slowly through the rich jade and emerald jungle of the Black Sea coast towards tall mountains to the northeast that took on inconceivable peacock colors as the day declined. In the compartment we nibbled black bread and I tried to juggle French and German into a conversation. Someone was complaining of the lack of manufactured articles, paint and women's stockings and medicine and spare parts for automobiles and soap and flatirons and toothbrushes.

Someone else was saying that none of those things were necessary: The mountains will give us wool, the fields will give us food, the forests will give us houses; let every man bake his own and spin his own and build his own; that way we will be happy and independent of the world. If only they would not compromise with industrialism. But in Moscow they think, if only we get enough foreign machinery the revolution will be saved; we should be self-sufficient like the bees.

Strange how often they speak to you of bees. The order and sweetness of a hive seem to have made a great impression on the Russians of this age. Again and again in Tiflis people talked of bees with a sort of wistful affection, as if the cool pungence of bees were a tonic to them in the midst of the soggy bleeding chaos of civil war and revolution.

By this time it was night. The train was joggling its desultory way through mountain passes under a sky solidly massed with stars like a field of daisies. In the crowded compartment, where people had taken off their boots and laid their heads on each other's shoulders to sleep, hordes of bedbugs had come out of the stripped seats and bunks, marching in columns of three or four, well disciplined and eager. I had already put a newspaper down and sprinkled insect powder in the corner of the upper berth in which I was hemmed by a solid mass of sleepers. The bedbugs took the insect powder like snuff and found it very stimulating, but it got into my nose and burned, got into my eyes and blinded me, got into my throat and choked me, until the only thing for it was to climb into the baggage rack, which fortunately is very large and strong in the Brobdignagian Russian trains. There I hung, eaten only by the more acrobatic of the bugs, the rail cutting into my back, the insect powder poisoning every breath, trying to make myself believe that a roving life was the life for me. Above my head I could hear the people on the roof stirring about.

At about midnight the train stopped for a long while at a station. Tea was handed round, made in great samovars like watertanks; their fires were the only light; you could feel that there was a river below in the valley, a smell of dry walls and human filth came up from some town or other. Huge rounded shoulders of hills cut into the stars. Enlivened by the scalding tea, we all crawled into our holes again, the bunches of people holding on at the doors reformed, and the train was off. This time I went very decently to sleep listening to the stirring of the people on the roof above my head, to the sonorous rumble of the broadgauge wheels and to a concertina that wheezed out a torn bit of song now and then in another car.

In the morning we look out at a silver looping river far below in a huge valley between swelling lioncolored hills. The train casts a strange shadow in the morning light, all its angles obliterated by joggling, dangling figures of soldiers; on the roofs are the shadows of old women with baskets, of men standing up and stretching themselves, of children with caps too big for them. On a siding we pass the long train of the second tank division of the Red Army; a newpainted engine, then endless boxcars, blond young soldiers lolling in the doors. Few of them look more than eighteen; they are barefoot and scantily dressed in canvas trousers and tunics; they look happy and at their ease, dangling their legs from the roofs and steps of boxcars and sleepers. You can't tell which are the officers. Out of the big clubcar decorated with signs and posters that looks as if it might have been a diner in its day, boys lean to wave at the passing train. Then come flatcars with equipment, then a long row of tanks splotched and striped with lizard green.—A gift of the British, says the man beside me. The British gave them to Denikin, and Denikin left them to us.

Our train, the windows full of travelgrimed faces and the seats full of vermin, gathers speed and tilts round a bend. The sight of the green tanks has made everybody feel better. The man beside me, who used to be a banker in Batum and hopes to be again, exclaims fervently: All these words, Bolshevik, Socialist, Menshevik, have no meaning any more. . . . Conscious of it or not, we are only Russians.

6. The Relievers

Members of the N.E.R. sign a pledge not to drink fermented or distilled liquors. A private car full of members of the N.E.R. is in Tiflis trying to decide whether starving people or people with full bellies are more likely to become communists. In Tiflis twenty people a day die of cholera, forty people a day die of typhus, not counting those who die where nobody finds them. At the N.E.R. headquarters we all sleep on canvas cots and gargle with listerine to avoid infection and to take the vodka off our breaths. Headquarters swarms with miserable barons and countesses who naturally sigh for the old régime and color the attitude of even the honest men among the relievers. What American can stand up against a title, much less against a refugee title in distress? Why, she might be the Princess Anastasia in disguise! The Russian government understands all that but wisely argues that a live White child is better than a dead Red child; so it gives the relievers a free hand to decide what sheep shall live and what goats shall die.

But the real energy of the relievers goes into the relief of Things. To a casual eye Tiflis is bare of Things, nothing in the shopwindows, houses empty as the tents of arabs, but towards the N.E.R. there is a constant streaming of diamonds, emeralds, rubies, silver-encrusted daggers, rugs, Georgian, Anatolian, rugs from Persia and Turkestan, watches, filigree work, silver mesh bags, furs, amber, the Mustapha Sirdar papers, cameras, fountain pens. My dear, the bargains! For a suitcase full of roubles you can outfit yourself for life. I guess the folks back home'll be surprised when I tell 'em what I paid for that sunburst I bought the wife.

And, carrying the things, greyfaced people, old men and women terribly afraid of the Cheka of brigands of the cholera, of their shadows, débris of a wrecked world, selling for a few days' food, Things that had been the mainstay of their lives up to 1917; swaggering young men who had picked the winning team and were making a good thing of it; professional speculators, men who were usually but not always Greeks, Armenians, or Jews, men with sharp eyes and buzzard beaks, dressed in shabby overcoats, humpbacked with respect and politeness, rubbing their hands that never let go a banknote however depreciated the currency was, men who will be the founders of great banking houses in the future, philanthropists and the founders of international families. The bargains, the bargains!

And the pride and virtue of the members of the N.E.R. who had signed a pledge not to drink alcoholic or fermented liquors, who are relieving the sufferings of humanity at the risk of their lives, who are exposing themselves to the contamination of Bolshevism, communism, free love, nationalized women, anarchy and God knows what—their virtuous pride in the dollar king of the exchange as they paw over the bargains; rugs stolen out of the mosques, lamps out of churches; pearls off the neck of a slaughtered grand duchess; the fur coat of some poor old woman who sits hungry in her bare room looking out through a chink in the shutters at this terrible young people's world, a world jagged and passionate and crude that she can never understand, an old woman looking out through the shutters with the eyes of a cat that has been run over by an automobile.

7. *Funicular*

The inevitable Belgian Company still runs the funicular. You pay your fare to a little Polish girl neat as a mouse in a white dress. On her legs a faint ruddiness of sunburn takes the place of stockings. She complains of the lack of talcum powder and stockings and wonders what she's going to do when her shoes wear out. The car creaks jerkily up the hill. Above the shelter of the town a huge continual wind is blowing.

Back from a walk over the hills, I sit at a table outside a little shanty, drinking a bottle of wine of Kakhetia no. 66. Old Tiflis, dustcolored with an occasional patch of blue or white on a house, is loosely sprinkled in the funnel out of which the copper-wire river pours into the plain. Out of the defile rises a column of steam from the sulphur springs. Farther down, the enormous grey buildings of the Russian town straggle over the plain. From the valley bulge row after row of vast stratified hills, ochre and olivecolor, that get blue into the distance until they break into the tall range of the Caucasus barring the north. The huge continual streaming wind out of Asia, a wind so hard you can almost see it streaked like marble, a wind of unimaginable expanses, whines in the mouth of my glass and tears to tatters the insane jig that comes out of the mechanical piano behind me. I have to hold the bottle between my knees to keep it from blowing over.

We used to dream of a wind out of Asia that would blow our cities clean of the Things that are our gods, the knick-

knacks and the scraps of engraved paper and the vases and the
curtain rods, the fussy junk possession of which divides poor
man from rich man, the shoddy manufactured goods that are
all our civilization prizes, that we wear our hands and brains
out working for; so that from being an erect naked biped,
man has become a sort of hermit crab that can't live without
a dense conglomerate shell of dinnercoats and limousines and
percolators and cigarstore coupons and eggbeaters and
sewing machines, so that the denser his shell, the feebler his
self-sufficience, the more he is regarded a great man and a
millionaire. That wind has blown Russia clean, so that the
Things held divine a few years ago are mouldering rubbish in
odd corners; thousands of lives have been given and taken
(from where I sit I can make out the square buildings of the
Cheka, crammed at this minute with poor devils caught in the
cogs) a generation levelled like gravel under a steamroller to
break the tyranny of Things, goods, necessities, industrial civilization. Just now it's the lull after the fight. The gods and
devils are taking their revenge on the victors with cholera and
famine. Will the result be the same old piling up of miseries
again, or a faith and a lot of words like Islam or Christianity,
or will it be something impossible, new, unthought of, a life
bare and vigorous without being savage, a life naked and god-
less where goods and institutions will be broken to fit men,
instead of men being ground down fine and sifted in the service of Things?

Harder, harder blows the wind out of Asia; it has upset the
table, taken the chair out from under me. Bottle in one hand,
glass in the other, I brace myself against the scaring wind.

8. *International*

The eastbound American had dinner of caviar and tomatoes
and Grusinski shashlik and watermelon washed down with the
noble wine of Kakhetia in the pleasant gone-to-seed Jardin des
Petits Champs, where nobody thinks of cholera or typhus or
the famine along the Volga. Afterwards strolling through unlit
streets, you met no old people, only crowds of young men in
tunics and dark canvas trousers, some of them barefoot, young
girls in trim neatly cut white dresses without stockings or hats,

strolling happily in threes and fours and groups, filling the broad empty asphalt streets.

The night was warm and a dry wind drove the dust. The Grusinski garden, that used to be the Noblemen's Club, was crowded with the new softly laughing youngsters. A band was playing Light Cavalry. A few colored electric bulbs hung among the waving trees. There was nothing particular to do. In spite of famine and cholera and typhus everybody seemed nonchalant and effortlessly gay. A certain amount of wine was being sold, illegally, I think, at a table in a corner, but nobody but the Americans seemed to have any roubles to buy it with. Gradually the crowd was trickling into a theater that had great signs in Russian and in Georgian over the door. The eastbound American found himself in a narrow corridor being addressed as Amerikanski Poait and before he knew what was happening he found himself being settled in a seat in a curiously shaped room; as he was reaching for someone who spoke a known language one wall of the room rose and he found that he was on a stage facing an enormous auditorium packed with people. In the front row were broad grins on the faces of certain companions he had been with earlier in the evening. Then somebody behind his chair whispered in French into his ear that it was an international proletarian poetry festival and that he was expected to recite something. At that news the E. A. almost fainted.

The proceedings were splendid. Not more than ten people present ever understood any one thing. Poems were recited, chanted and sung in Armenian, Georgian, Turkish, Persian, Russian, German and God knows what else. Everything was received with the greatest enthusiasm. The E. A. managed to stammer out as his own a nursery rhyme by William Blake, the only thing he could remember, which revolutionary outburst was received with cheers. The E. A. retired in confusion and in a muck of sweat, feeling that probably he had mistaken his vocation. Certainly *Oh Sunflower weary of time* can never have been recited under stranger conditions. After a long poem in Russian by a thin young soldier with a conical head shaved bald that made everybody roar with laughter until the building shook, the meeting broke up amid the greatest international merriment and singing and everybody started streaming home through the pitchblack streets, young men in white tunics, bareheaded girls in white dresses, strolling about without restraint in this empty world like children playing in an abandoned house, gradually swallowed up by the huge black barracklike buildings.

On the way up the hill we passed the Cheka. The pavements round it were brilliantly lit. There was barbed wire in the windows. Sentries walked back and forth. As we walked past, trying to close our nostrils to the jail smell, the idyll crashed about our ears.

Up at the N.E.R. there was considerable excitement. One of the relievers was with difficulty being got into his cot. Others were talking about typhus and cholera. One man was walking round showing everyone a handful of heavy silver soupspoons.—Five cents apiece in American money, what do you think of that?—Are you sure they're not plated?—Genuine English sterling silver marked with the lion; can't get anything better'n that.—Because Major Vokes bought a necklace in Batum and it turned out to be paste.

I lay curled up on my cot listening to all this from the next room; the uneasy smell of the summer night came in through the open window with a sliver of moonlight. The street outside was empty and dark, but frailly from far away came the sound of a concertina. The jiggly splintered tune of a concertina was limping its way through the black half desert stone city, slipping in at the windows of barracks, frightening the middleaged people who sat among the last of their Things trembling behind closed shutters, maddening the poor devils imprisoned in the basement of the Cheka, caught under the wheels of the juggernaut of revolution, as people are caught under the wheels in every movement forward or back of the steamroller of human action. The jail is the cornerstone of liberty, thought the E. A. as he fell asleep.

V. One Hundred Views of Ararat

1. Tiflis

The train was made up of one small passenger car jammed with soldiers and many boxcars. I sat on my bag on the station platform as it pulled in and stared ruefully at the grandiloquent order for a compartment in the sleeping-car they had given me at the office of the Commissar for Foreign Affairs. The usual ragged crowd that haunts all railway stations in the Caucasus was scuttling up and down, dragging bags and gunnysacks from one side to the other, a sweating threadbare medley of peasants and soldiers. The Sayyid (that means descendant of the Prophet or of Ali, son of Abu Talib) strode about and made a great speech in Persian and Turkish to everyone who would listen on the rights and appurtenances of a diplomatic passport. At last, after much prodding of a weary interpreter and seeing of dignitaries at desks, it was decided that the nearest equivalent to a sleeper would be the freightcar that carried the newspapers and that the instructive company of great bundles of the *Isvestia* and the *Pravda* would be even superior to a compartment and a berth, that was, if the Commissar in charge consented. More commissars at desks were interviewed. Of course the Commissar was only too delighted. . . . The car was opened and one Samsoun, an Armenian, was discovered therein, to whom the Sayyid addressed a fervent allocation in Turkish on the virtues of cleanliness and hygiene, with the result that water was brought and lysol splashed to the very roof and new copies of all Moscow's most famous newspapers spread on the floor for us to sit on. At that point the Sayyid drew his knife and began to massacre a watermelon, and Samsoun effendi, or more properly Tavarishch Samsoun began to make a lustful gurgling noise in his thoat and brazenly asked for cognac. We put him off with a promise of wine later and with a slice of melon. At that point the two grimy youths who were Samsoun's underlings climbed aboard and the train, late only by some five hours, rumbled out of the station.

A curious sort of existence people lead along the railroad tracks in the Caucasus and, I suppose, all over Russia; the dilapidated arteries of communication exercise an uneasy sort of attraction. In all the stations there are crowds and even at crossings that seem very far from any village, groups of men and women stand and watch the train go by. Perhaps they feel a vague ownership over the endless gleaming rails and the oilsmeared locomotives, feel that somehow by this means their hungry frustrate lives are linked to great happenings far away. Then so many people seem to live all their lives along the tracks. The soldiers of the Red Army are in many cases permanently quartered in passengercars and freightcars fitted up with bunks that fill up all the sidings joined in long trains with staffcars and clubcars and hospitalcars and with cars loaded with the black bread and salt herring that form the staple rations. Then there are the special armored trains that have been one of the features of each of the campaigns of the civil war. Furthermore, particularly near towns, there are hundreds of freightcars fitted up with windows and stovepipes, used as houses by all manner of families—refugees from Lord knows where, people who repair the railroad, minor officials, gypsies, vagabonds of all sorts. And as the train goes by all this population cranes from between sliding doors and from the little windows of cabooses and scrutinizes with mild insolence the soldiers and peasants and civil employees who sprawl on the roofs and dangle their legs from the open doors of jerkily moving boxcars.

2. Karakliss

Moonlight sifts through tall poplars by the railway track and mingles strangely on the floor of the boxcar with the glimmer of the candle in my corner. The Sayyid has contrived a sort of bed out of his suitcase and the provision box and is somewhat uneasily asleep. Probably he's dreaming of Pan-Islam and driving off the attacks of hundreds of little British devils with cloven hoofs and pith helmets. At the other end of the car the Georgian and Samsoun and his myrmidons have made beds for themselves among the piles of newspapers. Outside, the station platform is deserted, drowned in moonlight. There is the sound of a stream. All along the picket fence are the shadows of people asleep. Along with the clean smell of the river and the mountains that rear spiny backs into the sheer moonlight behind the poplars, comes occasionally a miserable disheartening stench of cold sweat and rags and filthy undernourished bodies huddled somewhere in the sheds about the station.

Ever since sunset we've been in Armenia, having crossed the neutral zone where the Georgians and Armenians burnt each other's villages till the British stopped them, back in 1918. At the last Georgian stations before we started to climb this long valley up into the Little Caucasus everybody on the train invested largely in watermelons, which could be bought for a couple of thousand roubles apiece. Up here in the mountains and in the famine area, they sell for ten thousand or more.

At about dusk we had great excitement. Shots were fired and whistles blown all down the train. Samsoun effendi drew an enormous revolver and began to whirl it about with great heroism, and sent off the smallest boy to find out what was the matter. First the news came that a woman had fallen off the top of a freightcar and been killed, but it eventually transpired that it was only a bag of flour that had fallen out of the American relief car. So the flour was picked up and everybody got back to his place, in the cars or on the roof or on the rods, and the train started wheezing its way up the grade again. Samsoun effendi was put in high spirits by the accident and started telling us of past deeds of valor, pointing the revolver absentmindedly at each person in turn as he did so. To get the revolver back into its holster the Sayyid and I had to crack a bottle of our best wine of Kakhetia. The effect was magical. The smallest youngster, a curious boy with a face as careworn as a monkey's, began to sing songs of the Volga in an unexpectedly deep voice. The Georgian tightened his belt and slapped his thighs and began to dance, and a broad grin divided the rugged features, partly like those of a camel and partly like those of the Terrible Turk of the cartoons, of Samsoun effendi himself.

3. Alexandropol

Dusty soldiers and freightyards jammed with freightcars of which the paint has peeled under the hot sun. The little

Armenian girl has picked up her basket and gone. She appeared somewhere in the night in tow of a white-whiskered station master. Caused quite a stir. The Sayyid sat up on his valise, and noticing that she had on her chin the mole so admired of Orientals, put on an air of the most splendid doggishness and cried out Quel théâtre! in a loud voice. Samsoun effendi lit a candle and started smoothing his hair, looking at himself with great satisfaction in a small pocket mirror the while. But the Armenian girl was quite unmoved by all these manifestations and went calmly to sleep with her head on her basket.

As it grew light we crossed the watershed of the Little Caucasus. On the north side the villages, scattered collections of square houses of volcanic stone, roofed with turf and often topped by tall hayricks, were intact, and wellfed peasants were already in the fields getting in the crops, but from the moment the train started winding down the southerly slope, everything was sheer desert. The last Turkish attack, in 1920, had wiped the country clean; not a house intact in the villages, no crops, even the station buildings systematically destroyed, and everything movable carted away. Ghengiz Khan and his Tatars couldn't have laid waste more thoroughly. Alexandropol itself, though warseedy to the last degree, had evidently been spared. It straggles among railway yards on a yellow scorched plain, where the wind blows the dust in swirling clouds from one side to the other; the most outstanding buildings are the great rows of grey barracks where orphans are housed by the Near East Relief. On the station platform the usual crowd, ragged peasants and soldiers, Russian and Armenian.

Ararat, when I first saw it, was as faintly etched against a grey sky as is Fuji in some of Hokusai's Hundred Views, a tall cone streaked white against pearly mist. The train was winding round a shoulder of the hills through reddish badlands that glistened in the flat spaces with alkali. Some time before the Georgian had pointed up over dry hills and said—Ani. Somewhere in the rocky wilderness to our left there had been the capital of the ancient kingdom of Armenia. I was as excited at the sight of Ararat as if I could see the Ark still balanced on the peak of it, and made an attempt to stir the Sayyid's enthusiasm on the subject.

But he refused to budge from where he was tending an elaborate engine of sticks and bits of twine that was intended to keep
the tiny teapot from falling off our tinier alcohol lamp. When he
did finally get to his feet, he looked at the mountain appraisingly
for a long time, taking little sips from a tin cup of tea, and then
shook his head and said:—Damavand is higher and more
pointed.—But the Ark and Noah and the elephant and the kangaroo and all the rest of the zoo didn't land on Damavand!—
They used to say that there were divs on Damavand, said the
Sayyid, and considering the argument to have been brought to
a satisfactory conclusion, he squatted in his corner again and began brewing a new pot of tea.

We were coming down from the hills into an irregular
basinlike valley at the end of which the streaky white peak of
Ararat soared on two great strongly-etched curves above the
bluish mass of the mountain. In the foreground for a moment
were the roofless stone walls of a village; from behind one of
the huts drifted up a little woodsmoke from a campfire, but
nowhere in the whole landscape of tortured hills and livid
white alkali plains was anything alive to be seen. Then a squall
that for a long time had been gathering up indigo fringes
above the mountains to the west swept across and hid everything in oblique sheets of rain and hail.

At a station on the plain we sent Samsoun effendi to get water for tea, and instead he brought back, to the Sayyid's extraordinary delight, what the Sayyid always calls a Mademoiselle.

We sat on the mysterious packing case and looked out over
the plains at Ararat, that now, much nearer, stood erect and luminous above the dusk that was already seeping into the plain.
We had given the Mademoiselle a cup of tea and some black
bread and caviar from our provision box, and she seemed
vaguely content and expansive, like a cat tickled about the
ears. Evidently she had been taut on the defensive all the journey. She had come from Tiflis in a car full of soldiers. She had
a pleasant Teutonic face, with rounded cheeks and steel-blue
eyes, like Vermeer's women, and was dressed with a faint reminiscence of style in a soiled white suit. She wore stockings, a
distinction in these parts, and little rope sandals. She started to
talk gradually, remembering her French with effort—Yes, I am
going to Erivan. I work there as a stenographer in an office.

. . . Of course a government office; there are no others. No, things aren't so bad there. People are starving. . . . Certainly it's worse than Tiflis, but, do you know? we are so used to it all now. We don't notice those things any more. We have a nice house and roses in the garden and I have dogs. . . . I even take horseback rides. Still, it's a miserable existence, and all because my father and mother took fright when the Germans were getting near to Riga. You see we are Esthonians, not Russians. We lived in Riga, and when it seemed as if the Germans would bombard the town we fled into Russia. Many other people fled, too. And then our troubles began.—She laughed.—What a time we live in!

The train had stopped at a station. The plain was marshy now. In front of us, beyond a canebrake, was Ararat, at the base indigo, cut across by level streaks of mist, and on the summit bright rose. Behind it like a shadow was the smaller cone, all dark, of Little Ararat. Mosquitoes whined in swarms about our ears.

—But as I was telling you, went on the mademoiselle,—oh, these mosquitoes! You can't live a week in Erivan without coming down with malaria; really it's a frightful place. . . . Everybody there is dying. . . . But anyway, although I was just a child then—you see I'm not awfully old now—I kept begging mother and father not to go. We had such a lovely big old house with linden trees round it and a garden full of overgrown shrubs where I used to play. You've never been in Riga? The Baltic is so beautiful in summer out among the islands. . . . My grandmother wouldn't leave. I think she's still alive, living in our old house. I'm going back there if I die in the attempt. . . . I have already applied for a passport, and I have seen the Esthonian consul in Tiflis. . . . That's what I went up for. But it's so difficult to get anything done here. They get so in the habit of prohibiting.—She laughed again.—Oh, they make me so angry. They just go about and if they find anybody wants to do anything, they cry: Stop it, stop it.

The Sayyid in his corner was boiling a new pot of water for tea. A lurch of the train upset pot and lamp and everything, so I left the mysterious packing case to help reconstruct the scaffolding on which depended the frequency of our cups of tea. A moment later I saw that Samsoun effendi, who had been at his little pocket mirror again, had taken my place and was deep in conversation with the Mademoiselle. She looked at me over his shoulder and wrinkling up her nose like a rabbit's, said: Il me fait la cour. Pensez!

The Sayyid looked from one to the other and suddenly let out a stentorian: Quel théâtre! Then laughing he reached for the last watermelon, sliced it deftly with his penknife, and handed me half of it as a peace-offering.

Through the little upper window of the boxcar I caught a last glimpse of Ararat for that day, as I sat on my suitcase with my teeth in the sweet dripping melon, three streaks of watermelon pink converging against a sky of solid indigo.

4. Erivan

Long straight grassgrown streets full of a sickly stench of dung and ditchwater. Half-naked children with the sagging cheeks and swollen bellies of starvation cower like hurt animals in doorways and recesses in the walls. Over grey walls here and there an appletree with fruit on it. Up above, the unflecked turquoise of the sky in which from every little eminence one can see the aloof white glitter of Ararat. They say, though I haven't seen it, that a dead wagon goes round every day to pick up the people who die in the streets. People tell horrible stories of new graves plundered and bodies carved up for food in the villages. Yet on the Boulevard, the down-at-the-heels central square of the place, people stroll about looking moderately well fed and well dressed. There is plenty of fruit in the fruitshops, and meat and cheese and wretched gritty black bread in the bazaars. The Russians have started a cinema and an Armenian theater, that flaunts gaudy posters opposite the Orthodox church.

It was there the Sayyid found a Persian who kept a shop. He was a Mussulman and told how the Armenians had massacred and driven out the majority of the Mohammedan inhabitants of Erivan. We bought a watermelon and ate it on the spot, while the Sayyid and the Persian chattered happily in *turki*. I heard the word *Americai* coupled with Ararat a couple of times, and asked the Sayyid what was being said.—This man says that last year an American, an American journalist, went up to the top of Ararat and died there. He was poisoned by an Armenian. This man was his servant.

I was asking for details when several people came into the shop.—He won't talk now, said the Sayyid mysteriously. We never heard the rest of the story.

Opposite the station a crumbling brown wall. In the shade of it lie men, children, a woman, bundles of rags that writhe feverishly. We ask someone what's the matter with them.— Nothing, they are dying. A boy almost naked, his filthy skin livid green, staggers out of the station, a bit of bread in his hand, and lurches dizzily towards the wall. There he sinks down, too weak to raise it to his mouth. An old man with a stick in his hand hobbles slowly towards the boy. He has blood-filled eyes that look out through an indescribable mat of hair and beard. He stands over the boy a minute and then, propping himself up with his stick, grabs the bread, and scuttles off round the corner of the station. The boy makes a curious whining noise, but lies back silently without moving, his head resting on a stone. Above the wall, against the violet sky of afternoon, Ararat stands up white and cool and smooth like the vision of another world.

5. Bakh-nurashin

We got out of Erivan last night on a private and specially cleaned boxcar, procured after long confabs with the station master and other officials and not a little crossing of palms. The Sayyid was superb, and used his Courrier Diplomatique style to great effect. When we were settled and waiting for the train to decide to leave, he gave me a great lecture on the theme of tell 'em nothing and treat 'em rough as a method of travel in Russia and the Orient generally. Promised to store up the pearls of his wisdom. Furthermore he attached to himself one of the men who swing lanterns, by name Ismail, a Muslim, who ran about fetching water and melons and even produced some rather withered cucumbers. We sent two boxes of sardines to the engineer and a package of tea to the conductor. Then, feeling our position on the train assured we closed our doors and opened our little square windows and got ready our

usual meal of tea, cheese, bread and caviar, and after some
hours' delay the train started.

This morning found us halted in a fertile but weedgrown
valley between two ranges of bare pink hills. Behind us the
two Ararats stood up tall in the gold shimmer of the dawn. Beside the track was a lean melonpatch that a skinny brown man
in ragged Persian costume was trying desperately to protect
from the inroads of the passengers on the train. We washed in
an irrigation ditch and breakfasted hopefully, but it was noon
and blisteringly hot before the train got under way. The Sayyid
passed the time making great pan-Islamic speeches to little
groups marshalled by the faithful Ismail, who collected round
the door of the car and told of the atrocities of the Armenians
and the sufferings of the Muslims. Meanwhile, out the other
door I talked ragged French and raggeder English with an Armenian who told me the frightful things the Turks and Tatars
had done. When the train eventually started it was only to run
a couple of miles to this ruin of a town on the frontier of Armenia and Adjerbeidjan. And here we are, in an evil-smelling
freightyard full of trains, beside a ruined station. As usual there
is no house standing in the town. The Muslims say it was destroyed by the Armenians, and the Armenians that the Turks
did the job. Every now and then Ismail comes to assure us
that in two hours the train will start for Nakhtchevan and
Djulfa, the frontier town of Persia that is our goal.

The Sayyid has gone to visit a woman who is sick in the next
car. He comes back saying she has typhus, too far gone, nothing to do, will die in a couple of hours. We watch the other
people in the car stealing away one by one. Then they bring
her out and lay her on a little piece of red and yellow carpet
beside the railroad track. She is a Russian. Her husband, a lean
Mohammedan with a scraggly beard, sits beside her occasionally stroking her cheek with a furtive animal gesture. Her face
is dead white, greenish, with a putrid contracted look about
the mouth. She lies very still, her bare legs sticking awkwardly
out from under a dress too short. Not even the red light of
sunset gives any color to her skin. And the sun is sinking in
crimson fury behind Ararat. From a triangular space between
the slopes of the two mountains a great beam of yellow light
shoots into the zenith. A man is standing beside the dying

woman, awkwardly holding a glass of water in one hand. From the other end of the station comes the whining jig of a Georgian tune played on bagpipe and tomtom, to which soldiers are dancing. The woman's face seems to shrivel as you look at it. Behind Ararat a triangular patch of dazzle that rims with silver the inner edges of the two peaks is all that is left of the sun. On the wind comes a sour smell of filth and soldiers and garbage. The Sayyid, hunched dejectedly on the mysterious packing case in the middle of the boxcar, cries out feebly, shaking his head, Avec quelle difficulté.

Then without a word he gets up and closes the door on the side where the dead woman lies on the red and yellow mat beside the track.

Late that night, when I was wandering about in the moonlight with a glass of wine—the faithful Ismail had got us a bottle from the Lord knows where—trying to avoid the swarms of mosquitoes, I heard the Sayyid's voice raised in shrill discussion and often reiterated the phrase Courrier Diplomatique. Not being partial to discussions, I lengthened my walk up the track. When I returned everything was quiet. It appeared that certain people had tried to invade the sanctity of our private boxcar, but that in the middle of the discussion they had all been arrested for travelling without proper passes, which, according to the Sayyid, was an example of the direct action of Providence.

6. Nakhtchevan

Another freightyard, empty this time, except for a long hospital-train. Flies swarm in the stifling heat. The town is several miles away at the end of a scorching sandy road. The engine has disappeared and the few boxcars still remaining on the train seem abandoned. People lie about limply in the patch of shade under the cars. The cars themselves are like ovens. An occasional breath of wind stirs the upper branches of a skinny acacia on the platform beside the shed where tea used to be served out in the old days, but none of the breeze ever seems to reach the freightyard. The Sayyid, sweating at every pore, is slicing a watermelon that we have to gobble hastily under handkerchiefs to keep the flies from getting ahead of us.

Meanwhile the Sayyid delivers a lecture on the virtue and necessity of patience for those engaged in occupations cognate to that of courrier diplomatique. Having eaten all the melon possible, and having definitely discovered that we are due to stay in Nakhtchevan some eight hours more, I climb into the car and cover my head with a sheet against the flies with the faint hope that the heat will stupefy me into sleep. Baste it in the Dutch oven; the phrase somehow bobs up in my mind and the picture of a small boy watching fascinated the process of pouring gravy over the roast chicken, while it is placed against the front of the grate of the stove in a shiny tin onesided contraption. I wonder vaguely if I'm getting the rich sizzly brown the chickens used to get in their Dutch oven. Flies drone endlessly outside the sheet. Their droning resolves itself into the little song they sang in the Paris streets round the time of the signing of the so-called peace:

I' fallait pas, i' fallait pas, i' fallait pa-as y-aller.

Then from outside comes the voice of the Sayyid in his best style holding forth on pan-Islam and the resurrection of Persia. He must have found a Mussulman. One's head is like a soupkettle simmering on the back of the stove. Thoughts move slowly about in a thick gravy of stupor. Armenia. A second's glimpse of a war map with little flags, Russian, Turkish, British. What a fine game it is. The little flags move back and forth. Livelier than chess. Then the secret intelligence map. Such extraordinary cleverness. We'll exploit the religion of A to make him fight B, we'll buy up the big men of D so that they'll attack A in the rear, then when everybody's down we'll neatly carve up the map. The flies are droning: Carve dat turkey, carve him to de heart. Call the sections Armenians, Georgians, Assyrians, Turks, Kourds. But somehow when everybody's down they can't find the carving knife. So everybody just stays down and when they get tired of massacring each other they find they are starving. And death and the desert encroach, encroach. Where last year was a wheat field, this year is a patch of thistles, and next year not even thistles will grow there. And the peasants are beggars or bandits. And that's all there is of the map game in the East for the present. But the sheet's in a knot and lets in the flies. I'll climb down to see what the Sayyid's telling his audience.

The Sayyid is saying that the East must settle its own problems, that the Mohammedans of the world must wake from their stupor of acceptance, that they must drive out the foreigners who exploit them, and organize their nations themselves. He says many fine things, but he does not say how the little ragged children, tiny wide-eyed skeletons with hideous swollen bellies, shall be fed, or how the grain shall be bought for the autumn sowing.

There are a dozen of these little children, in all stages of starvation, crawling about under the cars looking for scraps; they are not like animals, because any other animal than man would have long since been dead. The Sayyid has talked to some of them in *turki*; some are of Muslim parents from Erivan; some are Christians from the Lake of Van; some don't know whether their parents were Christian or Muslim, and seem to remember nothing in all their hungry lives, but this freightyard and the scraps of food the soldiers throw to them.—This is the eighth month, says the Sayyid. In three months, winter, and they will all die.

7. Djulfa (*August 21, 1921*)

That evening politik, as the Sayyid calls it, waxed furious. It came out that the engine could pull only two cars at a time up from Nakhtchevan to Djulfa. The contending parties were the Sayyid and a group of vaguely official Armenians. The station master was enticed into our car and fed tea and cigarettes and, when the doors had been closed to keep out prying eyes, was slipped a couple of paper Turkish pounds. Even then, the thing was not assured until, by a brilliant coup, a doctor, the most important member of the other party, was detached and offered a place in our car. The foiled looked daggers at us as we clanked out of the station behind a spluttering little engine. The moon was almost full. The track wound up through a craggy gorge beside a stream through cool intensely dry mountain air. I sat most of the night on the mysterious packing case beside the open door breathing in the cleanness of the sheer desert rock. Not a blade of grass, no life, no suffering anywhere, only cliffs and great escarped mountains and the stony riverbed, and beyond every upward turn of the valley crouched unimaginably new things, Persia.

And Adjerbeidjan that night slipped from out the shaggy present into the neat daintily colored past, as Armenia had the night we left Bakh-nurachin, and at another station of which I never knew the name, saw, while our nostrils were full of the stench of starving people asleep, and a pipe played sighingly somewhere teased our ears, the last glimmer in the moonlight of the tall disdainful peak of Ararat.

VI. Of Phaetons

1. Garden of Epicurus

—The phaeton is ready, mssiou, said the longnosed waiter with a wave of the hand across the samovar. As he spoke the street outside filled suddenly with the jingling of bells.

When I suggested that the springs stuck into my back the Sayyid was offended in his national pride and sulked until on our way through the bazaar we upset a donkey loaded with clay pots that fell on a heap of watermelons and put everybody in a good humor. The phaeton was vaguely like a small victoria perched above a perilous system of ropes and wheels. It was driven by a stocky man in a white wool cap named Karim. In a little sling behind there crouched among some bags of oats an obscene broadfaced imp that Karim was continually shouting at under the name of Maa'mat. Thus with our legs stuck out over the baggage and our laps full of green and yellow melons and the springs of the seat cunningly gouging the marrow out of our spines we jingled, dragging a great bellying dustcloud like a comet's tail, past the Blue Mosque and out of Tabriz.

The entry into Persia had been made at Djulfa on the Araxes some days before. After the rawness of the death things and birth things of Russia, the balm of an old and feeble and graceful civilization was marvellously soothing. I remember scrambling off the locomotive that had brought us across the international bridge into the tremendous glare of sun of the valley of Djulfa where not a green tree grew among the pink and yellow cliffs that swayed like stage scenery in the heat that boxed it in on every side. Almost immediately we were ushered into a cool room with mud walls of a pinkish puttycolor on which were hung a couple of rugs, and little copper ewers of water were brought, and the Sayyid and I sat with our shoes off before an enormous and epoch-making watermelon being waited on by a tiny little man named Astulla Khan who had one side of his face swollen with toothache and his whole head bound about with a white cloth tied at the top so as to leave two long pointed ends the way people's faces used to be done up in the picturebooks of a hundred years ago. Then after lunch when mattresses had been brought

179

and great pink cylindrical pillows, we lay drowsily through an endless afternoon, looking at the smooth mud ceiling and at the portrait of the Shah woven in one of the rugs on the wall, and out into the court where a tame partridge strutted about the edge of a little pool and where a kitten lay prone on a patch of blue and crimson rug in the sunlight. There was not a sound except for very occasionally the discreet bubbling of Astulla Khan's water-pipe from the next room. One felt endless ages of well-modulated indolence settling like fine silk cloths over one's restlessness. Perhaps this was the garden beyond pain and pleasure where Epicurus whiled away passionless days. At last the kitten got up, stretched each white leg in turn and strolled without haste over to the pool. The sunlight was already ruddy and cast long shadows. The hills beyond the Araxes were bright rose with purple and indigo shadows. The Sayyid got to his feet, dusted his trousers and muttered meditatively—Quel théâtre! Whereupon Astulla Khan appeared staggering under an enormous shining samovar and the business of the day was on again.

Out of the plain of Tabriz we climbed a dry pass and ate our own dust up a long incline until another valley full of poplartrees and mudwalled villages opened up at our feet and we found ourselves rattling and bouncing down hill again. At Basmich where we lunched there was a memorable garden. It was there the Sayyid first got lyrical. We sprawled under silvery aspens in a garden full of green grass and little shining watercourses and a boy with his hair cut a little below the ears like a pageboy out of the Middle Ages, wearing a tight belted tunic and straight loose pants of bright blue, brought us tea and a lapful of red apples. Then the Sayyid sat bolt upright and half closed his eyes and chanted in droning cadence the poem of Hafiz I have since found in Miss Bell:

> "A flower-tinted cheek, the flowery close
> Of the fair earth, these are enough for me—
> Enough that in the meadow wanes and grows
> The shadow of a graceful cypress tree.
> I am no lover of hypocrisy;
> Of all the treasures that the earth can boast
> A brimming cup of wine I prize the most—
>   This is enough for me!"

—Quel théâtre! cried the Sayyid when he had finished and put a piece of sugar in his mouth and lay back with his hands spread in the soft grass.

2. The Shah's Wrestler

That night after a run through valleys sheening with poplars with a long range of eroded crimson mountains always to the left of us, we stopped in a dilapidated khan beside a very large beautifully built brick caravanserai, ruined now, of the type the road people always ascribe to the good Shah Abbas. The name of the place was Shibli and there we found a company of roadguards under the leadership of a mighty man of war, Hakim Sultan. Hakim Sultan was a stocky man wreathed in cartridge belts. He squatted in the most honorable corner of the room, pulling on a waterpipe, and looked out benignantly at us from small piglike eyes embedded in flesh. His hair and his drooping moustaches were dyed crimson with henna. Between prodigious suckings that made the water in the galian bubble like mad he told us that he had once wrestled before the Shah during Ramadan and had thrown all his opponents. With a rifle he was a dead shot. And Hakim Sultan's subordinates, fine lanky nomads a little less swathed in cartridge belts than their captain, who squatted about at a respectful distance, nodded confirmation like so many Chinese toys. Why, just five days ago in this very khan he had beaten off untold numbers of the Shahsivan. We were duly shown the bulletholes in the wall. It was admitted that the raiders had managed to make off with all the cattle in the place.—But I drove them back into the hills. I sat and shot from this very place. One could imagine him squatting with his rifle, handling it as he handled his galian. Ah the Shahsivan, they were mighty men! Eleven of them had once disarmed a thousand Russian soldiers sent against them with artillery. They lived so far in the mountains a man who knew the road would have forgotten it by the time he reached their country. Their teacups and their youghourt bowls were of solid gold and they never counted the number of their camels. Such were the men, he, Hakim Sultan, spent his life in fighting.

At this point the oration was interrupted by the appearance of the host with a squawking chicken in each hand. Alternately

they were presented to the Sayyid, who prodded and pinched
them with a look of unearthly wisdom on his face. At last one
was chosen and one rejected and the squawks brought to an
abrupt end by the penknife of one of the nomads. Then, while
from outside came hopeful sizzlings, the Sayyid took his turn.
He described the countries of the earth from Berlin to Stamboul and their state and the condition of their politik, and how
some were good and others bad and others, notably Turkey
and the Bolsheviki, *tamaam*, finished.

Later he explained to me that he did not think either Turkey
or the Bolsheviki *tamaam*, but that he wanted to counteract
their propaganda.—Diplo-o-omatik! he said, drawing out the
word with the wave of an extended brown hand. When we had
eaten bread and youghourt and cheese and chicken washed
down with many tiny swagbellied glasses of tea, we rolled up in
our blankets on the floor beside the window, through the
unglazed lattice of which whistled the good keen air of mountain passes. I noticed the Sayyid sitting up after I had turned in,
looking apprehensively back and forth between his moneybag
he held in his hand and the prone form of Hakim Sultan. But
we slept undisturbed in the Shibli pass.

3. Politik

Next day lunched at Shishmedosh, a famous place for hold-
ups, a lonely khan of one room perched on the summit of a hill
in the midst of a long desolate valley. More tales of the Shahsivan, of villages attacked and flocks and women driven off.

Night in a most beautiful village, Gareh Chaman, built on
the flanks of a burnt-orange gorge on either side of a small
sparkling river, full of trees and well defended by round watch
towers. Carpets were spread for us on the roof of a house at
the edge of the village under two enormous silver-trunked
poplars; a samovar was brought, chickens produced for pinch-
ing, little ewers of water for washing, and the Sayyid, in his capacity of doctor, held a regular clinic, lancing boils and slitting
ulcers and feeling pulses and distributing pills until supper-
time. Then while we ate a lordly meal set out on chased
pewter trays, the Sayyid delivered to the mollah and the owner
of the village and the cook and the little boy who waited on us

the usual allocution on the ingliz and the français and the americai and the osmanli in general and on the politik of Persia in particular, to the effect of Iran for the Iranis and beat the farangi at his own game. That night the wind rustled in the poplars and the stars sparkled with constantly shifting facets and in the distance jackals yelped.

On the road between Gareh Chaman and Tourkemanchai, where, by the way, was signed the first of Persia's disastrous European treaties, we caught up with the caravan of some of the grandees of Tabriz on the pilgrimage to the tomb of the Imaum Riza at Meshed. Such a prancing of white horses and a shouting of donkey drivers and a bouncing of panniers full of brighteyed children and ladies invisible under their cheddars! A fine whitebearded mollah with the blue turban of a Sayyid, descendant of the prophet, led the way on a well-groomed grey horse of which the tail and mane had been dyed with saffron. Not only the living but the dead were enjoying the benefits of the pilgrimage; at the end of the caravan came a long train of mules with coffins strapped to them on their way to reburial on sacred soil.

—If they worried as much about the living as they do about the dead, said the Sayyid, when we had got away from the dust and the shouting, Iran would be one of the finest countries in the world. If they would save the money they spend on pilgrimages and invest it in fabriks and railroads . . .

—But why factories and railroads. . . ?

—Have you been in Germany?—Not for a long time?—Oh, but the commodité. . . . Everything is so convenient. Here things are done with such difficulty. Our peasants, if you knew how hard they worked, and nothing for it but to die of starvation when there is a famine in order that some grandee may make a fortune. . . .

Conversation was interrupted by the phaeton sticking firmly in the mud in the bottom of a gulch. We had to clamber out and Maa'mat had to be waked up and made to push behind and the horses had to be lashed and shouted at until at last the phaeton bounced, careening perilously, out of the mud and came to rest halfway up the rocky hillside. The opportunity was pronounced an excellent one for the eating of a melon, a long yellow one, milky inside with a flavor like almonds. It threw the

Sayyid into a haze of rosy reminiscence, and when we had got settled in our pumpkin coach again, he started talking slowly:

—How well I remember when I first arrived in Leipsig from Constantinople. . . . Ah quelle commodité! It was so quiet at the hotel with thick carpets on the floors, and when you ordered anything, zut, it was brought! I dined there very well with wine, such good wine, and the waiter spoke French—I hadn't learnt German then—and was very amiable. When I had finished he asked me if there was anything more I should like. And I spoke my thoughts aloud and said without knowing it, Yes a mademoiselle. The waiter smiled and said he'd see what he could do, and I thought he was joking and went up to bed. When I was half undressed, who should appear but the waiter saying that the mademoiselle was waiting for me downstairs. I said send her up, but the waiter said that wouldn't do at all. And that is the whole difference between Oriental and European women. So I got dressed again and went down. I was so ignorant then of the ways of civilization; and the mademoiselle was very charming and took me to a cabaret where we drank champagne and there was music and she taught me many things. . . . Ah quelle commodité!

4. The White Bedbugs of Mianej

From Tourkemanchai on there was no appreciable road. The phaeton rattled over rocky hillsides, doubled itself up and leapt chasms like a flea, charged along the crests of ridges, dived into rocky defiles where at every instant we expected the whole contraption to do the trick of the one-horse shay. At a deserted caravanserai of the Shah Abbas sort, a road-guard, a most villainous-looking redheaded giant, met us and told us that last night a traveller had been sabred from the shoulder to the navel by robbers on that very spot. We gave him two krans and he went his way. The sun was hot like a lash in your face, we had eaten all our melons, and the water jar broke, and for all that day's farsachs we saw no living thing. Quel théâtre! cried the Sayyid at every lurch.

—Précautions. Toujours des précautions, was the burden of the Sayyid's cry as he superintended the cleaning of the roof in the caravanserai outside the gates of Mianej, a town famous for its flies, its gnats, its mosquitoes and especially its white bedbugs which breed a private fever of their own which has made the town's name renowned in the annals of medicine.

That afternoon we fought the flies and drank tea and discussed politik to the effect that Persia's policy should be to encourage European penetration from any countries that did not touch her borders, but to look with constant suspicion on her two great neighbors. That had been the reason for the pro-German tilt of the Democrats and Nationalists during the war.—So far we have been saved by the fact that Britain and Russia can't agree. For a moment they did agree in the early part of the war and we went under, trampled like the grass of a battlefield. . . . But now they don't know us. They don't know what we will do next, and we don't tell our thoughts. Now is the moment to assure our independence. To do that we must have capital and foreign help, but not from our neighbors, from more disinterested countries. . . . But we must work slowly, cautiously, keeping our aims secret, toujours avec précautions, avec beaucoup de précautions. . . . As he spoke, the Sayyid wrinkled his face into an expression of almost superhuman cunning; then neatly catching a fly off his forehead, he said conclusively, Diplomatik!

The night was the first of Moharram, the month of mourning for Hussein, the great martyr of the Shiah faith. The mosquitoes and sandflies were so thick it was impossible to sleep. The Sayyid was oppressed by the fear of a lurking bedbug and lay in a small disinfected patch on the floor, moaning from time to time Quel théâtre! in the most dismal fashion. I covered my head and face with a bandana and walked up and down a little balcony smoking and watching good old Orion climb slowly into the sky. From the town came a roll of drums and in constant breathless rhythm cries of Hussein, Hassan, Hussein, Hassan. In the intervals dogs barked deafeningly. The air from the courtyard had a sodden putrid smell, and I could hear the bells of our horses jingling as they fought off the mosquitoes and continually came the sound of men moving in unison and shouting with all the hard-muscled ferocity of Islam, Hussein, Hassan, Hussein, Hassan.

5. The Humpless Camel of Djemalabad

In the morning Khouflankou, a jolly broadbacked pass crossed by a paved road built, I suppose, by the indefatigable Shah Abbas. Clear thyme-scented air to blow away the miasmas of Mianej. But the Sayyid refused to be comforted. He assured me with tears in his eyes that he had been bitten and would probably fall sick and die. Et après tellement de précautions, he ended sadly, as we breasted the last upward curve. Neither the scenery nor a new stock of melons nor seedless white grapes of ambrosial fragrance would distract him. He had diagnosed himself as sick and it was due to his professional reputation to prove it, so sick he was; malaria, it turned out.

Discussed matters of religion at lunch in a rather mournful tone under an appletree in the ruined village of Djemalabad while a very old camel mangy and humpless looked at us fixedly with a They'll come to a bad end expression from the next field. The Sayyid said that all prophets had a little truth and that their followers should unite rather than squabble, since le Dieu was le Dieu by whatever name you called him. No, he was not a Baha'i, but he thought in many ways as the Baha'is thought, and they were good people, honest and tolerant and anxious for progress and education; he only wished there were more of them in Persia. But the poor people were very ignorant and fanatic and believed whatever the mollahs told them.—Think, he said, suddenly sitting bolt upright,—I might have been a mollah instead of a doctor and a man of science. . . . My father was a mujtahid, a very holy man, and if the American missionaries had not talked to my father and induced him to send me abroad to study, I should certainly have worn a beard and a blue turban and became a mujtahid. Do you wonder I like the things of America?

Then the Sayyid got to talking with a very ragged man who sat a little way off from us and ate our melonrinds. It turned out that his father had owned this field and many more, but that the Russians had come and the Turks had come and they had destroyed the crops and burnt the house and killed his father, and now he was a beggar. He told the story cheerfully as part of the divine order of things. Islam is truly self-surrender.

6. The Robin's-egg Domes of Zendjan

At Tarzikand the only place we could get to sleep was a contraption of planks perilously balanced over a cistern full of croaking frogs. The cistern was in a little walled garden of almondtrees. A terrific wind blew so that the coals would not stay in the samovar, and bits of the paperthin bread at supper kept being carried away. As I lay on my back carefully balanced on the shaky planks the stars were like silver balls, Christmas-tree ornaments, hung on the swaying branches of the almondtrees.

During these days the Sayyid was silent, took quinine and watched his temperature. We spent another night at Yekendje, a glen full of huge poplars that grew along the pebbly riverbed like those silvery trees in Piero della Francesca's Baptism. There we took up our abode on the roof of the khan where was a little mud room into which retired the Sayyid and his malaria. We were waited on most charmingly there by a little boy named Kholam-Hussein who had run away from his home in Zendjan because, as he said, he did not like his father any more. When we asked him in the morning if there was anything we could do for him, he said that perhaps the Sayyid, who was a doctor, a hakim, could give him some medicine to make his complexion light, for he was very black.

In Zendjan the Sayyid perked up under the influence of a very aromatic drink named bidmesh, that had an odor a little like orange blossoms and slipped down one's gullet with a delicious drowsy smoothness. We made an attempt to dine in a restaurant in the bazaars but were told with brutal firmness Farangi nadjiss: A foreigner is unclean. The Sayyid could not even convince them that he himself was a good Mussulman and a descendant of the prophet, for he was wearing at the time a European felt hat. So we dined ignominiously at the inn and had a furious argument about industrialism. As we had walked through the bazaar, the Sayyid had made a great clamor about how hard the men who made copper kettles and the silversmiths worked and how much better it would be to have it all done by machinery. He seemed to have the idea, universal in these parts, that machinery worked itself. I tried to tell him that the life of an industrial worker in Europe and America was not all beer and skittles, and even wondered whether those people hammering away at their copper pots, miserably underpaid as they were, might not get more out of life than, say, the steelworker in Germany, for all his moving pictures and bierhalle with which to amuse himself. But he snowed me under with a long list of famines and extortions of grandees and mujtahids and governors.—No, he said at last, we must have fabriks and railways. Then we shall be a great nation.

The next morning we left the holy and dilapidated city of Zendjan. The sun glittered entrancingly on the dome of the mosque that was the color and shape of a robin's egg. The nadjiss business came up once more that afternoon. We were drinking tea in a little roadhouse when a hadji with a huge crimson-dyed beard who was sitting in the corner smoking a thick-stemmed pipe saw fit to object to our presence. But the Sayyid was on his mettle. He shot out a verse of Saadi's on the subject of courtesy to strangers, and without taking breath delivered himself of an enormous passage of the Koran from the chapter entitled The Cow. Then he stopped suddenly and challenged the hadji to go on from where he had left off. The hadji stuttered and stammered, but made no headway, and finally had to admit that the Sayyid was a good Mussulman and a learned man. He even handed him his pipe as a peace offering.

From then on the Sayyid's malaria was virtually cured. When we reached Kasvin he was chipper as a sparrow, and full of regretful reminiscences of the German mademoiselles.—I shall marry a German, he said—I have a girl friend there who is a doctor, the daughter of a colonel. I think she will marry me when I am ready. I could not marry a Persian. They are very pretty but they are not developed. It would be like marrying an animal. . . . But all that will change; you will see!

7. The Guest Room at Kasvin

Kasvin was full of tall planetrees where perched enormous quantities of crows, that at dusk flapped cawing about the streets. We stayed with the Sayyid's brother and were royally wined and dined, although it was Moharram, in which month the Persians don't drink wine or allow any sort of amusement.

There is something very pleasant about the simplicity with which middleclass Persians live. The rooms are often bare except for rugs and a few chairs and couches. There are no servants about; the sons of the house bring the pewter trays at meals and wait upon the guests. There are no beds or ornaments of any sort; at night and at siesta time mattresses and quilts are brought out of cupboards and unrolled. Everything seems to go on strangely quietly and without fuss. Out of the patterns of rugs and cups of tea and softvoiced subtle talk and the vaguely cloying taste of sweet drinks is woven an extraordinary harmony of indolence. In Persia—I suppose it's the same throughout Islam—life gives me the impression of having no surge and torrent to it. It is like a dry watercourse that has once been a swelling river, but is reduced to a few quiet pools that deflect the blue and the clouds, that within their limits perhaps contain more intensity of wriggling intricate life than ever the river did, but that are troublingly discontinuous, intermittent.

It seems to be the custom in Persia to turn in immediately after supper, and that night in Kasvin when I was left alone with my bedding in one of the upper rooms of the house, I was seized with an uncontrollable desire to walk about the streets. No use, for the house door was sure to be locked and I was afraid if I wandered out of my room I'd get into the women's apartments. As a substitute I managed to crawl through my tiny window on to a little roof from which I could see the flat roofs and the inky-shadowed courtyards of the town stretching away in every direction under the moon. Opposite me was the fat dome and the stumpy tiled minaret of the Friday Mosque. On many of the roofs one could see figures in blankets rolled up asleep; occasionally there was some movement in a courtyard. I thought of a story of de Maupassant's in which a girl stands up darkly naked in the moonlight on the flat roof of a house in Morocco. And for some reason a spasm of revolt against the romantic Morris Gest sort of Orient, and there's tons of it even in the East, came over me to the point of climbing in through the window again and filling up pages of my notebook about it. Admitting the spectacle, the crimson beards and the saffron beards and the huge turbans and the high-domed hats of felt and the rugs and the gaudily caparisoned white horses and the beautiful gestures of old men and the shrouded ghosts of women and the camels with their long soft strides and the dim richness of the lofty vaulted storerooms in bazaars, was not all this dead routine, a half-forgotten rite learned ages ago? It is in the West that blood flows hot and that the world is disorderly, romantic, that fantastic unexpected things happen. Here everything has been tried, experienced, worn out. Wishing myself at Broadway and Forty-second Street I lay down on my soft mattress. As soon as I was quiet I heard a drumbeat in the distance and voices throaty, taut, ferocious, shouting in quick alternate rhythm Hassan, Hussein, Hassan, Hussein, as if it had been yesterday that Hussein, the gentle grandson of the prophet, had died thirsty at Kerbela.

In the morning before we left Kasvin the Sayyid performed an operation; then we jingled off in state, escorted by several officers of gendarmerie on their horses, leaving the victim bloody and groaning through his ether on a rickety table in the governor's dispensary. We ate grapes as the phaeton dragged with impressive slowness through dusty roads and the Sayyid talked about the revolt of Asia. First, he said, it was the collapse of Russia in the war with Japan that made Asia wonder whether it had been eternally ordained in the books of fate that her people should be slaves of Europe. Then the Turkish Constitution and the Persian Constitution had shown that the shady and dilapidated groves of the Orient had not been entirely withered under the killing blast of energy out of the west. And during the war, while Europe was fighting, Asia was thinking. Things moved very slowly in Asia, so slowly Europeans did not notice and said they moved not at all, but the time would come when the exploiting powers would suddenly find they did not know the road they were walking on. That was how things moved in Asia.—Look at me, said the Sayyid shrilly,—when I was a small boy, I thought the Europeans a superior race, they seemed to have done so much five or six years ago; I thought the best thing that could happen to Persia was to be ruled by the British. But now. . . . I have seen all countries, I have heard all their propaganda, I have seen the money they gave in bribes, and their methods of fighting, all these highly civilized exalted races of Europe, and I know what I know. And what I know the muledrivers know, and the makers of clay pots and the men who rub you down in the baths and the farmers and the nomads. No, I will die gladly before my country is dominated by any European nation. And I am not the only one.

—As for the British here in Persia. . . . yes, I know they are a great people. I spent three days in London once; it rained all the time, but I went about and saw the people, and I knew then that they were braves gens. But here it is not so, not towards us, and for that reason I shall fight against them, avec diplomatik, as long as I live. And among the Turks it is the same, and among the Arabs it is the same, and among the Afghans it is the same. First we liked the British because they were better than the Russians, but now there is no pressure from Russia, and the British have changed. And there is not so much resignation in Islam as there used to be. Europe is teaching us, giving us weapons.

8. The Little People in Persia

Later as we drove before dawn on the last stage to Teheran, the Sayyid said again:—What is the mistake all the European powers make with regard to Persia? I will tell you. They think only of the great personages. They do not realize that there are little people, like me, doctors, mollahs, small merchants, and that even the peasants talk politik in the teahouses along the roadside. They know they can bribe and threaten the great personages and they think they have the country in the palm of their hands. But they cannot bribe us, the little people, because we are too many. If they buy me over or get me killed there will be hundreds of others who think just like me to take my place. What good will it do them?

It was just dawn; the sharp upward angle of Damavand, the great mountain that overlooks Teheran, was edged with a brittle band of gold. The wind had a sharpness almost of snowfields about it.

—And when you go back to your country, said the Sayyid,—do not forget to tell the Americans that there are little people in Asia.

VII. Moharram

For Z. C. B.

---

1. Darvish

Outside the gate where the dusty road winds off under the planetrees towards the hills sits an old man dressed in white with a blue turban. His beard is dense as if moulded out of silver. He sits motionless, staring straight ahead of him out of frowning hawkeyes. In one hand he holds up a curved sword, in the other hand resting in his lap he holds a book. The sword or the Koran. The horns of the swelling crescent drawing together on the world. People as they pass leave coppers on the corners of the prayer rug he sits on. The old man sits without moving, regardless of the swirling dust, squats beside the road on a piece of Manchester carpet with the face of an emir leading Islam into holy war.

In Persia there is a sort of holiness in the very fact of beggary. A beggar is an instrument by which a believer may lay up for himself treasures in heaven. In Mianej at the khan there was a merchant whose caravan had been plundered by bandits. He had a certificate from some mujtahid that Allah had bereft him of worldly goods and was sitting in the upper chamber patiently waiting for travellers to make him presents so that he might eventually start in business again. He had the face of a very happy man, of one who had stopped struggling against adverse currents. Not for nothing does Islam mean submission, self-abandonment.

And in every teahouse along the road you find merry fellows, ragged and footsore, men of all ages and conditions who have given up working and drift along the highroads, exploiting as best they can the holiness of poverty. They are certainly the happiest people in Persia. They have no worry about tax collectors or raids from the hilltribes or bandits in the passes. They go about starving and singing prayers, parched by the sun and wind, carrying epidemics and the word of God from the Gobi desert to the Euphrates. Tramps exist everywhere, but in what we can vaguely call the East, going on the bum is a religious act.

All madness, all restlessness is from God. If a man loses his only child or his loved wife or suffers some other irreparable calamity he strips off his clothes and runs out-of-doors and lets his hair grow long and wanders over the world begging and praising God. A man becomes a dervish as in the Middle Ages in Europe he would have gone into a monastery.

I used to think deeply of all these things on my way back and forth to the telegraph station during those weeks in Teheran when my bag of silver krans had dwindled to a handful and my hotel bill grew and grew and every cable for money cost a week's board. It was in the early days of Moharram, the month of mourning, when there is no music or dancing, the month of the passion of Hosein, the son of Fatima, daughter of the Prophet. Every day Teheran was filling more and more with beggars and religion and hatred of foreigners. I used to wonder how it would be to sit under a planetree beside the road telling the story of the Shiah martyrs to a circle of villagers while people brought you tea and a bowl of rice with tears running down their faces at the tales of the sufferings of the great Imaum, son of Ali, whose flesh was infused with the substances of God, done to death by the falseness of the men of Kufa, dogs and sons of dogs, and by the wiles of Sheitan, the stoned one.

With the name of Allah for all baggage you could travel from the Great Wall of China to the Niger and be fairly sure of food and often of money, if only you were ready to touch your forehead in the dust five times a day, and put away self and the glamorous West.

And yet the West is conquering. Henry Ford's gospel of multiple production and interchangeable parts will win hearts that stood firm against Thales and Democritus, against Galileo and Faraday. There is no god strong enough to withstand the Universal Suburb.

Within our time the dervish, the symbol of mystery errant on the face of the world, will become a simple vagrant as he is in civilized countries.

2. The Teahouse

Hot afternoons the E.A. sat in a covered courtyard beside a fountain where goldfish swam, drinking glass after glass of tea and eating a curious cool jelly flavored with roses. There were few people in the teahouse: an occasional Armenian in European clothes, a Turk in fez and frock coat. In the month of mourning people stay in their houses. In a far corner the serving boys talked in low whispers. A fountain tinkled; there was the buzz of an occasional fly. The few sounds were flaws in the bright crystal silence.

Caught tight in the intent stillness of autumn afternoons, the E.A. used to wonder and puzzle on a continual jerky roundabout of ways and means. At the bottom of a vast still contentedness something miniature kept going round and round: how to get to Isfahan, how to get to Khorasan eastward, eastward to Kabul, to the Afghan mountains, to Canton, to Frisco. He pulled off ring after ring, but never the brass ring that carries the prize.

But what do I want to drag myself round the Orient for anyway? What do I care about these withered fragments of old orders, these dead religions, these ruins swarming with the maggots of history? Old men, toothless eunuchs asleep in the sun. It's in the West that life is, terrible, destroying sprouts of the new among the litter of Russian trainyards, out of the smell of burnt gasoline in Detroit garages. To hand Samarcand on a platter to that little Polish girl in the funicular at Tiflis.

As a sideshow it's still pretty fine, this vanishing East. The inexpressible soft, lithe swinging length of a two-humped camel's stride; the old men with crimson beards, the enormous turbans, white, blue, black, green, perched on shaved polls, boys with their hair curling troubadour-fashion from under their skullcaps, the hooded ghosts of women, the high-domed felt hats, the gaudy rags, the robes of parrot-green silk, trees the violent green of manganese spurting out of yellow hills, quick watercourses, white asses, the robin's-egg domes, the fields of white opium poppies.

If one were old enough and one's blood were cool enough there would be the delight of these quiet gardens of poplartrees, the deferential bringing of the samovar, the subtle half smiles across the rim of tiny glasses of tea, the glint of scurrying water in the runnel in the center of the room, the bright calm of sunny changeless courts, the effortless life of submission to the Written.

But there are things worth trying first.

The E.A. gets to his feet dizzy with a sudden choked feeling of inaction and walks out into the broad street where the twilight flutters down like scraps of colored paper through the broad leaves of the planes. Hassan, Hosein. Hassan, Hosein. . . . To a sound of drums a procession is passing, gruff voices savagely passing, the warlike banners and standards of Islam, the hand of Fatima, the mare's tails, the crescent. It is the caravan of Hosein, sweetbearded trusting old man, leaving Medina for Kufa on the last journey. There is no grief yet, but a sense of something circling overhead, wings of doom that plane above the dimming twilight, through the streets the drumbeat and the tramp of feet and the gruff cry of triumph, Hassan, Hosein.

After all are these gods so dead?

3. *Malaria*

The Russian engineer who said he owned a Ford looked at the thermometer and shook his head. Then he fetched his wife, who looked at the thermometer and shook her head. The room was full of people looking at thermometers and shaking their heads; a voice travelled from an immense distance and said: Nonsense, I feel fine. The bed was strangely soft, billowy, soaring above the heads of the Russian engineer who said he owned a Ford and his wife and the Hôtel de France and the cries beating out of brass throats, Hosein, Hassan.

There was a chasm. The City Without Bedbugs stood on the edge of the chasm. Insh'allah, said the Russian engineers, the city will not fall into the chasm, which is a hundred and five degrees deep. Then there arose a great prophet and he said, Ah mon ami, j'ai trouvé un poux. Avec le typhus qu'il a c'est très dangereux. Bismillah, cried the villagers. The city is going to fall into the chasm. Then spake the prophet: The City Without Bedbugs is doomed to slide into the gulf. Bismillah, cried the villagers. We must fill up the gulf or chasm. Whereupon they began throwing in their furniture and their possessions and their houses and their wives and children and lastly themselves. Intra venos, said the Sayyid rolling his eyes and shot in a tumblerful of quinine.

Then I was lying very long and cold and brittle on the stony tundra of my bed, and the Russian engineer who said he owned a Ford was explaining his plans to me in careful French. In a day or two the road would be open to Recht on the Caspian. Riza Khan was at this moment cleaning up the remnants of the Republic of Ghilan. Then we could drive the Ford to Recht, there load it with caviar that can be bought for nothing on the Caspian and drive back to Kasvin, Hamadan, Kermanshah and Baghdad, where the British would pay through the nose and buy by the grain what we had bought by the kilo. The only thing that stood between us and riches was a few hundred pounds capital to buy gasoline with. Now if I spent the sum I would eventually spend on the fare to Baghdad on gasoline and caviar, we would all get to Baghdad for nothing and have a substantial profit when we got there.

—But do you really own this voiture Ford?—Virtually. It's as good as mine.

Outside the wind howled and shrieked about the house. You couldn't see the courtyard for dust. Dust seeped into the room through every crevice. There was a half an inch coating of fine white dust on my pillow. The ramshackle building of the Hôtel de France shook and rattled as if it were coming down about our ears. At last the din grew so terrific that I couldn't hear the suave voice of the Russian engineer who said he owned a Ford.

There was a ripping crash and a shriek from somewhere in the hotel. The Russian engineer ran out and came back in a jiffy with his wife in his arms. Her hair hung snakily over her face and she was chirruping excitedly in Russian. The end of the roof over their room had blown off. It was a tin roof and waved in the wind with a sound like stage thunder. Surely the whole house would be down before night. I lay in the bed with the sheet over my nose to keep out the dust, and the sheet over my ears to keep out the noise, feeling very long and cold and weak and tired, and slid effortlessly into sleep like a trunk going down a chute.

4. Baha'i

The three American women were Baha'i Missionaries, one from New York, one from Chicago and the youngest one perhaps from some small town in the Dakotas. They all had the same eyes, spread, unblinking, with dilated pupils. We sat in a long dark room furnished in European Persian style, looking at each other constrainedly. The eldest women spoke of the persecutions of the followers of Baha'ullah in Persia, since the time of El Bab, the precursor, martyred in Tabriz: how they were not allowed to be buried, and how they could not meet, and how many of them held their faith in secret. She was old with tired grey hair puffed over her forehead and grey unfirm lips and a face full of small tired wrinkles. The Presbyterian missionaries who lived in the big mission at the other end of town would not speak to them because they were not Christians. They do not know that the service of our lord El Baha'ullah includes the service of Christ who was also a great prophet and the emanation of God.

Another of the women was a doctor. Her face was firm and thin and she was neatly dressed. She spoke of the sufferings of the women, of their flabby ignorance, their wilted lives in the candied gloom of the anderun, the sickness among them and the difficulty with which they had children.

The youngest one had come recently to Teheran. Her talk was full of miracles. She had come up from the coast in winter. They had told her it was death to attempt such a thing. Death has no power on the servant of everlasting light. She had crossed alone a great snowy pass that even the Kourds didn't dare pass in winter; when she came to a ford the swollen river would shrink within its banks; bandits had killed all the other travellers on the road but her; at every step she had felt the hand of God bearing her up, keeping her mule from stumbling, turning away the designs of wicked men.

It was dark when I left them. Outside, a procession was passing, first a few men dressed as Arabs on horses, then travellers on camels gaudily caparisoned, then men with heavy many-branched lamps of brass, then, behind a steel standard like a great flexed sword, weighted down at the tip by a brass tassel, flashing in the lamplight, penitents in fours beating their breasts in unison, tall dark men with bloodshot eyes, beating their breasts in unison to the agonized breathless cry Hosein, Hassan.

That was the thumping beat I had heard in the distance, that had made me restless sitting in the house listening to the missionaries talk of Baha'i gentleness and tolerance and fraternal love. From my room at the hotel where I sat reading an old and phony French translation of Euripides I could hear it still, sometimes from one direction, sometimes from another, shuddering through the dustladen air of the autumn night, the beating of the breasts of the mourners who followed the caravan of Hosein.

5. Hosein

Hosein, the son of Fatima and Ali, grandson of the Prophet, left Medina for Kufa, city of the first doctors of Islam, where his father, Ali, Lord of all the World, had been stabbed to death. Yezid was khalif in Syria and was plotting to poison Hosein as he had poisoned his lazy brother Hassan. The people of Kufa had invited him, the only surviving grandson of Mahomet, to be their khalif. On the first day of Moharram the small party of the imaum Hosein was met by Harro, who had been sent from Kufa by the khalif's officers to announce that Yezid was master of the city and that Hosein's adherent Muslim had been killed. Hosein was travelling with a few slaves and his sister and his wives and children. One of his wives was a Persian, daughter of the last Sassanid King. Harro, shameful of his errand, went back to Kufa to beg that the imaum be allowed to return to Medina. Hosein's party travelled on slowly by night, for the weather was excessively hot. Hosein said: Men travel by night and the destinies travel towards them. This I know to be a message of death.

Arab-fashion they continued parleying back and forth until, the ninth, Hosein's caravan encamped at Kerbela, a little hillock beside the Euphrates. The army of Amr ben Saad surrounded them, under orders from Yezid to kill the men and bring the women to Damascus. At the last moment Harro and his men came into the camp to die with the holy ones. That night they corded their tents together and made a ditch full of fagots around them so that they could be attacked only from the front. Hosein bitterly regretted that he had brought the children and the women. They had no water.

In the morning Amr ben Saad attacked. Hosein's party was hopelessly outnumbered. At midday, tired from fighting, Hosein sat down for a moment beside his tent and took his baby son Abdullah into his lap. An arrow killed the child. Their thirst became unbearable. Ali Afgar and Ali Asgar, Hosein's two half-grown boys, tried to make a dash to the river to bring back water. They were killed. At last Hosein himself went down to the river. For a while the men of the khalif did not dare attack him, but as he was stooping to drink an arrow struck him in the mouth. Then the khalif's men rushed him from all sides. Thirty spears went through him and Amr rode his cavalry back and forth over the body until it was mashed into the mud of the riverbank. The head was sent to Damascus.

And on the last day Allah, about to hurl all mankind into hell, unmoved by the supplications of Mahomet and Isa ben Miriam and Moses and the two hundred and seventy thousand prophets, will remember the sufferings of Hosein, his agony of mind and the wailing of his women and the death of his sons and his thirst in the tents at Kerbela, and his eyes will fill with tears and whoever has wept for Hosein, whoever has bled for Hosein, whoever has suffered pain for Hosein will be saved, and will enter the gardens, the well-watered gardens where the houris eternally virgin wait under the trees eternally green.

In Teheran the tenth of Moharram dawns in terror and dismay. All night the streets have been turbulent with torches and chanting and the hollow sound of bare breasts beaten in unison. In the early halflight the streets are full of water-carriers offering cups of water to passersby in memory of the terrible thirst they suffered in the tents at Kerbela. Now Hosein is receiving the first charge of the horsemen of Amr, the first flight of arrows.

In a big square in the bazaars the crowd is densest. On a roof chairs have been set for the diplomatic corps, Europeans in frock coats and uniforms, in white flannels and Palm Beach suits as if for a garden party, ladies in pastel-colored dresses, all guarded by a small contingent of Riza Khan's gendarmes. In every direction out of the covered alleys of the bazaars muffled drums and the gruff breathless shout Hassan, Hosein, Hassan, Hosein.

Officers of the cossacks and gendarmerie walking very slowly are passing with bowed heads, followed by led horses.

Occasionally you can see tears running down a tobacco-colored cheek. Harness clinks, standards glisten in the sun, the hand of Fatima, the crescent with the mare's tail, green banners and orange banners, penitents in black tunics beating their bare breasts fill the square with a strange gruff hollow sound of pain. Then behind the device of huge steel blades weighted down at the tip by brass ornaments come men stripped to loincloths with skewers and daggers stuck into their flesh, spiked ornaments hung from their bare shoulders, men seemingly spitted by lances and arrows, sweating and dusty in the sun. Then after them, two long lines of men and boys in white shrouds belted with chains, each with his left hand holding the belt of the man ahead and with his right hand beating himself on his bare shaven head with the flat of a sword. The line moves forward slowly, swaying, groaning, beating in time. The blood runs down faces and necks and clots with dust on the white shrouds. There's a smell of blood and agonized sweat. From everywhere comes the gruff continual choking cry, Hosein, Hassan, Hassan, Hosein. The sun directly overhead flashes on the swords, on the swaying blades of the standards, festers in the blackening blood. Hassan, Hosein. Whoever weeps for Hosein, whoever bleeds for Hosein, whoever dies for Hosein. . . .

VIII. On the Pilgrim Road

I DARIUS KING OF KINGS begins the inscription on the great rock carvings at Bisitun. In the dimming afternoon light we could barely see the huge outlines of the figures. The great mountain rises to a peak at either end, each cut off sheer, making, the Kourds say, the silhouette of a house with a broken ridgepole. On the higher cliff, ochre-stained and rusty with lichen, you can make out the gigantic figures of bearded men. Archæologists hung in baskets from the top of the cliff can still read the bragging cuneiform inscription: I Darius King of Kings . . .

This road, from Hamadan that may have been Ecbatana to Kermanshah and the pass of Taqi Garra that is a vast stair leading down into Iraq, is one of those roads where have marched all the great parades of history. The rocks are worn and grooved by the shuffling of the feet of countless generations of men and animals. Everywhere people have scribbled on the rocks. A curious awe of history hangs over these valleys and cliffs, these stony riverbeds. In the echoing gorges the shouts of the Elamites and the soldiers of the Great King seem still to rumble in the distance among the cursing of the Tommies and hoofbeats of Russian cavalry.

In these last years History has revisited these regions in the shape of three devastating armies. The Turks and the Russians fought back and forth here all through the war. In 1918 the British pushed through here in their campaign for oil, building, or rather rebuilding the road as they went. The result is that there is hardly a khan or a village standing, that the desert, heir of the great parades of history, has nibbled away all the arable land, that in a day's run in a broken-down Ford you can't find a thing to eat except a bowl of sour milk, if you're lucky, in the tent of a migrating family of Kourds.

The road is full of pilgrims from Persia and all the Shiah world, for this is the good time for travelling; the rivers are dry, and there is no snow yet in the passes and it is beginning to be cool in the lowlands of Iraq. I can't imagine how they eat, particularly the merry and dust-stained families you see going it on foot, because the Armenian and I, for all our jin-gling of silver, count ourselves lucky if we scrape up one meal a day. These pilgrims are on their way to the Holy Cities of Iraq, Kazimain and Samarra and Nedjef and Kerbela, burial places of imaums, men who cast no shadows, whose souls are God's body. Rich people on horses and mules, women jolting in camel-litters, poor people on donkeys or on foot, caravans of small white coffins of the dead being taken for reburial in sacred earth. All day we pass them, splashing them where the road is muddy, giving them dust to eat, the Ford hopping and choking along like a dog on three legs, for the Armenian who drives talks English and wears a thinly disguised English offi-cer's uniform and he feels as his the triumph of the Cross and the Allies over the turban and the Hun.

One night in the caravanserai of a ruined town I don't re-member the name of, we had a little cell of which we had blocked the door with the car. The Armenian had left me there to guard the stuff and had gone off to scare up some food. I squatted on the low roof, ducking my head to keep from knocking down any of the fragile glittering glass balls the stars that hung down from the intense blueglass ceiling of the sky. The courtyard was full of little fires round which sat motionless figures of pilgrims; their talk was so low you could hear the munching of the mules and horses in the stalls. Oc-casionally a camel growled. In my face came a smell of dry sticks burning and from the kahwe under the gate a drowsi-ness of opium. Everything was spun of glass or ice; you hardly dared breathe in the intense fragility of the moment.

East and west and north and south were intense and bodi-less presences like the being you used to imagine behind the windowcurtains when you were a kid. The four directions were torturing points spitting you through like the swords of Our Lady of Pain. Why is going east so different from going west; why is southward happy and northward miserable?

There was a whiff of singed meat in the air and the Armenian appeared below me with some skewers of kebab in his hand, a fold of bread and a white melon under his arm. We ate and fell fast asleep in our tracks.

Next morning the courtyard was empty. The pilgrims had all slipped away before light. We swallowed some tea and were

off. This was the day we were going to drop four thousand
feet over the great pass that leads into the Messpot. I felt itchy
and depressed. Names of the cities I hadn't seen hummed like
gnats round my ears: Kaboul, Herat, Khorasan, Isfahan, Shiraz. Baghdad would never make up for them. Besides it had a
German sound, smacked of articles in the *Nation* on the Near
East Question, of the Winter Garden. Oh, those pink Arabian
nights.

> And the ladies of the harem
> Knew exactly how to wear 'em
> In Oriental Baghdad long ago.

After all, what was the use of going to a place that had established itself so definitely in Berlin and New York? Baghdad
was in the locked-up plans of the German general staff, in
Jake and Lee Shubert's storehouse, in the vaults of the Anglo-
Persian. Why go messing round after it on the banks of the
Tigris? After all, between the rivers they still showed strangers
the wreck of the Garden of Eden and the actual figtree from
which Adam and Eve pulled the leaves out of which they fashioned decency, morality and vice. That was something to look
forward to.

Meanwhile the Ford was bowling along. We passed all the
pilgrims who had spent the night in the caravanserai. The dry
rolling plain was getting uneasy, breaking into gulches. Suddenly the plain began to flow through a gap in the hills. The
road was drawn with it and we were going down a broaden-
ing, steepening valley. The valley narrowed to a gorge and we
were zigzagging down the huge face of a mountain. Below us
the hills dropped away in folds like enormous steps into a series of blue streaked horizontals. The Sea?—The Messpot,
said the Armenian.—Over there, Baghdad.

At Kasr Shirin everybody seemed to think I was in a great
hurry. It was a pleasant pink and white town with porches
held up on thin white-daubed columns. I wanted to wait and
eat something, to sit around and see the town, but everyone
seemed to think I would miss the train if I waited a second,
so before I could help myself I was put in a vehicle with three
gendarmes with rifles and packed off, as I thought towards
Khanikin.

This vehicle was drawn by two mules and looked a little like the pictures of the ox-drawn beds of the Merovingian kings you used to get on little *bon point* cards they gave you when you knew your French lesson. It was the shape of a spring wagon—it had no springs—with a top and delicately looped side curtains. The woodwork was painted with pink and blue and purple flowers. In it the officer of gendarmerie and I lay at full length back to back, our heads elegantly resting in the palms of our hands, while the two men at arms squatted at our feet. The driver walked alongside and cursed at the mules.

So in reluctant and Shebalike splendor I was conveyed out of Kasr Shirin and out of Persia.

Across a crazy tumbled region of pink and violet and eroded orange hillocks, vermilion badlands, and the great pebbly bed of a river. Not a spear of green anywhere, nothing but this confusion of crumbling mineral color in the clangor of the afternoon sun. The vehicle plunged and lurched in the ruts of the fissured track; pink dust hung about us, and at last, shaken and thirsty and hungry and buffeted, we arrived at the railhead, a jumping-off place of jumping-off places. Yellow barrack sheds surrounded a patch of wheel-tracked dust where a few old men sat selling watermelons; beyond were some more sheds beside a track where stood three uncoupled freight cars. All this was penned off by fence after fence of barbed wire. This was the station and quarantine of the Iraq border.

The Persian gendarmes carried the hippo and escorted me gravely into the station building and then left me; the vehicle drove off and I was alone with the flies. After hours I found the babu stationmaster. He was pompous and severe. The time was different from Persia, the money was different; this wasn't Khanikin; there was nowhere to get anything to eat. So I sat on the hippo in the shade outside the station door, trying to eat my watermelon before the flies did, getting stickier and stickier and dustier and dustier, and lonelier and lonelier. Down the track a vague squatting of "natives," characterless natives out of Kipling.

At last a wheezy black locomotive arrived, towing three grey cars with sunshutters, giving out from every crack the smell of steam and machine oil that brought all terminals back to my mind, the old Seventh Street Depot in Washington and the Grand Central and the South Station and the Gare St. Lazare and the Gare d'Orléans and the Gare de Lyon and the Estacion del Mediodia and the Bahnhof in Strasbourg. Oh, the meals eaten in station restaurants and the coffee and drinks at midnight in the little bars across the street! The oyster stew at the Grand Central and langoustes opposite the Gare St. Lazare, the bolted meals at Bobadilla and the chestnuts and churros at the end of the Calle Atocha, the pickled partridges and the snails washed down with manzanilla, all the last meals in all the terminal cities, meals mixed with the smell of steam and the thump hiss, thump-hiss, thumphiss of engines. Candy cigars cigarettes. . . . Have a nice chicken sandwich, individual brick of pure homemade Horton's icecream. . . . Nothing sold after the train leaves. . . . Oh, even the paper sandwiches and the smell of diapers on the New York, New Haven, & Hartford.

And all I could do was sit there in the dark amid screaming memories and stuff myself with watermelon, and watch, in the dim light of the single lamp on the station, the pilgrims from Persia who had lost, in crossing the magic line of British dominion, their merriment, their dignity of feature and gesture, the elegance of their rags and their tall felt hats, and had become as they crowded into the sweaty train mere featureless natives out of Kipling.

At last in great distress in the midriff from overmuch watermelon and alarmed by what a French doctor had told me, Monsieur en Iraq il ne faut pas abuser des pastèques, I curled up in the striped Tabriz blanket and went to sleep.

I woke up to find an Englishman offering a drink; the train was in Khanikin; he had ridden down from some oil borings somewhere to the north. We sat up drinking in the dim light of the sleeping compartment talking about the Yezedis. All his workmen were Yezedis, devil-worshippers. He was trying to collect data about them, though it was very hard to find out anything very definite about them. The cult centered about a town or a tomb near Mosul, named Sheikh Aadi. They were supposed to be the last fragments of some Manichæan sect. They had a sacred book, but writing and reading were forbidden them. The name of Sheitan was holy and all the s and sh sounds were cut out of their language. They were supposed to have promiscuous love feasts on certain nights like those the Romans liked to ascribe to the early Christians. They always did the lowest possible kind of work, they were roadmenders and scavengers, and, a few of the richest of them, truck-gardeners. They were supposed to believe in the gnostic sevenfold emanation of God, but Sheitan they worshipped as lord of this world in the form of a golden peacock.

Eventually there was no more whisky and no more watermelon and no more about the Yezedis, and we went to sleep. When I woke up the Englishman had gone. The sun was rising over a vast plain dusty and treeless as a New York backyard that stretched an even battleship grey in every direction, without hills or houses or faintest hope of breakfast.

IX. Baghdad Bahnhof

1. Angels on Wheels

You sit in a garden outside of the American Bar on Tigris bank under some scrawny palms. At the foot of the grey mud bank the Tigris runs almost the color of orangepeel in the evening light. At a fire of palmstalks an Arab with his skirts girded up is frying Saratoga potatoes in a huge pan of boiling grease. As fast as he fries them he hands them out on plates to vague khakied Anglo-Saxons who sit limply drinking Japanese beer and talking about malaria, sandfly fever and dysentery. Round boats of wickerwork and skins (see Xenophon) navigate the swift river, spinning as they go. An occasional long wherry with a lantern in the bow shoots out from under the bridge of boats modelled on the one with which Cæsar crossed the Rhine. In the drinking of a glass of Japanese beer the day flares up yellow like a guttering lamp and goes out, leaving night, the scudding lanterns of the wherries, the arclights on the bridge and the dense Chaldæn sky embossed with stars.

From far away across the river come the hoot of a locomotive and the banging of shunted freightcars. The Baghdad Railway. The mazout-burning locomotives hoot derisively beyond the mud horizons. Oh, never-to-be-finished Baghdad Bahn that was to have joined the Sultan Shah Mulay Wilhelm Khan Pasha to his Eastern dominions, bogey of queasy-livered colonels in the Indian service, Moloch well fattened with young men's lives, phantom on lurid wheels that ran mad expresses through the eighteen-nineties up the steep years of the new century, only to smash up once and for all in the great bloody derailment of the War. Even now the apocalyptic vision of flaming wheels linking India with Constantinople, Vienna, Zurich, Berlin, Ostend, hovers over our heads like a greedy and avenging angel as we sit in the dark on Tigris bank drinking Japanese beer and eating Saratoga chips made by an Arab over a fire of palmstalks. Above our heads out of the dense sky the old gods of Chaldæa stare with set unblinking eyes at the river and the bridge of boats and the staffcars and the barracks and the littered trainyards and the fences of barbed wire and the trenches and the sodawater factories and the gutted bazaars and the moving-picture theaters and the great straggling stinking camps of refugees.

—Well, says the fat man from Illinois who is here to buy guts for the sausage factories of Chicago,—may be the Chicago of the Near East some day. . . . Still it'll take some booming before I invest in any real estate. . . .—Dunno, if I had a chance on some lots near the station, said the Armenian from St. Louis. . . .

There are no more Saratoga chips. We are tired of Japanese beer. Inside, cocktail time is beginning at the bar. I'm alone in the dark under the scrawny palms. From the distance comes the crazy hooting laughter of locomotives.

And Ezekiel too by the river Chebar in the midst of the great mudflats saw angels on wheels:

Their appearance was like burning coals of fire and like the appearance of lamps . . . and the fire was bright and out of the fire went forth lightning. . . . The appearance of the wheels and their work was like the color of a beryl, and they four had one likeness: and their appearance and their work was as it were a wheel in the middle of a wheel.

As for their rings they were so high that they were dreadful, and their rings were full of eyes about them four.

And when the living creatures went the wheels went by them.

2. Waters of Babylon

The Scotch engineer very kindly stopped the train for Kut to let me off at Babylon. In the grey plain the single track was two long flashes of sun. In every direction were gravelly hillocks of dust and potsherds that you could imagine to be the traces of walls, blocks of building, ziggaruts. This must have been about 125th Street. Jeremiah certainly had the right dope about Babylon:

And I shall dry up her sea and make her springs dry. And Babylon shall become heaps, a dwelling place for dragons, an astonishment and an hissing, without an inhabitant.

And Isaiah:

And Babylon the glory of kingdoms, the glory of the Chaldees' excellency shall be as when God overthrew Sodom and Gomorrah.

It shall never be inhabited, neither shall it be dwelt in from generation to generation; neither shall the Arabian pitch his tent there;
neither shall the shepherds make their fold there:

But wild beasts of the desert shall lie there; and their houses shall
be full of doleful creatures; and owls shall dwell there and satyrs shall
dance there.

And the wild beasts of the islands shall cry in their desolate
houses; and the dragons in their pleasant places. . . .

How hath the oppressor ceased, the golden city ceased.

—Morgen, said the leader of a ragged and dusty group of
urchins who started to lead me into the downtown district.—
Bonjour . . . Babylon me know. . . . Bloody no good. The
others kept up a chorus of Floos, meester, and danced round
me with grimy palms upturned, undoubtedly the satyrs of Isaiah. So we proceeded to scramble over rubbishpiles for hours
under the noon sun until at last we came, in the region of
Times Square, to the Lion Gate and foundations of great
paved halls that are supposed to be where Balthazar had his
famous feast.

At last, dripping with sweat and with my mouth stopped
with dust, I sank down under a palmtree in front of the still
backwater that was once the main stream of the Euphrates,
wondering at the peculiar effectiveness of the curses that Jeremiah had ordered the "quiet prince" Seraiah to write in a
book and tie to a stone and cast into the Euphrates so that
the luck of Babylon might sink as the stone sank. Jez I'd like
a glass of beer, I muttered half aloud to myself. The urchins,
their palms still outstretched, sat in a circle round me.—Glas
bier, cried the leader of the gang,—subito. And he ran off in
the direction of the mud village among the palms.

A little later he came back with a bottle of Münchner Ex-
portbier, cool and beaded, and some dates tied up in a pink
bandana. That was one on Jeremiah all right. And it was no mirage. When I had finished that bottle the urchin said hopefully,
Noch einmal, and ran off to fetch another. Revivified by
Münchner, the hanging gardens began to shake themselves free
of the dust. Bel and Mardruk sat once more in their starry
chambers at the tops of their skyscraper temples. The sweetvoiced girls of Ishtar began to sing again among the palms. The
song they sang was "Deutschland, Deutschland, über alles."

After all, if the mere hope of the Baghdad Bahn can make the dustheaps of Babylon flow with Münchner beer . . . But that certainly was one on the Hebrew prophets.

3. *Declaration of Independence*

As in ancient Rome, dawn is the calling hour in Baghdad. Yawning, my guide led me through many lanes that still had the chill of night in them, through narrow crumbling arches, along passages between fissured mudwalls until we came to a flight of steep steps in the thickness of a wall. At the head of the steps I waited in a little dark chamber while the guide went ahead through a Turkish door of inlaid work. He came back in a moment and let me into an empty carpeted room.— And the Sheikh Whatshisname? He patted the air with his hand—Shwaya . . . shwaya.

We sat down in the embrasure of a little window. Below, the Tigris flowed fast and brown, filmed with blue mist.—To-day, he went on, it is very dangerous for a patriot in Iraq. . . . We were glad to help the English fight the Turks. But now it is different. The English are like the old man of the sea: at first they are very light, but they get heavier and heavier. And if an important man is opposed to them . . . shwi . . . Cokus invites him to tea . . . and tomorrow he wakes up on the way to Ceylon. This great man we go to see this morning is very much afraid to be invited to tea with Cokus.

At length a boy with a red kerchief on his head ushered us into a long plain hall with rugs on the floor and long cushions round the edges. After the required hesitancy and mamnouning we were settled against the wall at the far end near an old gentleman in dove-grey robes with a beautiful gold and silver beard; we drank coffee and eventually he began to address me through the guide. He spoke in a low warm voice with downcast eyes, occasionally bringing long brown fingers down his beard without touching it. When he paused for the guide to translate he looked hard at us and I noticed that his eyes were blue.

In America, he had heard, we had had a great Sheikh Washiton who had written a book declaring the independence of America from the Inglizi many years ago. Since then we had so far followed the precepts of the Prophet as to believe in one God only and to prohibit the drinking of wine. All this was very good. And now in the big European powderplay we had sent another great Sheikh, Meester Veelson, who had declared in the Fourteen Points at Baries that all nations were free, equal and independent. This was good, too. If such had not been the will of God he would have created one nation and not many.

The Arab nation, made up of believers dwelling in Baghdad and Damascus, had gladly helped the Inglizi and Fransawi to drive out the Osmanli who were oppressors and now were anxious to remain at peace and friendly with all the world, according to the words of Meester Veelson. But the Allies had not acted according to the words of Meester Veelson nor according to the principles of Sheikh Jurij Washiton. This was not good. Arab patriots had been driven out and imprisoned by the Fransawi in Damascus, and now the Inglizi, breaking their plighted word, were trying to make slaves of the people of Iraq. The Inglizi thought they could treat the Arabs of Baghdad and Busra and Damascus as they had treated the people of Hind. They would find that the Arabs were of stiffer stuff. They had tried to deceive them with mock kingdoms, when the lowest porter in the bazaars knew that Feisul and Abdullah, even the King of the Hedjaz himself for all his holding the holy cities, had no power outside of the guns of the Inglizi.

The Americai must tell his countrymen that the people of Iraq would continue to struggle for their freedom and for the principles announced by Sheikh Washiton and Meester Veelson. The last revolt had failed because it had been ill prepared. Next time . . . His voice rose ever so slightly.

When we got up to go he led us to the door. I asked my guide to ask about the plebiscite. The old man laughed. Oh yes, they had given out papers in the bazaars, but they were already printed with the vote for the mandate, so that the ignorant should vote for the government without knowing it. But only the Jews had voted and a few ignorant people; what man who knew his letters and the law would demean himself by voting anyway?

Oh, self-determination, where is thy sting?

4. Misadventures with a Consul

What with the mirage and the difficulty of following the road through the breaks in old watercourses the representative of the Screaming Eagle and myself arrived in Samarrah very late, after driving the Ford all afternoon over the naked pebbly plain of *the land the rivers have spoiled*, where you continually pass the mounds of crumbled cities and towers. It was almost dark when we crossed on the crazy ferry and saw in the distance the silhouette of the great ziggurat, like the tower of Babel in ancient illustrated bibles. Close on our heels came the Adviser in his high-powered car to find out what the devil we were up to. We all went to the house of the kaimakom, where we were given rooms freshly furnished in chintzy European style by Maple's. Dinner was a splendid affair. The climax of the evening came when the kaimakom, much exhilarated by ardent spirits (it is wine the Koran forbids) anointed all our heads with brilliantine. The representative of the Screaming Eagle was a very tall man who neither drank nor smoked. He sat bolt upright with an untasted glass of arrak in his hand and brilliantine running down his face while the kaimakom gave him a shampoo. The adviser, who had brought his own whisky and had submitted cheerfully to the operation, leaned back in his chair as red as a turkeygobbler. It was a fine dinner.

It was on the way back to Baghdad the next afternoon that we definitely lost the way. When night came on our gas had run out. We were stalled in some tracks that might have been a road, somewhere between the Tigris and the Euphrates. After a great deal of palaver, for it was not supposed to be safe outside of the towns after nightfall, we left the representative of the Screaming Eagle eating a watermelon and went off in search of a fairly mythical village where we could perhaps find a can of gasoline.

Go, ye swift messengers, to a nation scattered and peeled, to a people terrible from their beginning hitherto: a nation meted out and trodden down, whose land the rivers have spoiled.

It's fantastic how this country is saturated with the Bible, how these desolate mudflats and rubbishheaps are scorched and seared by the cursing tongues of the Hebrew prophets.

Well, the consular servant, Abdullah, and I started out to look for a can of gas. He was a weazened brown worriedfaced man with a long crouching stride. We walked east away from the road towards some faint lights that might be a village. It was curious, walking over the pitted surface of the plain. There were stars, but they didn't seem to give any light. A cool dusty wind occasionally blew in our faces, a wind that smelled of nothing. Through vacancy from which shape and color and smell had withdrawn as a snail withdraws into its shell we walked and walked. Without speaking we walked and walked. Abdullah put his hand on my arm. We stopped dead. The ground dropped away under our feet. I remembered having seen some quarries or limepits somewhere on the ride up the day before. Through the gloom we made out a flicker of light. We smelled woodsmoke. Slipping and scrambling, we got down the incline into a muddy bottom of some sort, Abdullah walked ahead and I followed as best I could. We stopped before a burning kiln. The smoke eddied about us. Not finding anybody, we went on climbing up to the level of the plain again. We began to hear the barking of pariah dogs; as we drew nearer the village the dogs got our wind and came towards us, yelling in a pack. We made out some mud huts and walked among them with the dogs yapping and snarling at our heels.

An old man stuck his head sleepily out of a door and showed us the track towards Kazimain. For a long while we followed the road until it disappeared and left us stumbling over the jagged surface of the plain again. This was discouraging. It may have been an hour before we found ourselves walking along a railroad track. Good old Baghdad Bahn! It might have been the Willimantic Air Line. Eventually we came to a station. It was dark, but a road led east again from it. The road went through a Sepoy bivouac. To pipe and muffled drum, soldiers were dancing among the high-flaring campfires. Kazimain, said Abdullah, putting one hand on my shoulder and stretching the other towards the horizon.

At Kazimain we made a knocking to wake the dead on the portals of the Persian Consulate. At length the Consul himself, in carpet slippers, backed up by his retainers with lamps, appeared in the door. He must have thought the perfidious

Inglizi were coming to assassinate him. When he heard of the plight of his colleague of the Screaming Eagle he wrung his hands and ordered out his own limousine. We sped along the road to take help to the stranded consul and stopped only when the road ended at the edge of a deep pit. The Persian consul's chauffeur shook his head between his hands. He could go no farther. So the relief party started out on foot again, scrambling through gullies and ravines until, very tired, and each with a bidon of gas in one hand, we came again to the burning limekiln. At last we found the tracks of the Ford on a path. We shouted and yodeled. The yelling packs of dogs answered us from the horizons. Abdullah picked up a water-melon rind. The car had gone. Undoubtedly this was where it had been. Slowly, with a sense of gathering doom, he pieced together the whole melon. We strained our eyes to make it out in the starlight. Yes it had the markings of the melon the Consul Sahib had been eating when we left him. The car had gone, carried off by raiders, maybe. Abdullah squatted by the side of the road. He would wait there till the morning. I left him sitting beside the two bidons of gasoline and started to walk into Baghdad.

Walking along the dusty tracks, taking care to follow the ruts, is like walking through a dream you can't remember. The multitude of unfamiliar stars. The plain is terribly dark and empty in spite of the stars. The plain is crowded under its emptiness. Noise is shivering under the silence, ready to burst into the crazy yelling of pariah dogs. *Land shadowing with wings . . . a nation meted out and trodden down, whose land the rivers have spoiled.*

X. The Stony Desert of Damascus

—What, you never ate a prairie oyster? cried the Major. Never.—Then you shall by heaven, before the evening's out. And so it happened after we had given everybody airplane rides blindfolded on a board, even to the cook and all the bearahs and one little man they dragged in off the street, and while we were swallowing our prairie oysters and taking a last nip of Scotch, rifle shots started snapping somewhere towards the edge of town. Someone looked out of the window into the rainy square and said,—Dear me, they seem to be firing. After I had gone to bed above the lisp of rain trickling down mudwalls I could hear an occasional shot shiver the cadence of the rain like a breaking glass.

At breakfast over the bacon and eggs it transpired that a raid had been made on the sarai, the government house, and that the safe had been carried away.—Never mind, I know who did it, said the Adviser; he's a good friend of mine. I'll have him locked up before night. Those damn native levies are probably in league with him. I'll settle him. We had hardly finished our last cup of tea when a young man dressed in a fine Persian aba of camel's hair, with an expensive pink agal so heavily bound with gold thread that it would not stay straight but balanced ridiculously awry on his head, came stamping in with much ceremony. He said he was the son of the naqib of Madina and a relative of Malik Feisul, and gave what was afterwards explained to me to be an animated description of the heroic stand the caravan camp had made against the raiders. He also said it was too wet for the camels to start and that we were to spend yet another day looking at the crumbled mud-walls and the date gardens of Romadi. Tomorrow if God willed. . . . Bukra insh'allah.

Then the Aviator and the Intelligence Man and myself were prevailed upon to visit the young man with the pink-gilt agal in his tent and I was made to ride out on a led horse with red tassels on the bridle. In the tent, that was an English tent bought in Baghdad, we sat on sheepskins and drank tea and ate Turkish paste and I fingered my list of Arabic words like a breviary. Bronzefaced people gradually seeped in, made polite ejaculations and were silent. Tallow smell of sheepskins. Flash of eyes, teeth, brown toes along the edges of a Persian rug and lean dry hands motionless among the folds of abas, and a rakish man with a black beard passing little swell-bottomed glasses of tea, that the young man with the pink-gilt agal, who turned out to be the Sayyid Mohamet, clogged with condensed milk with his own hands as an especial treat. Eventually we escaped to the open air again after a great deal of bowing and scraping on both sides and went back to chairs, whisky and soda and luncheon. In the afternoon the indefatigable Sayyid Mahomet reappeared and dragged me round to the coffee houses and cigarette shops of the small brick bazaar down towards the Euphrates. We squatted on cane benches, grinning at each other, speechless as apes, and watched the flies glinting in the sun above a muddy alley outside, and drank tiny cups of coffee black as night and perfumed with some herb or other, the herb of delay perhaps that induces the bittersweet drowse into which one falls waiting for steamers to coal and roads to dry and streams to become fordable and caravans to start. Tomorrow, insh'allah, if God willed, we would start for Damascus across the desert.

And what should appear, wheezing and popping through the ruts and puddles, but the rusty Ford that had brought me from Baghdad across the mudflats that lie between the rivers? The Sayyid was immediately agog with it and after a great deal of discussion we set out through drizzly rain, lurching and clattering through puddles, spluttering down narrow lanes, frightening old women and chickens, making horses rear and break their halters. Half the population of the café had piled in, grave men in brown robes with beards like Micah and Ezekiel stood on the runningboards, little urchins hoisted up their gowns about their shoulders and ran after us, and every time the motor backfired everybody rolled up his eyes and cried, alham'd'ullah, Praise be to God. At last when we had twice circumnavigated the walls and date gardens and the tumbled cemeteries of Romadi, the engine gave a final frantic explosion, there was a horrid buckling snarl from the differential, and the car stopped. The driver took off his tarboosh and wailed and everybody roared with laughter. Took the opportunity to slip back into Europe through a breach in the wall to the British officers' mess, where I sat reading the *Strand* until it was time for whiskys and sodas again.

After dinner and talk about irrigation schemes and uprisings I set out with two men with lanterns to find the caravan camp. A rainy wind was howling in our faces and continually blew out the lanterns, and we expected to find a raider in every patch of grey in the shrill blackness of the night. Eventually we heard a man singing and there came on the wind the growl and sharp smell of camels. The Britishers' servants left me in my tent in the care of an obsequious and soiled man named Fahad who set up my bed with great skill and bowed himself out. Then one Saleh, a crookednosed youth in an English army coat, came in and said with a fine cockney twang:—Me speak bloody English, messboy bloody English camp. Me boy take care seecamels. Then he stopped and with the greatest delicacy and good humor began to say it over again.—Do we go tomorrow? I interrupted him. He rolled up his eyes, gargled an insh'allah and left me. I sat on my cot and looked about. The tent was crimson inside, with little decorations of hearts and diamonds on the flaps. It was round at the top, tapering to a single pole, and hexagonal at the bottom and gave me the feeling of being a worm in a fuchsia flower. Rain had come up and beat a gentle tattoo on the roof. I got undressed slowly, listening to the extraordinary bubbling and groaning of the camels. At last here was an end of colonies and whisky and soda and the *Strand* and canned goods and the American Bar on Tigris bank and the soldier-littered rail-scarred dumping grounds of the West. I wrapped myself in my striped Tabriz and blew out the candle. The rain beat harder on the sag of the tent over my head. People on guard round the camp called to each other at intervals with a long gruffening call. Once there were some shots far away. And just outside my tent someone was crooning a frail circular snatch of song over and over again. Something about Ali Asgar, Ali Afgar, dead at Kerbela. The word dead, Miut, I recognized because coming up from Baghdad we had passed the body of a Hindoo boy beside the road lying on its back with a stony smile, and Jassem had come back to the car from looking at it, had shaken his beard and said, Miut, and we had driven on. And listening to the song and the bubbling of the camels and the beat of the rain I went to sleep.

First Day: Woke up and crawled out of my tent to find everything else struck and everyone bustling and shouting at a tremendous rate. My delull (dromedary) that I'd been introduced to the day before and whose name I had thought to be Malek stood waiting, and her tasselled saddlebags they dragged the ground O! The datepalms in the gardens of Romandi stood kneedeep in mist that was just beginning to sop up gold in premonition of the sun. While I grasped the silver-encrusted pommels of the saddle everybody gathered round anxiously to see if I would fall off when Malek jerked to her feet. The hobble was loosed. Malek gave a grunt and opened herself like a jackknife. My head poked above the mist into the sunlight that stung red in my eyes. Then we turned round and followed the long string of baggage camels down the ruddy trail that led north and west towards Kubaissa, and for the first time I noticed round the shadows of my head and Malek's nodding head and Fahad's head the halo that so excited Cellini.

There's already excitement about safety money. It seems certain Bedawi of Toman are going to attack us if we don't come across with five pounds Turkish per head of cattle. We are being guarded by some fine hardboiled men on ponies, henchmen, if I got the name right, of one Abdul Aziz, head sheikh of the Delaim. From the moment we got out of gunshot of the sarai at Romadi we were on our own. During the afternoon I had lagged behind the main body of the caravan and was brewing tea with the Sayyid Mahomet and Hadji Mahomet, his cook, and a fauneyed brown youngster from Damascus named Saleh, over a fire of wormwood sticks, when there appeared suddenly over a pebbly hill to the west a bunch of men riding their camels hard. They stopped when they saw us and the wind brought us the groaning and gurgling of their beasts as they dismounted. The Sayyid grabbed his gun and began talking big, and the cook hastily packed the tea things, and we all rode hard after the caravan, saddlebags bouncing and rattling, dromedaries slobbering and snorting. Marvellous how not knowing the language takes away all sense of responsibility. I followed the rest without the vaguest idea of who was friend and who foe, calm in the recollection that my watch had gone by airplane mail. Of course it was a false alarm, but it made your blood tingle just the same. Almost as much as the air and the larks that rose singing from under the camels' feet and the uproar and shouting when a rabbit loped off into the thorny underbrush.

Second Day: We camped in a place called Sheib Mahomedi near a running stream. On the horizon to the north there are smudges of black smoke from the bitumen pits of Kubaissa. This morning I had to dress up in aba and ismak as Jassem made Saleh tell me that the sight of a European hat would make the caravan unpopular—English hat no bloody good. Arab hat good. So I am lying in all the pomp of a new Bagh-dad aba on a rug in front of my tent under a shining sky streaked like turquoise matrix. Beside my tent the big bales that load Jassem er Rawwaf's camels are piled in a semicircle round a fire about which all the gravest people of the caravan squat and drink coffee. Opposite is the English tent of the Sayyid Mahomet, which is where gilded youth seems to gather. The circle is completed by the bales of the six or seven other outfits that make up the caravan, arranged like Jassem's in a halfmoon to windward of the fire. Besides the Sayyid and my-self and the dancing girls on their way to Aleppo there is only a Damascus merchant effete enough to pitch a tent. Everyone else squats on rugs round the fires under the blue. The camels have been driven off to pasture on the dry shrubs of the hills round about the waterhole and stand dark in curious attitudes against the skyline. Occasionally you catch sight of a guard with his gun aslant his back, motionless, watching from the top of one of the tawny and steely violet hills that break away in every direction like a confusion of seawaves.

Down by the waterhole where I had been bathing I had a long talk in seven words and considerable pantomime with one of the Sayyid Mahomet's retainers, a tall chap with very slender feet and hands, named Souleiman. He was asking about an Englishman named "Hilleby" with whose outfit he had been cameldriver in the Nejd. Hearing that I knew about "Hilleby" excited him enormously. He too dressed like an Arab and liked the sweet air of the desert.—Air of desert sweet like honey. Baghdad air filth. Souleiman plucked a sprig of an aromatic plant and made me smell it, some sort of rosemary perhaps it was.—Desert like that, he said; then he screwed up his face in a spasm of disgust.—Ingliz Baghdad like that. "Hilleby" friend of Arab, not afraid of the desert, good. Then he took me by the hand and led me to the Sayyid's tent and sat me down in the seat of honor and brought me coffee and dates. After sitting there a long time trying to pick up a word here and there in the talk that seemed to be about the Nejd and how smoking was forbidden there and how great and goodly a person was ibn Saoud whom even the English called Sultan, Fahad my cameldriver appeared to tell me that my supper was ready. From him and Baghdad Saleh I got the impression that I was thought by the peple of Jassem's outfit to be frequenting low company in sitting so much in the tent of the Sayyid Mahomet. Saleh said as much when he drove the camels home at sunset:—Sayyid he bloody no good. Social life in the desert seems to be as complicated as it is everywhere else.

So I sat alone in my tent eating rice and canned sausage, kosher sausage at that. I peered out through the half-closed flap—Fahad always had the idea I ought to eat in secret and used to shut me up carefully every time he went out—and tried to size up the other outfits in the caravan. Round Jassem er Rawwaf's campfire were my tent and the tent of the dancing girls, from which came a faint wailing of babies, and the little campfires of people with only a few camels who seemed to have attached themselves to Jassem's outfit. Then opposite was the Sayyid's khaki tent and the big tent of the merchant from Damascus and the two wattled litters in which squatted without ever moving a little Turkish merchant and his wife. At one end of the oval was the big encampment of the people who are driving the young camels over to sell in Syria, and at the other the outfit made remarkable by the presence of a fine old gentleman with a green turban and a beard like snow and a dark blue umbrella.

Blue smokespirals uncoil crisply from the campfires through the amethyst twilight. Camels stroll towards the camp in a densening herd, sniffing the air and nibbling at an occasional cluster of twigs, urged on by the long labial cry of the driver. The mollah is chanting the evening prayer. The men stand with bare feet in a long rank facing the southwest, make the prostrations slowly, out of unison. Gradually the camels fill the great oval place between the campfires, are hobbled and fold themselves up in rows, chewing and groaning. The stars impinge sharply like flaws in the luminous crystal-dark sky. My blankets smell of camel and are smoky from the fire. Once asleep, I am awakened by two shots that ring on the night like on a bell. There's a sound of voices and pebbles scuttling under naked feet. Saleh sticks his head in the tent and says proudly,—Haremi, bang, bang, imshi, go away. And I'm asleep again rocked like by waves by the soft fuzzy grumbling noise of five hundred camels.

Third Day: After a couple of hours' riding we saw palms in a shallow ravine and came upon the little desert port of Kubaissa huddled into its mudwalls among rocky ledges and sandhills. Was taken to see the Mudir and wasted most of the day in mamnouning, coffee, and civilities. In front of the city gate children were playing with a tame gazelle. Was carried off to his house by a fine fat sheikh and fed a wonderful meal of eggs and rice and fried dates and chicken. The fat sheikh is coming with us to terrify the bedawi by the augustness of his presence.—All friends, he says, slapping himself on the chest. Was made to taste nine or ten different kinds of dates and not allowed to go to the bazaar, all sorts of attendants being sent to buy things I wanted instead. All this high society is rather trying. Eventually escaped with a book up a long rocky gulch to a deep basin in the hills full of mineral springs that steamed and bubbled out of potholes in yellow rocks. A very Sinai sort of a place. Jehovah used to come here in the old days.

Fourth Day: Great complication of social events. The Mudir came out to call on Jassem and the Americai, but was lured to the tent of the Sayyid Mahomet, who's a great little social climber, instead. Excitement and dark looks. Then apologies. Visit made all over again, interminable mamnouning. I squatted and grinned and nodded like a damned porcelain figure. Still the Sayyid carried off his infamy in fine style, spreading rugs and abas on the ground and then strewing on them with a grandiloquent gesture a basket of dates and a bag of Turkish paste that the Mudir distributed to his attendants and to the maimed and halt and blind who crowded round. A great day for the Sayyid. Bukra insh'allah, we are off.

Fifth Day: Malek has bushy eyelashes and eyebrows she can wiggle. Extraordinary how dainty camels are about their food. Some luscious-looking dry shrubs she won't touch and there are occasionally little rosettes with thistly leaves that make her eyes pop out of her head with greediness, that no amount of beating will drive her past.

Off first thing in the morning with considerable pomp, with the sun right in our backs and our shadows incredibly long, topped by crowns of bright rays. Rode with the fat sheikh, who kept producing legs of chicken out of his saddlebags. This is the order of our going: the outfits each start separately, with Jassem's usually first, and gradually fall into line along the trail; then as they get the sleep jounced out of them and the sun thaws their dromedaries the grandees of the caravan ride ahead. A couple of the Agail can usually be seen scouting far off among rocky hillocks on the horizon. At lunch the grandees squat about saucepans of rice and drink coffee and the caravan gets ahead and is caught up to during the afternoon.

This evening we're camping in a flat basin full of low aromatic plants, shiah and ruetha. Ruetha, that's probably the aromatic stuff Xenophon's always talking about in the Anabasis, seems to delight the camels beyond anything. Water must stand here in the rainy season. That rainy season, incidentally, must be about on us, for great showers are piling up to northward to everybody's delight, as they say a day's rain will mean plenty of food for camels. Also it keeps the Bedawi in their tents.

Sat in the tent of the Sayyid, in spite of Baghdad Saleh's remonstrances,—Sayyid he bloody loosewiler, whatever that meant,—and drank tea clogged with condensed milk I'd given the Sayyid in a moment of expansiveness, and listened to Souleiman, the man who went to the Nejd with "Hilleby," play wailingly on a tiny little lute.

Sixth Day: Enteuthen exelaunei a good bunch of parasangs with a general feeling of climbing up on a plateau. The trail, made up of many little paths padded soft by the feet of centuries of camels, wound around pinkish ledges here and there dotted with dry plants. In one place we passed the traditional skeletons. In a bottom we found the tracks of a Ford, the tracks of Leachman's car, they said. Leachman was shot during the revolt by the son of an old man he'd insulted. A delicious camping place at length at the edge of a basin where the dry shiah was tall as your waist. Three big rabbits broke cover as we were folding up our camels and everybody shouted and shot off guns in a most cheerful manner.

In the afternoon passed a small square stone tower.

Walked abroad after supper at the hour when they were bringing home the camels. A Bedawi whom I'd seen before riding on a white dromedary came up to me and said he was a friend of Malik Feisul's. We walked out into the desert together, he sniffing the air and saying that the air of the desert was sweet. His name was Nuwwaf. His tents were in El Garrá halfway over to Damascus. I taught him to say north, south, east and west, and he pronounced the words perfectly at once; while my pronunciation of the Arabic equivalents was so comical that he laughed until the tears filled his kohl-pencilled eyes. He took me to have coffee with the people who are bringing over the herd of young camels to sell in Syria. The Hadji, the old gentleman with the umbrella, was sitting at their campfire holding forth about something.

Back in my tent I found Baghdad Saleh and Jassem's little boy rolling me cigarettes. They tried to explain some terrible fate that had almost swooped down on the camels, but I couldn't gather anything definite except that it had been averted by Baghdad Saleh's single-handed prowess. It's very difficult to discover what Saleh means when he tries to speak English because, having worked in the Anglo-Indian camp in Baghdad, he has the deplorable notion that Hindustani and English are the same language.

It's the finest thing in the world to have no watch and no money and to feel no responsibility for events. Like being a dervish or a very small child.

Seventh Day: The mail plane passed overhead, flying high. Everybody looked at it scornfully without comment. Goddam cold and rainsqualls lashing in our faces. Everything more or less wet. Never have seen such exquisite distaste expressed by any animal as by Malek in the rain. Insh'allah the wind will go down with the sun. Sitting in chilly splendor in my gold-embroidered aba in my hearts and diamonds tent that lets in the wind most damnably for all its crimson lining. But who ever shivered in a broader wind?

The Sayyid's stock seems to be very low in the caravan. Souleiman had a fight with him about something, hit him in the face, so Baghdad Saleh says, climbed on his camel and made off for Baghdad. I shall miss the faint wail of his lute stealing through the bubbling, grumbling sound of camels across the camp at night.

Eighth Day: There never was invented a leisurelier, more soothing way of travel than this. The swaying of the camel is just enough to tire you out gradually, gently. You beat him just enough to keep your thoughts in a faint doze. You ride first with one person, then with another, looking back at the long trailing caravan like a kite's tail behind you; parts of it go out of sight in depressions, curve round hills. It's the way clouds travel, rivers flow. There are no orders given. Everyone knows what to do, as when birds migrate.

The sky is an immense sphere of clouded glass balanced on the bit of piecrust the earth; today it shines with occasional ruddy flaws of winter sunshine.

Towards evening, at the hour when your legs ache and your belly yaps like a dog with hunger, we came into a vast shallow valley running north and south. At the other rim of it was a row of long black things like beetles, the tents of the Delaim.

Ninth Day: Sweet wind and clear sky. A small party of Agail with a dozen or so baggage camels passed us coming from Aleppo. Very much like speaking a ship at sea.

We sat all day in our tents, O Israel.

Spent the day roaming about restlessly, trying to talk Arabic with Nuwwaf and reading Molière. There's some hitch. The fat sheikh from Kubaissa seems rather low. Much talk of a certain sheikh Mohamet Turki of the Kubain wanting an incredible amount of safety money.

Tenth Day: Still in the same place. Strange people keep filtering into camp, Delaim dressed in white, very large white-skinned men with waxed whiskers and their hair in pleats over their ears. They are friends of the Agail and the caravan is more or less under their protection.

From the first crack of dawn tremendous tumultuous speechifying went on at the campfire of Jassem er Rawwaf and has kept up all day; people jump to their feet and shout and wave their arms. The fat sheikh seems to be the general mediator. Jassem er Rawwaf is tall with prominent teeth and a beard slightly lopsided like the beard of Moses, he wears two head-cloths that fall amply over his shoulders, one white and one purple, and mostly sits silent directing the making of coffee with little movements of his long hands or strokes a string of amber beads. Once he got angry and leaned forward across the fire and said something slowly and deliberately that made everyone quiet down and nod his head. Later I asked him what the row was about. He smiled and shrugged his shoulders, at the same time rubbing his thumb and forefinger together with a gesture incredibly Semitic, and said gently, Floos, money.

All the desert seems to be prowling about greedily and ap-praisingly, waiting to pounce on our bales of Persian tobacco and the tempting herd of young camels.

Nuwwaf came and sat in my tent and talked a great deal about how the Ingliz were united and used their guns only to shoot strangers, while the Arabs were always squabbling among themselves and were very nice to strangers. At least so I understood. I agreed with him vigorously.

There's a great deal of polishing of guns going on.

Eleventh Day: Last night happened the first great rumpus.

I'd gone to my tent and closed myself in to read by can-dlelight when across the camp there began a great deal of shouting. Everybody started tripping over my tent ropes and rushing about. Baghdad Saleh rushed in to get his gun that he'd left there for safe keeping. Fahad appeared tremendously excited and kept shouting something equivalent to Man the boats. I stood in the door of the tent without being able to see anything, as it was very dark, but Fahad insisted I go in again, shaking his head in a most lugubrious manner. Mean-while the candle had been knocked over, so I sat a minute in the dark on my cot, listening to the growing tumult outside. I had been plentifully nourished with horrors of Baghdad so I began to form pictures like the waxwork at Madam Tous-saud's of Gordon at Khartoum. I thought of lithographs I'd had in my childhood of explorers in pith helmets being trans-fixed by assegais. The unfortunate death of the Prince Napoleon. Thank God I didn't have a pith helmet.

Finding that I was trembling and chilly, I went to the door of the tent again and lit a cigarette. Immediately a man I did not know ran by shouting something. I gave him the cigarette. He went off with it, seeming much encouraged. Then the Sayyid came up bareheaded and shaking and breathless, saying something about a gun. No, I didn't have a gun, but I gave him my cigarette. By the time I'd given away a handful of cigarettes the shouting had begun to recede in the distance. I kept wondering when the rifles would begin, not knowing how extremely careful with firearms the Arabs are. Then a great many people came and began to explain what had happened, all more or less unintelligibly. Did manage to gather, though, that the fight had started by one of ibn Kubain's men trying to steal the Sayyid's rifle. The rifle had been got back but there had been a fight and heads had been broken.

There were double sentries posted and everybody lay down heroically to sleep.

This morning we moved north across a thorny slope noisy with larks, to a camping place near a waterhole in front of the tents of the Delaim.

Went over with the fat sheikh to visit the Delaim. Their tents are very large, open on the lee side, divided in the middle by a curtain that screens off the women's part. To anyone born in a way of life given over to cult of Things they seem incredibly bare; a few rugs, some saddles and guns and a couple of piles of sheepskins, some cooking-bowls and the black ragged walls of their tents, are all the Delaim have to swaddle themselves in between the naked earth and the inconceivable sky. We squatted on rugs that were spread for us, coffee was brought, and I stared across the plain that stretched away indefinitely southward, where grazed great herds of sheep with men in brown robes walking among them like in illustrations to the Old Testament, while the fat sheikh talked gravely with the people we were the guests of. Then a woman brought a flat wooden dish that had in it a cake of unleavened bread, steaming hot, swimming with melted ewe's butter. Must be such butter that Jael brought forth in a lordly dish. A boy poured water over our hands from a little copper ewer, and the head of the house broke a piece out of the middle of the dish with a loud Alham'd'ullah. Then we stretched out our right hands and did eat.

In the afternoon went round and sat at people's fires and drank coffee and tried to find out how long we were expected to stay in the tents of the Delaim. Everybody said we'd go bukra insh'allah, but they said insh'allah so many times and rolled up their eyes so fearfully as they said it that it seemed pretty sure that the responsibility for leaving tomorrow was being foisted on Allah and that we'd stay where we were.

Twelfth Day: Terrific cold wind. Too cold to do anything but crouch over the fire with your eyes full of smoke.

Went to call on the Damascus merchants who brought me over the cakes the other day. Their little boy produced, to everyone's pride and delight, two or three phrases of excellent English. His elder brother knows about five words of French so we had a roaring conversation. Their father seemed extremely gloomy about our prospects and suggested that we'd probably turn back to Baghdad. But the little boy, who can't be more than ten, heartened everybody by saying,—We weel shoot Bedawi with the gun and keel him.

I don't entirely like the enthusiasm with which these Delaim people look over my possessions. Three superb rascals have just left my tent. They sat there a long time with baksheesh on the tip of their tongues. They felt of the canvas and of my aba and poked at the hippo and asked what was inside it, and their eyes sparkled with greed at the sight of the silver-incrusted saddle El Souadi lent me. I tried to glut them with cigarettes.

Bad. About noon. The wind's like a razor, and the camp is knocked flat with dismay. The merry men of ibn Kubain have called our bluff and driven off our camels from the grazing grounds. From the little hillock with the cairn I saw them disappearing behind the horizon. People rushed out from camp and shot off guns, but the Kubain people are stronger than we are, or at least they have more nerve.

Baghdad Saleh has just come in without his British army coat or his new red ismak, dragging his feet and looking very dejected:—Bloody Bedawi, bloody loosewilers steal bloody seecamels. He explained that he was asleep at the time or it would never have happened. He was beaten up and his gun was stolen and his coat and his new head-cloth.—Bedawi no good.

I went and found Jassem, who was sitting in the lee of some bales of tobacco, beside the ashes of a fire. He smiled gloomily and nodding to the horizon made a gesture of coins running through his fingers and said with great emphasis, Floos, floos ketir, money, much money. So I went sulkily back to my tent. Well, the walking was probably excellent. It would be farewell to the hippo and its nonsensical contents. Perhaps we'd all be carried off into servitude in some lost oasis. So long as I don't lose my glasses, I was thinking. I lay shivering on the camp bed wrapped up in the Baghdad blanket. Molière had lost his flavor and drawing seemed a futile occupation. All the wind of heaven whistled round my legs. The tent was no more protection than a sieve. The leaden day was already shattered into tumultuous twilight when I heard a familiar delicious *cupalaoop* in the distance and the grumbling of camels. The camels were being driven home. They drifted one by one into camp, craning their necks absentmindedly from side to side until the whole space between the fires was full of their roaring and bubbling.

Thirteenth Day: It's all a farce played according to rules. The Delaim went after ibn Kubain's people and brought back the camels, and everything is where it started. We'll pay the safety money and I suppose the Delaim will get some of it for their trouble. The insh'allahs about leaving tomorrow are pretty feeble so I guess we'll round out the week in this accursed spot. My only amusement is sitting on the cairn and watching the flocks of the Delaim move slowly among the scrub-littered valleys round the waterholes. I'm sick of Molière. *And the stars in their courses fought against Sisera.*

Yesterday afternoon, after the crisis was over, the camp became very social. Groups of the Delaim and the Fede'an roamed about from campfire to campfire. I sat in state on my camp bed and everyone came and sat on the floor of my tent and was silent. Got very chummy with a young man of ibn Kubain's people who wore his hair in two little plaits neatly looped in front of his ears. He showed me his Turkish rifle and said he was the Osmanli's own man. Feeling it was up to me to do something to promote the Christmas spirit, I gave everybody cigarettes and handfuls of tobacco. The man with the little plaits I liked so much, I gave a box of matches.

Whereupon he offered to go with me to Esch Scham or over the sea or anywhere. Then I would give him many gold pounds Turkish. I tried to explain that I was a fakir, a poor man, and had no floos of any sort, but he would not believe me. At that point Nuwwaf came in. Now Nuwwaf is a friend of Feisul's and a deadly enemy of the Fede'an and was much annoyed to find me so friendly with a mere bandit. I didn't have enough Arabic to explain to him that I liked these little brown hardboiled people better than the big white Delaim with their waxed moustaches, even if they were holding us up. He went off looking very hurt.

It's a cloudy stagnant day. The elders of Israel sit round Jassem's fire where Fahad is cooking disgustedly pots and pots of rice to feed this multitude. Now and then a gust of dispute rises and is caught up by other groups round other smoky fires, or there is an impressive clink of moneybags.

Fourteenth Day: Rained cats and dogs in the night, so we have to wait another day before starting, as camels are as helpless in mud as a giraffe on skates. That's five days going in two weeks. Damn all delays. I have the immortal itch to be gone from these cheezy hills where the sheep graze dully as maggots and the tents of the Delaim lie like dead beetles along the horizon. Was called on today, right after my lunch of oatmeal and condensed milk, by my Osmanli friend and the little crosseyed boy who is sheikh of the ibn Kubain crowd and a great mob of our yesterday's enemies. The little sheikh showed me with pride a German trench periscope he had; several of his men had field glasses. Everybody was having a social time when the fat sheikh and Jassem er Rawwaf came and drove them all away. Evidently the caravan does not approve of the way I get on with our enemies. That's the hell of being a hakim and sitting in a crimson tent. Everything you do has political significance. Nuwwaf came to see me later, looking very offended and making various unfriendly comments about the Fede'an. I cheered him up by having Jassem's little boy bring us coffee, and then we walked up to the cairn and he pointed westward along the marked trail. Five days that way to El Garrá where his flocks were. If I could stay with him he'd have a sheep killed for me. I should stay with him many days, very many days, always; and for a moment, leaning against the enormous ceaseless wind that whined and rattled among the little stones of the cairn, I thought I would. To live always in a tent of black felt eating unleavened bread and ewe's butter, with the wind always sheer in your nostrils, moving south in winter, north in summer, for the grazing of the camels and sheep; to take a shrill-voiced Bedawi woman for a wife, to die of a rifleshot in a raid and be buried under a pile of stones beside the ashes of your fire and the round dungheaps of your last camping ground. Will the world hold anything to make up for the not living of that life?

I came back very hungry to my tent and had Fahad cook me my last can of kosher sausage. The tent soars like a balloon in the wind.

Fifteenth Day: Crawled out of my cocoon a couple of hours before dawn to find the stars crackling with cold. Everything had been struck. The camping ground was a struggling confusion of camels and drivers holding their necks to the ground while the packs were being fastened on their backs. The camels were struggling and groaning and roaring, the drivers were cursing and kicking. Jassem, always quiet, crouched over the last embers of the fire, warming his long hands. He was laughing quietly to himself when I sat beside him. He handed me a last drop of coffee in one of his thimble cups and then packed up the three pots and the cups and the pestle and mortar in his red saddlebags. Malek was brought by Fahad and nakhed; she lurched to her feet with such a jump that my head almost tangled in Orion, and we were off, everything at a jog trot due north towards the Dipper. A superb ride through the dawn across grass-sheening uplands to the great canyon of the Sheib Hauran, down round the face of red sandstone cliffs, Malek leaping like a mountain goat from rock to rock, to the water bed, where remained a few muddy pools from the last week's rain. There the camels were watered quickly and we were off again, scattering up the steep paths of the north side, I riding beside the old Hadji with the umbrella who rolled his eyes and cried Alham'd'ullah in the most groaning tones every time his camel took a leap. Then when we had scrambled up the last squared cliff of the canyon rim we were off under sparkling showers across the vastest, most pancake flat desert we have yet come to. Travelled eleven hours at top speed, and made camp in the dark, wolf-hungry and dog-tired. Wow!

Sixteenth Day: Reclining Roman fashion on my couch and looking out between the loopedup tentflaps at Fahad pottering very tired and cross among the cooking-pots from which steam rises silvery against a pistachio-green twilight. Up above the sky loosens into scrolled clouds of platinum and feathery purple. Barefoot Ali walks slowly across behind the fire, leading home a strayed camel. Ali, the most skillful of our camel drivers, is built like a beechtree, never says anything, and walks with incredible majesty.

The journey was long and splendid. Gazelles were sighted. We rode through patches of scrub full of larks where now and then a rabbit broke cover under the camel's feet and sat watching a second with twitching nose before loping off into the blue ruetha again. White tablelands to the north that pinked to amethyst in the afternoon. And now the evening cry of *cupallyouawp, cupallyouawp* of the drivers calling the camels home from pasture.

After eight hours of the saddle my legs began to drop off.

It seems that the war in the Nejd is over. Ibn Saoud has captured Hael and ibn Raschid and all his wives and followers and is now supreme ruler of Central Arabia. There is a man in our caravan of the Shamar, a lean man with crazy eyes who gets to his feet beside his campfire after evening prayer every day and calls a challenge to any man who is enemy of his tribe to come out and fight. Every night his voice rises in a challenging cry that unfurls like a banner above the bustle and the camelnoises of the camp.

Seventeenth Day: Still headed a little west of north, wandering through gulches and between eroded tablelands. Camped about midafternoon near a waterhole in the dry bed of a sheib. To the south of us are high mesetas like those between Madrid and Toledo. Warm sunny afternoon. People retire modestly behind rocks to wash themselves and change their clothes. Wandered off over a hill and lay on a broad stone in the sun reading Martial. I have never been so happy. In the evening sat beside Hassoon at Jassem's campfire for a long while watching the balled flames of ruetha, listening to talk I could not understand, and looking at the moon through the fragrant dark-green smoke. Drank endless little cups of coffee, the black unsweetened coffee of the desert, three times distilled, flavored with an herb that makes it bitter as quinine, as pervading as one of Wagner's great pilings up of the orchestra, as restful to the aching wind-rasped body as morning sleep. These people from the Nejd, Jassem and Hassoon and Ali, and the two little black men with the camel colts are the finest people in the world. Later I lay awake looking out at the moonlight, listening to the crunch, crunch of the camels' cud and the soft bubbling of Fahad's waterpipe. If I had any sense I'd stay with Nuwwaf in El Garrá and never go any farther. Anyhow I don't care if it takes up a thousand years to get to Damascus.

Eighteenth Day: Nuwwaf and his friend went off today on their big white dromedaries. There had been discussion for several days as to whether the caravan should go through El Garrá or no. I suppose Nuwwaf wanted fat safety money in return for his protection. Anyway we are going northward still, probably to Aleppo instead of Damascus. They went off angry without eating bread. I might have gone with them. As I saw the two white specks growing smaller and smaller among the jagged folds of the hills I felt very bitter at my decision. It was during the noonday rest. I was eating rice out of the Sayyid's bowl with the Sayyid and Saleh, squatting in a patch of shiah. Our three hobbled camels stood above us, dripping green slavver from their mouths as they crunched and swallowed the succulent young growth of the shiah.

During the afternoon we veered more to the west into the teeth of a great wind cold as frozen razorblades. We are crossing a flat flint-strewn plain of a rusted purple color across which the camel tracks stretch straight and smooth like the path of a ship at sea. In the evening entertained myself with a touch of that damned Teheran fever. Ate quinine in great quantity for supper.

Nineteenth Day: Chilly dawn; hoarfrost on the bare flints, followed by a warm delicious day riding sleepily through gorges and dry watercourses and over rolling flinty hills. Tremendous numbers of rabbits wherever there's a patch of vegetation, and pernickety-looking grey-crested birds; I wonder if they are hoopoes. The Hadji bit the dust this afternoon. One of those mules of Abdullah's that are always causing trouble bit his camel's tail and the camel gave a great leap and twisted himself in thirteen directions and off went saddle and Hadji and umbrella and a vast diversity of little packages and cookpots. The old gentleman lay groaning and crying Al-ham'd'ullah until everybody picked him up and cursed Ab-dullah and his mules, and the bent umbrella was straightened. Then he perked up and was set upon his beast again without seeming very much the worse.

When we made camp one of the camels that had gone hope-lessly lame was killed. He seemed to know what was coming and stood tottering in the center of the camping ground, look-ing from side to side out of bulging eyes. Then one of the lit-tle black men from the Nejd, with his sleeves rolled up and his tunic girded high at the waist, jerked him off his feet and neatly cut his throat. Before the last twitches of life were out of the carcass it was skinned and, amid tremendous excitement and shouting, cut up. Fahad, all bloody up to the elbows, came back to our outfit staggering under the liver and several ribs. The liver was immediately grilled by being set among the em-bers, and the rest of the meat was stewed. I sat reading the elaborate idiocies of L'Amant Magnifique and made a noble supper at sundown off porridge and gobbets of camel meat fried with onions. Those onions are really the making of my larder. Went to sleep and dreamed of the sun-king and red heels tapping to the slow time of sarabands.

Twentieth Day: The sunrise was straight in our backs when we started out this morning, an unbelievable firework of grey and gamboge and salmon color; and so on sleepily swaying on Malek hour after hour, under a sky so intense that you seemed to see through the blue light of the world into the black of infinite space. Camped in the evening in a flat plain full of ruetha. Walked far out away from the caravan full of its noises of cookery and tent-pitching until a roll of the hills hid even the camels scattering to graze. There was no wind. The only sound was the occasional crunch or scuttle of a pebble under my feet. Suddenly I thought of the demons that Marco Polo tells about that dwell in deserts and whisper soft in trav-ellers' ears, coaxing them away from their tents and their caravans over another and another hill, until they lose the north and wander in the waste until they die. It was almost dark. Condor clouds hovered thicker and thicker above the bleeding west. A little wind came up and hissed, whispered soft among the flints. My name, almost, hissed soft among the flints. Hoisting the skirts of my aba about my waist, I ran and ran until against the last twilight I could see the tents and piles of bales and the ring of fires and the confused long-necked crowd of camels being nakhed for the night.

Some people compute eight, others fifteen days to Esch Scham.

Twenty-first Day: There are two little conical mountains to the west. One of them I think is called Jebal Souab. The group of grandees riding far ahead of the caravan came suddenly across the crest of a low hill into view of a great herd of gazelles. For several minutes they did not see us. Everyone had a rifle ready. Then like surf breaking on a ledge the nearest gazelles jumped straight in the air and were off. In the click of a trigger the whole herd was out of sight. Hard luck, because my larder is quite exhausted and I'm living on rice and fried dates I get from Jassem. My cigarettes are all gone too, and the news seems to have got about the caravan because these fine people never let me stir abroad without smoking. People I've never been particularly chummy with appear with the makings on every side so that I have to smoke more than I want to keep up with their generosity. As for Hassoon, he seems to want me to smoke them two at a time. Funny sensation being hungry all the time. Am attended for hours by visions splendid of roast goose and canvasback duck and hors-d'œuvre at the Bristol. When I wake up I find the air round my bed crowded with corn muffins and waffles. The descriptions of food in Mr. Martial's epigrams bring tears to my eyes.

Twenty-second Day: Splendid morning's ride through finest country ever, prairies of dry aromatic shrubs full of rabbits and strange white softly flying birds. Skirting the two little mountains, Souab and Damlough, under a sky piled high with rose and amber-glinting cumulus clouds, I was riding ahead with the grandees. Everyone seemed a little uneasy as one of the Agail had picked out a man on horseback watching the caravan from a shoulder of the mountain. Then all at once there was a cry of Haremi, bandits, and we all rode full tilt back to the caravan with clanky rattling of saddlebags and a waving of guns. Far away towards the mountain men on white ponies were loping down the hills like rabbits. Jassem rode up to his outfit and halted it in a little ravine. The camels groaning and roaring with their loads on them were nakhed and hobbled in a flash. The dancing girls tumbled squeaking out of their litter. The other sections of the caravan nakhed as they came up, until the camels were all sitting down squeezed together tight in an uneasy square. The pebbly bed of the ravine was full of shouts and squealing of women. The two horses were mounted, one by the Sayyid who annoyed everybody very much by stopping to put on his best aba for the occasion, the other by Abdullah; and the Agail and all the other combatant members of the caravan took up positions on the little hillocks round about. The Damascus merchant and his son took firm hold of me by either arm and sat me down between them in the deepest part of the gully, whether for their protection or mine I never made out. The little Turk's fat wife lay in a heap like soiled clothes at her husband's feet and now and then let out a long curdled shriek. Fahad pottered about scowling, tightening hobbles on camels, picking up things that had fallen out of saddlebags, muttering complaints as if this were all just another whim of Jassem's. Everybody sat hunched with expectation for a long while and I began to think again of the unfortunate death of the Prince Napoleon, but nothing happened. So I managed to get loose from my Damascus friends and climbed up on to the hillock above the ravine. There I found the Sayyid riding round and round like mad with his long sleeves floating behind him in the wind and his silver-encrusted gun flashing in the sun.—Baruda Ketir Ketir. Guns many many, bandits many many, Bedawi on horseback many many, he shouted when he saw me. I replied that in Frankistan I had seen guns so big that the whole caravan could ride through one. That seemed to settle him for a while. The Agail were coming back from scouting about the hills. It was a fine sight to see them gird up their loins and tie up the long sleeves behind each other's backs. Jassem was quiet and smiling as ever. With one hand he held his gun, with the other he stroke his beard. The purple and the white headcloths fluttered behind him as he walked. There was a big body of men on horseback advancing towards us; nobody knew who they were. The Agail with extra cartridge belts scattered towards the hills again, and I joined the circle of the less timorous noncombatants who sat smoking on a little mound, presided over by the Hadji, who nursed in his lap his cherished umbrella and invoked Allah at every batting of an eyelash. We must have sat that way for an hour when suddenly a rifleshot and then another rattled in the hollows of the hills. Two men on white ponies appeared on the slope in front of us, riding licketysplit and occasionally shooting. A few bullets whirred over our heads. The group of the less timorous broke up in confusion. I have a distinct impression that the Hadji raised his umbrella. Somehow I found myself engaged in a long conversation with a Turkish camel driver. What language we talked I have no idea, as he knew no more Arabic than I did, but we managed to convey the most complicated ideas to one another while the Agail fell back towards the camels and more and more men on white ponies appeared on the hills from every direction, riding round and round us, shooting as they rode like the Indians in Custer's Last Stand that used to be the last number in Buffalo Bill's great show.

This Turk did not like the Arabs a bit, said they were a low and shifty lot. Neither did he like History nor the Germans nor Baghdad nor the British. He had been in the Turkish army during the war, had deserted, had three times been stripped naked and left for dead by the Bedawi. He had wandered to all sorts of inconceivable places, always trying to get home to some village near Brusa. Everywhere everybody had too many guns and there was no law.

All this went on for a long time, and nobody seemed much the worse for it, until at last Jassem stood on the mound and waved a long white sleeve in the direction of the attackers and everybody began to say that they were friends after all.

The raiders rode into camp on their lolloping ponies, gaunt men tanned black by the wind, riding in pairs, singing as they came. Their clothes were ragged and dirty, looped up with cartridge belts. Ibn Haremis is their name or the name of their sheikh and they belong to the Fede'an.

I sit shivering among my baggage in a cold wind that has just come up to spite us. Opposite me the Damascus merchants are dejectedly raising their tent. Tall desert people stalk haughtily through the camp. They have just made off with a rug belonging to the Damascus people who are setting up a great outcry. Fahad is cooking me supper, cursing under his breath. Jassem and Hassoon sit impassively by their fire grinding coffee. Their eyes shining under their headcloths follow every movement of their friends of ibn Haremis the way the eyes of a cornered cat will watch a dog.

Twenty-third Day: This is goddam tiresome. Here we are sitting on our tails again, discussing safety money. This ibn Haremis gang is a rare one. They've all been sitting in my tent looking at me and my blankets and the hippo, and numerous other things that people have brought to my tent for safe-keeping. Such a set of walleyed, crooknosed, squinting, oneeyed, scarfaced cutthroats and slitpurses I have never seen. They go through all my possessions with gimlet eyes, and their hands feeling my blankets seem glued with greed to every fiber. I made a fatal error; they invited me to go see their sheikh and for some reason I was sore at them and refused. I don't know why, because I imagine they'd be very good fellows if you got to know them. May have unpleasant consequences, though. So I sulk in my tent with all the blankets wrapped about me and curse the wind and this blithering plateau and think of hot baths and steaks smothered in onions. Still it was worth it to hear their carolling song as they rode in pairs on white lolloping ponies into the conquered camp.

Twenty-fourth Day: Five camels and five pounds Turkish as ransom for the hippo was the khowa decided on, and now ibn Haremis is our friend and brother. Incidentally last night several old women appeared and sat round the fire and raised their voices in the discussion equally with the men. This morning the merry men saw us on our way. Great relief was manifested on all sides when our friends and brethren ceased to protect us and returned to their tents. During the day we kept crossing rocky wind-tortured ridges between flat patches of sandy desert. At sunset I thought I saw the mountains of Syria lying purple athwart the sun, but at dawn there was no sign of them.

Twenty-fifth Day: We were navigating splendidly this morning in the face of the perpetual westerly wind when some of Abdullah's ridiculous mules had to get lost in a tangle of dry watercourses. So we sat down beside a waterhole in a delicious sheltered valley, the Sheib War, with only half a day accomplished. Had the first wash in a week in a smooth sun-filled cave in the cliff where I lay a long time on the warm rock while my clothes were airing, reading Juvenal, to whom I don't kindle, notwithstanding his gorgeous turgid flow of indignant imagery. I smell rhetoric in him. Hope I left a few fleas behind in that rocky cave. It's terribly annoying to be cold and fleabitten at the same time. The mules are caught again and come with a great scampering and clattering up the canyon. Bukra insh'allah, we'll see the mountains of Syria and the Jebal Druse.

Twenty-sixth Day: Feel rather like the anonymous Wise Man who got there too late to offer myrrh or frankincense. Goddam cold and I don't care who knows it. Doubt if I was ever colder in my life. All day rode in a bitter wind under a bright sky over terrific uplands of sharp glinting flints. About the first real continuous desert; no trace of vegetation. All our fires are of dry camel dung, jelle, collected from an old camping place we passed. Here we are camped under a cairn at the head of Wadi Mia which is diversely said to be four and eight days from Damascus. Shiver and pray for supper. Fleas.

Twenty-seventh Day: Have a sort of suspicion that this is Christmas Day, but as I'm not quite sure what the date was when I left Baghdad, I may have calculated wrong. Ate kastowi for lunch, rice with my last onions for supper. Cold as blazes. Long desolate ride over purple hills strewn with sharp flints into a wind colder and sharper than all the flints from here to Jericho. This must be the highest part of the hogback, as there comes in the rain an occasional spit of sleet. Put my foot in it terribly this evening. Was taking my habitual before-supper stroll to the highest hill round about the camp, and had paused on the crest to look down through grey smudges of mist into the vast putty-colored wilderness ahead of us. In front of me, standing out against the last silvery light like monsters of an eocene world, two camels were making love, twining their snaky necks together with flopping slobbering lips and groanings through yellow teeth. Clumsily, sensitively under the aluminum twilight the act was accomplished. I had climbed on a rock to see further, when I saw Jassem running up the slope with his fieldglasses in his hand, hallooing desperately. I went down to him and found him wild. All day the caravan had been manoeuvring to keep out of sight of some black tents pitched in the next valley and there I was standing like a monument on top of the hill, visible for a day's journey in every direction. He vented his wrath, and I my shame, by throwing stones at the camels and driving them back to camp.

Twenty-eighth Day: Bitter rain in misty squalls. A North Sea day with nary a glimpse of sun. Rode from before dawn till after dark through howling flinty wilderness. The Agail laugh at me at night sitting round the fire because the stinging smoke of jelle makes my eyes water. Hassoon can hold his face almost to the flame in the thickest of the smoke without a flicker of his eyelids. Held high discourse about America. It seems that some of the Agail have been there and come back with the word that it was a land full of floos. The coffee we were drinking came from Santos, so everybody thought I lived where the coffee came from. Everyone wondered at the great iron ships going over the sea; and sitting there in the desert round the glowing fire of cameldung under a night of unfathomable misty blackness, we felt the suction of the great machine, the glint of whirring nickel, the shine of celluloid and enamel, the crackle of banknotes fingered in banks, the click and grinding of oiled wheels. I made a great speech and said that if I had any sense I would live in the desert with the Agail and never go back; but they took it as a compliment and did not understand. Jassem asked me, then, what kind of a hakim I was in my country, a great man like Cokus? No not quite.

The Hadji has no luck. He slept in my tent last night as it was very wet outside, and naturally the tent had to blow down and half the camels to stampede, so that the poor old gentleman was forgotten and trampled on and finally picked prone and groaning from under the collapsed bed. And the umbrella underwent further injuries.

My shoes are split and I have chilblains.

Twenty-ninth Day: Stuck again. Fifteen camels lame from the heavy going of the last few days. Shivered in wet tents all day. Sat all afternoon in the tent of the Sayyid, while his cook Hadji Mahomet told stories. I could not follow them at all, but they began with such pomaded suaveness of Once upon a time there lived . . . and worked up to such pitch of excitement where everybody cried Ei Wallah and Allah and wallowed in such smutty chortlings when all hands wriggled in their places and curled up their brown toes with delight that it was almost as if I had understood the words. Then the Damascus merchant's little boy sang and everybody ate dates and drank tea. Between the verses of love-songs everyone cries Allah and groans in a most melancholy manner.

Thirtieth Day: Began in mist and despair. Then phantom hills to the west seemed to promise Syria and its fleshpots, and the sun came out and the immense disk of purple flint shone like a shattered mirror.

Thirty-first Day: Splendid frosty morning. Interminably westward across this petrified sea of flints. Continually hungry. Hours before noon I start thinking of the taste of kastowi, a delicious molasses-brown concoction of ewe's butter and dates fried up together, and in the evening I massacre the rice and bread almost without tasting it. Last night I dreamed of dining at the Bristol in Marseilles, of eating the crackly brown skin of roast goose. It makes me feel terribly soft. No one else seems to mind half rations. The Arabs are the most frugal people I ever consorted with.

Thirty-second Day: Half day on. Camels low, as there has been no food for several days. Let 'em take a thousand years to get to Damascus. I don't care. I'll never sit about such fragrant fires again, or with such fine people. Christ, I feel well, bearded, fullblooded, all the bile out of my belly, all the wrinkles ironed out of my mind by the great cold purple flinty flatiron of the desert.

The Sayyid and Damascus Saleh have had a row, I don't know what about.

Thirty-third Day: A new wind has come up, Hawa Esch Scham, the wind of Damascus, they call it. Everything is pink and warm colored like the ears of a jackrabbit seen for a second against the sun. We have made a splendid camp on a shiah-covered slope. At the end of a trough to the northwest are tall promontory hills jutting into the desert, the actual hills of Syria. Beyond them is Tidmor that I am not fated to see—Alas, Zenobia. Shoes split, feet chilblained, hands stiff with cold, but jolly as a lark. Wish I had a rum punch, hot, with a slice of lemon and two cloves.

Thirty-fourth Day: Through rocky defiles and over patches of sandy desert with the hills of Syria gathering like a herd of cattle to the west. This afternoon we were almost held up again. Two of the Agail sighted guns and headcloths at the opening of a deep ravine the trail leads through, so in a jiffy the caravan did a right-about-face, and went off to the south, while the grandees on their dromedaries rode on towards the ambuscade with their guns cocked. These people wore various-colored headcloths and were from the Jebal Druse. I don't think they were actually Druses, but rabble from the outskirts, half Bedawi and half Druse. They asked to see the mad Frank who was wandering about the desert, and upon my being produced looked at me critically but amiably. A lot of big talk followed. They were finally bought off with fifteen pounds Turkish and a sack of dates. I don't think they could have done us much mischief anyway as few of them were mounted.

Thirty-fifth Day: We are riding between two ranges of barren mountains, pink and ochre and purple and indigo in the shadows, reflected in long streaks of stagnant water that leaves where it dries the sand cracked and mottled like alligator hide. Now that we are out of danger from the Bedawi everybody is worried about the French camel corps, as there is a duty on tobacco and camels and the game is to smuggle through. How a caravan of five hundred camels can slip into Damascus unnoticed is beyond me, but one should never deny wonders. Everybody is restless and excited like the last day out on an ocean liner.

Thirty-sixth Day: All things have come to pass. We are camped over against Dmair, huddled in a little hollow of the hills. We are in Syria. Blue smoke goes up from the village and is lost in the blue of the ridges in front of Lebanon. Further south the Jebal Sheikh sits hunched and hoary. There are goats and flocks of sheep grazing round about the camp. I'd like to go to Dmair, but Jassem won't let me for fear of waking the drowsy customs officers. Various inhabitants of Dmair are coming out to us on camels and donkeys, however. I almost wish we were still out in the desert, leaving instead of arriving, but oh, for a hot bath and food, food, food.

Thirty-seventh Day: O those Sayyids. The unforgettable entry into Damascus.

Last night the caravan camp was full of goings and comings, deep talk round Jassem's fire, and groaning and bubbling of camels. The last thing I heard as I went to sleep was the clink of money, gold pounds Turkish being counted from palm into palm. In the morning when I woke up the camp looked as if a cyclone had struck it. Half the camels, most of the bales of tobacco and rugs and, I imagine, opium had vanished in blue haze. Jassem sat quietly grinding his coffee, occasionally stroking his black beard. As I was drinking coffee with him he gently insinuated the thought that when I talked with the French in Damascus I should not know how many camels nor how we had come. I told him I had a bad head for figures.

Then Abdullah's white stallion was brought up and I perched my galled posterior on an execrable saddle and we were off towards Damascus, I on my stallion, the Sayyid on his dromedary, the Sayyid's cook on a skittish white camel, and one of the Agail on foot to put us on the road. That morning seemed endless. We kept losing the road, first over shaggy uplands and then in a fat valley full of pasture lands, patches of green sesame and alfalfa, apple orchards, pink adobe houses. Eventually the Sayyid took pity on my agonized bouncing on the stirrupless stallion and let me ride his dromedary. The white camel did not like the smell of civilization and kept trying to bolt back to the desert. At last, deliriously hungry, galled, limping, tired to a frazzle, we got to a village where we left our beasts in the inn, ate all too frugally of beans and cheese and kebab, and then drove, lolling like Zeus in his chariot of eagles, in a landau into Damascus. Then before I could put food to my mouth or water to my skin I had to go to see all the Sayyid's relatives, old men with beards in the Scribes' bazaar, people in mysterious courtyards who were adherents of Feisul's and plotting against the French, a tailor in a tailor shop, the keeper of a café frequented by the Agail; with all these, interminable scraping and mamnouning, until at last we found ourselves in contact with the forces of civilization. We had left the cab outside a café where we were palavering busily, I too dazed with hunger and unwashedness to know what was going on; on coming out we found a drunken French officer sitting in it. The Sayyid protested that it was our cab and the Frenchman started spouting abuse, and the Sayyid drew his little dagger and there would have been the devil to pay if the Frenchman had not hazily realized that I was talking French to him. He immediately apologized profusely and embraced the Sayyid in the name of the Allies and we all rode off together singing "la Madelon de la Victoire" to a most Parisian ginmill in the main square. The Sayyid sat outside while we Occidentals went in and drank I don't know how many glasses of absinthe in the name of Liberty, Fraternity and Equality. In a pink indeterminate and vaguely swishing cloud I drove to the hotel, somehow got rid of the Frenchman and the Sayyid, and at last was alone sprawling buoyant in a warm bath that tasted of absinthe, smelled of absinthe, swished and simmered drowsily, tingled pinkly with absinthe.

XI. Table d'Hôte

1. The wind blows up the tent like a balloon.
   The tent plunges tugging at pegged ropes,
   about to wrench loose and soar
   above wormwood-carpeted canyons
   and flinty sawtooth hills,
   up into the driven night
   and the howling clouds.
   Tight
   as a worm curls wickedly
   round the stamen of a fuchsia,
   a man curls his hands round a candle.
   The flame totters in the wind,
   flares to lick his hands,
   to crimson the swaying walls.
   The hands cast shadows on the crimson walls.

   The candlelight shrinks and flaps wide.
   The shadows are full of old tenters—
   men curious as to the fashion of cities,
   men eager to taste newtasting bread,
   men wise to the north star and to the moon's phases,
   to whom East and West
   are cloaks pulled easily tight,
   worn jaunty about the shoulders:
   Herodotus, Thales, Democritus,
   Heraclitus who watched rivers,
   parian-browed tancheek travellers,
   who sat late in wineshops to listen,
   rose early to sniff the wind off harbors
   and see the dawn kindle the desert places,
   and went peering and tasting
   through seas and wastes and cities,
   held up to the level of their grey cool eyes
   firm in untrembling fingers
   the slippery souls of men and of gods.

The candle has guttered out in darkness and wind.
The tent holds firm against the buffeting wind,
pegged tight, weighted with stones.
My sleep is blown up with dreams
about to wrench loose and soar
above wormwood-carpeted canyons
and flinty sawtooth hills,
up into the driven night
and the howling clouds.

Perhaps when the light clangs
brass and scarlet cymbals in the east
with drone and jangle of great bells,
loping white across the flint-strewn hills,
will come the seeking tentless caravans
that Bilkis leads untired,
nodding in her robes
on a roaring dromedary.

2. Képis, two caps, a felt hat and a derby, headless on the rack; a muffler dangles, an umbrella. My hat among them. The doors swing. . . .

Table, two rows of green white jowls (*comme on s'ennuie*) munching razorscraped jaws face the catsup bottles, picklepots; collars constrict the veins on flabby necks; knives and forks tinkle with little zigzag acetylene glints (*dans ce sale pays*). Eyes in sideglances (*comme on s'ennuie*) purse minds in tight (*dans ce sale pays*) like clasps on the mouths of pocketbooks.

My shoes creak as fed I make discreetly for the swinging door.

And yesterday
I rode a grey stallion
into the first olive garden
and day before yesterday
squatted in the full wind
I ate dates fried in ghee
at the right hand of Jassem er Rawwaf
in the red cave of firelight,

and watched Hassoon staunch the blood
from his cut foot in hot embers
and leaned my head back on the bale
of stringy yellow Persian tobacco
eyes gashed by the sharpscented smoke
legs pricked by the sharp desert flints,
and listened to Saleh
teach his frail thirsty song
of parched Hosein and Kerbela
to slenderwaisted Ali
whose walk when calling and calling
he led back to camp the fortytwo camels
was a procession of kings returning darkly
carved on a mountain
in triumph,
and wondered
watching the barbed flames of wormwood
why Nuwwaf rode off that day
on his great whitebearded dromedary
without eating bread
curlybearded Nuwwaf,
wind lover, cunning in the four directions,
who when he laughed brandished steel
out of kohlblackened eyes.

Esch Scham

Chleuh

Teheran: The Bath of the Lion

Mogador

Traintime: Beni Ounif

Teahouse: Teheran

Trebizond

The Golden Horn

Baghdad: The Bazaars That Burned

XII. Homer of the Trans-Siberian

AT the Paris exposition of 1900—but perhaps this is all a dream, perhaps I heard someone tell about it; no, it must have happened—somewhere between the Eiffel Tower and the Trocadero there was a long shed. In that shed was a brand-new train of the Trans-Siberian, engine, tender, baggage coach, sleeping-cars, restaurant-car. The shed was dark like a station. You walked up wooden steps into the huge dark varnished car. It was terrible. The train was going to start. As you followed the swish of dresses along the corridor the new smell gave you gooseflesh. The train smelled of fresh rubber, of just-bought toys, of something varnished and whirring and oily. The little beds were made up, there were mirrors, glittering washbasins, a bathtub. The engine whistled. No, don't be afraid; look out of the window. We were moving. No, outside a picture was moving, houses slipping by, bluish-greenish hills. The Urals. Somebody says names in my ear. Lake Baikal. Irkutsk. Siberia. Yangtse, Mongolia, pagodas, Pekin. Rivers twisting into the bluish-greenish hills and the close electric smell of something varnished and whirring and oily moving hugely, people in boats, junks, Yellow Sea, pagodas, Pekin.

And the elevator boy said the trains in the Metro never stopped; you jumped on and off while they were going, and they showed magic lantern slides and cinematograph pictures in the Grande Roue and at the top of the Eiffel Tower . . . but that must have been years later because I was afraid to go up.

I've often wondered about the others who had tickets taken for them on that immovable train of the Trans-Siberian in the first year of the century, whose childhood was full of *Twenty Thousand Leagues* and Jules Verne's *sportsmen* and *globe-trottairs* (if only the ice holds on Lake Baikal) and Chinese Gordon stuttering his last words over the telegraph at Khartoum, and Carlotta come back mad from Mexico setting fire to a palace at Terveuren full of Congolese curiosities, fetishes of human hair, ithyphallic idols with shells for teeth and arms akimbo, specimens of crude rubber in jars; and those magnates in panama hats shunted slowly in private cars, reeking with mint and old Bourbon down new lines across the Rio Grande, shooting jackasses, prairie dogs and an occasional greaser from the rear platform, and the Twentieth Century and Harvey lunchrooms and Buffalo Bill and the Indians holding up the stage and ocean greyhounds racing to Bishop's Rock and pictures of the world's leading locomotives on cigarette cards. O Thos. Cook and Son, here's grist for your mill. Uniformed employees meet all the leading trains. Now that Peary and Amundsen have sealed the world at the top and the bottom and there's an American bar in Baghdad and the Grand Lama of Thibet listens in on Paul Whiteman ragging the Blue Danube and the caterpillar Citroëns chug up and down the dusty streets of Timbuctoo, there's no place for the Rover Boys but the Statler hotels and the Dollar Line (sleep every night in your own brass bed) round the world cruises.

That stationary Trans-Siberian where the panorama unrolled Asia every hour was the last vestige of the Homeric age of railroading. Now's the time for the hymns and the catalogues of the ships. The railsplitting and the hacking and hewing, the great odysseys are over. The legendary names that stirred our childhood with their shadow and rumble are only stations in small print on a timetable. And still. . . . Or is it just the myth humming in our drowsy backward-turned brains?

Does anything ever come of this constant dragging of a ruptured suitcase from dock to railway station and railway station to dock? All the sages say it's nonsense. In the countries of Islam they know you're mad.

In the countries of Islam they know you're mad, but they have a wistful respect for madness. Only today I was fed lunch, beef stewed in olives and sour oranges, couscous and cakes, seven glasses of tea and a pipe of kif, by the extremely ugly man with a cast in his eye and a face like a snapping turtle who hangs round the souks buying up fox skins, in the company of his friend the tailor, a merry and philosophic individual like a tailor in the *Arabian Nights*, all because I'd been to Baghdad, the burial place of our lord Sidi Abd el Kadr el Djilani (here you kiss your hand and murmur something about peace and God's blessing) and they feel that even a kaffir passing by the tomb may have brought away a faint whiff of the marabout's holiness. So a pilgrim has a certain importance in their eyes.

They may be right, but most likely this craze for transportation, steamboats, trains, motorbuses, mules, camels, is only a vicious and intricate form of kif, a bad habit contracted in infancy, fit only to delight a psychoanalyst cataloguing manias. Like all drugs, you have to constantly increase the dose. One soothing thought; while our bodies are tortured in what Blaise Cendrars calls the squirrelcage of the meridians, maybe our souls sit quiet in that immovable train, in the darkvarnished newsmelling Trans-Siberian watching the panorama of rivers and seas and mountains endlessly unroll.

Now's the time for the Homeric hymns of the railroads. Blaise Cendrars has written some of them already in salty French sonorous and direct as the rattle of the great express trains. Carl Sandburg has written one or two. I'm going to try to string along some inadequately translated fragments of *Prose du Transsiberien et de la Petite Jeanne de France.* It fits somehow in this hotel room with its varnished pine furniture and its blue slopjar and its faded dusteaten windowcurtains. Under the balcony are some trees I don't know the name of, the empty tracks of the narrow gauge, a road churned by motortrucks. It's raining. A toad is shrilling in the bushes. As the old earthshaking engines are scrapped one by one, the mythmakers are at work. Eventually they will be all ranged like Homer's rambling gods in the rosy light of an orderly Olympus. Here's the hymn of the Trans-Siberian:

In those days I was still a youngster
Only sixteen and already I couldn't remember my childhood
I was sixteen thousand leagues away from my birthplace
I was in Moscow, in the city of a thousand and three belfries
    and seven railroadstations
And the seven railroadstations and the thousand and three belfries
    were not enough for me
For my youth was then so flaming and so mad
That my heart sometimes burned like the temple of Ephesus,
    and sometimes like the Red Square at Moscow
At sunset.
And my eyes lit up the ancient ways.

And I was already such a bad poet
That I never knew how to get to the last word.
    .   .   .   .

I spent my childhood in the hanging gardens of Babylon
Played hookey in railwaystations in front of the trains that were going
     to leave
Now, all the trains have had to speed to keep up with me
Bale-Timbuctoo
I've played the races too at Auteuil and Longchamp
Paris-New York
Now, I've made all the trains run the whole length of my life
Madrid-Stockholm
And I've lost all my bets
And there's only Patagonia, Patagonia left for my enormous gloom,
     Patagonia and a trip in the South Seas.

I'm travelling
I've always been travelling
I'm travelling with little Jeanne of France
The train makes a perilous leap and lands on all its wheels
The train lands on its wheels
The train always lands on all its wheels.

"Say Blaise are we very far from Montmartre?"

We are far, Jeanne, seven days on the rails
We are far from Montmartre, from the Butte that raised you, from
     the Sacred Heart you huddled against
Paris has vanished and its enormous flare in the sky
There's nothing left but continual cinders
Falling rain
Swelling clouds
And Siberia spinning
The rise of heavy banks of snow
The crazy sleighbells shivering like a last lust in the blue air
The train throbbing to the heart of lead horizons
And your giggling grief . . .

"Say Blaise are we very far from Montmartre?"

The worries
Forget the worries
All the cracked stations katicornered to the right of way
The telegraph wires they hang by

The grimace of the poles that wave their arms and strangle them
The earth stretches elongated and snaps back like an accordion
    tortured by a sadic hand
In the rips in the sky insane locomotives
Take flight
In the gaps
Whirling wheels mouths voices
And the dogs of disaster howling at our heels . . .

And so he goes on piling up memories of torn hurtling metal, of trains of sixty locomotives at full steam disappearing in the direction of Port Arthur, of hospitals and whores and jewelry merchants, memories of the first great exploit of the Twentieth Century seen through sooty panes, beaten into his brain by the uneven rumble of the broad-gauge Trans-Siberian. Crows in the sky, bodies of men in heaps along the tracks, burning hospitals, an embroidery unforeseen in that stately panorama unfolding rivers and lakes and mountains in the greenish dusk of the shed at the Exposition Universelle.

Then there's *Le Panama ou Les Aventures de mes Septs Oncles*, seven runaway uncles, dedicated to the last Frenchman in Panama, the barkeep at Matachine, the deathplace of Chinamen, where the liveoaks have grown up among the abandoned locomotives, where every vestige of the de Lesseps attempt is rotten and rusted and overgrown with lianas except a huge anchor in the middle of the forest stamped with the arms of Louis XV.

It's about this time too that I read the history of the earthquake at
    Lisbon
But I think
The Panama panic is of a more universal importance
Because it turned my childhood topsyturvy.
I had a fine picturebook
And I was seeing for the first time
The whale
The big cloud
The walrus
The Sun
The great walrus
The bear the lion the chimpanzee the rattlesnake and the fly
The fly

The terrible fly
"Mother, the flies, the flies and the trunks of trees!"
"Go to sleep, child, go to sleep."
Ahasuerus is an idiot

      .   .   .   .

It's the Panama panic that made me a poet!
Amazing
All those of my generation are like that
Youngsters
Victims of strange ricochets
We don't play any more with the furniture
We don't play any more with antiques
We're always and everywhere breaking crockery
We ship
Go whaling
Kill walrus
We're always afraid of the tsetse fly
Because we're not very fond of sleep. . . .

Fantastic uncles they are; one of them was a butcher in Galveston, lost in the cyclone of '95; another washed gold in the Klondike; another one turned Buddhist and was arrested trying to blow up the Britishers in Bombay; the fourth was the valet of a general in the Boer War; the fifth was a cordon bleu in palace hotels; number six disappeared in Patagonia with a lot of electromagnetic instruments of precision; no one ever knew what happened to the seventh uncle.

It was uncle number two who wrote verse modelled on de Musset and read in San Francisco the history of General Sutter, the man who conquered California for the United States and was ruined by the discovery of gold on his plantation. This uncle married the woman who made the best bread in a thousand square kilometers and was found one day with a rifle bullet through his head. Aunty disappeared. Aunty married again. Aunty is now the wife of a rich jam-manufacturer.

And Blaise Cendrars has since written the history of General Johann August Sutter, *L'Or*, a narrative that traces the swiftest leanest parabola of anything I've ever read, a narrative that cuts like a knife through the washy rubbish of most French writing of the present time, with its lemon-colored gloves and its rose-water and its holy water and its *policier-gentleman* cosmopolitan affectation. It's probably because he really is, what the Quai d'Orsay school pretend to be, an international vagabond, that Cendrars has managed to capture the grandiose rhythms of America of seventy-five years ago, the myths of which our generation is just beginning to create. (As if anyone ever *really was* anything; he's a good writer, leave it at that.) In *L'Or* he's packed the tragic and turbulent absurdity of '49 into a sky rocket. It's over so soon you have to read it again for fear you have missed something.

But the seven uncles. Here's some more of the hymn to transportation that runs through all his work, crystallizing the torture and delight of a train-mad, steamship-mad, plane-mad generation.

I'm thirsty
Damn it
Goddam it to hell
I want to read the *Feuille d'Avis of Neufchâtel* or the *Pamplona Courrier,*
In the middle of the Atlantic you're no more at home than in an editorial office
I go round and round inside the meridians like a squirrel in a squirrel cage
Wait there's a Russian looks like he might be worth talking to
Where to go
He doesn't know either where to deposit his baggage
At Leopoldville or at the Sedjerah near Nazareth, with Mr. Junod or at the house of my old friend Perl
In the Congo in Bessarabia on Samoa
I know all the timetables
All the trains and their connections
The time they arrive the time they leave
All the liners all the fares all the taxes
It's all the same to me
Live by grafting
I'm on my way back from America on board the *Volturno*, for thirtyfive francs from New York to Rotterdam

Blaise Cendrars seems to have rather specialised in America, in the U.S. preferring the happier Southern and Western sections to the Bible-worn hills of New England. Here's a poem about the Mississippi, for which Old Kentucky must have supplied the profusion of alligators, that still is an honorable addition to that superb set of old prints of sternwheel steamboats racing with a nigger on the safety valve.

At this place the stream is a wide lake
Rolling yellow muddy waters between marshy banks
Waterplants merging into acres of cotton
Here and there appear towns and villages carpeting the bottom of
    some little bay with their factories with their tall black chimneys
    with their long wharves jutting out their long wharves on piles
    jutting out very far into the water

Staggering heat
The bell on board rings for lunch
The passengers are rigged up in checked suits howling cravats vests
    loud as the incendiary cocktails and the corrosive sauces
We begin to see alligators
Young ones alert and frisky
Big fellows drifting with greenish moss on their backs
Luxuriant vegetation announces the approach of the tropical zone
Bamboos giant palms tuliptrees laurel cedars
The river itself has doubled in width
It is sown with floating islands from which at the approach of the
    boat waterbirds start up in flocks;
Steamers sailboats barges all kinds of craft and immense rafts of logs
A yellow vapor rises from the toowarm water of the river
It's by hundreds now that the 'gators play round us
You can hear the dry snap of their jaws and can make out very well
    their small fierce eyes
The passengers pass the time shooting at them with rifles
When a particularly good shot manages to kill or mortally wound
    one of the beasts
Its fellows rush at it and tear it to pieces
Ferociously
With little cries rather like the wail of a newborn baby.

In *Kodak* there are poems about New York, Alaska, Florida, hunting wild turkey and duck in a country of birchtrees off in the direction of Winnipeg, a foggy night in Vancouver, a junk in a Pacific harbor unloading porcelain and swallowsnests, bambootips and ginger, the stars melting like sugar in the sky of some island passed to windward by Captain Cook, elephant-

hunting in a jungle roaring with torrents of rain; and at the
end a list of menus featuring iguana and green turtle, Red
River salmon and shark's fins, sucklingpig with fried bananas,
crayfish in pimento, breadfruit, fried oysters and guavas, dated
en voyage 1887–1923. 1887 must be the date of his birth.

Dix Neuf Poèmes Elastiques, Paris. After all, Paris, whether
we like it or not, has been so far a center of unrest, of the
building up and the tearing down of this century. From Paris
has spread in every direction a certain esperanto of the arts
that has "modern" for its trademark. Blaise Cendrars is an itinerant Parisian well versed in this as in many other dialects. He
is a kind of medicineman trying to evoke the things that are
our cruel and avenging gods. Turbines, triple-expansion engines, dynamite, high tension coils. Navigation, speed, flight,
annihilation. No medicine has been found strong enough to
cope with them; in cubist Paris they have invented some
fetishes and gris-gris that many are finding useful. Here's the
confession of an enfant du siècle, itinerant Parisian.

So it is that every evening I cross Paris on foot
From the Batignolles to the Latin Quarter as I would cross the Andes
Under the flare of new stars larger and more frightening
The Southern Cross more prodigious every step one makes towards
    it emerging from the old world.

I am the man who has no past.—Only the stump of my arm hurts,—
I've rented a hotel room to be all alone with myself.
I have a brand new wicker basket that's filling up with manuscript.
I have neither books nor pictures, not a scrap of æsthetic bricabrac
There's an old newspaper on the table.
I work in a bare room behind a dusty mirror,
My feet bare on the red tiling, playing with some balloons and a little
    toy trumpet;
I'm working on THE END OF THE WORLD.

I started these notes on the little sunny balcony at Marrakesh
with in front of me the tall cocoa-colored tower of the Koutoubia,
banded with peacock color, surmounted by three gilded balls,
each smaller than the other; and beyond, the snowy ranges of the
high Atlas; I'm finishing it in Mogador in a shutin street of

houses white as clabber where footsteps resound loud above the continual distant pound of the surf. It's the time of afternoon prayer and the voice of the muezzin flashes like brass from the sky announcing that there is no god but God and that Mahomet is the prophet of God; and I'm leaving at six in the morning and there's nothing ahead but wheels and nothing behind but wheels. O Thos. Cook and Son, who facilitate travel with long ribbons of tickets held between covers by an elastic, what spells did you cast over the children of this century? The mischief in those names: Baghdad Bahn, Cape to Cairo, Trans-Siberian, Compagnie des Wagons Lits et des Grands Expresses Européens, Grand Trunk, Christ of the Andes; Panama Canal, mechanical toy that Messrs. Roosevelt and Goethals managed to make work when everyone else had failed, a lot of trouble for the inhabitants of the two Americas you have damned up within your giant locks. The flags, the dollars and Cook's tours marching round the world till they meet themselves coming back. Here in Morocco you can see them hour by hour mining the minaret where the muezzin chants five times a day his superb defiance of the multiple universe.

If there weren't so many gods, tin gods, steel gods, gods of uranium and manganese, living gods—here's Mrs. Besant rigging a new Jesus in Bombay, carefully educated at Oxford for the rôle—red gods of famine and revolution, old gods laid up in libraries, plaster divinities colored to imitate coral at Miami, spouting oilgods at Tulsa, Okla., we too might be able to sit on our prayercarpets in the white unchangeable sunshine of Islam which means resignation. The sun of our generation has broken out in pimples, its shattered light flickers in streaks of uneasy color. Take the train, they're selling happiness in acre lots in Florida. So we must run across the continents always deafened by the grind of wheels, by the roar of airplane motors, wallow in all the seas with the smell of hot oil in our nostrils and the throb of the engines in our blood. Out of the Babel of city piled on city, continent on continent, the world squeezed small and pulled out long, bouncing like a new rubber ball, we get what? Certainly not peace. That is why in this age of giant machines and scuttle-headed men it is a good thing to have a little music. We need sons of Homer going about the world beating into some sort of human rhythm the shrieking hullabaloo, making us less afraid.

XIII. Kif

GARE ST. LAZARE. A man is sitting by the window of a restaurant eating alphabet soup. Outside through the twilight sifting pink sand over the grey-pilastered station, green omnibuses blunder, taxis hysterically honk, girls and young men with white twilight faces come up out of the Metro; there is a red-faced woman selling roses, a man with a square black beard unfolds *Paris-Soir*. From seaweed-garnished counters spread with seafood: oysters, scallops, seaurchins, mussels, clams, lobsters, snails, shrimps, prawns comes a surging tidal smell of the horizon. The man by the window of the restaurant eating alphabet soup against his will stirs the letters slowly with his spoon. Seven letters have come to the surface—GO SOUTH. Resolutely he eats them. Stirs with his spoon again; two letters left—G O.

What was the story of the Irishman with the false teeth who was a spy for the British Intelligence who was eating alphabet soup in the little restaurant at the back of the mosque of Nouri Osmanieh in Stamboul? He was shot by a woman supposed to be a Russian and they said he had read his doom in the alphabet soup. Why are there always so many X's in alphabet soup?

Among the crowds going in and out of the station stalk long resounding words of twilight. The city of gleaming asphalt is flat and tiny, desert under the last scaring expansion of the summer day.

The other station is full of light, a refuge from the empty dusk. The train is packed with people and valises. In the nick of time I slip into the eighth seat in a third-class compartment. There is not room in the compartment for sixteen legs of assorted sexes, for sixteen perspiring arms. In the aisle you can stand up and smoke and see the suburbs of Paris, devastated and smouldering with dusk, at last decently buried by the advancing night. The train rakes up a picturebook landscape with inquisitive fingers of light as it rattles along wailing like a banshee. The trucks rumbling over the rails sing a jiggly song: Mort aux vaches aux vaches aux vaches. Mort aux VACHES.

The train is racing neck to neck with another train, gaining; windows, faces, eyes blur and merge into memories gulped by the hollow roaring night, fade into other trains; the Congressional gnawing into the feverish Maryland springtime, slamming the picket doors of shanty yards full of the funeral swaying of lilacs; the Black Diamond; the nameless train from nowhere into nowhere, the bobbing tassels of the blueshaded lamp, the looking out through eyes stingingly weighed down with sleep at the red yellow vanishing flowers with twisting petals, dark bottle-shaped bulks and unexplained word, blastfurnaces; the train folding itself up into the ferry to cross the bright mica of the Gut of Canso; the speeding express of the Trans-Siberian speeding to Pekin that never left its shed. Too many trains, too many wheels clattering over crossings, strange names spelled out in the night, goodbys at ticket windows, last meals gulped hastily at lunchcounters, hands clasped over suitcases; the head of the girl at the crossing you see on the body of a trackwalker down the line, hungry eyes looking through grimed panes, smiling lips shattered into void at the next station, questioning eyes of brownarmed gangs resting on their picks.

I have slipped back into my place between the highbusted lady in serge who sleeps with a handkerchief over her face and the starched Annamite who sits bolt upright. Opposite, a newly married couple strangled by their new clothes are stickily asleep; her head leans against a pillow in the corner, her mouth is open; his red winedrinker's face is burrowed into her shoulder. The windows are closed. You could dent the air with your finger.

Waking up with the sun in my eyes I sit watching the long blue shadows of black cypresses. At a spick-and-span creamcolored station the air smells of roses and garlic and dust: le Midi.

At Beni Ounif the air was sheer white fire. It was scaring to stumble off the beer-sticky diningcar into such hugeness. A black boy in a red fez carried my bag to Madame Mimosa's. On a bed in a shuttered room I stretched out. The train was leaving the station, hooted, puffed, rumbled away into the rocky desert. From very far away the lessening sound of wheels over rails, then silence. Silence becoming dense with sleep.

The sun had set. The sky had hardened into flaming zones,

topaz, emerald, amethyst. Outside my door leaning against a pillar of the porch still warm from the sun, looking out into the vast desert square hemmed by low buildings with crumbling ochre-pink porches. In front of the crenelated station three toy freightcars. Nobody in sight, not even a dog. Size expands and contracts with the changing flare of the sky. Striding out of the tiny square, down the infinitesimal street, I trip over a purple mountain. I put out my hand to touch the white wall of a house; it is a mile away across the railroad tracks. The spiky cluster-headed grass is palmtrees striding in ranks through a gash in crimson rock. Beyond the houses the trodden stone falls away into an immeasurable canyon that turns out to be a sandy runnel made by irrigation water. Wondering whether I was still asleep I stumbled down a rocky path admiring the great river valley; I stepped in it. It was a little stream broad as my foot seeping through a crack in the mudwall of a dategarden. Meanwhile night was fast screwing down a glistening lid on a dimensionless chaos. A cool wind blew. Towards the town a few campfires were twinkling. A row of twitching mounds were camels asleep; there were muffled figures round the campfires. In doorways there were lamps, shadows about them. In a bare white room at a corner three Algerian soldiers were drinking against a green bar. They told me Madame Mimosa's was on the next corner. There walking through a small conglomerate store you came into an empty diningroom lit by a hanging lamp tightly shuttered to keep the light from trickling out into the night.

After a supper of turkey and desert truffles and white wine from Philippeville to stride out of doors again into the street without footsteps. The low flatroofed houses are obliterated under the stars. Silence is stretched taut across the night. I walk gigantic above the flattened houses, suddenly shrink with a drop like an express elevator from under the soaring stars, tiny manikin tottering on infinitesimal pins, to the tiny throbbing of a heart, frail squirts of blood through a tangle of infinitesimally tiny pipes. On the taut night comes a dribbling of watery notes from a reed, the softest drumming of two tired hands. The man who ate alphabet soup against his will is forgotten. The Irishman with false teeth is forgotten. The cool bright notes of the reed ripple out of everywhere; the drumbeat rising, deepening, is modelling breathless stately land-scapes out of darkness. The eastbound southbound American who ate alphabet soup against his will takes refuge in his room, beside the wide creaky bed, in the protection of the smoky lamp, out of the path of these moving dunes of sound. This is the solitude and the voices crying in the wilderness. He gets undressed, cleans his teeth, sorts his clothes, works out a few lines of Lucretius, pretends he's in Buffalo, Savannah, Noisy le Sec, Canarsie. The trickle of the flute has parched away into the hurrying driven dunes of the drumbeat. St. Anthony alone in the wilderness of dark flesh, the intricately throbbing wilderness.

But the Irishman with the false teeth wasn't killed in Stam-boul. He didn't dare go to a hospital, so the Russian woman and her husband took care of him in a shed in an old sheep corral in the outskirts of Top Hanep. They all three made jumpingjacks and the girl whose name was Olga sold them in the evening in front of the Tokatlian. She sold more than jumpingjacks, and all night the husband who had been an of-ficer in the Russian navy without ever going to sea sat polish-ing his high boots and groaning. The Irishman groaned on account of the pain in his shoulder and for the loss of his false teeth. They talked in French the rest of the time, lying in abandoned army stretchers they used for beds. The Irishman, whose name was Jefferson Higgins, was a Gaelic pantheist. In a broken-down creamery in County Cork, he had had long talks with the Little People in his youth. The Russian officer believed in chastity, in macerating the flesh with alcohol to burn the devil out of it. In spite of that he never drank. Olga believed in hunger, fear, and the Virgin Mary. She hated men except those she loved. Through the long August days they lay in their stretchers talking of these things while the ci-cadas shrilled and kites wheeled in the cloudless sky. She loved them both and bought them food and washed their clothes and hung them to dry on the roof of the shed. She loved them both and petted them and called them her little grandchildren.

The naval officer blamed the misery of their days on what he called the helpless Russian soul; the Irishman blamed it on the British government; Olga blamed it on mankind. The two men, if it hadn't been for their lice and for the difficulty of shaving, would have been completely happy.

One morning Olga came home with a copy of the Communist Manifesto. It was in three languages, Russian, Armenian and Georgian. It had been given her by a taxidriver from Odessa who had been an ornithologist. He had taken her to his room and set her up to a meal, but in the morning he had no money to give her, so he had given her a copy of the Communist Manifesto.

They translated it for Higgins the next day. The husband and wife cried and kissed each other. They must have a faith, they told each other. From now on they would work for Russia, for the communist Christ, savior of mankind. They must work to go home. Olga would have to give up the Virgin Mary, she was too much like the czarina. They would work as carpenters and make furniture for the new Russia. He would stop making jumpingjacks; she would never prostitute her body again. If necessary they would starve. Immediately he started building a kind of settee out of a few old boards, to get his hand in; she watched him with bright eyes.

Meanwhile Jefferson Higgins walked up and down gnawing his ragged sandy moustache with toothless gums. The wound wasn't healing properly; he suspected he had syphilis. He wanted a new set of false teeth, cleanliness and fresh linen and Piccadilly and the military club. He was sick of the unceasing chatter of the two Russians; if he'd had a gun he would have shot them both dead.

When he had Olga alone he asked her with tears in his blue eyes to take him to a communist meeting. There must be communist agitators among all the Russians in Constant'. His life had entirely changed since that night when she had shot him in the shoulder. Thank God she hadn't killed him, she broke in, kissing him on the forehead. He would never work for the British again. He would go home and fight for Irish freedom. He would hand over all the secret codes of the Intelligence Department to the Bolos. The naval officer came home and found them in each other's arms. He wants to join the communist party, she explained. The Russian grabbed the Irishman and kissed him several times on the head.

Next day Jefferson Higgins with a cigar in his mouth and a panama hat on the back of his head sat in a small room in the Pera Palace typing a report with one hand. He was clean

shaven, his moustache was neatly trimmed. He wore a neat
grey flannel suit. His arm was strapped to his chest with clean
bandages. He had a mouthful of teeth; they didn't fit very
well but they were teeth. He was typing out the description
of a Bolo plot to assassinate the High Commissioners, spread
mutiny in the Allied armies and with the help of the discontented Turks seize Constantinople for the Soviet government.
Occasionally he stopped typing and blew smoke rings. There
was a soft triple knock on the door.—Kitchener, said Jefferson
Higgins in a low voice. A stout grizzled man in the uniform
of a British colonel came in.—It's not Kitchener today, it's
Baden-Powell, growled the colonel.—But I knew your voice.
He picked up some typewritten sheets off the table and let
the breath go out in a whistle between his teeth.—It'll be a
jolly fine bag I'll tell you. . . . We'll clean the blighters up.
The High Commissioner'll feel pretty cheap when he sees
this. You know where to leave it?—Yes, sir. Without another
word the colonel laid on the table an American passport,
handsomely outfitted with visas and made out for Fernald
O'Rielly, travelling for a Chicago manufacturer of agricultural
machinery, and a letter of credit on Lloyd's Bank.—Report
December 15th in Shanghai according to orders 26b, was the
last thing the colonel said as he left the room.

Jefferson Higgins typed and typed. When he had finished
the cigar he rang the bell for a whisky and soda. The waiter was
a Bulgarian and read English perfectly. While he was making
change he glanced at the typewritten sheets. Certain names on
it were familiar to him. When he got down to the bar again he
sent out a compatriot of his who was washing glasses in back to
deliver a message to a bearded man sitting beside the mechanical piano in a small bar in a side street in Galata playing
backgammon with a onearmed Greek sailor. As a result when
the British military police went round at midnight to make the
arrests certain of the more weighty birds had flown.

But Jefferson Higgins was already far down on the Sea of
Marmora on the steamboat of the Lloyd Triestino. It was a
moonlight night. He felt molten and tender as he used to
feel as a boy when he thought of the Little People and the
high kings of Ireland. His Gaelic was a ladle skimming rich
thoughts off the milkwhite sky. The girl with the white arms

working the butterchurn. The way a white shoulder sometimes peeped out from her dress. He began humming "Kathleen Mavourneen," shouted to the barman to bring him a gin
fizz, went back to humming "Kathleen Mavourneen." Marseilles 'ld be the first place he could get a decent meal. The Bristol. He must find a nice sympathetic girl. Getting too old to
care for the wild ones. For a week he'd live like a sultan. Then
he'd settle down, look up Makropoulos and make some investments. About time he started thinking of the future, of his old
age. He sat watching the great dry curves of the hills shining in
the moonlight. The boat was going through the Dardanelles.

Meanwhile the British were combing Pera for Russians.
Several men shot themselves. Olga's husband knocked out a
sergeant with a blow in the stomach and was promptly shot
through the head by a nervous recruit. The Russian refugees
suspected of bolshevizing were herded into a basement. Most
of them didn't care what happened to them; many were glad of
the opportunity of getting a square meal. Then those considered most dangerous were weeded out and taken to detention
camps. The rest were loaded on a scow and towed up into the
Black Sea in the direction of Odessa. But Olga didn't go with
them. In the company of a French interpreter she got out of
Constantinople and eventually turned up in Algiers in the es-
tablishment of a certain Madame Renée, fifty francs to the girl
and fifty to the house. Wherever she went she carried her
zinc-white firmly modelled body carelessly as one might carry
a chair across a room.

No one ever knew how Olga managed to get to New
York—perhaps as somebody's wife. Anyway the dense clattering life all about her in the East Side tenement where she
lived made her feel happy although she was tired all the time.
Best of all she liked the Five and Ten Cent Stores and the
blue trolley cars on Second Avenue. She sang nights in a little joint far east on Seventh Street. But she looked too much
like a schoolgirl when she sang. The other girl, a dark Jewess
who had been to Panama, got all the applause with

> A thousand miles of hugs and kisses
> O . . . poppa . . . here we are
> O so far . . . from Omaha.

When we arrived in the open space among the crumbled houses of Findi the Caïd and his brother who had been a tirailleur came out to meet us. I presented my letter and black Mahomet made a little speech. We sat in the guestchamber, a tiny whitewashed room with a running blue border of grapeleaves interspersed with the imprint of a hand at regular intervals. They brought out dates and sour milk. They were people of the Beni Amour, pure-blooded Arabs whom the French had planted in the oasis left desolate by the flight of the native Haratine and Berber people who had originally built the ksar and tended the dategardens. The wells were filling up and the sand was encroaching on the palms. When the guest dish had been eaten up we walked slowly and with dignity around to see the notable things of the oasis, the place where the battle had been between the Joyeux and the ksourians, the old wells, the dam built by people in the olden time, the vegetable gardens, the place where a foreign lady had pitched her tent and remained for five days, the tumbledown monument to the French soldiers killed in the battle, the wheeltracks of the great autocar with six double wheels that had passed carrying officers in gold-braided hats to Timimoum. In the mountain that hemmed in the oasis to the south lived a demon named Dariuss, guarding a great treasure of gold. He rolled down rocks on people who tried to climb up there.

After dinner of ta'am with sweet milk poured on it and eggs we drank tea and sat long by the little light of two pigeon lamps talking. Eventually they forgot me and I leaned back against the wall, letting the great waves of Arabic eddy over my head. In pauses in the conversation you could hear no sound. The six or eight men who lived in the oasis were all in the room. Probably their wives were listening through chinks in the wall. Outside of the little patch of habitable houses were the broken houses of the old ksar, the tall datepalms and the immensity of sun-licked rock where only the demon Dariuss kept watch.

A great listless quiet was in men's faces, the energy of their words was mere ripples in quiet. In everything they sought the quiet that was the peace of Allah the merciful, the compassionate. It was what Achmed and his friend the tailor said in Marrakesh while Achmed was chopping the fresh hemp for the pipe of kif.—In America we drink stimulants to make us excited, I had said.—Here you smoke kif to make you feel peaceful. He couldn't make out what I meant. Excited was what he had been when the mule had run away and he ran after it and lost his slippers, a miserable feeling worse than sickness. I tried to explain Coney Island, people paying money to be shaken up, jostled, ruffled, to slide down chutes, to roll in barrels, to jiggle on broken-back bridges. Achmed decided we must be mad in the western lands, but there must be a baraka in our madness because we were very rich. He handed a pipe to the little tailor, who took it reverently, smoked it between sips of tea and sat quiet looking out through the tall door at the sky, a drowsy smile at the corners of his mouth. Then Achmed inhaled deep and sat looking at nothing with a blue glaze over his eyes. He handed the pipe to me. The Westerner, the eater of alphabet soup, drew in the pungent smoke perfunctorily. Was there enough kif in the world to drown the breathless desires, the feeling of headline events round the next corner, the terrible eagerness of railroad stations at dusk, the twilight madness of cities, the wheels, the grinding cogs, the sheets of print endlessly unrolling? For Achmed none of these things existed. Life lay in quiet submission, life's fulfilment was life's brother death.

That night at Findi in the little guestroom of the Caïd's house, sitting back listening to the longdrawn quiet talk, I thought of those things, and of graven images and alphabet soup and the torture of the four directions and the squirrelcage of the meridians, and of the train of the Trans-Siberian eternally about to leave, the engine whistling on the new train, shiny, smelling like new toys and rubberballs, that never left its shed at the Exposition Universelle. Who will find a name for our madness that has taken the place of glory and religion and knowledge and love, contagion subtler and more lasting and more full of consequences even than the pox Columbus brought back from the New World? Is it worth the drowsiness of kif and a man alone in the sheer desert shouting the triumphant affirmation: *There is no God but very God; Mahomet is the prophet of God*?

XIV. Mail Plane

In the lee of the tin shed squat an old man and two women muffled to the eyes in tallow-colored rags. A mechanic kneading a piece of waste between his hands is kidding them about pork in a gentle drawl of French mixed with pidgin Arabic. Everybody shivers in the huge flow of cold east wind. At last the plane comes skimming the roll of the bare Moroccan hills. The women giggle behind their veils. In the name of God, says the old man and looks impassively at the passenger and the bags of mail and at the propeller blades that jerk round more slowly and more slowly, become two and stop. The passenger climbs in and huddles facing a thinfaced melancholy man with goggles; they drop in the mail, then the engine roars, the tin shed runs away, the hills waltz slowly, and white Tangier and the Straits and the Atlantic and the black cloud-dribbling mountains of the Riff spin gradually away, dropping in a lopsided spiral. The plane bounces like a ball across a snowy floor of white clouds. You're very cold and a little sick and the hours trundle by endlessly until all at once you are being sucked into a vortex of flying mist and sunny red plowed land and yellow and white houses, you circle the bull ring and it's Malaga. No time for lunch.

At Alicante the passenger sits drinking Fundador with the pilot in a kind of cabaret. On the stage stout ladies out of the past stamp tiredly to castagnettes, but at the table Mercedes (1926 model) slips into an empty chair. Her little black head is shingled, she makes goldy-round eyes like a cat at the talk of speed and cold airpockets.

In the hangover at dawn with hot eyes and dry tongues they start off again, grinding into the north wind.

Valencia through rifts in a snowstorm; then hours of bronze-green sea and rusty coasthills and a double corkscrew into Barcelona. No time for lunch.

North of the Pyrenees the air is thick like white soup. Over Cette the clouds are spouting in gigantic plumes. Trundle and swoop and sudden sideways skidding in the blinding whirl of a storm. It's terribly cold. The earth is dissolved in swirling mist. No more restaurants, steamheated seats in trains, election parades, red fire, beefsteaks. Nothing but the speed of whirling cold over an imaginary sphere marked with continents, canals, roadribbons, real estate lots. An earth weird as Mars, dead cold as the moon, distant as Uranus, where speed snaps at last like a rubber band. Huddled in a knot, hard and cold, pitched like a baseball round the world. . . . Until you meet yourself coming back and are very sick into your old black hat.

IN ALL COUNTRIES

Contents

I. Passport Photo

SLIPPING unsurely with numb wet feet on the sleetslimed pavement the Amerikanski Peesatyel stumbled into the station and found his way dazedly to his compartment in the train. In the trainshed it was like the Moscow winter afternoon outside, only darker and greyer. The dim electric bulbs made no light in the December murk, cold and heavy and grey as pigiron. Only the steam rising from the engine and our breaths made a little fragile stir of whiteness. The A. Peesatyel was dead tired, his nose stuffed up with a cold, his stomach was full of cold herring and smoked fish, the vodka of many goodbyes had worked up into his head where it weighed and buzzed in an iron crown. All the day before, all night, all this day he'd slushed through the sleetpitted snow of the streets, climbed grey stairs, tried to explain, to understand explanations, to say things in foreign languages, to ask how, to tell why; had stood face to face with great healthy youthful people in formless grey clothes; had been warmed and moved by the warmth and movement of their faces so alive in the eyes and lips, eyes strained to see beyond the frontier, beyond next week and next century, lips always forming questions; had left the questions halfanswered, halfunderstood and had shaken hands. This shaking hands and saying goodbye was like shaking hands with a doctor you were friends with who had come to the door of the operating theatre for a moment to strip off his rubber gloves and smoke a cigarette and try to explain something to you before it was time to go back to the lights and the blood and the glittering instruments of the theatre where with desperate difficulty a baby was being born.

In the early morning there'd been a long drunkendrowsy trip in a taxicab to a suburb where you could hardly see the grey ramshackle houses against the long grey snowbanks disappearing under the grey sky, to visit an old peasant, a sharp-faced timeless man, who'd brought from some Volga villages a whole bagful of lacquered scraps of the middleages made up for sale into ashtrays and soupspoons and cigarette boxes, painted right today in the style of the Byzantine ikonpainters; and then back into the murk of Moscow, into the terrible jangling girderwork of the future again, and more unfinished talks, goodbyes, little glasses of vodka, goodbyes.

But all the old habits of thirty years of life are straining away towards the west and carpets and easychairs and the hot and cold bathwater running and the cheerful trivial accustomed world of shopwindows and women's hats and their ankles neat as trottinghorses' above the light hightapping heels, and the nonsensical lilt of advertisements and gimcracks and greenbacks. It's like waiting for the cage that's going to haul you up out of a mine, like getting out of a cementfactory, like climbing the long greasy ladder out of the stokehold of a steamboat, like getting away from the rotary presses of a newspaper and stepping out onto the disorganized jingling street.

Groggily the A. Peesatyel dropped his bags in his compartment (anyway made the train) and stepped out on the platform to smoke one more of too many last cigarettes, and stood stamping his numb feet in the grey iron cold of the trainshed under the spiralling beckoning vaguelyseen steam. The woman who was a theatredirector, the nice genial woman with the fine dark eyes, had come down to say goodbye; the company came with her, all the fifteenyearolds and eighteenyearolds I'd seen rehearsing the plays for the Sanitary Propaganda Theatre, the play about avoiding syphilis, the play about cleaning your teeth, the play about the world that will stand up so bright and shining when the dark murky scaffolding of today's struggle is torn away. "They want to say goodbye," she said as I was shaking the hard untrembly hands (they were all factoryworkers in the daytime and actors at night), under the probing of so many blue eyes curious and friendly, wanting to be told, to be with, to understand, to cross all these faraway frontiers. "They want to know," she said. "They like you very much, but they want to ask you one question. They want you to show your face. They want to know where you stand politically. Are you with us?"

The iron twilight dims, the steam swirls round us, we are muddled by the delicate crinkly steam of our breath, the iron crown tightens on the head, throbbing with too many men, too many women, too many youngsters seen, talked to, asked questions of, too many hands shaken, too many foreign languages badly understood. . . . "But let me see . . . But maybe I can explain . . . But in so short a time . . . there's no time." The train is moving. I have to run and jump for it. They are gone in a whirl of steam, rubbed out by the irongrey darkness. The train has pulled out of the station and is rumbling westward.

I fell into my bunk into the too stuffy, too rumbling, too drowsyhot compartment and rolled over and went to sleep.

II. Russian Visa

1. BROOKLYN TO HELSINGFORS

Rockall

In Brooklyn, in a few patches of grass, in the fuzzy antlers of the ailanthustrees that sprout beside garbagecans in back yards, it was beginning to be spring. There was something about the way the tugs hooted on the East River in the morning twilight, and the harbor wind had a new sniff to it; but the girl with the copper-rivetted henna rinse in the cafeteria was just the same, her face wore the same sleepwalker's never-asmile when she rang up your change or talked to somebody named Deary into the telephone or threw back a kidding remark or a Nice day, Bum day, Rainy day as if it had burned her; it was always the same in the subway, the echoing passage stinking of elevatorshafts and urinals, the scattering people in overcoats on the platform, hurried eyes that looked at you but never into yours (when eyes meet on the I.R.T. the airbrakes go on, the train stops with a crash), jostling bodies packed together through the long tunnel under the river, and the whiff of grit and burned gas in your face as you climbed out onto Seventh Avenue; and always the halfwop loafers at the corner of Bleecker, waiting for what?

In Manhattan there are no seasons and for a long time there hadn't been any days, only the little office with its perpetually clacking typewriter (when the typewriter stops in a New York office everybody's embarrassed; men start to quarrel or to make love to the stenographer or drop lighted cigarettes in the wastebasket), and the stuffy little theatre, and the stage lit for rehearsals and the empty rows of seats stretching into the dark; and upstairs the smell of the gluepot over the gasburner and the brushes that are so hard to keep from dripping and the dusty painted flats; and effort, hurry, delay to make a number of things understood that we are unable to make understood. And home hours after midnight, walking to walk off the shots of socalled rye at the saloon at the corner of Carmine Street through the scarywindowed downtown streets, past furtive doorways, occasional stonefaced cops, embers of bonfires the kids had made out of old packingboxes and then forgotten; frightened streetwalkers who grabbed your arm in the sidestreets off Second Avenue; men with grimy eyes stirring around under the L structure on the Bowery; the empty downtown with the shapeless shamble of scrubwomen going to work along windy pavements, pressmen and newsboys round City Hall, the tired crowd sodden with work waiting for the Flatbush Avenue car. Then to stride magnificently out on the old bridge soaring in the lift of delicately webbed cables into the sky, the smell of the harbor, the looking over your shoulder at the dark jagged tooth of buildings poised on the edge of the sky; the shuttle of the car and the footsteps, way up above the river, of somebody walking towards you across the bridge. . . . Who is he? What does he want? Where is he going? Who am I? What do I want? Where am I going? . . . and ten thousand young men in ten thousand hall bedrooms have escaped the drilling grind of the day and sit on the edges of their sour beds pulling off their clothes . . . and want.

Want maybe Madison Avenue and the smell of florists and newbought leather knickknacks and the plateglass shine and the brass, and Bacardi cocktails and speakeasy meals, the stiff white napkins and her leg in a silk stocking against yours under the table and the fiveoclock bustle of furs and the warm room smelling of the perfume the girl wears and the tinkle of ice in the glasses and the bright black of the piano and smell of the dressingtable in her bedroom and the sidelong hand pulling down the shade. (But mostly they go to bed alone in the last stale swirl of some bunches of wornout drinks.) In Brooklyn it was beginning to be spring, but in Manhattan there were no more days that rattled along towards five o'clock on Madison, only jangled nights of empty streets gone sour.

The other subway had a fresh powdery smell; Hoboken was all yesterdays melting forgotten into the grey vacant scentless cavern of the wharf. There is no sleep so good as sleep in a ship's bunk.

It was on that trip that we came out on deck one afternoon to shake off the choking afterluncheon sleep; the North Atlantic was smooth and mottled and grey as a sheet of zinc to eastward, there was something on the horizon. Somebody said it was a steamboat, somebody else said it was a fullrigged ship, somebody else said No it was a derelict; as we got near it we began to feel the swell; it was a rock. We passed close enough to hear the growling of the surf round its sheer cliffs.

Rockall stands alone in the North Atlantic, twentyfour hours steaming west of the Pentland Firth. It stands up tall as a large liner out of the empty ocean in cliffs that are reddish slatecolor above and seaweed green near tidelevel, that taper into jagged peaks covered solid white with birddroppings as a mountainpeak might be covered with snow. Gulls and gannets whirl constantly round it in a screaming cloud.

Mr. Hansen

Mr. Hansen was a small mild grey elderly man with manners so meticulously unobtrusive he was hardly noticeable in the cabin I shared with him. He was an accountant by profession and was going back to Denmark after twentyfive years in the States with a small amount of money saved up, a small amount but enough, he said almost coyly. He wore a grey suit the same color as his hair and a grey tweed overcoat. His suitcases were new and shiny. He had a new set of silverbacked military brushes with his initials on them. It was the first time he'd been home to the old country in all those twentyfive years. He'd told himself he wouldn't go home till he'd saved really enough. Now he was going home.

Rockall left Mr. Hansen cold, but when we sighted the Butt of Lewis and the Scotch coast next day his grey eyes seemed to water more than usual in the keen wind off the Orkneys, and he walked up and down the small Tourist Third deck with a lively step. Now that we were in Europe, he kept saying, now he would see his friends. The worst thing about Los Angeles had been that he'd made no friends there, he'd been accountant for a large bakery concern, and he'd boarded at a very nice home, but, perhaps he'd been a little shy on account of the language, yes he'd been on good enough terms with everybody, but it had been How do you do Mr. Hansen, A nice day Mr. Hansen, but never more than that, very respectable people you understand, of course he wouldn't have stood for the other kind, fast girls and all that, all they thought of was to make you spend your money.

Going through the Pentland Firth the tide ran so strong that the boat kept swinging round till she was almost amidships to her course. The Orkneys stood up tall and grassy against the bright north; to the south was the smoky Scotch coast, slate roofs and steeples, leaden inlets. Mr. Hansen was saying that of course it wouldn't do to be extravagant, but that now he would be able to afford a few pleasures. He'd never believed in drink and raising Cain. He was afraid his relations would think he was a millionaire, over here people still thought we could pick up money in the gutters in California. But now and then a glass of beer or ale hurt nobody, and he must learn to talk and discuss topics of interest. When a boy he'd been quite a talker. It worried him a little for fear he'd forgotten his Danish; at the village where he was born they spoke a dialect. He supposed it was speaking the language incorrectly that had made him have so few friends in the States. "In California I have been always a lonely man, now I must be careful that they don't marry me off to some woman who thinks I have money."

Mr. Hansen was in such a hurry to get to Denmark he got off the boat at Christiansand to cross on the ferry, and missed the long quiet trip up the fjord to Oslo through the pale glare of the white summer night, during which I woke at two in the morning with the red sun shining in my eyes and my nose full of northwoods birchbark wildstrawberry smell, like the smell of Maine.

A few days later I met him in front of the Tivoli amusement park in Copenhagen at the beginning of one of those endless summer evenings. He seemed a little too glad to see another American. He wore a new derby hat but he looked unhappy. I asked him to have a glass of beer with me; we sat a long time in the café opposite the empty amusement park. He told me he'd been back to his village and found that they didn't speak the dialect any more. Everybody he'd known had gone. He'd been to see some cousins in Copenhagen, but it hadn't been a success. He found it hard to speak good Copenhagen Danish, harder than English. But almost everybody here speaks English, I said. That wouldn't be the same, he'd wanted to talk the way he used to talk at home. He'd had a handsome headstone put on his father's and mother's grave. Now he didn't know what to do with himself; he supposed he ought to go to see the sights in Copenhagen, a museum, or Elsinore; did I know a nice restaurant where we could eat? We went to a restaurant and sat down in front of a mirror brimmed with the late pale light of the summer night. He wouldn't drink anything and he looked as if he would burst into tears at any minute. I couldn't think of much to say. Then he said maybe he'd go back to the States, they had told him that if he should come back he could have his same job again. The restaurant was empty; whatever time it was, it wasn't when people eat in Copenhagen.

Gare du Nord

The Paris Gare du Nord is a building large and colorless as a European summer twilight. It has a hotel in it where you can take a room that looks out on the grey columns and the darkgreen taxis and buses and the long streams of commuters and the stout spearpointed railings that are there to keep the Parisians from rushing the railroadstation if they happen to get sore at their government. From your room at the Gare du Nord you can go in and out of the Ville Lumière as if it were a museum of painting; you can shuffle through its views like going through a stack of old postal cards found in a trunk. Every time you come and go from your room you look through the long windows of the inside corridor down into the trainshed and smell the oily steamy smell of the locomotives. But mostly Paris isn't a museum or postalcards, these toohandsome June days with the horsechestnuts and the advertising kiosks all in bloom, often it's painful snapshots I seem to have taken myself some years ago; sometimes I can make out a few familiar squinting figures in the foreground; now who was that, could that have been me in that funny hat? There's the Tuileries and the dome of the Institut and the spring crop in the pictureshops along the rue La Boêtie and the Café de la Paix that used to be the corner of Bagdad and 42nd Street and the café all white and mirrors at the Porte Maillot and the little bars where so and so said such and such and the bright barges and towboats on the river and the little steamboats as old as the Eiffel Tower still announcing Maggi and Amer Picon and Chocolat Meunier and the whiskered senators still doddering over their croquet in the

Luxembourg Gardens; but where is the Ville Lumière, Paname, throbbing intersection of Bangkok and Buenos Aires, of Barcelona and Berlin? Surely not in the grands reportages in the Petit Parisien or in the quaintish restaurants people try to make you go to because a Somebody was once seen straining his soup through his whiskers in one corner, or in the spindly young men in dark suits who look like perfumery salesmen they tell you are surréaliste poets, or in the queasylooking hicks with hangovers who droop fidgeting at the Dôme in the American quarter, or in the anachronistic phonies with long hair who sit in the little square on the top of Montmartre where we were caught by an airraid once, or in the nocturnal whoopee ten years stale in the dumps in the side streets off from du Maurier's Boul' Mich' . . . well it may have been always like that. I keep a timetable in my pocket all the time. You and me, Mr. Hansen.

The Baltic

Looking out of the window across Germany is not half so entertaining as looking out of the New York New Haven and Hartford between Providence and New York, but it is fine going on board the Finnish boat at Stettin. The boat is enamelled and bright as a toy in a toyshop window, everybody's eyes are blue on top of clean shining freshsoaped faces; everybody talks languages I can't even pretend to understand, but is delighted to produce whenever necessary a few words of a neat copybook English. The midday meal was Valhalla brought down to earth (except alas for the mead); in the center of the diningsaloon there's a long table; down the center of the table lie two whole boiled salmon head to head, they are flanked by a good hundred dishes of smoked salmon, herrings smoked, pickled, salted and raw, haddock and whitefish in a number of forms, caviar, hot cheese dishes, salads, cole slaw, red cabbage, pickles, savories, spiced meat, smoked tongue, sugared ham . . . no wonder Veblen, the old Scandihoovian, understood the philosophy of conspicuous waste. When the whole long table is thoroughly gutted the passengers who have been darting about politely but briskly with loaded and reloaded plates in their hands, settle down to the spotless white table to eat a quiet solid fourcourse lunch, a lunch to put a sevenfoot lumberjack to sleep.

No wonder the bourgeoisie of these parts rose on its ear to defend its fleshpots.

Helsingfors was all right except that the sea isn't salt there and the town looks like a cleaner Duluth and they'd run entirely out of this year's supply of darkness. There was a big fuzzy park where two brass bands played cheerlessly through the livid night and stocky pinkfaced boys and girls walked round in fours and fives nudging and elbowing and stepping on each other's feet when they met. In the center of it was a chaletshaped restaurant where for a remarkably small sum you could be admitted to another Valhalla similar to the one on the boat.

The Sundays waiting for a visa in Helsingfors are the longest anywhere. You take a little steamboat and steam through endless birchcovered islands like islands in the Great Lakes, then you come back and walk out of town and go swimming in the chilly unsalt sea, then you come back and walk around in the elegant empty cleanasapin railroad station; it's nine o'clock but it's bright day; no place is open and there's nobody anywhere. Through the windows of the big hotel opposite the station you can at least see waiters moving about. The cavernous dining room is a chilly pink with lugubrious hangings held over from the old régime. The waiter speaks a little English, denies that he knows any place where I can get a drink. The food is like the food in a Maine summer hotel, no Valhalla here, nothing for the bourgeoisie to put up a scrap about. I sit munching alone; then a voice from home comes drawling out from some table behind the portières, emphasizing each pause with a rattle of phlegm: "The trouble with . . . European countries . . . is . . . now all these customs barriers. Well in the States . . . fortyeight of 'em . . . well sir there's nothing like that. A man in Connecticut can trade with a man in Louisiana with no difficulties whatsoever. . . . There everything is done to promote trade friendship, here you do everything you can to interfere with it. . . ." All of which was indubitably true. Eating the canned pears that ended the meal I formed a project to talk to the invisible speaker and his soundless companion; maybe they'd know where a man could get a drink. The voice honked and gurgled and then went on: "Now look at the great enormous city of New York . . . stretched over three states . . . fifteen

millions of inhabitants if you count the entire metropolitan district. Now look at that great metropolis. . . ." I had. The thing
to do was to go to bed and lie there in the colorless evening
light worrying about why the Russian visa hadn't come.

Two days later it came. In the clean and comfortable Finnish-
style station I went to bed in a clean and comfortable Finnish-
style third class sleeper. The train rambled out of the station and
on through endless grey birchwoods in the pale gloaming. It
was fine to lie half asleep looking out of the window joggling
towards the actual existing to-be-seen-with-my-own-eyes so
bloodily contested Frontier between yesterday and tomorrow.

2. RAINY DAYS IN LENINGRAD

Finland Station

The train ran into the station and stopped; an empty station
without bustle, broad clean asphalt platforms, grey ironwork,
a few porters and railroad officials standing around. Very
quickly the American conducted tours were absorbed and disappeared bag and baggage. I waited on the empty platform
for a man who was doing something about a trunk. This was
where Lenin, back from hiding in the marshes, had landed
and made his first speeches during the Russian October eleven
years ago. How could it be so quiet? I'd half expected to
catch in the grey walls some faint reverberation of trampling
footsteps, of machineguns stuttering, voices yelling: All Power
to the Soviets. Could it have been only eleven years ago?

At length we get into a muchtoosmall cab driven by a huge
bearded extortioner out of the chorus of Boris Godunov, and
start joggling slowly along the toowide streets under a low grey
sky. In every direction stretch immense neoclassic façades, white
columns, dull red, blue or yellow stucco walls, battered, silent,
majestic, and all like the Finland station, swept free, empty.
How could it be so quiet when only eleven years ago . . . ?

Hermitage

We ducked out of the chilly rain under a porch held up by
tiredlooking stone women that I suppose must have meant

something noble and artistic to somebody sometime, and through swinging doors into the vestibule of the museum. That vestibule full of people standing round waiting to check their coats and goloshes was a tower of Babel. A party of Americans was being conducted up the stairs, a few German students in windjackets and shorts stood round, a horde of dark people from southeast Russia were speaking Tatar, there were pale blueyed soldiers from somewhere in the north. A young man standing next to me asked me something and I tried him on English thinking he was a Chinaman. He turned out to be a Kirghiz.

We walked round together, and as he was as pleased to be talking to two men from America as we were to be talking to a Kirghiz, none of us saw any of the pictures.

He was a metalworker, an unskilled laborer. He'd been in Leningrad a year just making enough to live. He and his brother had left the tent of their fathers on the Kirghiz steppes and their herd of shaggymaned ponies, because they wanted to find out about the world and the revolution. His brother was a partymember and was studying at the university for eastern peoples. No, he himself wasn't a communist. Well, mostly because he had not seen enough yet, he had not made up his mind as to whether they were right or not. He didn't know. He was too young yet. He'd have to see the world and draw his own conclusions. Criticize? Yes the workers in his factory said about what they pleased . . . of course if someone made a habit of talking directly against the Party, the Gaypayoo might bring pressure to bear. He wasn't sure. As for him, it wouldn't convince him the Party was right if they locked him up, he thought they understood that. He had to see the world and find out for himself.

And his people, the nomad tribes of the great steppes of Central Asia, stockraisers still living in the age of Abraham, Isaac and Jacob? The ideas of the revolution were just beginning to reach them, through schools, through young men like himself who went to work in the Russian cities. They talked about the revolution in their tents at night, round their smoky fires. The old people still clung devoutly to Islam, but the young men were like him, they wanted to know what was right, what was good for the world. Perhaps five per cent of them were communists or comsomols. Many of the rest of them, like him, wanted to see for themselves.

We talked about books. He said he was reading Gorki and until he had read everything Gorki had ever written he wouldn't have time for any other books. It was only since the revolution that there had been books among the Kirghiz.

What about the position of women? At home it was very complicated, it was all a matter of money or cattle, getting a wife, neither party was free; but here among the Leningrad factory workers you could do pretty much as you pleased with your individual life, if a fellow and a girl liked each other well enough, they lived together, and then if they got very fond of each other, or if she was going to have a baby, they registered the marriage. The only place the police stepped in was if either party failed to chip in supporting the child.

But what about America? We must tell him everything about America, whether you could get work, how much pay you got, what the schools were like, whether life was good there, what kind of marriage we had, whether the workers had any power, how mighty was capitalism.

Yes he wanted to go to America, he must see as much as he could of the world, so that he could make up his mind.

Smolny

We had just come out from the bare stone corridors of Smolny Institute, huge austerelyproportioned colonnaded building that stood serenely athwart the grey drizzly afternoon; we had seen the little room where Lenin lived and worked from the time the Bolsheviki seized power in the name of the peasants and workers until the government was moved to Moscow, a bare room with a few chairs and a table and a little cot behind a partition: we walked down the road and out through the gate. Eleven years ago . . . and now Smolny was history, like the music of Bach, like Mount Vernon, like the pyramids.

We wanted to find a place to drink tea and asked two youngsters who had also turned round to look back at Smolny.

The question of tea was lost for a long while in the questions about America they peppered us with. They were communists, students at the university at Odessa, in Leningrad on an excursion run by Narkompros. Smolny for them was the beginning of everything. They were too young to have much memory of the old Russia of the Czar when Smolny had been a ladies' seminary for daughters of the nobility. To them the October days seemed as long ago as the fall of the Bastille. They had finished their two years in the Red Army and were studying to be teachers. It took a definite effort for them to imagine how things must be in the capitalist world outside. Our routine questions about freedom of opinion and the economic position of the peasants didn't interest them. It wasn't that they didn't care about these things, it was that their approach was from an entirely different side. For us October, Smolny, Lenin were in the future; for them they were the basis of all habits, ideas, schemes of life. It was as hard for them to imagine a time when Marxism had not been a rule of conduct as it would be for an American high school kid to doubt the desirability of the open shop or the Monroe Doctrine.

"Why," they kept asking us, "why can't they understand what we are trying to do, why can't the workers in America understand that we are building socialism, why can't the workers in England realize that we are working for them as much as for ourselves?"

Proletari

In the restaurant run by the cooperative "Proletari" you could get a dinner, consisting of a vast bowl of cabbage soup with meat in it and a plate of meat with vegetables, for forty kopeks. The waitress was a large melancholy woman who spoke French. Her husband had been a chef in aristocratic families and restaurants; she had lived in France. She was not enthusiastic about the way things were going, life was raw and grey and there were no more little elegances to make things plausible. You didn't have to work so hard; as a worker, she admitted, she had all the privileges, but the revolution had shattered all her dreams. She and her husband had been saving up, they wanted to open a small restaurant all their own, to cater to a purely distinguished clientele, strictly French cuisine, everything cooked with butter. They would have made it a success, she knew, they would have made money, and have had a little house in the European style. She'd never liked to live slapdash the way the Russians do, she was at heart a European. There were tears in her eyes when she took away the plates. When she came back with the stewed fruit and tea, she said: "I don't want you to think I'm against the revolution. It was necessary, but it's very hard."

Peter the Great

The man who was taking us round town that evening was the son of a rich man. He had joined the red guards and fought with them all through the October days. Later he had been head of a division in the Red Army through the civil war. He had gotten into trouble somehow, been expelled from the communist party and spent a year in jail. People told me afterwards that he wrote first rate poetry. He called himself, jokingly, a counterrevolutionary. He spoke English.

He showed us the great square where the monument to the October dead was and told us how it had been made on one of Lenin's Saturday Afternoons, when bunches of soldiers and factory workers would tackle some particularly unsightly corner of the city and dig it up into a park. He told us a little wistfully about the enthusiasms and comradeliness of those days. He showed us the streets where he had fought eleven years ago, the place where they'd held the barricade against a desperate attack from the cadets, squares where the red guards had camped for the night, houses they had taken shelter in. Maybe he almost wished things still were as they had been eleven, eight, six years ago, when it was still possible to kill and be killed for the revolution, and politics was as simple as the mechanism of a machine gun.

We came out on the bank of the Neva. It was about twelve. You could still see things dimly in a faint milky twilight. The stately palaces along the Neva, the spires of the Peter and Paul fortress, the wide bridges, the icy clear grey swift flowing river must have looked about the same as they looked to Pushkin a hundred years ago. We walked down the embankment until we came to a small park. A young man and a girl sat on a bench talking low. At the end of the park on a base of granite rock was a statue, a huge black mass rearing into the pale night, a man on a prancing horse. The man who had been showing us around pointed to it: "There's my favorite Russian in history," he said, "Peter the Great, who brought order out of chaos, the first Bolshevik."

Peterhof

When we got off the Ford bus at Peterhof a drunken man who said he was a chauffeur offered to show us the way to the palaces of the Empress Catherine. He tried to talk sensibly, there were things he wanted to know about Detroit, about the Taylor plan, but he was too drunk and had to submit to being led away by a little boy, probably his son, who tagged along at his heels. We walked off through dripping gardens full of fountains, eternally autumnal like some place in a story by Hans Andersen, along the edge of the grey sea and the grey sky of the Baltic. At the end of every vista one way was the sea, the other way a spouting fountain. Then we came to eighteenth century palaces in red brick. Inside you had to put on slippers over your shoes and walk through acre after acre of state apartments.

After a mile and a half of royal furniture we managed to get out through a side door, and went walking for a long time down a muddy country road and fell in with a man who told us to go to see the local rest house run by the Leningrad Trade Union Council. That was an immense gawky fakegothic building that had been the royal stables. In two directions enormous parks formed a backyard for the Leningrad workers.

One of the doctors in charge showed us around and set us up to an uncommonly good dinner. He was so wrapped up in his work he could talk of nothing else. He wasn't a party member, but he had no private practice, he never had time.

After dinner we saw the show gotten up by one two weeks' batch as it was leaving, to entertain the newcomers. There were musical numbers and recitations and a little farce about a mixup among people in the doctor's waiting room, and a physical culture expert made a speech suggesting that people ought to sleep with their windows open. This was too much for the audience that had eighteenth century ideas about the dangers of the night air, and he was howled off the platform. Then the doctor explained his aims and methods of work and was received with cheers for he was evidently very popular.

When we walked down to the station to catch the last train back to Leningrad, the responsible director of the institution walked part way with us. He was a big quietfaced man with grey hair who had been a baker before the revolution. He walked with big strides beside us, asking timidly what we thought of it, whether it was clean, whether we thought the food was good, whether we thought the people looked as if they were having a good time. Then he asked us to excuse him as there was still work to do (he worked eighteen hours a day), embraced Kittin, shook hands with me and left us.

Extinct Volcano

It still stays dusk all night. The nearest thing to darkness is a dense bluish gloaming between eleven and two. Not that the days are very bright either; occasionally there's a patch of sun, but mostly a low ceiling of grey cloud weighs on the long Italianate façades that stretch infinitely into the drizzle on either side of broad wornout cobbled streets. There's something gutted and gone about the city, it has the feeling of the ruins of a great setpiece the morning after the fireworks. We wander about, we talk to people, we ask questions. I'm weary all the time trying to hack my way through the dark magnificent thicket of the Russian language.

At the building of the Leningrad Soviet, that used to be the duma and before that a nobleman's palace, we talk to the doorkeeper, an aged party with manners of the old régime. He's had the job since 1906. He's not impressed by the hoarse statements of political leaders, not all human progress makes up to him the shine on a state carriage, and the coachman's hat, and the sleek cruppers of a pair of fat bays.

We take the train to a suburban station in a firwood. The framehouses scattered among trees and neglected gardens are like the houses in an American residential section of twenty-five years ago, except that the paint has worn off them. The critic my friend is taking me to see is a very charming man. His English is very good. He asks us to take tea and strawberries with him. (The Leningrad strawberries are the size of peaches and have as much taste as wild strawberries. Queen Victoria and the Kaiser William considered them the best in the world. Dear Nicky used to ship them to his relatives in

Germany and England every summer.) The critic is a man of humanity, refinement, real humor; he knows a great deal. Somehow he missed the red train that left one November. Other friends and associates of his, who also missed it, were able to catch it at stations further down the line. He was left where he stood eleven years ago. He asks with that timid feverish interest all Russians seem to feel, about the world across the Frontier. It's hard to explain how fast Europe is crumbling away, leaving a dreary madhouse instead of those pleasant parks where people talked about Verlaine as they let the foam settle on their beer, and those watering places where even the almost poor could live genially and idly. Life is hard for those who have lost the train; the authorities don't let them publish what they want, the Gaypayoo nags their relatives and children; they never know when they are going to be arrested or exiled. Still, he says, in the long run, it's better now for a writer than under the czar, at least you can argue with these censors, they give you reasons, they listen to what you have to say. In the old days you might as well try to argue with a gorilla as with the czar's police.

A long trolley ride takes you out to Red Putilov where you're shown through the locomotive works. There everybody you talk to is lively and hopeful, talks about studying engineering, literature, languages; it's more like going through a college than a mill. And across the road in towards the city rows on rows of new interesting looking comfortable white dwellings are going up. "The ground is levelled and dug out for the foundations," says the mechanic who knows French. "Now we're starting to build. That's how it's done."

In the evening the café under the Europskaya Hotel seems a great relief. Here's something a guy doesn't have to cudgel his wits to understand. It's like Europe, it's like the East Side of New York. Beer, jingly music, white tablecloths, shoddy whores. You can give your order to the waiter and he politely brings you a breaded cutlet. There are business men at the tables, tricky-looking articles who will assist you to buy a genuine antique ikon or a young lady's recumbent halfhour. There are speculators who will change your dollars for rubles in the black market. It's the kingdom of money again, the blessed land of valuta. After a while the nightlife begins to get a stale look, the beer begins to taste sour; best thing to do's to go to bed. It's too drearily obvious that the café's a grimy microcosm of the capitalist world across the Frontier, too obvious to be funny even. I'm no Y.M.C.A. secretary, but Red Putilov has somehow taken the edge off it. When I ask my Russian friends about it they laugh and say, "That's the underworld. The police let that place stay open so that they can always know where the criminals are when they want to put their hands on them."

Friends take us to the Aquarium, a center of businessmen's whoopee under the old régime. Now it's a movingpicture studio. Trauberg is directing a picture about the Paris Commune. It's entertaining there, women in Empress Eugenie dresses and men in sidewhiskers dancing the cancan under the glaring spotlights, the sort of place you'd pay money to go to back home, the 1870 costumes don't seem any more antiquated than many things you remember from the world across the Frontier. Why there's a good lively joint, you say to yourself, then it suddenly comes to you that it's all a show, that it's not happening at all, it's a movie studio. That's probably why, among antediluvians, actors are the happiest.

When the studio closes up, the directors and some of the actors take the visitors home to a little party. A small Valhalla of smoked and pickled fishes has been laid out, there's a samovar and vodka and warmly modulated talk in several languages. You don't have to understand more than one word in ten to feel the vivid and sometimes scary freedom of the Russian mind. On this side of the Frontier a man may live on potatoes and sour bread but he lives in a real world. If he puts up some stage scenery to keep the wind of too enormous spaces off him, he knows it's stage scenery because he had to paint it himself. People lie in the Soviet Union like any place else, but, in this primeval landscape swept clean of all the instituted lies-by-common-consent, a man damn well knows when he's lying and when he's telling the truth. Living in reality is a strain the human race has always done its best to avoid, so it is not surprising that Russians come up to you and ask you wistfully if Wiesbaden is as pleasant as it used to be.

Anyway this evening the people we were with seemed happy. Their work was in itself a transition between the antediluvian world they were brought up in and the new world where so many older people, no matter how deeply they believe in it, tend to feel cold and lonely; so they could live, breathe, think without strain, and give the best work they had in them to what they were doing. In spite of the language I never spent a pleasanter evening. The visitors were toasted and tossed in a blanket (which is a compliment in these parts) and walked home to the hotel through the early glare of a Leningrad summer morning. Peasantwomen in shawls were selling strawberries along the Nevsky.

Walking round Leningrad I have all the time the feeling that I'm walking around in the burntout crater of a volcano. Things I've read about it, Dostoyevski's St. Petersburg, and the Petrograd of Jack Reed's and Ransome's despatches still are more vivid in my mind than this huge empty city full of great handsome buildings (we'd call them Georgian or Colonial) that exaggerate as through a megaphone the last words of Vitruvian architecture. No town can make so much history as has been made by the city of Peter and Lenin and not wear itself out, I suppose. Still I kept wishing I'd been there eleven years before. When Kittin and I took the sleeper to Moscow it was once again like going to bed to wake up a few years forward in the future.

3. BETWEEN THE TWO ROADS

The Caspian

The trip down the Volga had been restful to a degree; the wide green river; the silver onion domes of the old monasteries; the ramshackle towns with names full of literature, Nijni, Samara, Kazan; the quiet breakfasts of caviar, black bread and tea; the almost wordless conversations with the other passengers; the continual dreary association with Mr. Hugo's Russian Made Easy and the attempt to read in paroosky a life of Jack London for children, had made five days go gradually jerkily by. The one eventful moment had been climbing flights and flights of wooden steps up a bluff one black night in the rain to walk for an hour around the muddy streets of

the town where Lenin was born; there was something about
the way the raw wooden steps and the board walks resounded
underfoot, something about the smell of the river and mudflats in the rain, that brought up a town on a bluff on the
Mississippi so vividly it couldn't be shaken off. Nothing foreign about Lenin.

Rarin' to go, the Amerikanski found himself in Astrakhan
with a day to waste, somewhat shaken by the discovery that
Astrakhan is as far from the Caspian as New Orleans is from
the Gulf of Mexico; the effort to get something out of Astrakhan resulted in a great deal of walking and sweating in the
sizzling sun and a thick coating of silty dust in the eyes, nose,
ears and mouth. The summer night had come on comfortably
black and the Amerikanski was beginning to worry about the
bed he'd have to sleep in at the morguelike empty hotel,
when a man walking past him on the sidewalk asked him
where he was going, in English.

He was a youngish man in the uniform of a ship's officer
who had once spent six months in England, he was mate of a
steamboat anchored down at the eightfathom anchorage. He
took me, and a silent and soiled young man he had with him,
into a joint to have a drink. The joint was a sort of little cook-
shop full of a smell of rancid muttonfat and droning with big
old drowsy flies. From somewhere a bottle of vodka was procured. The joint was as sordid as a speakeasy in Redhook. A
grumpy and unclean Tatar presided over it. The man who
spoke English was a Pole. He was on the verge of suicide, he
said. All his life as a youngster he'd dreamed of going to sea,
of seeing all the ports in the world, talking all the languages,
of seeing in what varied colors and shapes men and women
were produced. Now he was a navigating officer all right, but
where? I allowed that the Caspian might be an interesting sea
and that Astrakhan was full of people in assorted shapes and
colors. He said I'd never seen it or I wouldn't speak so foolishly, it wasn't a sea, it was a dreary trough full of slime.
Think of the horrible fate of a new wellbuilt steamer being
launched into the Caspian, what future did it have in store?
The Caspian was a prison, it smelt like a purge, like Epsom
salts, where could a boat go if it got its start in the Caspian?
Why the northern part was so shallow half the time you

couldn't get near the ports and had to load and unload five miles out, out of sight of land. What was the use of keeping a boat in good shape if you never went into port? Steamers rotted and rusted if there were never any new ports to go to. "And I myself rot and rust. I dream of a great red merchant marine. If I were not a red I would go back to Poland; I am not a communist but I am a red . . . but how can great navigators come out of the Caspian? The Caspian Sea is one of nature's mistakes."

When the vodka was finished the Tatar closed up his place (the flies had all gone to sleep on the ceiling) and threw us out. The last I saw of the disappointed seafarer he was going along the wide dark empty street in search of more to drink and calling back to me over his shoulder, "Perhaps tonight I shall kill myself . . . no hope for a seaman on this bloody Caspian Sea."

The Caucasus

It turned out that the Caspian did smell like Epsom salts and that the anchorage where you changed from the riverboat to the seagoing steamer was out of sight of land; what the seafaring Pole hadn't mentioned was the swell, a huge black endless tarry swell in which the incredibly rusty stinking and delapidated whaleback (a little like the oldstyle Great Lakes wheatboats) rolled soddenly like a log. Every family had brought a chamberpot to be sick in; the set of Levantine oddlots (people of all colors and shapes), Armenians, Adjerbeidjan Turks, Tatars, Georgians, Kalmuks, Persians and the few pale Russians, vomited continually from the time they set foot on the boat till we tied up at the dock at Makhach Kala next day, and their cousins and aunts vomited, and their wives and children vomited. I shared a cabin with two bearded gents who spoke less Russian than I did and who lay groaning all night in the opposite bunk. They had filled the cabin with watermelons that bounded around in the rolling like cannonballs.

At Makhach Kala I looked up at the mountains; it was like being in another planet; nobody spoke any language I'd ever heard of; nobody belonged to any nation or race I'd ever heard of; it was Daghestan. From the train, where a compartment full of Russians, deliriously pleased to be on their vacations, were talking what seemed by comparison to me my native tongue (at least I knew what it was), I caught sight, with my hands and mouth full of the beautiful seedless green grapes of the region, amid a volley of vots and khawrashaws and krasivies, of the great blue and white snowy range of the Caucasus.

At Grozny I found that the bunch I'd hoped to meet had already gone up into the mountains. Next day after a feverish morning spent in trying to rent a car a cab a horse a guide, anything to get started with, and being told that the mountains were too far, too high, too lonely, too dangerous; that there were white guard brigands in the passes; that the road was impassable; that the bridges were down, I ran into a Russian engineer who was on a similar quest and together we induced a cabdriver, after having invoked everything from the secretary of the revcom to American dollars and the onward march of the world proletariat, to take us. As the shadows grew long and the evening purpled into dusk we drove up a broad wooded valley that got deeper and narrower as it cut into the first wooded range of the high mountains. Every verst the country was vaster and emptier. It was dark when we reached the village amid the barking of fierce white sheepdogs as large as St. Bernards. As I stepped into the light of the schoolhouse where the exploring party was settled for the night one of these Caucasian sheepdogs tried to take a nip out of the calf of my leg, but all he got was a mouthful of woolly puttee.

Next day we started off on scraggly ponies with a guide. We rode for two weeks through the mountains through a country as varied as the southern Pyrenees, as gigantic in scale as Mexico, over pass after pass, over cold uplands and into deep hot valleys. The rivers were spanned by ancient swinging bridges of logs built on the cantilever principle. The villages were incredibly varied in architecture; the country had such a variety of races and languages that the guides would never go more than a couple of days with us, or three at the most. The last day the guide usually had to find an interpreter to ask the way.

In Botlikh they had the best pears in the world. On the steep trail down we met an old man who'd never heard of

Moscow or America. The president of the revcom put on a dance for us that night. The girls wore long flaring black dresses with long flaring sleeves, tight at the wrist, and mediæval wimples. In the dance they whirled around the room like tops, the dresses spreading out bellshape so that you couldn't see their feet.

In other places we found villages of Mohammedans who'd been converted from Judaism, villages of Jews converted from Mohammedanism, villages of great stone houses where the people were said to be Jews from the time of the Babylonian captivity. We rode all day and ate cornbread and occasionally some eggs or a little mutton. At night, when it wasn't too cold we slept on roofs or in the porches of the houses; one night we slept in the rain very high on a misty pasture full of tinkling sheep. The rawwool blankets and coats of the Caucasus are so greasy that even after hours the rain doesn't penetrate. After that we rode all morning along a steep hogback with the mist thick as milk on either side. A man we rode with showed us a lake where two shepherds and their dogs and three thousand sheep had been drowned a few weeks before. The sheep had started running down the steep slope and the dog and the shepherds had cut in in front of them to try to turn them and had been carried along with them into the lake. On the last and highest pass, where we had to haul the ponies behind us by their bridles through the sunrotted snow, we saw a flock of ibex that sniffed at us for a second, laid their horns back on their shoulders and were gone along the high shaly ridge. Going down the steep valleys into Adjerbeidjan the clay of the trail had been here and there undercut by the torrent; we rode through huge cedars and cypresses, the landscape under a thundery lowering sky was like a Japanese print. We hurried to escape the rain in the dangerous gorge.

It was a relief to be alone on the cosily rumbling train again. The names of the villages and their languages had been too hard to pronounce, the geography too intricate to keep in my head, the people and the houses too oddlooking, the sense of timelessness too nerveracking; by the time I'd reached the big station at Tiflis I was forgetting where I'd been. I could only remember that all one day we'd followed the winding cañon of a river, the path veering in some places under caves and natural bridges, and that the water of the river was salt as the sea.

The villany you taught me . . .

The bus stopped at an inn for lunch before crossing the highest pass on the Georgian road. The stoutish gentleman with a beard was a technician, what kind he didn't say. He spoke some English and some French and too much German. He asked me to sit at the table with him and ordered my lunch for me. He looked at me severely through his nose-glasses over the bortsch. "Of course," he said, "you have invented the best industrial technique in the world . . . Taylor, Ford, Firestone. . . . There has never been anything like it in history." I bashfully assented that there never had. "But in your hands," he pointed at me with his spoon, "it can only lead to disaster . . . a period of horror for the human race such as has never been seen in history." I agreed that we were in for a period of horror, but that perhaps it was not entirely our fault. "It is the fault of the capitalist system and the plundermadness of the business men. . . . But you Americans are to blame. . . . You have no feudalism, you boast of being free, you should have gotten control of the system during the lifetime of Marx. . . . But we are learning your system. . . . It is like arithmetic, once it is invented anybody can learn it. What did your Shakespeare say? *The villany you taught me I shall execute.*" "Then there's something about better the instruction," I said hurriedly, relieved to be on what seemed that non-controversial ground so popular with magazine editors at home.

He was quiet for a moment. We were eating a hard local goaty cheese with butterbrod. He swallowed and cleared his throat. "Shakespeare," he shouted. "You have no right to Shakespeare. He belongs to the civilized world. He belongs to us because we understand him, we love him." I tried to put in a word for American taste for writing. After all our classics were built on a Shakespeare base, look at our oratory. The glasses danced on his nose. "It is nothing," he said. "I have read your Upton Sinclair Lewis. It has no soul. The soul of America is in industrial technique."

It was time for the bus to go. We were each trying to get outside of a glass of boiling hot tea so we couldn't talk any more. He insisted on paying for my lunch. As we settled back into our seats in the bus, he turned to me fiercely. "And tell me meester, why are you so cruel to the Negroes?" "That will take a lot of explaining," I said, but the bus rattled so and the low gear made such a racket climbing the winding road to the pass that it drowned out anything I could say.

From the Georgian Road to the Mamison Pass

The inn in the little alp on the north side of the divide was like an inn in Gogol. The samovar was shining, the food was good, there were curtains in the windows; it was pleasant after the hard beds made of boards at Kasbek. Coming up we'd walked through the grassy valley and bathed in a sodawater spring that made your whole body tingle as it dried in the sun afterwards. After that we had stretched out our legs, breathed the incredibly sweet upland air and walked happily. The little inn, the hot tasty cornbread, the good butter, the flowered teapot sitting so fragrant on top of the samovar, the cosy accustomed feeling of the past, of things read of in books, was like oil on chapped knuckles after the days of riding, the raw braincudgelling country, where everything was too old or too new. It would have been pleasant to spend the night there, but we'd already hired the Terrible Turk and his cart to take us to Zaramag on the Ossetine road.

The cart consisted of four wheels and a couple of boards laid between the axles that you sat on with your feet dangling. The road west up the valley south of the great buttressed snowy mass of Kasbek mountain was very stony indeed, so it was more comfortable to walk ahead and let the two young Russians from Leningrad ride on the cart. The valley wound between enormous ranges. The brook in the bottom of it was yellow with sulphur deposits, every now and then a hot spring sent up a column of steam; the air was full of mineral smells. The afternoon was wearing on; no signs of Zaramag, a village we'd found on the map and that we'd decided must be on the Ossetine road. In Kasbek nobody had been able to tell us how far it was to Zaramag, whether there was any road to it, whether it was best to go there in a cart on horseback or on foot. But the Terrible Turk had claimed he could take us there.

Towards evening we came to a village of cubical houses linked together with walls and turrets. We were dropping into the eleventh century. Was it Zaramag? The Terrible Turk didn't seem to know, the people in the village didn't seem to understand what we wanted. By the time they'd gotten us some extraordinarily tough muttonscraps to eat, it was night, and we'd understood that the village wasn't Zaramag. To go to Zaramag you had to cross a high pass, you could go on foot or with horses. The Terrible Turk said he was frightened, he was too far from home; he began to ask big money, so next morning the cart, and the Russians, who had discovered they wanted to be in Tiflis right away, turned back. The doctor and I rented horses from the son of the head man in the village and pushed on.

We passed walled village after walled village with small ogival gates, crenellated castles on hills. Century after century dropped away from us. We crossed a steep shaly pass that brought us face to face with a ring of huge silent snowpeaks, we wandered through a maze of high valleys, we crossed a divide and came down into a broad stream lined with trees. At dusk we got to a goodsized village. Was it Zaramag?

The guide shook his head. We would spend the night there in the house of a widow who was a relative of his. Next day it would be easy to walk to Zaramag. How about riding? He shook his head. He had never been to Zaramag, he couldn't take the horses any further, his father would be missing him, he must go back that night. So we slept in the house of the widow and next day we set out with our packs on our backs. We were told to follow the valley until the river ran into a bigger stream. There we'd find Zaramag. And sure enough we found it in the early afternoon in the middle of a brisk rainstorm. The schoolteacher put us up in the schoolhouse (turned into a tourist depot for the summer) and lent us a gasoline stove. Unfortunately he said he had nothing he could give us to eat. This matter of eating was a sore subject. As far as we could find out, nobody was eating that day, or any of the days of our travels. At the widow's house we hadn't even been able to get hot water for tea. It was explained that it was the custom only to light a fire once a day. At Zaramag we found nothing but five eggs and some very old sweet crackers. We bought the five eggs and boiled them when we made tea. They were fine eggs and very appetizing. Then as we were curling up for a nap, the officials of the village came to see us. We had for a moment a mad hope they'd come to invite us to dinner, but they had come to explain for us the mineral wealth of Zaramag and the vicinity. They brought us a list of ore deposits susceptible of development. There was copper and lead and zinc, and various mineral waters. Would we like to go out and see the deposits so that we could write about them in the foreign press? Zaramag had a great future as a mining center, but they had to have mining engineers. Perhaps we were mining engineers. We said no we weren't mining engineers, what we were was tired and very hungry. When the road was repaired, they said, and the mines were open, there would be restaurants and resthouses. It would become a magnificent restcenter too. It was dark when they went away.

Next day was clear. With our packs in a small twowheeled springless cart, we started up the Mamison Pass on an empty stomach. At a sodawater spring below the road we met a carter who spoke English. He was an Ossetine, a very cheerful man, he had been in Canada, and in the Yukon goldrush and now he was back driving a cartload of wheat over the pass to Vladykavkass. No he hadn't brought back any gold, but it was just as well what with the revolution. He was a fine man, I should have liked to have talked to him more, but we were going in different directions.

On top of the pass we got one of the most magnificent views in the world over the valleys of Georgia, and, what was more surprising, a magnificent dinner of mutton soup, cooked up by an old man who kept a resthouse for carters and muledrivers. By evening we were hungrier than ever, trying to reach the market town of Oni. What we reached was a village we didn't know the name of where we had to sleep supperless on the floor (due to fear of the bed the family had kindly vacated for us) of a new frame house. Next day at the crack of dawn we started on in another little cart behind a fat pony, and rattled down another valley through wooded country full of cedars, bouncing over treeroots and boulders along the banks of a clear splashing river that looked like a trout-stream. After noon we got to Oni, where there was a cleanish hotel and a restaurant where they had more than one thing. It was hot in Oni, we stayed there a couple of days, bathing in the river and sunning ourselves and eating pilaf and shash-lik and drinking the Georgian wine. A bus took us to Kutaïs, a stucco town with cypresses and tiled roofs that looked like Italy. The rooms at the Hôtel de France weren't so bad and it had a lovely garden, but there was no way of escaping the reek of the all too centrally located water closet, that was something to write home about. Kutaïs was very gay. A band played in the park, there were dramatic performances and red flags everywhere. But the fact that everything took place in Georgian made it hard to figure out what was going on.

I sat that night alone in an untidy restaurant, full of food at last but full, too full, of braincudgelling impressions. Was the poverty and desolation the ground being cleared for future building, or was it just the result of oldfashioned ignorant centralized oppression? Were the Georgians inveterate small proprietors or was it just the two or three innkeepers I'd car-ried on painfully inadequate conversations with? Were the Ossetines procommunist because they were poor or because they were intelligent, and what were all the people the names of whose languages I didn't know? Was this waiter with a dirty apron happier now than under the czar? Was he a better waiter, a better citizen, more socially minded, did he have more chance to study languages (it was French he wanted to speak), play checkers, make love to his wife, raise clean healthy brighteyed children? How can you answer these ques-tions when you don't know the names of the birds or the rivers, when you can't speak the languages or make out the al-phabets, when you've lost the slip of paper where you noted down the names of the villages and the mountainpasses?

I had several glasses of wine with a sallowfaced man with large treacherous eyes who seemed interested to know who I was, where I came from. What could I tell him? We struggled for a long time in a tangle of incomprehension. When we fell back on slogans we could drink our wine and be happy. You can always shout Hooray for our side and feel fine. But sup-pose you feel a slogan can only be used once, suppose you

want to know what's in the package under the label? And
where are you going to get your information? Where are the
facts, how do you know them when you run into them? Is a
fact a town or is it a road or is it a mountainpass, or is it a
child or a man or a woman that needs to eat or to drink and
to wear clothes and to know the way and to love and be loved
and be happy? It's not that foreign languages are hard to understand, it's that language is hard to understand. My companion accompanied me, full of questions, to the door of my
hotel. I hope he was satisfied.

Walking to my room I had to struggle through the tremendous reek of the waterless closet. Stink is a fact, the same to
an Eskimo as to an Andaman Islander or a banker from Mil-
waukee. Write that down, cable that home to Mr. Newswriter.
But who made the stink? The Soviets or the old inveterate
Adam?

Next day leaving Kutaïs unsolved, the Amerikanski Peesatyel
took the train to Baku. Baku is an oil town, a new town, maybe
that'll be simpler, more like home. But speaking of home, how
much do you know about home, Mr. A. Peesatyel?

4. SOME SLEETY NIGHTS ROUND MOSCOW

The Great Switchboard

There are traces of other Moscows still to be seen under this
tremendous November Moscow of our day, humming overcrowded city that is the key switchboard to which all the wires
lead that hold together the forces that are building socialism
over one sixth of the world. Of course there is the startling remnant of the Red Square and the very visible and operatic mediæval shell of the Kremlin that brings to your mind the music of
Boris and Khovanchina, but beyond that, across the river
stretches a less showy region of streets of eighteenth and nineteenth century merchants' houses, the Moscow of Ostrovsky's
plays, Zamoskvarekya. These streets have a particularly desolate
and forlorn appearance but there still lingers in them a faint
flavor of the life of the counting houses in the days when the
Russian businessmen, for all their bushy whiskers and their aba-

cuses, were getting rich fast and easily. I don't know why they should have attracted me (perhaps because the life in them had resembled so much American life) but I seemed to feel their imprint in walking round the city more than that of the ferocious furlined boyars who built the Kremlin. Not that the merchants were any less ferocious than the boyars or that I've ever personally felt very deeply for the heady excitement of buying cheap and selling dear to which their lives were dedicated; maybe it's that the hope of something for nothing is in the American blood. You can still see the last remnants of these businessmen in the old markets, where, trodden underfoot by the new order, always at the risk of being nabbed as speculators, they still manage to find a few odds and ends to haggle and chaffer over. Another place you see them is in the beerrestaurants and in the café near the postoffice where the gypsies sing at night. They sit there in their leather jackets with their beady eyes and predatory faces, a crumpled cartoon of the bankpresidents and realestate agents and bondsalesmen and speculators for whose benefit the game is always rigged at home. Here these people make up the down and out disinherited and criminal class. Penal institutions reform some of them, they say.

The people not even the revolution seems able to reform are the gypsies. They sing and strum for the moneyless debris of the businessman's world with the same passionless aloof enthusiasm with which they strummed and sang for rich drunken landowners and sentimental barflies in the old days. In one café we had a talk with an old gypsy. The man I was with wanted to get up an oldfashioned entertainment for me at some place outside of town where the gypsies lived. For some reason the authorities at that time frowned on such performances. The gypsy was an old fellow with a scarred tobaccocolored face and a bawdily twinkling eye and the manners of an oldfashioned diplomat. I couldn't follow very well what was being said. The gypsies wanted to go away. There were no more gentry to pay for entertainments. The government kept interfering with them, trying to induce the young men to work in factories. Soon they would move away to Rumania. The gypsies were very poor. They could put on a singing and dancing show but it would be very dangerous. The sum of a hundred rubles was mentioned. As no one wanted to put up the hundred rubles the matter was dropped. The old man left us, saying with a bow, that he would think of the problem. With wisdom things could always be arranged. He would be glad to talk with us again when we cared to bring the matter up.

The most grotesquely irrelevant of all Moscows is the Moscow of the hotels where a rather threadbare reflection of luxurious bourgeois life is kept up for the benefit of tourists and foreign experts and the still ruling businessmen of other countries. In the Grand Hotel there is not only jazz music, nightlife and course dinners, but it is possible to see a roomful of American newspapermen with a hush of awe in their voices politely trying to pump out of Ivy Lee the lowdown on the latest plans of the Tsik. Here the life of the foreign correspondents goes on like life in a besieged city. Not that some of them haven't considerable sympathy for the besiegers, but they are all afraid that they'll catch bolshevism and have to rearrange their lives. They come, they say, to get the news, but they can't really get the news because the news is socialism and that's propaganda, so they buy furs and fake ikons and listen to the grim pathetic stories of the disinherited and of the intellectuals who found themselves in the wrong camp during the civil war, and the pressure of dread grows on them day by day, and they live counting the days until they can get out across the Frontier, away from the crushing imminence of change. It's not funny to be in the camp of the enemy in the middle of a major engagement.

But the Moscow of now, the Moscow of today, the Moscow of the new order, how can you get hold of it? I can't do anything about it. I hear the tramp of it under my window every morning when the Red Army soldiers pass with their deep throaty singing, I see it in the kindergarten I sometimes go to see that's so far away at the end of a trolley line, I see it most among the youngsters who run the Sanitary Propaganda Theatre where Alexandra directs the plays, energy, enthusiasm, selfeffacement (it's not at all like the Y.M.C.A.) and that fervid curiosity and breadth of interest that is the magnificent earmark of the Russian mind. I see it in the communist friends I make who are all the time working, arguing, organizing, teaching, doing office work and who, no matter how pale and haggard from overwork they are when they come home to those late afternoon Moscow dinners, are always ready to talk, explain, ask questions. But an onlooker in Moscow is about as out of place as he would be in the assembly line of a Ford plant. If you are an engineer or a mechanic or a schoolteacher you can do something but if you're a writer you're merely in the unenviable position of standing round and watching other people do the work.

Well you're a reporter, you tell yourself. You're gathering impressions. What the hell good are impressions? About as valuable as picture postalcards or the little souvenir knickknacks people who'd been on trips used to bring home to set in rows on the glass shelves of the parlor cabinet. Worthwhile writing is made of knowledge, feelings that have been trained into the muscles, sights, sounds, tastes, shudders that have been driven down into your bones by grim repetition, the modulations of the language you were raised to talk. It's silly to try to report impressions about Moscow; you can stay there and work or you can go home and work.

That's why the best thing to do if you're in Moscow is to go to the theatre. Here's as much as you can digest at a sitting put into digestible form. Not knowing the language is hardly a barrier at all. You can look at the stage all the better for not following all the lines. You can look at the audience. You are part of the audience.

Moscow: 7 P.M.

A New York theatre is a large, too fancylooking building put up on a realestate speculation for the purpose of getting people to pay more than they can afford to come in and sit in the dark to see actors moving round on a stage (lit brightly or bluely according as the production aims for the box office or for "art"), saying lines they've learned off typewritten sheets without knowing what the play's about, making gestures taught them by a director with jumpy nerves. A lot of expert electricians and stagehands change the lights and move round the scenery. Everybody except the technical staff and the audience is there on speculation, hoping against hope to cash in on the various forms of exhibitionism involved, to see their names in electric lights, to make a million dollars. The author, the director, the actors, the boxoffice man, the manager, the promoter who introduced the manager to the angel that put up the original capital, stagestruck girls, culturefuddled old women, ticket speculators, officeboys, playdoctors, scenedesigners, all think that this time they've matched the buffalo and will wake up famous and rich, or just rich, which is more important.

Underneath that there's a complex of needs and glamors not entirely connected with the dollar symbol. People want to be in the swim, to get out of their cubbyholes, to feel what others feel, to get vicariously sexual excitement, adventure, cocktails, money. They want to have others look at them with admiration and envy for having seen or written a good show, made money, spent money. It even occasionally happens that the writers, actors, scenedesigners, directors, have something on their chest they want to get rid of; the poor devils who pay their money at the box office want to be dragged out of themselves onto the gaudytawdry stage to feel themselves part of the imperial American procession towards more money, more varnish, more ritz, that obsesses all our lives.

In Moscow people go to the theatre to feel part of the victorious march through history of the world proletariat.

Most of the American critics who've been to Moscow enjoy coming home to report that the Russian theatre isn't any good, but they are wrong. What happens to them is this: in the first place, they're scared all the time they're in the Soviet Union by the thought that they are going to be caught and chopped up into mincemeat by the Gaypayoo. Then, they are flustered by the different living habits of the Russians; the show begins just about when the critic would ordinarily be eating dinner; if he didn't eat, he's hungry and if he did, it was probably in a hurry and he's getting a touch of indigestion. None of the audience is much dressed up; he wonders anxiously how often these dirty Russians bathe. The theatre building looks raw and crude, probably an old theatre stripped of its decorations, barny, painted in plain white or grey. He's worried.

The play begins without much formality; usually the house goes dark and the stage lights go on; bright nervous spotlights point out the action dogmatically, like the ferrule of a schoolteacher pointing out equations on a blackboard. Somebody's trying to translate for the American; he can't understand Russian or the translator's English very well. The American is worried for fear he's hearing propaganda and will be converted to communism without knowing it. The play lasts a long time, the intermissions are too long, the seats are hard; he misses the sense of luxury even the smallest movingpicture house gives him at home; he goes back to the hotel yawning and tired, afraid he may have picked up lice, and writes back to the folks at home that the Russian theatre is much overrated and that it's all bolshevik propaganda anyway.

These gentlemen are completely wrong. It ought to be obvious to anybody that while the American theatre is dying, the Russian theatre is at the beginning of a period of enormous growth. Historically they are of about the same age. Both of them branched off from the stem of the European stage towards the end of the eighteenth century. There is the difference that Russia got its influences direct from what was most lively in the French, German and Scandinavian theatres in the late nineteenth century, while in America we got the same influences strained through the respectabilities and the caponized Shakespeare tradition of the English stage. In Russia, as in America, moving pictures are a strong opponent, but in Russia the theatre doesn't seem to be giving any ground. Quite the contrary, every year more plays are acted, more theatres open up.

For one thing, each theatre organism has a permanent tradition behind it. Every Russian theatre has a corporate existence, like a college. Individual directors and policies come and go, the staff of actors changes a little from year to year, as does the repertory of plays, but the institution is an organism with a memory. Acting and directing are considered reputable professions requiring long conventional training. Workers in any particular theatre are signed up for a season at least; and they usually think of themselves as being permanently part of it. Since the October revolution everybody (in the left theatre at least) has some say in the policies, the choice of directors and plays. Contrary to the general impression, the revolution did not interrupt the tradition in many of the theatres. Naturally, existing in a new society has modified them, as it has modified the lives of individuals, but there has been no memoryless break with the past, such as every season brings to New York, where each batch of new speculators is profoundly ignorant (except for vague traditions, such as that *Ben Hur* was a hit) of what has been done before. In Moscow today you can still see audiences weep rivers at the Small Theatre (Maly Teatr) over the original productions of Ostrovsky's plays that were first put on in the eighties of the last century. At the Second Art Theatre (MXAT 2) they still occasionally do *The Cricket on the Hearth* in a sugary production that was popular in 1914. At the Vakhtangoff Theatre you can still see Vakhtangoff's original *La Princesse Turandot* that had such an influence on the whole European stage. At the Moscow Art (MXAT 1) they still do *The Blue Bird, The Lower Depths* and Ostrovsky's *Men of Heart* in productions that date back to the beginning of their existence. It's as if in New York you could still see *The Yellow Jacket* or *The Girl with the Green Eyes* or *In Old Kentucky* or a couple of Hoyt farces.

Another thing that insures the vitality of the Russian theatre is the opportunity for experiment offered by the subsidiary studios that shoot up around the roots of the big theatres. These studios are the germs of new theatres and at the same time the tryout grounds for new methods and ideas. It costs so little to run them that they are not dependent on the public, and there are so many of them that every conceivable line of ideas has a chance to get practical application.

Of course, it might as well be admitted right here that the Russian theatres are subsidized, like most of the important theatres of Europe. There is a central committee (Glavniskoostva) under the Department of Education that subsidizes theatres and turns over sums of money from time to time to studios and amateur club theatres that it considers deserving. There are theatres like the M.G.S.P.C. in Moscow that are subsidized by the Central Trade Union Councils. Then there are factory theatres, almost any organization is likely to run or sponsor a theatre. Before the revolution the theatres were supported by the government, or, as in the case of the Art Theatre, by a group of wealthy angels. American theatre people have a way of throwing up their hands and rolling their eyes heavenward at the mention of the word subsidy, but they ought to begin to realize that the theatre is not a business, at best it's a very poor business, from which big money can only be extracted by various sorts of sharp practice along the edges of it. Even in America, where more fortunes have been dug out by playwrights and managers and parasitic racketeers than in any other country, I doubt that if the industry was balanced up as a whole, and the entire capital invested compared with the profits, it would be found solvent at all.

The Russian theatre has never been a business; now more than ever it is thought of as a public service.

Terror

Englishmen who have lived many years in foreign countries get a crazy look in their eyes like the look in the eyes of Van Gogh's selfportraits. This man had asked me to come to see him. As soon as I came in he poured me out a glass of Kakhetian wine. It was good wine, a little like port; he apologized for the wine, said he had to take what he could get. His wife came in, a nervous, unhappylooking Russian woman. They both seemed nervous and uneasy. I sat looking at them, looking round the apartment. It was a small apartment crowded with furniture, oldfashioned heavy carefully polished mahogany furniture. The furniture was crowded in the room. It had evidently been made for much larger rooms. There was a great deal of Dresden china, and cutglass decanters on the sideboard. The things in the room looked huddled together like stuff saved from a fire. Everything was clean and polished but there was an air of hurry and dread about the way the things were arranged in the room. We sat there uneasily at the fine oval mahogany table while the wife fussed nervously about, coming in and out from the other room. It was evident that he wanted to tell me something and that the wife was trying to keep him from saying it.

All at once he started to talk: "I used to believe in them as you do," he said, "sometimes I still do, but most of the time it's a nightmare. I came here to work full of idealism because I believed in them, now I'd go away anywhere, but I can't make any money. They won't let her go out of the country. We don't dare make enquiries about leaving for fear they'll arrest her." "It can't be as bad as that," I started to say. He broke in and talked on and on. He hadn't believed in the terror either, but now he lived under it. She was a member of the old intelligentzia; there was nothing she could do to put herself right. They were doomed unless they could get out. After all let them stamp on the old nobles and the middleclass social revolutionaries if they got in their way, it was war, he could understand that; it was how they treated their own people . . . now it was the Trotzkyites, the old revolutionaries who had created the Soviet Union, friends and co-workers with Lenin; it was anybody who fell under the wheels. Did I know about Kronstadt? It was learning the truth about Kronstadt that had turned it all into a bitter nightmare for him. The sailors who revolted at Kronstadt were the men who had made the October days, among them were members of the crew of the *Aurora*, they were real revolutionaries but they were misled by crazy anarchists and S.R.'s, very likely there were paid English agents there too. There was no doubt that the revolt was a great danger. In Petrograd they got the wind up terribly. Undoubtedly it had to be suppressed. The loyal troops recaptured the fortress after fierce fighting. The sailors capitulated on terms. The Tcheka agents had run like rabbits at the first sign of danger. They didn't dare come back until three days after the troops had recaptured the place. But then the prisoners were turned over to the Tcheka, the Tchekists had many of them been members of the old Okhrana, czarists, sadists, perverts of every hideous kind—"there's no cruelty like Russian cruelty, not even Chinese. They butchered even the miserable prostitutes in the brothels of Kronstadt. Some of the Tcheka agents had with them copies of *Le Jardin des Supplices* written by that filthy Frenchman to use as a textbook when their imagination failed. It's a nightmare, I tell you."

I got to my feet a little dizzily. It was terror I'd seen in the man's eyes, in the huddle of the oldfashioned furniture moved into this choked apartment, in the woman's nervous step. I felt sick. I cleared my throat. "But the Tcheka's gone. . . . They had most of them shot. The terror is over."

"You can say that. . . . You can come and go when you please. It'll never be over for us till we die or they get us, unless we can get out. We are doomed. You know they always come at night. No arrests are ever seen. No one who sees them ever dares tell anyone. Nothing is ever known."

It was a relief to get out into the casual street, to look into everyday faces, to see the streetcars crowded with people coming home from the theatres, to feel the soft brush of snowflakes in my face. But that night I couldn't sleep on account of the man's creaking voice and the crazy look in his eyes, and the terrified huddle of the old middleclass mahogany furniture in that choked room.

The Story of the Persian Merchant and the Red Army Soldier

The country round Moscow looks like the rolling part of Wisconsin, only occasionally in a clearing you catch sight of a landlord's house, often with white Georgian columns like a southern plantation mansion, but usually on a bigger more princely scale. The mansions that weren't burned down by the peasants in the first flare of the revolution are now resthouses or schools or sanitariums. It was to one of these resthouses, the Writers', that I was being driven by an eightfoot grizzled izvoshchik when he asked me if I was a German. I said I was an American. "Americans are civilized but Germans are more civilized," he said. "Here in Russia what we need is more Germans. Now we have too much liberty. Every barefoot noaccount in the village thinks he's as good as the next man. There is no discipline, too much liberty. With liberty everything goes to hell. Hindenburg, he's what we need. He's a great man. But the young men now they do nothing but talk about liberty. That will not make a great nation. To become a great nation Russia should have a great man to put every man in his place, a man like Hindenburg."

The Writers' Resthouse was a frame building like a small American summer hotel. Behind it there were beeches and a scattered birchwood. If you get a bunch of writers together without any other kinds of people the effect is dreary in any country. Socialism doesn't seem to have made us any more entertaining as a class. Like the leech a writer is a varmint that can't get any sustenance from his own kind. Probably you can enjoy their company more when what they say is strained through the incomprehension of a foreign language. Of course you can't help getting to be friends with some of them; then you stop thinking of them as writers and it's all right.

A couple of Russian writers I had come to think of as friends took me for a walk through secondgrowth woods that made me think of Connecticut except for the terrible lead sky of Russia clamped down over our heads. The wet autumn leaves, the little patches of snow under the birchtrees, the brook and the little grassy glades all looked like home; but the smell of the fall was more sodden and colder. There was none of the flare and the excitement of the American autumn. As we walked they were telling me a story that had happened in Batum when one of them was working there: A Red Army soldier hurt himself working on the parallel bars in the gymnasium so that the doctors at the hospital thought it necessary to remove one of his testicles. The surgeon there was interested in experiments in glandular transplantation and just happened to have on hand an elderly Persian merchant who was suffering from impotence. So he transplanted some of the tissue removed from the Red Army soldier into the Persian merchant. When the Red Army soldier came to and heard about it he was extremely indignant. As soon as he got out of the hospital he hurried to the Gaypayoo and denounced the surgeon as a counterrevolutionary and demanded his immediate arrest. The Gaypayoo arrested the surgeon and demanded explanations. The surgeon insisted that he had performed a scientific experiment of great use to the state. The Red Army soldier stormed and said it wasn't the experiment he minded but it was having his proletarian tissue, and a very important type of tissue, being transplanted into the hide of a dirty bourgeois. The other doctors and technical workers in Batum went on strike and paraded in protest to the Gaypayoo, claiming that the liberty of scientific experiment was being infringed and demanded the surgeon's release. The whole town was in an uproar. There was a public trial at which it was brought out that the surgeon had received a large sum of money from the Persian merchant. Without the money it would have been science, with the money it was counterrevolution. So the surgeon was sentenced to jail, but as he was a very good surgeon and they needed him at the hospital he was soon let out. In spite of every effort of the Red Army soldier and the Gaypayoo the Persian merchant was nowhere to be found. He had slipped out of bed and vanished across the border. So the result of this counterrevolutionary experiment will never be known.

The Village

In Russian when you want to say you're going to the country you say you're going to the village. The village where I went to visit the parents of a friend was not very far from Moscow. The village straggles for a long way over the rolling plain. The houses are set out in rows a hundred or more feet apart and far back from the road. The houses are built of logs, thatched with bark, with smallpaned doublewindows. Inside, a huge stove, built of earth and plastered fills up the center of the house. Sometimes there are no partitions, but often the house is cut up into a series of small rooms in which the strapping people in their padded winter clothes crowd incongruously big. In the enormous plain, under the enormous sky, packed with the big hulking redcheeked men and women, the houses and everything in them look small as dollhouses. Back of each house there are outbuildings, a pigsty, a yard enclosed by a rail fence, a woodpile, a strip of garden or the beginning of a narrow field that stretches away out of sight over the next hill. If you're a guest or a foreigner the samovar starts to steam and you have to sit in the stuffy front room full of the fragrance of the tea and the sweetsickly smell of the charcoal, drinking tea and eating bread and butter and raspberry jam interspersed with little glasses of plum brandy. People talk with that same softvoiced innocence of manner and speech you find among farmers in outoftheway parts of the middle west. You feel that at last you're learning the truth.

It is a very simple truth. The village needs seed, clothing, agricultural implements, scientific knowledge about stockraising, poultryfarming and the care of children, a doctor and a schoolteacher, books, radios, contact with civilization, that heady enthusiastic participation in the march of human history that is being substituted for the calendar of saints, the ikons and the onion domes and the deep bearded voices of the churchsingers. The revolutionary bureaucracy needs grain, potatoes, cabbages, sunflower seeds, pork, support against reactionaries whose whole habit of life is buying cheap and selling dear, intelligent workers who will carry out the changing policies of the center, even helpful hardheaded criticism sometimes. We are Russia, we believe that the Communist Party will eventually benefit us, that the Communist Party is putting

us in the forefront of history. But it is not easy for the bureaucracy and the peasant to learn to work together. It is not
easy, but we will learn.

When my head was bursting with the stuffiness and the
smell of the charcoal and the maddening prismatic puzzle of
the Russian language I slipped out and walked away from the
house over the hill. It was dark and the sleet had made a light
crust on the snow. Overhead I could barely make out the low
even lid of clouds. In a few steps the tiny string of lights of
the village was lost in the snowy folds of the plain. The raw
wind threw an occasional handful of sleet in my face. Everywhere the endless northern plain at the beginning of night, at
the beginning of winter. No sense of locality; no ingrained
quaintness of ancient local histories and customs. It might be
Alberta or the Dakotas or Tasmania or Patagonia, any un-
trampled unfenced section of the earth's surface where men,
tortured by the teasing stings of hope, can strain every apprehension of the mind, every muscle of the body to lay the
foundations of a new order. It's a tremendous thing to walk
alone, even a short distance, at night at the beginning of winter over the Russian plains.

Moscow, December, 1928

III. Land of Great Volcanos

1. RELIEF MAP OF MEXICO

In the center holding up the bluebrittle changeless sky are the three tall volcanos, white at night, pink at sunset, Orizaba, Popocatepetl, Ixtaccihuatl. Only Popocatepetl smokes an everlasting cigar that greys the snow of his steep flanks with the falling ash. From the volcanos spread northward, patterned with endless checkerboards of maguey, the rimmed plains that are Anáhuac, the high valley, the core of Mexico.

Under the brittle cold sky, under the invariable sun, Mexico City stretches out its gridiron of streets, the green squares full of flowers, the low red vaults, and the towers leaning this way and that, of dusty colonial buildings. On the streets old men with spectacles, young girls, old women in shawls, barefoot children sell lottery tickets, candied cactus and sweetpotatoes, chiclets, cigarettes, lottery tickets, chiclets, lottery tickets, chiclets. In the stores the storekeepers, Gallegos, Catalans, Jews, Germans, Frenchmen, shake their heads over the morning paper. Business is bad, depressed, stagnant. In Sanborn's tearoom, drugstore, department store, citadel of Yanquilandia, travelling men from the States talk about bad business, scare each other with a new revolution every day, and at last apply to their hopes the healing balm of "eventually we'll intervene."

In the bar of the Regis the correspondents drink and talk about the power of Andrew Mellon, occasionally sniffing at the fire and brimstone that continually emanates from the American Embassy against all things Mexican from tacos to the labor laws.

Along the street shuffles an Indian in old wornout sandals, a dusty silent man in whitish rags, bowed under a crate he carries by a strap across his forehead. He walks with his eyes on the ground and says nothing. Politicians of all colors go by in pink limousines, purple roadsters, monogrammed speed cars.

"In Mexico more people die from worry than from bullets," a man said to me.

On the map you can see Mexico being pushed into the small end of the funnel of North America with the full weight of Yanquilandia crushing it down. It's like Poe's pit and pendulum, the pressure from the North increasing, increasing. And the silent Indian shuffling along bowed under the weight of exploited centuries.

"Mexico is a pyramid," a man said to me, "a pyramid under a piledriver. The top of the pyramid is Calles, strong enough to stand up under any impact, but under him are politicians and generals, some working and some looting, a squirming mass. Under them the masonry becomes firm again, more than a million organized workmen, the C.R.O.M. And at the bottom is the peon with his eyes on the ground."

The churches are open. You can still see country people on their knees painfully dragging themselves across the floor towards the Virgin Who Gives Help. In Guadalupe Hidalgo a child saw a Face in a treetrunk and they had to call out the fire department to clear the street. Masses and sacraments are bootlegged to the faithful for enormous sums in back rooms. In the hills that rim the valley there are merry men ready to slit throats and purses to the cry of *Viva Cristo Rey.* The *Cabelleros de Colón* are said to furnish them two pesos fifty a day and what they can pick up in the way of livestock from the country people. Saviors arise for the cross and the collection box. There was the Prince Pignatelli, last descendant of Cortés, duellist and fascist; he was rumored to be giving the warcry of *Ave Maria Purissima* in Oaxaca, but it turned out that he'd fled to Nicaragua leaving a trail of bad checks. There is the fighting Archbishop of Guadalajara supposed to have taken to the bush in Jalisco. There's a certain Capistran Garza, mighty man of valor before the Lord, who is panhandling American capitalists and the K. of C. and posting up proclamations in jerkwater Texas towns. There's the estimable Adolfo de la Huerta, president in Los Angeles. Then there were all the clericals netted by the police the other day at the archbishop's palace in Mexico City, along with two cursing American newspapermen. Against all that there is the Laborista Government, the C.R.O.M., bastard of the A. F. of L., but a pretty lively bastard, even its enemies will admit, certain syndicalist outfits, the agrarian associations, a few communists and the peon with his eyes on the ground.

Give a peon a gun and he becomes an *agrarista*, agricultural banks appear, cooperatives, rural schools. Give Juan Sin Tierra a gun and he becomes a small image of his murdered leader, Zapata.

Fifteen million Mexicans against a hundred and twenty million, of those fifteen million perhaps five hundred thousand are vagabonds, without visible means of support, two million are wild Indians in the hills. Ten million Mexican peasants and workmen, disunited, confused by political rows, sleeping on a straw mat on the floor, eating off a few tortillas a day and a speck of chile to take away the raw taste of the corn, standing up in their fields against the Catholic Church, against the two world groups of petroleum interests, against the inconceivably powerful financial bloody juggernaut of the Colossus of the North.

Which side are you on, on the side of the dollar, omnipotent god, or on the side of the silent dark man (he has lice, he drinks too much pulque when he can get it, he has spasms of sudden ferocious cruelty), Juan Sin Tierra, with his eyes on the ground?

Mexico, D. F., February, 1926

2. ZAPATA'S GHOST WALKS

Morelos

The State of Morelos (named after the revolutionary patriot, José Maria Morelos) with a population of 160,500 and an area of 7,184 sq. kilom., is bounded on the North by the Federal District, on the West and Northwest and Southeast by the State of Mexico, on the East and Southeast by the State of Puebla and on the South and Southwest by Guerrero. Magnificent mountain chains cross the region, which is marked by tall peaks, deep valleys, gorges, waterfalls, luxuriant tropical vegetation, fine sugar-haciendas, Indian temples, towns and citadels. . . .

—From Terry's *Mexico*

The sun is hot and white on the dust of the market, on the small square awnings in the blue shade of which the Indian women, heavy as granite idols, squat behind minute piles of peppers or oranges or onions. There's a heavy smell of fat from the pork crackling that seethes in a huge cauldron in front of the cantina. From inside, on the sour cool rankness comes an old man's voice singing to a guitar. He is singing a corrido called *The Ghost of Zapata*. People stop talking when they hear the name of the song. Brown faces, yellow faces, are motionless under the huge pushed back straw hats. This is Morelos where Zapata ruled.

> *Pero su alma persevera*
> *en su ideal Libertador*
> *y su horrenda calavera*
> *anda en penas . . . oh terror . . .*

> You can hear the jingle of his spurs
> his scaring voice once again
> as, teeth gritted in a curse
> he shouts the orders to his men

> and raising a limp hand in command
> he leads a white and silent host
> of dead men across the southern land,
> dead Zapata's walking ghost.

This is Yautepec, blue, white, pink and lilacsplotched streets rambling among humped shiny mangotrees. All the big houses have been burned or are falling to ruin. They keep sheep in the parlors of the old haciendados, chickens and turkeys go pecking between the tiles of abandoned courts, there are ducks setting in the counting houses where the overseers used to keep the accounts and figure out how much the peons owed the landlords. In a square where everyone walks round in the evening, you don't see any foreign clothes, men wear white cotton suits like pyjamas, and broad petate hats, and girls wear dark shawls and full skirts.

One afternoon I climbed the hill. Two men were sitting at the foot of the cross. We stood smoking together and looked over the plain towards the huge barrier of reddish jagged hills that culminate to the northeast in the shadowy smoking peak of Popocatepetl. The fat man pointed out the churches and the abandoned sugar factories. "See, *señor*," he said, "the green squares where there is cane planted, and the brown squares where there is none. In the old days it was all green. See those sheds, those are the mills where they crush the cane. There used to be eighteen in the district here and several refineries. Now they are all idle. There are no machinists to run them. The machines are all rusted. But then eleven men, Spaniards most of them at that, *gachupines*, maybe one or two of them were *gringos*, owned the whole state."

"Well, aren't you better off without them?"

"*Quien sabe, señor?*"

The man who was talking was a fat man in a threadbare khaki suit with bushy moustaches that had a melancholy droop to the tips. He addressed himself mostly to his friend, a little wiry coppercolored Indian with a few streaks of whisker at the corners of his mouth, who squatted on his heels and smiled and said nothing. The fat man was of a yellowish color and enjoyed talking.

"Hernan Cortés was a wise and great man, one of the ancients, the great conqueror," he went on greasily. "When he came to Morelos he founded the first church and the first sugarmill side by side in Tlaltenango near Cuernavaca. Who knows, maybe he knew what he was doing." The little Indian almost laid his hand on my knee, then he pointed with it to the town that shone in the dusk among the mangotrees. "There was too much fighting here in the time of the Zapatistas, but now the priests have gone, the landowners have gone, the middlemen have gone, there are no bandits in the hills or in the cities, we are all united." "United to starve," said the fat man, "and the governor in Cuernavaca is a *sinverguenza* and the managers of the cooperatives are *sinverguenzas*, and the next revolution will be against the *sinverguenzas*." The little Indian looked up deferentially at his fat friend and smiled and said nothing.

That night I was sitting in the doorway of the hotel. There was an old brown man with a white beard with whom I had been dickering about the horse I was hiring in the morning. When we had settled about the horse he sat beside me and started talking. He talked so low into his beard I could not catch all he said. " 'Good Don Porfirio,' they say, 'in the good old days' . . . . That is not true. Those days were very bad . . . good for the rich maybe, but there were very few rich men, in this town perhaps five or six and their families. . . . For the poor . . . I had a wife and three children and suddenly they came and took me away. Nobody would say why, maybe it was all a mistake, because I have always been a quiet peaceful man. Maybe it was about a horse Don Abundio wanted to buy . . . I never knew. In the box car there were other poor people, old men and boys, some of them were criminals from the jail. We were shut up in the box car for days and days and then in the boat. I couldn't eat or sleep thinking of my wife and the littlest child who was a little girl. I thought every day I was going to die. Then when we got to Yucatan we were marched many days across a trackless country with foul water to drink and those who got tired fell down and the wild Indians killed them, and every day I thought I was going to die. . . . We stayed there for years building roads and every night they flogged someone. Then they told me to go home and I had to beg my way to Merida. My son who was already a grown man came and fetched me home. He found me sitting in the street in Merida. I didn't know him because I had remembered him as a little boy. You see they had sent me letters, but every time I tried to read the letters my eyes filled with tears so that I couldn't read them."

The state of Morelos is the great example for all the dollar-minded of the failure of the agrarian revolution. The sugar-landlords and their families have filled two continents with their lamentations over the ruin of its rich industries. They have formed an association and probably most of them live richly in Neuilly and on the Riviera; meanwhile their interests have fallen into the hands of three banks, the Banco de Londres y Mexico, the Banco Nacional de Mexico, and the Banco Germanico de la America del Sur. These banks are constantly sponsoring projects to "put Morelos on its feet" and certainly their faces are not unknown in the various claims commissions that hover on the outskirts of Mexican politics always ready to back a revolution or hinder the operation of a useful reform. The government has tried to remedy the situation by promoting the culture of rice, as sugar is a crop that with the present markets can only be grown under slave conditions. There are various "enlightened capitalist" projects in the air to reorganize the whole state on an industrial basis, of which the most favorably seen in Mexico City is that of the Honolulu Ironworks Company to centralize irrigation and the refineries, at the same time leaving the land in the hands of the peasants. Naturally the land, without water or factories, won't do the peasants much good, so they do not look with great enthusiasm at these foreign projects. Meanwhile, as in the bad times in the Bible, every man lives as best he can under his own vine and fig tree and is a law unto himself, and the state is bankrupt and the roads and ditches and towns are falling into weedy ruin, and the great hopes of Zapata and his men still stalk the land unappeased.

Yautepec, February, 1926

In the Hills

It was sleeting in our faces as we crossed the last rocky gulch. Some cultivated land, a few trees, adobe cubes of houses, the top façade of a church hove in view on the soaring slope above us as we floundered through the slimy mud of the track. Broadfaced men standing in the lee of the low houses in the hardtrampled courtyards received us with shouts: *"Vivan los Agraristas, Viva Zapata."* Antonio and his father and all his family came out and embraced us and made us sit in the house that was one long room with a broad bed of boards at one end and a sort of altar in front of the door. Outside the sleet had turned into a downpour and the young men were shooting off skyrockets into the rain.

A dozen people told us the story over bowls of warm *pulque*. The village from time immemorial had owned an *ejido*, a tract of common land, part of it pasture, part of it worked in common by the families of the village that inherited its compactness from the Indian tribe that had settled it some time in the distant past. In the days of the good Don Porfirio the owners of the neighboring ranch with the help of lawyers and gendarmes had gradually encroached on the village lands, first claiming the right to pasture and eventually forcing the villagers out entirely. They had to eat, so having no lands of their own to work they were forced to work for the ranchowners, who would generously cede them the use of corn patches and advance them credit. So from free villagers they became, in two generations, peons. This until the "bandit" Zapata started riding through the south with the warcry of "Land, Water, Schools." The Mexican owners of the ranch had long ago gambled it away to an absentee Spanish company. At the first ping of the bullets the overseers fled and the villagers quietly installed themselves in their birthright. Then divisions began within the village. The priest and a small group who had made a little money in towns or by dealing in cattle stood out against the rest of the village. They owned bits of communal land themselves and were quite content to let things ride as they were. The priest went off with documents stored in the church showing the ancient boundaries. The landless villagers sent delegations to the capital, received promises from one *politico* and the other, but as soon as the *politicos* were elected they were all for letting things ride. Meanwhile nothing was settled. Government engineers came and made surveys that somehow always came out in favor of the landowners who were working through a powerful lobby in Mexico City. *Politicos* came and went. Nobody had a clear title to the land so nobody dared work it. While the Indians stood guard with guns in their hands, the hard won fruits of the revolution were melting away behind their backs. There was little corn for the *tortillas*, beans were almost unknown; the young men were slipping away to the cities or taking up highway robbery. What were they to do? Now we had come, two men and a woman dressed in store clothes, speaking foreign languages, versed in the great movements all over the world, friendly with the Russians (in Morelos they called the Bolsheviks "the Zapatistas of the east"). Now we would help them; they were children lost in a lonely village, far from roads and railroads and they wanted to feel that they could work their land in safety, and they needed help.

The rain had stopped. They walked us up the hill through a scattering of houses to see a great cypress surrounded by a little fence that seemed to be the sacred tree of the village. Everyone spoke very respectfully of it as if it were a person; at Christmas they celebrated the nativity of Christ in the little wellswept enclosure round the trunk. They showed us from a distance the

Church and the priests' house and the houses of the enemies, as they called the small landowner faction. "I bet they're looking out of the doors wondering what we're doing with visitors from the capital," said Antonio and gave out a tremendous shout of *Vivan los agraristas, vivan los communistas.*

As we were winding down the little lane again we had a scare. A party of men with guns came striding towards us out of the hilly pastureland. The boys didn't set off any more rockets, everyone was quiet until they came within hail. Then the strangers shot their guns in the air and let out a great cry of *Viva Zapata*; they were agraristas from the next village. At the shout all tension vanished. The men from Amonalco were not alone any more. In hundreds of villages they had brothers who stirred to the same cry, men who dressed, starved and drank *pulque* the way they did. Their leader was dead, but his name had power to bind and to loose.

What they lacked, the old men said as they all crowded back together into the house, was a leader, a leader who thought and lived as a countryman. They were tired of trusting engineers and surveyors and lawyers, men in black suits and Stetson hats, from the capital. They were very disappointed the next day when we started on our walk back into the Valley. They had hoped we would stay and help them with advice and counteract the wiles of the surveyor who was at the moment trying to whittle down the size of the *ejido*. The communist said that he would send them back comrades to advise them. *Vivan los communistas*, they cried. We left them at the edge of the glen, a little group of men in white cotton suits, uneasy, hungry, leaderless, isolated, a fragment of a defeated nation, standing blinking, dazed in the light like a man just broken out of jail. When the Carranzistas killed Zapata they thought the agrarian movement was dead; his ghost walks uneasily and until it is laid Mexican politics will be perpetually unstable.

> But his soul still perseveres
> in the will to liberate
> and his skull goes out in tears
> his dead bones walk. . . .

Cuernavaca, March, 1926

3. EMILIANO ZAPATA

I will not say what is not true
for never can I tell a lie,
as I don't want when I am dead
carpers to say he told a lie.

Those who like to hear my rhymes
telling things just as they came about,
must never lay the blame on me
for the shortness of my witless brain.

I don't pronounce Castilian right,
my words are just the common kind;
but it's my experience that every time
the clear way to tell the thing is the best.

> —Song by Marcianito Silva, of Cuautla,
> popular corridosinger in Zapata's army.

Emiliano Zapata was the son of a householder in San Miguel Anenecuilco, a hamlet in the village of Ayala in the state of Morelos; all through his childhood the Indian villagers lived under the shadow of the great hacienda of Chinameca; every year the hacienda pared more land off the commonlands of the village. Sugar was money in those days. Morelos was the richest sugar land in Mexico. If the Indians worked their own lands they wouldn't go to work for the sugarmills. The sugarmills needed the land and they needed the Indians. Sugarcane needs plenty of water. They took the land and they took the water and they took the Indians.

Eleven families in the state of Morelos became enormously rich exploiters of sugar, the Indians became peons.

The sugar exploiters were cientificos, they were friendly with North American capitalists and railroad builders; that was what they called progress in the days of Don Porfirio.

The state of Morelos is a set of rich plains and broad ravines gouged out of the southern flanks of the great volcanos that close the Valley of Mexico. Its boundaries are high arid mountains snowy in winter, but the plains are fat tropical land, alluvial soil mixed with volcanic ash, wherever there's water the soil will grow anything, tomatoes, peppers, figs, guavas, aguacates, cane, maize, huge mangotrees, chirimoyos, papayas.

Morelos was the richest state in Mexico in the days of Don Porfirio. The villages were well off, they hired lawyers to go to the capital to defend their land, they brought suit, they hired the services of men in black clothes and stiff collars. But somehow the sugar exploiters always won the suits. They sent delegations to talk to Don Porfirio about it; but somehow the sugar exploiters were always sitting beside him when the delegations came in.

Wherever a sugarfactory sent up its tall stacks from a mass of tin roofs among the canefields, there the villages lost their commonlands, there the Indians were always in debt to the exploiters' stores, there the Indians were peons.

They're not fit for anything else, have to handle them like dumb animals with a whip, the overseers said; the cientificos left the peons and the crushers and the storeaccounts to the overseers; their sons gambled away the money at the Jockey Club in Mexico City and spent it on badtempered French mistresses in Neuilly and villas on the Riviera. When old Indians crawled into their hovels to die, they told their sons: You must get our land back.

Morelos was a rich bowl of sugar hemmed in by high mountains, the owners were few and powerful and greedy; sugar was money in those days.

While Zapata was growing up the last lands were being taken away from the village of Ayala by the great hacienda of Chinameca; every year more of the land went into cane. When Zapata was a young man he went to work for the exploiters as a charro, a cowhand, a crack rider who took care of the stock. His father before him had had a bad reputation among the millowners and overseers of the great hacienda of Chinameca as a man who stood up for the rights of his people. Emiliano soon had a worse reputation. In the opinion of the sugar exploiters and the hacienda owners and of Diaz's government the place for a bad Indian was the army. Yucatan or the fever country of Tabasco soon took the meanness out of a bad Indian, usually he left his bones there. So Emiliano was drafted into the ninth cavalry regiment.

But he was a valuable hand, they missed him on the ranch where he worked, after leaving him six months to cool off the rancher bought him out of the army again. This was in 1909. The old order was getting shaky. Don Porfirio was old, the sons of the cientificos were shot through with drink and syphilis and even with a few liberal ideas. In Morelos the liberals even put up a rich young man named Leyva to run against Escadon, Don Porfirio's nominee for governor. Even Don Porfirio was not crushing opposition as ruthlessly as in the old days; people needed a little harmless politics to keep them out of mischief. Zapata organized furiously for Leyva whom he thought was a man who would stand up for the rights of the villages.

Emiliano Zapata's politics were not so harmless as the liberals'. He kept talking about land. He began to have influence in Ayala and the towns around. When Don Porfirio's nominee was elected Zapata had to leave the state. He went to Chietla in the state of Puebla, where he broke and trained horses for a rancher.

Meanwhile Madero, another liberal son of the cientificos, was speaking in the north. In November 1910 Aquiles Serdán started the revolt all alone in the town of Puebla. On the eighteenth he was shot down by the government troops. But already Madero was in San Antonio organizing his revolution, and all over Mexico liberals were taking to the hills, calling on the peons to revolt against the oppressor Diaz.

From Ayala Pablo Torres Burgos travelled to San Antonio to offer Madero the rebellion of the South, and got a commission for himself as second and for young Leyva as first in command of the Revolutionary Army of the South. In all their white adobe houses the Indians were getting their guns ready, sharpening knives and scythes, patching up their harness and saddles.

The revolt was set for immediately after the fair that was held in Cuautla the second Friday in Lent. There at the crowded market among the booths of pottery and toys and the dust and the cockfights and the smell of peppers and chiles and fried crackling it was easy for the leaders to get together, talk to their men, distribute guns and cartridges.

At the first rising Leyva scuttled back to Mexico City and offered his services to Diaz. The first leader of the revolution in the section round Ayala was a sanguinary old man named Tepepa. Torres Burgos found he had no control over his soft-voiced Indians, who burned canefields, pillaged stores, massacred the storekeepers, overseers, moneylenders, gachupines, sacked and destroyed everything that the exploiters had touched. First Tlaquiltenango was taken and sacked, then Jujutla, then Yautepec.

Everywhere the government troops were wiped out after desperate resistance, everywhere the politicos and generals ran as fast as they could back to Mexico City.

After he found he was powerless to stop the sacking of Jujutla, Torres Burgos who was a humane man, a reader of books, who dreamed of liberty and peace, resigned his command and left the force. He and his two small sons were surprised by the government forces, resting under a tree on the roadside, and killed.

By the time the rebels were besieging Cuautla Zapata had arrived with a new force, riding over the mountains from Chietla. Already the Indians were calling themselves Zapatistas. They had organized a force that they called the dinamiteros, who made hand grenades out of old tin cans full of scrapiron. Each dinamitero went into action with a cigar in his mouth, and a supply of fuses. They threw the grenades with a fibre sling and lit the fuses from their cigars like people setting off fireworks. They blew themselves up as often as not. But they took Cuautla. The city of palaces, as the rich men of Morelos liked to call it, was fired in the course of the battle and a large part of it ruined.

In Cuautla the news came to Zapata of the flight of Diaz and Madero's victory. Madero came to Cuautla to get the arms away from the Indians. He is said to have offered Zapata a large sum of money and a trip abroad if he would disband his army; but Zapata wanted to know when the Indians would get their land back.

Madero embraced Zapata in public and made some fine speeches about justice and liberty and went back to Mexico City like the other men in stiff collars and black suits who had taken the Indians' money and their lives and promised to get them their rights. But nothing was done about the land, nothing was done about the waterrights, nothing was done about schools.

Zapata believed Madero and went back to Ayala to attend to his own business. Many of his men scattered to their homes to raise their crops.

Then one day he was suddenly attacked in Ayala by a force of government troops. He saddled his horse and took to the hills with the schoolteacher of the primary school, Otilio Montaño. The two of them hid in a shepherd's hut up in the Sierra de Ayoxustla for three days with paper and pens and wrote up the Plan de Ayala in which Zapata proclaimed that he would not lay down his arms until the Indians of Morelos were given their lands, their waterrights and their schools.

He called his men together and laid the papers on a little wooden table in front of the hut. Then the schoolteacher read the plan and Zapata said in his soft drawling Indian speech, "Whoever has got the nerve to sign, come forward and sign it."

Signing gave them a feeling that they were linking themselves to the great movements of history; the Indians of his little force waved their hugerimmed coneshaped hats and cheered. Boys ran down to the little villages below in the valley and rang the churchbells. Rockets went up and left their white blobs of cottonwool in the blue glittering sky.

Then Zapata sent down to the little town of Cuautla to get the priest, who owned a typewriter, to come up into the sierra with some carbonpaper and copy the document for him. The priest came and did the copying and was given some bottles of wine for his pains. The copies were sent to all the revolutionary groups in Mexico. With Madero's special permission (he remained a liberal till his death) the plan was printed in the paper in Mexico City, "so that people could see what a madman this fellow Zapata was," Madero said.

From that time on Zapata's headquarters were in the sierra; sometimes he had a large army, sometimes a small guerrilla force. His men had to go home from time to time to plant their crops. After the flight of Huerta he helped the Carranzistas capture Mexico City. But neither by force nor by his letters to revolutionary leaders could he get the winners in the civil war to set to work honestly to give the Indians their lands, their waterrights, and their schools. So he stayed in the field under arms.

I am a rebel from the state of Morelos,
I keep my faith in the promise of San Luis.
I am a rebel. I'll fight against old man Carranza
who in the end is sure to break his word.

Two cartridgebelts, my winchester and my horse
are all I've got, and the Virgin of Tepeyac,
to make them respect the plan we signed in Ayala,
though every valiant liberal bite the dust.

The mountain is my bulwark, yes indeed,
and always true Zapatista I must be
waiting for the Carranzistas I'll stand firm
with my darling 30-30 in my hand.

If in the long run luck turns against me
and a hostile bullet finds its mark
I'll take my bad luck and die firmly repeating:
Long live the heroes of the south. Long live Zapata.

is a corrido that was common in those days among his soldiers.

In 1918 Zapata, who for a long time had had his capital at
Tlaltizapán, was driven up into the high mountains again by the
invasion of Morelos by the Carranzista general Pablo Gonzalez,
who aimed to destroy the roots of Zapata's army by laying the
country his men lived on waste with a savagery extraordinary
even in Mexican civil wars. With Pablo Gonzalez the sugar exploiters, the ranchers, the overseers and the owners of the great
haciendas came back. It was their turn. When the troops of
Pablo Gonzales captured a Zapatista they made him dig his
own grave. "So you wanted the land," they'd say. "Well take
it," and then they'd shoot him. This was considered a great
joke among the ranchers and sugar exploiters.

The Zapatistas had their jokes too, as when they captured
and destroyed a railroad train and shot the escort and took all
the clothes off the citydressed passengers.

But Zapata tried to keep his men in order, tried to keep
their minds fixed on getting their land, their water, and their
schools. We are not bandits, he would say, all we demand is
our rights. Continually he tried by messengers and letters to
unify the revolutionary forces against Carranza and to set up

an agrarian commonwealth in Mexico where the Indian in his white cotton suit and his blanket and his sandals would not be at the mercy of the men with black clothes and stiff collars and heavy boots who always managed to rig the forces of law and order against him. He was in correspondence with Villa and Obregón, and the agrarian forces all over the country.

This is how the men in black suits and the ranchers and the exploiters of sugar finally answered him, at the hacienda of Chinameca:

A certain Colonel Guajardo who had been murdering and burning in the northern part of Morelos let it be known that he was on the outs with Pablo Gonzalez and was ready to change sides and join the agrarians against Carranza, and invited Zapata to come down to Tepaltzingo to take command of his troops. To prove his sincerity Colonel Guajardo shot fiftynine of his own men who had been accused by the Indian villagers of rapes and pillage in the villages and whose punishment was demanded by Zapata. Even so Zapata was uneasy on account of the warnings of his friends and the bad reputation of Colonel Guajardo, but the opportunity of winning over an important body of troops was too important to be neglected. Before he left his camp in the hills he is said to have told his wife how tired he was of all this warfare. "I suffer a great deal," he said. "Few men have as much pain and trouble as I have. Others get a chance to rest. I'd like to get on my horse right now and ride and ride, and settle down and go to work quietly some place far away."

As they were riding down to Tepaltzingo he said to one of his companions: "You must tell them in the villages, that so long as I live, the land is theirs, but that when I die, they must trust nobody but themselves and defend the commonlands with arms in their hands."

Here is the account of a man who was present at the assassination of Zapata:

"Guajardo was in Jonocatepec, which place he claimed to have captured from the enemy (the Carranzista troops of Pablo Gonzalez). When we heard this, we went to the railroadstation of Pastor, and there Palacios was ordered by the Chief (Zapata) to write him to meet us in Tepaltzingo, to which place General Zapata would repair with thirty men, and that he should do the same. The Chief ordered his men to retire and with thirty men we went to Tepaltzingo, where we waited for Guajardo. He presented himself there round four in the afternoon, but instead of with thirty soldiers with sixhundred cavalrymen and a machinegun. When the column reached Tepaltzingo, we went out to meet it. There we saw for the first time the man who the next day was to be the assassin of our General-in-Chief, whom, with all nobleness of soul, he received with open arms. 'Colonel Guajardo, I congratulate you sincerely,' he said smiling. At 10 P.M. we left Tepaltzingo for Chinameca, which was occupied by Guajardo and his column, while we spent the night at a place called the Duck Pond. Around eight in the morning we went down to Chinameca. Once there, the Chief ordered his men (a hundred and fifty men who had joined us in Tepaltzingo) to form up in the square of the place, while he, Guajardo, Generals Castrejón, Casales, and Camaño, Palacios and the undersigned should go to a quiet place and discuss plans for the future campaign. A few minutes later rumors began to circulate that an enemy force was drawing near. The Chief ordered Colonel José Rodriguez of his escort to go out scouting with some men in the direction of Santa Rita. As they were leaving, Guajardo, who had gone out to give orders to his men, came back saying, 'General, you give the orders, shall I go out with infantry or cavalry?' 'The plain is very much broken up, you'd better send out infantry,' replied General Zapata, and we retired. From Piedra Encimada we looked over a wide stretch of country, but not seeing any sign of enemy troopmovements in any direction we went back to the hacienda buildings of Chinameca. It was approximately half past twelve in the afternoon. The Chief had sent Colonel Palacios to talk to Guajardo, who was going to turn over five thousand cartridges, and when he arrived at Chinameca immediately asked for him. There presented themselves Captain Ignacio Castillo and a sergeant, and in the name of Guajardo, Castillo invited the Chief to come into the inner court of the hacienda buildings where Guajardo was arranging the subject of the munitions with Palacios. We chatted for about half an hour with Castillo, and after reiterated invitations the Chief assented. 'We'll go to see the colonel. Let only ten men come with me,' he ordered. And jumping on his horse—a sorrel that Guajardo had presented to him the day before—he started for the gate of the hacienda. Ten of us followed him as he had ordered, the rest of our people remaining confidently stretched out in the shade of some trees with their rifles stacked. The guard drawn up at the gate made as if to get ready to do him the honors. The bugle sounded the salute three times and as the last note died out, just as the General-in-Chief arrived at the threshold of the gate, in a most miserable villainous cowardly way, point blank, without giving us time even to draw our pistols, the soldiers who were presenting arms twice discharged their rifles, and our general Zapata fell never to rise again. His faithful assistant, Augustín Corres, died at the same time. Palacios must have been assassinated inside the hacienda. The surprise was terrible. The soldiers of the traitor Guajardo, entrenched in the heights, in the plain, in the ravine, from all directions (there were about a thousand men), discharged their rifles on us. Resistance soon proved to be useless. On one side we were a mere handful of men in consternation over the loss of our Chief, on the other side a thousand enemies taking the advantage of our confusion to punish us unmercifully. Thus was the tragedy. Thus did the perfidious Guajardo repay the noble confidence of our General-in-Chief. So died Emiliano Zapata, so die brave men, men of honor, when their enemies, unable to defeat them any other way, have recourse to treason and crime. As I said before, my General, enclosed are all the documents relating to the event. And offering you my deep and sincere condolences for the death of our fellowcitizen, the General-in-Chief, who can never be mourned enough, let me repeat to you, my General, the assurances of my subordination and respect.

Reform, Liberty, Justice and Law

At the revolutionary camp at Sauces,
State of Morelos
April 10, 1919

> The private secretary
> Major Salvador Reyes Aviles."

4. THE DEPUTY AND THE INDIAN

Just before we caught sight of Lake Atitlán, coming up from Antigua, we found ourselves face to face with an almost obliterated stone idol on the side of the road. In front of it was a bunch of fresh flowers. The faraway lake through the mist looked like a steel engraving of "Volcanos" in an old geography book. At the end of the lake was a tall volcanic mountain plumed with clouds and a range of towering grey cones flanked it on either side. Streaks of denser mist cut the long bright tawny shimmer of the sun on the water. It wasn't till later, where the road wound down into a deep tropical valley, that we began to see the Indians on their way to the Sunday market at Chichicastenango. They straggled up the road in groups in their blue, white and green cotton clothes. They are solidly built, but not stocky, with grave features and soft twittering speech and very small hands and feet. They are a light ruddy color between bronze and copper and the boys and girls have very red cheeks. The women's dresses are, some of them, voluminous, with great scarfs into which are woven silk threads in peacock blue and green; others, close-fitting gowns of a deep scarlet caught tight with a knot at the hip. They carry their babies on their backs. Their tunics and the short drawers of the men are embroidered with figures of animals and birds. Some of the men have folded up their clothes on top of their packs and walk naked except for their clean breechclouts. The costumes must vary from village to village because each group we pass seems to have a different outfit. Men and women and even the little children (and one of the dogs) carry a pack caught by a band across the forehead. Some of the men have bulky packingcases on their backs, or little cupboards with shelves on which are arranged cheeses and fruits and vegetables. The women have smaller packs and the children the smallest of all. They fill the steep road, advancing fast with a regular trotting step. On the grassy patches among the enormous pinetrees in the pass we catch sight of little circles of them squatting to rest, talking in low quiet even voices.

The market place at Chichicastenango was crowded but there was no hubbub. In the dense fastmoving crowds nobody ever brushed against you. Buyers and sellers bargained slowly and shyly with few words and long regretful glances. The tall portals of the two churches were high above the heads of the crowd, reached by steep threesided flights of steps like the steps in front of the pyramids at Chichén and Teotihuacan. Half way up the steps was a stone altar for incense. A continuous blue crinkling fume of incense went up before the glittering white façades of the churches. On all the steps there were Indians praying in Quiché with smoking censers in their hands. Inside the churches a lane of roseleaves led from the portal to the high altar. Small candles had been stood on the floor among the roseleaves and beside them squatted the diviners making little patterns in the roseleaves with their brown hands.

Beside the main church was the Padre's house with a fine courtyard and tall white rooms with beamed ceilings and pineneedles on the floor. At lunch the Padre was entertaining his guests with a fine meal of lamb and aguacates and little copitas of cognac. The Padre was a German who had been ordained a priest in Manchester, N.H., an archæologist, a student of Indian languages who had the reputation of being much loved by the Indians. He had lived thirty years among them. His guests were some local mestizos, a pair of casual travellers, a couple of students of folklore from the U.S., and some newsreel men who had brought with them a pair of little Hollywood blondes who ate nothing drank nothing said nothing and seemed to be worried about fleas. Probably they were wishing they were back at the Brown Derby.

After lunch the visitors thronged into the church to see the Padre baptize a round half dozen of squalling brown babies. Then they scattered to take photographs. Their raucous voices could be heard above the quiet murmur of the crowd as they bargained for strips of handwoven cotton and embroideries among the marketbooths.

Going down to Guatemala City a local politico who was a deputy asked permission to ride in the front seat of the car we had hired. He was going down for the opening of Congress. He was a stoutish yellowfaced man with a greedy-looking upperlip. He had with him his son, a spindly silent little pale yellow boy whom he stuffed with fruit and candy until he got carsick. After that the car had to stop every few miles so that the little boy could get out and upchuck timidly on the side of the road. Then everybody said "Pobrecito" and the politico said "It is nothing" and the car started off again.

The politico explained to us that the Indians were hard to deal with. They resented progress, they wouldn't learn to understand the modern world. They wouldn't change their customs or sell their land. They'd buy very little because they were so lazy they made everything they needed for themselves. Unless they were starving they wouldn't come to work for you. And then when they'd made a little money they were so lazy they'd quit work and walk back fifty or sixty miles into the mountains to their villages. Some of them held rich coffee lands but they wouldn't plant coffee. They were too reactionary and stubborn to do anything like that.

He told us a story about the trouble a friend of his, also a deputy to Congress, had had with an Indian over coffee land. (He didn't say that this deputy was himself but it may have been.) Just to show how exasperating they were. There was an old Indian on the other side of the lake, on the warm slopes below Santa Maria, who had started a coffee plantation. Now a coffee plantation takes endless work and trouble to get started. The trees that are to shade the coffee have to be of just the right height and thickness and it takes the sapling coffee trees from five to seven years to come into bearing. Then there is the coffee fly that comes from the running streams and ditches in that section and causes sickness and blindness among the people who cultivate the coffee plantations. This old Indian had been through all this and the plantation was beginning to produce some magnificent coffee. The deputy went over it and saw that it was a magnificent plantation and worth a great deal of money. We were to understand that the Indians are a shiftless and lazy people, reactionary to the greatest degree, who wouldn't understand an important commercial enterprise like that. They are priest-ridden, few of them can read and write and they rarely have legal title to their lands. So the deputy thought he'd better go to court and get title to the coffee plantation, he was an educated man and a deputy and understood commercial enterprises.

Just to show what exasperating reactionaries these Indians are, no sooner had the deputy gotten title to the land than the Indian and his family went out at night and cut down every single coffeetree. Seven years' hard work cut down in one night.

5. THE MALARIA MAN

Quirigua is in the lowlying banana land along the east coast. Along the railroad United Fruit has set out a row of greenishyellow frame buildings like buildings some place in Ohio. The damp night comes on enormously hot under the tall gawky trees whose names we don't know. The last of the frame buildings is a boarding house, dingy and crowded like a railroad boarding house at home. It's hot in there, smells of sweaty bedclothes and flit. A few foremen and overseers, from Texas or Oklahoma by their talk, are getting supper. They have guns on their hips. The sweat glistens on their necks and in the hollow of the collarbone under their open shirts. It's too hot to eat. We step out of the squalid light and the protecting screens of the boarding house into the breathless hot dripping dark. The nightinsects aren't as noisy as we'd expected, shriller, but no noisier than katydids at home. There's an occasional thin whine of a mosquito in our ears. The hospital is empty and dark. The patients have been put away for the night. The lights are shaded in the wards. The corridors are dim. It's completely quiet in the hospital, but you can feel a faint crowded stirring behind the white walls. "Yes the Señor Doctor would like to see you. He is free now."

We sit drinking coffee at a round table in a small room under a dim electric light with the Malaria Man and another doctor. Through the screens in the crowding darkness comes a little soft feeling not of coolness but of moisture. From somewhere far away the onecylinder motor of a waterpump gives your skull sharp regular taps as with a metal rod. It's hard to talk, it's too dark outside, the light's too dim.

Yes, they know about the attempted revolution in El Salvador. It's the communists. The Malaria Man (he is a Scotchman, he is a scientist of distinction, he is an employee of United Fruit) has seen the confidential report of the Guatemala police. It was a very dangerous rising. They captured Santa Ana and several other towns and held them for several days. Many Americans and people of prominence fled to Guatemala. No, there was no danger here, the police had acted in time, arrested eleven leaders, shot some of them. Nothing had gotten out to the press at all. That was efficient action. In Salvador it had been terrible though. From there the thing might have spread to all Central America. The extraordinary thing about it was that there had been many educated people involved. They had stirred up the masses against the army officers and coffee-planters. There'd almost been a massacre of army leaders in Santa Ana. Even in San Salvador, the capital, there'd been trouble. The communists had stirred up the wild Indians and the town workers and part of the army. Prominent officers had been shot, some of them tortured, eyes burned out with cigars. What the doctors couldn't understand was that men of education like themselves had been mixed up in it, agitating against imperialism, demanding land for the Indians, higher wages for plantation workers. In fact they were planning to expropriate all the coffee and banana land. It was the communists behind it, agents from Moscow undoubtedly. Too bad that the leader in Guatemala, he'd probably been shot by this time, had an English name. He was a Honduran, the son of an Englishman, no not a real Englishman of course. Anyway, thank God, it was over now. The army was in control. The government of El Salvador was making a thorough cleanup. They'd been shooting two or three hundred people a week. All kinds of people, doctors, lawyers, students, people of education and breeding that you wouldn't have expected to be mixed in a criminal business like this. They're keeping a firm hand on the situation. "Now that they've got communism stamped out," said the Malaria Man, "I suppose the government of the United States will feel more like recognition."

The pump kept up its steady tapping on our skulls out of the crowding blackness. It was good to get out of the dim hospital where the steam of the night seemed to be always crowding in round the dim electric bulbs. There was little sleep in the black stuffiness of the boarding house.

Next morning we went down the little rickety line of the banana railroad on a motor sectioncar through banana plantations gutted and ragged from the cutting of the crop, to the ruins of the Old Empire city. The ruins had been cleared of jungle a year before but already saplings rose eighteen or twenty feet high from the crumbled terraces and pyramids. Here stands the row of enormous stelæ that have furnished the date that links the Mayan calendar to ours. These stones standing grimly in line, swelling with the enormous strength of their halfobliterated carvings, still give you, through all the confusion of races and empires long dead, of languages and writings that can never be understood, a feeling of serene order and form that is an actual refuge like a strong stone house, cool against the sun, in the midst of the terrible silent carnage of the tropical rainforest; so that, after seeing them, the railroad and the guns of the overseers and the loading sheds and the uptodate malaria hospital, all the carefully organized machinery for efficiently squeezing out of the spongy soil and the sweat and the blood of the yellow brown and white mongrel race of workers who live in the rows of company shacks and whose arms belong to United Fruit, bananas and dollars for the north, seems feeble and flabby, not organization at all, not order at all.

On the way back up to Guatemala City there was a woman in the observation car whom an unhappylooking man, evidently her husband, was very tenderly taking up to a sanitarium in the capital; she was a pleasantfaced middleaged woman; she was crazy, she lay back in her seat and screeched like a parrot all the way.

Guatemala City, March, 1932

IV. The Republic of Honest Men

I. DOVES IN THE BULLRING

It was a hot Sunday morning in July. Members of the Socialist party had come from all over northern Spain for the big meeting in Santander. They had come with their red goldlettered tradeunion banners, with their wives and children, and lunches in baskets, and canteens of wine. They had come in special trains and in buses and in mulecarts and on bicycles and on foot. The bullring held about ten thousand people; every seat was full, agreeable intelligentlooking people mostly, mechanics, small storekeepers and farmers, shoemakers, tailors, clerks, schoolteachers, bookkeepers, a few doctors and lawyers, for this part of the world a quiet characterless crowd, but a big crowd.

The proceedings began by the singing of the *Internationale* by a bunch of schoolchildren in white dresses with red bows. They sang it very nicely. It passed the time while we waited for the speakers to arrive. The more important dignitaries seemed to be late. Then when the speakers filed onto the stand set up in the broiling sun in the center of the bullring, everybody sang the *Internationale* again standing, red bunting waved.

Somebody had gotten the idea that it would be effective to send up two white pigeons with red ribbons round their necks, but (maybe it was the heat or that the ribbons were tied too tight or that the pigeons were sick) the pigeons couldn't seem to fly. They fluttered groggily over the heads of the crowd, and crashed against the wall of the bullring. Eventually one of them managed to rise over the roof of the stands and vanished into the sizzling sunny sky, but the other fell back into the crowd. People tried to coax it to fly, to give it a starting toss into the air, but it was too weak. It finally came to rest in the middle of the bullring, right in front of the speaker's stand. All through the speaking it stood there, a very sicklooking pigeon indeed. We kept expecting it to flop over dead, but it just stood there with its head drooping.

The first speakers were local leaders, working men or tradeunion officials. They spoke simply and definitely. The fight at home, as all over the world, was between socialism and fascism, the kind of order the workers and producers wanted and the kind of order the exploiting class wanted. The Socialist Party had no choice but to go ahead and install socialism right away (cheers) . . . through a dictatorship if need be (more cheers). When the deputy to the cortes spoke he was a little vaguer, he talked more about world conditions and the course of history and economic trends, but in the end he could think of no other way of finishing his speech than by promising socialism (wild cheers). But when the Socialist Minister spoke (cheers, cries of *Vivan los hombres honrados*, Hurray for honest men) things became very vague indeed. It was very hot by this time, he was a stout man with a neat academic beard. Neither the heat nor the fact that he was sweating terrifically under his black broadcloth suit brought a single tremor into his long carefully modulated sentences. He used the classical form of address, subjunctives and future subjunctives and future conditional subjunctives and conditional subjunctive futures, he brought in history and literature, philosophy and the fine arts, as if he were speaking to his students at the university, and he ended with a throaty oratorical period that quite took the audience's breath away. The gist of it was that he called for moderation and ponderation; the Socialist Party was the party of discipline and order and the best thing sincere Socialists could do was stay at home and pay their dues and leave talk about attaining a socialist state in the interest of the worker to their betters, their political leaders who had the interest of all humanity at heart and understood the need for law and order and were honest men besides. The interests of all humanity demanded confidence and discipline from the Socialist Party.

When the speaking stopped the sick pigeon was still teetering in the center of the bullring. With as much discipline, but perhaps with less confidence than they'd had that morning, the members of the Socialist Party grouped themselves for the parade through the center of town. Everybody was telling everybody else that the watchword was order.

By that time it was afternoon and very hot indeed. The paraders with their banners and their children and their lunchbaskets marched without music through the center of town to the beach, mild, straggling, wellmannered and a little embarrassed. All the cafés were full. The people sitting at the cafés were the type of Spaniard who's hated in Mexico as a *gachupin*, people with gimlet eyes and greedy predatory lines on their faces, jerkwater importers and exporters, small brokers, loan sharks, commissionmerchants, pawnbrokers, men who knew how to make two duros grow where one had grown before. They'd never been much before under the monarchy, mostly they'd had to scrape up their livings in America, at home the hierarchy, the bishops, the duchesses, the grandees and the Bourbons high-hatted them off the map, but now the feudal paraphernalia was gone, the *gachupines* were on top of the world. They sat silent at their tables looking at the embarrassed Socialists straggling by. There were a great many Socialists; it took them a long time to pass with their banners and their children and their red ribbons and their lunchbaskets. The silent hatred of the people at the café tables was embarrassing. They filed on by as innocent as a flock of sheep in the wolf country.

2. TOPDOG POLITICS

The Royal Palace

When Don Alfonso finished sorting out and burning papers in his office on the side of the palace towards the city, he walked round to the other side of the immense pilastered greystone building; through the tall state rooms ornate with overweening pomp of scrolling designs in stucco and gilt and bronze and crystal and damask and velvet; through the throne room with its lions and its crowded black busts of antique Romans; under the huge ceiling where, for the first of the Bourbons in the gaudy days of the Sun King, the Venetian, Tiepolo had painted, in that daze of blue empyrean light that was his specialty, the grandiloquently draped abstractions of Government and Power; under the tasseled portières, through the inlaid eighteenthcentury doors to the room where the Englishwoman his wife was having tea. It was a narrower room with an open fireplace, that instead of looking out on the

strident masculine city, looked out on the boxhedges of the
royal gardens and on that magnificent stretch of rolling tawny
country tufted with blue evergreen oaks that rises to the
foothills of the Guadarrama, that Velasquez invented as a
background for the sallow faces and jutting wolfjaws of the
members of the house of Austria. Don Alfonso, too, had the
face for that background. Tourists smuggled on gala days into
palace functions in the tooearly bright light of the Madrid
morning had often cried out how like a Velasquez he looked,
passing against the sweeping voluted draftsmanship of the figures on the tapestry, a step ahead of the mass of uniforms,
decorations, colored ribbons, stars, chokers, sunbursts, stom-
achers of the grandees of Spain and the ladies of the court;
there were the dead bored eyes, the sallow skin, the humble
haughty set of the mouth of Philip IV without his easy assurance and his poise, all dulled by the halfwit leer the painter saw
on the face of the helpless Carlos II the Bewitched, who so feebly ended the great line of the house of Austria, and gave the
French monarchy a chance to impose a Bourbon as the head of
the vast bureaucracy that Philip II had fitted together out of
the chaotic straggle of conquests, covering half Europe and all
America, the Emperor Charles and the conquistadors had left
behind them.

The last of the Bourbons brusquely told his wife that he'd
packed his trunk and was off for the border. He could trust
the navy. He was going to drive. There was a battleship waiting in Cartagena. She could wind up her affairs and follow
him to France when she was ready. He left and he lost no
time about it.

It may have been the crowd crying "Death to the king.
Live the republic" as they ran from under the hoofs of the
horses and the flailing sabres of the Civil Guards; it may have
been the uneasy recollection of Ramon Franco's airplanes
within an inch of unloading their bombs over the palace; or
the strikes, or the parades of university students, or the
changed attitude of his friends the armyofficers, or the frown
on the face of General Sanjurjo who commanded the Civil
Guard, or a fit of pique because everybody was telling him
what to do; or it may have been just that the fruit was ripe to
fall from the tree. Anyway the last of the Bourbons left Madrid

as stealthily as a defaulting bank cashier. Next morning the Queen, who had learnt her profession in the stern vocational school of Victoria, left with more dignity by train, accompanied by her children, forty trunks and four carloads of furniture and knickknacks. The crown of Spain was found poked into a green baize bag, in a wardrobe in the palace.

The Republic of Honest Men

Meanwhile in the streets and cafés of Madrid the citizens were celebrating the republic. You could shout "Viva la Republica" right into the moustaches and the mausers of the Civil Guard without being arrested. Trucks paraded the main thoroughfares crowded with armyofficers and sailors and workingmen in blue denim singing the *Marseillaise* together. In the Puerta del Sol an artillery officer appeared on the balcony of the Gubernacion (the ministry that traditionally has charge of breaking the heads of dissenting citizens) and hoisted the new tricolor, red yellow and purple, to the flagpole. Spain was a republic. The Bourbons had gone back to France where they came from.

The grandees trod on each other's heels crowding across the border at Irún and Port Bou, not a few generals and politicos who'd made themselves unpopular under the old régime suddenly found that they needed to take the cure in French and German watering places. Wealthy businessmen stayed at home with shutters closed and doors barred till they found out how a liberated Spain was going to behave. Even the dyedinthewool republicans were uneasy when they stepped out of doors that morning and found themselves in the middle of the glorious republic of honest men they'd so long talked about.

But the republic of honest men was very well behaved indeed. Property and persons were respected. Everybody was for law and order in the shape of the now republican Civil Guard led by the now republican General Sanjurjo. The only outrages were the chipping off of the royal arms wherever they could be reached on public buildings and the upsetting of the magnificent bronze statue of Philip III in the Plaza Mayor. A couple of grandees were hissed and a few nuns were hustled but everything passed off with the greatest good humor. *Vivan los hombres honrados.*

On back streets and in the workingclass quarters there may have been a little singing of the *Internationale* but in the Puerta del Sol it was the *Marseillaise* and the *Hymn of Riego* that greeted Alcala Zamóra, the whitehaired and silver-tongued head of the new government when he addressed the people from the balcony draped with the new red yellow purple bunting. The liberal and socialist junta of hombres honrados that had been in exile and in jail was hastily dusted off and presented as a ministry.

The generals had lost their nerve and failed. It was the turn of the intellectuals to spring to the defense of order, progress and the rights of private property.

The Ateneo

The leading republicans were doctors, lawyers, college professors, literary men; the republic was rooted in the Ateneo.

The Madrid Atheneum was one of those agreeable organizations that grew out of the enthusiasm for the arts and sciences that boiled up among the rising middle classes in the early nineteenth century. Some time in the eighties it was established in its present dark and musty building. Downstairs there are quiet parlors with deep carpets and cavernous armchairs that might belong to any club anywhere, and a lecturehall. Upstairs there's an excellent library. It might be in Boston or London, except that the members talk more, smoke more and are permitted to drink coffee at their desks in the library and are rather more varied in dress and feature than they would be in an Anglo-Saxon country. For many years, in talk and lectures and debates the opposition of the professional classes to the church, the army and the monarchy that formed a triple lid over their heads, stewed and steamed. With the first republic under Pi y Margall that lid blew off only to be promptly clamped down again; this time it looks as if it had blown off for good.

It's no accident that Manuel Azaña, the dominant political leader of the liberal republicans, was president of the Ateneo before he was president of the council of ministers.

When the first republican cortes that was to write the constitution for a liberal Spain was elected it was no accident that very many of its member were Ateneistas. They moved their

debates, their habits of thought and their academic aloofness
to the roomier and more gaily decorated congresshall around
the corner. (At the congress the coffee's better, the seats are
more freshly upholstered, the attendants are more elderly and
courtly, and the speakers are refreshed by large glasses of a
soothing and nonalcoholic drink made from burnt sugar and
water. It is the best café in Madrid and Madrid is above all the
city of cafés.)

The Ateneo is the finest flower of the free thought of the
rising middle classes in the nineteenth century and Madrid is
the very special soil in which it grew.

Madrid, City of Cafés

Madrid has a peculiar position among European capitals.
Like Washington it is an invented city. It was invented by
Philip II. He picked out a crumbling mudfort left by the
Arabs on the banks of the Manzanares as his capital because it
was square in the center of Spain and because it was far from
any of the old cities where intense local feeling still smouldered against the centralizing monarchy of the Austrias.
When Charles the Emperor tired of the pompous velvets and
the smiles of ambassadors and the deferential voices of secretaries reading the reports of victorious generals from Mexico
and Italy and Peru (most of which reports ended by asking
for money), and the difficulties in collecting taxes and the rich
colors of Venetian painting and the classical gimcracks and the
weight of the engraved armor and the chafing of the saddle
and the buttery voices of archbishops and the pointed beards
of his courtiers and all their lies, he abdicated in favor of his
son and retired to Yuste in the wild oakforests of Extremadura
where he spent the rest of his life mending clocks and thinking about God.

Hardly a half century had gone by since the Catholic Kings
had entered Granada and driven the last of the Moslems into
Africa and Columbus had come back from his voyages; only
thirty years since Cortés had sent back the golden shield of
the sun from Tenochtitlán; less since Pizarro and Valdivia had
sacked the temples of Peru and Chile.

Philip had been born and brought up in Valladolid amid the
enormous turmoil of the early conquests. Moorish artisans were

building church façades in the pagan style of the Italian renaissance tortured into crazy richness by memories of Granada and of the sculptured pyramids of America. There were Jews everywhere in their long gowns. Ideas of human liberty were seeping down from Flanders and Germany where Luther had discovered the individual conscience. The Church, choked with its own pomp and riches, was shaken with contagion of the pride of this world. Priests as well as nobles thought and whored and hunted and read Greek texts. The European spirit had broken out of the walls of humbleness and poverty and obedience built for it by the mediæval clergy. Men were dizzy with America. There was no limit to power or to pleasure for human life now, today. The kings were building palaces instead of castles. Mechanical invention had begun.

Philip was a man of order. His tastes were simple and severe. He hated and feared liberty and richness and lushness. These things were only for kings who exhibited them as symbols of the glory of God. In the Escorial, his great monastery-palace on the slope of the Guadarrama, he built his mind in quadrangles of grey granite. That was to be the spiritual center of the sober enormous Christian kingdom. Madrid was to be the lay capital, a city of clerks who would organize, annotate, file the records of a subject world that stretched north to Flanders, east to the two Sicilies, west as far as the imagination of man could conceive. Madrid was the nail he drove in to hold down the scattered empires. Then the Inquisition could weed out the unorthodox, the unruly, the too rich, the too thoughtful, the too intelligent. Philip II established in Madrid the first great bureaucracy in the modern world.

Philip and his holy office did their work so well, levelled their subjects so successfully to their measure of conformity and faith, let so much blood in the doing of it, that the whole great empire died. Only the bureaucracy went on giving out reflex motions like the legs of a dead frog. Louis XIV of France managed to drag the great carcass glittering with gold and steaming with incense in the wake of his weltpolitik for a while until his own dominion sickened with the same diseases. Everywhere the trading classes were putting kings and priests in their places. The French Bourbons themselves were thrown on the dustheap. Faced with the invasion of the modern world in the shape of Napoleon and the French the Spanish spirit flared up out of a century's long drowse. Madrid produced the revolt of the Dos de Mayo and the feverish pencil of Goya.

The nineteenth century in Spain was a period of further contraction with intermittent flares of new life. Cuba and the Philippines were the last outlet for easy jobs for the sons of landowners and successful bureaucrats. The bureaucracy was admittedly nothing but a jobholders' paradise. All concrete thought of service to the commonwealth had long ceased to be connected with it. So long as there were jobs to hold, cozy niches in the weatherworn edifices of church and state, there were traditionalists to defend them, and abstractions of honor duty loyalty to give them a sympathetic drapery. But there was always a section of the professional class left out in the cold. These were the people who kept breaking through the traditional crust that the secure bureaucrats had levelled over the country. There were always more ideas of generosity, honor, patriotism, easy living, liberalism than there were salaries to give them form and content. When Cuba and the Philippines were broken away under the shadow of Manifest Destiny, there was a final lopping off of opportunities for young men growing up. As a result came the revolting generation of '98, Kraussist idealism, and socialism from the top, enthusiasm for renovation: an effervescence of Europeanizing ideas.

All this meant a great deal of talk; jobholders who go to their offices at ten and leave at one and then look in again from five to seven, have a great deal of time for talk, and people who have no jobs at all have more yet. Hence the magnificent, and civilized in the Athenian sense, institution of Madrid cafés.

The cafés are as important a source of the Second Republic as the Ateneo. They are always open, they are always cheerful. A man can sit brooding over a single cup of coffee from the time he gets up till it's time to walk home in the greyness of the early morning, or else he can talk with a group of friends or with a casual stranger. He's not on the make, there's nothing to be gained; jobs come from family pull, money comes from a salary or a stipend, or from the lottery or roulette; to have no money is no disgrace. Talk is a pure art. Its only limits are the patience of the listeners who, when they get tired, can always pay for their coffee or charge it with a friendly waiter and walk out. The only place of entertainment that can compare with a Spanish café in cheapness and democracy is an American movie palace. But at a movie we pay for forgetfulness, darkness, soft seats and the stupor induced by a narcosis of secondhand daydreams. In his café the madrileño pays for his mild stimulant and has free entrance to the agora of concepts and ideas where he can make his way on his own. As the Stock Exchange is the central nervous system of New York, the cafés are the brains and spinal column of Madrid.

Las Constituyentes

The cortes that made up the republican constitution was ever so much like a tertulia at one of the best cafés. It failed to live out its constitutional span largely because its members got bored with the conversation there and moved to other cafés, and it follows naturally that Manuel Azaña, head of the government it created, exbureaucratic jobholder, president of the Ateneo, was the star of several famous tertulias. There lay the republic's strength, but also its weakness. The trouble was that the life of a professor, of the holder of a sinecure in a government office, or an entertaining talker in a café, offers little training in dealing with the grim coarse hardtoclassify and often deadly realities of the life of a country day by day. They never could span the distance between word and deed. This genial group of wellintentioned gentlemen who talked so well and so wittily, and so goodnaturedly exchanged their various ideas about liberty, education, transportation and farming, who arrived so late and sat so late polishing the phraseology of the constitution for the Republic of Manual and Intellectual Workers, helped create a Spain that they certainly did not intend.

They legalized the disappearance of Don Alfonso and his family, they gave Spain liberal divorcelaws and disestablished the Church, they abolished titles of nobility and confiscated (giving bonds in return) the estates of the grandees, but they also doubled the wages of the Civil Guard, established a new corps of strongarm men, the Assault Guards, whose business it is to break up demonstrations hostile to the Republic of Workers and to private property, and passed a Law of Public Order and a

Law against Vagrancy that would have made old Fernando VII, the Bourbon who got most pleasure out of shooting down his subjects, stand aghast. They sanctioned casual arrests of batches of citizens, mass deportations of working men and shootings of the rebellious in a way that must have made that genial old lowlife, the benevolent dictator, Primo de Rivera, turn in his grave. Don Alfonso, in his cosy retreat in Fontainebleau must have had more than one bitter thought about the trickiness of history's lotteries, when he read about the events in the Llobregat, at Villa de Don Fadrique, at Pasajes and Castilblanco and Casas Viejas. He'd been put on the skids for carrying out the death penalty against two mutinous army officers, and here were the honest men of the republic, in the name of progress and socialism, shooting down their fellowcitizens by the hundreds. They busted up the old glass case of feudalism, also in the name of liberty and justice; in so doing they destroyed Spain's only protection against its own growing capitalist class and against the international bourgeoisie.

How was it that these honest men, lawyers, doctors, socialist professors and lecturers, that finer element of the population that it is the dream of reformers the world over to get into positions of power, found themselves so situated that it was easy for them to vote approval of the deportations on the *Buenos Aires* or the shootings at Casas Viejas as it had been for their ancestors, the scholarly gentlemen, so full of Christian unction and unworldly thought we know in the portraits of El Greco, to approve of the stranglings and burnings of heretics and Jews in the days of good King Philip? What has happened to them since they went to visit their friends at the Model Jail under Primo, and gathered to conspire so idealistically in the Café del Leon opposite the postoffice?

For one thing, the scene changed faster than they realized. Spain has for centuries been acting out a very old and very beautifully arranged play: the ancient Christian pagan Mediterranean myth acted out day by day by the Church. The local festivals, the bullbaitings, the nuns and priests, the state coaches, the beggars were all part of it. The story of the redeemer coming to life in the spring, and the virgin mother goddess sorrowful and merciful, repeated in variants in the local saints and martyrs, pride and center of the civic life in each village, was deeply embedded in men's habits, if not in their minds. In matters of religion it is always hard to know how much is the alive core of feeling and how much is a merely mechanical incrustation of habits. Perhaps it was the prosperity and the sense of freedom the country got from keeping out of the last war, or the growing pressure of industrial life, or the influence of the American movies, or Ortega y Gasset's "*revolt of the masses,*" or all of them together, that suddenly broke up the processions and scattered the actors and turned Our Lady of Sorrows into a collector's item.

The disappearance of the Bourbons, in a thin whiff of smoke, like an old puffball when you step on it, was only an incident in the nationwide collapse of timeworn (and how delightful to the tourist) stage properties.

Whenever these deputies to the first cortes of the Second Republic stepped out of their comfortable and gaudily decorated clubhouse, they found themselves faced by a Spain older and newer than any they knew. Steeped in that academic ignorance of life that besets the intellectual and professional classes the world over, they found themselves, like any panicstricken human group, facing the unknown according to the lowest common denominator.

Almost to a man they called for jails and mausers and machineguns to protect the bureaucracy that was the source of the easy life and the hot milk and the coffee and the Americanmade cars, and order, property, investments.

They smelt danger. Maybe the new Spain wasn't the Spain of the Madrid bureaucracy, or the Spain of those who weren't holding jobs yet: the honest men.

So the Republic of Manual and Intellectual Workers turned out to be the Republic of those who work others so that they shan't have to work themselves.

3. UNDERDOG POLITICS

History

To the Romans Spain meant Saguntum. In the Punic Wars an Iberian town on a hill overlooking the Mediterranean and the rich plains, that are in our time the orangegardens of Valencia, held out for months against the enormous army of Hannibal; then when the cisterns were dry and the granaries empty, the people of Saguntum, to a sound of pipes and drums, set to work to build bonfires out of the doors and roofbeams of their houses, and burnt themselves up with their wives and children and their town. As Saguntum was on their side, the Roman historians handed down its defense to posterity as one of the great heroic exploits of all time. It is a happening that has been repeated again and again in the history of the peninsula. Zaragoza and Gerona are famous for the heartbreaking sieges they stood from the French; the history of the workers' struggle in the last century is full of strikes carried on and on by small groups to the point of starvation.

Lope de Vega cashed in on this local heroism in a play that has been very popular in Russia in the last few years. *Fuente Ovejuna* is the story of the revolt of a small town in the mountains of the province of Cordova. (The fact that the town revolted from the Knights of Calatrava, allied to the Portuguese, and submitted to the Catholic Kings, made it a good patriotic subject.) The townsmen, led by their alcalde and urged on by the womenfolk, rise and murder the local tyrant and his retainers. In the inquest conducted by a military judge to find out who is responsible for this infraction of law and order, men women and children are put to torture. The judge and the executioners wear themselves out working the rack. All that anyone will answer, when asked who is the murderer, is "Fuente Ovejuna killed the Commendador." Fuente Ovejuna was one of the towns that declared itself a free canton at the time of the Federalist revolution of 1873, and its daylaborers were involved in revolutionary anarchist strikes in the first decade of this century. From Saguntum and Fuente Ovejuna you can run a straight line through recorded history to the shootings at Casas Viejas in January, 1933.

Geography

If you fly over any part of Spain in an airplane the country you look down on is ridged like a walnut shell. Even the plateau section of Aragon and the two Castiles is crossed by small ranges and wavy rolling hills, all the rest is a tangle of mountains through which wind a net of more or less narrow and canyonlike or broad and fertile rivervalleys. That is why, in spite of the great imperial steamrollers that have worked for centuries to flatten it out, Spain remains a country of independent towns. There still survives in people's minds and in the economic setup the original Mediterranean unit of society, the citystate. Probably the act of most actual historical significance in connection with the collapse of the monarchy has been the restoration to Barcelona and its Catalanspeaking hinterland of its position as an autonomous citystate.

Spain seen from Madrid is a very different country than Spain seen from the small towns. The provincial capitals are, it is true, administered by small pools of bureaucrats that reflect the colors of Madrid, but under that thin veneer the people have not yet come to think of themselves as Spaniards. They are Gallegos or Catalans or Valencians. Working people and small storekeepers are more likely to make the jump out of the mediæval church and town life in the direction of America. When they can't make a living in their native places, they tend to emigrate to Havana or Buenos Aires instead of to Madrid (or did until the depression clamped down its iceage on international travel and trade). Only professional people and students and the sons of officials enter the mandarin circle of the capital within which is all the surface of political and intellectual life. The gentlemen who made the republic live within that circle. Few of them seem to know the many and diverse Spains that exist under the surface. Or if they know them, they don't feel them in their bones.

The monarchy had long since ceased to mean anything to these Spains. It had come to be an incident in the life of Madrid like the Fountain of Cibeles or the Puerta del Sol. So far, the republic that has replaced it means very little, either, to the country as a whole. The liberal group of wellintentioned gentlemen, who moved the witty conversations of the Buffet Italiano and La Granja to the congressbuilding and the debates of the Ateneo into the government offices, were elected, it is true, by a genuine revolt of the voters given their chance by the first national election in years that hadn't been rigged. They overflowed with ideas of liberty democracy and service, but they had no thought of trying to jolt the basic structure of the nation onto any new track. The vested interests, except for the obsolete nobility, were untouched. They boasted that the rights of property would be respected. They made no effort to change the basic setup of power. They did not turn out the local bosses, they merely turned them in a few cases upsidedown. It was only a new track that could have saved them.

The Caciques

The cacique is a Tammany wardboss Iberian style with some traces left of a feudal commendador. Sometimes he rules over a small town and sometimes over a whole region, like the gentleman who runs Murcia, or the picturesque Don Juan March whose fief is the Balearic Islands. Under the monarchy his business was to turn the votes of his section to whatever political combination made it worth his while. Often time and money were saved by not letting the citizens vote at all, the cacique just announcing to Madrid how many votes he controlled. In return the cacique was buttered up with contracts and sinecures, and controlled the local patronage. In the old days his politics were liberal or conservative according as he played with La Cierva or Romanones, the supercaciques in Madrid; in the days of Primo he was a member of the Union Patriotica; it was only natural that when the king fled he should undergo an overnight change of spots into a republican or into a socialist or into that curious type of politico on the French model, a radical socialist (with radical meaning conservative and socialist on the make). The election in the fall of 1933 showed how these fresh colors on the caciques were already wearing thin.

The old type of cacique was not very active outside of his home town, tended to sit in the casino receiving friends and retainers and settling business and would only stir out for an occasional drive around his estates or a trip to a balneario for his health or to Paris to see life.

Juan March, who was the public enemy No. 1 of the Azaña régime and was one of the major architects of Azaña's fall, has had a livelier career. His life sounds as if it had been made up by Blasco Ibañez. He was a thrifty young Mallorquin sailor who made a good thing of tobacco smuggling and of selling supplies to the Allies and gasoline to the German submarines during the war. By the time of Primo his tobaccosmuggling business in Morocco had so undermined the trade of the legal monopoly that the elderly dictator very realistically handed the monopoly over to him. He became one of the wealthiest men in Spain. The Azaña government clapped him into jail on his tobacco deals but didn't quite manage to bring him to trial. In jail he became a deadly enemy of the liberal group, bought up papers of all shades of opposition opinion, including *La Libertad*, that had been, under the monarchy, virtually the organ of that same group, and managed to get his faithful Mallorquins to elect him to the Tribunal of Guarantees, a new high court that is to perform some of the functions of our Supreme Court. The man who went to Mallorca to campaign against him for a seat in the cortes found that there wasn't a single automobile in Palma he could hire for his speaking tour. Every driver he caught up with told him he'd been hired by Don Juan March until after the election. March escaped from what was supposed to be the most breakproof jail in Spain, appeared in Gibraltar in the company of one of the wardens, drinking his coffee with a group of exiled grandees, and went from there to France, was elected to the second cortes by an enormous majority in the Balearic Islands, and returned to Spain a very powerful man indeed.

The Casas del Pueblo

Outside of the caciques, the republic's contact with the basic elements of the peninsula was maintained, up to the fall of the Azaña régime, through the Socialist Party, that has the only really modern organization of any Spanish political party. The Socialist Party was built up by Pablo Iglesias, a Spanish Gene Debs, who filled the more skilled section of the working class with the Debs tradition of orderly humane careful progress through idealist organizations. The liberal socialism of Spanish workers was in many ways a reaction against the romantic confusion and the use of terror by the predominant anarchists. Its leaders believed blindly in all the liberal cultural values of the nineteenth century and gladly accepted the political help of doctors and lawyers and professors who thought they were socialists because they didn't like to hear of children starving to death or to see men in blue workclothes ridden down in the street by the Civil Guard. Through a sort of truce with Primo de Rivera, the Socialist Party became the strongest republican party in Spain and built up a compact trade union organization, the U.G.T., under Largo Caballero, a dogged working-class bureaucrat of the Gompers type. So, when the monarchy crumbled, leaving the old line politicos paralyzed with terror, it was natural that the Socialist Party with its power to call general strikes in Madrid and Bilbao, its 800,000 organized workers, and its many sympathizers among students and desk workers, should be the strongest prop of the new régime. The Socialists with 115 votes were the majority party in the Constituent Cortes.

The Casas del Pueblo were started way back as political and cultural centers for the workingclass. Under the old régime the first thing a provincial governor did when there was any kind of trouble in the air, was close up the local Casa del Pueblo. Many were under nonpolitical or anarchist leadership, but in the flush of republican victory, the Socialist group in any town usually got control. They are a real element of cohesion, in contact with the diverse populations of the country; at the Casa del Pueblo a miner can talk to small peasants or trolley conductors or construction workers or storeclerks, or listen to sympathetic members of the professional classes make speeches, recite poetry or lecture on hygiene.

His enemies claim that under the Azaña government Largo Caballero, holding the Ministry of Labor, turned them into small Tammanies, building up the power of the Socialist Party by distributing doles and jobs, meanwhile using the forces of law and order to crush the anarchist and syndicalist-controlled labor organizations and to force working people into his camp. Certainly everything possible was done to build up socialist influence among the peasants and in the small towns and through the mixed boards (of employers and employees) to arbitrate strikes. In the cortes the Socialistas always threw their vote for central authority and repressive machinery.

The repressive machinery of compulsory arbitration was all very well while the Socialistas were in control. It was at least used for the benefit of one section of the working class. The trouble is that it can so easily be thrown into reverse. As soon as the gentlemen upstairs got control they used it to close the doors on the advance of the workers and producers into the well-lighted upper world of comparative ease and power. For this now triumphant socialism in reverse, Mussolini a few years ago invented the intensely selling label of fascism. The gentlemen upstairs are now sitting happily at the wheel.

The Port of Seville

The situation in Seville is typical. Since Seville had the biggest boom, when Primo de Rivera tried to go American at the time of the exposition and turn the señoritos into realestate boosters, it has suffered the worst slump of any Spanish town. A great many unskilled workers attracted there by the boom in building and shipping found themselves jobless and starving when the republic was proclaimed. The strongest working class organization there was the Longshoremen's Union built up by Manuel Adame and affiliated to the Third International. Alongside it were more or less crumbling anarchist organizations and a few socialist outfits. The owners and boosters were broke and demoralized. By a magnificent show of workingclass unity and force the reds put over the general strike that nipped General Sanjurjo's uprising in the bud. The señoritos were badly frightened again. Nothing but the habit of submission stood between the workingclass organizations and control of the city. What happened? The communist leader Adame was discovered by Moscow to be heretical and was thrown out. He went over to the left wing of the Socialistas but his authority was much diminished. Meanwhile the government rightwing socialists were filling the jails with the very communists and syndicalists who had just gone out on the street to defend them against the monarchists. What resulted was the crushing of the Longshoremen's Union, the buildingup of a small weak Socialista Tammany, a bitter triangular fight between socialists, communists and anarchists, all equally threatened with unemployment and starvation, shooting, gangsterism and bleak discouragement. It's not surprising that the propertyowners, backed up by the unsleeping everunited organization of the church, carried the day.

Libertarian Communism

In Spain as everywhere else in Europe, the function of the Socialist Party has been to give disorganized capitalism a breathingspace. Of course the socialists never intended to find themselves in this predicament, what they wanted was justice for all and orderly and humane progress toward a socialized state. What happened was that they were more scared of a slogan that had got into the mouth of the underdog than they were of a monarchist restoration; for the monarchists at least believed first in the sanctity of moneypower, property and investments, as the socialists did deep down under their humanitarian skins. The terrifying slogan was Libertarian Communism.

The Spanish working class awoke to the modern world under the spell of Bakunin. In fact the Congress of Córdoba in 1872 gave international anarchism a typically Spanish cast that it has not lost to this day. Both the communal autonomy and the personal Quixotism that have been the distinguishing marks of anarchist movements all over the world have a distinctly Iberian tang.

The Spanish peasant and worker in industry tends to be narrowly sectionalist in his home town and internationalist outside it. The tenants and daylaborers of Andalusia and the millhands of Catalonia have staged again and again great revolutionary strikes that have failed through lack of cohesion among the local groups. Almost always there was perfect solidarity within any given village, but complete lack of organization on a national scale. The history of Spain since the middle of the last century has been a series of these revolutionary waves, spaced about ten years apart, with the crests alternating between Andalusia and Catalonia. In each case the owning class has been forced into temporary unity by the fear of losing lands and factories and has been able to crush the revolt with the help of the central government's troops. As the wave receded, the beaten workers and peasants tended to emigrate to America or to drop into the outlaw class, affirming their defiance of the world and its wrongs by individual acts of terrorism.

January, 1933, was one of these times. In spite of the growing power of the carefully organized socialist movement the anarchist syndicates loosely organized in the C.N.T. still have a great many more members than the U.G.T., something like a million and a half to the U.G.T.'s eight hundred thousand. These syndicates are under the influence of two groups of agitators, the exponents of immediate action and any kind of action in the F.A.I (Federacion Anarchista Iberica) and the socalled Thirty who, under the influence of Angel Pestaña, are urging a more moderate policy of massacre and nonviolence similar to that of the communists. The anarchist syndicalists of all colors tend not to vote, and to consider all political action as spurious and deluding. However, as they constitute a power within the state, they have been unable to escape being involved in more than one political combination. In Catalonia they have tended to be friendly with Macia's romantic nationalist party of the Esquerra, and in national politics fierce persecution by the Socialistas has thrown them into connection with the unsavory demagogic fringes of Lerroux's Radicals (anticlerical conservatives). What resulted was that the January wave of peasants' and workers' revolts and the succeeding waves throughout 1933 found not only the socialists cooling the ardor of their adherents, but anarchist leaders as well sending out messages that the great day of el reparto (the division of lands and wealth) had not yet come.

But somehow in January, 1933, the word got around that the great day had come. The landless peasants who live like serfs on the great Andalusian estates, and millhands in Catalonia ground down between rising prices and lowering wages, had been excited by the ease with which the bourgeoisie of the big towns had run out the king and at least temporarily paralyzed the power of the church. Their economic condition was becoming more and more desperate, as the landlords and millowners were quietly sabotaging the new deal social legislation of the liberals in Madrid by leaving their lands uncultivated or closing down their factories. So a series of strikes and popular disturbances began to break out, more or less isolated one from the other, in various parts of Spain.

The Saguntum of the 1933 movement was Casas Viejas.

Benalup

Benalup, the old name of Casas Viejas, has an African sound. It is a small hamlet on a hill in the township of Medina Sidonia (a town that dates back to the Phœnicians; it was the Duke of

Medina Sidonia who commanded the Invincible Armada that
Philip II sent in his capacity of King of England to bring
Queen Bess to her senses), in the province of Cádiz. The
province of Cádiz is the part of Spain nearest Morocco. It's a
country of arid eroded mountains, yellow sunbleached hills and
riverbottoms fertile and green so far as the scarce water can be
eked out. The people, like the Berbers, have their skin tanned
to leather by the sun and wind, are dead shots with the rifle,
and in the poorer hilltowns near Gibraltar, like Casas Viejas,
live largely by poaching and smuggling tobacco. The houses
are of stone and adobe, enormously clean, whitewashed several
times a year. The houses of the storekeepers and landowners
have tiled roofs, balconies and shady patios full of plants in
pots. The houses of the poor have hardly any windows and are
thatched with straw. Nearly always they have a little paved
court and a grapevine on a pergola outside the front door.
Most of the arable land is in the hands of large landowners and
the landless live from hand to mouth as daylaborers. Like the
laborers in the Bible they go each morning to the main square
of the town to wait to be hired. Twentyfive cents a day is considered a good wage. Their complete poverty is mitigated by
the fact that the sun is hot most of the year, and that bread, oil
and wine and tomatoes are cheap and good.

That winter there was no work. In many towns the entire
population of hired hands and their wives and children were
on the municipal dole. That meant that most of the week they
went hungry. In the local syndicates they had plenty of time
to talk about a better arrangement of society. In Casas Viejas
the leading spirit of the anarchist union (their little meeting-
place with a portrait of Bakunin on the wall, next to the
wineshop, was known to the local storekeepers and respectable people as the Madhouse) was an old man known as
Seisdedos (sixfingers) who had been the village rebel for so
long that rebellion had come to be a sort of tradition in his
family. He and his sons and sonsinlaw were known in the village as the Libertarians. He was said to have a good deal of
that vigor and refinement of mind, expressed in rare salty
speech, that is common among Andalusian countrypeople.

The socialist and republican orators in the days before Don
Alfonso had fled had gone around promising to find land for

every landless man. The members of the anarchist unions had been too canny to believe them, but they had used those promises as a talkingpoint among the countrypeople to win adherents. Only the revolt of men of kidney would bring the day of el reparto and the reign of justice; the politicians had been given time to make good their promises; now it was time to seize the municipalities and distribute the land. It was only a question of waiting for the day when all the towns in Spain would run out or shoot the Civil Guard and declare themselves free communes. Then, if the bourgeoisie resisted, up and at them with the sharpened sickles; if they didn't resist let them take their share with the rest. That was the program of Libertarian Communism. In Casas Viejas every member of the syndicate had his gun oiled and ready and his collection of knives and sickles carefully sharpened and waiting for the day.

In the early days of January a series of strikes and riots took place in Barcelona and Valencia and Lerida, in connection with a strike of railroad workers called by some of the anarchist-syndicalist unions. In Catalonia several townhalls were seized and the red and black anarchist flag raised on them. In the province of Cádiz word went round that the time for el reparto had come. There was to be a march of countrypeople on Jerez, a strike in Cádiz, everywhere the workers were to seize the towns. On the tenth there'd been scattered shooting in Medina Sidonia; a group of armed men tried to ambush the alcalde's automobile, and exchanged volleys, in which no one was hurt, with the Civil Guard. The same day the little union (numbering at the outside a hundred and fifty members) at Casas Viejas got word that Libertarian Communism had been proclaimed all over Spain and that it was up to them to do their parts.

The morning of the eleventh was clear and very cold. At dawn the members of the union met with all their arms and raised the red and black flag over their meeting place. Then they routed the sleeping alcalde, a peaceable sort of a man who'd been appointed to the job because he was the only socialist in the village, out of his bed and told him to come with them to the barracks of the four Civil Guards who represented law and order in Casas Viejas. He must explain to them that Libertarian Communism had been proclaimed and that the best thing they could do was to surrender their arms; in that case nobody would hurt them.

By this time the sun was up filling the whitewashed town with a white glare against which shadows moved sharp and black. Hungry men who had been shivering in their thin denims began to feel warmer and more confident. Grouped up in the street in front of the barracks of the Civil Guard they began to lay plans about how they would divide the land. Women gathered around them bringing bowls and saucepans. Their men had told them that everybody in town would eat meat that day. But the alcalde came back saying that the Civil Guard would die rather than surrender. Libertarian Communism wasn't going to be so easy.

The guards barricaded their door. Their terrified wives began picking a hole through the wall into the next house. Reports conflict as to who started shooting; they always do. The men of Casas Viejas were crack shots. Two of the guards were shot in the head when they tried to take aim through the windows.

After that there was a lull. The alcalde got permission to go into the barracks again to argue with the guards some more, and seems to have slipped out of the back door of the barracks and gone home, and so far as anybody knows, back to bed.

Meanwhile Seisdedos had sent a detachment to cut the telephone wires and to barricade the road from Medina Sidonia. Others raided the store for cartridges and guns and seized some foodstuffs there to satisfy the women. When the storekeeper protested that he was a poor man and that they were ruining him, they paid him for the food out of the syndicate's scantily furnished cashdrawer. Another bunch went to the office where the titledeeds to property and records of loans and mortgages were kept and burned all the papers they could find. When the better people of Casas Viejas woke up to what was going on, they piled their heaviest furniture against their doors and huddled trembling in the darkest part of their houses. Their terror was increased by groups of boys walking around the streets and shooting into the air, crying "Viva el comunismo libertario."

Every little while Seisdedos sent somebody to the upper part of the town to look for the train. If the morning train didn't go past in the valley it meant that the general strike was on; if it passed at its regular time it meant that Casas Viejas stood alone against all the forces of the owners of Spain. They saw the train, a little black caterpillar winding through the valley, the smoke white as cotton in the cold morning light. They heard it whistle. From then on they knew their revolt was hopeless.

Before the wires were cut the guards had managed to call Medina Sidonia. At two o'clock reinforcements arrived. At the entrance to the village they had a brush with the syndicalists, who broke and ran for the hills.

In the square Seisdedos and his friends were arguing about the division of the land. When a boy came breathless to tell him the syndicalists had run, he turned and went up the hill to his house. "Come in with me whoever wants to die," he said. Five men, two women and his small grandson stayed with him. They say he begged the women to leave and take away the child, but they wouldn't. They piled the place with rifles and ammunition and barred the stout wooden door.

Meanwhile the forces of law and order were pulling themselves together. The wounded guards were sent to the hospital, where one of them later died. The Civil Guard held the approaches to the square but waited for more help before mopping up the rebels. The village was deathly quiet, shuttered white houses with big closed wooden doors; nobody stirred on the streets.

At five twelve the Assault Guard arrived under a lieutenant who took charge of the situation. They began searching the poorer houses to make arrests. First the lieutenant ordered a cheer for the republic and had the red and black flag taken down from over the union hall. In one house they found four or five men whom they beat up with sticks to teach them respect for the republic, but as the one unwounded Civil Guard left who'd been in the fight that morning vouched for them they were let go. Next they arrested a man named Quijada, who the guard claimed had fired on the barracks. They put the handcuffs on him and continued on up the street.

The thatched hut of the Libertarians was one of the highest in the place; as it was on a steep slope, part of it was dug into the hillside. In front of the door was a little paved court with a vine on a pergola and a huge pricklypear. When the Assault Guards tried to break down the door, a volley broke out from the hut, killing one man and wounding another, who fell into the little courtyard. The lieutenant and his guards prudently took cover, and began shooting at the hut from behind a wall.

Then from behind the wall the lieutenant called to the people in the hut to surrender, and sent in the handcuffed Quijada to argue with them. The door closed on Quijada.

After half an hour, in the company of still more reinforcements, from La Linea this time, the lieutenant ordered the firing to begin again. He himself went down to the square and telegraphed to Cádiz for handgrenades. The men of Casas Viejas are crack shots. Their huts have thick adobe walls.

At ten o'clock that night, the Assault Guards were still firing volleys into the hut.

Then at two in the morning Captain Rojas, an exarmy-officer with experience in Morocco, arrived with a full company of Assault Guards. By this time there had been several more guards wounded by the sharpshooting from within the hut, but no answer to more demands to surrender. Captain Rojas took charge and deployed a full military attack with rifle-fire, machine guns and handgrenades, with no result. In the small hours of the morning a telegram arrived signed Governmental Delegate, ordering the captain to raze the house to the ground at once at any cost. (The governmental delegate had decided that he could best watch developments from the hotel at Medina Sidonia.) So the captain gave orders to burn the house down. His men soaked cotton wool in gasoline and wrapped it round stones and threw them onto the dry thatch. In a few minutes the roof was burning, soon it fell in; the space between the adobe walls was a furnace. Before the roof fell in the door opened and Maria and the child ran out. Josefa, with her dress in flames, and one man tried to follow but were drilled through by a volley from the Assault Guards. Even as the thatch burned round them the men in the hut kept up their shooting.

When there were no more shots and the fire had burned down a little, Captain Rojas led his men to the square for two hours' wellneeded rest. They were too jumpy to rest; they saw syndicalists behind every barred door. At dawn they began going through the streets in groups, breaking down doors and arresting and handcuffing any man they found. In one house they shot an old man seventythree years old because he didn't open up soon enough to suit them. In some of the houses they reassured the women and children when they arrested the men, saying that they were only taking them to give testimony.

This is Captain Rojas' own account of what followed: "These prisoners, when we got them up the house of Seisdedos, to show them what they had done, I made them go down into the court to see what they'd been responsible for, the lousy mess they'd made; and as the situation and the moment were very grave and I was completely unnerved, because it wasn't only the situation in Casas Viejas, but in the whole province in revolt that worried me; and that there were five hundred armed men in my rear along the road and the people in arms in Medina Sidonia, and the people in the village, and the whole thing in a state of anarchy, not only on account of myself, but on account of the danger to the Republic, that if I didn't give them a powerful lesson, there was danger that anarchy might break out in the whole region, and the men chased into the sierra might come down again, which would have been bad.

"So for this reason and for the Republic, and for the sake of the government and the safety of my own men; when we got there to the house, there wasn't anything else to do. The thing is that these orders when they'd been given to the officers had seemed to some of them a little strong and hard to carry out; but seeing that it was the only solution for the defence of the Republic and the government and my own men I decided to do it; so on getting to the little court, when they'd gone down in there (although what I'd planned to do to the prisoners was to use the ley de fuga on them at the entrance to the village) there was one of them who looked at the dead guard whose body lay charred in the doorway and said something to another of them and gave me a dirty look. . . . Well I couldn't stand his insolence and I shot him and immediately the others fired and all those who were looking at the charred body of the guard fell, and then we did the same with the others who hadn't gone down to look at the body, I think there were two of them. That way I obeyed orders and saved Spain from the anarchy that was rising on all sides and saved the Republic. . . ." They shot down sixteen of the village men and threw their bodies into the burned hut.

After that the Assault Guards and the Civil Guards who had been engaged in this work were drawn up in formation in the square in the sunlight and the governmental delegate, who had finally gotten up his nerve to come on from Medina Sidonia, made them a speech complimenting them on their courage and energy, asked for a minute of silence in honor of the dead and then for a good rousing cheer for the Republic.

The Ghost of Casas Viejas

The story of the death of Seisdedos went all over Spain, although, except for Ramón Sender's account in *La Libertad*, the press softpedalled it as much as possible. At first the government denied that any such thing had happened, but gradually as the fear of a syndicalist revolt faded, the fact became apparent that some pretty dirty business had gone on. Eventually Ortega y Gasset read a detailed account of the whole thing, with statements of all concerned, to the cortes. The cortes voted that the government was not responsible; even at a meeting of the Ateneo, home of humanitarian liberalism, a vote of censure was defeated. Here is Captain Rojas' account, read to the cortes by Ortega y Gasset, of what happened when he got back to Madrid.

". . . On my return to Madrid I told him (the Director-General of Security) everything that had happened and he told me that it would be inconvenient for the government if I told how we had killed the prisoners and that absolutely no one ought to find out about it, as it would be sure to get out; he asked me to give my word of honor to tell nobody, which I did, giving my word of honor.

"When His Excellency the Minister of Government called me to his office to give him an account of what had happened Señor Menendez (the Director-General of Security) was there with him. It was he who introduced me, and on going into the room I whispered to him, should I tell everything, but he said everything except about the shootings, and that's what I did, being congratulated by his excellency the minister.

"But when they began to talk so much about the shootings in the cortes I went to see Menendez again in his office, and told him I feared that Lieutenant A—— ... knowing his character, I was scared he'd tell everybody, and then Menendez said I should go right away to Seville using my military pass, and that I should say I was going to Jerez to see what the Assault Guards were up to in their barracks in Jerez and that I should see Lieutenant A—— and tell him to buck up and not tell the truth to a living soul. I did that and returned to Madrid the same night. For the trip, as I hadn't any money, I told his secretary Señor G—— to give me twenty duros, which he did, with which money I took the trip. On my return to Madrid Señor G—— was waiting for me at the station with two detectives: we got into Señor G——'s car and he said we'd breakfast together, which we did in a café in the Calle de Alcalá, near the Puerta del Sol. While we were breakfasting he talked to me of many things, telling me in the end that he had gone to meet me because the government was in danger, and that it was going to fall on account of what happened at Casas Viejas, and that, so that the President of the Council shouldn't fall the Minister of Government had to, and so that he shouldn't fall the Director of Security had to; and that he came to say to me wouldn't I, as a friend of his, he being my co-worker and director, and in view of what everybody else was doing, wouldn't I sacrifice myself for him? Right away I answered Yes, that I was ready for anything and would do whatever he said. From the café I went to Pontejos to leave my bag, and then to the office, where they all told me that they'd known all along I was a man, and things like that. Menendez told me to write out an account of the whole business as Señor G—— suggested and dictated in relation to what I'd told him, and that I shouldn't put down anything about the orders he'd given me, a copy of the said account being enclosed with this writing.

"When the other captains got wind of this business they all told me plenty about the director, that I didn't believe at the time, but that opened my eyes; and as it happened one night while we were writing up the account, they introduced me to the Señora Menendez, who with one thing and another, said to me that this was how it was, sometimes we had to make sacrifices one for another, and that when another government came they'd make a hero of me; and also another day when Señor G—— sat writing at my left, he said that they were going to give me a month's leave right away to go any place I wanted, and a big mound of hundred peseta notes to spend on parties, and again the other night at the dance for 'Miss *Voz*,' the Superior Chief of Vigilance, accompanied by Señor L—— and the State's Attorney Señor F——, told me not to worry about anything, and that if anything happened to me now, they'd fix it up afterwards and see I got a good job; it's on account of all this that I came to understand that they were doublecrossing both the Government and me, and that's why I refused to sign the account of what had happened unless they let me put in the orders they had given me.

"And that is why I'm making this declaration in my own handwriting, and putting it in somebody's care, so that if what Señor Menendez says is really for the good of Spain, it may be torn up; but if the contrary is true, that it may serve to make the facts clear, as a beginning of the task I am undertaking to uncover the traitors who are working against the republic.

"God grant that these notes may be torn up and that my sacrifice may really be for the good of Spain and the republic; but if all this is being worked up by one man merely to hold his position, without attention to the evil he is doing, may these notes come into the light of day, so that they may be fairly judged.

"Today, 1st March 1933 (signed)
"Assault Captain Manuel Rojas Feijeuspan."

Ortega y Gasset's reading of these documents resulted in the arrest of the Director of Security and a volley of resignations all down the line. But the ghosts of Casas Viejas continued to walk, and became a factor in the crushing defeat of the government of honest men in the November election. Whether it was the shooting of the daylaborers of Casas Viejas, or the repudiating of it afterwards that turned out most unluckily will be a matter for historians to decide. Anyway the hour has struck for the liberals and the day of the reactionaries has come.

This was the reply of Señor Azaña, President of the Council, to the reading of the documents about Casas Viejas.

"Not a word came from the government, not a bat of an eye that could justify the circulation of such orders, the result of which the government contemplates with horror. If I had been told that one man had fallen unduly in Casas Viejas, one single victim, I should have doubted it. But they told me that fourteen or sixteen men had been shot, and that constituted such an enormity, such an absurdity that I refused to believe it."

Is it the historic mission, as Trotsky would put it, of well-meaning liberals and social democrats the world over to be left helplessly "contemplating with horror" the collapse of the very civilized life they prize so highly?

Madrid, August, 1933

V. Stamped with the Eagle

1. 300 RED AGITATORS INVADE PASSAIC

The people who had come from New York roamed in a desultory group along the broad pavement. We were talking of outrages and the Bill of Rights. The people who had come from New York wore warm overcoats in the sweeping wind, bits of mufflers, and fluffiness of women's blouses fluttered silky in the cold April wind. The people who had come from New York filled up a row of taxicabs, shiny sedans of various makes, nicely upholstered; the shiny sedans started off in a procession towards the place where the meeting was going to be forbidden. Inside we talked in a desultory way of outrages and the Bill of Rights, we, descendants of the Pilgrim Fathers, the Bunker Hill Monument, Gettysburg, the Boston Teaparty . . . *Know all men by these presents.* . . . On the corners groups of yellowish grey people standing still, square people standing still as chunks of stone, looking nowhere, saying nothing.

At the place where the meeting was going to be forbidden the people from New York got out of the shiny sedans of various makes. The sheriff was a fat man with a badge like a star off a Christmas tree, the little eyes of a suspicious landlady in a sallow face. The cops were waving their clubs about, limbering up their arms. The cops were redfaced, full of food, the cops felt fine. The special deputies had restless eyes, they were stocky young men crammed with sodapop and ideals, overgrown boyscouts; they were on the right side and they knew it. Still the shiny new doublebarrelled riot guns made them nervous. They didn't know which shoulder to keep their guns on. The people who had come from New York stood first on one foot then on the other.

Don't shoot till you see the whites of their eyes. . . .

"All right move 'em along," said the sheriff.

The cops advanced, the special deputies politely held open the doors of the shiny sedans. The people who had come from New York climbed back into the shiny sedans of various makes and drove away, except for one man who was slow and got picked up. The procession of taxis started back the way it had come. The procession of taxis, shiny sedans of various makes, went back the way it had come, down empty streets protected by deputies with shiny new riot guns, past endless façades of deserted mills, past brick tenements with illpainted stoops, past groups of squat square women with yellow grey faces, groups of men and boys standing still, saying nothing, looking nowhere, square hands hanging at their sides, people square and still, chunks of yellowgrey stone at the edge of a quarry, idle, waiting, on strike.

New York, October, 1925

2. THE WRONG SET OF WORDS

Fishpeddler

About dawn on Monday, May 3rd, 1920, the body of Andrea Salsedo, an anarchist printer, was found smashed on the pavement of Park Row. He had been arrested for deportation eight weeks before in the tail end of the anti-Red raids of the Department of Justice then running amok under A. Mitchell Palmer. The man had jumped or been thrown from a window of the offices of the Department of Justice on the fourteenth floor of the Park Row building. What happened during those eight weeks of imprisonment and third degree will never be known.

At that time Bartolomeo Vanzetti was peddling fish in the pleasant little Italian and Portuguese town of North Plymouth. He was planning to go into fishing himself in partnership with a man who owned some dories. Early mornings, pushing his cart up and down the long main street, ringing his bell, chatting with housewives in Piedmontese, Tuscan, pidgin English, he worried about the raids, the imprisonment of comrades, the lethargy of the working people. He was an anarchist, after the school of Galeani. Between the houses he could see the gleaming stretch of Plymouth Bay, the sandy islands beyond, the white dories at anchor. About three hundred years before, men from the west of England had first sailed into the grey shimmering bay that smelt of woods and wild grape, looking for something; liberty . . . freedom to worship God in their own manner . . . space to breathe. Thinking of these things, worrying as he pushed the little cart loaded with eels, haddock, cod, halibut, swordfish, Vanzetti spent his mornings making change, weighing out fish, joking with the housewives. It was better than working at the great cordage works that own North Plymouth. Some years before he had tried to organize a strike there and been blacklisted. The officials and detectives at the Plymouth Cordage, the largest cordage in the world, thought of him as a Red, a slacker and troublemaker.

Shoemaker

At the same time Nicola Sacco was living in Stoughton, working an edging machine at the Three K's Shoe Factory, where star workmen sometimes made as high as eighty or ninety dollars a week. He had a pretty wife and a little son named Dante. There was another baby coming. He lived in a bungalow belonging to his employer, Michael Kelly. The house adjoined Kelly's own house and the men were friends. Often Kelly advised him to lay off this anarchist stuff. There was no money in it. It was dangerous the way people felt nowadays. Sacco was a clever young fellow and could soon get to be a prosperous citizen, maybe own a factory of his own someday, live by other men's work.

But Sacco, working in his garden in the early morning before the whistles blew, hilling beans, picking off potatobugs, letting grains of corn slip by twos and threes through his fingers into the finely worked earth, worried about things. He was an anarchist. He loved the earth and people, he wanted them to walk straight over the free hills, not to stagger bowed under the ordained machinery of industry; he worried mornings working in his garden at the lethargy of the working people. It was not enough that he was happy and had fifteen hundred or more dollars in the bank for a trip home to Italy.

The Red Menace

Three years before Sacco and Vanzetti had both of them had their convictions put to the test. In 1917, against the expressed votes of the majority, Woodrow Wilson had allowed the United States to become involved in the war with Germany. When the law was passed for compulsory military service a registration day for citizens and aliens was announced. Most young men submitted whatever their convictions were. A few of those who were morally opposed to any war or to capitalist war had the nerve to protest. Sacco and Vanzetti and some friends ran away to Mexico. There, some thirty of them lived in a set of adobe houses. Those who could get jobs worked. It was share and share alike. Everything was held in common. There were in the community men of all trades and conditions: bakers, butchers, tailors, shoemakers, cooks, carpenters, waiters. It was a momentary realization of the hope of anarchism. But living was difficult in Mexico and they began to get letters from the States telling that it was possible to avoid the draft, telling of high wages. Little by little they filtered back across the border. Sacco and Vanzetti went back to Massachusetts.

There was an Italian club that met Sunday evenings in a hall in Maverick Square, East Boston, under the name of the Italian Naturalization Society. Workmen from the surrounding industrial towns met to play bowls and to discuss social problems. There were anarchists, syndicalists, socialists of various colors. The Russian revolution had fired them with new hopes. The persecution of their comrades in various parts of America had made them feel the need of mutual help. While far away across the world new eras seemed to be flaring up into the sky, at home the great machine they slaved for seemed more adamant, more unshakable than ever. Everywhere aliens were being arrested, tortured, deported. To the war heroes who had remained at home any foreigner seemed a potential Bolshevik, a menace to the security of Old Glory and liberty bonds and the bonus. When Elia and Salsedo were arrested in New York there was great alarm among the Italian radicals around Boston. Vanzetti went down to New York to try to hire a lawyer for the two men. There he heard many uneasy rumors. The possession of any literature that might be interpreted as subversive by ignorant and brutal agents of the departments of Justice and Labor was dangerous. It was not that deportation was so much to be feared, but the beating up and third degree that preceded it.

On May 3rd Salsedo was found dead on Park Row. The impression was that he had been murdered by the agents of the

Department of Justice. There was a rumor too that a new raid was going to be made in the suburbs of Boston. There was a scurry to hide pamphlets and newspapers. Nobody must forget that people had even been arrested for distributing the Declaration of Independence. At the same time they couldn't let this horrible affair go by without a meeting of protest. Handbills announcing a meeting in Brockton were printed. Vanzetti was to be one of the speakers.

On the evening of May 5th, Sacco and Vanzetti with the handbills on them went by trolley from Stoughton to West Bridgewater to meet a man named Boda who they thought could lend them a car. Very likely they thought they were being trailed and had put revolvers in their pockets out of some confused feeling of bravado. If the police pounced on them at least they would not let themselves be tortured to death like Salsedo. The idea was to hide the handbills somewhere until after the expected raid. But they were afraid to use Boda's car because it lacked a 1920 license plate and started back to Stoughton on the trolley, probably very uneasy. When they were arrested as the trolley entered Brockton they forgot all about their guns. They thought they were being arrested as Reds in connection with the projected meeting. When they were questioned at the police station their main care was not to implicate any of their friends. They kept remembering the dead body of Salsedo, smashed on the pavement of Park Row.

Underworld

About this time a young fellow of Portuguese extraction named Madeiros was living in Providence. From confidence games and the collecting of money under false pretences he had slipped into the society of a famous gang of professional criminals known as the Morelli gang. They lived mostly by robbing freightcars but occasionally cleaned up more dangerous jobs. Gerald Chapman is supposed to have worked with them once or twice. In the early morning of April 15, Madeiros and four other members of the Morelli gang went over to Boston in a stolen touring car and at a speakeasy on Andrews Square were told about the movements of the payroll of the Slater-Merrill factory in South Braintree, which was to be shipped out from Boston that day by express. They then went back to Providence and later in the morning back again towards South Braintree. In the outskirts of Randolph they changed to another car that had been hidden in the woods. Then they went to a speakeasy to wait for the time they had chosen. Madeiros' job was to sit in the back seat and hold back the crowd with a revolver while the other two got the payroll. Everything came out as planned, and in broad daylight in the most populous part of South Braintree they shot down two men and carried off the satchel containing some $5,000. The next day when Madeiros went to a saloon on North Main Street, Providence, to get his share of the swag, he found no one. In his confession made at the Dedham jail he says he never did get paid.

The Trap Springs

When Sacco and Vanzetti were first grilled by the chief of police of Brockton they were questioned as Reds and lied all they could to save their friends. Particularly they would not tell where they had got their pistols. Out of this Judge Thayer and the prosecution evolved the theory of "the consciousness of guilt" that weighed so heavily with the jury. After they had been held two days they were identified, Sacco as the driver of the car in the South Braintree holdup and Vanzetti as the "foreign looking man" who had taken a potshot at a paytruck of the L. Q. White company at Bridgewater early on the morning of Christmas eve, 1919.

In spite of the fact that twenty people swore that they had seen Vanzetti in North Plymouth selling eels at that very time in the morning, he was promptly convicted and sentenced to fifteen years in the Charlestown penitentiary. The fact that so many people testified to having bought eels was considered very suspicious by the court that did not know that the eating of eels on the fast day before Christmas is an Italian custom of long standing. Later Vanzetti was associated with Sacco in the murder charge. On July 14, 1923, both men were found guilty of murder in the first degree on two counts by the Norfolk County jury, a hundred per cent American jury, consisting of two realestate men, two storekeepers, a mason, two machinists, a clothing salesman, a farmer, a millworker, a shoemaker and a lastmaker.

New England Town

Dedham is the perfect New England town, white shingle-roofed houses, polished brass knockers, elmshaded streets. Dedham has money, supports a polo team. Many of the wealthiest and oldest families in Massachusetts have houses there. As the seat of Norfolk County it is the center of politics for the region. Dedham has always stood for the traditions of the Bay State. Dedham was pro-British during the war; even before the *Lusitania* the people of eastern Massachusetts were calling the Germans Huns. Dedham has always stood for Anglo-Saxon supremacy, and the white man's burden. Of all white men the whitest are those descendants of Puritan shipowners and brokers and ministers who own the white houses with graceful colonial doorways and the trim lawns and the lilac hedges and the elms and the beeches and the barberry bushes and the broad A and the cultivated gesturelessness of the New English. When the Congregational God made Dedham he looked upon it and saw that it was good.

But with the decline of shipping and farming a threefold population has grown up in the ring of factory towns round Boston, among which Dedham itself sits primly disdainful like an old maid sitting between two laborers in a trolley car. There is the diminished simonpure New England population, protestant in faith, Republican in politics and mostly "professional" in occupation. Alongside of that is the almost equally wealthy Irish Catholic element, Democratic, tending to make a business of politics and of the less severely respectable trades and industries. Under both of these is the population of wops, bohunks, polacks, hunkies, dagoes, some naturalized and speaking English with an accent, others unnaturalized and still speaking their native peasant dialects; they do the work. These three populations hate each other with a bitter hatred, but the upper two manage to patch up their rancor when it becomes a question of "furriners." In industrial disputes they find that they are all hundred per cent Americans. Meanwhile the latestcome immigrants are gradually gaining foothold. The Poles buy up rundown farms and get the tired and stony land back to the point of bearing crops. The Italians start truck gardens in back lots, and by skilful gardening and drudgery bring forth fiftyfold where the Americanborn couldn't get back the seed they sowed. The Portuguese work the cranberry bogs and are reviving the shore fisheries. The Americanborn are seeing their own state eaten up from under their feet. Naturally they hate the newcomers.

The war exalted hatred to a virtue. The anti-Red agitation, the Ku Klux Klan, the activities of the American Security League, and the American Legion have been a sort of backwash of hate dammed up by the signing of the peace. It was when that pentup hatred and suspicion was tumultuously seeking an outlet that Sacco and Vanzetti, wops, aliens, men who spoke broken English, anarchists, believing neither in the Congregationalist nor the Catholic God, slackers who had escaped the draft, were arrested, charged with a particularly brutal and impudent murder. From that moment the rightthinking Puritanborn Americans of Massachusetts had an object, a focus for the bitterness of their hatred of the new young vigorous unfamiliar forces that are relentlessly sweeping them onto the shelf. The people of Norfolk County, and of all Massachusetts, decided that they wanted these men to die.

Bird in a Cage

The faces of men who have been a long time in jail have a peculiar frozen look under the eyes. The face of a man who has been a long time in jail never loses that tightness under the eyes. Sacco has been six years in the county jail, always waiting, waiting for trial, waiting for new evidence, waiting for motions to be argued, waiting for sentence, waiting, waiting, waiting. The Dedham jail is a handsome structure, set among lawns, screened by trees that wave new green leaves against the robinsegg sky of June. In the warden's office you can see your face in the light brown varnish, you could eat eggs off the floor it is so clean. Inside, the main reception hall is airy, full of sunlight. The bars are cheerfully painted green, a fresh peagreen. Through the bars you can see the waving trees and the June clouds roaming the sky like cattle in an unfenced pasture. It's a preposterous complicated canary cage. Why aren't the birds singing in this green aviary? The warden politely shows you to a seat and as you wait you notice a smell, not green and airy this smell, a jaded heavy greasy smell of slum, like the smell of army slum, but heavier, more hopeless.

Across the hall an old man is sitting in a chair, a heavy pear-shaped man, his hands hang limp at his sides, his eyes are closed, his sagged face is like a bundle of wet newspapers. The warden and two men in black stand over him, looking down at him helplessly.

At last Sacco has come out of his cell and sits beside me.

Two men sitting side by side on a bench in a green bird cage. When he feels like it one of them will get up and walk out, walk out into the sunny June day. The other will go back to his cell to wait. He looks younger than I had expected. His face has a waxy transparency like the face of a man who's been sick in bed for a long time; when he laughs his cheeks flush a little. At length we manage both of us to laugh. It's such a preposterous position for man to be in, like a man who doesn't know the game trying to play blindfold chess. The real world has gone. We have no more grasp of our world of rain and streets and trolleycars and cucumbervines and girls and gardenposts. This is a world of phrases, *prosecution, defence, evidence, motion, irrelevant, incompetent* and *immaterial.* For six years this man has lived in the law, tied tighter and tighter in the sticky filaments of lawwords like a fly in a spider web. And the wrong set of words means the chair. All the moves in the game are made for him, all he can do is sit helpless and wait, fastening his hopes on one set of phrases after another. In all these lawbooks, in all this terminology of clerks of the court and counsel for the defense, there is one move that will save him, out of a million that will mean death.

If only they make the right move, use the right words.

But by this time the nagging torment of hope has almost stopped, not even the thought of his wife and children out there in the world, unreachable, can torture him now. He is numb now, can laugh and look quizzically at the ponderous machine that has caught and mangled him. Now it hardly matters to him if they do manage to pull him out from between the cogs, and the wrong set of words means the chair.

Nicola Sacco came to this country when he was eighteen years old. He was born in Puglia in the mountains in the heel of Italy. Since then up to the time of his arrest he has had pretty good luck. He made good money, he was happily married, he had many friends, latterly he had a garden to hoe and rake mornings and evenings and Sundays. He was unusually powerfully built, able to do two men's work. In prison he was able to stand thirtyone days of hunger strike before he broke down and had to be taken to the hospital.

In jail he has learned to speak and write English, has read many books, for the first time in his life has been thrown with nativeborn Americans. They worry him, these nativeborn Americans. They are so hard and brittle. They don't fit into the bright clear heartfelt philosophy of Latin anarchism. These are the people who coolly want him to die in the electric chair. He can't understand them. When his head was cool he's never wanted anyone to die. Judge Thayer and the prosecution he thinks of as instruments of a machine.

The warden comes up to take down my name. "I hope your wife's better," says Sacco. "Pretty poorly," says the warden. Sacco shakes his head. "Maybe she'll get better soon, nice weather." I have shaken his hand, my feet have carried me to the door, past the baggy pearshaped man who is still collapsed half deflated in the chair, closed crinkled eyelids twitching. The warden looks into my face with a curious smile. "Leaving us?" he asks. Outside in the neat streets the new green leaves are swaying in the sunlight, birds sing, klaxons grunt, a trolleycar screeches round a corner. Overhead the white June clouds wander in the unfenced sky.

Bartolomeo Vanzetti

Going to the Charlestown Penitentiary is more like going to Barnum and Bailey's. There's a great scurry of guards, groups of people waiting outside; inside a brass band is playing *Home Sweet Home*. When at length you get let into the Big Show, you find a great many things happening at once. There are rows of benches where pairs of people sit talking. Each pair is made up of a free man and a convict. In three directions there are grey bars and tiers of cells. The band inside plays bangingly *If Auld Acquaintance Be Forgot*.

A short broadshouldered man is sitting quiet through all the uproar, smiling a little under his big drooping moustache. He has a domed, pale forehead and black eyes surrounded by many little wrinkles. The serene modelling of his cheekbones and hollow cheeks makes you forget the prison look under his eyes. This is Vanzetti.

Bartolomeo Vanzetti was born in Villa Faletto, in a remote mountain valley in the Piedmont. At the age of thirteen his father apprenticed him to a pastrycook who worked him fifteen hours a day. After six years of gruelling work in bakeries and restaurant kitchens he went back home to be nursed through pleurisy by his mother. Soon afterwards his mother died and in despair he set out for America. When, after the usual kicking around by the Ellis Island officials, he was dumped on the pavement of Battery Park, he had very little money, knew not a word of the language and found that he had arrived in a time of general unemployment. He washed dishes at Mouquin's for five dollars a week and at last left for the country for fear he was getting consumption. At length he got work in a brick kiln near Springfield. There he was thrown with Tuscans, first learned the Tuscan dialect and read Dante and the Italian classics. After that he worked for two years in the stone pits at Meriden, Connecticut. Then he went back to New York and worked for a while as a pastrycook again, and at last settled in Plymouth where he worked in various factories and at odd jobs, ditchdigging, clamdigging, icecutting, snowshovelling and a few months before his arrest, for the sake of being his own boss, bought a pushcart and peddled fish.

All this time he read a great deal nights sitting under the gasjet when everyone else was in bed, thought a great deal as he swung a pick or made caramels or stoked brick kilns, of the workmen he rubbed shoulders with, of their position in the world and his, of their hopes of happiness and of a less struggling animallike existence. As a boy he had been an ardent Catholic. In Turin he fell in with a bunch of socialists under the influence of De Amicis. Once in America he read St. Augustine, Kropotkin, Gorki, Malatesta, Renan, and began to go under the label of anarchist-communist. His anarchism, though, is less a matter of labels than of feeling, of gentle philosophic brooding. He shares the hope that has grown up in Latin countries of the Mediterranean basin that somehow men's predatory instincts, incarnate in the capitalist system, can be canalized into other channels, leaving free communities of artisans and farmers and fishermen and cattlebreeders who would work for their livelihood with pleasure, because the work was itself enjoyable in the serene white light of a reasonable world.

Sweet Land of Liberty

And for seven years, three hundred and sixtyfive days a year, yesterday, today, tomorrow, Sacco and Vanzetti woke up on their prison pallets, ate prison food, had an hour of exercise and conversation a day, sat in their cells puzzling about this technicality and that technicality, pinning their hopes to their alibis, to the expert testimony about the character of the barrel of Sacco's gun, to Madeiros' confession and Weeks' corroboration, to action before the Supreme Court of the United States, and day by day the props were dashed from under their feet and they felt themselves being inexorably pushed towards the chair by the blind hatred of wellmeaning citizens, by the superhuman involved stealthy soulless mechanism of the law.

Boston, June, 1926

3. HARLAN COUNTY SUNSET

As the afternoon wore on a curious lonesomeness came over the speakin' in the new gymnasium of the school at Wallins Creek. Miners and their wives, who had sat in their faded and threadbare Sunday clothes with a look of quiet and intentness on their pale lined faces, began to slip quietly out of the hall and start for home. An old miner had been speaking, striding up and down the platform and banging his fist on the table like a backwoods preacher. He'd stride up and down and then pause with his fist clenched over the table; then he'd stare into the crowd and let out a sentence. "Your laborleaders has led you into captivity; they git the money and you git the beans and bread," and bang would go his fist down on the table and he'd be off again. "I love my chillun a thousand times better today than I love Herbert Hoover." Then bang would go his fist on the table. "The prettiest thing I'd like to see in Harlan County would be to see the laborin' man all stand together as one." Then bang would go his fist. "We don't aim to git rich, but we aim to make our livin' out of it; today the moneyed man in Harlan town is tryin' to press the workin' man down into an aggregation of poverty and sin. . . . Dear companions there's things happened in this state and county you couldn't believe could happen in civilized Ameriky. . . . We're on that lonesome road between starvation and heathenism." Then he sang an old time strike song about seventy cents a ton and sat down.

Aunt Molly Jackson sang her moaning blues:

> I am sad and weary, I've got the
>   hongry ragged blues,
> Not a penny in my pocket
>   to buy one thing I need to use.
> I was up this mornin'
>   with the worst blues ever had in my life,
> Not a bit to cook for breakfast
>   or for a coalminer's wife.
>
> When my husband works in the coalmines
>   he loads a car on every trip,
> Then he goes to the office that evenin'
>   an' gits denied of scrip;
> Juss because it took all he had made that day
>   to pay his mine expenses,
> Juss because it took all he had made that day
>   to pay his mine expenses.
> A man that'll juss work for coal light and carbide
>   he ain't got a speck of sense.
>
> All the women in this coalcamp
>   are sittin' with bowed down heads,
> All the women in this coalcamp
>   are sittin' with bowed down heads,
> Ragged and barefooted and their
>   children acryin' for bread.
> No food no clothes for our children;
>   I'm sure this ain't no lie,

If we can't get no more for our labor
  we will starve to death and die.

Please don't go under those mountains
  with the slate ahangin' over your head,
Please don't go under those mountains
  with the slate ahangin' over your head,
An' work for juss coal light and carbide
  an' your children acryin' for bread;
I pray you take my council
  please take a friend's advice;
Don't load no more, don't put out no more
  till you get a livin' price.

This minin' town I live in
  is a sad an' lonely place,
This minin' town I live in
  is a sad an' lonely place,
For pity and starvation
  is pictured on every face,
Everybody hongry and ragged,
  no slippers on their feet,
Everybody hongry and ragged,
  no slippers on their feet,
All goin' round from place to place
  bummin' for a little food to eat.
Listen my friends and comrades
  please take a friend's advice,
Don't put out no more of your labor
  till you get a livin' price.

Other women spoke about the flux and how the Red Cross wouldn't help the family if the man went on strike. Bright young men from the *Daily Worker* made stirring speeches about China and the international proletariat and the defence of the Soviet Union. Members of the Writers' Committee assured the strikers a little shakily that public opinion the whole country over was being aroused in favor of the striking miners of eastern Kentucky. A collection was taken up. But all the time a curious lonesomeness was coming over the hall.

There had been warnings that the gunthugs were coming from Black Mountain to break up the meeting, that Sheriff Blair and his deputies were coming over to arrest everybody present. People were listening to the speeches with one ear cocked for noises outside. Once somebody thought he heard a shot outside and a dozen men ran out to see what the trouble was. The clear fall afternoon light through the gymnasium windows was becoming stained with blue. Slowly and lonesomely the afternoon wore on. At last the speakin' broke up.

On the hillside outside people were melting away into the violet dark. The lights were pumpkincolor in the little stores along the road in the creekbottom. The west flared hot with a huge afterglow of yellow and orange and crimson light against which the high dark hills that hemmed in the Cumberland River cut a sharp razoredge.

Walking down the hill we felt the scary lonesome feeling of the front lines in a lull in the fighting. By the time we got to the road the cars had all gone back to Pineville. We went up to a garage a little piece up the road. Dreiser was standing in the door of the garage looking out into the fading flare of the evening. The garageman said a taxi would be coming back soon. We stood a long time in the door of the garage. I could feel the wonderful breathless hush I'd felt years ago on post in the Avocourt wood. This was war all right.

This time the day before we'd been standing shamefacedly in the door of Alec Napier's cabin way up Straight Creek. "Be keerful when you step in," the women had said and pointed out the places where the floor had caved in. The man was propped up in a chair in front of a flaring coal fire. His belly was so swollen from the infected wound he couldn't fasten his trousers. "A piece of coal fell on me when I was workin under the tipple. You can see here it's all swelled up and stuff comes out like water. My sister paid the doctor. We don't pay him regular now but he hasn't quit comin'. He says he thinks I'll git well. I always paid my doctor bills before." There was nothing in the tworoom house but a bed covered with rags where a little half naked girl sat shivering. The two women who were taking care of the wounded man were haggard. The man was very weak, his eyes glittered in the firelight. He was obviously going to die.

The members of the Writers' Committee had talked for-
lornly about the Red Cross, the hospital in Pineville, accident
insurance. He'd worked five years for the coal company but
hadn't carried insurance as he was an outside worker. It was
obvious that the man was going to die.

The meeting in the Straight Creek Baptist Church had been
cosy and friendly. The miners were in a bad way for food and
the only house in the settlement that was tight against the winter was the barn where the coal company kept its mules, but
they felt good, they were unanimously for the strike and the
N.M.U., and the sheriff of Bell County had not yet turned
strikebreaker, so there had been no disorder. The farmers who
lived on the upper slopes were with the miners too, and gave
them pumpkins and all the stuff from their gardens they didn't
need themselves. They had their soup kitchen and a truck that
went around collecting food. The mineowners weren't showing themselves much. The miners felt good in Straight Creek.
They even talked of taking the mines away from the owners
and running them on their own hook and building themselves
decent houses and a good school and hiring a doctor who
didn't work for the company. The only dissenting voice at the
N.M.U. meeting had been that of a big fat woman, the company bookkeeper, who must have been tight because she stood
in the aisle with her arms akimbo scowling and kept shouting
at the chairman, a young fellow who also did a little preaching
Sundays: "You big bum you owe me ten dollars, now don't
you tell me it ain't so, you owe me ten dollars."

On the way to the meeting at Straight Creek I had walked
down the road with a young miner of about twenty. The way
the eyes looked out of his white lean mountaineer's face made
me think of the desert arabs I'd been with in Syria years before. The coaldust sticks in the lashes and eyebrows when a
softcoal miner washes; it gives the same intent look to the eyes
as the kohl the Bedawi decorate their faces with. These people
too have the same direct affectionate manners. Their pure un-
modernized English lilts in the air like reading Elizabethan
lyrics. I'd asked this boy how he liked the communist's
speeches about the international workingclass, their struggles in
Germany and China, miners' life in the Soviet Union. He said
he liked them, there was a great deal of learning in them, every

time he listened to them he learned something new. "Here in Bell County we lack learnin' and eddication. It's the greatest thing ever happened to the laborin' man in eastern Kentucky. Why if it warn't for the N.M.U. we'd be on our knees before the coal company beggin' for a glass of water right now."

Then he turned to me and said, "Are you in this business too?" I said I was a writer, writers were people who stayed on the sidelines as long as they could. They were sympathizers. He looked disappointed. "I thought maybe you was a lodge-member, in for a revolution too . . . because I'm in it . . . up to the neck."

It was entirely dark now. I stood in the doorway of the garage beside Dreiser who stood with his hands in his coat pockets looking out into the quiet breathless night, not saying anything. I was wondering what he was thinking. Headlights of cars passed along the road. It seemed a long time before the taxi stopped and we got in. Sure he'd drive us to Pineville. We couldn't see his face in the darkness of the sedan; his voice was cheerful. He was a redneck himself. We got in and he started down the road. "These coal companies and the rest of the money interests, they can't go on forever puttin' it over on us. My neck's gettin' so red I swear it's like to burn up." The car was purring downhill, swinging easily round the curves where the road followed the winding Cumberland.

Pineville, November, 1931

4. DETROIT, CITY OF LEISURE

Debating Society

The sun is hot on the fresh green of Grand Circus Park, but the wind that combs through the leaves of the trees and shrubs has a smack of the north woods in it. All round, the windows of the skyscrapers of the boom town stare out with dusty vacancy at the summer afternoon. Unemployed men lie out on the grass in a hundred helpless attitudes of sleep. Nearly all of them spread out newspapers before they lie down; got to keep that suit decent as long as possible. On the benches men sit talking unhurriedly, all the time in the world. Around the livelier benches groups stand, listening in; occasionally someone from the back pops off with a remark. Towards the eastern end it's more shady and the crowd is thicker; there are *Daily Workers* and *Labor Defenders* for sale; in an easy wellpitched voice (the traffic isn't so thick in the street behind him that he has to yell) a young man with a touch of an Italian accent is making a speech:

"If a lot of fellers go to walk through the woods, through real heavy woods, they'll all walk in single file, won't they? Well, suppose they walk an' walk an' the trail gets worse an' worse, all rocks an' brambles an' then deep swamps an' then no trail at all maybe; by an' by one feller yell out to the guys in front, 'Where the hell you boys leadin' us?' An' then they all begin to worry an' think maybe they've lost the road. Well, the American workin' class is just like that. Everybody say, 'Step along, Johnny, keep in line, pretty soon we have prosperity.' But the trail get worse and worse. Pretty soon we got to ask, 'Where the hell are they leadin' us to anyway?' You bosses lead us into the swamp; our turn to lead the way now."

Behind some bushes two perspiring bandylegged Germans are having a private argument. "These here Reds they say a voman she just as good as a man, thot's foolishness." . . . "Sure she is, comrade, sure she is, if she does a man's vork she ought to get a man's vages." . . . "But she can't do the vork so good." . . . "Sure she can, look here, ven you go hunting, you take along a male dog and a female dog, one no good without the other." . . . "I don't know nutten about huntin', what I say is voman's vork not worth man's vages. Vomen ain't no account." . . . "But, comrade, just for the sake of the argument, suppose you did go huntin'. You'd take along a male dog and a female dog, wouldn't you?" "Thot's all foolishness, never go huntin'," the other man spluttered as he walked off red in the face.

Closing up Fisher Lodge, the giant emergency flophouse conducted in one of the unused buildings of the Fisher Body plant—officially it was closed through lack of money, but actually, because the homeless men living there were getting too interested in their forum and the place was getting to be a "nest of Reds"—has turned several thousand workless men out onto the streets and parks of Detroit. They are everywhere, all over the vast unfinished city, the more thrifty living in shacks and shelters along the waterfront, in the back rooms of unoccupied houses, the others just sleeping any place. In one back lot they have burrowed out rooms in a huge abandoned sandpile. Their stovepipes stick out at the top. All along the wharves and in the ends of the alleys that abut on the waterfront you can see them toasting themselves in the sun, or else patiently fishing. A sluggish drowsy, grimy life, of which Grand Circus Park is the social center and the One Cent Restaurant operated by some anonymous philanthropist on Woodward Avenue is the Delmonico's. In the evening they stroll up and down Woodward Avenue and look at the posters on the allnight movies and cluster around medicine shows and speakers in back lots where you hear the almost forgotten names of oldtime labor parties like the Proletarian party and the Socialist Labor party. One man was trying to sell to a large but unmoved crowd a parlor trick by which, if you can find a man who has a dollar bill to start with, you can make a quarter and have the pleasure of putting one over on him besides. You get him to wrap up his dollar bill in various different-colored sheets of paper and then bet him a quarter you can make it vanish. You unwrap the papers and hey, presto, instead of the dollar there's seventy-five cents in change. A man yells from the back of the crowd, "Hey, buddy, where do you expect us to get the six bits?"

Direct Action

In a blind pig a newspaper man is talking. It's cool and dark in there at the small tables. The radio roars so loud it blows the foam off our beer. We get the radio turned off so we can hear the newspaper man telling what isn't in the papers. "Here's a story that keeps coming in that we don't dare touch. A bunch of men, sometimes forty or fifty of them, go into a chain grocery store, usually the store where they're accustomed to deal, and ask for credit. The clerk tells 'em the business is on a cash basis. Then they tell him to stand back, they don't want to hurt him, but they've got to have some groceries. They take what they need and go off quietly. In the case

I'm thinking of, the clerk didn't phone the police, he phoned the general manager. The general manager told him he did right, the less anybody heard about stuff like that the better."

"You mean if others heard about it, they'd get the same idea?" The newspaper man nodded.

We drive out through miles of partly built-up subdivisions. Ten miles out we are still within the skeleton of streets and avenues. In a roomy suburban house like the houses that have filled the boom developments of every other American city, there's gathered a group of people with the standard clothes and faces of the whitecollar class. We sit around sipping California wine and gradually, unhurriedly, talking. What are we talking about in this early summer evening? About a moonlight steamboat ride being gotten up to raise money for unemployed relief, about Soviet Russia and about the style of revolution we shall have in America. Somebody brought up the Red terror. "Well if you're using force, you're using force," said a sweetvoiced woman in a pale blue dress. "And when they're changing the social system, I guess they'll have to use force. Ford's service men are using force all right."

Social Club

Some old radicals have organized a communal boarding house in an old brick dwelling near the river that used to be Detroit's House of Mirrors. Upstairs the rooms are fitted up with cots, on the ground floor there's a social room where you can read or play pinochle or checkers, in the basement there's a thoroughly organized kitchen and lunchroom where you can get meals for five cents or ten cents, according to the state of your brokeness. I ate a darn good meal there. The kitchen was clean and the food fresh. The secret of their success is that they never buy any provisions. They keep track of stores and markets that can't sell their surplus and bum it. If a dealer gets in an extra large shipment of onions, say, they keep an eye on it, and if they don't seem to be selling, manage to bum a case or two off him that otherwise would spoil and have to be thrown out. These men understand that in a depression caused by overproduction of goods, no one need starve if he'll organize with his fellows and forget about money. One said he was living better now than he did when he worked.

Whitecollar Man

There was nobody in the entry of the huge new office building, nobody in the elevator going upstairs. The lawyer sat and talked to us from behind his wide glasstopped desk, now and then glancing out the window at the sunny back lots, the street where crowds moved slowly, the ranks of automobiletops like dominoes face down. "I don't know what it is," he was saying, "but something is happening. I used to be a union worker and a radical and all that when I was a kid, but it's something different now. None of the political parties catch it, nobody believes in the old parties and the socialists and communists don't fit in somehow. In the men out of work, in the crowd everywhere, I can feel something I can't explain, something that's going to burst out. It makes you want to give up everything you've been working and hustling and sweating for, this kind of life at a desk, and go back where you came from, where you belong, with the men on the street. It sounds goofy and I can't explain it. It has something to do with these men on the street, laying around in the parks, what are they going to do when they get so they won't stand for it any longer? . . . The only trouble is I've got four families to support."

"Well, you can always look on, you can observe the show."

"I can't. I've been a man of action all my life. I'd be in this now if I only knew what was happening."

Rationalization

Out in the Rouge Plant colored men are all the time washing the windows. A collegiatelooking young man takes visitors through. From the primal cell of the magneto they follow the new V-8 motor along the line until it's complete, then follow the chassis through from its first appearance as a castiron wishbone, through the big climaxes of its junction with the motor and then with the body, until they see the new glistening insect crawl off the end of the line under its own power.

A whistle blew and the men knocked off for lunch. "A halfhour for lunch," says the collegiate young man. "He's lying, they only get fifteen minutes," whispers the man next to me. The men have slumped down in their tracks and are eating their food with bent heads, no laughing or talking. The visitors are piled into a bus and safely deposited outside the mainoffice gates.

Back in Grand Circus Park men lie out asleep in the morning sun or else sit talking drowsily on the benches. A man's auctioning off *Daily Workers*, groups are arguing. In one group a middleaged roundfaced Negro with bright eyes is trying to convince a lanternfaced yellow boy with gold teeth. "Lemme reason with ye, lemme reason with ye," he keeps saying. They are arguing as to whether the workers could run the banks. The yellow boy keeps saying no, they don't know enough. He keeps trying to get away. The older man has hold of the lapel of his coat. "Look here, boy, lemme reason with ye, lemme reason with ye."

At last in desperation he kneels down on the pavement and draws two sides of a triangle with his finger in the dust. "Look here, boy, this here's one foot and this here's one foot, ain't it?"

"Mebbe," grumbles the yellow boy.

"Well, we'll jus 'low that it is." . . . "Well, you don't know how long that third side is?" . . . "No, nor you neither." . . . "Well, that don't mean that nobody don't know. See what I mean? That don't mean that nobody don't know."

Detroit, July, 1932

5. THOSE BOATS

Old Dick, the frozenfaced bosun, is at the wheel. Cap'n John, the mate, is leaning out of the window to knock his pipe on the lee rail. The skipper is still in his bunk in the little cabin back of the pilothouse. We're towing along the southerly edge of Lahave bank. The winter afternoon sky is flecked with little ragged clouds of silver and zinc. Wherever a wave breaks the wintrycolored sea is stained with green. Aft of us, where the net is towing, there stretches a long trail of gulls, neat blacktipped bonapartes plump as pigeons, sooty young herringgulls and scrawny gannets. Against the bright aluminum band of the horizon abreast of us comes another steam trawler exactly like our trawler, towing the other way, belching smoke as the fires are stoked, and dragging another long trail of gulls.

Old Dick is telling about some place up above the Bay of Islands where he was as a boy. A young man who lived at the place was coming home late one Christmas eve from a time at one of the houses over the hill. Right where the path crossed the high hill he met an old man with a jug of rum. He was the lad for the liquor so he asked the old man for a drink. As soon as he'd taken the drink he began to look odd so the lad who was with him ran home as fast as he could. He never came back home. Next Christmas eve at the same time in the same place some people coming home met the young man wandering on the hill singing and drinking out of a jug of rum. He offered them all drinks, but he acted so odd they all ran away and left him. Next day they hunted all over the hill for him but they couldn't find him. The next year his wife was up there waiting for him early in the evening and sure enough at the same time he came over the hill singing and playing funny music on a fiddle. His wife took him by the hand and made him come home with her, but he was dazedlike and had lost all sense and never got his sense back all the rest of his life. The old people said he'd been with the fairies on the hill, but he never could tell what had happened to him. Anyway after that nobody liked to cross the high hill after dark.

Old Dick asked Cap'n John for a chew of tobacco when he turned the wheel over to him and went below. Cap'n John drooped tiredly as he leaned over the wheel talking back over his shoulder to the skipper about old doryfishing days, Cap'n Soandso who'd taken his schooner across George's Shoal in an easterly gale and beaten the fleet into a record high Boston market, and about the sailing qualities of the schooner he'd skippered out of Gloucester about that same year, until it was time to toot the whistle to get the crew out to haul the net.

The winch sang as the trawler came round with her head into the sea. As she lost steerageway the gulls filled the sky around us like snowflakes. The watch piled out on deck in their shiny green and yellow oilskins. It took a lot of yanking at the viciously swinging ironbound "doors" to get them hooked on the gallus when they leaped dripping and draped

in seaweed out of the water. The winch sang again reeling in
the wires. The belly of the net rose and floated in the green
water to leeward. "Pollock," somebody shouted. The boat
was rolling in the trough now, an occasional curl of a frothy
wave slapping over the rail on the windy side. It took all five
of them to haul the net inboard clawing at the mesh with
their hooks. Then the belly of the net was swung in over the
checkers on the slippery deck, the sliprope on the cod end
was pulled and the catch came slithering out on deck with a
thump, pollock mostly with the red bladder puffed up in their
mouths, a glittery wave of fish, eyes staring, distended gills
quivering, toothed mouths gasping, with here and there a
sponge or a shiny sealemon or a red starfish.

Then the net was set again, and the boat put back on her
course, and the crew set to work gutting and sorting the catch.
The skipper was sitting on the edge of his bunk pulling on his
boots. "What is it John?" he called. "Pollock," said Cap'n John
over his shoulder in a colorless voice. "Ain't worth the ice to
pack 'em in," said the skipper lurching forward into the pilothouse. "Lucky if they get seventy-five cents a hundred . . . a
hundred pounds, not a hundred fish," he said making a pass
with a big flipper at the passenger. "All right John."

Cap'n John knocked out his pipe, went carefully down the
ladder to the deck and aft to the galley to get something to
eat. The skipper stuck his head out of the pilothouse door to
see if all the gear was clear and then fastened the wheel with
a becket and accepted a cigarette.

"Those boats," he said, ". . . if you're going to write in the
papers about those boats you better tell the truth. Put in that
there's no living in them any more. I don't get anything in
the captain's lay, not enough to keep the old lady going and
the boy in school, so how you expect those poor devils in the
forecastle" (Newfoundlanders pronounce the word out) "to
get anything out of it? I guess the company don't split even
either but that's not so bad as for a man that's got his living
to make from day to day. I've been working eight years in
those boats, and on schooners ever since I was a lad. I've seen
plenty of slack times and times when you could put by a little
money, but never anything like this. If they could get anything else to do wouldn't be a man would make the trip on

those boats. Put in about the rackets too, put in about the
amount we have to pay the pilot's association. Put in that you
can't sell a pound of fish in Fulton Market in New York without fixing it up, put in about how every skipper that goes into
New York has to pay fifteen dollars to a Greek named George
who comes aboard to collect so that the gangs won't smash
things up and ruin your catch. It's the rackets that's ruining
fishing as much as anything else."

Sparks came in with a slip of paper in his hand. The skipper
looked at it. "It's Boston for Tuesday," he said. "Well we
might as well be in there as out here. Those boats ain't going
to be making anything this winter," and he tooted the whistle for hauling the net.

There's a deadspot south of Halifax, so Sparks couldn't get
his radiobearing, but the skipper checked up with this fath-
ometer, looked at the water, sniffed the wind and said with
a sly look, maybe he could hit Boston Light in the eye anyway, after all they used to do it before they had the radio. The
watch on deck mended the net where it was torn, stowed the
gear and lashed everything down because the trawler was
sticking her nose into a choppy rising sea lashed up by a westerly wind. Then everything on board settled down, quiet in
the gathering brinesplattered dark.

From the forecastle came the sound of a Scotch jig on the
Icelander's phonograph; there the seas rattle against the plates
of the bow, the stove purrs, the men are all stretched out in
their tiny bunks chatting in their flat Newfoundland voices
before they turn in. Old Dick, who never sleeps, is making
himself a pair of slippers out of variouscolored twine. Up in
the radio room Sparks, who is a Dane, sits opposite his photo-
graph of Greta Garbo and tunes in on Amos and Andy. Amidships the Chief has just been told by the skipper down the
speakingtube that it's up to him whether they make Boston in
time for the market or not and is sore as a crab. He's a Massachusetts man. "It's always the same goddam thing," he's
growling. "They always wait till the last minute and then they
say it's up to me to take 'em in for the market. Why the hell
should I care if they make their goddam market or not?" The
second makes out he's sore too, but all he wants to talk about
is deerhunting. The silent squarehead fireman has just dumped

the ash and is leaning out of his black hole sniffing the salty cold wind. In the galley in the afterhouse, the Portugee cook is cleaning up after the last mess, complaining about the lousy flour that won't rise they sell you in New York, and saying he wouldn't be leading this dog's life if he could get a job on a yacht like he did once. Beside the stove two lanky Newfoundlanders sit swigging the inky tea that's boiled all day and saying nothing.

Eighteen hours later the skipper hits Boston Light dead in the eye.

Provincetown, February, 1932

6. VIEWS OF WASHINGTON

The Hill: December, 1931

Washington has a drowsy look in the early December sunlight. The Greco-Roman porticoes loom among the bare trees, as vaguely portentous as phrases about democracy in the mouth of a southern senator. The Monument, a finger of light cut against a lavender sky, punctuates the antiquated rhetoric of the Treasury and the White House. On the hill, above its tall foundation banked with magnolia trees, the dome of the Capitol bulges smugly. At nine o'clock groups of sleepylooking cops in well brushed uniforms and shiny visored caps are straggling up the winding drives. At the corner of Pennsylvania Avenue and John Marshall Place a few marchers stand round the trucks they came in. They look tired and frowzy from the long ride. Some of them are strolling up and down the avenue. That end of the avenue, with its gimcrack stores, boardedup burlesque shows, Chinese restaurants and flophouses, still has a little of the jerkwater, outinthesticks look it must have had when Lincoln drove up it in a barouche through the deep mud or Jefferson rode to his inauguration on his own quiet nag.

Two elderly laboring men are looking out of a cigar store door at a bunch of Reds, young Jewish boys from New York or Chicago, with the white armbands of the Hunger Marchers.

"Won't get nutten thataway," one of them says. "Who's payin' for it anyway, hirin' them trucks and the gasoline. . . . Somebody's payin' for it," barks the clerk indignantly from behind the cash register. "Better'd spend it on grub or to buy 'emselves overcoats," says the older man. The man who first spoke shakes his head sadly. "Never won't get nutten thataway." Out along the avenue a few Washingtonians look at the trucks and old movingvans with *Daily Worker* cartoons pasted on their sides. They stand a good way off, as if they were afraid the trucks would explode; they are obviously swallowing their unfavorable comments for fear some of the marchers might hear them. Tough eggs, these Reds.

At ten o'clock the leaders start calling to their men to fall in. Some tall cops appear and bawl out drivers of cars that get into the streets reserved for the marchers to form up in. The marchers form in a column of fours. They don't look as if they'd had much of a night's rest. They look quiet and serious and anxious to do the right thing. Leaders, mostly bareheaded youngsters, run up and down, hoarse and nervous, keeping everybody in line. Most of them look like city dwellers, men and women from the needle trades, restaurant workers, bakery or laundry employees. There's a good sprinkling of Negroes among them. Here and there the thick shoulders and light hair of a truck driver or farmhand stand out. Motorcycle cops begin to cluster around the edges. The marchers are receiving as much attention as distinguished foreign officials.

Up on the hill cordons of cops are everywhere, making a fine showing in the late fall sunshine. There's a considerable crowd standing around; it's years since Washington has been so interested in the opening of Congress. They are roping off the route for the Hunger Marchers. They stop a taxicab that is discovered to contain a small whitehaired Senator. He curses the cops out roundly and is hurriedly escorted under the portals.

Inside the Capitol things are very different. The light is amber and greenish, as in an aquarium. Elderly clerks white as termites move sluggishly along the corridors, as if beginning to stir after a long hibernation. The elevator boy is very pale. "Here comes the army of the unfed," he says, pointing spitefully out of the window. "And they're carrying banners, though Charlie Curtis said they couldn't." A sound of music comes faintly in.

Led by a band with silvery instruments like Christmas tree ornaments that look cheerful in the bright sunlight, the Hunger Marchers have started up Capitol Hill. Just time to peep down into the Senate Chamber where elderly parties and pastyfaced pages are beginning to gather. Ever seen a section of a termite nest under glass?

There's a big crowd in the square between the Capitol and Congressional Library. On the huge ramps of the steps that lead to the central portico the metropolitan police has placed some additional statuary: tastefully arranged groups of cops with rifles, riot guns and brandnew teargas pistols that look as if they'd just come from Sears, Roebuck. People whisper "machinegun nests" but nobody seems to know where they are. There's a crowd on the roof around the base of the dome, faces are packed in all the windows. Everybody looks cheerful, as if a circus had come to town, anxious to be shown. The marchers fill the broad semicircle in front of the Capitol, each group taking up its position in as perfect order as if the show had been rehearsed. The band, playing *Solidarity Forever* (which a newspaper woman beside me recognizes as *Onward, Christian Soldiers*), steps out in front. It is a curious little band, made up of martini-horns, drums, cymbals and a lyre that goes tinkle, tinkle. It plays cheerfully and well, led by a drum major with a red tasseled banner on the end of his staff, and repeats again and again. *The Red Flag, Solidarity,* and other tunes variously identified by people in the crowd. Above the heads of the marchers are banners with slogans printed out: IN THE LAST WAR WE FOUGHT FOR THE BOSSES: IN THE NEXT WAR WE'LL FIGHT FOR THE WORKERS . . . $150 CASH . . . FULL PAY FOR UNEMPLOYMENT RELIEF. The squad commanders stand out in front like cheerleaders at a football game and direct the chanting: We Demand—Unemployed Insurance, We Demand—Unemployed Insurance, WE DEMAND—UNEMPLOYED INSURANCE.

A deepthroated echo comes back from the Capitol façades a few beats later than each shout. It's as if the statues and the classical revival republican ornaments in the pediment were shouting too.

A small group leaves the ranks and advances across the open space toward the Senate side. All the tall cops drawn up in such fine order stick out their chests. Now it's coming. A tremor goes over the groups of statuary so tastefully arranged on the steps. The teargas pistols glint in the sun. The marchers stand in absolute silence.

Under the portal at the Senate entrance the swinging doors are protected by two solid walls of blue serge. Cameramen and reporters converge with a run. Three men are advancing with the demands of the Hunger Marchers written out. They are the center of a big group of inspectors, sergeants, gold and silver braid of the Capitol and metropolitan police. A young fellow with a camera is hanging from the wall by the door. "Move the officer out of the way," he yells. "Thank you. . . . A little back, please, lady, I can't see his face. . . . Now hand him the petition."

"We're not handing petitions, we're making demands," says the leader of the Hunger Marchers.

Considerable waiting around. The Sergeant-at-Arms sends word they can't be let in. Somebody starts to jostle, the cops get tough, cop voices snarl. The committee goes back to report while the band plays the *Internationale* on martini-horns and lyre.

Meanwhile in the Senate Chamber everybody stands while the chaplain asks Almighty God to instill into the hearts of the Senators "a Christlike tenderness for the overborne and heavy-laden." The Senators' heads are bowed over their desks, their faces are, as they used to say in oldtime magazine stories, a study. A thin yellow mantislike Senator, to the obvious disgust of many of his colleagues, starts reading a report of the committee on elections to the effect that no conclusion has been reached in regard to the two contested seats. As for Senator Heflin, he seems to be sitting in his seat in spite of the contest, large as life in a white vest, a patent medicine salesman if I ever saw one. He has a look of placid doggedness on his face. The other termites will have trouble ejecting him from the hill.

Over in the House, things are more animated. The representatives are electing their speaker. On the Democratic side they are licking their chops. Every new vote for John Nance Garner (they say he squirms whenever he hears his middle name) brings the fleshpots nearer. The lean years are over. When he's elected the Democrats break out in whoops. "The rebel yell," giggles a newspaper man. "Don't cheer, men, the poor devils are dying," cries a reporter with a breath like a distillery. In the press gallery they are laughing. Down on the floor the Republicans are taking the gentlemanly attitude. At length, amid cheering and applause, a stocky whitehaired freshfaced man, who looks like a prosperous wheatfarmer, is led down the center aisle by four of his colleagues. The gentleman from Texas has a determined, mean mouth, set in a countenance strikingly devoid of warmth, generosity, intelligence, feeling, whatever it is that makes the human features better to look at than a paving stone. From the press gallery you can see the faces of the representatives all too clearly. Except for a few women and a couple of little girls brought by their papas, there are not more than a dozen faces you can look at with pleasure out of almost five hundred; everywhere the closeset eyes full of lawyer's chicanery, the pursed, selfrighteous mouth drawn down at the corners, the flabby selfsatisfied jowl.

After the representatives of the sovereign wardheelers, even the ladies of the W.C.T.U., who are holding "exercises" among the frightened statuary downstairs, look charming and warmhearted. They are hanging a wreath on a large white lady in a flowing gown modeled in castilesoap, whose name I believe was Willard. They are in Washington to make a last stand against the demon rum.

A. F. of L. Building

Out of the termite hill, the Washington streets are unusually cheery. People seem to have gotten a sort of release out of the parade of the Hunger Marchers and the toodletinkle of the lyre and the martini-horns. It's a magnificent cloudless day. We follow the parade in a taxi. The taxidriver said they'd already been to the White House and had yelled their demands at President Hoover through a megaphone. The Washingtonians seem to feel about it like children in class when somebody from outside has come in and sassed the teacher. Even the cops are smiling.

We catch up outside the A. F. of L. building. The band is there and the marchers are lined up chanting and singing. A delegation has gone in to beard Green in his den. Marchers shout for the key of Billy Green's cellar, somebody starts the chant, "WE DON'T WANT BOOZE, WE WANT BREAD." One man keeps yelling, "Down with William Green, the lady miscellaneous." Everybody feels that the serious part of the show is over, now for the comedy relief. The motorcycle cops and the big shots in gold braid want their dinner, but they're smiling. Everybody's out for a good time, although the wind's beginning to blow up cold. Finally the delegation comes out, announces that William Green was sore as a pup, bawled them out for a lot of dirty communists with their pockets full of Moscow gold, and told them to get the hell out. The marchers boo and march on.

Washington Auditorium

A meeting in the Washington Auditorium. A good many Negroes. The marchers have huddled into their seats tired, many of them have fallen asleep where they sit. Out in the lobby Brigadier-General Glassford, who handled the police end of the program, stands around beaming. On the platform the marchers' leaders looked pleased too. When the band plays the *Internationale* all the newspapermen get to their feet. Speeches go on and on, though the speakers are hoarse from days of riding in springless trucks and much shouting of slogans. For the first time, in the faces of the men and women sitting drowsily in the dimly lit auditorium, you can see something that reaches out of the curious neverneverland of Washington, D.C. It is hope, hunger, despair, the mills, the mines, the train yards, the brokers' offices back where these people have come from, that are real, not this antiquated mirage of a Greco-Roman republic set among the fine lawns and the magnolia trees of the Washington parks. When I left the hall to catch a train, the Brigadier-General was sitting in the audience in mufti, placidly smoking his pipe, while Weinstone thundered a *Daily Worker* editorial into the mike.

Downstairs in the auditorium a dance marathon was going on. Surrounded by empty seats a few puttyfaced boys and girls were feebly jiggling their feet to lethargic jazz played by a discouraged orchestra. They'd been at it for ninety hours. A young man in a white sweater bearing the letters NATIONAL PRODUCTS

COMPANY had keeled over onto his platinumblonde partner's neck. She was holding him up as she danced and trying to revive him with an occasional pecking kiss. A boy in a green sweater was held up to the microphone and crooned breathlessly into it for a while, his feet still moving. The announcer announced a bargain matinée next day, when between eight and four two ladies would be admitted for the price of one. A girl got the mike next and sang a little, while the announcer put his arm around her enthusiastically. Then the faint gyrations of the couples started up again. Anyway the jazz age is dead.

Anacostia Flats, June, 1932

"Home, boys, it's home we want to be," we sang in all the demobilization camps. This was God's country. And we ran for the train with the flags waving and a new army outfit on and our discharge papers and the crisp bills of our last pay in our pockets. The world was safe for democracy and America was the land of opportunity.

They signed you up in the American Legion and jollied you into voting for Harding and the G.O.P. Beaucoup parades, beaucoup speeches, run the slackers and the pacifists and the knockers out of the country, lynch them Wobblies, tell the Reds to go back where they came from. The G.O.P. took care of the Civil War vets and the Spanish War vets, didn't it? Well, it'll take care of youse boys.

You went to work if you could get a job; some kinds of jobs you made big money on, on others the bosses gypped you, but anyway you could eat, you could save up a little, get married, start payments on a home; boom times ahead.

When things slackened and you began to look a little democratic around the gills, they handed you the bonus. The G.O.P. and the nation are behind youse boys. Well, we got some of it and we spent it and we didn't reckon on cyclic depression No. 8b. And now look at us.

A bunch of outofwork ex-service men in Portland, Oregon, figured they needed their bonus right now; 1945 would be too late, only buy wreaths for their tombstones. They figured out, too, that the bonus paid now would liven up business, particularly the retail business in small towns; might be just enough to tide them over until things picked up. Anyway, everybody else was getting a bonus; the moratorium was a bonus to European nations, the R.F.C. was handing out bonuses to railroads and banks, how about the men who'd made the world safe for democracy getting their bonus, too? God knows we're the guys who need it worst. Every other interest has got lobbyists in Washington. It's up to us to go to Washington and be our own lobbyists. Park benches can't be any harder in Washington than they are back home.

So three hundred of them started east in old cars and trucks, hitchhiking, riding on freight trains. (Maybe the words "direct action" still hovered on the air of the Pacific slope, left over from the days of the Wobblies.) By the time they reached Council Bluffs they found that other groups all over the country were rebelling against their veterans' organizations and getting the same idea. It was an army. They organized it as such and nicknamed it the B.E.F.

Now they are camped on Anacostia Flats in the southeast corner of Washington. Nearly twenty thousand of them altogether. Everywhere you meet new ragged troops straggling in. A few have gone home discouraged, but very few. Anacostia Flats is the recruiting center; from there they are sent to new camps scattered around the outskirts of Washington. Anacostia Flats is the ghost of an army camp from the days of the big parade, with its bugle calls, its messlines, greasy K.P.'s, M.P.'s, headquarters, liaison officers, medical officer. Instead of the tents and the long tarpaper barracks of those days, the men are sleeping in little leantos built out of old newspapers, cardboard boxes, packing crates, bits of tin or tarpaper roofing, old shutters, every kind of cockeyed makeshift shelter from the rain scraped together out of the city dump.

The doughboys have changed, too, as well as their uniforms and their housing, in these fifteen years. There's the same goulash of faces and dialects, foreigners' pidgin English, lingoes from industrial towns and farming towns, East, Northeast, Middle West, Southwest, South; but we were all youngsters then; now we are getting on into middle life, sunken eyes, hollow cheeks off breadlines, palelooking knotted hands of men who've worked hard with them, and then for a long time have not worked. In these men's faces, as in Pharaoh's dream, the lean years have eaten up the fat years already.

General Glassford again has played the perfect host; his entertainment committee of motorcycle cops has furnished iodine and CC pills, helped lay out the camps, given advice on digging latrines (the men call them Hoover Villas), and recently set out some tents and bedding. One of the strangest sights Pennsylvania Avenue has ever seen was a long line of ex-service men, hunched under their bedticking full of straw, filling up a long iron stairway in the middle of a partly demolished fourstory garage that the police department had turned over to them. The cops and the ex-service men play baseball together in the afternoon; they are buddies together.

In the middle of the Anacostia camp is a big platform with a wooden object sticking up from one corner that looks like an oldfashioned gallows. Speaking goes on from this platform all morning and all afternoon. The day I saw it, there were a couple of members of the bonus army's congressional committee on the platform, a Negro in an overseas cap and a tall red Indian in buckskin and beads, wearing a tengallon hat. The audience, white men and Negroes, is packed in among the tents and shelters. A tall scrawny man with deeply sunken cheeks is talking. He's trying to talk about the bonus but he can't stick to it; before he knows it he's talking about the general economic condition of the country:

"Here's a plant that can turn out everything every man, woman and child in this country needs, from potatoes to washing machines, and it's broken down because it can't give the fellow who does the work enough money to buy what he needs with. Give us the money and we'll buy their bread and their corn and beans and their electric iceboxes and their washing machines and their radios. We ain't holdin' out on 'em because we don't want those things. Can't get a job to make enough money to buy 'em, that's all."

When he was through speaking a congressman was hoisted up on the platform, a stout representative from Connecticut with that special politician's profile that's as definite in its way as the standardized face of a dick. He announced that the bonus bill had passed the House and that he was the only congressman from Connecticut that had voted for it. Everybody cheered. He added that he thought it would pass the Senate, but he doubted if the Lord Himself knew what the distinguished gentleman in the White House was going to do about it.

"Now I'm not a Red, God damn it," said somebody near me, "but . . ."

The arrival of the bonus army seems to be the first event to give the inhabitants of Washington any inkling that something is happening in the world outside of their drowsy sunparlor. Maybe it's the federal pay cuts that have made them take notice. In the Anacostia streetcar two mail carriers and the conductor started to talk about it. "Well, they say they'll stay here till they get the bonus if they have to stay here till 1945. . . . I guess they ought to get it all right, but how'll that help all the others out of work? . . . Terrible to think of men, women and children starvin' and havin' to beg charity relief with all the stuff there is going to waste in this country. Why up home . . ." Then began the stock conversation of this year 1932 about farmers not shipping apples, cabbage, potatoes, because they couldn't get any price, about loads of fresh fish dumped overboard, trainloads of milk poured out and babies crying for it. One of the mail carriers was from Texas and had just come back from a trip home. He'd seen them plowing under last year's unharvested cotton. "We got the food, we got the clothing, we got the man power, we got the brains," he said. "There must be some remedy."

7. ON THE NATIONAL HOOKUP

Spotlights and Microphones

Sitting up in the gallery at the Chicago Stadium behind a battery of Rosslite superspots. As the sweating electricians move round behind them, the black monsters (with the name of R. J. Duggan painted on their backsides) shake, a little like huge bellflowers on their delicate steel stems. Below bubbles a violet mass of delegates marked with white tickets like fruit in a pushcart. People are streaming back and forth around the edges like at Barnum and Bailey's during the Wild West show. The faces in the galleries shine blue in the smokefiltered daylight that streams in through the windows out of the clear sky outside. From somewhere comes a tapping like the noise trained sealions make tapping with their flippers on their circus-stands. Bells ring under the spots. Suddenly you discover that the battery next along the gallery has invented a little comic figure on a platform that's beating on a board with a mallet. From up here the neckless puppet that represents Mr. Snell looks much too much like a sealion waiting to do an act. The puppet balances on its nose an enormous smooth voice that politely asks everybody to rise and sing *America*.

Three bells. My spots and all the rest spring to attention. The center lights reveal a huge Old Glory hanging in the middle of all the other little Old Glories in the ceiling. The wailing begins to die. "Dim out," yells the guy at the phone to the guy at the switchboard.

Out of the blue haze the spots dextrously produce a little beaked figure in black. "It's a rabbi 'n' he's goin' to pray," says somebody behind me.

Full lights on invocation to Almighty God, then dim out on brief mention of "these dark days of confusion and despair." Cautiously the spots come on again as the rabbi lets a note of hope creep into the prayer. "Not so fast Joe," warns the man at the phone, the rabbi warms up through "brotherhood" into "guidance," "confidence in the future"; full lights come up everywhere.

The show goes on smoothly. In the speeches the Ship of State reels and shudders through such a hurricane of metaphors and is buffeted by such heroic waves of stale oratory that the captain, at the helm, on the bridge, in the pilot house (who's getting it all over the radio at the White House) must be feeling a bit seasick. At one place only, the wires get crossed for a few seconds, when the fat marionette of ex-Senator France appears on one side of the rostrum waving its little arms and attempting (as it turns out later) to nominate for President that sturdy rotogravure fisherman and columnist, Calvin Coolidge. We didn't get a chance to see what the spotlights would have done if they'd had to extemporize, because the offending marionette was immediately dragged off by the stagehands and the show continued according to the script.

The only other hitch occurred during the spontaneous celebration that took place when Mr. Scott, lifting himself hand over hand up an astonishingly long ladder of "becauses," reached the exalted name of Herbert Hoover. The delegates marched round all right, and the tin trumpets tooted and the little flags waved, and the toy balloons that had been coyly hiding in big nets in the ceiling all through the convention were released and floated down to give the delegates something to do with their hands. The ushers threw paper streamers from the galleries and the bands played, and the organ pealed forth *I'se Been Workin' on the Railroad*, but the grand climax, when His Master's Voice poured out of the loudspeakers and a moving picture of the rotund features of the Great Engineer flicked vaguely on two huge screens, was a flop, owing to bad lighting and stage management; or perhaps for other reasons. The Presence failed to materialize.

Out of the Red with Roosevelt

They came out of the Stadium with a stale taste in their mouths. Down West Madison Street, walking between lanes of cops and a scattering of bums, the crowds from the galleries found the proud suave voice of the National Broadcasting Company still filling their jaded ears from every loudspeaker, enumerating the technical agencies that had worked together to obtain the superb hookup through which they broadcast the proceedings of the Democratic Convention of 1932. Well, they did their part: the two big white disks above the speakers' platform (the ears of the radio audience) delicately caught every intonation of the oratory, the draggedout "gre-eats" when the "great Senator from the great state of . . ." was introduced, the deep "stalwart" always prefixed to "Democrat" when a candidate was being nominated, the indignant rumble in the voice when the present administration was "branded" as having induced "an orgy of crime and saturnalia of corruption"; the page with the portable microphone in his buttonhole had invariably been on hand when a delegate was recognized from the floor; the managers for the N.B.C. had been there all the time, stagemanaging, moving quietly and deftly around the platform, with the expression and gestures of oldfashioned photographers; coaxing the speakers into poses from which they could be heard; telegrams had been read giving the minutetominute position of the nominee's plane speeding west, the radio voice of Wally Butterworth had whooped things up by describing the adverse flying conditions, the plane's arrival at the airport, the cheering throngs, the jolly ride from Buffalo, the Governor's nice smile; but when Franklin D. Roosevelt (in person) walked to the front of the rostrum on his son's arm while the organ played *The Star-spangled Banner* and an irrepressible young lady from Texas waved a bouquet of red, white and blue flowers over his head, to greet with a plain sensible and unassuming speech the crowd that had yelled itself hoarse for an hour for Al Smith three days before, that had gone delirious over the Wet plank and applauded every phrase in the party platform, and sat with eager patience through the weeklong vaudeville show—nothing happened.

Courteous applause, but no feeling.

The crowd in the huge hall sat blank, blinking in the glare of the lights. Neither delegates nor the public seemed to be able to keep their minds on what the candidate, whom they had nominated after such long sessions and such frantic trading and bickering downtown in their hotel rooms, had to say. As he talked the faces in the galleries and boxes melted away, leaving red blocks of seats, even the delegates on the floor slunk out in twos and threes. After all, what is a man, a tiny bundle of nerves and muscles only six feet tall, compared to the giant muddling awesome blurs, a hundred times amplified, on the radio and screen?

Starting on Monday with *The Star-spangled Banner* and an inaugural address of Thomas Jefferson's read by a stout gentleman with a white gardenia in his buttonhole; through the Senator from Kentucky's keynote speech, during which he so dexterously caught his glasses every time they fell from his nose when he jerked his head to one side and up to emphasize a point; through Wednesday's all star variety show that offered Clarence Darrow, Will Rogers, Amos 'n' Andy, and Father Coughlin "the radio priest" (who, by the way, advised the convention to put Jesus Christ in the White House), all on one bill; through the joyful reading of the platform with its promise of beer now and a quietus by and by on prohibition snoopers and bootleggers; through the all night cabaret on Thursday, with its smoke and sweaty shirts and fatigue and watered Coca Cola and putty sandwiches and the cockeyed idiocy of the demonstrations: Governor Byrd's band in plumes and rabbit's fur (which he kindly loaned to Ritchie and to Alfalfa Bill when their turn came) and the pigeons and the young women who kept climbing up on the platform and bathing in the kleig lights like people under a warm shower, and the sleepy little Oklahoma girls in their kilties; and the grim balloting while the sky outside went blue and then pink until at last the sun rose and sent long frightening bright horizontal shafts through the cigarsmoke and the spotlights and the huddled groups of wornout politicians; through the nominating speeches and the seconding speeches and the oldtime tunes, *The Old Grey Mare, A Hot Time in the Old Town Tonight, I'se Been Workin' on the Railroad,* . . . through all the convention week and the flicker of flashlight bulbs and the roar of voices there had been built up a myth, as incongruous to this age as the myth of the keeneyed pilot at the helm of the ship of state that the Republicans tried to revitalize three weeks before:—the myth of the young American working his way by honesty and brawn, from Log Cabin to President.

This stalwart Democrat was to rise in his might, wrench the government out of the hands of the old bogey Republicans, Wall Street, Privilege, Graft and Corruption, return it to the people and thus in some mystic way give a job to the jobless, relieve the farmers of their mortgages, save the money the little fellow had deposited in the tottering banks, restore business to the small storekeeper and producer and thereby bring the wouldbe Democratic officeholders massed on the floor back to the fleshpots of power. A powerful myth and an old myth. But when, largely through the backstage efforts of Mr. McAdoo, the myth took flesh in the crippled body and unassuming speech of the actual Governor of New York, the illusion crashed. Too late.

You come out of the Stadium and walk down the street. It's West Madison Street, the home address of migratory workers and hoboes and jobless men all over the middle west. Gradually the din of speeches fades out of your ears, you forget the taste of the cigar you were smoking, the cracks and gossip of the press gallery. Nobody on the street knows about the convention that's deciding who shall run their government, nor cares. The convention is the sirens of police motorcycles, a new set of scare headlines, a new sensation over the radio. There are sixday bicycle races and battles of the century and eucharistic congresses and bigleague games and political conventions; and a man has got a job, or else he hasn't got a job, he's got jack in his pocket, or else he's broke, he's got a business, or else he's a bum. Way off some place headline events happen. Even if they're right on West Madison Street, they're way off. Roosevelt or Hoover? It'll be the same cops.

You walk on down, across the great train yards and the river to the Loop, out onto Michigan Avenue where Chicago is raising every year a more imposing front of skyscrapers, into the clean wind off the lake. Shiny storefronts, doormen, smartly dressed girls, taxis, buses taking shoppers, clerks, business men home to the South Side and North Side. In Grant Park more jobless men lying under the bushes, beyond them sails in the harbor, a white steamboat putting out into the lake. Overhead pursuit planes fly in formation advertising the military show at Soldiers' Field.

To get their ominous buzz out of your ears, you go down a flight of steps, into the darkness feebly lit by ranks of dusty red electric lights of the roadway under Michigan Avenue. The fine smart marble and plateglass front of the city peels off as you walk down the steps. Down here the air, drenched with the exhaust from the grinding motors of trucks, is full of dust and grit and the roar of the heavy traffic that hauls the city's freight. When your eyes get used to the darkness, you discover that, like the world upstairs of storefronts and hotel lobbies and battles of the century and political conventions, this world too has its leisure class. They lie in rows along the ledges above the roadway, huddled in grimed newspapers, grey sagfaced men in wornout clothes, discards, men who have nothing left but their stiff hungry grimy bodies, men who have lost the power to want. Try to tell one of them that the *gre-eat* Franklin D. Roosevelt, Governor of the *gre-eat* state of New York, has been nominated by the *gre-eat* Democratic party as its candidate for President, and you'll get what the galleries at the convention gave Mr. McAdoo when they discovered that he had the votes of Texas and California in his pocket and was about to shovel them into the Roosevelt band wagon, a prolonged and enthusiastic Boooo.

Hoover or Roosevelt, it'll be the same cops.

Herbert Hoover's Last Stand

So many people want to see Mr. Hoover that even Ninth Avenue is jammed, so crowded, indeed, that the cops can't get at the communist demonstrators come to jeer, and their boos are lost in the shuffle of the enormous crowd. Ducking through the ranks of brave boys in blue who seem bent on not letting anybody, with or without a ticket, get into the hall, you can catch a glimpse of the placards of the unemployed council, peaceably massed under the L. After working through five lines of cops I find myself in a rush of people up a stairway and am catapulted into an aisle that comes to an abrupt end in a bunch of men and women mashed against a rail. Beyond their heads is the hall, a pink mist of faces and American flags and spotlights.

They are singing something about Hoover to the tune of *John Brown's Body*. The flags wave, the pink faces roar: ovation. A small, dumplingshaped mannikin has appeared on the mannikin-packed platform in the middle of the hall. Through the glasses I can see as distinctly as in the newsreels, among the jowly faces of Republican magnates, the familiar jowls of Herbert Hoover. He's waving a hand in a short gesture, squinting from side to side into the glare.

That man's not the boss type; more the confidential foreman.

A drunk behind me yells, "Rah for Roosevelt!" There's a considerable scuffle as two sweating ushers and a cop try to clear the aisle. In the middle of it I see a printed sheet drifting down from the balcony. I reach for it, but a little fat man beside me who looks strangely like a dick has grabbed it. His companion, an identical little fat man who also looks strangely like a dick, snatches it out of his hand. Over their shoulder I can read the headline, MR. HOOVER YOU'RE A LIAR.

The second little fat man who looks strangely like a dick folds it and puts it in his pocket. "Vat," says the man who first grabbed it, "you will be taking from me my vatch next?"

At the other end of the hall a heckler is being ejected. That boo never had a chance. Everybody is quieting down. The Hoover mannikin has been set out by itself in a pool of white light. From where we jam against the rail we look intently into its left ear. A dry phonograph voice comes from the loudspeakers that hang from the shadowy ceiling in the center of the hall. Through the glasses I can see the mouth barely moving. The expressionless face when he turns our way is like the face of a ventriloquist. We are listening to Herbert Hoover's great speech in Madison Square Garden in the last week of the losing campaign of 1932, the speech about grass growing in the streets of a hundred cities. . . .

After it's over, everybody piles out to catch trains, go home to bed, meet friends in speakeasies, drink coffee in one arm lunch rooms. Streets still jammed. On a car stalled in the crowd down Eighth Avenue a group of young Jewish boys is chanting in unison, "We want Roosevelt." From brownstone steps on a cross street an elderly man is doing a big business selling *Daily Workers*. Nobody notices a few isolated sticks of red fire in the hands of organization stalwarts.

Motorcycle cops charge by, opening a lane in the crowd. A black limousine follows. To me it looks empty, but the skinny man on the curb beside me says he saw Hoover sitting in it. "Sure he was in it, all hunched up wid a black robe thrown over him. Oder cars all went out de oder way." I'm carried across the street by the push of the crowd. Faintly from far away comes the sound of a boo that is echoed by the bubbling noise an old drunken Irishman is making in his throat as he lurches out of the way of a policeman's horse.

Pink Tea

For the Socialists I sat in a box. Everything was very agreeable. The air was good. The hall was full, but there was room to move around. The speakers were ranked in chairs on a platform at the end of the hall. The speeches were very long. Judge Panken spoke a long time about the achievements of the socialist government of Vienna. A Negro from uptown spoke warmly and well; socialism was the only hope for the Negro people. Mr. Broun (in person) made a brief appearance. Everything was very agreeable.

Everybody agreed with what everybody said. The only novelty was the youngsters from Columbia, Hunter, City College, New York University who paraded around with placards, COLUMBIA VOTES SOCIALIST, and similar mottoes. Things dragged so that Norman Thomas did not begin to speak until around eleven. Here was a good speech, a handsome dignified presence, a graceful way of talking, smoothed by a faint reminiscence of the Episcopal pulpit, as if he were always on the edge of dropping into, "Dearly beloved brethren." When he first came on there was great animation among the cameramen. Flashlight bulbs flickered like heat lightning. He was posed with his hand in the air, holding a large red flag in the attitude of the resurrection angel, leaning over the desk and looking into the crowd. Everything was very agreeable. His speech was well put together (I thought I could detect a faint cloud cross Mr. Hillquit's face at the mention of a capital levy). Everybody wanted to hear the speech, but the Long Island Railroad and the Staten Island ferry are mightier than salvation by socialism, and the audience was melting away all through it.

When we got out we looked for the cheering crowds outside so feelingly described by the speakers. A lot of people but no real jam, as there had been to see Hoover. Not even a boo.

The Big Chief Sits in His Tepee

At the Democratic rally the attitude of the cops was quite different. Instead of keeping people out of the Garden, they were inviting them in. Again it was pink with American flags. A crowd, but not the eager jam there had been to see Hoover. A theatrical manager would have said, "A lot of paper in this house." The Democrats had a better band than the Republicans, but worse speeches. For a long time a procession of candidates appeared on the rostrum, making remarks that smacked a good deal of a high school commencement, each depositing a small identical bouquet at the feet of John F. Curry.

When they saw the face of Surrogate O'Brien even the two Greeks sitting in front of me, whose main anxiety had been to get hold of some of the American flags that were being distributed free, winced. Not a word of Jimmy Walker, not a

word of Acting Mayor McKee. Regularity on every face including the benign countenance that Colonel Lehman wears
below his genteel bald head.

People were pretty well choked with regularity by the time
Frank, preceded by the Roosevelt smile, and Al with "raddio"
on the tip of his tongue, came in to their Damon and Pythias
act. Their speeches gained a certain dignity from the fact that
they made no mention of the candidacy of Surrogate O'Brien
and dropped no incense before the noble Democratic leader,
Curry; but where are campaign speeches now?

Going out, it was a happy bunch of wardheelers and district
leaders that hurried to their beer. Seabury was stopped, McKee
was on the leash, the Tammany van was safely included in the
big Democratic parade to Washington. But the ordinary voter
was thinking of Hoover. Boo.

The Forgotten Man

Where was the forgotten man in all these meetings, the
citizen of Hooverville, the down and out guy you find
wherever you look for a second under the thinning veneer of
comfort and the American standard? Or is Al Smith right in
saying he doesn't exist? Depends on what you mean by exist.
Maybe a few of him went to stand outside and crane and
boo at Hoover, but the people you rubbed elbows with in
the campaign rallies were of the stiffest small respectability.
The forgotten man didn't go to the socialist meeting, and
he'd have been out of place among the Deserving Democrats. Where is he?

Maybe it's the rain or the fact that it costs fortyone cents to
get in, or maybe it's something else, but he isn't in evidence
at the communist rally and celebration of the Fifteenth Anniversary of the October Revolution, either.

The minute you step in the hall, though, you feel there's
more life in the air. People look younger and livelier than at
the other meetings. When they sing the *Internationale* they
sing it as if they meant it. The speeches are short, boiled
down to sets of slogans. The meeting starts at a high tide of
enthusiasm. Cheers for the Communist Party and the triumphant workers and peasants of the U.S.S.R., boos for
Hoover and for Norman Thomas and Morris Hillquit.

After the crowds of dignitaries of the other meetings, the wide empty platform, with its short row of speakers on spindly chairs and the big upsidedown 5 among the stage-properties behind them that are going to be used later in the pageant, gives you a feeling of almost ominous emptiness. The audience is cheerful, orderly, neatly dressed, fills all the seats; the ushers are livelylooking youngsters with wide red bands across their chests; the organized cheering is brisker than at the socialist meeting, but the voices of the speakers are small and dry and far away.

Foster is sick, broken down under the strain of bucking a hostile continent. His speech is going to be broadcast from his bedroom. The feeling of farawayness and emptiness is enormously intensified. Is it that we're ten thousand miles from Moscow? When his voice starts coming over, the accent and intonation of a native American workingman fills the hall for a moment with warmth. Hathaway has to finish reading it for him; his voice is American, too. It's a good speech, well put, with a New England canniness in the phrases that Foster has never quite lost, but it leaves the meeting with a sense of loneliness and abandonment that nothing can cure, not even the announcement that the cheering thousands outside are being beaten up by the cops. (I looked outside; about as big a crowd as the socialists had; no signs of busted heads.)

The chairman tells us to be sure to stay for the pageant and begins to read the results of the German elections. The German communists have won two million votes, eleven seats in the Reichstag. Cheering. We feel for a moment the tremendous intoxication with history that is the great achievement of communist solidarity.

Then Earl Browder begins to speak; a well thoughtout, carefully enunciated statement of the party's aims in the election. But there is something dry and pithy in his voice that fails to hold the crowd. Suburban trainschedules, the perennial hopeless struggle of the New Yorker to get ahead of the crush in the subway, begin to wield their enormous power. People are drifting out.

A series of resolutions is voted automatically, so automatically that nobody listens to them, and the pageant comes on. It describes the triumph of the Five Year Plan in Four. There's

a feeling of energy and youthfulness about it. But where's
Hooverville? Where's the forgotten man? Where's the great
boo of 1932?

We walk out between triple rows of chesty cops. The cops
look happy. It's their last massmeeting before the election.

The Radio Voice

Outside the tight framehouse there's a northeast gale blowing. The slanting rain drums on the roof and sloshes down
the windowpanes. The house is a tiny neat stable wooden box
full of dryness, warmth and light, in the enormous driving
drift of the night. It's full, too, of a lonely tangle of needs,
worries, desires; how are we going to eat, get clothes to wear,
get into bed with someone we love, raise our children, belong
to something, have something belong to us? After supper
people sit around in the parlor listening drowsily to disconnected voices, stale scraps of last year's jazz, unfinished litanies
advertising unnamed products that dribble senselessly from
the radio. A brisk deferential organizing voice from N.B.C.
breaks in. People wake up. People edge their chairs up to the
radio . . . in the Blue Room at the White House.

Then there is a man leaning across his desk, speaking clearly
and cordially to you and me, painstakingly explaining how
he's sitting at his desk there in Washington, leaning towards
you and me across his desk, speaking clearly and cordially so
that you and me shall completely understand that he sits at his
desk there in Washington with his fingers on all the switchboards of the federal government, operating the intricate machinery of the departments, drafting codes and regulations
and bills for the benefit of you and me worried about things,
sitting close to the radio in small houses on rainy nights, for
the benefit of us wageearners, us homeowners, us farmers,
us mechanics, us miners, us mortgagees, us processors, us
mortgageholders, us bankdepositors, us consumers, retail
merchants, bankers, brokers, stockholders, bondholders,
creditors, debtors, jobless and jobholders . . . *Not a sparrow
falleth but* . . . He is leaning cordially toward you and me
across his desk there in Washington telling in carefully chosen
words how the machinations of chisellers are to be foiled for
you and me, and how the myriadcylindered motor of re-

covery is being primed with billions for you and me, and you and me understand, we belong to billions, billions belong to us, we are going to have good jobs, good pay, protected bankdeposits, a new dealing out of billions to youandme. We edge our chairs closer to the radio, we are flattered and pleased, we feel we are right there in the White House. When the cordial explaining voice stops we want to say "Thank you Frank," we want to ask about the grandchildren and that dog that had to be sent away for biting a foreign diplomat . . . You have been listening to the President of the United States in the Blue Room . . .

Chicago, June, 1932
New York, November, 1932
Provincetown, March, 1933

8. MORE VIEWS OF WASHINGTON

Masonic Hall: February, 1934

The rule is seven minutes a speaker but it's hard as the devil to enforce. The speakers have so much to tell, the nine hundred delegates in the hall are so anxious to hear what the speakers have to tell. Time and again when the stroke of the chairman's gavel is heard, hands rise all over the hall, voices rise pleading for two more minutes. The speakers stand waiting for the decision too eager to tell their story to be shy or flattered or pleased. Nearly always a thundering Aye comes from the hall. The speakers have come a long way with these stories, some of them riding freights, some of them packed into chartered busses or borrowed cars. There's a Canadian and some Porto Ricans, men and women and young boys and girls from Texas and Oklahoma and Minnesota and Michigan and Maine and Illinois and Indiana and Wisconsin, from Missouri, Oregon, Washington State and Alaska, Pennsylvania, Ohio, Maryland, Idaho. (There'd be a California delegation if they hadn't been picked up for vagrancy in Memphis, where a police officer overheard one of them telephoning for some extra money. These days it's a prison offence for a citizen to be even temporarily without money in his pocket.) It's a cold winter. It's been a mean hard trip. And before they started, before their local Unemployed Councils elected them, they'd known a mean hard winter of grinding struggle. That's how winters are these days for the great mass of the American people.

But it's not to bellyache about how mean and hard things are that they have come. You get the meanness and the hardness of it only in indirect references. These speakers who have so much to tell that seven minutes is a pitiably short time for them, have come not to bellyache about their hunger and misery (though the words hungry, ragged, freezing occur again and again in their speeches) or to repeat the oldtime slogans of workingclass oratory (they have forgotten all the old May Day slogans; most of them never knew them); they have come to report their successes.

They have come to report as pithily and wittily as they can, even if they do run over the seven minutes, their successes in dealing with relief commissions, town councils, mayors, district attorneys, hardboiled officials, softboiled officials, liberal Democratic officials trimmed with all the beguiling apparatus of the New Deal. You can boil down what they have to say to a simple basic diagram. A middleaged negro woman with glasses from Houston, Texas, a schoolteacher from the Mesaba Range, a boilermaker from Denver, or a young Socialist who looks like a college football player from Hartford, Connecticut, or a tall blonde logger from Washington State have the same tale to tell. Things were bad; little by little through the first years of the depression everything that was worthwhile in the American standard—schooling, independence, the chance to travel around, fair food and housing—was withdrawn from them and their families. They found themselves helpless before corrupt politicians, loansharks, brutal charities. By the end of Hoover's presidency they were sick and tired of the way things were going; a lot of enthusiasm and revolt went into the ballot boxes that elected Roosevelt. Then came the various stages of hope and discouragement with the promises of the N.R.A. and its attendant organizations under the sign of the blue eagle, the honeymoon period, democratic talk, soft soap and pretty words from platforms draped in various shades of pink. Now, last summer, this winter, today, came the discovery that there was something more effective than talk or the complications of Washington red tape. There were the Unemployed Councils, there was mass action.

When the bailiff took the furniture out, the members of the councils carried it back in the house, or maybe made the bailiffs carry it back; if the bank foreclosed on a farm there was the Sears, Roebuck sale; if the relief was insufficient or charity supplies spoiled there was the delegation ready to make life miserable for the officials, the delegation that demanded demanded demanded, no matter how often the delegates were jailed and clubbed, until they got what they wanted. Through the Unemployed Councils these speakers had found that with organization and solidarity they could stop being worms and downandouts picking up a living out of garbage pails and relief kitchens, and be respected citizens again. They'd found it out, they'd made a success of it. What it took was organization, solidarity and nerve. They didn't pretend that they didn't feel good about it.

That is the tone of voice of the National Convention of Unemployed Councils. "We workers have been the yes men of the bosses too long, now is the time for us to learn to say No." . . . "We've been lettin' the preachers and politicians do our thinkin' for us. Now we're goin' to do our own thinkin'."

And who are these people who have managed to get to this convention over the snowy February roads from every corner of the country? To see them all together makes you feel like a kid on the Fourth of July. There are young men and old men, young woman and middleaged women, white people and negroes, Italians, Jews, Poles, Swedes, Finns and plain American towheaded farmboys. There's a Chinese laundryman. There are delegates from a Cleveland flophouse. There are bookkeepers, furworkers, cannery slaves, cotton pickers, granitecutters, printers, cigarmakers, carpenters, plumbers, painters, cooks, waiters, waitresses, automobile and airplane workers, writers, teachers, architects, chemists, artists, chauffeurs, miners, steelpuddlers, electric welders, cementpourers, bakers, and a diamond cutter. They represent something like twelve hundred councils. There are delegates from the Progressive Miners, from some A. F. of L. quarryman's unions, from an Aeronautical Workers Union, the Right to Live Club of Providence, farm organizations, Socialist unemployed leagues, the Farmer Labor Party of Minnesota, the League for Struggle for Negro Rights, several professional groups, and a Small Homeowners League in Ohio. They are the advanceguard of the rank and file that has come to grips with certain grim realities behind the rosy smokescreen of the New Deal.

These realities stalk through all their speeches: unemployment has come to stay, real wages are going down, America has few opportunities to offer young men growing up to take their places in the world. In spite of liberal efforts to spread round money and employment the New Deal has speeded up rather than retarded the growth of the allpowerful monopolies. The immediate remedy offered and endorsed by the convention is a drastic bill for Federal Unemployment Insurance introduced in the House on February 2nd by Representative Lundeen. But everybody knows it will take more than that. Everybody knows it will take organization, solidarity and nerve. Particularly the young men know it, the young men growing up full of wants and ambitions who are finding themselves lucky if they can get a job shovelling snow.

Snow is heaping up on the buses waiting to take the delegates home. Inside the last resolutions are being adopted, the constitution of the national organization has been voted, the last reports of the delegations that went to heckle public officials have been made. People are saying goodbye, getting ready to scatter into the snowy night out over the great continent rigid with winter. Everybody looks tired but very cheerful. They feel they've got a line on events, they feel that they're not alone in the tangle of frustrations that's the life of the moneyless man without a job. In a few days they'll be reporting back to the groups that sent them. They'll be reporting that there are victories to be won by organization, solidarity and nerve.

Opposite the Gompers Memorial

"We've been paradin' around the streets with our bellies rattlin' like a bunch of tin cans an' a flock of ideas in our heads," says the tall pinkfaced man with sparse yellow hair who is spokesman for the Aeronautical Workers Union in Buffalo. He is telling William Green how the old members of the In-

ternational Association of Machinists who are now airplane
workers feel that the leadership of the A. F. of L. is nearer to
the strawbosses and politicians than to the working man. The
trade union delegation from the unemployed convention lines
both sides of the handsomely lighted council chamber. Mr.
Green, a small genial greyhaired bureaucrat in round glasses,
who was a miner when he was young, sits at the head of a
long mahogany table. Next to him towers a great floursack of
a man with a whispy droop of white mustache towards the
bottom of a face as expressionless as an egg. The other members of the council, widely spaced down the long neatly-
ranged table, have ordinary wardpolitician's faces, a little
harder than the average perhaps (riding the laborunions is a
tough game, you need a good pair of bellows in your chest
and sometimes a pair of handy mits). Pastyfaced secretaries in
snappy dark suits hover round the table with an occasional
spiteful glance at the serious worried traveltired faces of the
rank and file delegates who fill the two sides of the room. The
bright wintry light pouring in through the windows behind
these men shows up all the wear on their old overcoats and
sweaters and leather jackets. They are a third of a century
younger than the men at the table, most of them; they are respectful before this great table with its neat piles of papers,
before these old men sitting powerful and leisurely in the
shining Washington morning; their faces are in shadow.

"Gentlemen," says Mr. Green ingratiatingly. "You mustn't
come here to lecture us."

The young man who tells how gangsters are in control of
the cleaners' and dyers' unions, and who demands that the
A. F. of L. actively support unemployment insurance, fight
racketeering and undemocratic methods in the unions and re-
mit dues to unemployed members, gets more of a rise out of
the council. "We're in charge of this organization," snarls a
heavyset man at the table. "And we know best what the mem-
bership wants."

"Gentlemen," says Mr. Green, "you mustn't lecture us."

When a miner from Shenandoah speaks about how the an-
thracite unions are threatened with extinction by the use of
strip mines and highpower steamshovels, Mr. Green shakes
his head and agrees with him that things are very bad indeed.

"When we don't know just what to do, we have to do the best we can."

"Yes you hang around the congressmen's offices and lobby and compromise, till you don't know whose interests you are serving," says a delegate. There's a certain tenseness along the counciltable.

The International President of the Plumbers' and Steamfitters' starts to light into the delegate of the Philadelphia plumbers. "Yes, we all know you've been to Russia. . . . And how far did you get with the union convention in Chicago? Your motion was defeated, wasn't it?"

It was Mr. Green's turn to lecture. "Why don't you go and lecture the bosses? We're doing the best we can. You don't know the difficulties we are up against. You are always ready to denounce us who are doing the best we can for the working class in this tremendous struggle with the employers. You go and denounce them for a change."

The spokesman for the cleaners and dyers had answered that a few minutes before when he told of trying to get into the convention of his union in Mecca temple in New York. He had to get into the convention before he could take the floor to denounce the racketeers and bosses. In the entrance hall a man had met him and stuck a gun in his ribs and warned him that he'd find the climate very unhealthy if he tried to attend the convention. That was why they had to start their housecleaning inside the unions.

Nobody wanted a row. The delegates began to shuffle their feet, to look out of the windows down into the snowy uncrowded Washington streets. "Well I guess that's all we have time for. . . . We have important business to consider, important business in the interests of the working class. . . . Goodbye," said Mr. Green hurriedly.

We filed out and scattered into the cheerful noontime of a crisp winter day.

The Big Tent

After all where else can a citizen see such a show free, gratis? On every street a colonnade capped by a pediment, the rhetorical grandeur that was eighteenth-century Greece and Rome; at the end of every vista, on this wintry day, above a haze of bare branches of trees, the white dome that stands for certain hopes held long ago, and for Congress, the delicately involved arcana of the Supreme Court, Republican and Democratic oratory. When you have seen one of the President's secretaries politely kidding a delegation from the unemployed convention in the vestibule of the White House, you can go up to the hill, where those pesky starlings have established themselves in the pediments and in the dome itself and fly around in a black chuckling cloud, endangering the hats and the dignity of the representatives of the people, and even of the august Supreme Court justices. Up on the hill you can examine the vast new building of the Supreme Court; in the Capitol you can climb the long flight of steps into the rotunda under the dome that houses, you are puzzled to find, exactly nothing. You can look up at the strangely flatulent effigies in the Hall of Statuary (their number is now limited by the fact that the floor threatens to cave in if any more great men are added), or you can hurry up the marble stairway of the House of Representatives, past the huge picture full of furry pioneers and smokes and mountainpeaks, that depicts, I believe, the Westward Course of Empire, into the galleries of the House. This year, however, nothing much goes on there. The representatives are so intimidated by the thought of what the Radio Voice from the Blue Room may do to them next fall that few of them dare to speak above a whisper; in fact, most of them seem to have stopped attending sessions at all. Better stroll over through the warm gilded light of the corridors, passing pursemouthed legislators who walk with selfimportance draped about them like a toga, into the Senate wing.

The Senate looks younger than it used to, or maybe the old warhorses aren't in their seats. The walls are hung with maps illustrating the St. Lawrence waterway treaty. Norris of Nebraska is on his feet explaining another phase of his long, often solitary, fight against the power monopolies. Even after all these years in Washington there is something square and unpretentious about him; he has the untired ease of a man who has found his job and settled down into it happily. If his job has been to fight a losing fight for the farmer and small businessman against the monopolies of finance and power, he can't help it; he's put the case as well as he could and he will continue to represent his clients as long as there is breath in him. Nye and La Follette seem to be the only senators listening to him. Huey Long is asleep in his seat; he looks, with his puffy face and the blue sags under his eyes, like an overgrown small boy with very bad habits indeed. Whitehaired Senator Gore's calm blind face gives an oldtime rustic dignity to things as he wanders in and out restlessly, led by a page, or feeling his way with his stick.

You leave the gallery to smoke a cigarette, or to look at *The Storming of Chapultepec* or that childhood favorite *Commodore Perry Transferring His Flag During the Battle of Lake Erie*, and, when you go back a pantagruelically paunched senator from Kentucky is telling a rambling tale, vaguely on the side of the powerinterests, about a taxistand in front of the depot of the Louisville and Nashville Railroad at Bowling Green. Better take a look at the sideshows.

In the basement the little monorail trolley takes you to the senate office building. Another rotunda, more marmoreal corridors. In a large room full of cigarette smoke Mr. Pecora is carrying on his investigation of the bankers. Witnesses, lawyers, newspapermen sit at long greenbaizecovered tables. Over each table is a loudspeaker. The loudspeakers are controlled by a worried looking thinfaced man at a keyboard. It takes you some time to make out who is speaking. The voices come from the ceiling. You have to watch their lips. First Pecora's lips move, then the lips of a pale and apologeticlooking Detroit banker in the witness chair. You try to listen, but it takes a long time to shake off the sense of unreality. Is this really Mr. Pecora, are these really Detroit bankers caught with the goods, is something really going to be done about it, or is it all a not entirely skillful marionetteshow arranged by that worriedlooking man at the keyboard?

Down the hall there's another inquisition going on that has drawn a bigger crowd: Airmail contracts. This room looks more like a courtroom. The inquisitors sit on a raised dais round three sides on one end of the long room. Below them and in the middle of them sits on a solitary chair, with his back to the press and the public, a certain Mr. Boeing. This gentleman used to have a small machineshop somewhere out in Washington State; he took up the manufacture of airplane motors, he became connected with certain genial gentlemen who had many friends in Washington, a grand began to grow for him where a dollar had grown before; a warm rain of subsidies refreshed Mr. Boeing's enterprises and they prospered. Mr. Boeing, on being asked to explain all this, looks as if he'd sat on a tack. He's squirming on his chair, he's perspiring freely, he seems to have ants under his collar, he looks wildly for help to the right and left. He keeps remembering things he's just forgotten, he makes damaging admissions, he stammers and squirms. Senator Black happily tightens the thumbscrew another notch and looks round smiling at the members of the committee, at the press, at the private citizens looking on. The trouble with the witness seems to be that he hasn't been a millionaire long enough not to feel guilty about it.

To go over to the House sideshows you have to walk across the park. A couple of small grey squirrels are scampering across the snowy paths. From the trees comes an occasional derisive whistle from a starling.

The room where the Military Affairs Committee of the House meets has armchairs as comfortable as the armchairs at Radio City. At either end of the dais where the committee sits is the bronze model of an airplane. General Mitchell is appearing to testify, dressed in tweeds as befits a country gentleman. He is surrounded by photographers. The silver crinkle in the flashlight bulbs flares and goes out to a milky white. The photographers are chased away. General Mitchell begs to state that from Langley to this day the high staff-officers of the army have fought the progress of aviation. During the war in spite of flying coffins and the Liberty motor we made great strides, then the merchants got hold of it. "When the merchants get hold of our government we might as well stop work." A funny look goes round the ring of pursedup politicians' faces. "What do you mean by merchants, general?" somebody asks nervously. "People who have something to sell. Hoover was a merchant. . . . The merchants have got all the honest aviation officers scared so that they don't dare call their souls their own . . . even army officers have to eat you know." A look of relief comes over the smalltime merchants' faces of the politicians on the committee when the chairman gets the general onto the subject of specific reforms. No more talk about merchants.

Back at the capitol you look into the Senate chamber again. You don't know how to explain the fact that the paunchy senator from Kentucky is telling the story about the taxicabs outside of the Louisville and Nashville depot all over again, or maybe he's still telling it.

You hurry out into the corridors to discover that the Supreme Court is in session. A sepulchral doorkeeper politely pulls the door open for you by a thick crimson cord. You slide in and sit on the elegant cushioned bench provided for the public. It's a different world. What magnificent staging. What fine lighting. What handsome makeups. Two elegantly trimmed chryselephantine beards, one in the center and one to one side, Brandeis's mop of steely hair and his lean thespian face, Cardozo's carefully cut lawyer's profile. Behind them against the crimson hangings, pageboys stand ready to fetch and carry. From the shadowy pit below the justices comes a halting voice reading a brief. You can only catch some of the words. "Therefore . . . therein . . . acquisition in a competitive situation . . . under such circumstances . . . parallel lines following parallel routes . . . therein . . . cause to appear . . . differing from the situation in other industries . . . a railroad is held by its rails." And suddenly it's all over. The justices are on their feet in their long robes. The clerk of the court is droning out a formula. Closing time.

As we came out of the Capitol we almost tripped over a mike on a stand. An N.B.C. truck was standing by and a group of N.B.C. young men. We asked them what it was for. Mr. Something, the presidential announcer, was coming to broadcast the shooting of the starlings by the War Department at six o'clock sharp. We began to get indignant. Are they really going to shoot the starlings? "Naw, they're shootin' 'em with blanks. They want to scare 'em away, that's all."

And sure enough at six o'clock several parties in uniform began blazing away in the direction of the dome of the nation's capitol. The blanks made a great racket. The starlings flew round and round the dome against the darkening lavender sky. They made a black chiding chuckling cloud in the last light. When the blanks were all shot off they settled back into their places again.

Any Hotel Ballroom

As there is no room for them in any government building the code hearings take place in the ballrooms of the Washington hotels. In some of them the management has supplied a decoration of flags and patriotic bunting. At a long table at the end of the room sits the board with the administrator or deputy administrator in the middle and his advisers and the representatives of the industry grouped about him like the apostles in Da Vinci's *Last Supper*. In front of that there is a press table, chairs for counsel and for representatives of interested concerns. The rest of the room is filled with rows of little caterer's chairs for the public. At one end of the table glitter the shivering magic circles of the mike. Loud speakers make it as easy (or as hard) to hear what is going on in the cloakroom as in the front row. The proceedings have that faintly holiday air, felt dimly through a dense mist of boredom, of a highschool commencement. The boredom is the reaction of actors and spectators to the endless trail of bewildering and uncoordinated detail that flows from the typewritten sheets of a great variety of spokesmen for special interests who pour their "remarks" all day into the mike. It's like trying to take an inventory of somebody else's house. Attention sags under the infinite complexity of industry and business. You find yourself following the seasonal difficulties of the sardinecanners of Eastport, Maine, of the Virginia and Carolina shrimp industry, of the producers of snap beans in the Ozarks; you hear that the women who pit maraschino cherries are overworked and underpaid; you hear the San José fruitgrowers put forward their side of the case; you discover that the producers of pipeorgans are in desperate straits; if a man could be found with the patience and application to listen, the whole pageant of American life would unroll for him in the pros and cons of the thousands of codes that unravel in such gentlemanly style in these tastefully decorated Washington ballrooms.

It's only when representatives of the workers appear that things lose their cosy tone of Washingtonian leisure. Then a certain bitterness enters into the discussion. The administrator sits up vigilant instead of leaning back drowsily in his chair. When the delegates of the automobileworkers' unions appeared, at the hearing of the body manufacturers' code in the sunparlor of the Washington Hotel, there was a cop in the end of the room, possibly to protect the dozen representatives of the manufacturers and the ten dignitaries at the table from violence at the hands of the three union spokesmen. These men spoke grimly about the rise in the price of living outstripping the slight rise in wages. They said that they were skilled workers at a trade that required long and difficult apprenticeship and that the code allowed them only the wages of unskilled workers. Women and negroes were paid less for doing the same work. It was time a halt was called on the manufacturers' attack on the American standard of living. The administrator pounded on the table and said, "I will not have you people making speeches here. . . . We are willing to listen to a statement of your views as to the facts, nothing more." "You'd better listen to us here than listen to us outside. . . . You read about the riots in Paris? Well, the automobile workers'll have to do something like that if they can't get listened to any other way."

The Brass Hat

General Johnson is the drummajor of this vast parade. He is meeting the press in his handsome office in the vast new white Commerce Building that stands as a bulky monument to the departed Herbert Hoover. Bright snowy sunlight pours in under the green venetianblinds, between the heavily draped curtains, onto the big desk and reflects on the big knobby rambunctious face of the general. The photographers' flashlights keep bringing everything into sudden sharp relief, and catch the shine on the thin head bald as an ostrich egg of one photographer who has climbed on the radiator in the corner. Among the crowd of correspondents there moves with a broad grin on his face a little man who has one of Dr. Solomon's buttonhole cameras hung round his neck. He is gleefully snapping everybody; the General, the secretaries, the reporters, even the solemnlooking eagle in basketwork that stands in the back of the room. The general talks leaning across a desk piled high with codes in blue covers. He is amused, cheerful, resentful, tired, enthusiastic. Questions and answers come on and off like flashlight bulbs. One remark hangs a moment in the air. Manufacturers are going to be told they can't pile up stocks ahead; an industry's got to make what it sells and sell what it makes.

An indiscreet reporter elicits the information that the general only reads digests of the codes; his secretary puts a digest on top of each code. The general doesn't read the code unless something catches his interest.

After all, how could he?

The Line of Talk

In the lobby of the hotel a whitehaired old lady with a manner of speech from far south of the Mason and Dixon line is saying to another whitehaired old lady: "My dear, the Senator has been so kind . . . he remembered dear Fred perfectly . . . he's going to take the matter up, this mornin' at eleven thirty. . . . He invited me to come to his office."

In the waiting room at the Union Station a colored man in a frayed overcoat is saying to another colored man in a frayed overcoat: "Jobs . . . man there ain't no use to think about it. . . . I doan know where you come from, but you better tun roun' an' go back there while the goin's good. A man of color ain't got no more chance to git a job widde democrats than he has to . . . to . . . to git to be president."

In the newspapermen's club they are eating spaghetti and talking about the association of reporters and editorial writers that is being formed, no of course it's not a labor union, it's a guild. But at another table they are talking about the real union that is organizing the N.R.A. employees. They discovered in one office that girls were being worked fourteen hours a day, seven days a week.

At the Metropolitan Club a tall man is talking over a plate of Chesapeake oysters: "But what government that has started on inflation has ever been able to resist the temptation to continue?"

At a Swedish restaurant bright young men from the economics department of the colleges are arguing late over a long table from which the meal has long been cleared away. "But can you see anything but brilliant improvisation and a juggler's skill in holding his audience?" "Well, I've seen Moscow and I've seen Germany, and I'm watching this Washington show as intently as I can, but for the life of me I can't tell the direction things are going." "You mean the left hand doesn't know what the right hand doeth?" "Neither does anybody else."

At a press conference an administrator is telling the reporters: "If the republicans publish any more pamphlets like the last one I'll believe Farley is subsidizing the Republican National Committee. . . . I mean their stuff is so dumb it's a great help."

A western senator getting out of a taxicab where he's been talking about the French revolution being driven down the snowy avenue through the zerocold night "Well it's a great and terrible time to be alive. Something is going to happen in this great country and we are going to see it. . . . I couldn't say just what."

Out of an armchair overlooking Lafayette Square: "Yes people actually seem to walk faster than they did in Washington. Even in the Cosmos Club you see new youthful faces."

A tall thin young farmerlaborite in lumberman's boots addressing the Unemployed Convention: "In Northern Minnesota we are slaves under the Steel Trust. The Steel Trust owns everything, runs everything. We know that Roosevelt says he is for the ordinary man, we try to believe in Roosevelt but what we see is the Steel Trust."

Delano the Magician

The ladies and gentlemen of the press stand around waiting or lounge on the leather settees in the creamcolored vestibule of the White House on the green carpets between the columns and the policeinspectors with brightly polished badges, in that peculiarly Washington atmosphere of space and quiet. Just before the time they form up in two lines on either side of the door. A secretary appears. The people in the lines get in first, the rest straggle after. In the executive office it's very light. There are electric lights in the octagonal glass and chromium chandelier overhead. Light pours in through the two tall windows behind the President's desk. You can't see him, you can only see the two flagstaffs with gold eagles on them that stand on either side of the desk. Then somebody moves his head. Through a canyon of cheeks, collars, ears, serge shoulders, you can see the desk. When the secretary into whose ear he has been whispering lifts his head you can see, beyond three pink carnations and a slight crinkle of cigarettesmoke Mr. Roosevelt's face. The glare of the snow on the lawn outside beats through the tracery of shrubs and treebranches and the oblong panes of the tall windows and glows on the broad carefullyshaved cheeks, and outlines the small nose, as delicately cut as Andrew Jackson's. There are heavy shadows under the eyes. The face has a soft powdered look, like an actor's face. His voice is fatherlyfriendly, without strain, like the voice of the principal of a firstrate boys' school. He is talking. He is producing unexpectedly out of the air a great piece of news. It's a bombshell. The ladies and gentlemen of the press lean forward happily. There's the headline for them, the front page spread. Dazzled they watch the exciting red white and blue streamers come out of the hat. Every pupil has a piece of candy to take home. When the President has briefly and concisely explained his piece of news, he leans back in his chair, takes a deep breath, puffs out his cheeks and lets the air out with the sudden puff of a man who's finished blowing up a toy balloon. The great headline hovers over the heads of the ladies and gentlemen of the press as they perfunctorily ask a few questions. Mr. Roosevelt answers them simply and unhurriedly as if he were sitting at a table talking to an old friend. He has the light unworried smile of a man who's working hard and enjoying his work. There's a pause. Somebody looks at his watch. "Thank you, Mr. President," say the ladies and gentlemen of the press as they file out. Faces hide the desk between the drooping silk flags. As you go out you get a glimpse of a set of early nineteenth century American prints round the walls of the tall spaciously lighted colonial office.

The Machine That Writes Cheques

In the office in the Department of Agriculture where they handle the allotments farmers get for refraining from the production of cotton, wheat, pigs and a great many other things that a great many people need, they have a set of machines to write cheques. With these machines about twenty girls and young men can send out eighty thousand cheques a day. First an orange card is run through a machine like a stencilling typewriter, which instead of writing leaves a set of perforations on the card that will indicate all the information needed in connection with the allotment: the name of the farmer, his serial number, state, county, acreage, minimum and maximum acreage in the specified crop, percentage of land uncultivated, amount of allotment, etc. This card is then run through another machine where the perforations are translated by an elaborate keyboard of electric contacts and written out on a cheque. At the same time another section of the mechanism enters the names and amounts on a payroll and adds them up at the bottom of each sheet. Another machine rechecks the Treasury drafts with the cards and stamps them with index numbers. A last machine stamps them with a special colored background to prevent forgery, and signs them with a die made from the signature of the Secretary of the Treasury. These machines will do the work of many hundreds of clerks.

A Spring Month in Paris

Montmartre Revisited

Running up the grimy steps of the metro at the Place de Clichy, it was hard not to feel in my ears the different ring the name had had other times, ten years back, twenty years back, the longago Paris-on-leave ring of barroom chatter, funny stories, comic prostitutes, all the sidewalk café Saturdaynight jingle that went with the gone mythological sound of Montmartre. But twenty years from war to war have somewhat eroded the venereal mount of martyrs of bidet and makeupbox, and taken the glitter out of the last lingering tinsel of nineteenthcentury whoopee. Those days the metro and the taxis stopped running early in the evening and after supper we used to walk up the steep cobbled streets and then the unlit stone stairs, past houses that reminded us of the stageset for the last act of *Louise*, to see the airraids from the top of the hill. Moonlight nights were the best. We would wait out of breath on the terrace in front of the lividlooking church, with its narrow domes that looked so naked in the moonlight, and wait for the Gothas to come over. Under the silvery haze the unlit city would stretch like an iceflow in tiers and ridges from under our feet into the long past (Lutetia, Julian the Apostate, Villon, St. Bartholomew, Henri Quatre's white plume at Ivry, the Bastille and the singing mobs, the wall of the Communards, the days of the grand dukes) and far away to the north an antiaircraft gun would start barking. The sirens would chill the spine and the whole ring of the barrage would go into action. Shrapnel would sparkle tinselly overhead, and gradually through the din the sound of airplane motors would fill our ears humming now soft now loud. Very soon would come the shriek and the red flare and the shattering growl where the bombs had hit. One time something made a flame and fluttered down like a piece of burning paper far to the east. The barrage would slacken, everything would get still, and as we'd start the long walk home to the hotel, we'd hear the *breloque*, merry quacking little fireengine, hurrying up and down the black streets announcing that the raid was over. The next morning Monsieur Poincaré with his derby and his gloves and his cutaway coat buttoned high under his little beard would be photographed felicitating the survivors or beaming on the wounded.

This is March, 1937. I'm headed for a different Clichy, the industrial town outside the city limits of Paris. It's a long walk from the Place de Clichy, out a long crowded thoroughfare of little gimcrack stores, rundown movietheatres, jerry-built bars and cafés that blow a stale breath of *pernod* in your face as you pass, and haberdashers and noveltyshops shoddier than Fourteenth Street and not so much fun. It's a long walk out to Clichy. Where the Franco-Prussian War fortifications used to be there are weedy buildinglots. Now Paris's fortifications are the Maginot line along the north frontier. The street crosses a temporary bridge of unpainted wood. Big trucks slither through the coating of mud on the pavement. The glum darkgrey buildings of a factory town close in on either side. The sidewalks fill up with soberlooking middleaged men coming home from work. In skimpy meatmarkets broadbeamed women are counting out the change to buy the family supper. People look sober and their clothes are drab, but they are not down yet. The young girls aren't pretty but their eyes are bright, and sturdyseeming young men skim in and out among the trucks and the big green buses on their bicycles. The talk you hear has the throaty drawl of the workingclass suburbs.

The street opens up into a square set with young trees. Across it stands the grey townhall, looking like every other townhall in every other French small town. This is where the riot was and the shooting that gave this new resonance to the name of Clichy. Under the stunted barelybudding trees the square is thick with knots of workingmen. In the middle of each knot a couple of men are arguing, soberly enough, or else an eyewitness is telling for the hundredth time his story. Not many women, a few families that have come, kids and all, from other parts of Paris to see for themselves. Hardly anybody is excited. People listen gravely to what others have to say. One tall man with a red hatchet face is making a speech, that doesn't go so well with the crowd, about how the workingclass must arm and answer bullets with bullets. The older men have all been through one war. They know about bullets. Now and then a man nudges another man and whispers, "Look out for provocateurs."

There's a feeling of uneasiness in the crowd. People are trying to work out the story for themselves. They look at the broken windows and the bulletmarks on the grey stone of the townhall, and at the boardedup corner café and the butchershop wrecked by the crowd during the scrimmage. That was the window over the tobaccostore the shooting started from. No, the first shots were fired from the roof of the movingpicture theatre. No, this is how it happened.

They point out the broken windows and the scars where police bullets made little pits in the grey stone walls. People shake their heads. They don't talk much. They'd rather let the other fellow speak first. People feel insecure. It's only two nights ago at this time that nothing had happened yet; the wounded were still walking around feeling good, the young blood was pumping through the bodies of the dead.

That night Mr. Léon Blum, the parliamentary medicineman whose spells had so far kept off civil war, had dressed himself in his best soup and fish and had gone to the opera to hear the London Philharmonic play a Haydn symphony. *Perfide Albion.* He is called out of the concert by the news that a firstclass riot is going on at Clichy. A crowd has tried to storm the Olympia movietheatre where the Fiery Crosses, under their new name of French Social Party, are giving each other the creeps with speeches about the Moscow menace. The police have fired into the crowd.

While Mr. Blum went home to his quiet literary man's apartment on the Ile St. Louis to change into an outfit more suitable for the occasion, his secretary, Mr. Blumel, and his bearded Minister of the Interior, Mr. Marx Dormoy, were trying to quell the storm. The Fiery Crosses had given up their meeting and had been shepherded by the police out of the movietheatre by the back door at the first catcalls and were by this time well on their way to their respectable homes. Mr. Blumel was shot down by the police as he stood in the middle of the fracas with his arms raised trying to get a hearing, and both the mayor of Clichy and Mr. Marx Dormoy got their heads broken. The crowd took cover in the townhall; the police took the townhall by storm. At last, the shock troops tired of beating up the townspeople, the wounded were taken to hospitals, the dead went to the morgue, newspapermen staggered groggy out of their telephonebooths, the presses started clanking out the story, and the battle was history.

Two days later the people of Clichy are still talking it over gravely, standing in knots, shivering a little in the chill of the gathering twilight. The truce has been broken; no telling now; anything can happen now. People begin to scatter to their suppers. The last little groups of arguers break up shaking their heads as they go.

Front Populaire

The French are great hands for a funeral. The next Sunday the funeral procession of the young men shot down at Clichy crossed the northern quarters of Paris. We saw the head of it start from near the Gare de l'Est at ten in the morning, with the plumed hearses and the cars full of flowers and the red goldlettered tradeunion flags and the lettered streamers of crafts and trades and political parties, and at seven in the evening the tail of it was still pouring through the square in front of the townhall at Clichy five miles away. Young men, old men, young women, families, the great sober middleaged mass of the French people. They are not handsome, they're not very lively, even the young people have an old look, but it's hard not to feel that they embody, just as they did twenty years ago during the frenzy of wholesale war, a stubborn, unfanatical, live-and-let-live habit of mind, a feeling in every man and woman of the worth of personal dignity that is, for better or for worse, the unique contribution of Western Europe to the world. Twenty years ago seeing Frenchmen during gasattacks, under shellfire, in dressing stations, in bombarded cities, standing grumblingly in line, bumbling helplessly like flies in flypaper in the effortdestroying gum of their governmental red tape, I used to have the same feeling of respect. Now, walking all day under the leaden sky in the slowmoving unhurried crowds, even listening to the speeches of the popular leaders that ranted out of the loudspeakers (all for the popular front, down with the Fascists, support the exposition, boys) I couldn't help feeling with a certain relief (these are days when a man wonders sometimes how long any spot on the globe will be left fit to live in) that this would be a tough people to wipe out. It's easy to forget how central the French people are in everything we mean when we say Europe.

Croix de Feu

The next time I climbed up the stairs at the Place de Clichy metro station it was again late afternoon. I was on my way out to see a member of the French Social Party, the converted Fiery Crosses, a nicemannered young man who was managing his family trucking and warehousing business. When I got there a quavery middleaged lady was in his office talking about the cause. She was a charity worker who helped on the social service end. Handouts, distribution of old clothes, medicine and tracts for the sick, a little cash for the deserving; it turned out that some of the deserving had been unmasked as communists in sheep's clothing and as money was none too plentiful there had been suggestions from higher up that only the faithful be relieved. The deserving poor. They'd damn well better be deserving. Afterwards my friend took me upstairs to a dark middleclass diningroom that had the look of the family being away for the summer, although it was not summer, and rummaged in a big old walnut sideboard to find me a drink. He found a bottle of kümmel and poured me but a small glass. For himself he put a few drops in a glass of water. I couldn't help thinking that whoever had arranged this stiff room devoted to proper heavy meals, properly served at the proper time by a maid in a starched apron, would not have approved of our sitting there drinking the wrong drink at the wrong time. My friend spoke lovingly of *Le Patron* as he called the good colonel Casimir de la Rocque, spoke of the need for a moral revaluation, for the spiritual resurgence of France etcetera, etcetera, said politicians were disgusting. There I agreed with him. The Fiery Crosses were opposed to class hatred; Le Patron had supporters in all walks of life; he was for the union of all Frenchmen. Especially the small artisans were for him. As for Blum and the Front Populaire, they were ruining business. They were endangering the franc. They were the lackeys of Moscow. The firm's profits had been cut in half. The packers and the truckdrivers kept demanding more wages. The forty-hour week. Paid vacations, good God. He hadn't been able to buy a new car. There was a trip to America he'd been planning that he hadn't been able to take. True Frenchmen understood that that sort of thing had to stop. What was the use of raising wages if the price of living went up faster than the increased purchasing power? It was time the working classes got it through their heads that their standard of living was too high already. It would be the ruin of business.

He was perfectly rational, hardly violent; again and again he denied that the P.S.F. had started the shooting at Clichy, and he was certainly telling the truth so far as he knew it. But my friend had not a suspicion in the world that big profits for him were not also the best possible thing for the workingclass, la belle France, civilization and the human race in general.

At the office of *Flambeau*, the good colonel Casimir's newspaper, where I went the next afternoon to enquire for an editor I'd been recommended to, things didn't seem so rational. There was nobody in the vestibule but the doorman and a little redeyed hunchback in a derby hat who looked mad-hatter mad. The doorman didn't look any too sane either. He opened the door by inches when I knocked and closed it after me with a bang and turned the key. "That's orders," he said mysteriously. No, the editor wasn't there, nobody was there. Except enormous poster photographs of the good colonel Casimir hung around the vestibule. "Le Patron, le voilà!" he shouted with a sweep of his arm. "Magnificent," he said, rubbing his hands. "Magnificent," said the hunchback in the derby hat. Then like alarmclocks going off they started in, one into each ear, on the regular line; nobody but Le Patron could save France from Blum and the other Jews and the thieving freemasons and the communists, who were going to take everybody's property away, ruin the franc, burn the churches, rape the nuns and your wife and mine, turn the French farmer over to the minions of Moscow to be collectivized and his daughters nationalized and everything sold to the Jews, murderers, thieves, Jews. That's the first thing; they'd have to drive out the Jews. It was hard to get them to stop talking long enough to unlock the door and let me out. Before they let me go they pointed again to the huge hawknosed haughtylooking face on the poster. "Remember his face! Go to hear him speak. He's the savior of France," they shrieked.

Odysseus Among the Shades

We went in through the dank cobbled court of an eighteenthcentury house on the Left Bank near the river. Across the court we went through a carriage gate with boxtrees in tubs on either side into an open garden very green in the drizzly gaslight. At the back was a little stone house with tall shuttered windows. We stepped from the dark hall into a feebly lit room with a big coal fire. There, among potted palms and little curleycue tables and burnished brass and silver objects with complicated surfaces that caught the firelight, over Dresden coffeecups, sat politely benign the characters in a novel Henry James unluckily didn't live long enough to write, one of those chronicles of gradually diminishing interest, of the marriage of the prejudices and inhibitions of Back Bay with those of the Faubourg St. Germain. The talk was about the Spanish Civil War. Voices were gradually growing more tense. The last warmth in these fading fictions that had unhappily survived their inventor was in their hatred. It was natural enough that they should be for Franco because they were people well along in life and encrusted with dividends and possessions that they felt only policing armies could hold for them against the rising hordes of the workingclass. As for the cost of the policing, that would be taken out of the hides of the wageslaves once they'd been taught manners again. What was surprising, as it is always surprising, was the bloody personal violence of their feelings. They were gentle and refined people, the sort of people who would be moved by finding a hurt cat, or even a hurt child, in the street, and would probably put themselves out to find a remedy. Their quiet and assured lives seemed as far from the bloody fighting round Madrid as the ghosts Odysseus visited in the underworld were far from the cities and the pitchblack ships and the oarsmen and the booty that were his seaman's life. A woman who bore the name of a nineteenthcentury literary figure was retailing the stories of a Spanish lady of title who had recently escaped from the embassy at which she had taken refuge in Madrid with not only her life but a large sum of money and the family jewels. As bloody atrocity of the Reds followed bloody atrocity, these fading lady and gentleman ghosts from a world that the deaths of James and Proust have left without a master, began to swell and grow warm and ruddy with life, like the ghosts that Odysseus that crafty navigator poured out the blood for. Odysseus kept the ghosts off him with a sword. He was a wise man, because the only life of those dead was hatred of life. A curious thing about atrocity stories is that they mirror, instead of the events they purport to describe, the extent of the hatred of the people that tell them.

Still, you can't listen unmoved to tales of misery and murder. You know that only too many of them are true, and women who see those they love butchered before their eyes suffer the same whether they are duchesses or the wives of bankers or trolleyconductors. I was beginning to feel pretty nightmarish when they shifted to the chapter of the destruction of art by the Reds. A story was unfolded that seemed to be covering events and people vaguely familiar. It was about how the Reds were selling the arttreasures of Spain, and about an American woman who was an international Red of the bloodiest type and the mistress of the American ambassador who was a Red too (a Democrat is the same as a Red). She had recently arrived in Paris with a trunkload of stolen Grecos to sell to the highest bidder. By that time it was hard not to laugh. The nightmare figures sank back into the innocent dodder of the perpetually misinformed. The Red adventuress was an innocent and extraordinary kindly spinster whom I had known years ago in Madrid and who was helping get up an artexhibition for the benefit of Spanish hospitals. But was there any use in trying to explain? What could Odysseus say to the shades?

Workers' Housing

Out in Suresnes, the working people's suburb beyond the Bois de Boulogne, I had been walking around one morning with the mayor, Henri Sellier, who has been the leader of a newdealish program of municipal housing that in ten years has transformed the living standards of a whole section of Paris suburbs. He's a stocky sanguine bearded man with the bluff unassuming manners of an army doctor. He had taken

to the Kremlin. The new social legislation is going to ruin the small businessman. He talks on and on amid the cheers of his supporters and an increasing racket from the Left. Old man Herriot, the president of the Chamber, who towers over the deputies from his high desk in the middle, a loosepaunched huge pale man with a teddybear haircut who leans from side to side over his desk like a figure in a Punch-and-Judy show, glaring or smiling at his charges with the manner of an indulgent schoolmaster, has to rap more and more for order. Under the heckling and jeering from the Left Mr. Ybarnégaray loses his head and finally lets a big indiscreet cat out of the bag. "Berlin will never allow communism in France," he shouts. Pandemonium.

This gives Mr. Blum his chance to do the handsome thing and to get to his feet and suggest that the gentleman from the Pyrenees can't mean what he seems to mean. Mr. Blum can handle his opponents in the Chamber with one hand tied behind his back. Mr. Ybarnégaray finishes his speech under Mr. Blum's protection. It is obvious that he has made a fool of himself.

After supper the stage is all set for Mr. Blum's speech in defense of his policies. The speech is clear, to the point and seemingly frank; there's no doubt but that Mr. Blum has more brains than his colleagues. His speaking is rather spoiled for me by the almost whining apologetic tone of his voice. He has a curious trick of clasping and unclasping his hands when he speaks, and then bringing them together as if to shake hands with himself, but instead clasping and unclasping each one separately. But in his speech there are moments of unexpected dignity and force. You remember that people of all parties have told you that Mr. Blum is no Ramsay MacDonald. After all there's nothing in France that corresponds to a Duchess. At the end of his speech Mr. Blum let loose a little trial balloon in the shape of a slip of the tongue in which he called the Front Populaire the Front Nationale. I guess the Front Nationale is the Duchess.

The Key Word is National

The significance of the phrase came to me sharply when a newspaperman who was playing Virgil to my Dante among

French politicians took me to see the editor of the official Socialist Party paper, who was minister without portfolio with his office in the Ministry of Justice next to the Ritz on the Place Vendôme. He was a small brown wryfaced man with a bush of white hair. When we were ushered in he was talking over the telephone at his desk in the middle of his huge ancient régime office, arguing in a sour meridional voice with someone at the other end of the line. We couldn't help hearing what he was saying, "*Amis ou non, il faut les mettre dédans.* . . . Put them in the cooler whether they're friends or not. No, confiscation is better, saves the trouble of a lawsuit." "After all," he said, looking sharply at us as he laid down the receiver, "we've got to govern." When we got outside we found out what he must have been talking about. The police had just confiscated an issue of *Jeune Garde*, the young socialist paper, at the same time as they confiscated an issue of *Flambeau*, the good colonel Casimir's sheet. National seems often to be a key word when a new group of politicians attain power. All the time he talked to us about the program of the Socialist Party, Monsieur le Ministre was playing with little gold paper seals out of a box he had on his desk, the gold paper seals that are affixed to the bottom of official documents.

Paname

But Paris in the spring is pleasant as a song in a musical comedy, if you can get away from the chore of interviewing politicians and waiting for them in their gloomy antechambers where the furniture and carpets and the palefaced attendants with not very clean starched shirts and white ties and unbrushed liveries look as if they hadn't been changed since the days of the Sun King. The horsechestnuts are sprouting. It's spring. Now and then the sun comes out. Rosytinted clouds mass and scatter little showers of rain in the broad sky above the Place de la Concorde and then roll away again. It's not the keyedup international Paris, capital of the world, of the great days of the Peace Conference, or the old Ville Lumière of the grand dukes, that they are trying to bring back to life with artificial respiration for the Exposition, but it's an agreeable chilly springlike Paris that has the cosy feeling of every old much lived in city. The city gives you the feeling of

being something stable and permanent in a changing world of violence. It's almost the mediaeval feeling of a city protected by its walls. The feeling of being encrusted with the vagaries of generations of Parisians. In the Tuileries gardens one Sunday we met an elderly conciergelooking woman leading a fox on a string. An old yellow dog ran beside the fox keeping the other dogs off him. At the Samaritaine department store they sell anacondas by the meter. In one window there was a large sign, LES VAMPIRES SONT ARRIVES. "Bats are lovely pets," said a lady we were lunching with; "they fold up like little umbrellas. *C'est tellement gentil.*"

Paris, March, 1937.

Coast Road South

Le Midi

Getting off the train from Paris early in the morning at Perpignan, I stood on the platform blinking from the violet impact of the clear light of the Mediterranean coast; there were the planetrees with their sunmottled trunks, the light dust, the creamy rusty colors of the stucco houses, the violet brightness dazzling after the dim greys of northern Europe. It's a light that goes with the smell of figs and dust and rancid oliveoil. The man in the baggageroom was old and brown. I checked my rucksack that was bulging and heavy with cakes of chocolate and soap and sausage for the trip, and walked down the long empty early morning street towards the town.

Perpignan still had the sleepy but not quite dead look of the small Mediterranean citystate with its narrow streets and its ancient gate and its Catalan gothic exchange building now turned into a café, but the people looked different. There were more Spaniards, a considerable ragged refugee population that obviously didn't belong to the town. At the café in the old exchange there were groups of men in dusty *boinas* talking Catalan in low voices. What the devil are they doing in Perpignan? Beside me when I sat down to eat my breakfast a thinfaced livid young man was waiting for somebody, staring down the street the yellow trolleycars came from, tapping a tattoo with two grimy fingers on the marble tabletop. Under the planetrees along the little river, where an old man was scything the long fragrant grass, I passed a sunburned blond man, obviously a squarehead German, who gave me a sharp gimlet secretserviceman's stare. What the devil is he doing in Perpignan? I turned into the town and walked up the stone streets with shuttered houses that went beyond picturesqueness into the dull stagnant look of poverty. Up on the hill in a dusty square, outside of what must have been the castle in the old days, a regiment of Senegalese was lined up, their faces black and shiny in the sun. Makes me hot to look at them in their woolly khaki.

The sun's burning the morning away. Time to find the Café Continental.

The Café Continental turns out to be a fine place, a regular operatic smugglers' cave of a place. It's where the local buses stop. There's bustle and bundles and baskets and sacks of potatoes stacked out in front of the long scaling stucco front with grapevines on it. Inside you find yourself in a narrow room with the bar and tables. When I ask about the trucks and show the letter to the barman, I'm introduced to a stout absentminded man dressed in dusty black with glasses askew on a broad face. Yes, the drivers are there. They are asleep. They are leaving at noon. The waiter shows me into a little back room where I can leave my bag when I bring it from the station. On the wall is a map of Spain with the fronts marked out with little flags. "Ours," he says, smiling, pointing to the loyalist side. We look at each other smiling, we have a feeling of being among friends. When we go out into the front room, the waiter closes the door carefully behind us.

At noon the drivers were there, both French, one a lighthaired man of thirty from the north, a husky laughing guy who'd been a sailor, the other a stocky Parisian in his forties who'd been an upholsterer and had taken up truckdriving because he'd lost two fingers in a furniture factory and couldn't upholster any more. We drank our *apéro* and then they took me to their hotel to eat lunch, a remarkably good lunch. We all ate a lot because we weren't so sure of what we'd get across the border. We said goodbye, a little lingeringly perhaps, to the bigbosomed Frenchwoman at the cashregister and walked across town to the garage where the trucks were, huge and shiny with new grey paint. We stopped for gas and were off down the white road that ran straight down an avenue of planetrees towards mountains that bulked grey under billowing piles of clouds; the Pyrenees.

Nonintervention

The driver was telling me how he'd been left an orphan at nine and stowed away on a freighter bound for the Black Sea and been taken care of by the captain until he could get his apprentice's papers, and was beginning to tell about the Toulon mutiny in the French fleet, when on the ramp of a bridge over a small river a gentleman with a gallows face waved to us to stop. *Le controle*. The gendarme was certainly no beauty. He had only a couple of teeth and no hair and a long wrinkled face full of liverspots hung over a crooked lantern jaw, but he turned out not so tough as he looked; he was going to let us by after squinting for a long time at our papers, when a patrol of the *Garde Mobile* came up and the officer insisted on seeing the inside of the packingcases with which our trucks were loaded. One of the trucks was loaded with cases of gasmasks for Madrid. The other had some diemaking machinery and boxes and boxes of field telephones. The patrol seemed to get bored by the time they had opened a couple of cases and found them as indicated, but they held us up while they sent our handsome friend on his bicycle to the next village to phone headquarters for instructions. Meanwhile they smoked our cigarettes and told us about how many volunteers attempting to cross the border had been arrested. The clouds on the mountains spread over the whole sky and it came on to rain. Maybe it was the rain or maybe it was headquarters but they finally grudgingly let us go on, telling us that they were phoning Cerbère, where we were planning to cross the border, and that we'd be held there.

Frontier of Violence

At Cerbère, while the drivers dickered with the authorities, I sat a long time on a bench in front of a grey shingle beach in the light drizzle, smoking sour cigarettes, watching a little group of Spanish refugee children under the care of a gentle forlornlooking young man playing an endless slow dance and song game. The drizzle stopped, the green and slategrey headlands that hemmed in the little harbor cleared. On the headland towards Spain the pointed vaults of a cemetery stood out sharp against the sky in the washed glassgrey light. Between the fishing boats painted blue and yellow and dull red and black drawn up on the shingle a couple of thin hounds were rooting for dead fish.

An airplane passed flying low far out towards Spain. A few old men came out of the café and looked apprehensively at the plane, shading their eyes with their hands although there was no sun. Loyalist? Fascist? The plane disappeared behind the headland and the cemetery. A train came hooting out of the tunnel. It came on to rain again. A sadfaced woman in black came down to the beach and shepherded the children off somewhere. I went into the bar where the old men were and drank a glass of flat sour beer and then went and sat in the truck and read.

When the drivers came back they said that the truck with the gasmasks would have to be left. The sailor, who had no visa on his passport, would have to stay with it. We said goodbye to him, and the upholsterer and I ground slowly in the truck with the field telephones through the pouring rain up the steep hill to the Spanish border. At the border post we had another long wait while the officer in charge phoned Cerbère and tried to pin on the officer there the responsibility for letting us through. At last negotiations broke down and it looked as if we'd be there all night until the upholsterer sagely suggested that the official draw up a paper, and have all the officials sign it. The paper stated that he was letting us through only in accordance with instructions and not upon his own responsibility. It seemed to relieve his mind. Everybody signed it and shook hands and we were off.

At the Spanish border post things were more cheerful. A group of healthylooking boys in militia uniforms of various shades of green and khaki raised their clenched fists to us in the Popular Front salute. We offered them cigarettes, everybody shook hands and wished us a pleasant journey and waved as we drove away. In Port Bou the buildings looked neat and paintedup after the soggy grey look of Cerbère, in spite of the fact that it was raining harder than ever. We had quite a search for the representative of the Valencia Ministry of War who was to give us an order for gasoline along the road, but when we found him he was energetic and cheerful. He was a small plump baldheaded man more or less of the business class. When we told him the other truck with the gasmasks had been stopped he smiled and said he'd get it through next day. I asked him how. "Combinations," he said. "At the border everything is combinations."

The Upholsterer

It was dusk when we left Port Bou and started along the endless hairpin curves of the coast road south. The upholsterer, who was a Communist Party member, told me as we rode along of the difficulties he'd had other trips with the local anarchist committees who all wanted to hold meetings as to whether they ought to requisition the truck or not. The Valencia government meant nothing to them; each committee considered itself sovereign. Once he'd had to bring out his gun and drive off while he held the spokesman covered. "Folly," he said, shaking his head. "And the waste of good machinery." Every time we passed the wreck of a car along the side of the road, and there were certainly plenty of wrecks, he'd slow up and shake his head and mutter, Imbeciles. He told about how he'd taken up truckdriving when he'd had to give up upholstering and how he'd been one of the founders of a truckdrivers' union, and was blacklisted by all the big concerns, so that now he was working for the Spaniards. He'd made nine trips to Madrid. On one trip a Fascist spy had stolen his papers and he'd been almost shot for a spy himself, would have been if one of the Party responsibles hadn't known him, because while he was away some fifth column guy shot a militiaman from the window of his room at the hotel.

We drove into Gerona late at night in the dark. The upholsterer was talking about the care and training of cagebirds. That was his hobby, it turned out. He and his wife had a blackbird, two nightingales and some specially trained Hartz Mountain canaries. From all over the quarter people brought him sick birds to doctor. He fixed them up with cayenne pepper and a drop of cognac and water fed through an eyedropper. You had to hold the bird in the palm of your hand and open its beak very carefully so as not to frighten it.

Cooperative Commonwealth

The night was so black we could see nothing of Gerona when we got there. For fear of airraids only an occasional blue light showed. We left the truck in the army garage and walked along the river to a hotel. The hotel had been taken over by the C.N.T. but except for the sign announcing that fact in the hall it seemed entirely normal. Everything had evidently been recently repainted in a neat but gloomy battleship grey. We were so sleepy we could hardly keep our eyes open. We had hot baths, an excellent Spanish hotel dinner, plenty of good red Catalan wine and went up to our rooms in the elevator.

In the morning we spent a long time scrambling up and down the steep streets of the stately old town in the hot sun to find the right man to give us a new order for gasoline. A few churches had been ruined and the walls everywhere had been plastered with warposters signed by every imaginable committee and political party. The shopwindows were covered with thin strips of paper tape to keep them from breaking from the concussion of airplane bombs. On some of them the paper tape was in plain crisscrosses but in most of them it had been worked into all kinds of designs. The spiderweb with a spider in the middle of it was popular, as were fish, monograms of CNT and UGT, and linked squares and rays and interlacing triangles. We finally found our official in an infantry barracks in the old citadel clear up at the top of the pre-Roman hilltown. At least we found his office. We had to wait for him three-quarters of an hour while my Frenchman cursed at Spaniards, anarchists and disorder generally under his breath.

It was noon when we scampered back down the long flight of stone stairs to fill up the tank with gasoline and to be off, down a wide macadam road through a broad valley of rich farmland and vines and umbrellapines, towards the coast and Barcelona again. We came out on the coast road along the beach and drove through a series of blue and yellow and white seaside suburbs that looked normal enough except that here and there trenches and machinegun nests had been built to repel landingparties, and into Barcelona. By that time the offices were all closed for the middle of the day and there was no hope of getting any more of our famous orders for gasoline until two or three in the afternoon. We ate and went to drink our coffee on the Ramblas.

A certain number buildings I had known on other trips had been destroyed, banks all had signs on them: *Taken Over By The Generalitat.* Most of the big stores had signs, *Employee Control* or *Taken Over By The C.N.T.*, and the trolleycars and buses had been neatly repainted black and red with C.N.T. in small letters on them, but the city looked neat and busy and the flowermarket was as fine and fragrant as ever down the center of the Ramblas.

Again it was late before we argued our way past Barcelona officials, who wanted us to leave the truck and the field telephones there instead of taking it to the Ministry of War in Valencia to which it was consigned, and we lost a lot of time looking for the converted church school which was the central warehouse for machineparts where we were to leave our diemaking machinery, so that again it was dark before, honking our way through a long crowded industrial street full of carts and children and mules and motorcycles, we got out onto the coast road south again. My friend the upholsterer wanted to make Sitges, where he knew a place where he could get a really French meal, before eating supper.

Supper Behind the Lines

Sitges was pitchblack so we couldn't see what the town was like but the little bar and restaurant in front of which we stopped was brightly lit. Two men and a heavyfaced woman behind the bar greeted the upholsterer as an old friend and set us up to a drink while our supper was being cooked. The place was crowded and lively. The man, who spoke French and had lived in France, had been wounded on the Aragon front and was back at work again, after convalescence. At the bar there was a greenfaced man busy getting himself drunk, who came over to us and made us try on a pair of metal eyeprotectors he used when he threw handgrenades. He too was from the Aragon front. The woman, a big sexy blackeyed meanlooking woman, was definitely the boss. The son had been a waiter in London and spoke English. I had a feeling that business was good. They were optimistic about the war, felt that the Fascists would soon be licked. The man who had been at the front was strong for the Valencia government and against Barcelona and all the local committees and tradeunions. We must have a central command, he said.

When we'd had our drink we went into a beautiful little blue and white tiled diningroom with blue rafters to eat our supper. We ate broadbean soup and veal *escalopes* and some fresh sardines and salad thrown in illegally (restaurants are supposed only to serve two dishes to a meal) because we were friends. The wine was good, the woman came out from behind the counter and threw insolent smutty remarks at us that nobody seemed to know just how to take; there was a feeling of warm coastal richness and plenty.

There'd been a tableful of rosyfaced noisy cheerfultalking young men in the corner of the diningroom when we came in. When they got up to leave we noticed that one of them was on crutches. He had only one leg. After supper, after a lot of kidding back and forth with the woman, we got aboard our truck to push on towards Tarragona. As we were leaving the village to hit the coast road again we saw in the glare of our headlights on the whitewashed walls five young men cross the road in front of us. There was something curious about their walk. They were hopping on crutches. Each of them had lost a leg.

Night on the Road

After leaving Sitges we got our first smell of orangetrees in bloom, coming in streaks through the cool night. My friend the upholsterer was hellbent for Tarragona where he knew another Frenchman, at least a man who spoke French, who kept a hotel. The night was very dark, with stars, and chilly, but the good meal and the farewell cognacs at Sitges kept us warm. At Tarragona our first stop was the filling station, a big modern filling station just before the road entered the town. In the glassedin office back of it, some men were sitting round a table in the light of a couple of candles. "It's because the electric light is too bright," they explained. We asked where we could get an order for gasoline. "Right here," they answered proudly. "We keep open all night. . . . Here in Tarragona we're trying to do things right."

When we asked about beds they sounded doubtful. "The town is jammed with troops in training," they said. We went to find the upholsterer's Frenchman. Nothing doing. He offered to let us sleep on the floor of his hotel office. We decided to push on to Perelló, an hour or so south. With us we took a militiaman who was on his way home for a threeday leave to Castellón de la Plana. He'd been a sergeant in the regular army, quartered at the seacoast Sahara fort of Ifni. When the officers of his outfit joined the July movement he and some others escaped across the desert to the French patrol. It was easy because they were at an isolated border post at the time. The French had helped them across Morocco and let them get back to Spain to join the troops loyal to the government. He was grateful to the French and asked me to include his thanks to the French detachment in anything I might write. He wanted the officers and noncoms to know he was grateful. Now he was a lieutenant, on the front at Teruel. I asked him if the enemy could break through there. "Let them try," he said.

Perelló was a long dusty stucco street that we saw dimly by the blue bulbs of the streetlights. Long lines of trucks and carts were parked against the houses. We knocked at various doors of what we had been told were fondas but got no answer except voices grumpy with sleep saying, "Full up." At a café that had one shaded light in it and where all the tables were full of country people asleep with their black heads on their tanned thickfingered fieldworkers' hands we were told what the trouble was. People from Tortosa had filled up the town on account of the airraids there. "Fine," said the militiaman. "We'll go on to Tortosa and sleep quietly."

First we woke up the fat and drowsy proprietor of the café to get him to heat up some coffee for us. It was about three in the morning. We sat in the shuttered room stuffy with the breath of huddled sleepers, drawing on coarse cigarettes with mouths raw from too much smoking during the evening, talking in whispers while we waited for the coffee to heat. I don't know what we talked about, outside of the sour taste of the cigarettes. It was that time of night when the first drowsiness of overpast bedtime wears off and you feel alert and solitary. "It's absurd to leave a good bed on account of airraids . . . first thing you know they'll drop a flare and see all the trucks and raid here," said the militiaman. After we had drunk our coffee we got up and left after one more glance around the room at the grimed helpless sleepers. On the benches there were shapeless bundles of women in full skirts covered with shawls, in the chairs men and boys were nodding curled up in all the attitudes of sleepy ingenuity. From the shadows came heavy breathing, snores, the whimper of a child.

Once outside the air filled our lungs sweetly again and on the road out of town the night felt clean and dry. The road wound between rocky hills among the rounded shapes of olivetrees that shone silvery when the headlights swept them. We went through villages where not a light showed. Cocks were crowing to beat the band when we dove into a leafy dark avenue that led into Tortosa. At the hotel everything was quiet, an old man with a drooping white moustache who was cross as a hornet about something led us up interminable tiled stairs to clean bare rooms. Greyness of dawn was coming through the shutters. At first the sheets were cold and the eyes hot and the ears pricked for the old wellknown bumble of raiding bombers in the air. The cocks crowed incessantly. Then suddenly sleep came on like a warm blanket pulled up over you.

The House of the Wise

Next morning the trip was virtually over, we were barely four hours from Valencia. We drove fast through the sunlight under the pale blue levantine sky, bordered by white and lilac-tinted clouds piled above jagged desert hotcolored mountains, through the brightgreen fields and the orangegroves and the white villages with baroque churches with bluetiled domes I'd seen from the sea four years before scudding effortlessly down the coast on a schooner. Some of the churches were closed, some had been turned into markets or storehouses; one was a café. In most of the squares recruits were drilling under the small trees.

In Castellón we said goodbye to our militiaman who, not content with having paid for our lodgings for the night, insisted on setting us up to some magnificent glasses of cold beer accompanied by two kinds of big roasted prawns. Then too soon after leaving Castellón we found ourselves passing the great alligatorbacked hill from which the old walls of Saguntum cut into the sky, and tearing into the dusty pink and yellow suburbs and the glistening greener than ever huerta of Valencia. Then the bridge, the mediaeval gates and the clatter and jangle of the town.

Valencia didn't look very different from other times I'd been there. There was still something about the look of it that grated on the eyes, a jumble of ancient mellowly ornate buildings, scarred with new construction elaborately hideous under the sharp searching sun. The streets were crowded with miscellaneouslooking people and peddlers and signs almost like at the time of the annual fair, the only difference was the sprinkling of assorted military uniforms and the rifles and the pistolholsters and the tasseled militiamen's caps. Instead of bullfights the posters announced civil war. We drew up in front of the Hotel International next to the station where the upholsterer had another friend who spoke French. Again it was the dead time of day when all the offices would be closed; as there was no chance to deliver the truck until later in the afternoon we decided we'd better settle down to eat. The hotel seemed to be a sort of headquarters for international brigades; in the swelter of heat and the clatter of dishes of the hotel diningroom, scattered among the local militiamen at the crowded tables among which sweating waiters scooted desperately were Frenchmen, Belgians, Germans, Poles, Jugoslavs, Italians; a cross section of Europe in arms. After lunch the upholsterer and I separated. He was to deliver his truck and to go back to Paris by train.

Valencia still centers around the Plaza Castelar with its underground flowermarket and its yellow trolleycars and its Coney Island buildings now hung with bunting and republican flags and plastered with posters, but instead of the old afternoon quiet every inch of the city is packed with a rambling crowd in which young men enormously predominate. There's the feeling that the town's been turned inside out like an old coat and that all the linings show.

At the office of the censor of the foreign press it's cosy and a little embarrassing, like a club. You meet old friends, you read the mimeographed sheets telling you what the government wants you to know. You snap at rumors. Inside, beyond a roomful of typewriters, the censor himself sits owllike in his big glasses at a little desk under a blue light.

The newspapermen are tendered a lunch by the Minister for Foreign Affairs at the restaurant at the Grao, the big old restaurant on the beach where years ago . . . the rice was just as good. Through the windows of the glassedin porch you could see a warship hulldown on the blue horizon. Nonintervention. The Minister with his curious whistling diction makes an excellent speech, a heart to heart talk in two languages. There's no question about our feeling that he has the right on his side. The wine is good. It's the old famous *paella* and the shrimps and the little clams. But the food at official luncheons does not digest. It stays in a hard lump in your throat. You think of those who are being led. It all depends whether your heart is with the hounds, or the hares. Official luncheons are hunt breakfasts.

Afterwards two Frenchmen and an American stroll round the port. A sentry politely shoos us off the wharves. The port is crowded with freighters. As we turn away from the port to walk up the long dusty road full of carts and trucks to Valencia, we see a darkgrey bow nosing past the breakwater, a big darkgrey steamship is slipping silent into the harbor: a Mexican.

We walk back to Valencia talking about the mysteries of the Mediterranean these days, the unannounced blockades, the unreported sinkings, the freighters with their names painted out that run without lights slipping through the blockades, the Mexicans as they are called; some of them are Russians but they can't all be Russian. One of the Frenchmen tells of a contract through a Czechoslovakian intermediary, between the Loyalist government and Krupp. Europe is a tangle these days that nobody has yet unravelled. There's rarely been a time when the wise guys knew so little.

Back in the town I meet an old friend who takes me to see the place where the paintings from the Prado are stored. Double cement vaults have been built under the already strong stone vaulting in a chapel of a high renaissance church. That's where the paintings are. A huge collection of tapestries from the royal palace in Madrid has just arrived. They are being unpacked before being put away by an old man and two young men. A couple of experts, museum directors in black suits, hover around. It's quiet under the frescoed dome. They unfold the tapestries for us on the clean marble steps of the chancel, the magnificent crucifixion that Charles V always took with him on his campaigns, a Marriage at Cana, some enormous apocalypses. We spell out the ornate symbolic figures, the horseman of war, pestilence, famine and death. "It's like that now," the old man says. "These are the days we are living." The young men look at the tapestries and at us and shrug their shoulders.

Casa de los Sabios is what people call the converted hotel where the government has put up some college professors and literary people who have lost their homes and have nowhere else to go. Its real name is the House of Culture. It's dreary in the parlor there, dinner is a gloomy function there. It's like being in quarantine. We feel like old trunks in somebody's attic. There in every mouthful in every lowvoiced conversation in every gesture you feel the choking strands of the tangle that nobody dares unravel. It seems hours before the oranges come that signify the end of dinner.

It's a relief to get out on the pitchblack streets where there are unstrained voices, footsteps, giggling, the feeling of men and women walking through the dark with blood in their veins. We turn into a narrow street and walk towards a dim blue light. In the narrow stone street the smell of orangeblossoms from the groves outside the city is intolerably sweet. We duck into a narrow door and through a dank stone passage enter a little litup bar. There are militiamen, a couple of sailors, a sprinkling of civilians. It smells of coffee and brandy. As we settle at a small table a frogfaced soldier comes up and introduces himself. He's a Serb serving in the International Brigade. He wants to tell his story. We piece it out with a little English, a little French, a little Spanish. He's a political exile living in Brussels. He was living with a Belgian girl who had a little boy by a former divorced husband. It's not his child but he loves it as his own, such a smart little boy. He couldn't help it, he had to leave them to come to Spain to join the International Brigade to help save Madrid from the Fascists. And now the former husband is trying to take the child away from the girl because they are Reds. The court has granted the child to the husband. What can he do? He's heartbroken. It's all in a letter. He shows us the letter. What can he do? What can we do? We tell him he's a good guy and he goes away.

Thoughts in the Dark

It's quiet at night in the Casa de los Sabios. Lying in bed it's hard not to think of what one has heard during the day of the lives caught in the tangle, the prisoners huddled in stuffy rooms waiting to be questioned, the woman with her children barely able to pay for the cheap airless apartment while she waits for her husband. It's nothing they have told her, he was just taken away for questioning, certain little matters to be cleared up, wartime, no need for alarm. But the days have gone by, months, no news. The standing in line at the policestation, the calling up of influential friends, the slowgrowing terror tearing the woman to pieces.

And the hostages penned in the tarpaper barrack eating the cold rice with a piece of stale meat in it, playing cards on gritty blankets in corners of the floor, and the sudden hush when the door opens and the officer steps in, behind him two soldiers with guns. He tries to keep his voice steady when he reads the names. Eyes stare out of pale faces. Feet scuffle on the dirty floor of the office. "I am obliged to inform you that you have been ordered to be shot . . . at once."

And the man stepping out to be courtmartialed by his own side. The conversational tone of the proceedings. A joke or a smile that lets the blood flow easy again, but the gradual freezing recognition of the hundred ways a man may be guilty, the remark you dropped in a café that somebody wrote down, the letter you wrote last year, the sentence you scribbled on a scratchpad, the fact that your cousin is in the ranks of the enemy, and the strange sound your own words make in your ears when they are quoted in the indictment. They shove a cigarette in your hand and you walk out into the courtyard to face six men you have never seen before. They take aim. They wait for the order. They fire.

Valencia, April, 1937.

Valencia–Madrid

THE Big Hispano the Generalitat furnished the famous
French journalist in Barcelona was standing outside the
Hotel Victoria. That nest of newspaper correspondents, governmental agents, spies, munition salesmen and mystery
women is empty and quiet now. A pale boy in a green baize
apron is sweeping the stairs down. It is seven in the morning.
We pile in with our packages of food and our bags and our
boxes of chocolate and extra cigarettes and spin out of town
over the bridge. As the road climbs up out of the green plains
of the huerta of Valencia into the dry mountains of the
province of Cuenca we tell each other our surprise at the lack
of military traffic on the road and at the fact that it is in such
excellent condition. With the railway cut this road is the main
feeder of Madrid in munitions and food. We pass the map
from hand to hand. We talk knowingly about a number of
things we know very little about.

Towards noon the famous French journalist began to call
for an *apéritif.* We stopped in a dry dilapidated village where
we found homemade vermouth in the café run by the U.G.T.
and with the help of some little boys tried to rustle up some
ham to go with it. There was nothing to eat in any of the little stores or at the *posada*, but we eventually fell on a completely equipped pastryshop. We bought the woman out and
the famous journalist photographed the little boys and everybody exclaimed about the excellence of Castilian spongecake.
When we asked the little boys what the sores on their faces
came from the woman said it was because they'd been scared
by the Fascist bombers flying over the village.

Thirty miles further along the road in another greystone
town clustered round a towering greystone church we stopped
for lunch. In a small inn an old man and two girls were most
cheerfully and seeming tirelessly serving a meal of fried eggs
with tomatoes and little steaks with fried potatoes, accompanied
by good bread, washed down by a fine dense wine, to roomful
after roomful of officers, soldiers, truckdrivers, political party

officials. This was far from the famine we had been warned to expect.

Then we were off chugging up over bare huge faintly green slopes of ranked hills that rose against indigo distances under continuously changing clouds, and down into the broad canyon of the Tagus; then up again over continually bolder hills until the road crossed a ridge with two towns with square towers on it. From the winding downward slope beyond we could look down into the valley of the Jarama and the red brick walls and the pointed slate spires of Alcalá de Henares and beyond over the strawcolored plain with cloudshadows moving across it at the great white barrier of the Sierra.

In the outskirts of Alcalá we begin to see troops, field-kitchens, youngsters in illfitting tin hats, some in the mush-room German shape and others in the more elegant French shape with a keel down the middle. There were many trucks and men marching in formation on the broad road into Madrid, but nothing like what memories of the Western Front had led us to associate with a road leading up to an army. Then suddenly the outskirts have closed in on us and we are in Madrid, passing the big terracottacolored bullring, honking our way through a broad crowded asphalt street un-der an enormous steely twilight sky.

As we drive into the great stone city with its broad streets and squares and avenues where the skimpy trees are just com-ing into leaf the twilight deepens fast on the cues of women in shawls and men with mufflers standing in line for bread and oil and beans outside the halfshuttered foodstores, the young men and girls strolling, the crowds coming out of movingpicture theatres. The unlighted houses are dark. Their windows stare blankly in the last light. A raw wind blows dust and newspapers among the crowds and flutters the edges of hastily putup posters. The city has a grim look as if stamped out of iron. In spite of the cries of newsboys and sellers of lot-tery tickets and the clang of streetcars and the roaring motors of trucks and automobiles all lettered with names of brigades or political parties, there's a grim silence about the city. For some reason we have an idea we ought to report to an offi-cial. We go to a public building and rub our behinds on red plush in a chilly anteroom for a while. Everything in there is delay, red tape and obstruction, just like old times. The official wouldn't think of seeing anybody till next week. We head for the Hotel Florida. It's too dark to see anything on the Gran Via. The driver is getting nervous. He wants to get his car in a garage. It's quiet and black in the Plaza de Callao. While we are piling our bags on the pavement we stop suddenly. The noise that went on when the motor stopped was machineguns. We listen. Not very near but getting nearer; up the street from the front night, shattered and dented with gunfire, pours into the city.

Madrid, April, 1937.

Madrid Under Siege

Room and Bath at the Hotel Florida

I wake up suddenly with my throat stiff. It's not quite day. I am lying in a comfortable bed in a clean wellarranged hotel room staring at the light indigo oblong of the window opposite. I sit up in bed. Again there's the hasty loudening shriek, the cracking roar, the rattle of tiles and a tinkling shatter of glass and granite fragments. Must have been near because the hotel shook. My room is eight or nine stories up. The hotel is on a hill. From the window I can look out at all the old part of Madrid over the crowded tiled roofs, sootcolor flecked with pale yellow and red under the metalblue before dawn gloaming. The packed city stretches out sharp and still as far as I can see, narrow roofs, smokeless chimneypots, buff-colored towers with cupolas and the pointed slate spires of seventeenth-century Castile. Everything is cut out of metal in the steely brightening air. Again the shriek, the roar, rattle, tinkle of a shell bursting somewhere. Then silence again, cut only by the thin yelps of a hurt dog, and very slowly from one of the roofs below, a smudge of dirty yellow smoke forms, rises, thickens and spreads out in the still air under the low indigo sky. The yelping goes weakly on and on, then stops.

It's too early to get up. I try going to bed again, fall asleep to wake almost immediately with the same tight throat, the same heavy feeling in my chest. The shells keep coming in. They are small but they are damn close. Better get dressed. The water's running in the bathroom, though the hot's not on yet. A man feels safe shaving, sniffing the little customary odor of the usual shaving soap in the clean bathroom. After a bath and a shave I put on my bathrobe, thinking after all this is what the madrileños have been having instead of an alarm-clock for five months now, and walk downstairs to see what the boys are up to.

The shells keep coming in. The hotel usually so quiet at this time is full of scamper and confusion. Everywhere doors fly open onto the balconies round the central glassedover well. Men and women in various stages of undress are scuttling out of front rooms, dragging suitcases and mattresses into back rooms. There's a curlyhaired waiter from the restaurant who comes out of several different doors in succession each time with his arm round a different giggling or sniveling young woman. Great exhibitions of dishevelment and lingerie.

Downstairs the correspondents are stirring about sleepily. An Englishman is making coffee on an electric coffeepot that speedily blows out the fuse at the same time melting the plug. A Frenchman in pajamas is distributing grapefruit to all and sundry from the door of his room.

The shells keep coming in. Nobody seems to know how to get at the coffee until a completely dressed woman novelist from Iowa takes charge of it and distributes it around in glasses with some scorched toast and halves of the Frenchman's grapefruit. Everybody gets lively and talkative until there's no more coffee left. By that time the shelling has died down a little and I go back to bed to sleep for an hour.

When I woke up again everything was quiet. There was hot water in the bathroom. From somewhere among the closepacked roofs under the window there drifted up a faint taste of sizzling oliveoil. Round the balconies in the hotel everything was quiet and normal. The pleasantfaced middleaged chambermaids were there in their neat aprons, quietly cleaning. On the lower floor the waiters were serving the morning coffee. Outside on the Plaza de Callao there were some new dents in the pavement that hadn't been there the night before. Somebody said an old newsvendor had been killed outside. Yesterday the doorman at the hotel got a spent machinegun bullet in the thigh.

Metropolitan Stroll

The midmorning sunlight was hot on the Gran Via in spite of the frigid dry wind of Castilian springtime. Stepping out of doors into the bustling jangle of the city I couldn't help thinking of other Madrids I'd known, twenty years ago, eighteen years ago, four years ago. The streetcars are the same, the longnosed sallow madrileño faces are the same, with the same mixture of brown bullet-headed countrymen, the women in the darkcolored shawls don't look very different. Of course you don't see the Best People any more. They are in Portugal and Seville or in their graves. Never did see the Best People at this time of the morning. The shellholes and the scars made by flying fragments and shrapnel have not changed the general look of the street, nor have the political posters pasted up on every bare piece of wall, or the fact that people are so scrappily dressed and that there's a predominance of uniforms in khaki and blue denim. It's the usualness of it that gives it this feeling of nightmare. I happen to look up at the hotel my wife and I stayed in the last time we were here. The entrance on the street looks normal and so does the department store next door, but the top floor with the balconies where our room was is shot as full of holes as a Swiss cheese.

Nobody hurries so fast along the street, and hardly anybody passes along the Gran Via these days without speeding his pace a little because it's the street where most shells fall, without pausing to glance up at the tall NewYorkish telephone building to look for new shellholes. It's funny how the least Spanish building in Madrid, the proud New York baroque tower of Wall Street's International Tel and Tel, the symbol of the colonizing power of the dollar, has become in the minds of the madrileños the symbol of the defense of the city. Five months of intermittent shellfire have done remarkably little damage. There are a few holes and dents but nothing that couldn't be repaired in two weeks' work. On the side the shelling comes from the windows of several stories have been bricked up. The historically exact ornamentation has hardly been chipped.

Inside you feel remarkably safe. The whole apparatus of the telephone service still goes on in the darkened offices. The elevators run. It feels like Sunday in a New York downtown building. In the big quiet office you find the press censors, a cadaverous Spaniard and a plump little pleasantvoiced Austrian woman. They say they are going to move their office to another building. It's too much to ask the newspapermen on the regular services to duck through a barrage every time they have to file a story, and the censors are beginning to feel that Franco's gunners are out after them personally. Only yesterday the Austrian woman came back to find that a shellfragment had set her room on fire and burned up all her shoes, and the censor had seen a woman made mincemeat of beside him when he stepped out to get a bite of lunch. It's not surprising that the censor is a nervous man; he looks underslept and underfed. He talks as if he understood without taking too much personal pleasure in it the importance of his position of guardian of those telephones that are the link with countries technically at peace, where the war is still carried on with gold credits on bankledgers and munitions contracts and conversations on red plush sofas in diplomatic anterooms instead of with sixinch shells and firing squads. He doesn't give the impression of being complacent about his job. But it's hard for one who is more or less of a free agent from a country at peace to talk about many things with men who are chained to the galley benches of war.

It's a relief to get away from the switchboards of power and walk out in the sunny streets again. If you follow the Gran Via beyond the Plaza de Callao down the hill towards the North Station, stopping for a second in an excellent bookshop that's still open for business, you run into your first defense barricade. It is solidly built of cemented pavingstones laid in regular courses high as your head. That's where men will make a last stand and die if the Fascists break through.

I walk on down the street. This used to be the pleasantest and quickest way to walk out into the country, down into the shady avenue along the Manzanares where the little fat church is with Goya's frescoes in it, and out through the iron gate into the old royal domain of El Pardo. Now it's the quickest way to the front.

At the next barricade there's a small beadyeyed sentry who smilingly asks to see my pass. He's a Cuban. As Americans we talk. Somehow there's a bond between us as coming from the western world.

There are trenches made with sandbags in the big recently finished Plaza de España. The huge straggling bronze statues of Don Quixote and Sancho Panza look out oddly towards the enemy position in Carabanchel. At a barracks building on the corner a bunch from the International Brigade is waiting for chow. French faces, Belgian faces, North of Italy faces; German exiles, bearded men blackened by the sun, young boys; a feeling of energy and desperation comes from them. The dictators have stolen their world from them; they have lost their homes, their families, their hopes of a living or a career; they are fighting back.

Up another little hill is the burned shell of the Montana Barracks where the people of Madrid crushed the military revolt last July. Then we're looking down the broad rimedge street of the Paseo de Rosales. It used to be one of the pleasantest places in Madrid to live because the four- and fivestory apartmenthouses overlooked the valley of the Manzanares and the green trees of the old royal parks and domains. Now it's noman's land. The lines cross the valley below, but if you step out on the paseo you're in the full view of the enemy on the hills opposite, and the Moors are uncommonly good riflemen.

With considerable speed the sightseers scuttle into a house on the corner. There's the narrow hall and the row of bells and the rather grimy dark stairs of the regular Madrid apartmenthouse, but instead of the apartment of Señor Fulano de Tal on the third floor you open a groundglass door and find . . . the front. The rest of the house has been blown away. The groundglass door opens on air, at your feet a well opens full of broken masonry and smashed furniture, then the empty avenue and beyond, across the Manzanares, a magnificent view of the enemy. On the top floor there's a room on that side still intact; looking carefully through the halfshattered shutters we can make out trenches and outposts at the top of the hill, a new government trench halfway up the hill and, closing the picture, as always, the great snowy cloudtopped barrier of the Guadarramas. The lines are quiet; not a sound. Through the glasses we can see some militiamen strolling around behind a clump of trees. After all it's lunchtime. They can't be expected to start a battle for the benefit of a couple of sightseers.

Walking back to the hotel through the empty streets of the wrecked quarter back of the paseo we get a chance to see all the quaint possibilities of shellfire and airbombing among dwelling houses. The dollshouse effect is the commonest, the front or a side of a house sliced off and touchingly revealing parlors, bedrooms, kitchens, diningrooms, twisted iron beds dangling, elaborate chandeliers hanging over void, a piano suspended in the air, a sideboard with dishes still on it, a mirror with a gilt stucco frame glittering high up in a mass of wreckage where everything else has been obliterated.

Afternoon Call

After lunch I walk out into the northern part of the city to see the mother of an old friend of mine. It's the same apartment where I have been to visit them in various past trips. The same old maid in black with a starched apron opens the door into the dim white rooms with the old oak and walnut furniture that remind me a little of Philip II's rooms in the Escorial. My friend's mother is much older than when I saw her last, but her eyes under the handsomely arched still dark eyebrows are as fine as ever, they have the same black flash when she talks. With her is an older sister from Andalusia, a very old whitehaired woman, old beyond conversation. They have been in Madrid ever since the movement, as they call it, started. Her son has tried to get her to go to Valencia where he has duties but she doesn't like to leave her apartment and she wouldn't like the Fascists to think they'd scared her into running away. Of course getting food is a nuisance but they are old now and don't need much, she says. She could even invite me to lunch if I'd come some day and wouldn't expect to get too much to eat. She tells me which papers she likes, then we fall to talking about the old days when they lived at El Pardo and her husband the doctor was alive. I used to walk out to see them through the beautiful park of liveoaks that always made me feel as if I were walking through the backgrounds of Velasquez's paintings, still full in those days of the Bourbons of mantraps and royal gamekeepers in Goya costumes. Over the big white cups of hot tea and the almond paste cakes we used to talk about walks in the Sierra and skiing and visits to forgotten driedup Castilian villages and the pleasure of looking at the construction of old buildings and pictures and the poems of Antonio Machado.

Street Life

As I stepped out into the empty street I heard shelling in the distance again. As a precaution I walked over to the metro station and took the crowded train down to the Gran Via. When I got out of the elevator at the station I found that there weren't so many people as usual walking down towards the Calle de Alcalá. There was a slight tendency to stand in doorways. I was thinking how intact this part of the town was when, opposite Molinero's, the pastryshop where we used to go in the intermission of the symphony concerts at the Price Circus and stuff with almond paste and eggyolk and whipped-cream pastry in the old days, I found myself stepping off the curb into a pool of blood. Water had been sloshed over it but it remained in red puddles among the cobbles. So much blood must have come from a mule, or several people hit at one time. I walked around it.

But what everybody was looking at was the division El Campesino in new khaki uniforms parading with flags and Italian guns and trucks captured at Brihuega. The bugles blew and the drums rattled and the flags rippled in the afternoon sunlight and the young men and boys in khaki looked healthy and confident walking by tanned from life at the front and with color stung into their faces by the lashing wind off the sierras. I followed them into the Puerta del Sol that, in spite of the two blocks gutted by incendiary bombs, looked re-markably normal in the late afternoon bustle, full of shoeshine boys and newsvendors and people selling shoelaces and bri-quets and papercovered books.

In the island in the middle where the metro station is an elderly man shined my shoes.

A couple of shells came in behind me far up a street. The dry whacking shocks were followed by yellow smoke and the smell of granite dust that drifted slowly past in the wind. There were no more. Perhaps a few more people decided to take the metro instead of the streetcar. An ambulance passed. The old man went on meticulously shining my shoes.

I began to feel that General Franco's gunner, smoking a cigarette as he looked at the silhouette of the city from the hill at Carabanchel, was taking aim at me personally. At last the old man was satisfied with his work, and sat down on his box again to wait for another customer while I walked across the halfmoonshaped square through the thinning crowd, to the old Café de Lisboa. Going in through the engraved glass swinging doors and sitting down on the faded chartreusecolored plush and settling down to read the papers over a glass of vermouth was stepping back twentyone years to the winter when I used to come out from my cold room at the top of a house on the other corner of the Puerta del Sol and warm up with coffee there during the morning. When I come out of the café at closing time and head for the Hotel Florida it's already almost dark. For some reason the city seems safer at night.

The Nights Are Long

The correspondents take their meals in the basement of the Hotel Gran Via almost opposite the Telephone Building. You go in through the unlit lobby and through a sort of pantry and down some back stairs past the kitchen into a cavelike place that still has an air of pink lights and nightclub jippery about it. There at a long table sit the professional foreign correspondents and the young worldsaviours and the members of foreign radical delegations. At the small tables in the alcoves there tend to be militiamen and internationals on sprees and a sprinkling of young ladies of the between the sheets brigade. This particular night there's at a special table a group of British parliamentary bigwigs, including a duchess. It's been a big day for them, because General Franco's gunners have bagged more civilians than usual. Right outside of the hotel, in fact under the eyes of the duchess, two peaceful madrileños were reduced to a sudden bloody mess. A splatter of brains had to be wiped off the glassless revolving doors of the hotel. But stuffed with horrors as they were, the British bigwigs had eaten supper. In fact they'd eaten up everything there was, so that when the American correspondents began to trickle in with nothing in their stomachs but whiskey and were fed each a sliver of rancid ham, there was a sudden explosion of the spirit of Seventy-Six. Why should a goddam lousy etcetera duchess eat three courses when a hardworking American newspaperman has to go hungry. A slightly punchdrunk little exbantamweight prizefighter, who was often in the joint wearing a militiaman's uniform and who had tended in the past to be chummy with the gringo contingent who were generous with their liquor, became our champion and muttered dark threats about closing the place up and having the cooks and waiters sent to the front, lousy profiteers hiding under the skirts of the C.N.T. who were all sons of loose women and saboteurs of the war and worse than Fascists, *mierda*. In the end the management produced a couple of longdead whitings and a plate of spinach which they'd probably been planning to eat themselves, and the fires of revolt died down.

Still in Madrid the easiest and most sustaining thing to get, though it's high in price, is whiskey; so it's on that great national fooddrink that the boys at the other end of the wires tend to subsist. One of the boys who'd been there longest leaned across the table and said plaintively, "Now you won't go home and write about the drunken correspondents, will you?"

Outside the black stone city was grimly flooded with moonlight that cut each street into two oblique sections. Down the Gran Via I could see the flashlight of a patrol and hear them demanding in low voices the password for the night of whoever they met on the sidewalk. From the west came a scattered hollow popping lightly perforating the horizon of quiet. Somewhere not very far away men with every nerve tense were crawling along the dark sides of walls, keeping their heads down in trenches, yanking their right arms back to sling a handgrenade at some creeping shadow opposite. And in all the black houses the children we'd seen playing in the streets were asleep, and the grownups were lying there thinking of lost friends and family and ruins and people they'd loved and hating the enemy and hunger and how to get a little more food tomorrow, feeling in the numbness of their blood, in spite of whatever scorn in the face of death, the low unending smoulder of apprehension of a city under siege. And I couldn't help feeling a certain awe, as I took off my clothes in my quiet clean room with electric light and running water and a bathtub and lay down on the bed to read a book, but instead stared at the ceiling and thought of the pleasantfaced middleaged chambermaid who'd cleaned it that morning and made the bed and put everything in order and who'd been coming regularly every day, doing the job ever since the siege began just as she'd done it in the days of Don Alfonso, and wondered where she slept and what about her family and her kids and her man, and how perhaps tomorrow coming to work there'd be that hasty loudening shriek and the street full of dust and splintered stone and instead of coming to work the woman would be just a mashedout mess of blood and guts to be scooped into a new pine coffin and hurried away. And they'd slosh some water over the cobbles and the death of Madrid would go on.

Madrid, April, 1937.

The Fiesta at the Fifteenth Brigade

D RIVING across the rolling parklands of the old royal hunting preserve shaded by scattered clumps of liveoaks and huge corktrees the young lieutenant colonel who was taking me to the field headquarters in the foothills near the Escorial, told me about his life. Up to last July he had been a pianist and composer. He had lived a great deal in Paris. He'd felt that his days didn't tie up to anything. When the military revolt began he'd put himself under the orders of the Communist Party and been put in charge of an arms depot. They found he had an organizing mind so first thing he knew he was in the field as an officer of the Fifth Regiment. Now he was in command of a brigade. He said he was happier than he had ever been in his life.

At a crossroads at the edge of the village, among the ugly summer villas of welltodo madrileños that deface the high boulderstrewn foothills of the Guadarramas, we got out of the car and stood at the edge of the road waiting in a little crowd of guests. There were officers of various nationalities in various uniforms and campaign clothes, newspapermen from Madrid, Loyalist staff officers, and the mayor and a group of leading citizens from the village, the schoolteacher, the doctor, the pharmacist. We stood around in the hot sun. Opposite us a couple of companies of internationals, Frenchmen mostly, were drawn up waiting. Somebody suggested that there'd be mighty good pickings for Franco's airmen if they chose this moment to attack this particular crossroads. A Russian newsphotographer was raking the group with his camera.

While I was waiting a stout little sunblackened Frenchman, the sergeant of one of the companies, came over and handed me the typewritten words of a song in French about *la victoire* and *la gloire* and *les sales fascistes* and *mauvaise piste* which his commanding officer had made up and which he wanted me to give to the press of the world. I put the song in my pocket though I told him that my command over the press of the world was slight to say the least. We got to talking. He'd been in Spain since November, he had been wounded twice and had lost a finger but he was still full of enthusiasm for the fray. He was a man in his late forties, at home he'd owned two grocerystores. His business had gone on the rocks since he'd enlisted but he said he didn't care: Fascism had to be destroyed.

While we were talking the staffcars drove up with General Miaja and a Russian staffofficer who goes under the name of General Walter and Colonel Rojo and various functionaries from the Ministry of War. The little Frenchman trotted back to his company. The companies presented arms very snappily. The band played the *Hymn of Riego*. The mayor of the village made a small speech welcoming the heroic-defenders of Madrid and the heroic foreigners who were giving their lives to drive the Fascist traitors and the foreign invaders from the soil of Spain, and then everybody got into his car. "The Fascists have supporters everywhere," said my friend the musician, "but their espionage service is lousy. They ought to be bombing us this minute."

We drove out a little way down a dusty road into the hills and parked in a row of cars. While the band played the *Hymn of Riego* again and then the *Marseillaise* we walked through groups of countrypeople looking on, into a clearing among great boulders and stonepines where the brigade was formed in a hollow square round a truck hung with bunting arranged for the speakers. The band sounded brassy and merry, the keen wind rippled in the red purple and yellow flags of the Republic and carried dust out from under the restless hoofs of the calvary. Behind rose great boulders and pines and the bare blue folds of the foothills and the snowy wall of the sierra.

The speeches, some in French and some in Spanish, were translated sentence by sentence. A new phase had come in the history of the International Brigades. They had played a heroic rôle independently. Now the time had come for them to add their experience and knowledge of the business of war to the fresh cadres of the new Spanish people's army. They had come as antifascists. They had helped save Madrid. Now they were to help build up a victorious army that would fight for democracy and liberty until the peninsula was cleared of the tyrant and the invader. The old Fifteenth was dissolved, hurray for the new Fifteenth Brigade of the victorious Army of the Center under General Miaja. Hurray for the Army of the Center. Hurray for General Miaja.

After the speechmaking the guests and the general and his staff moved back to the road, where a rough stand had been built, and reviewed the march past of the troops. First the internationals marched by with a firm step, their stained uniforms carefully brushed, worn cartridgebelts scrubbed, rifles cleaned, battered helmets cocked jauntily over leathery faces ribbed and lined by six months of war; in this brigade there were French and Belgians mostly with a sprinkling of German and Italian exiles; it was surprising how many of them were middleaged men; here and there the face of a new young boy stared out startlingly pale. Next came the brown and ruddy newlytrained Spanish youths in new uniforms, cavalry, artillery, trucks, ambulances. And in the tailend two old tobaccocolored countrymen on donkeys. The tiny feet of the little grey donkeys moved in a dainty trot over the white dust of the road.

There's a certain restrained elation about the staffofficers grouped round the elderly figure of General Miaja that it's hard for a bystander not to share. After all Guadalajara was not so very long ago. The Loyalists had started to move on the Cordova front. And here they see their new army, their real army coming to life before their eyes out of the old makeshift militia and the foreigners. In the center of the group stands Miaja, a stout elderly man with a round Sancho Panza face and a fatherly bearing. There's a vague kindliness about his manner that seems not entirely a matter of surfaces. He strikes you as being a man who is all of one piece. Looking at him you can understand the story commonly told that when in November the members of the government were fleeing Madrid in considerable panic he was found sitting at his desk in the Ministry of War saying mildly, "I am staying. . . . If anybody wants to stay with me we'll see what we can do." Just as the review was beginning the officer of the guard of honor or whatever you call it that was drawn up on either side of the staffofficers and guests began to bustle around shooing away a bunch of countrypeople, mostly old men and women, who were standing in front of the reviewing stand. The old general saw what was happening and shook his finger at the officer with a halfsmile and a kind of a deprecatory shrug. The officer went back crestfallen to his position and the old people stayed where they were.

When the last band and the last pennant and the last ambulance had passed we all got into our cars again and were driven to the handsome new stucco villa, decorated with arches of pine and firboughs for the occasion, that was the brigade's headquarters. The officers' mess had invited the guests to lunch and two long tables were arranged in an ell under a canvas awning and backed with pineboughs. The band, sweating by this time under the hot afternoon sun, played away manfully with tunics unbuttoned, and sweat trickling down their faces.

At the head of the table sat Miaja with his indulgent paterfamilias air and the shavenheaded weatherbeaten Russian who went under the name of General Walter. Behind General Walter's chair while everybody else was getting seated stood his aidedecamp, a young man with popping black eyes and sleek black hair in an overtailored green uniform with a brand new mapcase over his shoulder who tended to move in jerks like a jumpingjack. The cook was a Frenchman, the meal was extraordinarily good, including some tough little steaks, that had probably been walking around that morning, garnished with a sauce Béarnaise that you couldn't have gotten at Foyot's. There was red and white wine and beer, and very soon another round of speeches began in French, Spanish, and this time with one in German. General Walter, after a little crack in pidgin andaluz, spoke in Russian, which his little bantamcock of an aidedecamp, who followed his every word with deferential devotion, translated into excellent schoolbook Spanish. Then three soldier representatives from the old internationals came up and presented a gold watch to the tall grave Frenchman who had been their commander and who was leaving the brigade for the general staff.

The best speech was Lister's. Lister is the gallego stevedore and stonemason who has risen to be one of the most brilliant commanders in the young republican army. He's a man in his late twenties, built like a welterweight with a mane of black hair above a very white face that looks like a prizefighter's until he speaks; he spoke frankly of the difficulties they had to face and the need for criticism and for learning from past mistakes and ended up calling for victory for their new world with cascading eloquence that carried everybody away. After him one young man after another was called on. As they spoke it was hard not to feel mounting enthusiasm for these youthful commanders, most of them in their twenties, who less than a year ago had been carpenters, blacksmiths, musicians, doctors, some of them businessmen even, who had had to learn the whole business of war from the ground up, and who were learning it out of the mistakes and the terrible disorganizing slaughter of the first months of civilian resistance against the military revolt. Writing several months after that fine April afternoon in the foothills of the sierra, I wonder how many of them are still alive.

In the middle of the speechmaking, General Miaja and his staff left and with them the Russian followed by his little aide-decamp strutting one or two paces behind him. The table began to fill up with the rank and file, and speeches became more personal and humorous. Some very bad warm champagne appeared and with it a good deal of kidding back and forth. Then I heard someone say, "Here they come." The tall pleasantfaced young man who had been a carpenter in Huelva until the fortunes of war had placed him in command of an army corps went out into the sunlight to meet them. He came back ushering two women in broad strawhats with silk shawls drawn over their faces into the comparatively cool shade under the awning. He placed them in the chairs at the head of the table that the generals had left empty. They sat down panting and fanning. There followed them into the shade a little group of lean yellowfaced Andalusian men who had that look of undertaker gravity peculiar to singers of the *canto jondo*. When the women took off their hats and pushed back their shawls from their sleek black heads we could see that they were Pastora Imperio and Niña de las Peñas. Pastora is one of the greatest Spanish dancers there has ever been and Niña de las Peñas is one of the very good singers. They were going to give a performance for the soldiers that evening. Everybody clapped and a little speech of greeting was delivered. They sat at the end of the table smiling and bowing with that mixed expression of pain and pleasure that so becomes their carefully madeup pale tobaccocolored gypsy faces. Then with great grace Pastora got to her feet and made a little speech. "I can't make speeches, but when I see you young men and how you are fighting for our liberty and when I think of my Spain . . . my heart breaks." Tears filled her eyes. She pressed her hand over her mouth and sat down. People brought her wine and tried to get her to drink a little cognac but she sat there shaking her head with the tears running down her face. Niña de las Peñas wouldn't drink anything either. "A little water," she said in a choked voice. Pastora reached for the earthen waterjug on the table with her small hand, still, after all these years, as delicately moulded as a child's at the end of the thick arm of a stout woman in late middle age, and poured out a glass. She asked for sugar. As she carefully stirred the lump around in the water with a spoon she began to smile. She took out the spoon and laid it on the table with a little precise tap and handed the glass to the singer, who took it almost laughing. "You see she's going to sing tonight," Pastora said with a black flash of her eyes round the table.

After we'd drunk our coffee we walked down to a field where boxing and horseracing and a soccergame were going on simultaneously. The afternoon was pure sunlight under a sky full of big cottonwhite clouds. Not a plane was in the sky. From the frontline posts there came not a sound. Around five o'clock my friend the musician called his car and said he'd have to be getting back to his outfit. I said it had been a fine day. He wrinkled up his face. "I've wasted my time. I should have been at work," he said.

Madrid, April, 1937.

The Villages Are the Heart of Spain

First it was that the driver was late, then that he had to go to the garage to get a mechanic to tinker with the gasoline pump, then that he had to go somewhere else to wait in line for gasoline; and so, in pacing round the hotel, in running up and down stairs, in scraps of conversation in the lobby, the Madrid morning dribbled numbly away in delay after delay. At last we were off. As we passed the Cibeles fountain two shells burst far up the sunny Castillana. Stonedust mixed with pale smoke of high explosives suddenly blurred the ranks of budding trees, under which a few men and women were strolling because it was Sunday and because they were in the habit of strolling there on Sunday. The shells burst too far away for us to see if anyone were hit. Our driver speeded up a little. We passed the arch of Carlos Third and the now closed café under the trees opposite the postoffice where the last time I was in Madrid I used to sit late in the summer evenings chatting with friends, some of whom are only very recently dead. As we got past the controlposts and sentries beyond the bullring, the grim exhilaration of the besieged city began to drop away from us, and we bowled pleasantly along the Guadalajara road in the spring sunlight.

In a little stone town in a valley full of poplars we went to visit the doctor in charge of the medical work for the Jarama front. He was a small dark brighteyed young man, a C.P. member, I imagine; he had the look of a man who had entirely forgotten that he had a life of his own. Evidently for months there had been nothing he thought of, all day and every day, but his work. He took us to one of his base hospitals, recently installed in a group of old buildings, part of which had once been a parochial school. He apologized for it; they had only been in there two weeks, if we came two weeks later we'd see an improvement. We ate lunch there with him, then he promptly forgot us. In spite of the rain that came on, we could see him walking up and down the stony court inside the hospital gate with one member of his staff after another talking earnestly to them. He never took his eyes off whoever he was talking to, as if he were trying to hypnotize them with his own untired energy. Meanwhile we tried to stimulate our driver, a singularly spineless young man in a black C.N.T. tunic, the son of a winegrower in Alcazar de San Juan, to fix the gasoline pump on the miserable little Citroën sedan we had been assigned to. At last the doctor remembered us again and as our driver had gotten the pump into such a state that the motor wouldn't even start, he offered to take us to the village to which we were bound, as he had to go out that way to pick a site for a new basehospital. We set out in his Ford, that felt like a racingcar after the feeble little spluttering Citroën.

Rain was falling chilly over the lichengreen stone towns and the tawny hills misted over with the fiery green of new wheat. Under the rain and the low indigo sky, the road wound up and down among the great bare folds of the upland country. At last late in the afternoon we came to a square building of lightbrown stone in a valley beside a clear stream and a milldam set about with poplars. The building had been a monastery long ago and the broad valley lands had belonged to the monks. As we got out of the car larks rose singing out of the stubby fields. The building was a magnificent square of sober seventeenthcentury work. In the last few years it had been used as a huntingclub, but since July none of the members of the club had been seen in those parts. A family of country people from Pozorubio had moved out there to escape the airraids and to do some planting. They invited us in with grave Castilian hospitality and in a dark stone room we stood about the embers of a fire with them, drinking their stout darkred wine and eating their deliciously sweet fresh bread.

With his glass in his hand and his mouth full of bread the doctor lectured them about the war, and the need to destroy the Fascists and to produce as much food as possible. Wheat and potatoes, he said, were as important as machinegun bullets in war.

"I am an illiterate and I know more about driving a mule than international politics. That is all my parents taught me," the tall dark thinfaced man who was the head of the family answered gravely. "But even I can understand that."

"But it's so terrible, gentlemen," the woman broke in.

"There are no more gentlemen or masters here," said the man harshly. "These are comrades."

"How soon will it be stopped? It can't last all summer, can it?" asked the woman without paying attention to the man. Tears came into her eyes.

"The war will stop when the Fascists are driven out of Spain," said the doctor.

Then he explained how the countrypeople must tell everybody in the village to send to Madrid to the Department of Agriculture for free seed potatoes and that they must use the milldam to irrigate the fields. Then we gravely wished them good health and went out to the car and were off into the rainy night again.

Village Bakery

We stopped at their village, Pozorubio, to load up on bread. We went into the bakery through a dimly lit stone doorway. The baker was at the front, so the women and young boys of the family were doing the baking. The bread had just come out of the oven. "Yes, you can buy as much as you want," the women said. "We'd have bread for Madrid if they'd come and get it. Here at least we have plenty of bread." We stood around for a while talking in the dry dim room looking into the fire that glowed under the ovens.

As we got back into the car with our arms piled high with the big flat so sweet loaves the doctor was saying bitterly, "And in Madrid they are hungry for bread; it's the fault of the lack of transport and gasoline . . . we must organize our transport." Then he snapped at his Belgian chauffeur, "We must get back to headquarters fast, fast." You could see that he was blaming himself for the relaxed moment he'd spent in the warm sweetsmelling bakery. As the car lurched over the ruts of the road across the hills furry black in the rainy night there went along with us in the smell of the bread something of the peaceful cosiness of the village, and country people eating their suppers in the dim roomy stone houses and the sharp-smelling herbs in the fires and the brown faces looking out from the shelter of doorways at the bright stripes of the rain in the street and the gleam of the cobbles and the sturdy figures of countrywomen under their shawls.

Socialist Construction

Fuentedueña is a village of several hundred houses in the province of Madrid. It stands on a shelf above the Tagus at the point where the direct road to Valencia from Madrid dips down into the river's broad terraced valley. Above it on the hill still tower the crumbling brick and adobe walls of a castle of Moorish work where some feudal lord once sat and controlled the trail and the rivercrossing. Along the wide well-paved macadam road there are a few wineshops and the barracks of the Civil Guard. The minute you step off the road you are back in the age of packmules and twowheeled carts. It's a poor village and it has the air of having always been a poor village; only a few of the houses on the oblong main square, with their wide doors that open into pleasant green courts, have the stone shields of hidalgos on their peeling stucco façades. The townhall is only a couple of offices, and on the wall the telephone that links the village to Madrid. Since July, '36, the real center of the town has been on another street, in the house once occupied by the pharmacist, who seems to have been considered hostile, because he is there no more, in an office where the members of the socialista (U.G.T.) Casa del Pueblo meet. Their president is now mayor and their policies are dominant in the village. The only opposition is the C.N.T. syndicalist local which in Fuentedueña, so the socialistas claim and I think in this case justly, is made up of small storekeepers and excommissionmerchants, and not working farmers at all. According to the mayor they all wear the swastika under their shirts. Their side of the story, needless to say, is somewhat different.

At the time of the military revolt in July the land of Fuentedueña was held by about ten families, some of them the descendants, I suppose, of the hidalgos who put their shields on their houses on the main square. Some of them were shot, others managed to get away. The Casa del Pueblo formed a collective out of their lands. Meanwhile other lands were taken over by the C.N.T. local. Fuentedueña's main cash crop is wine; the stocks in the three or four bodegas constituted the town's capital. The Casa del Pueblo, having the majority of the working farmers, took over the municipal government and it was decided to farm the lands of the village in common. For the present it was decided that every workingman should be paid five pesetas for every day he worked and have a right to a daily litre of wine and a certain amount of fire-wood. The mayor and the secretary and treasurer and the treasurer and the muledrivers and the blacksmith, every man who worked was paid the same. The carpenters and masons and other skilled artisans who had been making seven pesetas a day consented, gladly they said, to taking the same pay as the rest. Later, the master mason told me, they'd raise every-body's pay to seven pesetas or higher; after all wine was a valuable crop and with no parasites to feed there would be plenty for all. Women and boys were paid three fifty. The committees of the U.G.T. and the C.N.T. decided every day where their members were to work. Housing was roughly dis-tributed according to the sizes of the families. There was not much difficulty about that because since the Fascist airraids began people preferred to live in the cavehouses along the edges of the hill than in the big rubble and stucco houses with courts and corrals in the center of town, especially since one of them had been destroyed by a bomb. These cavehouses, where in peacetime only the poorest people lived, are not such bad dwellings as they sound. They are cut out of the hard clay and chalky rock of the terraced hillsides facing the river. They have usually several rooms, each with a large coneshaped chim-ney for light and to carry off the smoke of the fire, and a porch onto which narrow windows open. They are whitewashed and often remarkably clean and neat. Before the civil war the housedwellers looked down on the cavedwellers; but now the caves seem to have definite social standing.

The village produces much wine but little oil, so one of the first things the collective did was to arrange to barter their wine for oil with a village that produced more oil than it needed. Several people told me proudly that they'd improved the quality of their wine since they had taken the bodegas over from the businessmen who had the habit of watering the wine before they sold it and were ruining the reputation of their vintages. Other local industries taken over by the collec-tive are the bakery and a lime kiln, where three or four men worked intermittently, getting the stone from a quarry imme-diately back of the town and burning it in two small adobe ovens; and the making of fibre baskets and harness which people make from a tough grass they collect from the hills round about. This is a sparetime occupation for periods of bad weather. After wine the crops are wheat, and a few olives.

The irrigation project seemed to loom larger than the war in the minds of the mayor and his councillors. Down in the comparatively rich bottomland along the Tagus the collective had taken over a piece that they were planning to irrigate for truck gardens. They had spent thirteen thousand pesetas of their capital in Madrid to buy pumping machinery and cement. A large gang of men was working over there every day to get the ditches dug and the pump installed that was going to put the river water on the land before the hot dry summer weather began. Others were planting seed potatoes. An old man and his son had charge of a seedbed where they were raising onions and lettuce and tomatoes and peppers and artichokes for planting out. Later they would sow melons, corn and cabbage. For the first time the village was going to raise its own green vegetables. Up to now everything of that sort had had to be imported from the outside. Only a few of the richer landowners had had irrigated patches of fruits and vegetables for their own use. This was the first real reform the collective had undertaken and everybody felt very good about it, so good that they almost forgot the hollow popping beyond the hills that they could hear from the Jarama River front fifteen miles away, and the truckloads of soldiers and munitions going through the village up the road to Madrid and the fear they felt whenever they saw an airplane in the sky. Is it ours or is it theirs?

Outside of the irrigated bottomlands and the dryfarming uplands the collective owned a considerable number of mules, a few horses and cows, a flock of sheep and a flock of goats. Most of the burros were owned by individuals, as were a good many sheep and goats that were taken out to pasture every day by the village shepherds under a communal arrangement as old as the oldest stone walls. Occasional fishing in the river is more of an entertainment than part of the town economy. On our walks back and forth to the new pumping station the mayor used to point out various men and boys sitting along the riverbank with fishingpoles. All members of the

C.N.T., he'd say maliciously. You'd never find a socialista going out fishing when there was still spring plowing to be
done. "We've cleaned out the Fascists and the priests," one of
the men who was walking with us said grimly. "Now we must
clean out the loafers." "Yes," said the mayor. "One of these
days it will come to a fight."

Cooperative Fishing Village

In San Pol, so the secretary of the agricultural cooperative
told me with considerable pride, they hadn't killed anybody.
He was a small, schoolteacherylooking man in a worn dark
business suit. He had a gentle playful way of talking and intermingled his harsh Spanish with English and French words.
San Pol is a very small fishingvillage on the Catalan coast perhaps thirty miles northeast of Barcelona. It's made up of several short streets of pale blue and yellow and whitewashed
houses climbing up the hills of an irregular steep little valley
full of umbrellapines. The fishingboats are drawn up on the
shingly beach in a row along the double track of the railway
to France.

Behind the railway is a string of grotesque villas owned by
Barcelona businessmen of moderate means. Most of the villas
are closed. A couple have been expropriated by the municipality, one for a cooperative retail store, and another, which
had just been very handsomely done over with a blue and
white tile decoration, to house a municipal poolparlor and
gymnasium, public baths and showers, a huge airy cooperative barbershop and, upstairs, a public library and reading-
room. On the top of the hill behind the town a big estate has
been turned into a municipal chickenfarm.

The morning I arrived the towncouncil had finally decided
to take over the wholesale marketing of fish, buying the catch
from the fishermen and selling it in Barcelona. The middle-
man who had handled the local fish on a commission basis
was still in business; we saw him there, a big domineering
pearshaped man with a brown sash holding up his baggy cor-
duroys, superintending the salting of sardines in a barrel.
"He's a Fascist," the secretary of the cooperative said, "but
we won't bother him. He won't be able to compete with us
anyway because we'll pay a higher price."

He took me to see a little colony of refugee children from Madrid living in a beautiful house overlooking the sea with a rich garden behind it. They were a lively and sunburned bunch of kids under the charge of a young man and his wife who were also attending to their schooling. As we were walking back down the steep flowerlined street (yes, the flowers had been an idea of the socialista municipality, the secretary said, smiling) it came on to rain. We passed a stout man in black puffing with flushed face up the hill under a green umbrella. "He's the priest," said the secretary. "He doesn't bother anybody. He takes no part in politics." I said that in most towns I'd been in a priest wouldn't dare show his face. "Here we were never believers," said the secretary, "so we don't feel that hatred. We have several refugee priests in town. They haven't made any trouble yet."

He took me to a fine building on the waterfront that had been a beach café and danceplace that had failed. Part of it had been done over into a little theatre. "We won a prize at the Catalonia drama festival last year, though we're a very small town. There's a great deal of enthusiasm for amateur plays here." We had lunch with various local officials in the rooms of the choral society in a little diningroom overlooking the sea. Far out on the horizon we could see the smoke of the inevitable nonintervention warship.

And a fine lunch it was. Everything except the wine and the coffee had been grown within the town limits. San Pol had some wine, they said apologetically, but it wasn't very good. First we had broadbeans in oliveoil. Then a magnificent dish of fresh sardines. My friends explained that the fishing had been remarkably good this year, and that fish were selling at war prices, so that everybody in town had money in his pocket. The sardine fishing was mostly done at night with floating nets. The boats had motors and great batteries of acetylene lights to attract the fish to the surface. After the sardines we had roast chicken from the village chickenfarm, with new potatoes and lettuce. Outside of fish they explained new potatoes were their main cash crop. They sold them in England, marketing them through a cooperative. My friend the secretary had been in England that winter to make new arrangements. The cooperative was a number of years old and a member of the Catalan alliance of cooperatives. Of course now since the movement they were more important than ever. "If only the Fascists would let us alone." "And the anarchists," somebody added . . . "We could be very happy in San Pol."

We drove out of town in the pouring rain. As the road wound up the hill we got a last look at the neat streets of different colored stucco houses and the terraced gardens and the blue and white and blue and green fishingboats with their clustered lights sticking out above their sterns, like insect eyes, drawn up in a row along the shingle beach.

The Defeated

Barcelona. The headquarters of the P.O.U.M. It's late at night in a large bare office furnished with odds and ends of old furniture. At a big battered fakegothic desk out of somebody's library a man sits at the telephone. I sit in a mangy overstuffed armchair. On the settee opposite me sits a man who used to be editor of a radical publishing house in Madrid. We talk in a desultory way about old times in Madrid, about the course of the war. They are telling me about the change that has come over the population of Barcelona since the great explosion of revolutionary feeling that followed the attempted military coup d'état and swept the Fascists out of Catalonia in July. They said Barcelona was settling down, getting bourgeoise again. "You can even see it in people's dress," said the man at the telephone, laughing. "Now we're beginning to wear collars and ties again but even a couple of months ago everybody was wearing the most extraordinary costumes . . . you'd see people on the street wearing feathers."

The man at the telephone was wellbuilt and healthylooking; he had a ready childish laugh that showed a set of solid white teeth. From time to time as we were talking the telephone would ring and he would listen attentively with a serious face. Then he'd answer with a few words too rapid for me to catch and would hang up the receiver with a shrug of the shoulders and come smiling back into the conversation again.

When he saw that I was beginning to frame a question he said, "It's the villages. . . . They want to know what to do." "About Valencia taking over the police services?" He nodded.

"Take a car and drive through the suburbs of Barcelona, you'll see that all the villages are barricaded . . ." Then he laughed. "But maybe you had better not." "He'd be all right," said the other man. "They have great respect for foreign journalists." "Is it an organized movement?" "It's complicated . . . in Bellver our people want to know whether to move against the anarchists. In some other places they are with them. . . . You know Spain."

It was time for me to push on. I shook hands with Andrés Nin and with a young Englishman who also is dead now, and went out into the rainy night. Since then Nin has been killed and his party suppressed. The papers have not told us what has happened in the villages. Perhaps these men already knew they were doomed. There was no air of victory about them.

Over the Short Wave

The syndicalist paper had just been installed in a repaired building where there had once been a convent. The new rotary presses were not quite in order yet and the partitions were unfinished between the offices in the editorial department. They took me into a little room where they were transmitting news and comment to the syndicalist paper in the fishingtown of Gijon in Asturias on the north coast, clear on the other side of Franco's territory. A man was reading an editorial. As the rotund phrases (which perhaps fitted in well enough with the American scheme of things for me to accept) went lilting through the silence, I couldn't help thinking of the rainy night and the workingmen on guard with machineguns and rifles at sandbag posts on the roads into villages, and the hopes of new life and liberty and the political phrases, confused, contradictory pounding in their ears; and then the front, the towns crowded with troops and the advanced posts and trenches and the solitude between; and beyond, the old life, the titled officers in fancy uniforms, the bishops and priests, the pious ladies in black silk with their rosaries, the Arab Moors and the dark Berbers getting their revenge four hundred and fifty years late for the loss of their civilization, and the profiteers and wop businessmen and squareheaded German travelling salesmen; and beyond again the outposts and the Basque countrypeople praying to God in their hillside trenches and the Asturian miners with their sticks of dynamite in their belts and the longshoremen and fishermen of the coast towns waiting for hopeful news; and another little office like this where the editors crowded round the receiving set that except for blockade-runners is their only contact with the outside world. How can they win, I was thinking? How can the new world full of confusion and crosspurposes and illusions and dazzled by the mirage of idealistic phrases win against the iron combination of men accustomed to run things who have only one idea binding them together, to hold on to what they've got.

There was a sudden rumble in the distance. The man who was reading stopped. Everybody craned their necks to listen. There it was again. "No, it's not firing, it's thunder," everybody laughed with relief. They turned on the receiver again. The voice from Gijon came feebly in a stutter of static. They must repeat the editorial. Static. Black rain was lashing against the window. While the operator tinkered with the adjustments the distant voice from Gijon was lost in sharp crashes of static.

Antibes, May, 1937.

A PUSHCART AT THE CURB

TO THE MEMORY

OF

WRIGHT MCCORMICK

WHO TUMBLED OFF A MOUNTAIN

IN MEXICO

My verse is no upholstered chariot
Gliding oil-smooth on oiled wheels,
No swift and shining modern limousine,
But a pushcart, rather.

A crazy creaking pushcart, hard to push
Round corners, slung on shaky patchwork wheels,
That jolts and jumbles over the cobblestones
Its very various lading:

A lading of Spanish oranges, Smyrna figs,
Fly-specked apples, perhaps of the Hesperides,
Curious fruits of the Indies, pepper-sweet . . .
Stranger, choose and taste.

Dolo

Contents

Contents

Winter in Castile

The promiscuous wind wafts idly from the quays
A smell of ships and curious woods and casks
And a sweetness from the gorse on the flowerstand
And brushes with his cool careless cheek the cheeks
Of those on the street; mine, an old gnarled man's,
The powdered cheeks of the girl who with faded eyes
Stands in the shadow; a sailor's scarred brown cheeks,
And a little child's, who walks along whispering
To her sufficient self.
                    O promiscuous wind.

Bordeaux

I

A long grey street with balconies.
Above the gingercolored grocer's shop
trail pink geraniums
and further up a striped mattress
hangs from a window
and the little wooden cage
of a goldfinch.

Four blind men wabble down the street
with careful steps on the rounded cobbles
scraping with violin and flute
the interment of a tune.

People gather:
women with market-baskets
stuffed with green vegetables,
men with blankets on their shoulders
and brown sunwrinkled faces.

Pipe the flutes, squeak the violins;
four blind men in a row
at the interment of a tune . . .
But on the plate
coppers clink
round brown pennies
a merry music at the funeral,
penny swigs of wine
penny gulps of gin
peanuts and hot roast potatoes
red disks of sausage
tripe steaming in the corner shop . . .

And overhead
the sympathetic finch
chirps and trills
approval.

Calle de Toledo, Madrid

II

A boy with rolled up shirtsleeves
turns the handle.
Grind, grind.
The black sphere whirls
above a charcoal fire.
Grind, grind.
The boy sweats and grits his teeth and turns
while a man blows up the coals.
Grind, grind.
Thicker comes the blue curling smoke,
the moka-scented smoke
heavy with early morning
and the awakening city
with click-clack click-clack on the cobblestones
and the young winter sunshine
advancing inquisitively
across the black and white tiles of my bedroom floor.
Grind, grind.

The coffee is done.
The boy rubs his arms and yawns,
and the sphere and the furnace are trundled away
to be set up at another café.

A poor devil
whose dirty ashen white body shows through his rags
sniffs sensually
with dilated nostrils
the heavy coffee-fragrant smoke,
and turns to sleep again
in the feeble sunlight of the greystone steps.

Calle Espoz y Mina

III

Women are selling tuberoses in the square,
and sombre-tinted wreaths
stiffly twined and crinkly
for this is the day of the dead.

Women are selling tuberoses in the square.
Their velvet odor fills the street
somehow stills the tramp of feet;
for this is the day of the dead.

Their presence is heavy about us
like the velvet black scent of the flowers:
incense of pompous interments,
patter of monastic feet,
drone of masses drowsily said
for the thronging dead.

Women are selling tuberoses in the square
to cover the tombs of the envious dead
and shroud them again in the lethean scent
lest the dead should remember.

Difuntos; Madrid

IV

Above the scuffling footsteps of crowds
the clang of trams
the shouts of newsboys
the stridence of wheels,
very calm,
floats the sudden trill of a pipe
three silvery upward notes
wistfully quavering,
notes a Thessalian shepherd might have blown
to call his sheep
in the emerald shade
of Tempe,
notes that might have waked the mad women sleeping
among pinecones in the hills
and stung them to headlong joy
of the presence of their mad Iacchos,
notes like the glint of sun
making jaunty the dark waves of Tempe.

In the street an old man is passing
wrapped in a dun brown mantle
blowing with bearded lips on a shining panpipe
while he trundles before him
a grindstone.

The scissors grinder.

Calle Espoz y Mina

V

Rain slants on an empty square.

Across the expanse of cobbles
rides an old shawl-muffled woman
black on a donkey with pert ears
that places carefully
his tiny sharp hoofs

as if the cobbles were eggs.
The paniers are full
of bright green lettuces
and purple cabbages,
and shining red bellshaped peppers,
dripping, shining, a band in marchtime,
in the grey rain,
in the grey city.

Plaza Santa Ana

VI

BEGGARS

The fountain some dead king put up,
conceived in pompous imageries,
piled with mossgreened pans and centaurs
topped by a prudish tight-waisted Cybele
(Cybele the many-breasted mother of the grain)
spurts with a solemn gurgle of waters.

Where the sun is warmest
their backs against the greystone basin
sit, hoarding every moment of the palefaced sun,
(thy children Cybele)
Pan a bearded beggar with blear eyes;
his legs were withered by a papal bull,
those shaggy legs so nimble to pursue
through groves of Arcadian myrtle
the nymphs of the fountains and valleys;
a young Faunus with soft brown face
and dirty breast bared to the sun;
the black hair crisps about his ears
with some grace yet;
a little barefoot Eros
crouching to scratch his skinny thighs
who stares with wide gold eyes aghast
at the yellow shiny trams that clatter past.

All day long they doze in the scant sun
and watch the wan leaves rustle to the ground
from the yellowed limetrees of the avenue.
They are still thine Cybele
nursed at thy breast;
(like a woman's last foster-children
that still would suck grey withered dugs).
They have not scorned thy dubious bounty
for stridence of grinding iron
and pale caged lives
made blind by the dust of toil
to coin the very sun to gold.

Plaza de Cibeles

VII

Footsteps
and the leisurely patter of rain.

Beside the lamppost in the alley
stands a girl in a long sleek shawl
that moulds vaguely to the curves
of breast and arms.
Her eyes are in shadow.

A smell of frying fish;
footsteps of people going to dinner
clatter eagerly through the lane.
A boy with a trough of meat on his shoulder
turns by the lamppost,
his steps drag.
The green light slants
in the black of his eyes.
Her eyes are in shadow.

Footsteps of people going to dinner
clatter eagerly; the rain
falls with infinite nonchalance . . .
a man turns with a twirl of moustaches

and the green light slants on his glasses
on the round buttons of his coat.
Her eyes are in shadow.

A woman with an umbrella
keeps her eyes straight ahead
and lifts her dress
to avoid the mud on the pavingstones.

An old man stares without fear
into the eyes of the girl
through the stripes of the rain.
His steps beat faster and he sniffs hard suddenly
the smell of dinner and frying fish.
Was it a flame of old days
expanding in his cold blood,
or a shiver of rigid graves,
chill clay choking congealing?

Beside the lamppost in the alley
stands a girl in a long sleek shawl
that moulds vaguely to the curves
of breast and arms.

Calle del Gato

VIII

A brown net of branches
quivers above silver trunks of planes.
Here and there
a late leaf flutters
its faint death-rattle in the wind.
Beyond, the sky burns fervid rose
like red wine held against the sun.

Schoolboys are playing in the square
dodging among the silver tree-trunks
collars gleam and white knees
as they romp shrilly.

Lamps bloom out one by one
like jessamine, yellow and small.
At the far end a church's dome
flat deep purple cuts the sky.

Schoolboys are romping in the square
in and out among the silver tree-trunks
out of the smoked rose shadows
through the timid yellow lamplight . . .
Socks slip down
fingermarks smudge white collars;
they run and tussle in the shadows
kicking the gravel with muddied boots
with cheeks flushed hotter than the sky
eyes brighter than the street-lamps
with fingers tingling and breath fast:
banqueters early drunken
on the fierce cold wine of the dead year.

Paseo de la Castellana

IX

Green against the livid sky
in their square dun-colored towers
hang the bronze bells of Castile.
In their unshakeable square towers
jutting from the slopes of hills
clang the bells of all the churches
the dustbrown churches of Castile.

How they swing the green bronze bells
athwart olive twilights of Castile
till their fierce insistent clangour
rings down the long plowed slopes
breaks against the leaden hills
whines among the trembling poplars
beside sibilant swift green rivers.

O you strong bells of Castile
that commanding clang your creed
over treeless fields and villages
that huddle in arroyos, gleaming
orange with lights in the greenish dusk;
can it be bells of Castile,
can it be that you remember?

Groans there in your bronze green curves
in your imperious evocation
stench of burnings, rattling screams
quenched among the crackling flames?
The crowd, the pile of faggots in the square,
the yellow robes. . . . Is it that
bells of Castile that you remember?

Toledo—Madrid

X

The Tagus flows with a noise of wiers through Aranjuez.
The speeding dark-green water mirrors the old red walls
and the balustrades and close-barred windows of the palace;
and on the other bank three stooping washerwomen
whose bright red shawls and piles of linen gleam in the green,
the swirling green where shimmer the walls of Aranjuez.

There's smoke in the gardens of Aranjuez
smoke of the burning of the year's dead leaves;
the damp paths rustle underfoot
thick with the crisp broad leaves of the planes.

The tang of the smoke and the reek of the box
and the savor of the year's decay
are soft in the gardens of Aranjuez
where the fountains fill silently with leaves
and the moss grows over the statues and busts
clothing the simpering cupids and fauns
whose stone eyes search the empty paths

for the rustling rich brocaded gowns
and the neat silk calves of the halcyon past.

The Tagus flows with a noise of wiers through Aranjuez.
And slipping by mirrors the brown-silver trunks of the planes
    and the hedges
of box and spires of cypress and alleys of yellowing elms;
and on the other bank three grey mules pulling a cart
loaded with turnips, driven by a man in a blue woolen sash
who strides along whistling and does not look towards
    Aranjuez.

XI

Beyond ruffled velvet hills
the sky burns yellow like a candle-flame.

Sudden a village
roofs against the sky
leaping buttresses
a church
and a tower utter dark like the heart
of a candleflame.

Swing the bronze-bells
uncoiling harsh slow sound through the dusk
that growls out in the conversational clatter
Of the trainwheels and the rails.

A hill humps unexpectedly to hide
the tower erect like a pistil
in the depths of the tremendous flaming
flower of the west.

Getafe

XII

Genteel noise of Paris hats
and beards that tilt this way and that.
Mirrors create on either side
infinities of chandeliers.

The orchestra is tuning up:
Twanging of the strings of violins
groans from cellos
toodling of flutes.

Legs apart, with white fronts
the musicians stand
amiably as pelicans.

Tap. Tap. Tap.
With a silken rustle beards, hats
sink back in appropriate ecstasy.
A little girl giggles.
Crystals of infinities of chandeliers
tremble in the first long honey-savored chord.
From under a wide black hat
curving just to hide her ears
peers the little face of Juliet
of all child lovers
who loved in impossible gardens
among roses huge as moons
and twinkling constellations of jessamine,
Juliet, Isabel, Cressida,
and that unknown one who went forth at night
wandering the snarling streets of Jerusalem.

She presses her handkerchief to her mouth
to smother her profane giggling.
Her skin is browner than the tone of cellos,
flushes like with pomegranate juice.

. . . The moist laden air of a garden in Granada,
spice of leaves bruised by the sun;
she sits in a dress of crimson brocade
dark as blood under the white moon
and watches the ripples spread
in the gurgling fountain;
her lashes curve to her cheeks
as she stares wide-eyed
lips drawn against the teeth and trembling;
gravel crunches down the path;
brown in a crimson swirl
she stands with full lips
head tilted back . . . O her small breasts
against my panting breast.

Clapping. Genteel noise of Paris hats
and beards that tilt this way and that.

Her face lost in infinities of glittering chandeliers.

Ritz

XIII

There's a sound of drums and trumpets
above the rumble of the street.
(Run run run to see the soldiers.)
All alike all abreast keeping time
to the regimented swirl
of the glittering brass band.

The café waiters are craning at the door
the girl in the gloveshop is nose against the glass.
O the glitter of the brass
and the flutter of the plumes
and the tramp of the uniform feet!
Run run run to see the soldiers.

The boy with a tray
of pastries on his head
is walking fast, keeping time;
his white and yellow cakes are trembling in the sun
his cheeks are redder
and his bluestriped tunic streams
as he marches to the rum tum of the drums.
Run run run to see the soldiers.

The milkman with his pony
slung with silvery metal jars
schoolboys with their packs of books
clerks in stiff white collars
old men in cloaks
try to regiment their feet
to the glittering brass beat.
Run run run to see the soldiers.

Puerta del Sol

XIV

Night of clouds
terror of their flight across the moon.
Over the long still plains
blows a wind out of the north;
a laden wind out of the north
rattles the leaves of the liveoaks
menacingly and loud.

•   •   •   •

Black as old blood on the cold plain
close throngs spread to beyond lead horizons
swaying shrouded crowds
and their rustle in the knife-keen wind
is like the dry death-rattle of the winter grass.

(Like mouldered shrouds the clouds fall
from the crumbling skull of the dead moon.)

Huge, of grinning brass
steaming with fresh stains
their God
gapes with smudged expectant gums
above the plain.

Flicker through the flames of the wide maw
rigid square bodies of men
opulence of childbearing women
slimness of young men, and girls
with small curved breasts.

(Loud as musketry rattles the sudden laughter of the dead.)

Thicker hotter the blood drips
from the cold brass lips.

Swift over grainless fields
swift over shellplowed lands
ever leaner swifter darker
bay the hounds of the dead,
before them drive the pale ones
white limbs scarred and blackened
laurel crushed in their cold fingers,
the spark quenched in their glazed eyes.

Thicker hotter the blood drips
from the avenging lips
of the brass God;
(and rattling loud as musketry
the laughter of the unsated dead).

•   •   •   •

The clouds have blotted the haggard moon.
A harsh wind shrills from the cities of the north
Ypres, Lille, Liège, Verdun,
and from the tainted valleys
the cross-scarred hills.

Over the long still plains
the wind out of the north
rattles the leaves of the liveoaks.

Cuatro Caminos

XV

The weazened old woman without teeth
who shivers on the windy street corner
displays her roasted chestnuts invitingly
like marriageable daughters.

Calle Atocha

XVI

NOCHEBUENA

The clattering streets are bright with booths
lighted by balancing candleflames
ranged with figures in painted clay,
Virgins adoring and haloed bambinos,
St. Joseph at his joiner's bench
Judean shepherds and their sheep
camels of the Eastern kings.

Esta noche es noche buena
nadie piensa a dormir.

The streets resound with dancing
and chortle of tambourines,
strong rhythm of dancing
drumming of tambourines.

Flicker through the greenish lamplight
of the clattering cobbled streets
flushed faces of men
women in mantillas
children with dark wide eyes,
teeth flashing as they sing:

La santa Virgen es en parto
a las dos va desparir.
Esta noche es noche buena
nadie piensa a dormir.

Beetred faces of women
whose black mantillas have slipped
from their sleek and gleaming hair,
streaming faces of men.

With click of heels on the pavingstones
boys in tunics are dancing
eyes under long black lashes
flash as they dance to the drum
of tambourines beaten with elbow and palm.
A flock of girls comes running
squealing down the street.

Boys and girls are dancing
flushed and dripping dancing
to the beat on drums and piping
on flutes and jiggle
of the long notes of accordions
and the wild tune swirls and sweeps
along the frosty streets,
leaps above the dark stone houses
out among the crackling stars.

Esta noche es noche buena
nadie piensa a dormir.

In the street a ragged boy
too poor to own a tambourine
slips off his shoes and beats them together
to the drunken reeling time,
dances on his naked feet.

Esta noche es noche buena
nadie piensa a dormir.

Madrid

XVII

The old strong towers the Moors built
on the ruins of a Roman camp
have sprung into spreading boistrous foam
of daisies and alyssum flowers,
and sprout of clover and veiling grass
from out of the cracks in the tawny stones
makes velvet soft the worn stairs
and grooved walks where clanked the heels
of the grave mailed knights who had driven and killed
the darkskinned Moors,
and where on silken knees their sons
knelt on the nights of the full moon
to vow strange deeds for their lady's grace.

The old strong towers are crumbled and doddering now
and sit like old men smiling in the sun.
About them clamber the giggling flowers
and below the sceptic sea gently
laughing in daisywhite foam on the beach
rocks the ships with flapping sails
that flash white to the white village on the shore.

On a wall where the path is soft with flowers
the brown goatboy lies, his cap askew
and whistles out over the beckoning sea
the tune the village band jerks out,
a shine of brass in the square below:
a swaggering young buck of a tune
that slouches cap on one side, cigarette
at an impudent tilt, out past the old
toothless and smilingly powerless towers,
out over the ever-youthful sea
that claps bright cobalt hands in time
and laughs along the tawny beaches.

Denia

XVIII

How fine to die in Denia
young in the ardent strength of sun
calm in the burning blue of the sea
in the stabile clasp of the iron hills;
Denia where the earth is red
as rust and hills grey like ash.
O to rot into the ruddy soil
to melt into the omnipotent fire
of the young white god, the flamegod the sun,
to find swift resurrection
in the warm grapes born of earth and sun
that are crushed to must under the feet
of girls and lads,
to flow for new generations of men
a wine full of earth
of sun.

XIX

The road winds white among ashen hills
grey clouds overhead
grey sea below.
The road clings to the strong capes
hangs above the white foam-line
of unheard breakers
that edge with lace the scarf of the sea
sweeping marbled with sunlight
to the dark horizon
towards which steering intently
like ducks with red bellies
swim the black laden steamers.

The wind blows the dust of the road
and whines in the dead grass
and is silent.

I can hear my steps
and the clink of coins in one pocket
and the distant hush of the sea.

On the highroad to Villajoyosa

XX

SIERRA GUADARRAMA

TO J. G. P.

The greyish snow of the pass
is starred with the sad lilac
of autumn crocuses.

Hissing among the brown leaves
of the scruboaks
bruising the tender crocus petals
a sleetgust sweeps the pass.

The air is calm again.
Under a bulging sky motionless overhead
the mountains heave velvet black
into the cloudshut distance.

South the road winds
down a wide valley
towards stripes of rain
through which shine straw yellow
faint as a dream
the rolling lands of New Castile.

A fresh gust whines through the snowbent grass
pelting with sleet the withering crocuses,
and rustles the dry leaves of the scruboaks
with a sound as of gallop of hoofs
far away on the grey stony road
a sound as of faintly heard cavalcades
of old stern kings

climbing the cold iron passes
stopping to stare with cold hawkeyes
at the pale plain.

Puerta de Navecerrada

XXI

Soft as smoke are the blue green pines
in the misty lavender twilight
yellow as flame the flame-shaped poplars
whose dead leaves fall
vaguely spinning through the tinted air
till they reach the brownish mirror of the stream
where they are borne a tremulous pale fleet
over gleaming ripples to the sudden dark
beneath the Roman bridge.

Forever it stands the Roman bridge
a firm strong arch in the purple mist
and ever the yellow leaves are swirled
into the darkness beneath
where echoes forever the tramp of feet
of the weary feet that bore
the Eagles and the Law.

And through the misty lavender twilight
the leaves of the poplars fall and float
with the silent stream to the deep night
beneath the Roman bridge.

Cercedilla

XXII

In the velvet calm of long grey slopes of snow
the silky crunch of my steps.
About me vague dark circles of mountains
secret, listening in the intimate silence.

Bleating of sheep, the bark of a dog
and, dun-yellow in the snow
a long flock straggles.
Crying of lambs,
twitching noses of snowflecked ewes,
the proud curved horns of a regal broadgirthed ram,
yellow backs steaming;
then, tails and tracks in the snow,
and the responsible lope of the dog
who stops with a paw lifted to look back
at the baked apple face of the shepherd.

Cercedilla

XXIII

JULIET

You were beside me on the stony path
down from the mountain.

And I was the rain that lashed such flame into your cheeks
and the sensuous rolling hills
where the mists clung like garments.

I was the sadness that came out of the languid rain
and the soft dove-tinted hills
and choked you with the harsh embrace of a lover
so that you almost sobbed.

Siete Picos

XXIV

When they sang as they marched in step
on the long path that wound to the valley
I followed lonely in silence.

When they sat and laughed by the hearth
where our damp clothes steamed in the flare
of the noisy prancing flames

I sat still in the shadow
for their language was strange to me.

But when as they slept I sat
and watched by the door of the cabin
I was not lonely
for they lay with quiet faces
stroked by the friendly tongues
of the silent firelight
and outside the white stars swarmed
like gnats about a lamp in autumn
an intelligible song.

Cercedilla

XXV

I lie among green rocks
on the thyme-scented mountain.
The thistledown clouds and the sky
grey-white and grey-violet
are mirrored in your dark eyes
as in the changing pools of the mountain.

I have made for your head
a wreath of livid crocuses.
How strange they are the wan lilac crocuses
against your dark smooth skin
in the intense black of your wind-towseled hair.

Sleet from the high snowfields
snaps a lash down the mountain
bruising the withered petals
of the last crocuses.

I am alone in the swirling mist
beside the frozen pools of the mountain.

La Maliciosa

XXVI

Infinities away already
are your very slender body
and the tremendous dark of your eyes
where once beyond the laughingness of childhood,
came a breath of jessamine prophetic of summer,
a sudden flutter of yellow butterflies
above dark pools.

Shall I take down my books
and weave from that glance a romance
and build tinsel thrones for you
out of old poets' fancies?

Shall I fashion a temple about you
where to burn out my life like frankincense
till you tower dark behind the sultry veil
huge as Isis?

Or shall I go back to childhood
remembering butterflies in sunny fields
to cower with you when the chilling shadow fleets
across the friendly sun?

Bordeaux

XXVII

And neither did Beatrice and Dante . . .
But Beatrice they say
was a convention.

November, 1916–February, 1917.

Nights at Bassano

I

DIRGE OF THE EMPRESS TAITU OF ABYSSINIA

And when the news of the Death of the Empress of that Far Country did come to them, they fashioned of her an Image in doleful wise and poured out Rum and Marsala Sack and divers Liquors such as were procurable in that place into Cannikins to do her Honor and did wake and keen and make moan most piteously to hear. And that Night were there many Marvels and Prodigies observed; the Welkin was near consumed with fire and Spirits and Banashees grumbled and wailed above the roof and many that were in that place hid themselves in Dens and Burrows in the ground. Of the swanlike and grievously melodious Ditties the Minstrels fashioned in that fearsome Night these only are preserved for the Admiration of the Age.

i

Our lady lies on a brave high bed,
On pillows of gold with gold baboons
On red silk deftly embroidered—
O anger and eggs and candlelight—
Her gold-specked eyes have little sight.

Our lady cries on a brave high bed;
The golden light of the candles licks
The crown of gold on her frizzly head—
O candles and angry eggs so white—
Her gold-specked eyes are sharp with fright.

Our lady sighs till the high bed creaks;
The golden candles gutter and sway
In the swirling dark the dark priest speaks—
O his eyes are white as eggs with fright
—Our lady will die twixt night and night.

Our lady lies on a brave high bed;
The golden crown has slipped from her head
On the pillows crimson embroidered—
O baboons writhing in candlelight—
Her gold-specked soul has taken flight.

II

ZABAGLIONE

Champagne-colored
Deepening to tawniness
As the throats of nightingales
Strangled for Nero's supper.

Champagne-colored
Like the coverlet of Dudloysha
At the Hotel Continental.

Thick to the lips and velvety
Scented of rum and vanilla
Oversweet, oversoft, overstrong,
Full of froth of fascination,
Drink to be drunk of Isoldes
Sunk in champagne-colored couches
While Tristans with fair flowing hair
And round cheeks rosy as cherubs
Stand and stretch their arms,
And let their great slow tears
Roll and fall,
And splash in the huge gold cups.

And behind the scenes with his sleeves rolled up,
Grandiloquently
Kurwenal beats the eggs
Into spuming symphonic splendor
Champagne-colored.

Red-nosed gnomes roll and tumble
Tussle and jumble in the firelight
Roll on their backs spinning rotundly,
Out of earthern jars
Gloriously gurgitating,
Wriggling their huge round bellies.

And the air of the cave is heavy
With steaming Marsala and rum
And hot bruised vanilla.

Champagne-colored, one lies in a velvetiness
Of yellow moths stirring faintly tickling wings
One is heavy and full of languor
And sleep is a champagne-colored coverlet,
the champagne-colored stockings of Venus . . .
And later
One goes
And pukes beautifully beneath the moon,
Champagne-colored.

II

ODE TO ENNUI

The autumn leaves that this morning danced with the wind,
curtseying in slow minuettes,
giddily whirling in bacchanals,
balancing, hesitant, tiptoe,
while the wind whispered of distant hills,
and clouds like white sails, sailing
in limpid green ice-colored skies,
have crossed the picket fence
and the three strands of barbed wire;
they have leapt the green picket fence
despite the sentry's bayonet.

Under the direction of a corporal
three soldiers in khaki are sweeping them up,
sweeping up the autumn leaves,

crimson maple leaves, splotched with saffron,
ochre and cream,
brown leaves of horse-chestnuts . . .
and the leaves dance and curtsey round the brooms,
full of mirth,
wistful of the journey the wind promised them.

This morning the leaves fluttered gaudily,
reckless, giddy from the wind's dances,
over the green picket fence
and the three strands of barbed wire.
Now they are swept up
and put in a garbage can
with cigarette butts
and chewed-out quids of tobacco,
burnt matches, old socks, torn daily papers,
and dust from the soldiers' blankets.

And the wind blows tauntingly
over the mouth of the garbage can,
whispering, Far away,
mockingly, Far away . . .
And I too am swept up
and put in a garbage can
with smoked cigarette ash
and chewed-out quids of tobacco;
I am fallen into the dominion
of the great dusty queen . . .
Ennui, iron goddess, cobweb-clothed
goddess of all useless things,
of attics cluttered with old chairs
for centuries unsatupon,
of strong limbs wriggling on office stools,
of ancient cab-horses and cabs
that sleep all day in silent sunny squares,
of camps bound with barbed wire,
and green picket fences—
bind my eyes with your close dust
choke my ears with your grey cobwebs
that I may not see the clouds

that sail away across the sky,
far away, tauntingly,
that I may not hear the wind
that mocks and whispers and is gone
in pursuit of the horizon.

III

TIVOLI

TO D. P.

The ropes of the litter creak and groan
As the bearers turn down the steep path;
Pebbles scuttle under slipping feet.
But the Roman poet lies back confident
On his magenta cushions and mattresses,
Thinks of Greek bronzes
At the sight of the straining backs of his slaves.

The slaves' breasts shine with sweat,
And they draw deep breaths of the cooler air
As they lurch through tunnel after tunnel of leaves.
At last, where the spray swirls like smoke,
And the river roars in a cauldron of green,
The poet feels his fat arms quiver
And his eyes and ears drowned and exalted
In the reverberance of the fall.

The ropes of the litter creak and groan,
The embroidered curtains, moist with spray,
Flutter in the poet's face;
Pebbles scuttle under slipping feet
As the slaves strain up the path again,
And the Roman poet lies back confident
Among silk cushions of gold and magenta,
His hands clasped across his mountainous belly,
Thinking of the sibyll and fate,
And gorgeous and garlanded death,
Mouthing hexameters.

But I, my belly full and burning as the sun
With the good white wine of the Alban hills
Stumble down the path
Into the cool green and the roar,
And wonder, and am abashed.

IV

VENICE

The doge goes down in state to the sea
To inspect with beady traders' eyes
New cargoes from Crete, Mytilene,
Cyprus and Joppa, galleys piled
With bales off which in all the days
Of sailing the sea-wind has not blown
The dust of Arabian caravans.

In velvet the doge goes down to the sea.
And sniffs the dusty bales of spice
Pepper from Cathay, nard and musk,
Strange marbles from ruined cities, packed
In unfamiliar-scented straw.
Black slaves sweat and grin in the sun.
Marmosets pull at the pompous gowns
Of burgesses. Parrots scream
And cling swaying to the ochre bales . . .

Dazzle of the rising dust of trade
Smell of pitch and straining slaves . . .

And out on the green tide towards the sea
Drift the rinds of orient fruits
Strange to the lips, bitter and sweet.

V

ASOLO GATE

The air is drenched to the stars
With fragrance of flowering grape
Where the hills hunch up from the plain
To the purple dark ridges that sweep
Towards the flowery-pale peaks and the snow.

Faint as the peaks in the glister of starlight,
A figure on a silver-tinkling snow-white mule
Climbs the steeply twining stony road
Through murmuring vineyards to the gate
That gaps with black the wan starlight.

The watchman on his three-legged stool
Drowses in his beard, dreams
He is a boy walking with strong strides
Of slender thighs down a wet road,
Where flakes of violet-colored April sky
Have brimmed the many puddles till the road
Is as a tattered path across another sky.

The watchman on his threelegged stool,
Sits snoring in his beard;
His dream is full of flowers massed in meadowland,
Of larks and thrushes singing in the dawn,
Of touch of women's lips and twining hands,
And madness of the sprouting spring . . .
His ears a-sudden ring with the shrill cry:
Open watchman of the gate,
It is I, the Cyprian.

—It is ruled by the burghers of this town
Of Asolo, that from sundown
To dawn no stranger shall come in,
Be he even emperor, or doge's kin.
—Open, watchman of the gate,
It is I, the Cyprian.

—Much scandal has been made of late
By wandering women in this town.
The laws forbid the opening of the gate
Till next day once the sun is down.
—Watchman know that I who wait
Am Queen of Jerusalem, Queen
Of Cypress, Lady of Asolo, friend
Of the Doge and the Venetian State.

There is a sound of drums, and torches' flare
Dims the star-swarm, and war-horns' braying
Drowns the fiddling of crickets in the wall,
Hoofs strike fire on the flinty road,
Mules in damasked silk caparisoned
Climb in long train, strange shadows in torchlight,
The road that winds to the city gate.

The watchman, fumbling with his keys,
Mumbles in his beard:—Had thought
She was another Cyprian, strange the dreams
That come when one has eaten tripe.
The great gates creak and groan,
The hinges shriek, and the Queen's white mule
Stalks slowly through.

The watchman, in the shadow of the wall,
Looks out with heavy eyes:—Strange,
What cavalcade is this that clatters into Asolo?
These are not men-at-arms,
These ruddy boys with vineleaves in their hair!
That great-bellied one no seneschal
Can be, astride an ass so gauntily!
Virgin Mother! Saints! They wear no clothes!

And through the gate a warm wind blows,
A dizzying perfume of the grape,
And a great throng crying Cypris,
Cyprian, with cymbals crashing and a shriek
Of Thessalian pipes, and swaying of torches,

That smell hot like wineskins of resin,
That flare on arms empurpled and hot cheeks,
And full shouting lips vermillion-red.

Youths and girls with streaming hair
Pelting the night with flowers:
Yellow blooms of Adonis, white
scented stars of pale Narcissus,
Mad incense of the blooming vine,
And carmine passion of pomegranate blooms.

A-sudden all the strummings of the night,
All the insect-stirrings, all the rustlings
Of budding leaves, the sing-song
Of waters brightly gurgling through meadowland,
Are shouting with the shouting throng,
Crying Cypris, Cyprian,
Queen of the seafoam, Queen of the budding year,
Queen of eyes that flame and hands that twine,
Return to us, return from the fields of asphodel.

And all the grey town of Asolo
Is full of lutes and songs of love,
And vows exchanged from balcony to balcony
Across the singing streets . . .
But in the garden of the nunnery,
Of the sisters of poverty, daughters of dust,
The cock crows. The cock crows.

The watchman rubs his old ribbed brow:
Through the gate, in silk all dusty from the road,
Into the grey town asleep under the stars,
On tired mules and lean old war-horses
Comes a crowd of quarrelling men-at-arms
After a much-veiled lady with a falcon on her wrist.
—This Asolo? What a nasty silent town
He sends me to, that dull old doge.

And you, watchman, I've told you thrice
That I am Cypress's Queen, Jerusalem's,

And Lady of this dull village, Asolo;
Tend your gates better. Are you deaf,
That you stand blinking at me, pulling at your dirty beard?
You shall be thrashed, when I rule Asolo.
—What strange dreams, mumbled in his beard
The ancient watchman, come from eating tripe.

VI

HARLEQUINADE

Shrilly whispering down the lanes
That serpent through the ancient night,
They, the scoffers, the scornful of chains,
Stride their turbulent flight.

The stars spin steel above their heads
In the shut irrevocable sky;
Gnarled thorn-branches tear to shreds
Their cloaks of pageantry.

A wind blows bitter in the grey,
Chills the sweat on throbbing cheeks,
And tugs the gaudy rags away
From their lean bleeding knees.

Their laughter startles the scarlet dawn
Among a tangled spiderwork
Of girdered steel, and shrills forlorn
And dies in the rasp of wheels.

Whirling like gay prints that whirl
In tatters of squalid gaudiness,
Borne with dung and dust in the swirl
Of wind down the endless street,

With thin lips laughing bitterly,
Through the day smeared in sooty smoke
That pours from each red chimney,
They speed unseemily.

Women with unlustered hair,
Men with huge ugly hands of oil,
Children, impudently stare
And point derisive hands.

Only . . . where a barrel organ thrills
Two small peak-chested girls to dance,
And among the iron clatter spills
A swiftening rhythmy song,

They march in velvet silkslashed hose,
Strumming guitars and mellow lutes,
Strutting pointed Spanish toes,
A stately company.

VII

TO THE MEMORY OF DEBUSSY

Good Friday, 1918.

This is the feast of death
We make of our pain God;
We worship the nails and the rod
and pain's last choking breath
and the bleeding rack of the cross.

The women have wept away their tears,
with red eyes turned on death, and loss
of friends and kindred, have left the biers
flowerless, and bound their heads in their blank veils,
and climbed the steep slope of Golgotha; fails
at last the wail of their bereavement,
and all the jagged world of rocks and desert places
stands before their racked sightless faces,
as any ice-sea silent.

This is the feast of conquering death.
The beaten flesh worships the swishing rod.
The lacerated body bows to its God,
adores the last agonies of breath.

And one more has joined the unnumbered
deathstruck multitudes
who with the loved of old have slumbered
ages long, where broods
Earth the beneficent goddess,
the ultimate queen of quietness,
taker of all worn souls and bodies
back into the womb of her first nothingness.

But ours, who in the iron night remain,
ours the need, the pain
of his departing.
He had lived on out of a happier age
into our strident torture-cage.
He still could sing
of quiet gardens under rain
and clouds and the huge sky
and pale deliciousness that is nearly pain.
His was a new minstrelsy:
strange plaints brought home out of the rich east,
twanging songs from Tartar caravans,
hints of the sounds that ceased
with the stilling dawn, wailings of the night,
echoes of the web of mystery that spans
the world between the failing and the rising of the wan
        daylight
of the sea, and of a woman's hair
hanging gorgeous down a dungeon wall,
evening falling on Tintagel,
love lost in the mist of old despair.

Against the bars of our torture-cage
we beat out our poor lives in vain.
We live on cramped in an iron age
like prisoners of old
high on the world's battlements
exposed until we die to the chilling rain
crouched and chattering from cold
for all scorn to stare at.
And we watch one by one the great
stroll leisurely out of the western gate

and without a backward look at the strident city
drink down the stirrup-cup of fate
embrace the last obscurity.

We worship the nails and the rod
and pain's last choking breath.
We make of our pain God.
This is the feast of death.

VIII

PALINODE OF VICTORY

Beer is free to soldiers
In every bar and tavern
As the regiments victorious
March under garlands to the city square.

Beer is free to soldiers
And lips are free, and women,
Breathless, stand on tiptoe
To see the flushed young thousands in advance.

"Beer is free to soldiers;
Give all to the liberators" . . .
Under wreaths of laurel
And small and large flags fluttering, victorious,
They of the frock-coats, with clink of official chains,
Are welcoming with eloquence outpouring
The liberating thousands, the victorious;
In their speaking is a soaring of great phrases,
Balloons of tissue paper,
Hung with patriotic bunting,
That rise serene into the blue,
While the crowds with necks uptilted
Gaze at their upward soaring
Till they vanish in the blue;
And each man feels the blood of life
Rumble in his ears important
With participation in Events.

But not the fluttering of great flags
Or the brass bands blaring, victorious,
Or the speeches of persons in frock coats,
Who pause for the handclapping of crowds,
Not the stamp of men and women dancing,
Or the bubbling of beer in the taverns,—
Frothy mugs free for the victorious—,
Not all the trombone-droning of Events,
Can drown the inextinguishable laughter of the gods.

And they hear it, the old hooded houses,
The great creaking peak-gabled houses,
That gossip and chuckle to each other
Across the clattering streets;
They hear it, the old great gates,
The grey gates with towers,
Where in the changing shrill winds of the years
Have groaned the poles of many various-colored banners.
The poplars of the high-road hear it,
From their trembling twigs comes a dry laughing,
As they lean towards the glare of the city.
And the old hard-laughing paving-stones,
Old stones weary with the weariness
Of the labor of men's footsteps,
Hear it as they quake and clamour
Under the garlanded wheels of the yawning confident cannon
That are dragged victorious through the flutter of the city.

Beer is free to soldiers,
Bubbles on wind-parched lips,
Moistens easy kisses
Lavished on the liberators.

Beer is free to soldiers
All night in steaming bars,
In halls delirious with dancing
That spill their music into thronging streets.

—All is free to soldiers,
To the weary heroes
Who have bled, and soaked
The whole earth in their sacrificial blood,
Who have with their bare flesh clogged
The crazy wheels of Juggernaut,
Freed the peoples from the dragon that devoured them,
That scorched with greed their pleasant fields and villages,
Their quiet delightful places:

So they of the frock-coats, amid wreaths and flags victorious,
To the crowds in the flaring squares,
And a murmurous applause
Rises like smoke to mingle in the sky
With the crashing of the bells.

But, resounding in the sky,
Louder than the tramp of feet,
Louder than the crash of bells,
Louder than the blare of bands, victorious,
Shrieks the inextinguishable laughter of the gods.

The old houses rock with it,
And wag their great peaked heads,
The old gates shake,
And the pavings ring with it,
As with the iron tramp of old fighters,
As with the clank of heels of the victorious,
By long ages vanquished.
The spouts in the gurgling fountains
Wrinkle their shiny griffin faces,
Splash the rhythm in their ice-fringed basins—
Of the inextinguishable laughter of the gods.

And far up into the inky sky,
Where great trailing clouds stride across the world,
Darkening the spired cities,
And the villages folded in the hollows of hills,
And the shining cincture of railways,
And the pale white twining roads,

Sounds with the stir of quiet monotonous breath
Of men and women stretched out sleeping,
Sounds with the thin wail of pain
Of hurt things huddled in darkness,
Sounds with the victorious racket
Of speeches and soldiers drinking,
Sounds with the silence of the swarming dead—
The inextinguishable laughter of the gods.

IX

O I would take my pen and write
In might of words
A pounding dithyramb
Alight with teasing fires of hate,
Or drone to numbness in the spell
Of old loves long lived away
A drowsy vilanelle.
O I would build an Ark of words,
A safe ciborium where to lay
The secret soul of loveliness.
O I would weave of words in rhythm
A gaudily wrought pall
For the curious cataphalque of fate.

But my pen does otherwise.

All I can write is the orange tinct with crimson
of the beaks of the goose
and of the wet webbed feet of the geese
that crackle the skimming of ice
and curve their white plump necks to the water
in the manure-stained rivulet
that runs down the broad village street;
and of their cantankerous dancings and hissings,
with beaks tilted up, half open
and necks stiffly extended;
and the curé's habit blowing in the stinging wind
and his red globular face

like a great sausage burst in the cooking
that smiles
as he takes the shovel hat off his head with a gesture,
the hat held at arm's length,
sweeping a broad curve, like a censor well swung;
and, beyond the last grey gabled house in the village,
the gaunt Christ
that stretches bony arms and tortured hands
to embrace the broad lands leprous with cold
the furrowed fields and the meadows
and the sprouting oats
ghostly beneath the grey bitter blanket of hoarfrost.

Sausheim

X

In a hall on Olympus we held carouse,
Sat dining through the warm spring night,
Spilling of the crocus-colored wine
Glass after brimming glass to rouse
The ghosts that dwell in books to flight
Of word and image that, divine,
In the draining of a glass would tear
The lies from off reality,
And the world in gaudy chaos spread
Naked-new in the throbbing flare
Of songs of long-fled spirits;—free
For the wanderer devious roads to tread.

Names waved as banners in our talk:
Lucretius, his master, all men who to balk
The fear that shrivels us in choking rinds
Have thrown their souls like pollen to the winds,
Erasmus, Bruno who burned in Rome, Voltaire,
All those whose lightning laughter cleaned the air
Of the minds of men from the murk of fear-sprung gods,
And straightened the backs bowed under the rulers' rods.

A hall full of the wine and chant of old songs,
Smelling of lilacs and early roses and night,
Clamorous with the names and phrases of the throngs
Of the garlanded dead, and with glasses pledged to the light
Of the dawning to come . . .

O in the morning we would go
Out into the drudging world and sing
And shout down dustblinded streets, hollo
From hill to hill, and our thought fling
Abroad through all the drowsy earth
To wake the sleeper and the worker and the jailed
In walls cemented of lies to mirth
And dancing joy; laughingly unveiled
From the sick mist of fear to run naked and leap
And shake the nations from their snoring sleep.

O in the morning we would go
Fantastically arrayed
In silk and scarlet braid,
In rich glitter like the sun on snow
With banners of orange, vermillion, black,
And jasper-handed swords,
Anklets and tinkling gauds
Of topaz set twistingly, or lac
Laid over with charms of demons' heads
In indigo and gold.
Our going a music bold
Would be, behind us the twanging threads
Of mad guitars, the wail of lutes
In wildest harmony;
Lilting thumping free,
Pipes and kettledrums and flutes
And brazen braying trumpet-calls
Would wake each work-drowsed town
And shake it in laughter down,
Untuning in dust the shuttered walls.

O in the morning we would go
With doleful steps so dragging and slow
And grievous mockery of woe
And bury the old gods where they lay
Sodden drunk with men's pain in the day,
In the dawn's first new burning white ray
That would shrivel like dead leaves the sacred lies,
The avengers, the graspers, the wringers of sighs,
Of blood from men's work-twisted hands, from their eyes
Of tears without hope . . . But in the burning day
Of the dawn we would see them brooding to slay,
In a great wind whirled like dead leaves away.

In a hall on Olympus we held carouse,
In our talk as banners waving names,
Songs, phrases of the garlanded dead.

Yesterday I went back to that house . . .
Guttered candles where were flames,
Shattered dust-grey glasses instead
Of the fiery crocus-colored wine,
Silence, cobwebs and a mouse
Nibbling nibbling the moulded bread
Those spring nights dipped in vintage divine
In the dawnward chanting of our last carouse.

1918–1919

Vagones de Tercera

Hard on your rump
Bump bump
Hard on your bump
Bump bump

I

O the savage munching of the long dark train
crunching up the miles
crunching up the long slopes and the hills
that crouch and sprawl through the night
like animals asleep,
gulping the winking towns
and the shadow-brimmed valleys
where lone trees twist their thorny arms.

The smoke flares red and yellow;
the smoke curls like a long dragon's tongue
over the broken lands.

The train with teeth flashing
gnaws through the piecrust of hills and plains
greedy of horizons.

Alcazar de San Juan

II

TO R. H.

I invite all the gods to dine
on the hard benches of my third class coach
that joggles over brown uplands
dragged at the end of a rattling train.

I invite all the gods to dine,
great gods and small gods, gods of air
and earth and sea, and of the grey land
where among ghostly rubbish heaps and cast-out things
linger the strengthless dead.

I invite all the gods to dine,
Jehovah and Crepitus and Sebek,
the slimy crocodile . . . But no;
wait . . . I revoke the invitation.

For I have seen you, crowding gods,
hungry gods. You have a drab official look.
You have your pockets full of bills,
claims for indemnity, for incense unsniffed
since men first jumped up in their sleep
and drove you out of doors.

Let me instead, O djinn that sows the stars
and tunes the strings of the violin,
have fifty lyric poets,
not pale parson folk, occasional sonneteers,
but sturdy fellows who ride dolphins,
who need no wine to make them drunk,
who do not fear to meet red death at the meanads' hands
or to have their heads at last
float vine-crowned on the Thracian sea.

Anacreon, a partridge-wing?
A sip of wine, Simonides?
Algy has gobbled all the pastry
and left none for the Elizabethans
who come arm in arm, singing bawdy songs,
smelling of sack, from the Mermaid. Ronsard,
will you eat nothing, only sniff roses?
Those Anthologists have husky appetites!
There's nothing left but a green banana
unless that galleon comes from Venily
with Hillyer breakfasts wrapped in sonnet-paper.

But they've all brought gods with them!
Avaunt! Take them away, O djinn
that paints the clouds and brings in the night
in the rumble and clatter of the train
cadences out of the past . . . Did you not see
how each saved a bit out of the banquet
to take home and burn in quiet to his god?

Madrid, Caceres, Portugal

III

Three little harlots
with artificial roses in their hair
each at a window of a third-class coach
on the train from Zafra to the fair.

Too much powder and too much paint
shining black hair.
One sings to the clatter of wheels
a swaying unending song
that trails across the crimson slopes
and the blue ranks of olives
and the green ranks of vines.
Three little harlots
on the train from Zafra to the fair.

The plowman drops the traces
on the shambling oxen's backs
turns his head and stares
wistfully after the train.

The mule-boy stops his mules
shows his white teeth and shouts
a word, then urges dejectedly
the mules to the road again.

The stout farmer on his horse
straightens his broad felt hat,
makes the horse leap, and waves
grandiosely after the train.

Is it that the queen Astarte
strides across the fallow lands
to fertilize the swelling grapes
amid shrieking of her corybants?

Too much powder and too much paint
shining black hair.
Three little harlots
on the train from Zafra to the fair.

Sevilla—Merida

IV

My desires have gone a-hunting,
circle through the fields and sniff along the hedges,
hounds that have lost the scent.

Outside, behind the white swirling patterns of coalsmoke,
hunched fruit-trees slide by
slowly pirouetting,
and poplars and aspens on tiptoe
peer over each other's shoulders
at the long black rattling train;
colts sniff and fling their heels in air
across the dusty meadows,
and the sun now and then
looks with vague interest through the clouds
at the blonde harvest mottled with poppies,
and the Joseph's cloak of fields, neatly sewn together with
        hedges,
that hides the grisly skeleton
of the elemental earth.

My mad desires
circle through the fields and sniff along the hedges,
hounds that have lost the scent.

Misto

V

VIRGEN DE LAS ANGUSTIAS

The street is full of drums
and shuffle of slow moving feet.
Above the roofs in the shaking towers
the bells yawn.

The street is full of drums
and shuffle of slow moving feet.
The flanks of the houses glow
with the warm glow of candles,
and above the upturned faces,
crowned, robed in a cone-shaped robe
of vast dark folds glittering with gold,
swaying on the necks of men, swaying
with the strong throb of drums,
haltingly she advances.

What manner of woman are you,
borne in triumph on the necks of men,
you who look bitterly
at the dead man on your knees,
while your foot in an embroidered slipper
tramples the new moon?

Haltingly she advances,
swaying above the upturned faces
and the shuffling feet.

In the dark unthought-of years
men carried you thus
down streets where drums throbbed
and torches flared,
bore you triumphantly,
mourner and queen,
followed you with shuffling feet
and upturned faces.
You it was who sat
in the swirl of your robes

at the granary door,
and brought the orange maize
black with mildew
or fat with milk, to the harvest:
and made the ewes
to swell with twin lambs,
or bleating, to sicken among the nibbling flock.
You wept the dead youth
laid lank and white in the empty hut,
sat scarring your cheeks with the dark-cowled women.
You brought the women safe
through the shrieks and the shuddering pain
of the birth of a child;
and, when the sprouting spring
poured fire in the blood of the young men,
and made the he-goats dance stiff-legged
in the sloping thyme-scented pastures,
you were the full-lipped wanton enchantress
who led on moonless nights,
when it was very dark in the high valleys,
the boys from the villages
to find the herd-girls among the munching sweet-breathed
    cattle
beside their fires of thyme-sticks,
on their soft beds of sweet-fern.

Many names have they called you,
Lady of laughing and weeping,
shuffling after you, borne
on the necks of men down town streets
with drums and red torches:
dolorous one, weeping the dead
youth of the year ever dying,
or full-breasted empress of summer,
Lady of the Corybants
and the headlong routs
that maddened with cymbals and shouting
the hot nights of amorous languor
when the gardens swooned under the scent
of jessamine and nard.

You were the slim-waisted Lady of Doves,
you were Ishtar and Ashtaroth,
for whom the Canaanite girls
gave up their earrings and anklets and their own slender
      bodies,
you were the dolorous Isis,
and Aphrodite.
It was you who on the Syrian shore
mourned the brown limbs of the boy Adonis.
You were the queen of the crescent moon,
the Lady of Ephesus,
giver of riches,
for whom the great temple
reeked with burning and spices.
And now in the late bitter years,
your head is bowed with bitterness;
across your knees lies the lank body
of the Crucified.

Rockets shriek and roar and burst
against the velvet sky;
the wind flutters the candle-flames
above the long white slanting candles.

Swaying above the upturned faces
to the strong throb of drums,
borne in triumph on the necks of men,
crowned, robed in a cone-shaped robe
of vast dark folds glittering with gold
haltingly, through the pulsing streets,
advances Mary, Virgin of Pain.

Granada

VI
TO R. J.

It would be fun, you said,
sitting two years ago at this same table,
at this same white marble café table,
if people only knew what fun it would be
to laugh the hatred out of soldiers' eyes . . .

—If I drink beer with my enemy,
you said, and put your lips to the long glass,
and give him what he wants, if he wants it so hard
that he would kill me for it,
I rather think he'd give it back to me—
You laughed, and stretched your long legs out across the
    floor.

I wonder in what mood you died,
out there in that great muddy butcher-shop,
on that meaningless dicing-table of death.
Did you laugh aloud at the futility,
and drink death down in a long draught,
as you drank your beer two years ago
at this same white marble café table?
Or had the darkness drowned you?

Café Oro del Rhin
Plaza de Santa Ana

VII

Down the road
against the blue haze
that hangs before the great ribbed forms of the mountains
people come home from the fields;
they pass a moment in relief
against the amber frieze of the sunset
before turning the bend
towards the twinkling smoke-breathing village.

A boy in sandals with brown dusty legs
and brown cheeks where the flush of evening
has left its stain of wine.
A donkey with a jingling bell
and ears askew.
Old women with waterjars

of red burnt earth.
Men bent double under burdens of faggots
that trail behind them the fragrance
of scorched uplands.
A child tugging at the end of a string
a much inflated sow.
A slender girl who presses to her breast
big bluefrilled cabbages.
And a shepherd in the clinging rags of his cloak
who walks with lithe unhurried stride
behind the crowded backs of his flock.

The road is empty
only the swaying tufts of oliveboughs
against the fading sky.

Down on the steep hillside
a man still follows the yoke
of lumbering oxen
plowing the heavy crimson-stained soil
while the chill silver mists
steal up about him.

I stand in the empty road
and feel in my arms and thighs
the strain of his body
as he leans far to one side
and wrenches the plow from the furrow,
feel my blood throb in time to his slow careful steps
as he follows the plow in the furrow.
Red earth
giver of all things
of the yellow grain and the oil
and the wine to all gods sacred
of the fragrant sticks that crackle in the hearth
and the crisp swaying grass
that swells to dripping the udders of the cows,
of the jessamine the girls stick in their hair
when they walk in twos and threes in the moonlight,

and of the pallid autumnal crocuses . . .
are there no fields yet to plow?
Are there no fields yet to plow
where with sweat and straining of muscles
good things may be wrung from the earth
and brown limbs going home tired through the evening?

Lanjaron

VIII

O such a night for scaling garden walls;
to push the rose shoots silently aside
and pause a moment where the water falls
into the fountain, softly troubling the wide
bridge of stars tremblingly mirrored there
terror-pale and shaking as the real stars shake
in crystal fear lest the rustle of silence break
with a watchdog's barking.

O to scale the garden wall and fling
my life into the bowl of an adventure,
stake on the silver dice the past and future
forget the odds and lying in the garden sing
in time to the flutter of the waiting stars
madness of love for the slender ivory white
of her body hidden among dark silks where
is languidest the attar weighted air.
To drink in one strong jessamine scented draught
sadness of flesh, twining madness of the night.

O such a night for scaling garden walls;
yet I lie alone in my narrow bed
and stare at the blank walls, forever afraid,
of a watchdog's barking.

Granada

IX

Rain-swelled the clouds of winter
drag themselves like purple swine across the plain.
On the trees the leaves hang dripping
fast dripping away all the warm glamour
all the ceremonial paint of gorgeous bountiful autumn.

The black wet boles are vacant and dead.
Among the trampled leaves already mud
rot the husks of the rich nuts. On the hills
the snow has frozen the last pale crocuses
and the winds have robbed the smell of the thyme.

Down the wet streets of the town
from doors where the light spills out orange
over the shining irregular cobbles
and dances in ripples on gurgling gutters;
sounds the zambomba.

In the room beside the slanting street
round the tray of glowing coals
in their stained blue clothes, dusty
with the dust of workshops and factories,
the men and boys sit quiet;
their large hands dangle idly
or rest open on their knees
and they talk in soft tired voices.
Crosslegged in a corner a child with brown hands
sounds the zambomba.

Outside down the purple street
stopping sometimes at a door, breathing deep
the heady wine of sunset, stride with clattering steps
those to whom the time will never come
of work-stiffened unrestless hands.

The rain-swelled clouds of winter roam
like a herd of swine over the town and the dark plain.
The wineshops full of shuffling and talk, tanned faces

bright eyes, moist lips moulding desires
blow breaths of strong wine in the faces of passersby.

There are guards in the storehouse doors
where are gathered the rich fruits of autumn, the grain
the sweet figs and raisins; sullen blood tingling to madness
they stride by who have not reaped.
Sounds the zambomba.

Albaicin

X

The train throbs doggedly
over the gleaming rails
fleeing the light-green flanks of hills
dappled with alternate shadow of clouds,
fleeing the white froth of orchards,
of clusters of apples and cherries in flower,
fleeing the wide lush meadows,
wealthy with cowslips,
and the tramping horses and backward-strained bodies of
        plowmen,
fleeing the gleam of the sky in puddles and glittering waters
the train throbs doggedly
over the ceaseless rails
spurning the verdant grace
of April's dainty apparel;
so do my desires
spurn those things which are behind
in hunger of horizons.

Rapido: Valencia–Barcelona 1919—1920

Quai de la Tournelle

I

See how the frail white pagodas of blossom
stand up on the great green hills
of the chestnuts
and how the sun has burned the wintry murk
and all the stale odor of anguish
out of the sky
so that the swollen clouds bellying with sail
can parade in pomp like white galleons.

And they move the slow plumed clouds
above the spidery grey webs of cities
above fields full of golden chime
of cowslips
above warbling woods where the ditches
are wistfully patined
with primroses pale as the new moon
above hills all golden with gorse
and gardens frothed
to the brim of their grey stone walls
with apple bloom, cherry bloom,
and the raspberry-stained bloom of peaches and almonds.

So do the plumed clouds sail
swelling with satiny pomp of parade
towards somewhere far away
where in a sparkling silver sea
full of little flakes of indigo
the great salt waves have heaved and stirred
into blossoming of foam,
and lifted on the rush of the warm wind
towards the gardens and the spring-mad cities of the shore
Aphrodite Aphrodite is reborn.

And even in this city park
galled with iron rails
shrill with the clanging of ironbound wheels
on the pavings of the unquiet streets,
little children run and dance and sing
with spring-madness in the sun,
and the frail white pagodas of blossom
stand up on the great green hills
of the chestnuts
and all their tiers of tiny gargoyle faces
stick out gold and red-striped tongues
in derision of the silly things of men.

Jardin du Luxembourg

II

The shadows make strange streaks and mottled arabesques
of violet on the apricot-tinged walks
where the thin sunlight lies
like flower-petals.

On the cool wind there is a fragrance
indefinable
of strawberries crushed in deep woods.

And the flushed sunlight,
the wistful patterns of shadow
on gravel walks between tall elms
and broad-leaved lindens,
the stretch of country,
yellow and green,
full of little particolored houses,
and the faint intangible sky,
have lumped my soggy misery,
like clay in the brown deft hands of a potter,
and moulded a song of it.

Saint Germain-en-Laye

III

In the dark the river spins,
Laughs and ripples never ceasing,
Swells to gurgle under arches,
Swishes past the bows of barges,
in its haste to swirl away
From the stone walls of the city
That has lamps that weight the eddies
Down with snaky silver glitter,
As it flies it calls me with it
Through the meadows to the sea.

I close the door on it, draw the bolts,
Climb the stairs to my silent room;
But through the window that swings open
Comes again its shuttle-song,
Spinning love and night and madness,
Madness of the spring at sea.

IV

The streets are full of lilacs
lilacs in boys' buttonholes
lilacs at women's waists;
arms full of lilacs, people trail behind them through the moist
    night
long swirls of fragrance,
fragrance of gardens
fragrance of hedgerows where they have wandered
all the May day
where the lovers have held each others hands
and lavished vermillion kisses
under the portent of the swaying plumes
of the funeral lilacs.

The streets are full of lilacs
that trail long swirls and eddies of fragrance
arabesques of fragrance

like the arabesques that form and fade
in the fleeting ripples of the jade-green river.

Porte Maillot

V

As a gardener in a pond
splendid with lotus and Indian nenuphar
wades to his waist in the warm black water
stooping to this side and that to cull the snaky stems
of the floating white glittering lilies
groping to break the harsh stems of the imperious lotus
lifting the huge flowers high
in a cluster in his hand
till they droop against the moon;
so I grope through the streets of the night
culling out of the pool
of the spring-reeking, rain-reeking city
gestures and faces.

Place St. Michel

VI

TO A. K. MC C.

This is a garden
where through the russet mist of clustered trees
and strewn November leaves,
they crunch with vainglorious heels
of ancient vermillion
the dry dead of spent summer's greens,
and stalk with mincing sceptic steps
and sound of snuffboxes snapping
to the capping of an epigram,
in fluffy attar-scented wigs . . .
the exquisite Augustans.

Tuileries

VII

They come from the fields flushed
carrying bunches of limp flowers
they plucked on teeming meadows
and moist banks scented of mushrooms.

They come from the fields tired
softness of flowers in their eyes
and moisture of rank sprouting meadows.

They stroll back with tired steps
lips still soft with the softness of petals
voices faint with the whisper of woods;
and they wander through the darkling streets
full of stench of bodies and clothes and merchandise
full of the hard hum of iron things;
and into their cheeks that the wind had burned and the sun
that kisses burned out on the rustling meadows
into their cheeks soft with lazy caresses
comes sultry
caged breath of panthers
fetid, uneasy
fury of love sprouting hot in the dust and stench
of walls and clothes and merchandise,
pent in the stridence of the twilight streets.

And they look with terror in each other's eyes
and part their hot hands stained with grasses and flowerstalks
and are afraid of their kisses.

VIII

EMBARQUEMENT POUR CYTHERE

AFTER WATTEAU

The mists have veiled the far end of the lake
this sullen amber afternoon;
our island is quite hidden, and the peaks
hang wan as clouds above the ruddy haze.

Come, give your hand that lies so limp,
a tuberose among brown oak-leaves;
put your hand in mine and let us leave
this bank where we have lain the day long.

In the boat the naked oarsman stands.
Let us walk faster, or do you fear to tear
that brocaded dress in apricot and grey?
Love, there are silk cushions in the stern
maroon and apple-green,
crocus-yellow, crimson, amber-grey.
We will lie and listen to the waves
slap soft against the prow, and watch the boy
slant his brown body to the long oar-stroke.

But, love, we are more beautiful than he.
We have forgotten the grey sick yearning nights
brushed off the old cobwebs of desire;
we stand strong
immortal as the slender brown boy who waits
to row our boat to the island.

But love how your steps drag.

And what is this bundle of worn brocades I press
so passionately to me? Old rags of the past,
snippings of Helen's dress, of Melisande's,
scarfs of old paramours rotted in the grave
ages and ages since.

No lake
the ink yawns at me from the writing table.

IX

LA RUE DU TEMPS PASSE

Far away where the tall grey houses fade
A lamp blooms dully through the dusk,
Through the effacing dusk that gently veils

The traceried balconies and the wreaths
Carved above the shuttered windows
Of forgotten houses.

Behind one of the crumbled garden walls
A pale woman sits in drooping black
And stares with uncomprehending eyes
At the thorny angled twigs that bore
Years ago in the moon-spun dusk
One scarlet rose.

In an old high room where the shadows troop
On tiptoe across the creaking boards
A shrivelled man covers endless sheets
Rounding out in his flourishing hand
Sentence after sentence loud
With dead kings' names.

Looking out at the vast grey violet dusk
A pale boy sits in a window, a book
Wide open on his knees, and fears
With cold choked fear the thronging lives
That lurk in the shadows and fill the dusk
With menacing steps.

Far away the gaslamp glows dull gold
A vague tulip in the misty night,
The clattering drone of a distant tram
Grows loud and fades with a hum of wires
Leaving the street breathless with silence, chill
And the listening houses.

Bordeaux

X

O douce Sainte Geneviève
ramène moi a ta ville, Paris.

In the smoke of morning the bridges
are dusted with orangy sunshine.

Bending their black smokestacks far back
muddling themselves in their spiralling smoke
the tugboats pass under the bridges
and behind them
stately
gliding smooth like clouds
the barges come
black barges
with blunt prows spurning the water gently
gently rebuffing the opulent wavelets
of opal and topaz and sapphire,
barges casually come from far towns
towards far towns unhurryingly bound.
The tugboats shrieks and shrieks again
calling beyond the next bend and away.
In the smoke of morning the bridges
are dusted with orangy sunshine.

O douce Sainte Geneviève
ramène moi a ta ville, Paris.

Big hairy-hoofed horses are drawing
carts loaded with flour-sacks,
white flour-sacks, bluish
in the ruddy flush of the morning streets.

On one cart two boys perch
wrestling and their arms and faces
glow ruddy against the white flour-sacks
as the sun against the flour-white sky.

O douce Sainte Geneviève
ramène moi a ta ville, Paris.

Under the arcade
loud as castanettes with steps
of little women hurrying to work
an old hag who has a mole on her chin
that is tufted with long white hairs
sells incense-sticks, and the trail of their strangeness lingers

in the many-scented streets
among the smells of markets and peaches
and the must of old books from the quays
and the warmth of early-roasting coffee.

The old hag's incense has smothered
the timid scent of wild strawberries
and triumphantly mingled with the strong reek from the river
of green slime along stonework of docks
and the pitch-caulked decks of barges,
barges casually come from far towns
towards far towns unhurryingly bound.

O douce Sainte Geneviève
ramène moi a ta ville, Paris.

XI

A L'OMBRE DES JEUNES FILLES EN FLEURS

And now when I think of you
I see you on your piano-stool
finger the ineffectual bright keys
and even in the pinkish parlor glow
your eyes sea-grey are very wide
as if they carried the reflection
of mocking black pinebranches
and unclimbed red-purple mountains mist-tattered
under a violet-gleaming evening.

But chirruping of marriageable girls
voices of eager, wise virgins,
no lamp unlit every wick well trimmed,
fill the pinkish parlor chairs,
bobbing hats and shrill tinkling teacups
in circle after circle about you
so that I can no longer see your eyes.

Shall I tear down the pinkish curtains
smash the imitation ivory keyboard
that you may pluck with bare fingers on the strings?

I sit cramped in my chair.
Futility tumbles everlastingly
like great flabby snowflakes about me.

Were they in your eyes, or mine
the tattered mists about the mountains
and the pitiless grey sea?

1919

On Foreign Travel

I

Grey riverbanks in the dusk
Melting away into mist
A hard breeze sharp off the sea
The ship's screws' lunge and throb
And the voices of sailors singing.

O I have come wandering
Out of the dust of many lands
Ears by all tongues jangled
Feet worn by all arduous ways—
O the voices of sailors singing.

What nostalgia of sea
And free new-scented spaces
dreams of towns vermillion-gated
Must be in their blood as in mine
That the sailors long so in singing.

Churned water marbled astern
Grey riverbanks in the dusk
Melting away into mist
And a shrill wind hard off the sea.
O the voices of sailors singing.

II

Padding lunge of a camel's stride
turning the sharp purple flints. A man sings:

Breast deep in the dawn
a queen of the east;
the woolen folds of her robe

hang white and straight
as the hard marble columns
of the temple of Jove.

A thousand days
the pebbles have scuttled
under the great pads of my camels.

A thousand days
like bite of sour apples
have been bitter with desire in my mouth.

A thousand days
of cramped legs flecked
with green slobber of dromedaries.

At the crest of the road
that transfixes the sun
she awaits
me lean with desire
with muscles tightened
by these thousand days
pallid with dust
sinewy
naked before her.

Padding lunge of a camel's stride
over the flint-strewn hills. A man sings:

I have heard men sing songs
of how in scarlet pools
in the west in purpurate mist
that bursts from the sun trodden
like a grape under the feet of darkness
a woman with great breasts
thighs white like wintry mountains
bathes her nakedness.

I have lain biting my cheeks
many nights with ears murmurous
with the songs of these strange men.
My arms have stung as if burned
by the touch of red ants with anguish
to circle strokingly
her bulging smooth body.
My blood has soured to gall.
The ten toes of my feet are hard
as buzzards' claws from the stones
of roads, from clambering
cold rockfaces of hills.
For uncountable days' journeys
jouncing on the humps of camels
iron horizons have swayed
like the rail of a ship at sea
mountains have tossed like wine
shaken hard in a wine cup.

I have heard men sing songs
of the scarlet pools of the sunset.

Two men, bundled pyramids of brown
abreast, bow to the long slouch
of their slowstriding camels.
Shrilly the yellow man sings:

In the courts of Han
green fowls with carmine tails
peck at the yellow grain
court ladies scatter
with tiny ivory hands,
the tails of the fowls
droop with multiple elegance
over the wan blue stones
as the hands of courtladies
droop on the goldstiffened silk
of their angular flower-embroidered dresses.

In the courts of Han
little hairy dogs
are taught to bark twice
at the mention of the name of Confucius.

The twittering of the women
that hop like silly birds
through the courts of Han
became sharp like little pins
in my ears, their hands in my hands
rigid like small ivory scoops
to scoop up mustard with
when I had heard the songs
of the western pools where the great queen
is throned on a purple throne
in whose vast encompassing arms
all bitter twigs of desire
burst into scarlet bloom.

Padding lunge of the camel's stride
over flint-strewn hills. The brown man sings:

On the house-encumbered hills
of great marble Rome
no man has ever counted the columns
no man has ever counted the statues
no man has ever counted the laws
sharply inscribed in plain writing
on tablets of green bronze.

At brightly lit tables
in a great brick basilica
seven hundred literate slaves
copy on rolls of thin parchment
adorned by seals and purple bows
the taut philosophical epigrams
announced by the emperor each morning
while taking his bath.

A day of rain and roaring gutters
the wine-reeking words of a drunken man
who clenched about me hard-muscled arms
and whispered with moist lips against my ear
filled me with smell and taste of spices
with harsh panting need to seek out the great
calm implacable queen of the east
who erect against sunrise holds in the folds
of her woolen robe all knowledge of delight
against whose hard white flesh my flesh
will sear to cinders in a last sheer flame.

Among the house-encumbered hills
of great marble Rome
I could no longer read the laws
inscribed on tablets of green bronze.
The maxims of the emperor's philosophy
were croaking of toads in my ears.
A day of rain and roaring gutters
the wine-reeking words of a drunken man:
. . . breast deep in the dawn
a queen of the east.

The camels growl and stretch out their necks,
their slack lips jiggle as they trot
towards a water hole in a pebbly torrent bed.

The riders pile dry twigs for a fire
and gird up their long gowns to warm
at the flame their lean galled legs.

Says the yellow man:

You have seen her in the west?

Says the brown man:

Hills and valleys
stony roads.
In the towns

the bright eyes of women
looking out from lattices.
Camps in the desert
where men passed the time of day
where were embers of fires
and greenish piles of camel-dung.

You have seen her in the east?

Says the yellow man:

Only red mountains and bare plains,
the blue smoke of villages at evening,
brown girls bathing
along banks of streams.

I have slept with no woman
only my dream.

Says the brown man:

I have looked in no woman's eyes
only stared along eastward roads.

They eat out of copper bowls beside the fire in silence.
They loose the hobbles from the knees of their camels
and shout as they jerk to their feet.
The yellow man rides west.
The brown man rides east.

Their songs trail among the split rocks of the desert.

Sings the yellow man:

I have heard men sing songs
of how in the scarlet pools
that spurt from the sun trodden
like a grape under the feet of darkness
a woman with great breasts
bathes her nakedness.

Sings the brown man:

> After a thousand days
> of cramped legs flecked
> with green slobber of dromedaries
> she awaits
> me lean with desire
> pallid with dust
> sinewy
> naked before her.

Their songs fade in the empty desert.

III

There was a king in China.

He sat in a garden under a moon of gold
while a black slave scratched his back
with a back-scratcher of emerald.
Beyond the tulip bed
where the tulips were stiff goblets of fiery wine
stood the poets in a row.

One sang the intricate patterns of snowflakes
One sang the henna-tipped breasts of girls dancing
and of yellow limbs rubbed with attar.
One sang red bows of Tartar horsemen
and whine of arrows and blood-clots on new spearshafts.
The others sang of wine and dragons coiled in purple bowls,
and one, in a droning voice
recited the maxims of Lao Tse.

(Far off at the walls of the city
groaning of drums and a clank of massed spearmen.
Gongs in the temples.)

The king sat under a moon of gold
while a black slave scratched his back
with a back-scratcher of emerald.
The long gold nails of his left hand
twined about a red tulip blotched with black,
a tulip shaped like a dragon's mouth
or the flames bellying about a pagoda of sandalwood.
The long gold nails of his right hand
were held together at the tips
in an attitude of discernment:
to award the tulip to the poet
of the poets that stood in a row.

(Gongs in the temples.
Men with hairy arms
climbing on the walls of the city.
They have red bows slung on their backs;
their hands grip new spearshafts.)

The guard of the tomb of the king's great grandfather
stood with two swords under the moon of gold.
With one sword he very carefully
slit the base of his large belly
and inserted the other and fell upon it
and sprawled beside the king's footstool.
His blood sprinkled the tulips
and the poets in a row.

(The gongs are quiet in the temples.
Men with hairy arms
scattering with taut bows through the city;
there is blood on new spearshafts.)

The long gold nails of the king's right hand
were held together at the tips
in an attitude of discernment.
The geometrical glitter of snowflakes,
the pointed breasts of yellow girls
crimson with henna,
the swirl of river-eddies about a barge

where men sit drinking,
the eternal dragon of magnificence. . . .
Beyond the tulip bed
stood the poets in a row.

The garden full of spearshafts and shouting
and the whine of arrows and the red bows of Tartars
and trampling of the sharp hoofs of war-horses.
Under the golden moon
the men with hairy arms
struck off the heads of the tulips in the tulip-bed
and of the poets in a row.

The king lifted the hand that held the flaming dragon-flower.

Him of the snowflakes, he said.
On a new white spearshaft
the men with hairy arms
spitted the king and the black slave
who scratched his back with a back-scratcher of emerald.

There was a king in China.

IV

Says the man from Weehawken to the man from Sioux City
as they jolt cheek by jowl on the bus up Broadway:
—That's her name, Olive Thomas, on the red skysign,
died of coke or somethin'
way over there in Paris.
Too much money. Awful
immoral the lives them film stars lead.

The eye of the man from Sioux City glints
in the eye of the man from Weehawken.
Awful . . . lives out of sky-signs and lust;
curtains of pink silk fluffy troubling the skin
rooms all prinkly with chandeliers,
bed cream-color with pink silk tassles

creased by the slender press of thighs.
Her eyebrows are black
her lips rubbed scarlet
breasts firm as peaches
gold curls gold against her cheeks.
She dead
all of her dead way over there in Paris.

O golden Aphrodite.

The eye of the man from Weehawken slants
away from the eye of the man from Sioux City.
They stare at the unquiet gold dripping sky-signs.

Phases of the Moon

I

Again they are plowing the field by the river;
in the air exultant a smell of wild garlic
crushed out by the shining steel in the furrow
that opens softly behind the heavy-paced horses,
dark moist noisy with fluttering of sparrows;
and their chirping and the clink of the harness
chimes like bells;
and the plowman walks at one side
with sliding steps, his body thrown back from the waist.
O the sudden sideways lift of his back and his arms
as he swings the plow from the furrow.

And behind the river sheening blue
and the white beach and the sails of schooners,
and hoarsely laughing the black crows
wheel and glint. Ha! Haha!

Other springs you answered their laughing
and shouted at them across the fallow lands
that smelt of wild garlic and pinewoods and earth.

This year the crows flap cawing overhead Ha! Haha!
and the plow-harness clinks
and the pines echo the moaning shore.

No one laughs back at the laughing crows.
No one shouts from the edge of the new-plowed field.

Sandy Point

II

The full moon soars above the misty street
filling the air with a shimmer of silver.
Roofs and chimney-pots cut silhouettes
of dark against the milk-washed sky!
O moon fast waning!

Seems only a night ago you hung
a shallow cup of topaz-colored glass
that tilted towards my feverish dry lips
brimful of promise in the flaming west:
O moon fast waning!

And each night fuller and colder, moon,
the silver has welled up within you; still I
I have not drunk, only the salt tide
of parching desires has welled up within me:
only you have attained, waning moon.
The moon soars white above the stony street,
wan with fulfilment. O will the tide
of yearning ebb with the moon's ebb
leaving me cool darkness and peace
with the moon's waning?

Madrid

III

The shrill wind scatters the bloom
of the almond trees
but under the bark of the shivering poplars
the sap rises
and on the dark twigs of the planes
buds swell.

Out in the country
along soggy banks of ditches
among busy sprouting grass
there are dandelions.

Under the asphalt
under the clamorous paving-stones
the earth heaves and stirs
and all the blind live things
expand and writhe.

Only the dead
lie still in their graves,
stiff, heiratic,
only the changeless dead
lie without stirring.

Spring is not a good time
for the dead.

Battery Park

IV

Buildings shoot rigid perpendiculars
latticed with window-gaps
into the slate sky.

Where the wind comes from
the ice crumbles
about the edges of green pools;
from the leaping of white thighs
comes a smooth and fleshly sound,
girls grip hands and dance
grey moss grows green under the beat
of feet of saffron
crocus-stained.

Where the wind comes from
purple windflowers sway
on the swelling verges of pools,
naked girls grab hands and whirl
fling heads back
stamp crimson feet.

Buildings shoot rigid perpendiculars
latticed with window-gaps
into the slate sky.

Garment-workers loaf in their overcoats
(stare at the gay breasts of pigeons
that strut and peck in the gutters).
Their fingers are bruised tugging needles
through fuzzy hot layers of cloth,
thumbs roughened twirling waxed thread;
they smell of lunchrooms and burnt cloth.
The wind goes among them
detaching sweat-smells from underclothes
making muscles itch under overcoats
tweaking legs with inklings of dancetime.

Bums on park-benches
spit and look up at the sky.
Garment-workers in their overcoats
pile back into black gaps of doors.

Where the wind comes from
scarlet windflowers sway
on rippling verges of pools,
sound of girls dancing
thud of vermillion feet.

Madison Square

V

The stars bend down
through the dingy platitude of arc-lights
as if they were groping for something among the houses,
as if they would touch the gritty pavement
covered with dust and scraps of paper and piles of horse-dung
of the wide deserted square.

They are all about me;
they sear my body.
How very cold the stars are touching my body.
What do they seek
the fierce ice-flames of the stars
in the platitude of arc-lights?

Plaza Mayor, Madrid

VI

Not willingly have I wronged you O Eros,
it is the bitter blood of joyless generations
making my fingers loosen suddenly
about the full glass of purple wine
for which my dry lips ache,
making me turn aside from the wide arms of lovers
that would have slaked the rage of my body
for supple arms and burning young flushed faces
to wander in solitary streets.

A funeral clatters over the glimmering cobbles;
they are burying despair!
Lank horses whose raw bones show through
the embroidered black caparisons
and whose heads jerk feebly
under the tall nodding crests;
they are burying despair.
A great hearse that trundles crazily along
under pompous swaying plumes
and intricate designs of mud-splashed heraldry;
they are burying despair!
A coffin obliterated under the huge folds
of a faded velvet pall
and following clattering over the cobblestones
lurching through mud-puddles
a long train of cabs
rain-soaked barouches
old landaus off which the paint has peeled

leprous coupés;
in their blank windows shines the glint
of interminable gaslamps;
they are burying despair!

Joyously I turn into the wineshop
where with strumming of tambourines
and staccato cackle of castanets
they are welcoming the new year,
and I look in the eyes of the woman;
(are they your wide eyes O Eros?)
who sits with wine-dabbled lips
and stained tinsel dress torn open
by the brown hands of strong young lovers;
(were they your brown hands O Eros?).

—Your flesh is hot to my cold hands
hot to thaw the ice of an old curse
now that with pomp of plumes and strings of ceremonial cabs
they are burying despair.

She laughs and points with a skinny forefinger
at the flabby yellow breasts that hang
over the tarnished tinsel of her dress,
and shows me her brown wolf's teeth;
and the blood in my temples goes suddenly cold
with bitterness and I know
it was not despair that they buried.

New Year's Day—Casa de Bottin

VII

The leaves are full grown now
and the lindens are in flower.
Horseshoes leave their mark
on the sun-softened asphalt.
Men unloading vegetable carts
along the steaming market curb

bare broad chests pink from sweating;
their wet shirts open to the last button
cling to their ribs and shoulders.

The leaves are full grown now
and the lindens are in flower.

At night along the riverside
glinting watery lights
sway upon the lapping waves
like many-colored candles that flicker in the wind.
The warm wind smells of pitch from the moored barges
smells of the broad leaves of the trees
wilted from the day's long heat;
smells of gas from the last taxicab.

Sounds of the riverwater rustling
circumspectly past the piers
of bridges that span the glitter with dark
of men and women's voices
many voices mouth to mouth
smoothness of flesh touching flesh,
a harsh short sigh blurred into a kiss.

The leaves are full grown now
and the lindens are in flower.

Quai Malaquais

VIII

In me somewhere is a grey room
my fathers worked through many lives to build;
through the barred distorting windowpanes
I see the new moon in the sky.

When I was small I sat and drew
endless pictures in all colors on the walls;
tomorrow the pictures should take life
I would stalk down their long heroic colonnades.

When I was fifteen a red-haired girl
went by the window; a red sunset
threw her shadow on the stiff grey wall
to burn the colors of my pictures dead.

Through all these years the walls have writhed
with shadow overlaid upon shadow.
I have bruised my fingers on the windowbars
so many lives cemented and made strong.

While the bars stand strong, outside
the great processions of men's lives go past.
Their shadows squirm distorted on my wall.

Tonight the new moon is in the sky.

Stuyvesant Square

IX

Three kites against the sunset
flaunt their long-tailed triangles
above the inquisitive chimney-pots.

A pompous ragged minstrel
sings beside our dining-table
a very old romantic song:

I love the sound of the hunting-horns
deep in the woods at night.

A wind makes dance the fine acacia leaves
and flutters the cloths of the tables.
The kites tremble and soar.
The voice throbs sugared into croaking base
broken with the burden of the too ancient songs.

And yet, beyond the flaring sky,
beyond the soaring kites,

where are no voices of singers,
no strummings of guitars,
the untarnished songs
hang like great moths just broken
through the dun threads of their cocoons,
moist, motionless, limp
as flowers on the inaccessible twigs
of the yewtree, Ygdrasil,
the untarnished songs.

Will you put your hand in mine
pompous street-singer,
and start on a quest with me?
For men have cut down the woods where the laurel grew
to build streets of frame houses,
they have dug in the hills after iron
and frightened the troll-king away;
at night in the woods no hunter puffs out his cheeks
to call to the kill on the hunting-horn.
Now when the kites flaunt bravely
their tissue-paper glory in the sunset
we will walk together down the darkening streets
beyond these tables and the sunset.

We will hear the singing of drunken men
and the songs whores sing
in their doorways at night
and the endless soft crooning
of all the mothers,
and what words the young men hum
when they walk beside the river
their arms hot with caresses,
their cheeks pressed against their girls' cheeks.

We will lean very close
to the quiet lips of the dead
and feel in our worn-out flesh perhaps
a flutter of wings as they soar from us
the untarnished songs.

But the minstrel sings as the pennies clink:
I love the sound of the hunting-horns
deep in the woods at night.

O who will go on a quest with me
beyond all wide seas
all mountain passes
and climb at last with me
among the imperishable branches
of the yewtree, Ygdrasil,
so that all the limp unuttered songs
shall spread their great moth-wings and soar
above the craning necks of the chimneys
above the tissue-paper kites and the sunset
above the diners and their dining-tables,
beat upward with strong wing-beats steadily
till they can drink the quenchless honey of the moon.

Place du Tertre

X

Dark on the blue light of the stream
the barges lie anchored under the moon.

On icegreen seas of sunset
the moon skims like a curved white sail
bellied by the evening wind
and bound for some glittering harbor
that blue hills circle
among the purple archipelagos of cloud.

So, in the quivering bubble of my memories
the schooners with peaked sails
lean athwart the low dark shore;
their sails glow apricot-color
or glint as white as the salt-bitten shells on the beach
and are curved at the tip like gulls' wings:
their courses are set for impossible oceans

where on the gold imaginary sands
they will unload their many-scented freight
of very childish dreams.

Dark on the blue light of the stream
the barges lie anchored under the moon;
the wind brings from them to my ears
faint creaking of rudder-cords, tiny slappings
of waves against their pitch-smeared flanks,
to my nose a smell of bales and merchandise
the wet familiar smell of harbors
and the old arousing fragrance
making the muscles ache and the blood seethe
and the eyes see the roadsteads and the golden beaches
where with singing they would furl the sails
of the schooners of childish dreams.

On icegreen seas of sunset
the moon skims like a curved white sail:
had I forgotten the fragrance of old dreams
that the smell from the anchored barges
can so fill my blood with bitterness
that the sight of the scudding moon
makes my eyes tingle with salt tears?

In the ship's track on the infertile sea
now many childish bodies float
rotting under the white moon.

Quai des Grands Augustins

XI

Lua cheia esta noit

Thistledown clouds
cover the whole sky
scurry on the southwest wind
over the sea and islands;

somehow in the sundown
the wind has shaken out plumed seed
of thistles milkweed asphodel,
raked from off great fields of dandelions
their ghosts of faded golden springs
and carried them in billowing of mist
to scurry in moonlight
out of the west.

They hide the moon
the whole sky is grey with them
and the waves.

They will fall in rain
over country gardens
where thrushes sing.

They will fall in rain
down long sparsely lighted streets
hiss on silvery windowpanes
moisten the lips
of girls leaning out
to stare after the footballs of young men
who splash through the glimmering puddles
with nonchalant feet.

They will slap against the windows of offices
where men in black suits
shaped like pears
rub their abdomens
against frazzled edges of ledgers.

They will drizzle
over new-plowed fields
wet the red cheeks of men harrowing
and a smell of garlic and clay
will steam from the new-sowed land
and sharp-eared young herdsmen will feel
in the windy rain
lisp of tremulous love-makings
interlaced soundless kisses

impact of dead springs
nuzzling tremulous at life
in the red sundown.

Shining spring rain
O scud steaming up out of the deep sea
full of portents of sundown and islands,
beat upon my forehead
beat upon my face and neck
glisten on my outstretched hands,
run bright lilac streams
through the clogged channels of my brain
corrode the clicking cogs the little angles
the small mistrustful mirrors
scatter the shrill tiny creaking
of mustnot darenot cannot
spatter the varnish off me
that I may stand up
my face to the wet wind
and feel my body
and drenched salty palpitant April
reborn in my flesh.

I would spit the dust out of my mouth
burst out of these stiff wire webs
supple incautious
like the crocuses that spurt up too soon
their saffron flames
and die gloriously in late blizzards
and leave no seed.

Off Pico

XII

Out of the unquiet town
seep jagged barkings
lean broken cries
unimaginable silent writhing
of muscles taut against strangling
heavy fetters of darkness.

On the pool of moonlight
clots and festers
a great scum
of worn-out sound.

   (Elagabalus, Alexander
   looked too long at the full moon;
   hot blood drowned them
   cold rivers drowned them.)

Float like pondflowers
on the dead face of darkness
cold stubs of lusts
names that glimmer ghostly
adrift on the slow tide
of old moons waned.

   (Lais of Corinth that Holbein drew
   drank the moon in a cup of wine;
   with the flame of all her lovers' pain
   she seared a sign on the tombs of the years.)

Out of the voiceless wrestle of the night
flesh rasping harsh on flesh
a tune on a shrill pipe shimmers
up like a rocket blurred in the fog
of lives curdled in the moon's glare,
staggering up like a rocket
into the steely star-sharpened night
above the stagnant moon-marshes
the song throbs soaring and dies.

   (Semiramis, Zenobia
   lay too long in the moon's glare;
   their yearning grew sere and they died
   and the flesh of their empires died.)

On the pool of moonlight
clots and festers
a great scum
of worn-out lives.

No sound but the panting unsatiated
breath that heaves under the huge pall
the livid moon has spread above the housetops.
I rest my chin on the window-ledge
and wait.
There are hands about my throat.

Ah Bilkis, Bilkis
where the jangle of your camel bells?
Bilkis when out of Saba
lope of your sharp-smelling dromedaries
will bring the unnameable strong wine
you press from the dazzle of the zenith
over the shining sand of your desert
the wine you press there in Saba?
Bilkis your voice loud above the camel bells
white sword of dawn to split the fog,
Bilkis your small strong hands to tear
the hands from about my throat.
Ah Bilkis when out of Saba?

Pera Palace

UNCOLLECTED ESSAYS
1916–1941

Against American Literature

I F ANY MOOD predominates in American writing it is that of gentle satire. This tendency to satire, usually vague and kindly, sometimes bitter with the unconvinced bitterness of a middle-aged lady who thinks herself worldly wise, is the one feature pervading all that can be called American among the mass of foreign-inspired writing in this country. Washington Irving is typical of its least significant manifestation; Edgar Lee Masters, Edith Wharton and Katherine Fullerton Gerould of its modern—and bitter—form. Search as you may, you will find little not permeated by this tone, which, chameleon-like, changes with the variations of European thought, but remains in its fundamentals always the same. And there is no doubt that up to now it has well approximated the temper of the nation, has pretty faithfully represented that genial, ineffectual, blindly energetic affair, the American soul. Strange combination of words; for until recently we have troubled very little about our *âme nationale*, leaving that sort of thing to introspective and decadent nations overseas. But even if we are unconscious of it, we have a national soul, and it is this, or at least the external of it, which is so aptly reflected by the pervading tone of our literature.

This wholesome rice-pudding fare is, unfortunately, a strangely unstimulating diet; so we are forced to give it body—like apple jack—by a stiff infusion of a stronger product. As a result of this constant need to draw on foreign sources our literature has become a hybrid which, like the mule, is barren and must be produced afresh each time by the crossing of other strains. What is the reason for this state of affairs? Much of our writing, particularly in the upper realm of the novel, the region of Edith Wharton and Robert Herrick, is sincere, careful, and full of shrewd observation of contemporary life; yet I defy anyone to confine himself for long to purely American books without feeling starved, without pining for the color and passion and profound thought of other literatures. Our books are like our cities; they are all the same.

Any other nation's literature would take a lifetime to exhaust. What then is lacking in ours?

For one thing American literature is a rootless product, a cutting from England's sturdy well branched oak tree, nurtured in the arid soil of the New England colonies, and recently transplanted to the broad lands of the Middle West. In other countries literature is the result of long evolution, based on primitive folklore, on the first joy and terror of man in the presence of the trees and scented meadowlands and dimpled whirling rivers, interwoven with the moulding fabric of old dead civilizations, and with threads of fiery new gold from incoming races. The result is glamour, depth, real pertinence to the highest and lowest in man. It is to be found, in one form or another, beneath the temporary scum of every established literature. This artistic stimulus, fervid with primitive savageries, redolent with old cults of earth and harvest, smoked and mellowed by time, is the main inheritance of the civilizations, the woof upon which individual artists may work the warp of their own thoughts.

America lacks it almost completely. The earth-feeling, the jewelled accretions of the imagination of succeeding ages, so rich in old English writing, seem to have lost their validity in the transplanting. The undercurrent, rooted in the people, often voiceless for whole epochs, which springs from the chants of Druids, from fairy-tales and terror-tales recited in wattled huts about the smoky fires of the woad-daubed Britons, and which has time and again revivified the literature of England, saved it from artificiality and courtiership, has been cut off from us. We find ourselves floundering without rudder or compass, in the sea of modern life, vaguely lit by the phosphorescent gleam of our traditional optimism. A sense of landscape, or else an imported, flushed, *erdgeist* feeling, has taken the place of the unconscious intimacy with nature—the deeper the less reflective it is—which has always lain at the soul of great writings. No ghosts hover about our fields; there are no nymphs in our fountains; there is no tradition of countless generations tilling and tending to give us reverence for those rocks and rills and templed hills so glibly mentioned in the national anthem.

The only substitute for dependence on the past is dependence on the future. Here our only poet found his true greatness. Walt Whitman abandoned the vague genteelness that had characterized American writing, the stiff product of the leisure hours of a *petite noblesse de province*, and, founding his faith on himself, on the glowing life within him, shouted genially, fervidly his challenge to the future. But, although sensibly unconventional in manners and customs, the American public desires its ideas well disciplined according to the conventions of ten years back; Walt Whitman failed to reach the people he intended to, and aroused only a confused perturbation and the sort of moral flutter experienced by a primly dressed old bachelor when a ruddy smiling Italian, smelling of garlic and sweat, plumps down beside him in the street car. Still, the day of Whitman's power may be in a rosy future, when Americans, instead of smiling with closed eyes, will look keenly before them.

Then there is the cult of the abstract. Perhaps it too grows out of our lack of root, out of our lack of spiritual kinship to the corn and wheat our fields grow, out of our inane matter-of-factness. American life, as much as an unsuccessful inventor, is occupied with smiling abstractions. This is particularly true of our religion, which under multifarious forms of Protestant Christianity is actually a muddled abstract theism. We have none of those local saints—tamed pagan gods, most of them—that have tied the Church in Europe so tightly to the people, to the soil, to the eternal powers of corn and wine and resurgent earth. One by one we have pulled from our god the garments of concreteness, the human qualities. Even the abolition of hell and the devil may have done much to tear religion from people's souls, and to place it in the chilly soil of convention where it at present languishes. There was something tangible and human about hell-fire which cannot be found in the vague notion of future harp-twanging for all "nice" people, that symbolizes most current religious faiths.

What is true of religion is true of art and literature. Worse than its lack of depth and texture is its abstractness, its lack, on the whole, of dramatic actuality. Compare say "The House of Mirth," a fairly typical American novel, with Turgenev's "Spring Freshets." The Russian stirs eyes and ears and nose and sense of touch, portrays his story with vivid tangibility; the American leaves an abstract impression of intellectual bitterness. It is not so much a question of technique as of feeling. In the same way match the dramatic power of Couperus's "Small Souls" with Mary S. Watts's "The Legacy," a novel dealing with the corresponding class of people in this country. Why should not our writers be as vivid as the Russian, express their life as dramatically as the Dutchman?

It is significant that, quite unconsciously, I chose the works of two women to typify American novels. The tone of the higher sort of writing in this country is undoubtedly that of a well brought up and intelligent woman, tolerant, versed in the things of this world, quietly humorous, but bound tightly in the fetters of "niceness," of the middle-class outlook. And when the shackles are thrown off the result is vulgarity, and, what is worse, affectation.

In all this may lie the explanation of the sudden vogue of Russian literature in this country. It has so much that our own lacks. There is the primitive savagery, the color, the romance of an age of faith suddenly burst in upon by European science, the freshness, rank and lush as the vegetation of early May. No wonder it is a relief to us Americans to turn from our prim colonial living room of thought, where the shades are drawn for fear the sun will fade the carpet Puritan ancestors laid there, to the bizarre pains and passions, to the hot moist steppe-savour of a Russian novel.

And it becomes harder every day for any race to gain the lesson of the soil. An all-enveloping industrialism, a new mode of life preparing, has broken down the old bridges leading to the past, has cut off the possibility of retreat. Our only course is to press on. Shall we pick up the glove Walt Whitman threw at the feet of posterity? Or shall we stagnate forever, the Sicily of the modern world, rich in this world's goods, absorbing the thought, patronizing the art of other peoples, but producing nothing from amid our jumble of races but steel and oil and grain?

"Well, isn't that enough?" I hear someone say.

Is the "Realistic" Theatre Obsolete?

Many Theatrical Conventions Have Been Shattered
by Lawson's "Processional"

W E MAY as well admit that for our time there are no questions of æsthetics. Least of all in the theatre, where the
problem is now one of sheer existence. It is doubtful, anyway,
if the stage will long be able to compete with the movies and
radio and subsequent mechanical means of broadcasting entertainment and propaganda. Perhaps it will follow the bison and
the dodo and the wild swan. Certainly it is among the last survivors of what might be called the arts of direct contact.

If the theatre is to subsist, it must offer something that city-
dwelling people need extremely, something matchless, that
can't be found anywhere else. A century that has to snatch its
hasty life furtively between time clock and alarm clock re-
quires the stimulant of some human externalization, warm
and glamorous and passionate, that it misses in the chilly fan-
tasmagoria of the movies or in the slightly curdled strains of
radio music. Baseball, football, and prizefights fill the bill in
one direction; jazz dancing, in another. But as America is
racked more and more by the growing-pains of conscious
adolescence, we have got to have some more organized and
purposeful expression of our loves, fears, and rages. That is
the theatre's one chance to survive.

I don't think that the people who control the theatres of
New York today quite see their peril. They do understand that
a change is coming over their audiences and that there are
breakers ahead. The danger is freely admitted of the competition set up by the movies and, more recently, by the radio,
which makes it unnecessary for people to move out of their
pigeonholes in the evening. If the theatre were on firmer
ground, there wouldn't be any competition, any more than
there is competition between shoe stores and soda fountains. If
the people connected with the stage only have the energy and
imagination, the theatres can get back their own audiences—
and more. For the theatre more than anything else welds into

a sentient whole the rigid honeycomb of our pigeonholed lives. Since religion has failed humanity, the theatre is the focus of mass emotion.

Of course, nobody can deny that a great many serious and well-intentioned people have been trying all over these United States to create a theatre and audience for the last fifteen years. Mightn't the unhappy slimness of the results be due partly to the fact that most of these people's interests have been literary rather than theatrical? The theatres that have run a successful course in various parts of the world since people went out and sat all day on the stonecut seats of an Athenian hill have had various aims and motives, but none of them have been *literary*. The fact that a lot of good and bad plays have been preserved as literature is beside the point. The plays had their real being where they were acted and applauded and hissed by the populace as spectacular and emotional entertainment and nowhere else.

Various aspiring organizations that are trying to coax the American public into taking the theatre seriously, have never quite gotten away from the point of view that plays must be regarded primarily as masterpieces of literary effort, fraught with the culture of a by-gone age. As a result, their audiences consist largely of wistful and literary-minded people who seek in culture a dope to make them dream that they live in a Never Never Land, European, decorous, and unattainable to the Man-on-the-Street, in which the Beautiful and True hold sophisticated discourse in a Louis Quinze drawing room. As long as the theatre depends on that audience, it will be more occupied with the idiotic schism between Highbrow and Lowbrow than with wringing people's minds and senses and hearts. And an audience of unsophisticated hot-blooded people can't be got by whistling for it.

The result is that the few worthwhile plays being produced round New York don't fit the frames they are presented in. At best they do no more than generate a lot of articles by the critics and a lot of superliterary conversation. They are short-circuited by the non-theatrical state of mind in which they are presented and attended.

That doesn't mean that a great deal of very noble and arduous sweeping of the boards hasn't gone on. The throb of the drum in *The Emperor Jones* cleared many a pair of ears that had been until that time tuned only to suburban comedy. The chesty roar of *The Hairy Ape* made several people forget to read how The Well Dressed Man would wear his cravat. Among many frustrated searchers after messages a few people, at least, sat up and felt terror and awe and a speeding up of the blood from the Dead People's Ball in *The Crime in the Whistler Room*. On top of all these comes *Processional* (John Howard Lawson's jazz play, produced by the Theatre Guild) as the straw to break the camel's back of the literary drama.

First it must be admitted that the audience of the best people that gasped when the curtain went up on Gorelik's painted drop to the sound of the Yankee Doodle Blues was only restrained by its all-too-evident good breeding and its respect for ART, in whatever aspect that puzzling divinity might show itself—and perhaps a trifle by its natural inertia—from rising *en masse* and shouting this noisy gibberish off the stage. Many of those cultured and educated people, warmers of orchestra chairs six nights a week, had never seen theatre before. Naturally they were shocked. We have been brought up to believe that the first convention of the theatre is that the events take place in a room, one side of which is imagined to be transparent. The audience, by the power of illusion, believes that what it sees going on on the stage really exists in the world of actuality. The great triumph of the realistic theatre was when people put their umbrellas up coming out of *Rain*. I don't mean to underrate the things that have been done under that convention; a great many of its effects are more natural than nature—like glass flowers.

But there is another sort of theatre. On a wooden platform in a hall actors perform acts. Trained seals would be the simplest illustration of this; a ballet like Stravinsky's *Noces*, one more subtle, complex, and intensely humanized. Instead of the illusion of "reality", its aim is to put on a show which creates in a hall full of people its own reality of glamor and significance.

Processional is the first American play in our generation in which the convention of the invisible fourth wall has been frankly and definitely abandoned. In other plays, the subterfuge of a dream has been used to placate the critics whenever the author felt he needed to be positively theatrical. In *The Hairy Ape* we were told that it was all subjective, inside the man's mind. Meanwhile burlesque, musical comedy, and vaudeville have preserved, but more or less flippantly, the real manners and modes of the theatre. In *Processional*, these are employed with passionate seriousness. The actors are actors, you feel the boards of the stage in every line, events take place against painted scenery, behind footlights, in the theatre. There is no attempt to convince the audience that, by some extraordinary series of coincidences, they have strayed into a West Virginia mining town in the middle of an industrial war. They are in a theatre seeing a show.

But why, everybody asks, go back to the humdrum and hokum of the Ten-Twenty-Thirty when we are just beginning to convince intelligent people, readers of *The World*, subscribers to *Vanity Fair*, book buyers, theatre lovers, art collectors, that what they want is Adult Entertainment, real life honestly set down? Even the most friendly critics label *Processional*'s most genuinely theatrical moments as satire and think that the author is poking fun at them. Actually, crude and comic and grotesque as many of the scenes intentionally are, the play is a very unsophisticated attempt to invade the audience's feelings by the most direct and simple means that come to hand. The fact that it does move and excite us, and succeeds thereby in reinstating the stage, makes it extraordinarily important.

The movies have made the theatre of the transparent fourth wall unnecessary and obsolete, just as photography has made obsolete a certain sort of painting. The camera and screen can transport the audience into circumstances, in the ordinary sense, real. It can show you what people who have been there recognize as West Virginia. The theatre can only bungle at it clumsily. Therefore, if the theatre is going to survive, it has got to find for itself a new function. Of course it is perfectly natural that the first attempt to climb wholeheartedly out of the blind alley of realism should be received with horror and consternation. American audiences are pathetically afraid of being moved either in space or time or in their feelings. That invited crowd the first night at the Garrick had the face of a maiden aunt who has been unwillingly coaxed by a small boy to take a ride on a roller coaster. They felt sick and held on desperately and prayed that it would stop. But as a trip to Coney Island on a Sunday afternoon will show you, there are a great many people in New York who are crazy to ride on roller coasters. Most of them have given up going to the theatre because they don't feel they get their money's worth. So far, "advanced", "serious", "highbrow" plays have been aimed at the intellectual audience that wants something to talk about at a dinner or a tea. *Processional* is aimed at the people who like roller coasters. Perhaps in its whole run only ten people who genuinely desire motion will go to see it. Those ten people will be the nucleus of the audience of a theatre that will have nothing to fear from the competition of the radio or of the movies.

Processional is the Uncle Tom's Cabin of the new American Theatre.

Vanity Fair, May 1925

Paint the Revolution!

Even Cortez clanking across the dykes on his warhorse is said to have been struck by the beauty of the markets of Tenochtitlan. Your first morning in the City of Mexico. The sunlight and the bright thin air, the Indian women sitting like stone idols behind their piles of fruit or their bunches of flowers, the sculpture on old red colonial buildings and the painting on the pulque shops, all tie you up into such a knot of vivid sights that you start sprouting eyes in the nape of your neck.

Going to see the paintings of Diego Rivera in the courts of the Secretaria of public education straightens you out a little bit. They give a dramatic sequence to all this brightness and white glitter, to the terribly silent welling up of life everywhere. In tense earth colors that have a dull burnish to them he has drawn the bending of bodies at work, the hunch of the shoulders under picks and shovels of men going down into a mine, the strain and heave of a black body bent under a block of marble, men working at looms, in dye-vats, spooning out molten metal. Then there are the plodding dust-colored soldiers of the revolution, red flags and black flags of the Zapatistas, crowds in marketplaces, women hanging out washing, politicians making speeches, Indians dancing. Everywhere the symbol of the hammer and sickle. Some of it's pretty hasty, some of it's garlanded tropical bombast, but by God, it's painting.

Go round to the art galleries in New York. Look at all the little pictures, little landscapes after Cezanne, Renoir, Courbet, Picasso, Corot, Titian, little fruity still lifes, little modern designs of a stovepipe and a bisected violin . . . stuff a man's afraid to be seen looking at . . . a horrible picking up of crumbs from rich men's tables. Occasionally a work of real talent, but what's the good of it? Who sees it? A lot of male and female old women chattering round an exhibition; and then, if the snobmarket has been properly manipulated, some damn fool buys it and puts it away in the attic, and it makes a brief reappearance when he dies at a sale at the Anderson Galleries.

"A lotta hunk this revolution stuff in Mexico," said the salesman of brewing machinery coming down on the train from Laredo. "Peons don't know nothin' . . . It's only a lot of politicians fighting for the swag, when they're not hired by the oil companies. Why people down here don't know what the word means." He got off at Saltillo before I could find out from him what the word did mean.

And there's not only the Secretaria of education. When you're through looking at the three stories of frescoed walls, probably a good half mile of them, setting down in passionate hieroglyphics every phase of the revolution, you can go to the superb baroque building of the Preparatoria where Clemente Orozco is working. Orozco was a cartoonist and started with a bitter set of lampoons on the bourgeoisie; but as he worked he became a painter. His panels express each one an idea with a fierce concentration and economy of planes and forms I've never seen anywhere except in the work of the old Italian Cimabue. Again the revolution, soldiers and peasants and workingmen and the sibylline faces of old countrywomen. Over the doors the sickle and hammer. Imagine a sickle and hammer painted (in three dimensions, no Willy Pogany pastels of Progressive Evolution as in the Rand School), over the door of the Columbia University library.

And that's not all. Roberto Montenegro is filling the walls of another school with a sober and lilting decoration. There's a library dedicated to Ibero-American Unity decorated by him with a huge map of South America and Mexico where the U.S. is left in anomalous darkness. And everybody complains that the good old days are over, that nobody is painting any more.

As a matter of fact the Sindicato de Obreros Tecnicos, the painters' and sculptors' union, that was the center of this huge explosion of creative work, has broken up. Everything that happened, happened in two years. In 1923 Diego Rivera came back from Europe, full of Picasso and Derain and the plaint of artists pampered and scantily fed by the after-the-war bourgeoisie. (In New York at that time we were trying to be modern and see the beauty of the Woolworth Building and sighing for the first Independents and the days of the, oh, so lovely Sienese tablas of Spumone degli Spaghetti.) He found an

enormously rich and uncorrupted popular art in textiles and
pottery and toys and in the decoration of ginmills, a lot of
young painters fresh from the heartbreaking campaigns of
civil war and eager to justify the ways of Marx to man, and
José Vasconcelos as head of the department of education.

After Felipe Carillo, the great leader of Yucatan, had made
a speech to the liberated Mayas, outlining a Socialist commonwealth, someone went up to him and said the speech was
worthy of Lenin. "Fine," he answered, "who's he?"

It wasn't a case of ideas, of a lot of propaganda-fed people
deciding that a little revolutionary art would be a good thing,
it was a case of organic necessity. The revolution, no more
imported from Russia than the petate hats the soldiers wore,
had to be explained to the people. The people couldn't read.
So the only thing to do was to paint it up on the wall.

So some thirty painters started a union, affiliated themselves
with the Third International, and set to work. Everyone was to
get the same wage for painting, a cooperative studio was to be
started; "its fundamental aesthetic aim was rooted in the so-
cialization of art, tending towards the absolute disappearance
of individualism, characteristic of bourgeois epochs, thus ap-
proaching the great collective art of antiquity." As a basis of
study they took the remains of ancient Mexican painting and
sculpture. Easel painting they rejected as intellectual, aristocratic and onanistic. But this isn't the first time that painters
have issued a manifesto. The extraordinary thing about this
group is that they set to work and delivered the goods.

Xavier Guerrero went down to Teotihuacan and studied the
methods of the ancient Indian painters there. They made
chemical analyses of the pigments and varnishes used and after
much experimentation, began to paint. Diego Rivera's first big
decorative work had been in encaustica, in which he had been
experimenting in Paris. Vasconcelos, whose boast was that he
would spend as much on education as the war department
spent on the army, was ready to give any competent painter
wall space, a small wage, and materials. And so in an incredibly short time an enormous amount of work, not only in the
capital, but in Jalapa and Guadalajara as well, was under way.

All this time there had been growing opposition. The
students of the Preparatoria, sons of haciendados and oil-

splattered politicians, objected to this new style of painting, and set about destroying the frescoes. The hammers and sickles over the doors made them uneasy. Intellectuals and newspaper writers, whose idea of painting was a chic girl drawn a la *Vie Parisienne* with sensually dark smudges under the eyes, kept up a continual hammering under which the Government began to weaken. Vasconcelos left the ministry of education. The Union broke up in personal squabbles, largely owing to the fact that to continue working under the Laborista government it became necessary to give up the Third International. Now Rivera, Orozco and Montenegro are the only three painters subsidized by the Federal government. The rest of them pick up a living as best they can in the provinces. Several of them are carrying on lively communist propaganda, through *El Machete*, which started as the Union's mouthpiece.

But, even if nothing more is done, an enormous amount of real work has been accomplished. Even if the paintings were rotten it would have been worth while to prove that in our day a popular graphic art was possible. Maybe it's not possible anywhere but in Mexico. As it is, Rivera's paintings in the Secretaria, Orozco's paintings in the Preparatoria, Montenegro's decorations are a challenge shouted in the face of the rest of the world. You're a painter? All right, let's see what you can do with a wall a hundred by sixteen and a lot of homely doors and windows in it.

All we have in New York to answer with are a few private sensations and experiments framed and exhibited here and there, a few watercolors like Marin's, and a lot of warmed-over truck, leavings of European fads.

If it isn't a revolution in Mexico, I'd like to know what it is.

New Masses, March 1927

A City That Died by Heartfailure

C ITIES are like men except that they live longer. Like men
they suffer from diseases, they are carried off young by
consumption; in old age they die slowly of cancer or hardening
of the arteries. Sometimes heartfailure or murder does them in
in a few days. That's what we debated walking under the empty
grey colonnades of Savona: was it murder or heartfailure?

X, Y and Z had found themselves as a result of a train of
circumstances running in a rakish twenty foot sloop before a
heavy wind that became a gale fit to read about in the papers.
X like Jesus was asleep in the cabin. By the time they were all
awake and had got over their sense of speed and the joy of
skimming through the moonlight between sea and sky it was
too late to take in the balloon jib and the clouds had buried
the moon. Eventually they found themselves at anchor in an
L in the breakwater of Savona in the full sweep of the wind,
yelling in various languages for a tugboat. The trouble was
that they were outside instead of inside the breakwater. The
tugboat came and the sloop, drenched and shuddering, was
towed into the harbor.

The harbor was full of gaunt steamers under the driving
rain. Here and there an arclight hung over the rainpocked
water. They had lost their author outside, so they had to tie up
against a bulky bark. Then, feverish with fatigue, they crowded
into the gutted cabin and rolled as best they could in damp
blankets and each fell down his individual elevatorshaft into
sleep.

In the morning dragging ourselves unshaven out of the
overwarmth of damp beds we climbed over the slippery rail of
the pale green bark we were tied up against, staggered across
a plank and were standing in the full untiring rain on a long
empty quay in front of big black houses with staring windows.
We walked along sniffing the wind for breakfast, turned hopefully up a long imposing arcaded street. It was as empty as
one of those painted perspectives you see on the off side of
old Lombard buildings. Then it was that X up and spoke out
his mind: The trouble with this town is it's dead.

From that time on it was an autopsy. Once warmed with coffee they asked the waiter why the street was so deserted. It wasn't deserted, the waiter replied, pointing to a thin and knockkneed black kitten that was padding across the car track. At the same moment at the end of the street a trolleycar appeared. All watched it breathless. It drew near and rattled past and turned a corner. It was empty.

Y had been in Savona during the war and had made lengthy speeches coming up the coast on its gaiety and charm, the crowded streets, the painted facades. As they followed the interminable arcade towards the station and the Albergo Diurno, he was razzed about it. He played for time; it was too early, he said, and at any rate it was raining.

In the Albergo Diurno they fell on our necks. They ran hot baths, they unlocked the doors of waterclosets, they offered to clean our shoes. The cashier was thin as a rail, had a touch of jaundice and spoke a few words of the language of Brooklyn. No, he admitted, business wasn't good, too much politics. Then there was the boycott.

Not even Sunday brought much change. A few automobiles turned out, there were people outside the movie theatres. What movement there was rattled round in the big arcaded streets. X noticed that the storekeepers sat with their backs to the doors, discouraged fat women knitting or dosing. When you went in they got up with a start. Gradually it began to seep in to us that everybody started when you spoke to them, people walked as if they were being followed, talked as if they felt they were being overheard; it was a town with the heebyjeebies.

Sunday afternoon we took to architecture. We were staring at the doorway of an old house where probably some rich shipowner had lived before the town had knuckled down to Genoa, when a pale sparrowlike little man whom we all immediately knew to be a schoolteacher, spoke to us in French. Round the corner of the next street there were more doorways and entrancehalls and ceilings. He would show them to us. From that we fell talking and little by little he made us look at all there was of antique splendor, a few old towers, carved staircases, a couple of painted ceilings, by the sea a huge fortress rising out of the rusty litter of a partly deserted foundry. In the fort we waited a long while in an upper court-yard very daintily painted and decorated with colored lights for the regimental festa while officers in skyblue cloaks, after a great deal of talking and scraping and bowing on the part of our little professor, fetched us a permit from the colonel to see the dungeon where Mazzini had been imprisoned, and from which he escaped. Coming out of the fortress X popped the question: What's the matter with the town? The little pro-fessor winced and said that there was nothing the matter with the town. Of course there was not quite the movement there used to be, but . . . And that was all we could get out of him.

One night a travelling circus performed manfully before the thinnest sprinkling of people in a cavernous mouldy green hall that had probably once been a vaudeville theatre. The ring was in the orchestra. There were chairs on the stage and round the edges. All the performers doubled; they worked like demons. The ushers reappeared as clowns. The man who did the bicycle trick sold seats and was the Swiss bellringer, the hind legs of the elephant did a dog and pony act. The Spartans that died at Thermopylae never stood up more proudly in a chilly, cringing world than did that circus. X, Y and Z came out warm and tingling from the company of heroes and walked gaily through the long, discouraged streets towards the harbor.

They stopped in front of an unexpectedly shining cafe that was crowded with people, that had bay trees in front of it. A smell of brasspolish and prosperity and rum punch came out of it. They went in past a resplendent bar. The room was full of young men with long frizzy hair, intellectual-looking young men playing chess. From upstairs came a sound of billiards. Everybody had an air of assurance that this cafe was *the right place.* They had no sooner sat down than a stout, redfaced, pigeyed, young man came over to them, with a big hand outstretched, a big hand unexpectedly soft when you shook it.

"Shake the hand that this morning shook the hand of Il Duce . . . at Parma. Yes we know who you are. It was a fascista who saved your lives by telephoning for the tug-boat. A nasty storm, a ticklish situation . . . No, thank you, couldn't drink anything . . . Well . . . Tonio, a creme de menthe . . . You see I'm very hoarse, worn out . . . Thirty five hours on the train . . . It was a magnificent manifestation. You see I had to go, I'm chief of a squadron of blackshirts . . . No I didn't speak, not this time. Ah what a man, Mussolini, what a handshake he has, he draws you towards him when he shakes your hand."

"Ask him," said X, "what's the matter with the town, why are all those freighters laid up in the habor, why aren't there any automobiles."

"Automobiles, there are thousands of automobiles . . . Ah the port. There's been a little trouble there. It was boycotted by the syndicate of maritime workers. There were a great many communists. It's only recently that the purification of the city has been complete."

"I should say it was."

"Yes, it was a fascista saved your lives. Last summer at Alassio an American was saved from drowning by a fascista. He paid a thousand lire into the party treasury to show his gratitude."

There was a silence. The chief of the blackshirt squadron sipped his creme de menthe, and looked at us with lire in his eyes.

"You understand we have many expenses. We have to travel all the time to go to conventions and manifestations. That all costs money. We have to keep up the dignity of our position. The rich people here are stingy, they stay in their houses, they never come out. Why the owners of casini 'll give more in contributions than the bankers. We get something out of the shopkeepers though." He leaned back in his chair and laughed showing all his teeth. "They have to give . . . The workpeople here are rotten with foreign ideas; they'd rather emigrate to France. But things are improving." He tapped himself on the chest. "We have borne the brunt of the work of purification . . . Colonel come over here," he called to a one-legged man in a long tightwaisted raincoat who stood at the bar. "There are the Americans."

The colonel stumped over to our table leaning on a heavy cane. He had stringy, black hair cut straight below his ears, and a gaunt twisted face. "He's listed for complete disability from the war. Show them . . ." The colonel held up a crimson, clawlike hand. The wrist had a hole through it between the two bones. At the same time he jiggled his wooden leg. "He's very brave and a dead shot with a revolver. He's bagged more communists than anybody."

Walking back to the boat through the silent purified streets of Savona, Z, who was from Odessa, said, "That man is exactly the type of a local Bolshevik boss." That was a hard morsel to swallow for one member of the party. After gagging a little he said it was a damn lie.

"When honest men start shooting each other up, it's always the things come out on top," said X in a philosophical tone.

"Pretty raw though about the thousand lire."

"If we don't get out of here soon they'll try to purify us," said Y, and recalled the itching palm that had been pressed to Il Duce's.

The tiny white cabin of the boat was snug and separate from the gaunt empty town, pleasant to go to bed in. The great hulks of abandoned freighters stood up all round cutting into black oblongs and upsidedown triangles the diffuse glare of scattered arc lights. It was pleasant to snuggle under the blankets in the narrow bunk and think that tomorrow we'd haul up the anchor and show a dainty pair of black heels to that great mass of brokenhearted stone and iron, and to the blackshirts who had purified it until there were no more workers.

The Lantern, February 1928

Edison and Steinmetz:
Medicine Men

Edison, His Life and Inventions, by Frank Lewis Dyer, Thomas Cummerford Martin and William Henry Meadowcroft. New York: Harper and Brothers. 2 vols. 1036 pages. $10.

Loki: The Life of Charles Proteus Steinmetz, by Jonathan Norton Leonard. New York: Doubleday, Doran and Company. 291 pages. $2.75.

Forty Years with General Electric, by John T. Broderick. Fort Orange Press. 218 pages. $2.50.

THE BOOK on Edison is the old-fashioned perfunctory two-volume life, evidently first published about 1910 and now revamped. In spite of much meaningless bombast and chapters so badly written that they convey no idea whatsoever, it has a full account of Edison's inventions, and contains much information (a little too much on the Horatio Alger side perhaps) about Edison's early life that should be interesting to anybody who wants to know about the personalities that created the world we live in today.

"Loki" is the up-to-date version of the same sort of thing. It attempts to be pithy and epigrammatic and to have the fashionable air that now seems to be considered necessary in biographies. The book contains some extremely interesting photographs that make it almost worth owning and are infinitely more informative than the text. A good deal of time is spent in glossing over Steinmetz's eccentricities, of which Socialism seems to have been the most sinful and glaring.

"Forty Years with General Electric" is as uninstructive as a book could well be. Still, the report of several conversations with Steinmetz gives it a certain historical value.

If the foregoing paragraphs seem grouchy and impertinent, it is due to the bitterness of a great many futile hours spent grubbing in the literature of the last fifty years of American industrial development. You have to read these books to believe how muddle-headed, ill-written and flatly meaningless they can be. You'd think that any youngster in a high-school composition course could do better with the material in hand.

For one thing, the writing was usually left to hired hacks and publicity men. The people who were actually doing the work had no time and no inclination to put themselves down on paper. But even if they had, I doubt if the result would have been very different. The men who counted in our national development during the last half-century seem hardly to have used the analytic or coordinating centers of their brains at all. They carried practicality to a point verging on lunacy.

Thomas Edison, who played the lead the other day in that amazing charade at Dearborn, where in the presence of Henry Ford and Harvey Firestone and Mr. Hoover and Mr. Schwab and Mr. Otto Kahn, and the regimented microphones of the world, he reconstituted the incandescent lamp as he had first built it at Menlo Park fifty years ago, is one of the two or three individuals most responsible for the sort of world we live in today. It would be more exact to say that thousands of men of the Ford and the Edison type are its builders. Politicians made more noise, financiers and industrial organizers and bankers got more personal power and ate bigger dinners, but it was the practical mechanics who were rebuilding the city the capitalists lived in while they blustered and gambled with the results of other men's labor. When you think that Edison was partially or exclusively connected with putting on the market the stock ticker, the phonograph, the moving picture camera, the loud-speaker and microphone that make radio possible, electric locomotives, vacuum electric lamps, storage batteries, multiple transmission over the telegraph, cement burners, it becomes obvious that there is no aspect of our life not influenced by his work and by the work of men like him. Reading his life, you feel that he never for a moment allowed himself to envisage the importance of the changes in the organization of human life that his inventions were to bring about. And he would have resented it if anyone had suggested to him that his work would destroy homes, wreck morals, and help end the individual toiler's world he was brought up in. Henry Ford, less the mechanic and more the organizer, seems equally unconcerned with the results of his work in human terms. The newspaper accounts of the goings-on at Dearborn at the jubilee of the incandescent lamp, the press statements and the kittenish skipping-about in the limelight of all involved, make that appallingly clear. These men are like the sorcerer's apprentice who loosed the goblins and the wonder-working broomsticks in his master's shop and then forgot what the formula was to control them by.

I don't mean to minimize their achievements, which are among the greatest in history.

Good writing is the reflection of an intense and organized viewpoint towards something, usually towards the values and processes of human life. The fact that the writing that emanates even from such a powerful institution as General Electric is so childish is a measure of proof that the men directing it are muddled and unclear about their human aims. They know in a vague sort of way that they want to make money and to make good; most of them want to play the game according to the rules of their time and not to be a worse son-of-a-bitch than the next man, but the problem of the readjustment of human values necessary to fit their world is the last thing they think about. I suppose they would say it was none of their business.

That is why the little crumpled figure of Steinmetz stands out with such extraordinary dignity against this background of practical organizers, rule-of-thumb inventors, patent-office quibblers. Steinmetz felt every moment what his work meant in the terms of the ordinary human being.

Steinmetz was a hunchback, the son of a hunchback, a railroad lithographer in Breslau. He was born in 1865, and grew up under the pressure of the Bismarck steamroller that was grinding down the jumble of cities, states, nationalities, idealistic creeds and caste prejudices that was Germany, into a smoothly integrated empire for his masters, the Hohenzollerns. Steinmetz was a bright boy; mathematics for him was a compensation for poverty, for being deformed, for being a member of the under-dog class in the university. It was a closed garden, free from corruption and death as the New Jerusalem of the early Christians, where he was absolute god and master. If he'd been a less warm-blooded man, that would have been enough, but he wanted real life, too. So it was inevitable that he should become a social revolutionist. Chased out of Breslau, he fled across the border to Zurich; there he studied at the Politechnik and shook up the institution considerably with his ideas about electricity. He met a young Dane named Asmussen and with him came to America, in the flood-tide of European immigration to the Promised Land, in the days when men used to fall on their knees and kiss the soil of liberty when they landed in Castle Garden. He had the good luck to get a job with Rudolf Eichemeyer, who was an old German forty-eighter, electrical theorist and practical inventor, who had a plant in Yonkers for building dynamos and hat-making machinery. From then on, Steinmetz had no life outside of the laboratory—when General Electric bought out Eichemeyer, Steinmetz went along with the rest of the apparatus, first to Lynn and then to Schenectady.

At Schenectady for many years he was the bad boy of G.E. The directors of that organization soon realized that apart from enormous value as a technician, Steinmetz was a publicity asset. So the Sunday papers were filled with his gila monsters and his cactus plants and his unconventional ideas on various subjects, and they let him teach and talk Socialism and even write offering his services to Lenin. He was the little parlor-magician who made toy thunderstorms for the reporters and took dignitaries out to his summer camp and dumped them out of his canoe with all their clothes on. It was largely his work with the mathematics of electricity that made the large-scale use of alternating current possible and the use of high-tension electricity safe and easy. The transformers you see hunched in their little gabled houses along the lines of high-tension wires are all monuments to Steinmetz's formulas. The officials of G.E. had the attitude of Edison, who when he was asked whether he'd ever studied mathematics, said "No . . . I can hire a mathematician any time, but the mathematicians can't hire me." G.E. had hired its mathematician, and it was a funny, rare little animal and had to be allowed to range a good deal to be kept happy and contented.

Finally, he wore out and died. If he'd been living, he'd probably have been at Dearborn with his toy thunderstorm, grinning in the limelight with the rest of the grand old men.

On the whole, it's fitting that he should not have been there. Edison, Ford, Firestone have cashed in gigantically on the machine. They have achieved a power and a success un-dreamed of by Tamerlane or Caesar. America has cashed in gigantically on the machine, has attained in these fifty years since the day when Edison—having tried everything, even a red hair out of a Scotchman's beard, finally settled on the paper carbon filament for the electric light bulb—a degree of wealth and prosperity absolutely new in history. Steinmetz was not of the temperament to cash in on anything.

Reading Hammond's life and Leonard's and the various notes and articles published about Steinmetz since his death, you feel more and more that the men around him were not of the caliber to understand and appreciate him. They thought of him as a pet oddity and let it go at that. He was a man of a different race, the race of those who do not cash in. The average European view is that America does not produce first-rate men—men who do not cash in. We had Franklin and Jefferson, but that's a long time ago. In the great industrial parades of our day, it is the cashers-in who are at the wheel. Are the Europeans right?

That brings me to the preachment I started in with. The woods are full of young men who have enough sense of hu-man value, who have in their veins enough of the blood of those who don't cash in, to be pretty good writers; it seems a shame that instead of picking up the easy garbage of Euro-pean bellelettristic small-talk, they don't try harder to worm their way in among the really compelling events and person-alities that are molding lives.

It's about time that American writers showed up in the industrial field where something is really going on, instead of tackling the tattered strawmen of art and culture.

The New Republic, December 18, 1929

Grosz Comes to America

I N THE last twenty-five years a change has come over the visual habits of Americans, something like what must have happened to Winslow Homer when, after half a lifetime grinding out stifflydrawn imaginings of current events as a newspaper artist, he suddenly broke out in his watercolors into a new world of sunlight and clouds and ocean. From being a wordminded people we are becoming an eyeminded people.

As I remember how things were when I was a child, the people my parents knew had hardly any direct visual stimulants at all. There were engravings on the walls and illustrated magazines and reproductions of old masters even, but the interest in them was purely literary. The type of drawing current in the late nineteenth century had such meager conventions of representation that it tended to evoke a set of descriptive words instead of a direct visual image. I am sure that my parents enjoying a view from a hill say, were stimulated verbally, remembering a line of verse or a passage from Sir Walter Scott, before they got any real impulse from the optic nerve. Of course there were a few oil paintings in the upstairs bathroom, those mysterious little works done by forgotten members of the family that you used to find in the dark upper halls of family residences left over from the nineteenth century, little landscapes that people had been reluctant to throw away because they were "handpainted" oils, but that were kept out of sight in the less seen parts of the house. As I remember them in my mother's house in Washington they tended to include a millwheel and a patch of woolly blue water towards the center of the canvas. They meant a lot to children but no grown person ever thought about them: the graphic arts consisted of newspaper and magazine illustrations, illustrations of literature in a book or on the wall, portraits and old masters.

I must have been well along in college before I looked at a picture directly, and then it was because I'd been reading Whistler's *Gentle Art of Making Enemies* and went into the Boston Art Museum to see what his painting was like. It must have been at about the same time that I first heard the music of Debussy. My generation in college was full of literary snob-admiration for the nineties. I can still remember the fashion-able mood of gentle and European snob-melancholy the Whistler pastels produced, with their little scraps of red and yellow and green coming out of the dovecolored smudge. At that I think the titles affected me more than the pictures. Still I must have been somewhat stirred visually because I seem to remember getting hold of a box of pastels and making dove-colored smudges of my own. The trouble was that it soon became obvious that almost any combination of pastel blurs was as agreeable to look at as any other, and my enthusiasm for that sort of thing began to flag.

The Armory Show was a real jolt, though I can't remember any picture I saw there, and it is associated in my mind with a torn yellowbacked volume of Van Gogh's letters a friend lent me along with a very bad translation of *Crime and Pun-ishment*. In spite of all the kidding about the *Nude Descend-ing Stairs*, I didn't recognize it when I saw it again at the Modern Museum in New York. The most I got from cubism at that time was a tingling feeling that a lot of odd things I didn't know about were going on in the world. I imagine I still thought Andrea del Sarto, of whose works we had pho-tographs in the library at home, real top notch in the paint-ing line, that is if I thought about the matter at all. Through George Moore I'd learned the names of the French impres-sionists but thought of them as literary figments like the Goncourts. The first time I was in Madrid the Velasquez paintings gave me most pleasure. I remember being rather scared by the Goyas and Grecos in the Prado. One rainy day in Toledo, I did go in to see the Count of Orgaz, though, and it probably began to bite in without my knowing it.

Right after that, in short glimpses of Paris during the war, I found myself walking up and down the rue de la Boètie and the little streets on the left bank looking at pictures in the windows of the few dealers that weren't bolted and barred behind iron shutters, and really seeing them. Then in Italy, on leave the next winter, the frescoes on the walls became sud-denly more important than anything else.

What started me off was going into Giotto's chapel in Padua one fine wintry day after an airraid. A big domed church was burning on the other side of town sending up one long straight plume of smoke. The chapel was all banked up with sandbags and the fellow I was with and I were both eating some sort of round sausages of chocolate and filbertnuts, a Paduan specialty that seemed delicious to us at the time, and as we looked up at the walls, standing there with our caps in our hands, shivering in the cellar chill, we felt that feeling of great permanence. Perhaps it was enhanced by the knowledge that the chapel might be blown to hell the next moonlight night. It was a feeling of the permanence of the perfectly imagined forms colored and spaced with such sober magnificence. We felt good all day afterwards.

After that the appetite for painting grew fast. On leave I did hardly anything but look at frescoes and paintings, discovering Piero della Francesca and Uccello and the *Last Judgement* in the Orvieto Cathedral and the City Hall in Siena and the cemetery walls in Pisa and the paintings in the catacombs at Rome. Back in Paris after the armistice there were Cézannes to see and the bold inventions of Picasso and Juan Gris and the feeling that great days were beginning. Since then in spite of my early training being verbal I tend to take a painting visual end first.

I think something of the sort has happened to many Americans of my generation, and even in a greater degree to the generations younger than us, so that an appetite and a taste for painting is growing up in this country very fast. Display advertising and the movies, though they may dull the wits, certainly stimulate the eyes. In New York the visual attack of the showwindows of Fifth Avenue stores almost equals in skill and scope that of the windows of the picture dealers on the Rue de la Boètie in the heyday of the school of Paris. It's not entirely because we are considered the freest spenders that artists who find Europe more and more impossible to live in tend to settle in the U.S. There is growing up here—fifteen years ago how we wise guys would have sniggered at the suggestion—the sort of previous atmosphere of appetite and enthusiasm that might make great work possible if any painters should be found who were men enough to do it.

Thus far outside of purely domestic painting, whittling and ironwork, of which those little bathroom pictures I spoke about were the last representatives, American art (always excepting Winslow Homer) has been first English provincial, then French impressionist provincial, school of Paris provincial and now it leans towards becoming Mexican provincial. We haven't yet done anything important in that direction. Young Americans with a taste for that sort of thing have felt that they had to go abroad somewhere to do it and have come home devout faddists, useless to themselves and to the culture of their country. But now in the last few years Europe (due to the abundant sprouting of the dragons' teeth the old men so sanctimoniously sowed round the green baize at Versailles) instead of being the land of liberty and art young middlewestern highschool students used to dream about, has become so stifling to any useful and rational human effort that suddenly the tables are turned. In the arts as in science America has become the refuge of the traditions of western European culture.

One can't help wondering whether we'll muff our opportunity the way our bankers (provincials too) muffed their chance to take the financial primacy away from London after the armistice.

Anyway there's a Chinaman's chance that we may come to something. The fact that firstrate men who can't live in their own countries feel that they can breathe here makes you feel good about the country. The fact that George Grosz, the great visual satirist of our time, has come to live here, has taken out papers and considers himself an American makes you feel good about the country.

It was in Paris on the Boulevard St. Germain some time during the Peace Conference that I first saw a German booklet of drawings by Grosz. It must have been in a bookstore, I suppose, but I somehow connect it in my memory with a magnificent colored drawing of cirrhosis of the liver in the window of the Society for the Suppression of Alcoholism opposite the old abbey. I suppose it was because what Grosz was representing was cirrhosis of nineteenth century civilization.

It's hard to reimagine the feelings of savage joy and bitter hatred we felt during that spring. We were still in uniform. We still had to salute officers, to go into outoftheway bars to talk to our friends who happened to be wearing the bettergrade uniforms. But with the armistice each one of us had been handed his life back on a platter. We knew what dead men looked like and we weren't dead. We had all our arms and legs. Some of us had escaped G.O. 42.

The horsechestnuts were in bloom. We knew that the world was a lousy pesthouse of idiocy and corruption but it was spring. We knew that in all the ornate buildings, under the crystal chandeliers, under the brocaded hangings the politicians and diplomats were brewing poison, fuddled old men festering like tentcaterpillars in a huddle of red tape and gold braid. But we had hope. What they were doing was too obvious and too clear. It was spring. The first of May was coming. We'd burn out the tentcaterpillars.

We knew two things about the world (two things that most of us have since forgotten), we knew that unorganized industrial life was becoming a chamber of horrors, and we knew that plain men, the underdogs we rubbed shoulders with, didn't go out of their way to harm each other as often as you might expect, that they had a passive courage the topdogs had never heard about and certain ingrained impulses towards social cohesiveness, the common good. Loafing around in little old bars full of the teasing fragrances of history, dodging into alleys to keep out of sight of the M.P.'s, seeing the dawn from Montmartre, talking bad French with taxidrivers, riverbank loafers, workmen, *petites femmes*, keepers of *bistros*, *poilus* on leave, we eagerly collected intimations of the urge towards the common good. It seemed so simple to burn out the tentcaterpillars that were ruining the orchard. The first of May was coming.

We felt boisterous and illmannered. Too many sergeants had told us to wipe that smile off your face, too many buglers had gotten us out of our blankets before we'd slept our sleep out. The only restraint that had survived the war was this automatic social cohesiveness among men that seemed to come on whenever they slipped for a moment out from under the thumbs of the bosses. If the old edifice crashed the bosses who lived in all the upper stories would go with it. They had already shaken the foundations with their pretty war, their brilliant famines. Their diligent allies, typhus, cholera, influenza were working for them still. Now their peace would finish the job. A couple of heaves and down she'll go. When the dust clears we'll see whether men and women are the besotted brutes the gold braided bosses say they are.

Finding Grosz's drawing was finding a brilliant new weapon. He knew how the old men, the fat men looked. He drew them as they grewsomely were. Looking at his work was a release from hatred, like hearing wellimagined and properly balanced strings of cusswords.

May first came and went. And another. And another. Outside of Russia the edifice trembled but it still stood. In the great halls at Versailles, Locarno, Geneva generals and dignitaries clustered in front of the camera to pin medals on each other, seemingly unconscious of the rotten smell of corpses from the cellar.

At home we went in for normalcy and Teapot Dome. We kept cool with Coolidge. The automotive boom began. America was filling the world with jazz and Ford cars and electric iceboxes. Americans poured over Europe to buy up artobjects cheap in the devaluated currencies. Americans still felt whole enough to make wisecracks about the bloody farce. We felt we had good comfortable seats for the last act of the European tragedy.

Those who didn't have any seats at all, who were actors in fact, felt differently. George Grosz's drawings will show the future how Europeans felt while their culture died of gas gangrene, just as Goya's drawings show us the agony of Europe a century before under the last convulsive stamping of the ironshod heels of the feudal church and the feudal army. Their impression is not verbal; (you don't look at the picture and have it suggest a title and then have the title give you the feeling) but through the eye direct, by the invention of ways of seeing.

The impact naturally was much sharper on Europeans who came of age during the war years than on Americans and sharpest of all on Germans. The generation of Germans who had begun their schooling in the nineties and were in their twenties when war broke out found themselves under a pressure almost unequalled in European history. They grew up in a respectable, easygoing, beerdrinking, sausageeating, natureloving world where everybody went to hear the band play in the *tiergarten* Sundays and was delighted to shine the shoes of his superiors, and if he didn't like it he could go to America. They had hardly begun respectfully and agreeably to occupy the situations to which God and the Kaiser had called them when they were goosestepping to the railroad station and in another fortyeight hours were being slashed to pieces by the French seventyfives.

George Grosz was born in Berlin in '93 and spent most of his boyhood at Stolp in Pomerania. His parents were Prussian Lutherans. His life developed at the exact point of greatest strain in the European social structure, in the more impoverished section of the middle class. His drawings must have shown promise in school because he was sent to Dresden to learn academic pencilwork and charcoal from casts of the antique. He started making his living by drawing for comic papers. He studied in Berlin. The summer of 1913 he spent in Paris.

Grosz had too much Prussian and too much Lutheran in his bones to feel at home in Paris, but he must have been stirred by the fact that the full tide of European painting was running through the less prosperous studios of Montmartre and Montparnasse. *Bohème* was attaining real eminence under Guillaume Apollinaire, its last poet and king. Out of student traditions of the cult of oddity, the romantic libertarianism of *les bourgeois à la lanterne*, scraps of science and anthropology, and the pressures on sensitive young men of a social system tottering to collapse and its releases, the modern point of view towards painting was coming into being. In spite of the romantic bohemian tradition of spontaneous artistic flareup (the sideshow charlatan tradition) painting suddenly became a matter of experiments and theories followed up with almost scientific rigor. In the fads and isms of the painters and writers of that time there was a core of real effort to cope with reality. Grosz seems never to have espoused any of these causes but his work shows the influence of all of them, particularly of Italian futurism and cubism. He used what elements he needed out of all the various methods of seeing that flourished and disappeared. His interests lay not in the studio or in the metaphysics of color and form, but in the everyday life as he saw it of men and women sleeping, dressing, eating, going to work, drinking, making love, and in their dreams and their wants. He was a satirist and a moralist.

Like Swift in another age and working in another medium, Grosz was full of the horror of life. A satirist is a man whose flesh creeps so at the ugly and the savage and the incongruous aspects of society that he has to express them as brutally and nakedly as possible to get relief. He seeks to put into expressive form his grisly obsessions the way a bacteriologist seeks to isolate a virus or a microorganism. Until he's done that no steps can be taken to cure the disease. Looking at Grosz's drawings you are more likely to feel a grin of pain than to burst out laughing. Instead of letting you be the superior bystander laughing in an Olympian way at somebody absurd, Grosz makes you identify yourself with the sordid and pitiful object.

Experiments in the visual arts (the invention of new ways of seeing things), are made because, due to the way the apparatus that makes up the mind is made, old processes and patterns have continually to be broken up in order to make it possible to perceive the new aspects and arrangements of evolving consciousness. The great enemy of intelligence is complacency. The satirist in words or in visual images is the doctor who comes with his sharp and sterile instruments to lance the focusses of dead matter that continually impede the growth of intelligence. Without intelligence it is impossible to cope with the intricacy of nature or with the madhouse every man carries within him. No one with any sensitiveness to words who has read Swift can ever be so complacent again about his position as a human being. Grosz's work combines visual freshness with a bitter satirical intensity that few complacencies can survive. When complacency goes young intelligence begins.

Esquire, September 1936

Farewell to Europe!

THE PEOPLE of Western Europe are facing this summer a series of tragic dilemmas. Of the hopes that dazzled the last twenty years that some political movement might tend to the betterment of the human lot, little remains above ground but the tattered slogans of the past. These old slogans still have enough magic in them to make them useful to gang leaders with a knack for organizing and a will to power, but their appeal is now of a pie-in-the-sky order and tends to be enforced with the bayonet or, in the case of a friend, with the butt end of a rifle. Out of them is brewing a partisan fanaticism that equals in savagery that of the wars of religion. And the organizers of victory have at hand the greatest arsenal of destructive machinery that's ever been brought together on this planet.

If there are any of us left in America who really want liberty for ourselves and our fellows, it's time we started using our wits. The Atlantic is broad enough to protect us against air raids, but it can't protect us against the infectious formulas for slavery that are preparing in Europe on every side.

Certainly Great Britain, the ancient mother of civil liberties, is going to be very little help to the democratic idea in the near future. The impression I got, from a few days in an England still bedraggled with coronation bunting, was that the ruling class, now in the form of the heavy industry–big banking clique typified by Stanley Baldwin, has managed to reduce the middle and working classes to a point of physical and moral malnutrition where revolt is impossible. The tories are going to have their own way for a long time to come. The British Empire has reached that classical point in the development of empires where the interests of the ruling clique are definitely opposed to the interests of the aggregation as a going concern.

The only question is whether the victim will be devoured slowly, or whether death will be attended by violent convulsions. At the present it looks as if the ruling class anaesthetics had been so skillfully applied by Dr. Baldwin that dissolution would be a long twilight process. There is talk of reviving the Defence of the Realm Act but it will probably not be necessary. All possible opposition is paralysed by two great dilemmas; first, a left-labor policy in foreign affairs means war with the fascist powers, and the British workman is stolidly and with good reason pacifist; and second, Stalinist Russia's monopoly of the socialist hopes of the world has much slowed up the labor movement at home; the British workman would rather be mildly oppressed by Mr. Chamberlain's bluecoated flatfeet than shot without trial, or more gruesomely with a trial, by the Communist Party, and thank you very much, sir.

In European affairs England (Mr. Baldwin's heavy industry–big banking England), is still dominant, and the Metternich policy of fighting popular rule, or any change that affects property, by any means that arise, continues triumphant. From behind the stained liberal curtains the singularly unplausible puppet of Mr. Anthony Eden is from time to time stuck out to gibber nineteenth-century platitudes for the benefit of the office force at Geneva, the American press and the Anglican clergy. In France this Metternich policy has been ably seconded by the Quai d'Orsay. Whether Mr. Blum is himself a willing assistant at the Foreign Office guignol or is merely following the policy of the lesser evil will not be discovered until he writes his memoirs. Certainly the French people are not happy about their predicament. Nobody really feels that the Paris Exposition is going to solve the class war.

France gives you none of the feeling of a dead country that England does, though politically there is the same paralysis on the left. You feel that the stalemate there is due rather to a balance of vigorously opposite forces than to blood and bones ethnic breakdown. As in England the great dilemma that blocks social advance is that a socialist or a truly democratic policy can hardly avoid being a war policy, and that the only vigorous leadership on the left comes from the Communist Party which is in turn hogtied by the internal and international politics of the Kremlin. Ably seconded by the British, the heavy industry–banking block is able to keep a knife at Mr. Blum's throat by threatening civil war and a German and

Italian invasion. Meanwhile the French helplessly watch themselves slipping from the position of a first class power, watch the Italians occupying the Balearic Islands and ready to cut communications with the African empire, and the Germans fortifying Morocco and the Basque border.

It's hard to see what the solution can be other than a civil war deadlier than the civil war in Spain. Certainly sympathy with loyalist Spain is the one bond that is holding the French left together during Mr. Blum's *pause*, and the active help to Spain of the French Communist Party is the one policy that holds the esteem of the French working class. This has forced the Right into a pro-German policy that is headed straight for high treason, and has afforded Mr. Blum the opportunity for the complete ascendancy he enjoys in parliament and among purely politician circles. His fatal weakness is that this ascendancy stops short of the banks and the industries where high treason is part of the day's work. Once his assault on the Bank of France failed, and once he was manoeuvered by Mr. Metternich-Baldwin into tolerating the Fascist aggression in Spain he became helplessly part of the windowdressing of the banking and heavy industry forces that are out to crush the working class of Europe at whatever cost.

In Spain the working class has defended itself with a magnificent heroism that will remain one of the bloodstirring episodes of European history. Meanwhile behind the lines a struggle as violent almost as the war has been going on between the Marxist concept of the totalitarian state, and the Anarchist concept of individual liberty. More and more as the day to day needs of the army become paramount over the turbulent effort of the working class in revolt against oppression, the Communist Party forges ahead as the organizer of victory. The anarchists and the socialists with their ideas of individual and local freedom and selfgovernment have given way step by step before this tremendously efficient and ruthless machine for power.

It is the Communists who have been able to attract the young men who want to see the war won. It's the Communists who have been able to obtain and canalize the help of the other Communist Parties of Europe and of the antifascists from all over the world who threw themselves into the breach to save Madrid. It's the Communists who have been supple enough to ally themselves with whatever Anti-Franco forces, small proprietors, shopkeepers, or political adventurers might temporarily be useful to win the war. On the debit side, it must be admitted that they have brought into Spain along with their enthusiasm and their munitions, the secret Jesuitical methods, the Trotzky witchhunt and all the intricate and bloody machinery of Kremlin policy.

The question which cannot be answered now is whether the Spanish people will have paid too high a price for the fine new army they have organized, and whether the Communist Party, once its social objectives are gone or translated into pie in the sky, won't turn out to be only one more magnificent instrument for power, which means a magnificent instrument for oppression. Anyway the die is already cast. It will be impossible to turn the clock back entirely in Spain, because an immense amount of spontaneous social reorganization has gone on; but the chances are that further changes will be in the direction of a centralized military state, possibly somewhat modified in the direction of personal liberty by the need to conciliate the instinct against centralisation of the masses and to cope with the economically cellular character of the peninsula. That is, unless the fascist combination wins. In spite of the seemingly overwhelming forces on the fascist side such a victory seems inconceivable to anyone who has felt the spirit of loyalist Spain. It would mean the final blotting out of hope for Europe.

The Atlantic is a good wide ocean. An American in 1937 comes back from Europe with a feeling of happiness, the relief of coming up out into the sunlight from a stifling cellar, that some of his grandfathers must have felt coming home from Metternich's Europe after the Napoleonic wars, the feeling all the immigrants have had when they first saw the long low coast and the broad bays of the new world. At least we still have alternatives.

Sure, we've got our class war, we've got our giant bureaucratic machines for antihuman power, but I can't help feeling that we are still moving on a slightly divergent track from the

European world. Not all the fascist-hearted newspaper owners in the country, nor the Chambers of Commerce, nor the armies of hired gunthugs of the great industries can change the fact that we have the Roundhead Revolution in our heritage and the Bill of Rights and the fact that the democracy in the past has been able, under Jefferson, Jackson, and Lincoln, and perhaps a fourth time (it's too soon to know yet) under Franklin Roosevelt, to curb powerful ruling groups. America has got to be in a better position to work out the problem: individual liberty vs. bureaucratic industrial organization than any other part of the world. If we don't it means the end of everything we have ever wanted since the first hard winters at Plymouth.

Common Sense, July 1937

The Death of José Robles

S IR: I did not intend to publish any account of the death of my old friend José Robles Pazos (the fact that he had once translated a book of mine, and well, was merely incidental; we had been friends since my first trip to Spain in 1916) until I had collected more information and possible documentary evidence from survivors of the Spanish civil war, but the reference to him in Mr. Malcolm Cowley's review of my last book [The New Republic, June 14] makes it necessary for me to request you to print the following as yet incomplete outline of the events that led up to his death. As I do not possess the grounds of certitude of your reviewer and his informants, I can only offer my facts tentatively and say that to the best of my belief they are accurate.

José Robles was a member of a family of monarchical and generally reactionary sympathies in politics; his brother was an army officer in the entourage of Alfonso of Bourbon when he was king; one of the reasons why he preferred to live in America (he taught Spanish Literature at Johns Hopkins University in Baltimore) was his disagreement on social and political questions with his family. He was in Spain on his vacation when Franco's revolt broke out, and stayed there, although he had ample opportunity to leave, because he felt it his duty to work for the Republican cause. As he knew some Russian he was given a job in the Ministry of War and soon found himself in close contact with the Russian advisers and experts who arrived at the same time as the first shipment of munitions. He became a figure of some importance, ranked as lieutenant-colonel, although he refused to wear a uniform, saying that he was a mere civilian. In the fall of 1936 friends warned him that he had made powerful enemies and had better leave the country. He decided to stay. He was arrested soon after in Valencia and held by the extra-legal police under conditions of great secrecy and executed in February or March, 1937.

It must have been about the time of his death that I arrived in Spain to do some work in connection with the film "The

623

Spanish Earth," in which we were trying to tell the story of the civil war. His wife, whom I saw in Valencia, asked me to make inquiries to relieve her terrible uncertainty. Her idea was that as I was known to have gone to some trouble to get the cause of the Spanish Republic fairly presented in the United States, government officials would tell me frankly why Robles was being held and what the charges were against him. It might have been the same day that Liston Oak, a one-time member of the American Communist Party who held a job with the propaganda department in Valencia, broke the news to José Robles' son, Francisco Robles Villegas, a seventeen-year-old boy working as a translator in the censorship office, that his father was dead. At the same time officials were telling me that the charges against José Robles were not serious and that he was in no danger. Mr. Del Vayo, then Foreign Minister, professed ignorance and chagrin when I talked to him about the case, and promised to find out the details. The general impression that the higherups in Valencia tried to give was that if Robles were dead he had been kidnaped and shot by anarchist "uncontrollables." They gave the same impression to members of the United States embassy staff who inquired about his fate.

It was not until I reached Madrid that I got definite information, from the then chief of the republican counterespionage service, that Robles had been executed by a "special section" (which I gathered was under control of the Communist Party). He added that in his opinion the execution had been a mistake and that it was too bad. Spaniards I talked to closer to the Communist Party took the attitude that Robles had been shot as an example to other officials because he had been overheard indiscreetly discussing military plans in a café. The "fascist-spy" theory seems to be the fabrication of romantic American Communist sympathizers. I certainly did not hear it from any Spaniard.

Anybody who knew Spaniards of any stripe before the civil war will remember that they tended to carry personal independence in talk and manners to the extreme. It is only too likely that Robles, like many others who were conscious of their own sincerity of purpose, laid himself open to a frame-up. For one thing, he had several interviews with his brother, who was held prisoner in Madrid, to try to induce him to join the Loyalist army. My impression is that the frame-up in his case was pushed to the point of execution because Russian secret agents felt that Robles knew too much about the relations between the Spanish war ministry and the Kremlin and was not, from their very special point of view, politically reliable. As always in such cases, personal enmities and social feuds probably contributed.

On my way back through Valencia, as his wife was penniless, I tried to get documentary evidence of his death from Republican officials so that she could collect his American life insurance. In spite of Mr. Del Vayo's repeated assurances that he would have a death certificate sent her, it never appeared. Nor was it possible to get hold of any record of the indictment or trial before the "special section."

As the insurance has not yet been paid I am sure that Mr. Cowley will understand that any evidence he may have in his possession as to how José Robles met his death will be of great use to his wife and daughter, and I hope he will be good enough to communicate it to me. His son was captured fighting in the Republican militia in the last months of the war and, as there has been no news of him for some time, we are very much afraid that he died or was killed in one of Franco's concentration camps.

Of course this is only one story among thousands in the vast butchery that was the Spanish civil war, but it gives us a glimpse into the bloody tangle of ruined lives that underlay the hurray-for-our-side aspects. Understanding the personal histories of a few of the men, women and children really involved would, I think, free our minds somewhat from the black-is-black and white-is-white obsessions of partisanship.

Provincetown, Mass.

To a Liberal in Office

DEAR ————: No matter how good the intentions of a man in public service are when he starts out, I think you'll agree that it's exceedingly difficult for him to avoid leading a double life. While with one side of his mind he's trying to fulfil his duty to his fellow-citizens, with the other he's busy with his career and with the demands of the organized group he belongs to. Only too often the members of the aggregations of men that make up a government lose all contact with the public needs they were got together to serve. Whether a public servant shall be written down as an honest man or a scoundrel depends on what part of his energy and brains goes into selfless work for his constituents in proportion to the part he has to use to make his way in the competitive scramble. Naturally if I didn't think you were an honest man I would not be taking up your time and mine with this letter. Furthermore, I know that through a long train of years you have done your best to throw your weight on the side of free institutions. If I'm not mistaken, it is largely because you proved yourself a conscientious liberal that you reached a position of power and responsibility under the present Administration. I am writing to ask you to stop to think for a moment how your power is being used, and what kind of responsibility you have undertaken in this difficult time toward your fellow-citizens and toward yourself.

It has been said so often that democracy is at stake that the mere repetition of the words has dulled their meaning for us. Nevertheless, it's frighteningly true. It's another commonplace that we are living through one of those periods in history when old institutions are crumbling away and new institutions are being built up. The thing nobody tells us is that what these new institutions will be like depends upon how every man jack of us acquits himself today. It's up to us to ask whether we are letting ourselves be used to build jails or homes for free men.

As Americans our minds were formed in childhood to react favorably to such phrases as liberty, equality of opportunity,

626

freedom of speech, but unfortunately nothing in our schooling gave us any inkling how to apply them to the problems of
real life. They were the measuring sticks with which we ap-
praised the world we grew up in. In many cases they tallied so
little with the facts we encountered in that world that we tried
to rip them out of our minds as old, rotten, sentimental lum-
ber, and to put in their place one of the authoritarian creeds
that are turning civilization into a slaughterhouse today. A
few of us, and you were one, held on to the old traditions.
They took root again in our minds and grew strong enough
to become the underpinning of all our political hopes, and of
our system of personal ethics.

Now, after a period of reform and helterskelter reorganization that has been, in spite of many wrong roads taken, productive of real living good in the national life, the United
States finds itself virtually at war. The fact of being at war
tends to freeze normal social and political processes inside a
country. This freezing puts a very grave responsibility on the
men in office at the time. Great inflation of the power of the
state is inevitable. For the duration public opinion will be able
to make itself felt only feebly and negatively. The whole duty
of protecting the self-governing system and the liberties that
are supposed to be the watchwords of the battle will rest on
men already in administrative and political positions. This is
the responsibility I am asking you, as a liberal, to face.

The general run of men, organized into any group or gang
or institution or government, must necessarily be time servers
whose emotions and ideals will be colored by the stronger
minds among them. They will tend to behave as their leaders
behave. Democracy depends upon the active support of a minority just as much as dictatorship does. The difference is that
democracy depends upon a minority able to set for the rest
the example of that minimum of civic courage necessary to
make self-governing institutions work instead of upon a minority of goons ready to club down opposition to the boss's
orders.

We can thank our stars that the men who founded our system of government understood so well the corruption of
power, and that in the common law we have a storehouse of
inherited techniques for the protection of the individual man.

But institutions are continually changing as a result of the uses men put them to. Each temporary distortion leaves its mark. In a time of emergency the temptation to a man in office to get results no matter how is almost overwhelming. It is the business of liberals in positions of power to remember that free institutions depend on the "how" much more than on the results. Democracy is a method of social organization, not an end. War has always meant the triumph of authority; that is why all through our history our statesmen in war time have occasionally neglected efficiency in the totalitarian sense in order to secure liberties at home that were more important to them than transitory victories abroad. If in the present war, out of a blind desire to catch up to the Nazis, we neglect to preserve the democratic process, we shall wake up one morning to find that we've given our blood and paid our taxes in order to fasten on our necks the dominion of a bunch of war lords who speak American instead of German. A doubtful victory!

Already, before we've even started shooting at the enemy, the Administration, which I honestly believe is more devoted to the aims of democracy than any we have had for many decades, has committed a number of acts that tend to put the bases of self-government in jeopardy. The prosecution of the Minnesota truck drivers is so far the outstanding example. On July 15 a federal grand jury handed down in St. Paul, Minnesota, an indictment against twenty-nine men, some leaders and members of Local 544, a union of transportation workers powerful in the Northwest, and the rest members of the tiny group of the followers of the murdered Trotsky that goes under the name of the Socialist Workers' Party. The indictment was handed down under a Civil War statute that has never been brought out before, and under the new Smith Act, which I believe was aimed at the subversive activities of the agents of foreign governments. The men are charged with conspiracy to overthrow the United States government by force and violence.

Let's assume that it's all perfectly legal, that the Department of Justice believes these men intended to rise in insurrection, and that it has a right to stretch a point or two to accomplish the useful purpose of restraining them. Is it wise to take this moment, when the Administration is trying to unify the country for a mighty effort, for this particular prosecution? Let us even assume that a few thousand Trotskyist Marxist sectarians scattered over the country can be a danger to the government of the United States at a time when the Department of Justice itself has more employees than the Trotskyists have adherents. What I want to ask you is: which is more dangerous to that survival of the democratic process in this country for which I am sure you would gladly lay down your life—the uprising of a few fanatics who control a single local of a trade union or a situation in which the government undermines at home those four freedoms for which it is asking the nation to make every sacrifice abroad?

You must remember the Palmer raids, the deportations delirium, the crushing of the I.W.W., the Sacco-Vanzetti case, all the terrible perversions of justice after the last war that made American democracy a mockery to a whole generation of young men. Is it all going to happen again? Is the same lack of whole-hearted principle that wrecked Woodrow Wilson's crusade to set the world straight going to destroy the present Administration too? A great deal of the history of the next few years depends on whether the Administration will recognize that it has made a mistake in this one case. If it is allowed to go ahead, the prestige of government will become involved in getting these men in jail and keeping them there. And a precedent will have been set that bodes ill for this country's liberties.

Well, you say, suppose you are right, what can one man do about it? We must keep our eyes on the great aims of the Administration and admit that in war time we have to do things that we don't quite like. That argument has been the refuge of officialdom from Pontius Pilate down. It just does not hold water. It is to make these decisions that a man is chosen for the public service. During the last war while some officials were busy tearing down the American system, a few others were doing their best to build it up. In the end the structure of self-government was tough enough to stand those strains and the great depression too. Where the present moment differs from 1917 is that now the traditions of our system are weaker than they were then. Although there has been more vocal expression of them recently than in any period since the great years of this country's founding, the average man still has a hard time connecting the principles of democracy with his daily life. In this immensely confusing time it is impossible to evoke from the mass of unthinking men the passionate automatic response to the old war cries that came in 1917. Furthermore, the national life is honeycombed with political groups such as the Communists and the Coughlinites, highly confusing in their line of talk and vowed to the destruction of the democratic method. They will continue to be a danger until that method has had time again to prove its practical worth.

Meanwhile we can't afford to lose any ground. The great successes of the despotic systems have been based on the fact that the democracies did not have the single-mindedness or the courage to advance to the attack. For a long time to come we are going to continue fighting against despotism with one hand tied behind our backs. The conviction of these union leaders in St. Paul in a case where even the language of the indictment has the peculiar twist of Stalin's famous frame-ups in Moscow will be a severe moral blow to the American cause. The heavens won't fall, you say. It won't be the first time that men have been framed in this country or that the majority of men have stood by and seen injustice done. But the effects will snowball. We musn't forget that in France the heavens did fall. The great reason for the success of the despotisms has been that they are as wholehearted in their work as a gangster in the middle of a holdup. They can be routed by a democracy that is wholeheartedly, even recklessly, for freedom. Can't we be as reckless on the right side as they are on the wrong?

Perhaps I'm the one who is wrong in thinking it is because of their honesty and frank speaking that the defendants in this case now find themselves in jeopardy rather than because of anything really subversive in their actions. Perhaps the Department of Justice is right in contending that so small a group can really be a nuisance to American institutions. In any case the Administration is risking more than can possibly be gained. I am writing you this letter to try to get you to step for a moment out of the peculiar exigencies of your official position. At a time when we are asking our young men to give up the best years of their lives, and possibly their lives entire, to national defense, it is hardly too much to ask a public official to remember that he is a citizen before he is an official and that he must decide for himself whether his actions are tending to the defense or the destruction of the Republic. If this were not a time of grave peril it would be insufferable effrontery for me to sit here in a quiet room in a shady retired village writing a letter asking you to go sit on a park bench and make this decision—you who are working fourteen hours a day in a Washington office, straining every nerve to do what you can in that precarious daily piling of average on slippery average which is the best victory a man can hope for who is trying to accomplish something through the directed work of groups of other men. But in every train of events there is a moment when one decision determines a long future. This, it seems to me, is one of the times when a man has to speak his mind.

The Nation, September 6, 1941

LETTERS AND DIARIES
1916–1920

To Rumsey Marvin

Dear Rummy,   May 29

Although I am awfully busy—exams are coming so soon—my *last* exams, pensez à ça—that is if I don't go to Oxford or somewhere absurd, which is possible.

About Masefield, you go and read 'The Widow in the Bye Street,' young man, and see if you don't think it has really tragic beauty. Of course bits of it, taken by themselves are ugly and disgusting, but, *as a whole*, it seems to me to have a peculiar sort of pathetic beauty—and a marvellous feeling of life—

Your long letter was a joy, really, and *I don't get bored*, 'cep'n with myself and with magazines and periodical literature in general—

One minute—I must go back to my muttons, What in the name of Heaven are "life's meaner things"? To me they are stockbrokers and hypocritical clergymen far more often than they are women of the streets or prize fighters or any of Masefield's riff-raff, not that I prefer them in literature to "decent" people—but I think that one's ideas as to what decent people are can't go according to conventional lines, if they are going to be ideas at all—

Nevertheless you must read 'Dauber' you'll like that and it isn't "slummy"—

Before I forget, listen what I did the other afternoon. In company with several friends, a cold roast chicken, cheeses, jellies etc, I went out in to the country and we had a most delightful souper sur l'herbe on a hillside that fronted the sunset. I've never known anything so delightful—It was a wonderful red-orange sunset, fading gradually through rosy-purple and violet to a sort of dim lavender with a yellow sheen—

We climbed into a big oak tree—as if we were Bonnie Prince Charlie being pursued by the King's men, and watched it (when we'd demolished the eatables) and then walked back to Cambridge through the gloaming.

'My muttons' is an English expression, I fear; that comes, I suppose from the horrid habit of serving up a cold joint of mutton again and again—till Fido gets the bone!

Poor Kitchener! Still I suppose one can't have a better death than to go down at the height of your achievement with band playing, and colors flying.

Were'nt you excited over the great sea battle?

I'd like to have been there.

The little poem is in a delightful cadence

"And went away" is rather a smash—could you get it more into tune?

Don't you love "A Night Among the Pines" in *Travels with a Donkey*?—I knew you'ld like it. You make me feel like reading it over again—out of sympathy!

Plus plus tard
Jack

But Rummy, to come again to our muttons—(I argue in chorus—with interludes of description!) there isn't so much really distasteful—if you get the right point of view to it—on the breast of the teeming earth. You can find a sort of mad splendor in things, the ugliest, the filthiest things, if you really look for it—if you don't, as most people do, put up stone walls and bar the gate on it.

There's a wonderful religious poem of Francis Thompson I like to apply to beauty—

"I fled him down the nights and down the days;
I fled him down the arches of the years
I fled him down the labyrinthine ways
Of my own mind; . . . .

From those strong feet that followed, followed after.
But with unhurrying chase,
And unperturbèd pace,
Deliberate speed, majestic instancy,
They beat". . . .

It is a queer strangely fascinating poem which you'll have to read soon.

Speaking of rhythm in Masefield, can anything be more rhythmic than this:

"I heard a partridge covey call;
The morning sun was bright on all.
Down the long slope the plow team drove

> The tossing rooks rose and hove.
> A stone struck on the share. A word
> Came to the team. The red earth stirred" . . .

in a strange rather harsh way, to be sure, but still rhymic. However, I agree with you completely on the subject. All the poetry I love best is intensely musical.

By the way—speaking in un-realistic mood—do you read Maeterlinck? If not you must tackle "Pelléas and Mélisande" and some of his other plays—you'll like them—perhaps you've seen Debussy's opera—

I should at this moment be reading a very dull book for a philosophy course on the Neoplatonists. Speaking of them, I've also been reading a novel of Merezhkovski called "The Death of the Gods"—about Julian the Apostate—Do you like him—from earliest infancy, he's been one of my pet Roman emperors.

But this letter's degenerating (ink has given out) into a literary causerie—which is dull—so let's change the subject to baseball—

No let's not—

We must & we shall arrange our grand New York spree for before July 3rd—I dont know many queer restaurants in New York, but I can hunt for one. Now if it were Boston I could take you to a dozen—

I jabber Spanish a little & read it a little—have read "Don Quixote" vol 1 & 2 in original and I intend to study it violently in the near future—So you have the linguistic bug too? I've always been mad to know a lot of languages—it's so humanizing, don't you think so?

Have heard of, but never read "The Anvil of Chance"—I envy your English teacher his story in *Scribners.*

Gosh, but I envy you your five months at Capri—it must have been wonderful. It's rather funny but I have never achieved Capri—Three times I have tried and each time a storm has come up, or been up and the boat has had to turn back—isn't that maddening? Once we tossed about for five hours in the Bay of Naples—I sitting on the cabin floor with a very sick Italian baby's head in my lap. C'était gai je vous assure

And how I long to stretch my legs on a good piece of road and set off, like Gil Blas or Don Quixote and everyone amusing who's ever lived—videre mundum.

I always envied Satan in 'Job' who was coming "from going up and down the earth"—

Don't you want to go up and down the earth?

Adios

Jack

1916

To Rumsey Marvin

Dear Rummy,

I've just been on a tremendously long ramble through Boston—I love cities on a rainy night—The reflections of the orange and yellow lights are so gray on the wet streets— Particularly Saturday night—there's a wonderful atmosphere of gaiety & a sort of paganism about which always delights me— I mean in the cheaper parts of the city—those are the only parts of any city that are ever alive—The market was wonderful— all old women, young women, boys, old grizzled men, flashing eyed Italians buying vegetables and meats—and the reds and greens and yellows were so fresh in the rainy atmosphere— It is wonderful what beautiful faces you sometimes see at such times—ugly gargoyle-grotesques too, to be sure—Still it is all very alive and exciting—when not done up in stays like the life of us cotton-wool plutocrats—because we are plutocrats compared to those people—But enough romantic sociology!

Congratulations! Once long ago I got fourth in a hundred yard dash—but——You know I've spent my entire existence vowing that sometime in the future I should develop my body and become a young Hercules. You make me quite envious with your blue ribbons.

Gee, but I used to hate to be made to exercise when I was at school!

I'll be awfully interested to see McLane's poem—hope to meet him someday.

By the way—I like your smash in "And went away" but somehow it might smash a little more successfully—You must write more. It doesn't hurt a bit to imitate form in poetry—so long as you have your own ideas—you'll find, too, that squashing an idea into a given form so transforms it (no pun!) that it ends up by being yours anyway.

Next week I am going to take a little walking trip up Cape Cod with a couple of friends. We'll start from inland and walk out to Provincetown. It'll be great fun I think, particularly as we know nothing about roads or inns or anything. I'll write you all about it.

Do you know, Rummy? I think the pair of us ought to understudy Stevenson sometime—and go on a ramble with some volumes of verse & an indefinite objective. We'll have to try to manage it.

Au Revoir
Jack
c. Spring 1916

To Rumsey Marvin

Aug 24th

Rummy, I like you for liking Plum Island—It must have been great fun—I quite envy you rubbing shoulders with such a lot of fellows of all sorts and conditions. My main moan has always been the lack of it. At school I was a most unsocial friendless little beast—and it has been hard to shake off the habit of solitude—Something like Plum Island would have been awfully good for me—although you know there are people who sort of have solitude in their blood, who are just as lonely in a crowd or on a mountain top—I may be one of them: quien sabe?

However, I assure you that its damned unpleasant, particularly when you have instincts that desire the extremest sociability—From that point of view I approve awfully heartily of military service—because it would make young men rub shoulders more, get to know people outside of their class—be actually instead of theoretically democratic.

But the devil of it is that military affairs lead the other way—Just think of the insufferable snobbery of army officers, of the swagger everything in uniform puts on when it runs up against a poor civilian (why I expect to be shoved off the very pavement by the breadth of your shoulders—your chestiness when I see you again)—and the messy picture of a military democracy—poet and peasant, doctor and butcher, arm in arm, sweating together, marching together, heroizing together, to the tune of a patriotic song—sort of fades away. Et plus when you have an army you immediately want to use it—and a military population in a government like ours would be absolutely at the mercy of any corrupt politician who got into the White House, of any millionaire who could buy enough newspapers——mais je vous ennuie mon pauvre Rummy—

But look! I have a idee—you really must agree to it—by Mars and the Star Spangled Banner—

I shall be in New York for a couple of weeks in early september—Now attention, my plan is thus: I have never been in the Catskills—they are near—a couple of hours I guess—Have you?—Now supposing we go to some place there and say walk for two days and then come back to N.Y.—What do you think of it?—We may hit godforsaken holes but we can always get a train or car or something and move on.

And we could do wonders in two days. We'd learn all each others absurdities and would quarrel madly at every cross roads—as a result we'd know each other better than by four thousand letters—Write at once what you think of it. All we'll need to take is a toothbrush comb and clean socks and books of verse—of course—Dont you dare say you can't do it—because I am going abroad—where as yet undecided—at the end of the month, and may not be back for an age—You see I shall vow not to come back until I've come to grips with old lady adventure—sort of a search for the Holy Grail.

I quite envy your hangings on the edge of love—Good God, though, if one is feeling well and properly in tune with earth and sky—one is already in love with every man woman and child in sight—except for those few repulsive mummified corpses of people that freeze the very name of love—Eros is a great god—I like his beautiful Greek name better than his Roman one that makes you think of St Valentine's and Baroque interiors—But how few votaries he has compared to the banal gigglesome Cupid. And so few girls have any idea of him—of his supreme human dignity.

But I'm probably talking rot—If you really fall I shall send you Swinburne

Ecrivez bientôt

Jack

For the Lord's Sake remember that neatness is a minor virtue—often a vice, and that hesitation delay and worry (+ alcohol) are what high art feeds on—Finally, Rummy, man *is a thinking* animal—Describe *her* or them

Fair?
Fat?
Thin?
Dark?
Languid?
Vivacious?
Frank?
Piquante?
Mysterious?
Seductive?
Miscellaneous?

Cintra, Virginia, 1916

To Rumsey Marvin

Thanks awfully Rummy dear but I possess a French Oxford Book—it has lots of nice things in it, hasn't it?

Was awfully glad to get your delightfully long letter—It carried me all through breakfast this morning—I wish you could have enclosed yourself in the envelope with it, though, as I am still in this beastly New York—all alone in our dark sepulchral house—You see I can't get out of here until Oct 14th when I sail on the 'Espagne' for Bordeaux. That's more than two weeks to wait and nothing particular to do ('ceptin my everlasting reading & writing which is part of the day—sort of like cleaning my teeth.)

I'm awfully glad you like the Swinburne you've read so far. How about 'The Garden of Proserpine'? I also particularly like the Sonnet to "Mlle. De Maupin"—a strangely exotic book you must read someday, by Gautier—a combination of rather decadent beauty and real passion and smut of a very low order. I think the sonnet's one of the most beautiful in English.

The account of the analytical amours delighted me—and as I said before, I love the name of Peggy—Don't think that I am utterly unsusceptible. I often fall in love with a face or a glint of light on hair or an intonation of the voice . . . Rather hard too. I admit that the idea of marriages and engagements and all the conventional fluffiness of respectable mating doesn't attract me particularly—It rather spoils things—And two of my best friends are getting married this fall—awful thought—for a friend married is a friend lost—and when the commodity is so rare—so damnably rare—I like to hold onto them.

Facilis decensus est—the descent into limbo of writing is easy—but the ascent into print! . . . But you can't begin too soon—as the mere fact of writing improves ones outlook and sharpens ones style—and so much is a question of dexterity acquired by practice—that is if you've got the stuff internally—and most of us have—I believe—the trouble is in finding a medium of outlet.

Apropos of scenario—make flirtatious lady a German spy trying to blow up a shipment of chipped beef or something; hero disentangles himself—convoys chipped beef to France—is met by French Girl in a nurse's uniform—and you have done the trick—

Send it to the Vitagraph or the Famous Players Co. 57th Street (bet. 6th & 7th Ave) & *maybe* you'll get back the desired $25 . . . and maybe not!

I really am interested in architecture—and I think the grinding study necessary will be good for my lazy & undisciplined soul—The plan is this: I shall go right to Madrid where I have letters to a number of rather interesting people learn Spanish & meanwhile take architecture courses in the University—unfortunately I'll have to take some Math too, since architecture is not possible without it—horrid thought—then in the spring I shall go to Paris and try to get an Ambulance job of some sort. Après? Let us hope Berlin on General Joffre's sight seeing tour—I fear though that there will be nothing as exciting—For some reason I confidently expect peace next year—

Look here Rummy—you and I must take a trip together or something before long—We might go to Iceland or Montevideo or Clapham Junction—

About the Man on the Street: Collectively he's the forces of darkness—but taken one by one . . . You know, I rather divide people into those who see, and those who drift. There are people—you and I and Swinburne—who analyse, who observe, who think, and then there are people who merely follow the bandwagon—The people who are free, who are in revolt, and the people who are shackled by all convention— But the illuminati are not to be found in any one class of society—Lower than the stupidity of the uneducated is the stupidity of the educated whose education is nothing but a wall that keeps him from seeing the world—And most of our schools and college do that merely—Then there are so many other sorts of education—a farmer's boy who has never been to school may be beautifully deeply educated—again he may not But a stupid farmer is no lower on the scale than a stupid Harvard graduate—one who can't see beyond wealth and clubs and that abominable coverer up of things—*niceness*—See what I mean?—It is so hard to get away from the lingo, from the little habits of speech and action, from the petty snobberies of ones own class that it takes a distinct effort to see real 'illumination' and appreciate it, regardless of garlic or lavender water.

Undoubtedly the worst abomination and the commonest is snobbery——its so blinding to the human beauty that everything is warm with, that touches you like a friend's hand when you are walking through the dirtiest, slummiest streets or sitting in the most corsetted drawing room—

Forgive this young essay—this conte morale—(on second thoughts, it is about a third true)

But the greatest truths are thoroughly honey combed with lies, so I should worry—

I'd love to meet *your* Irishman—Do you like Irish legends? I quite dote on them.

I see you have your emotional thermometer in good working order—You'll be ready for a course of Russian novels in no time—I admit that I have the same disease and if I ever were to fall in love with a whole person—instead of with part of one—I should probably make out graphs of myself on ruled paper; like the statistics of an epidemic—

Write me again before I leave &
I'll send you my address—

Jack

September 28, 1916

To Rumsey Marvin

Bordeaux
Oct 24th

Rummy, Rummy, I meant to write you tons on the boat, but honestly I was in a state of complete coma—you've never seen anything like. I just lay around and looked at the sea and felt the damp caressing breath of it and sort of melted into it—gee it was wonderful!

But its result was nothing in particular—As for excitement—temps de guerre etc. There was unfortunately none—

I met a couple of people who confessed to having slept in their clothes, and was told of a man who slept in a life preserver—but everyone was astoundingly placid. Of course, there was nothing to make anybody anything else but placid, as not one thing happened and we only saw three cargo boats and a few lights all the time we were crossing. And under sea—nothing, not even a porpoise.

Still, at both ends of the trip we ran without lights and with portholes muffled, and the trip up the Gironde at midnight was very interesting as there were said to be floating mines there, and the captain would'nt let anyone go to bed until we were safe in the channel to Bordeaux.

Have you ever been here? It's an awfully nice city, with a couple of charming old churches and very many beautiful houses in High Renaissance style, very simply and charmingly built. Oh it's so nice to get to France again—so sort of cosy and homelike—

the long windows, the donkey carts full of vegetables, the odor of café au lait and fresh-baked bread in the early morning, the nice little écoliers with their bare legs and their black capes, the horse chestnut trees . . . if I had something with me to bubble over to I should be quite contented—as it is I am highly delighted and trying, as I wander about the cobbled streets, with the grass growing bright green in the chinks of the grey stone, to lash my poor brain into a state of productivity.

Its remarkable how soon, if I let myself, I relapse into a state of complete cabbagism, without thought of any sort, with merely sensual joy in the colors and scents of the world, or unreasoning discomfort in physical—not exactly physical either—rather in emotional disabilities of my own—Its so darn hard to get outside of oneself enough really to see clearly and to follow frankly your ideas to whatever rocky ground or shaky rope ladder they lead you.

By the way read by all means Hugh Walpole's "Fortitude"—I read it coming over on the boat. Most of it is simply ripping. One of the vividest—most forceful—novels I've read for an age——

How about your muse?

Verse?

Prose?

I leave here for Madrid tomorrow

Jack

c/o Banco Hispano Americano
1 Calle de Sevilla
Madrid Espagne

1916

Diary: November 13, 1916

Monday Nov 13

Where the week has gone the Lord only knows—

Downes & Jackson have turned up & the excitement of finding myself not all alone in the gloaming seems to have put the quietus on all forms of reading or writing. This sort of thing must stop.

Yesterday I had a most delectable day—took with Señor Rosada the morning train for Cercedilla—It's funny, but all Madrid seems to deck itself out in Alpine costume of a Sunday and betake itself to the Sierra. A morning of burning greenish blue sky—Well, walked to the "Twenty Club" where almuerzoed pleasantly—Well at twelve Señor R & his brother-in-law & little me in my beloved palegreen boots—started for the puerto (whose name, with incredible stupidity, I have forgotten) Well, when we got to the puerto we broke off to the left up the first peak of the mountain of the Siete Picos—a long range that waltzes all about you as the train takes its devious course from Madrid through the foothills. A long grind up through pine woods, lovely gnarled pines shaped like appletrees with the younger trunks of a pale brown, creamy color that contrasted wonderfully with the warming, purpling blue sky and the blackgreen needles in tight bunches. And the odor! A charming twittering little bird a bit like a sparrow kept hopping about us—When we got to the bald rockstrewn first summit a lovely view of the mountains and the bounding plain the warm yellow-reddish Plain of Castella la V. & the colder tinted Castella la N. We could see Madrid—Segovia, La Granja, Escurial & all this section of Spain as far as the Mountains of Toledo in the South, that hung in long stripes above a grey mist. Then on to the second peak where the end of the climb was up a rock-chimney and great fun: The north side was covered with snow frozen & blown into feather shapes by the wind as you scrambled up the snow on the tiers of feathers, above you was something—whiz! On the top we ate naranjas and manzanas & chocolate and bananas and had a glorious time. Right up against the blue, with all the world shadowed and misty, streaked with rich sienna of bracken and black of pinares below us. As we were going, by the devil's own luck, we saw two boys climbing up the vertical south face. As it was very hot, one of them had taken off all his clothes except boots & stockings and little drawers—and what did he do when we got down from the chimney and were on the next peak, but silhouetted himself, a marvellous brown figure, against the sky? All of which gave a finishing touch to the beauty of the mountains. Then we skirted the north side of the other peaks—walking at

times in rather deep snow and came down through a puerto
into a southward sloping valley full of lovely pines noisy with
streams—Beside a most nymphaic fountain we ate more bread
& chocolate and then trundled back to the train through a
beautiful, lucid—Peruginesque—evening——

Whee!

To Rumsey Marvin

Dec 4

Dear Rummy—Here are two letters from you within a
week—most joyful—You ask why I talked to you in California
on the numerous trains where—by the Devil's own luck—I
ran into you—Lord, I don't know exactly—except that your
"all together" sort of pleased me & then once started . . .
Do you know, I sometimes think one can tell congenial people a mile off—rather like Masons with highsigns!—the trouble with me usually is that they stay a mile off—You see in
California the luck was with me——

Is there anything on earth more wonderful than the 'silent
on a peak in Darien' feeling? You say in your first letter you
felt it about Walter L.'s book—I'm feeling it now about
Spain—and afterwards always comes the chilly mud-case sensation of complete ignorance—which I am also feeling now
about everything in general.

Hurrah for the touchdown! (I once caught a fly in a baseball game—that's the beginning & end of my athletic record).

You ask me to talk architecture—I'll try to be learned
about Spanish cathedrals someday—at present my architecture consists of drawing plaster casts in a man's studio for two
hours daily, and a jolly mess I make of it so far.

Oh—I must run to my lecture in Spanish phonetics—which
is at the other end of town—

A bientôt

Imagine me seated in a smallish room with pink shiny walls
on which I have plastered numerous photographs of my pet

Velasquezes & El Grecos—wrapped, as it is extremely cold & heating is unknown, in a large woolen manta I have bought— The peasants wear them, the women as shawls, the men as togas.

The wonderful thing about Spain, speaking of togas, is that it is a sort of temple of anachronisms. I've never been any where you so felt the *strata* of civilization—Celt-Iberians, Phoenicians, Greeks, Romans, Moors and French have each in turn passed through Spain and left something there—alive. Roman Italy is a sepulchre—Roman Spain is living—actuality— in the way a peasant wears his manta, in the queer wooden plows they use, in the way they sacrifice to the dead—not con- sciously of course, but with a thin veil of Catholicism. The pottery you see in the markets is absolutely Greek in shape. The music and the dances are strangely Semitic & Phoeni- cian Moorish—Even the little cakes in the pastry shops are Moorish—oriental—the sort of things odalesques with henna stained fingers eat in the Arabian Nights. Its the most won- derful jumble—the peaceful Roman world; the sadness of the semitic nations, their mysticism; the grace—a little provincial- ized, a little barbarized, of Greek colony; the sensuous dream of Moorish Spain; and little yellow French trains and Ameri- can automobiles and German locomotives——all in a tangle together!

Oh but Rummy you mustn't stop talking about yourself— to me at anyrate—and what is English between friends? Then, too, my letters are as full of 'I's as yours are and the paper ac- tually blushes at some of the grammar—If people got all the letters I composed to them, if all the plots I thought up in bed & then promptly forgot got turned into literature, if all the phrases that came bubbling up to the waterlevel of con- sciousness got written down. . . . well I don't know what would happen. Indeed I have often had the experience of composing letters to people or holding conversations with them (sort of subconsciously at first) while walking about—

Some day get hold of William James' 'Shorter Psychology' or his 'Varieties of Religious Experience' and I think you will have an awfully interesting time, as they are wonderfully fas- cinating books and not a bit dry. And they are the most interesting books on psychology I know. I suppose you haven't much time for them—but the time may some day be found—

The question of getting time to do anything in is constantly acute with me—I always have a feeling of running after a bus and never catching it. It is so hard to get half the desired things done—and particularly if, as I do, you waste time wandering about—

I'm quite settled in Madrid now, and shall probably be here until quite long after Christmas—when I shall go South and wander about Andalusia and Granada—but I really have no plans;—indeed, I still have a vague hope the Belgian Relief may produce something yet. Here enclosed are a couple of strange poetic sketches I'd like your opinion on—They are part of a running series of things on Spain—As you see they are very wild and irregular—Please write me what you think as I'm anxious to know—& do try & remember what it was you didn't like in the article.

V

Green against a livid sky
In their square dun-tinted towers
Hang the bronze bells of Castile.
In their square light brown towers
Rising from the furrowed hills,
Clang the bells of all the churches
The dust-brown churches of Castile.

How they swing the green bronze bells
Athwart olive twilights of Castile
Till their fierce insistent clangour
Rings down the long plowed slopes
Breaks against the leaden hills,
Fades amid the trembling poplars
Beside the silent swift green river.

Oh you bronze bells of Castile
That commanding clang your creed
Over treeless fields and villages
That huddle in arroyos, gleaming
With orange of lights in the greenish dusk,
Can it be, Bells of Castile,
Can it be that you remember?

Lurks there in your bronze green curves
In your imperious evocation,
Stench of burnings; ringing screams,
Quenched amid the crackling flames!
The crowd, the pile of faggots in the square,
The yellow robes . . . Is it that,
Bells of Castile, that you remember?

IX

"Die schöne Tage in Aranjuez sind nun zu Ende"
Schiller 'Don Carlos'

The Tagus flows with a noise of wiers through Aranjuez.
The speeding dark-green water mirrors the old red walls,
And the balustrades and close-barred windows of the palace,
And on the other bank, three stooping washer women,
Whose reddish shawls & piles of linen gleam in the green,
The swift dark green where shimmer the walls of Aranjuez.
There's smoke in the gardens of Aranjuez,
Smoke of the burning of the year's dead leaves;
The damp paths rustle underfoot,
Thick with the crisp broad leaves of the planes.

The tang of the smoke, and the scent of the box,
And the savour of the year's decay
Are soft in the gardens of Aranjuez,
Where the fountains fill silently with leaves
And the moss grows over the statues and busts,
Clothing the simpering cupids & fauns,
Whose stone eyes search the empty paths
For the rustling silk brocaded gowns,
And the neat silk calves of the halcyon past.

The Tagus flows with a noise of wiers through Aranjuez
And, slipping by, mirrors the brown silver trunks
of the planes and the hedges
Of box, and the spires of cypress and alleys of
yellowing elms,
And, on the other bank, three grey mules pulling a cart,

Piled with turnips, driven by a boy in a blue woolen sash,
Who strides along whistling, and does not look towards
    Aranjuez.

and another

IV
Difuntos (All Souls' Day)
Women are selling tuberoses in the square,
And sombre-tinted wreaths,
Stiffly twined and crinkly;
For this is the day of the dead.

Women are selling tuberoses in the square;
Their velvet odor fills the street,
Somehow stills the tramp of feet;
For this is the day of the dead

Their presence is heavy about us
Like the velvet scent of the flowers—
Incense of pompous interments,
Patter of monastic feet,
Drone of masses drowsily said
For the thronging dead . . .

Women are selling tuberoses in the square,
To cover the tombs of the envious dead
And shroud them again in the Lethean scent,
Lest they should remember . . .

Aranjuez is a sort of Spanish Versailles not far from Madrid
with a lovely palace of red brick & grey granite and most
wonderful gardens. (I mean the *outside* of the palace—The inside is as usual, a thing of horror).

Well I must stop this scrawly letter & get to work on a
story—

              Au Revoir or rather
              à la prochaine lettre
              Jack

                  1916

To Rumsey Marvin

Dec 12th

At the same time Rummy dear as you were writing your plaint of the passage of time and the not getting of anything done ever, I was scrawling the same thing to you—Isn't it a joke? Indeed I can sympathize—For my life is a mad scramble after a bus that I never can catch, and juggling oranges the while! Some day we ought both of us to go and live in an abandoned monastery after having left fictitious addresses for all the world, and try to make up for lost time. Or else a voyage round the Horn on a sailing ship with a box of books & a ream of paper, might help—When I sailed for Spain I certainly thought that, away from distractions and boredoms, I could get a pile of work done and also amuse myself immensely— and yet—here I am moaning the old moan—stealing time from this to do that, and finding that I absolutely can't loaf about as much as I'd like to—I mean, wander about the streets and sit outside cafés and watch the people and let Spain soak in.

Then there is something frightfully paralysing to me in the war—Everything I do, everything I write seems so cheap and futile—If Europe is to senselessly destroy itself—Its as if a crevasse had opened and all the fair things, all the mellow things, all the things that were to teach us in America how to live, were slipping in—a sort of tidal wave and blood and fire— I can't grasp the idea of conflict any more—it seems more some thing immense and malignant and living that is grinding the helpless nations—Oh those boys in Bordeaux—limping in and out of the hospitals— . . . It is the sort of feeling it gave me when I was awfully small and read somewhere of human sacrifices—The senseless grin of the brass idol—the stench and sizzle of the bodies in the flames—the cold, the blackness, the nauseous hideousness of it. I remember how I closed the history book feeling cold and sick all over—Would to God I could close this one. I sort of lose my nerve when I think of it. . . .

Rummy—I stopped your letter to write a poem & it's now one o'clock so as we say in Spain hasta mañana——P.S. The poem is damnably bad.

Its very cold in my room and I am anxiously awaiting the arrival of my coffee & roll—Enter said coffee & roll—Promptly to be engulfed—

The story of the pirate fight of the Italian Gardener ought to be fine—particularly as you'll be able to ring in a lot of local color Capri blues etc. Don't swab it on too thick though. In fact at this moment, when I ought to be doing other things I am reading a book about Arab pirates in the Mediterranean. Fancy your reading Le Cid—it's such a silly play—though of course beautiful velvety verse—the French classic tragedy does so amuse me—I don't think such boresome ranting was ever put into such perfect language—Still a little goes a long way—Poor Don Rodrigue—Imagine Mio Cid Campeodor, the champion of the Faith, the cruel sinister warrior—turned into a china shepherd!

Oh such a funny thing happened the other night. I was on my doorstep clapping for the sereno—a most medieval watchman with lantern and pike who keeps the keys to the outer doors of the houses—and when the door is closed you stand outside and clap lustily till he comes—when a rather passé painted lady in a shawl came up and said 'oiga, estoy muy simpatica' "Look, I'm awfully congenial!"—in the most coaxing tone. Poor woman. To get to the point where she had to be congenial! Fortunately the sereno came at that moment and let me in—but afterwards I couldn't help thinking how often I, like the Madrid dama, had wanted to go up to people and say "oiga, estoy muy simpatica"—

For the Lord's Sake, Rummy, don't complain of the frequency of ideas—You see the thing is that it takes a pound of internal idea to produce an ounce of really proper stuff, or at least I find it so—probably according to the law of degeneration of energy or something more complex still. But don't let school stand too much in the way of your education—though it's most meritorious to achieve marks etc, your real education is what you plug out for yourself—'tween times, don't you think so? And the atmosphere of the American school is numbing to the intelligence—at least so it seemed to me—I think one reason is that everything is so pleasant and well managed and healthy and godly that no one has a moment's time in which to think out a darn thing for himself. Everything is so predigested that the mental gastric juices disappear through pure inaction.

Sunday I went up to the mountains—the Sierra Guadarrama—with some Spanish friends and watched the winter sports! Skiing and the like. Moreover we went for a long walk and in one of the passes got into snow up to our thighs—it was wonderful, though bitterly cold with driving snow that nearly put your eyes out—Spain is indeed different than I had expected and Oh Rummy! so fascinating—Castile, all I know anything about (and that just a radius of thirty miles about Madrid)—is a dry dun-brown land of rolling hills—deep arroyos like in California and dry lead-grey mesas. Now the long slopes are powdered with delightful green of the sprouting wheat, and in the distance to the north, sometimes faint as clouds, sometimes sparkling like lumps of nibbled sugar is the Sierra Guadarrama—In the mountains it's very cold and even here in Madrid it goes down to freezing very often—is always chilly—And I had expected to lie in orange-gardens!

Have I told you about Toledo? Oh but that'll have to take a letter to itself. Suffice it that the entrance is over one of the most beautifully proportioned fortified bridges, old as the Moors and the rest of the city is the most wonderful conglomeration of gothic walls, Moorish palaces, Christian churches—all built of stone & brick in different shades of warm brown——

but I mustn't get started

Adiós
Jack
1916

To Rumsey Marvin

On board the S.S. *Touraine*
Hello Rummy!   Feb 20th

We have just started out of the Gironde—after having waited two days on the river between Bordeaux and the mouth.

Great excitement—You see, the Touraine is the first ship to sail since the closing down of the blockade—

Last night we lay with all lights out—and tonight passengers are not to be allowed to go to bed—and must sit with clothes and life-preservers on all ready to take to the boats— But we are to be convoyed—and it is blowing a little gale to boot—so I doubt if we have any trouble—still it is most interesting—The mouth of the Gironde is full of shipping— steamers, sailing vessels, waiting, I suppose, to get up their courage to go out—

The Touraine is an old slow and rather uncomfortable steamer—and I imagine will roll like a log—Strange to say, she is full up—first class, second class and steerage——2. PM.

21st

I *did* go to bed—and slept undisturbed by mines or submarines—And today I believe we are out of danger—

You can't imagine how amusing it was to see all the passengers roaming about with life-belts on—in the dark

About college—Don't go to Williams I beg—it is the home and original abiding place of the Y.M.C.A. young man—I'm rather cynical about American colleges anyway—Yale and Harvard are about even in my estimation—both having many faults and I suppose, virtues. Chicago is supposed to be good and Columbia They have the merit of having no "college life", and I imagine U of California and that other Californian college,—I cant think of its name at the moment—are good.

Of course I am personally tremendously fond of Harvard and Cambridge—and the Harvard kind of snobbery does not irritate me so much as the Yale kind—I mean the sort of thing those sacred 'frats' breed—

But the intellectual life in any of them is slim enough;—and they are all pleasant in their way and—if one doesn't take them too seriously—one can chug very happily through four years and emerge without having ones intellect utterly mossed over.

But, as I say, I am cynical about American colleges.

Do you know, Rummy, we must try and get together for a week or so somewhere sometime very soon—There are so many things to talk about and to do together. I want to read you all my favorite poems, make you read my favorite books, expound my favorite ideas—my favorite foods—and Heaven knows what besides. And all that'll take time you know.

I have not an idea in the world what my plans are, and shall not know until I have been some time in New York—

We are having a very mild and smooth passage for this time of the year—that is—so far—Off the Banks we shall probably strike dirty weather—as this is the worst part of the year on our coast.

Friday—Dear Rummy! Fire Island Light is now astern of us and, after a trip of 13 days we are pretty nearly in. I suppose we will dock tonight. Everything must be in wild excitement about War—The latest rumor that I've received is that a secret treaty has been made between Mexico and Germany deeding Mexico "the three southern provinces of the United States", whatever that means. But it's too absurd even for Germany Diplomacy; so it probably springs from the fecund brain of a New York reporter.

Drop me a line to 18 East 56th Street. It'll get to me even if I have gone to Washington, which I shall have to do before very long.

Oh, Rummy, I dread the arrival in New York and the sympatheticness of certain relatives I shall have to see. I wish people wouldn't make such a fuss about the most ordinary things like death and birth and marriage. There is enough incidental pain connected with them anyway, without cumbering them with conventions and childish trivialities—

If people would only look at life straight and sincerely without having to dim their sight—faulty enough, God knows—with colored glass of different sorts—with church windows and shop windows and the old grimy glass of outworn customs.

But I suppose ones own individuality is so much of a distortion of clear reality (and one can't see except with ones own eyes, can one?) that other little distortions don't matter much. And the glittering wonderfulness of it all bursts through somehow.

I've been reading Flaubert's "Tentation De Saint Antoine" coming over—it is a marvellous nightmare of religion and philosophy, a book positively seething with life and beauty and bitterness. As vivid as Salammbô and much deeper.

I'm having the bank in Madrid hold my letters—Eventually I suppose I shall collect quite a little budget of yours from there. Perhaps I'll go back.

But I really haven't a plan in the world——

Love—
Jack
1917

To George St. John

214 Riverside Drive
NY

My dear Mr. St. John,   May 15th

I hope you will forgive my long delay in answering your very kind letter—as I have been very busy doing all sorts of uninteresting things. But don't think that I haven't thought of you and of Choate.

And we too have entered the dance of death. It was inevitable—I suppose it would have been better had we done so earlier—but I can't quite reconcile myself to the thought yet. The whole condition is so hopeless. It seems as if all our energy—all this complicated civilization the European races have labored and murdered and cheated for during so many evolving centuries were frittering itself away in this senseless agony of destruction. Germany seems to me rather a symptom than the cause.

Oh but it is wonderful to live amid the downfall—and perhaps it is the birth-pangs too—

I really dont know why I should take up your most valuable time by disburdening myself of my half-baked ideas—please excuse them.

In three or four weeks I expect to sail for France—either as an Ambulance Driver with the Norton-Harjes people, or in some other capacity with the Red Cross.

I have been for a long while very anxious to see things at first hand—but circumstances have in every case interfered

This time, however, along with the rest of America—I think I shall get my taste of the war.

Please remember me to Mrs St. John and tell her that my Greek has, alas, improved very little since the days when she used to coach me in it in the parlor of the then "Horne House"—also to the other masters that date back to those prehistoric days—

Very sincerely yours

Jack Dos Passos

1917

To Arthur McComb

Dear Arthur—   Monday

Thanks for your note.

I fear I shan't get to Boston. So many things to do have come up that I shall not stir—alas—from the angularities of New York until I finally embark—

When are you coming down—all the family? Tomorrow? Next day? Do make it soon—

Of course you're passing your exams.

I've been spending my time of late going to Pacifist meetings and being dispersed by the police. I am getting quite experienced in the cossack tactics of the New York police force. I've been in a mysterious police raid, too; nearly piled into a black maria—Every day I become more red—My one ambition is to be able to sing the internationale—

What about Roger Sessions? Did he get arrested or anything?

I think we are all of us a pretty milky lot,—dont you?—with our tea-table convictions and our radicalism that keeps so consistently within the bounds of decorum. Damn it, why couldn't one of us have refused to register and gone to jail and made a general ass of himself? I should have had more hope for Harvard.

All the thrust and advance and courage in the country now lies in the East Side Jews and in a few of the isolated "foreigners" whose opinions so shock the New York Times.

They're so much more real and alive than we are anyway—I'd like to annihilate these stupid colleges of ours, and all the nice young men in them instillers of stodginess in every form, bastard culture, middle class snobism—

And what are we fit for when they turn us out of Harvard? We're too intelligent to be successful business men and we haven't the sand or the energy to be anything else—

Until Widener is blown up and A. Lawrence Lowell assassinated and the Business School destroyed and its site sowed with salt—no good will come out of Cambridge.

It's fortunate I'm going to France as I'll be able to work off my incendiary ideas—"Liberty what of the night?"

San culottely   Dos

Love to all the family and dependents

c. May–June 1917

To Rumsey Marvin

June 5th

Dear Rummy—   15 E. 33rd Street

You poor child—I thought that something of the sort had been up . . . I wonder if you hate to be sick as much as I do—that is, if they won't let you read.

Speaking of sickness, our correspondence is awfully ill and in need of a tonic. It'll pull through all right, but I fear it's temperature is low and that it is suffering from anemia and debility. But I miss it—an' I hope you do. Of course I've been as much to blame as you. I've been very busy, and a strange lethargic state has brooded over me—so that I haven't wanted to do anything. I have been darn depressed about the war and myself and everything.

Moreover I've been trying to pound out an article on Spain for the *Seven Arts*—I think they are going to publish it during the summer.

The loss of the chance to have a hike and a ramble with you— you damn lazy correspondent—has annoyed me amazingly.

When does your school close?

I sail the sixteenth for France as a driver with the Norton-Harjes Ambulance—I'll send you my Paris address later—

For God's sake write & cheer me up—and I'll try to answer with a little pep.

My only amusement has been going to anarchist and pacifists meetings and riots—Emma Goldman etc. Lots of fun I assure you. I am thinking of becoming a revolutionist!

For the love of Mike

    Write in the first mail

                          Jack

                          1917

To Rumsey Marvin

Honest I was delighted to get your letter—Rummy one——Is this your last year at St. Pauls? As I remember, ones last year at school is a strangely important performance while it is going on—which suddenly waxes big and bursts in the strange and chilly newness of being almost in college.

Shall it be Harvard or Yale? It really doesn't matter—if you dont take either of them seriously. If it weren't for the existence of President Lowell and other annoyances, I would urge my beloved Harvard more strenuously, and I wouldn't mind Yale a bit if it weren't for Tap Day.

But, mon ami, apropos of free verse—it's *meant* to have rhythm—its not the same rhythm as so-called metrical verse; but it's a perfectly definite and sometimes quite *regular* cadence. I'd like to read some of my stuff and other people's aloud to you to show you what I mean. Of course I very often don't succeed in getting any effect at all—but that's often the case with the regularest of verse!

Your suggestion of the swim is splendid. I've found another preventative of blues, however. An artist friend of mine here has found way down in the lower East Side a strange little restaurant—where are Arabs and Spanish Jews and a weird Arab orchestra and women in ordinary street-walkers' clothes who dance the most amazing half-Spanish, half-Egyptian dances, while Spanish Jews, Lascars and Turks sit about smoking hookahs and drinking bad beer—It's really too good to be true and reminds one more than anything of bits of the Port Said part of "The Light that Failed." The East Side is a wonderfully fascinating place anyway. After much wandering I've decided that the only nice and human parts of New York are the East Side and Greenwich Village.

But, darn it man, glory or no I refuse to be killed until I've hiked somewhere with you—I warn you that my ghost'ld haunt you and refuse to be exorcized except by being walked for days through soothing scenery.

From the mouth of the Ambulance, and from the jaws of Hell (ie War-vide Mr. Sherman) I cry to you one word apropos of God and man and all things on the teeming earth. Don't believe the New York Times. You see I live with a man who's on it and knows its inner workings. Believe rather the Call or Masses or the New Republic or the Ladies Home Journal—I vow before Jehovah that half the ills of the country are caused by the fact that all educated and intelligent Americans believe the New York Times as if it were Direct Revelation—or Tablets found on a Mountain by a reputable Brigham Young.

I'm sure that by the time I get back from the war you'll disown me entirely, I'll be so red, radical and revolutionary.

I've decided that the thigh or the ear are the two nicest places to get wounded. You should see the delightful equipment I have to get—wonderful big boots and duffle-bag and bed roll and hurricane lantern and pins and needles and a cake of soap and other wonders besides.

Did I tell you about sitting next to Emma Goldman's table in the café at the Brevort some time ago. It was wonderful—the people I was with knew lots of her myrmidons and we were the outer circle of her glory—She's a Bronxy fattish little old woman who looks like a rather good cook. She has a charmingly munchy fashion of eating sandwiches and pats her myrmidons on the head and kisses them in a motherly fashion.

I'm not leaving till Wednesday so Write—

Jack

June 1917

To Rumsey Marvin

On board the S.S. *Chicago*

Dear Rummy—   June 20, 1917

I'm awfully cut up about leaving without a glimpse of you—you old bigoted militarist—

You must write often—as I shall need cheering up I expect.

You see I dont believe in the "spiritual good" of war and I expect to have one hell of a time until I get accustomed to taking ambulance loads of pulverized people about—

I'll write as often as I can—

Do tell me what's going on with you—Why don't you learn to drive a car and come on over? You're not too young if you could get your parents to consent and you are certainly as efficient as I am—aren't you?

Hurrah—the whistle's blowing and the old tub is starting to move—Your letters'll be food and drink and ice cream sodas—to my dusty imagination.

My address is

    c/o The American Red Cross Ambulance

    7 Rue François Premier

    Paris—

Gee the river's glorious, pink and grey and pale orange with lights—

Love

Jack

To Arthur McComb

Dear Arthur—   June 28—

Grey opal clouds, grey opal sea and a complete nirvana of soft drowsiness. I've never enjoyed a passage so much. Until yesterday I neither thought a think or cracked a book. I lay on deck at the bow, my head pillowed by a life-preserver, and alternately slept, ate and entered into a grey cloudy nirvana.

We've had one submarine scare—the periscope turned out to be a very barnacly log.

The most unusual ship's company—general troopship atmosphere without the discipline. The military air becomes unbreathably dense through a combination of uniforms, two long guns a colored sergeant and Archie Roosevelt. One sings much about

> "God help Kaiser Bill
> Oh—old Uncle Sam
> He's got the infantry
> He's got the calvary
> He's got artillery . . . .
> Then, by God, we'll all go to Germany—
> God help Kaiser Bill

and other joys. The devil of it is that God seems to be helping Kaiser Bill again—by the very veiled and emasculated communiqués we get on the boat.

Again the converted, seen-the-glory-of-the-Lord, Saul turned Paul in me is coming out. I feel that I am going to pen an exhortation to the Thessalonians. Courage, messieurs, courage, there are five socialists on the boat. Imagine among what the steward tells me are *jeunes gens des meilleurs familles américains; et les Allemands, monsieur, aimeraient bien les torpiller* . . . Five socialists!—and there may be more—Glory Halleluja!

By the way—if the Monthly starts up next year at college—it can count on a hundred dollars from me—that is if I'm not dead broke by that time—But by God you must make it whiz. You ought to be able to print one red hot issue before getting suppressed anyway—I almost wish I were back in college—If I only had something to blow off steam in—I'd love to lambaste conscription and the daily press and the intellectual classes and Harvard's attitude—

You see here is St. Paul among us—and I've always thought that Saint Paul was the most unpleasant of that very unpleasant gang, the Apostles.

Overheard from Archie R. (honest)

"But it's not only for Germany"

"__ ____ _ _____"

Major R. "No, sir. . . . when this is over the U.S.'ll be one of the greatest military nations in the world."

A.R.— *The* greatest
Major R. Then we'll be all ready to . . .

Unfortunately I missed the context—but I think I heard enough to chew on for a while. And this from Princes of the Blood.

> Nearer Bordeaux
> 29th
> And still untorpedoed.

Learn to sing the Carmagnole

> Dos

Remember that my address is
    c/o American Volunteer Red Cross Ambulance, Paris
      7 Rue François Premier

> *1917*

Diary: June 20–July 2, 1917

Sailed June 20th 1917
Band playing hula hula on the wharf people dancing in and out among the luggage—

Man who wanted paper as a souvenir—"cause you see sir I'm seein' off my son. I don't reckon they'll mind do you, sir?"

"I don't reckon they'd mind" goes off mumbling.

La traversée—uniforms—smoking room crap games. Singing. champagne—

"For we're bound for the Hamburg shoal to see the elephant and the wild kangaroo"

"God help Kaiser Bill
God help Kaiser Bill
Oh old Uncle Sam,
He's got the infantry
He's got the cavalry
He's got the artillery . . .
Then by God we'll all go to Germany
And God help Kaiser Bill"

General atmosphere of expectation of raising hell in Paris.

June 26th
Where' we going boys?
"Oh we're bound for the Hamburg shoal
To see the elephant and the wild kangaroo
    And we'll all stick together
    In fair or foul weather
For we're going to see the damn show through"

At Sea June 27th 1917
    I have no more memories.
    Before,
    My memories with various strands
    Had spun me many misty-colored towns,
    Full of gleams of halfheard music,
    Full of sudden throbbing scents,
    And rustle of unseen passers-by—
    Vague streets rainbow glowing
    For me to wander in . . .

    Today,
    As if a gritty stinking sponge
    Had smeared the slate of my pale memories,
    I stand aghast in a grey world,
    Waiting . . .
    I have no more memories.
    Sea and the grey brooding sky—
    Two halves of a flameless opal—
    Glow soft and sullenly
    In a vast sphere about me
    As I, very drowsy, lie
    On the deck; by the rise and fall
    Of the sound of spumed water
    Lulled into dreaminess,
    Into a passionless mood
    Of utter lassitude,
    A dull Nirvana where stir
    Negations without stress.

    As the petals are stripped from a rose,
    Faded to grey by the rain

Of a sere autumnal day;
So, shrivelled, grey
The pale veils of pain
And pleasure skip from the morose
And bitter emptiness
Of the core of lives and deaths
But gently through the deck beneath my back
Pounds the rhythm
Of engines urging the ship on her track.
In the stoke hole
Shoveling coal, shoveling coal
Stokers are striving
And sweating in the heat and dust
Their hard bodies writhing
With the weight of great shovels of coal
While the sweat runs in white streaks
Through the black coal-dust
On their bare heat-singed flesh . . .

Pain, a dagger plunging
Tears the misty veil.
Strife, a red sword, lunging
Forward out of the pale
Blankness of despair,
Rings its tocsin-flare
Of life through the grey charnel air—

June 27

Old man rushes out to put a hat on the head of a fellow who has none while the ambulance section is walking through Bordeaux.

Whores—protection etc—Champagne

Poitiers—July *2nd*
Wide grey-green fields,
Dappled with swaying vermillion,
Everywhere glowing with stains of poppies,
Poppies sprung from old sad fields
Of a battle long fought out . . .

How many years, oh God,
Before the blood of battles springs up
Into the arrogant glowing youth
Of poppies?

Grey-green fields,
Wide dappled with swaying vermillion,
Everywhere stained with a glow of poppies—
Bleeding with poppies,
Poppies sprung from old sad fields
Of a battle forgotten . . .
How many years oh God
How many rains and suns,
Before the blood of battles springs
Into the arrogant glowing Youth
Of poppies?

To Rumsey Marvin

Dear Rummy— July 12
   I wonder where you are—and I hope you've been wondering where I am—But America seems infinitely far off now—I
can hardly imagine it exists at all. I've never experienced anything quite like the strange break with everything past that
has seemed to come over me since that sleepy quiet trip—of
which I remember nothing but sleeping in the sun on the
hard friendly deck.
   Life since then has been a grotesque—a jumble of swoon-
ingly pleasant and strangely sinister despairing times. A sort of
Alice in wonderland with the world at stake instead of the
March Hare's watch.
   (I'm a fiercer pacifist-at-any-price than ever)
   I'm still in training at a camp in the middle of heavenly
French hills within distant hearing distance of the big guns to
the north—and of course I am nearly bursting with impatience

to get to work—but I must wait for a new section to be made up—an affair of ten days or two weeks.

In Paris, by the wildest good luck—I ran into three of my best friends. We had a lovely time wandering about dark silent Paris, quite forgetting war and discipline and duty in our excitement at meeting.

Tell me what you're reading—and for God's sake don't believe what your prep-school teachers tell you. With this St Paul to the Thessalonians sort of an exhortation, I close

Love

Jack

Sandricourt, 1917

To E. E. Cummings

Hello Estlin!   Sandrecourt

I hear you are with section twenty-two, wherever that is. I got over here a little over a week ago on the Chicago, and am now in the training camp of Sandrecourt—hoping to be sent out in a couple of weeks—somewhere—and meanwhile drilling, eating watery soup, and listening with vague interest to the casual tomtoming of guns that you can barely hear to the North. The scenery, however, is delightful and most soothing. Of course there's no chance that we'll land in the same section, but perhaps we might get together on leave sometime—

Drop me a note as soon as you can—addressed 7 Rue François I

I've met already—Bobby Hillyer & Van den Arend, both of Norton's gang—and Dudley Poore—on the American Ambulance Field Service—

Au Revoir

Dos

Written on a hillside with larks.

July 13, 1917

Diary: July 31–August 15, 1917

July 31st St. Martin-les Prés—Definitely I must start jotting
things down——
Paris—A strange Paris of whores and tragically sad widows
—The abandon of complete misery—My God—how ridiculous
it all is—I think in gargoyles

The men of the Middle Ages had the right idea in their rol-
licking grotesque dance of Death—I want to write a novel
called the Dance of Death—or some such title—though I fear
it'll be much used and abused by the time I come to do it—

I'm dying to write—but all my methods of doing things in
the past merely disgust me now, all former methods are
damned inadequate—The stream of sensation flows by—I
suck it up like a sponge—my reactions are a constant weather
vane—a little whimsical impish—giggling—sneering at tragedy—Horror is so piled on horror that there can be no
more—Despair gives place to delirious laughter—

How damned ridiculous it all is! The long generations toiling—skimping, lashing themselves screwing higher and higher
the tension of their minds, polishing brighter and brighter the
mirror of intelligence to end in this—My God what a time—
All the cant and hypocrisy, all the damnable survivals, all the
vestiges of old truths now putrid and false infect the air, choke
you worse than German gas—The ministers from their damn
smug pulpits, the business men—the heroics about war—my
country right or wrong—oh infinities of them! Oh the tragic
farce of the world. Hardy's Arch satirist is more a bungling
clown than an astute and sinister humorist.

Châlons—

We left Paris early, and arrived there, marching from the
station through grilling hot streets full of powdery dust to a
big arid "park" of automobiles & camions—there we were
put up in a barracks—very hot—and "fraternized" with many
poilus—all told the same story of utter boredom—and desolation—Hate of the Germans is rung in now and then, con-
ventionally, without convictions—one is too tired to be

anything but bored. Oh the dull infinity of dead. Occasional flashes of the most charming and graceful spirit of comradeship liven the dry dustiness of it all.

Bobby & Van & I had a delightful time in Châlons—going in swimming in the Marne, arrayed in the delightfully abbreviated & striped French tights, finding things to eat and drink, nosing about the rather unimpressive cathedral & the lovely church of Notre Dame & the lovelier church of St Alpin—that has one of the loveliest square Gothic towers I've ever seen—over the crossing.

I'm enjoying myself vastly, though I have a dusty unfruitful feeling—shall I ever produce anything? I wonder. I'm so damned lazy—so damnably lacking in conviction. Perhaps I shall—

One thing I know however—all my past attempts are on the wrong tack—I've closed the book of them, thank goodness,—and I've cleared the space for the new edifice. At least I think I have—but I know in my heart that whatever I do will be along the old lines—I want these notes to really begin something—I wonder if they will.

I'm sitting in the old beer garden of the erstwhile inn we're using as a barracks—in an arbor—how many pleasant drinks have been drunk here! how many wedding parties flushed with champagne have laughed and giggled and blushed and felt the world soft and warm with the phallic glow!

Behind me the French cooks are assiduously preparing our supper with an inimitable air of Savarins cooking for Henry Quatre. The French have such a wonderful relish for simple eternal things—food, women, music, soft undulating scenery . . .

It's raining pleasantly and lucid pensive drops fall one by one from the smallish horsechestnut trees, falling with a faint kiss on the puddley gravel. A rather seedy arbor vitae in front of me has its lower branches fringed with the gleam of the raindrops.

How ridiculous that Bobby—Van and I should be here—Its so very pleasant in the sloppy untidy garden—with the Frenchmen preparing dinner in such a charmingly noisy manner, and the children in dirty blue pinafores crunching about in wooden shoes.

Then, too, I've had my hair all clipped off and it's wonderfully amusing to explore with my fingers the hills and valleys and bristling tablelands of my skull.

The fellows on the section are frightfully decent—all young men are frightfully decent. If we only governed the world instead of the swag-bellied old fogies in frock-coats that do! oh what a God-damned mess they have made of organized society, the bankers and brokers and meat-packers—and business men. Better any tyranny than theirs. Down with the middle aged!

Aug 15   Have been amusing myself in three ways
   1. Writing a novel in collaboration with Bobs

   2. Eating & drinking omelets & white wine

   3. Having wonderful naval fights with fleets of paper boats on the brook—
Tomorrow we go to the Front to a devilish hot section
Don't forget Athos, Porthos & d'Artagnan—

To Rumsey Marvin

Dear Rummy   Aug 23
I've been meaning to write you again & again—but I've been so vastly bitter that I can produce nothing but gall and wormwood

The war is utter damn nonsense—a vast cancer fed by lies and self seeking malignity on the part of those who don't do the fighting.

Of all the things in this world a government is the thing least worth fighting for.

None of the poor devils whose mangled dirty bodies I take to the hospital in my ambulance really give a damn about any of the aims of this ridiculous affair—They fight because they are too cowardly & too unimaginative not to see which way they ought to turn their guns—

For God's sake, Rummy boy, put this in your pipe and smoke it—everything said & written & thought in America about the war is lies—God! They choke one like poison gas—

I am sitting, my gas mask over my shoulder, my tin helmet on my head—in a poste de secours—(down underground) near a battery of 220s which hit one over the head with their infernal barking as I write.

Apart from the utter bitterness I feel about the whole thing, I've been enjoying my work immensely—We've been for a week in what they say is the hottest sector an ambulance ever worked—All the time—ever since our section of twenty Fiat cars climbed down the long hill into the shot-to-hell valley back of this wood that most of our work is in, we've been under intermittent bombardment.

My first night of work I spent five hours in a *poste de secours* under poison gas—Of course we had our masks—but I can't imagine a more hellish experience. Every night we get gassed in this sector—which is right behind the two points where the great advance of the 21st of August was made—look it up & you'll see that we were kept busy—we evacuated from between the two *big hills.*

It's remarkable how many shells can explode round you without hitting you.

Our ambulance however is simply peppered with *holes*—how the old bus holds together is more than I can make out—

Do send news of yourself—and think about the war—and don't believe anything people tell you—'ceptin tis me—or anyone else whose really been here.

Incidentally Jane Addams account that the soldiers were fed *rum* & ether before attacks is true. No human being can stand the performance without constant stimulants—

It's queer how much happier I am here in the midst of it than in America, where the air was stinking with lies & hypocritical patriotic gibber—

The only German atrocity I've heard of was that they sent warning to a certain town three days before they dropped aero bombs on it so that the wounded might be evacuated from the hospitals—

Even French atrocities that you hear more of—slitting the throats of prisoners etc.—sort of fade away in reality—We've carried tons of wounded Germans and have found them very pleasant & grateful & given just as much care as the French. The prisoners & their captors laugh & chat & kid each other along at a great rate.

In fact there is less bitterness about the war—*at the front*—than there is over an ordinary Harvard-Yale baseball game.

It's damned remarkable how universally decent people are if you'll only leave them to themselves——

I could write on for hours, but I'm rather sleepy—so I think I'll take a nap among the friendly fleas——

Love
Jack

SS.Ane 60
7 Rue François I
Paris France
Here's another page—

You should have seen the dive I took out of the front seat of the car the other day when a shell exploded about twenty feet to one side of us—We were trying to turn on a narrow & much bombarded road——C'était rigolo, mon vieux! The brancardiers in the dugout are practicing their German on a prisoner——So long—Write at once.

Near Verdun, 1917

Diary, August 24-26, 1917

August 24th

Seated in the garden, where I've been sleeping all the afternoon en repos—It is the most charming of gardens with what was once a pool of water with a fountain, at one end in front of the shell of the little pink stuccoed house the garden belonged to. We use it now as a dug out and dive into it when the shells the Germans persist in tossing into this blessed village get too close. It is just the sort of garden a pensive little French boy with large brown eyes & premature scepticisms should play in, a garden full of such plaisance with its white roses and its fat-juiced pears and its white blotches of phlox-flowers among evergreens that it makes one hate still more all the foolishnesses with which men try to disturb the rich ease of life—The soul of it is in the faint breath of box, musty with generations of tranquil closes, shutting out the turbid asininity of life about us, or of death & dullness.

Death, that should come tranquilly, like the dropping of an over ripe pear, brimming with sweetness, why should it come in the evil shriek of a shell? And what's it for, what's it for? Governments are only makeshifts—like patent toothpaste—less important perhaps—and who would die for toothpaste, or kill for it.

The gas waves of stupidity!

I wish I could write verses, but I cant concentrate my mind enough on any one rhythm or mood—My ideas come in little hesitant showers, like flower petals when a wind blows after rain.

I'm sitting in the garden amid the aroma of it, soothed by the pathetic ruined soul of it—and over across the river in our dusty barracks, the rest of the fellows—alas Americans have so little tea—are probably quarrelling over their food.

Why can't they learn the lesson of perfect camaraderie from the French?

At present America is to me utter anathema—I cant think of it without belching disgust at the noisiness of it, the meaningless chatter of its lying tongues.

I've been trying to read a copy of the New Republic that has come over—honestly I couldn't get through it. Its smug phraseology, hiding utter meaningless—was nauseous.

And away off the guns roar & fart & spit their venom & here I lie spitting my venom in my fashion—

A bottle of white wine & a jar of gooseberry jam & an evil memory of canned goods on your stomach—such is war.

For some reason one falls back constantly on profanity. I've never in my life sworn so many swears or thought so many swears as since I have been "doing my bit" in France.

The utter goddamned ridiculousness of things so takes your breath away that you have no other recourse than the lame one of profanity—

And then of course when artillery trains get in ones way & camions run amuck in gas-soaked valleys—there is nothing to do but swear.

Aug 26th Out of sheer desperation of laziness I have been trying to sleep—but as the flies & the fleas and the biting & nipping & crawling things that I have acquired in postes de secours are equally desperate in their resolution to bite & itch

The little doctor at PJ gauche bending interestedly over a piece of cheese—mais il y a des petites bêtes dedans—regardez donc les petites bêtes—Qu'elles sont grandes—
Meanwhile the shells fall snort snort all round & the brancardiers from the door of the abris shout in vain for him to come in

Also the doctor & the aumonier at PJ right—seated at dinner with the inimitable air of a function the blessed French give every meal while shells burst all round & spray them with small stones go on drinking from their petites verres (conserved heaven knows how and looking utterly fantastic among the tin mess kits) continue with perfect calm to discuss linguistics, I think—
Later, the delightful aumonier out looking for his glasses—without his helmet, chased by a brancardier who pops it on his head—
How wonderful they are those nonchalant priests who wander about under shellfire, never a bit preachy, always quiet and absent minded and mildly amused—They make things go marvellously smoothly & well. Imagine a troop of heroic American clergymen in their place—
The marvellous part of the French is how unheroic they are The despair of them is absolutely Greek in its calm beauty——
Curious how impossible it is for me to write any verse—prose comes rather well—but verse simply wont
I wish I'd kept this beastly diary up—as things slide by so far they lose their impressiveness—except those that outstand, which of course gain.
But, gosh, I want to be able to express, later—all of this—all the tragedy and hideous excitement of it. I have seen so very little. I must experience more of it, & more—The grey

crooked fingers of the dead, the dark look of dirty mangled bodies, their groans & joltings in the ambulances, the vast tomtom of the guns, the ripping tear shells make when they explode, the song of shells outgoing, like vast woodcocks— their contented whirr as they near their mark—the twang of fragments like a harp broken in the air—& the rattle of stones & mud on your helmet—

And through everything the vast despair of unavoidable death of lives wrenched out of their channels—of all the ludicrous tomfoolery of governments.

To Rumsey Marvin

Aug 27

By candlelight in a dug out—Outside it is raining & German shells falling sound like infinities of heavy chain dropped all at once

Dear Rummy—

I've wanted time after time to write you & have produced many unwritten letters—you know the kind—Also two delightful letters from you have spurred me on—

But I've had so much to say & so much of it will be so hostile to your ears, you old militarist, that I haven't known where to begin.

Let's see When did I last write? It seems that it was in Sandricourt, when I was enduring the sorrows of training camp— After that we formed our section, S.S. u60 in Paris & jaunted by easy & unwarlike stages to a town on the Sacred Way, a little above Bar le Duc of blessed reputation——Ah but I'll continue in the morning—Imagine me stretched out on a stretcher on the floor of the dugout listening to the German shells whistling overhead & wondering if a chance one'll hit our roof—

Aug 29th

I am sitting in the charming weedgrown garden of a little pink stucco house whose shell only remains & if fortune favors

I shall finish this letter. It is a delightful day of little sparkling showers out of thistledown clouds that the autumn-nipped wind speeds at a great rate across the sky. I've not been on duty today—so I've been engaged in washing off to the best of my ability the grime and fleas of two nights in a dugout. Nos amis les boches have been keeping us excessively busy too, dropping large calibre shells into this town; as if the poor little place were not smashed up enough as it was.

We stayed for two weeks with our feet in the mud at Erize la Petite—a puny & ungracious hole—There the only interest was watching the troops, loaded on huge trucks—*camions*— go by towards the front where an attack was prophesied.

For some reason nothing I've seen since has affected me nearly as much as the camion loads of dusty men grinding through the white dust clouds of the road to the front. In the dusk always, in convoys of twenty or more escorted by autos full of officers, they would rumble through the one street of the ruined village.

The first night we were sitting in a tiny garden—the sort of miniature garden that a stroke of a sorcerer's wand would transmute into a Versailles without changing any of its main features—talking to the schoolmaster and his wife; who were feeding us white wine & apologizing for the fact that they had no cake. The garden was just beside the road, and through the railing we began to see them pass. For some reason we were all so excited we could hardly speak—Imagine the tumbrils in the Great Revolution—The men were drunk & desperate, shouting screaming jokes, spilling wine over each other—or else asleep with ghoulish dust-powdered faces. The old schoolmaster kept saying in his precise voice—"Ah, ce n'était pas comme ça en 1916 . . . Il y avait du discipline. Il y avait du discipline."

And his wife—a charming redfaced old lady with a kitten under her arm kept crying out

"Mais que voulez vous? Les pauvres petits, Ils savent qu'ils vont à la mort"——I shall never forget that "ils savent qu'ils vont à la mort"—You see later, after the "victory", we brought them back in our ambulances, or else saw them piled on little two wheeled carts, tangles of bodies with grey crooked fingers and dirty protruding feet, to be trundled to the cemeteries, where they are always busy making their orderly little grey wooden crosses——

Its curious. Do you remember Jane Addams statement that everyone in America jeered at, about the French soldiers—all the soldiers in fact, being doped with rum? Its absolutely true—Of course anyone with imagination could have guessed anyway—(there went a shell—near our cantonment, too) that people couldn't stand the frightful strain of deathly—literally so—dullness without some stimulant—In fact strong tobacco very strong red wine, known to the poilus as Pinard, and a composition of rum & ether—in argot, agnol, are combined with the charming camaraderie you find everywhere—the only things that make life endurable at the front—

Having our headquarters in the much bombarded remnants of a village, we do our business in a fantastic wood, once part of the forests of Argonne—now a "ghoul haunted woodland"; smelling of poison gas, tangled with broken telephone wires, with ripped pieces of camouflage—(the green cheesecloth that everything is swathed in to hide it from aeroplanes), filled in every hollow with guns that crouch and spit like the poisonous toads of the fairytales. In the early dawn after a night's bombardment on both sides it is the weirdest thing imaginable to drive through the woodland roads, with the guns of the batteries tomtomming about you & the whistle of departing shell & the occasional rattling snort of an arrivée. A great labor it is to get through, too, through the smashed artillery trains, past piles of splintered camions and commissariat wagons. The wood before and since the attack— the victory of August 21st look it up & you'll know where I was—has been one vast battery—a constant succession of ranks of guns hidden in foliage, and dugouts, from which people crawl like gnomes when the firing ceases and to which you scoot when you hear a shell that sounds as if it had your calling card on it—

The thing is that we, on our first service, landed in the hottest sector ambulance ever ambled in. My first night out I was five hours under gas—of course with a mask, or I shouldn't be here to tell the tale——

But the whole performance is such a ridiculous farce. Everyone wants to go home, to get away at any cost from the hell of the front. The French soldiers I talk to all realize the utter uselessness of it all; they know that it is only the greed and stubbornness and sheer stupidity of the allied govern-ments &, if you will, of the German government, that keeps it going at all——Oh but why talk?——its so useless—There is one thing one learns in France today, the resignation of despair—

Still, I'm much happier here, really in it, than I've been for an age. People don't hate much at the front; there's no one to hate, except the poor devils across the way, whom they know to be as miserable as themselves. They dont talk hypo-critical bosh about the beauty & manliness of war: they feel in their souls that if they weren't cowards they would have ended the thing long ago—by going home, where they want to be. And lastly and best, they don't jabber about atrocities—of course, everyone commits them—though about one story in a million that reaches our blessed Benighted States is true.

But I really must shut up. More later—

Love—

Jack

Near Verdun, 1917

To Arthur McComb

Dear Arthur—   Aug 27

Van & I were sitting side by side in a pitiful forsaken gar-den we spend our hours off duty in, and he was just opening your letter when a shell shrieked over our heads & exploded with a vicious pang! in the hill behind us. Of one voice we cried 'how ridiculous'. Isn't it damned absurd that one of your serene epistles redolent of eighteenth century abbés pee-ing in their gardens after their morning cup of chocolate off flowered Sèvres and thinking sonorous cadences of liberty and the world enlightened, should be opened to the accompani-ment of a bursting shell

But absurdities are so multiplied in this macabre world of our day that the grotesque loses its gargoyl-force and all flattens out into one dull despair—

Oh Arthur can't we do something, we who still have eyes in our heads & thoughts in our minds? Can't we stop this wailing over the dead?—Our life is a wake over the corpse of an elaborately garbed Liberty that I suspect was purely mythical anyway. Like the Jews at their wailing place the Liberals cover their heads with their robes of integrity and wail, wail, wail—God—I'm tired of wailing. I want to assassinate.

The joy of being on the front is that one is away from the hubbub of tongues, from the miasma of lies that is suffocating the world like the waves of poison gas the French & Germans in this sector reciprocally honor each other with. Then too, the excitement of it is splendid—for us to whom it is new; it'll soon wear off, however, into the utterest routine.

"Pensez", said a stifled mule driver that lurched into a dugout we were lying in during a gas attack one night, 'Qu'il y a des gents qui boivent le café sur les boulevards'

The French are invincible. They don't chatter—they are utterly charming and much more concerned with the ravitaillement than with the German attacks & every man jack of them realizes the utter futility of it all. They have ceased to argue; they merely suffer & shrug their shoulders—

Like the Greeks the poilu has reached the sublime heights of despair—In him the classic is vindicated. For one for whom there is no hope, only the rhythmed fittness of tragedy, death and pain are conquered eternally.

Some of the essays in Brandes' The World at War are very good—The old critic makes a rather superb figure—and, God, how few they are, the prophets of reason—There is no sound of their voices heard amid the babble of the priests of Baal—

I shall never forget the frightened eyes of the horses—choking of gas, standing beside their overturned gun carriages, waiting for the shell that will finish them—

And the drunken troops we saw go by in camions towards the front, camion after camion passing with grind of gears amid the the white powdery dust, while the old schoolmaster in whose garden we were sitting (it was in a town far behind the lines) kept saying "Il n'était pas comme ça en dix neuf cent seize. Il y avait du discipline . . . Il y avait du discipline—" and his charming wife, hugging a kitten closer & closer to her, her black eyes full of tears—answering, "Mais mon cher que voulez vous, ils savent qu'ils vont à la mort, les pauvres petits, il savent qu'ils vont à la mort"—

Yea verily—ils savent qu'ils vont à la mort—And the only joys left in the world are alcohol & tobacco—I'm not joking: I mean it.

And all that I leave unsaid—I shall have to come home—to heave 'arf a brick into the temple of Moloch if nothing else—at least to disturb with laughter the religious halo of the holocaust. Will you join?

Love—

Dos

Near Verdun, 1917

To Rumsey Marvin

Paris

Nov 12th

Dear Rummy—

"In that part of the book of my memory, before which little could be said, may be found a rubrick, reading: Incipit Vita Nova"——and so begins Dante's Vita Nuova & my excursion into Italian——

For know that many things have been happening—The Volunteer Service on the French front has been, as was threatened, taken over by the American army. I gracefully retired and have been lazing in Paris ever since—an atrociously delightful month of wandering through autumn gardens and down grey misty colonaded streets, of poring over bookshops and dining at little tables in back streets, of going to concerts, and riding in squeaky voitures with skeleton horses, of wandering constantly through dimly-seen crowds and peeping in on orgies of drink and women, of vague incomplete adventures—All in a constant sensual drowse at the mellow beauty of the colors & forms of

Paris, of old houses overhanging the Seine and damp streets smelling of the dead and old half-forgotten histories.

And now, mon enfant, I'm going to Italy——

Therefore a Dante, panoplied with Italian grammars and dictionaries.

You see in view of the recent excitements, a hurry call has been sent out for more ambulances. A lot of the remnants of the old service have volunteered—and here we are, off day after tomorrow in a convoy of Fords for the Italian front—

God knows where it'll be by the time we get there!

Write voluminously & often—

c/o Morgan, Harjes & Cie

31 Boulevard Haussmann

Lots of love——Jack

1917

Diary: November 14–December 7, 1917

Nov 14th

In Cope's room waiting for him to awake & arise & dine. Have spent the afternoon reading Petronius & Dante's Vita Nuova—strange combination!

Then I wrapped my head in Dudley's "this-colored" comforter & went to sleep—a light charming sleep in which—as in a frieze in Livia's house on the Palatine, moved the little contorted episodes, the Priapus—figures, and the little flashing pictures are scenes of the Satiricon—all curiously illumined by the white liturgical light of the Vita Nuova—

Then to awaken & to leave Dudley who wanted to ruminate over solitary herbs—& to walk at a mad rate through the fog & the glaring lights & the little groups seen & lost again—all the while thinking of the marvellous life of the Satiricon—how far away they are in their unreformed joy of the flesh—how it brings out the tragedy of lust—all the yearnings & risings of the penis & phallic flashings—

The more you fan the flame of your desire—the more frothings of the lard there are—after a certain

Nov 17

>The present is an unmasticated thing
>The digested in the future.
>The past is the blood in your veins
>The harp the future plays upon

Nov 25th

The great excitement—followed by the resultant boredom & blues

The trip grows more exciting as one goes along—

The incomparable boy of Montelimar—and now a whore in Marseille have filled me with a perfect sheaf of marked memories. This, by the way, is the 27 of November 1917—

Marseille is a place of tinny exciting glitter & spangle of comic opera crowds of all sorts—Algerians, Morrocans, marvellous ebony gnarled faces of Senegalese—and all manner of scum & dirt & fleas & squabble & jabber—The Mediterranean world—

Yesterday *The fire*

The marvelous Moulin à Vent dinner with Fairbanks

The cafe of the acrobatic waitresses oh god oh Montreal what a *spectacle* (pron. à la boche)

The way they histed up their skirts & seized the pennies—all with the expression of a Boston Child's lady sympathetically bringing a fine cut piece out of her apron—

and the unshockingness of the performance—the utter casuality of it—Waitresses, bar maids picking up pennies in their cunts!

bah one has seen it every day of ones life—

Dec 7

Genoa's a glowing spot in the distance and I am in Milan—reached after a night in Pavia—Villainously cold. Milan is a cheerless ponderous town with lots of buildings that would be charming anywhere else but that here are dull & stodgy or like nervously ornate and meaningless—Una citta maledita—I am writing this in a very bad musical show.

I am too far away to hope to understand and I am sleepy and its dull and I wish I had the sense to amuse myself with literature—The people I'm with want to go whoring, I wish I did. It is such a simple naive way of amusing oneself—Why people think it is worth the trouble I can't imagine. Of course love, attraction, the most temporary sort of affair of that sort is different—a barrel with a bunghole in it seems to be their only idea of women. It isn't worth the trouble. I suppose its only by going out & getting them that one makes adventures—but good God—why not wait? Things do turn up in time—vide Cope's letter

Also the guide who came up to us in the Square—in very bad English almost singing this

> Nice girls
> Naked girls
> Open all the time
> Dancing

What a fine chorus for a troop of pandars in a mask of love

Saw The Last Supper—Christ has just said "one of you shall betray me" and is sitting with malicious smugness amid the rough house of excited apostles—a banal & sentimental smirk as the climax of a wonderful composition—Brr—I detest this play

To Rumsey Marvin

Hôtel Cavour
Milan
Dec 9th

Darn your hide Rummy—

I want to hear from you and a letter persistently refuses to come—For some reason Italy keeps making me think of you—and its the very devil not to have you around or at least an eidolon (an image of your soul) in the shape of a letter——Gawd, what a soul I must have if this letter's an eidolon of mine. But I feel irrepressibly writative tonight so you'll suffer for it. But first I am going out into the cold and clammy streets of the ponderously dull city of Milan, a city of bankers that might be Denver, Colo., for any charm or beauty—Still Italia and the south and the ancient dream does creep in. In one of the rawest streets there rises the solemn series of a Roman Colonade. In Sant' Ambrogio are exposed three brown skeletons of Saints, in gold crowns and with embroidered slippers on their feet. On the coldest days women go about the streets selling yellow Solferino roses and chrysanthemums and carnations that have split with their fatness the spathes of their calyxes.

I have been out & have eaten pasta al sugo and pesce frito and salata and violent formaggio in a small and mournful restaurant. It is snowing, and I am wondering where we will go at the front. If they send us into the Alps—it'll be the frozen hell of the inner circle of Dante's Inferno, how frozen you'll know if you try to crank a recalcitrant automobile on a cold day when the crank handle bites your fingers and every piece of metal you touch is colder than ice—But there is a chance that we shall go to the western Piave— where it'll be warmish and rainy, and far pleasanter. At any rate we are leaving Milan in four days for some unknown point on the front.

The trip up here was great sport. From Paris and across to the Loire through the Forêt de Fontainebleau, a marvel of faint color in the ashen greyness of winter; then up the Loire to the uplands at its source and down through the mountains into Mâcon in the valley of the Soâne; then down the Soâne to Lyon and Vienne and out into the warmth and sunlight of the valley of the Rhone, where the roads were dusty with the white dust of the Midi and where cypresses rise in solemn exclamation marks among the vines.

In Montélimar, a white town full of plane trees above Orange, I met one of the most charming people I ever hope to run into—a boy of about thirteen whose passion was to faire le piano, and who was an amazingly vivid and fiery young person. We talked while I was ministering to the wants of my car and later walked together about the little town, he pointing out the interesting things with a wonderful contemptuous familiarity. He was one of those people who leave a glow in your memory for ever. I dont think there is anything on earth more wonderful than those wistful incomplete friendships one makes now and then in an hour's talk. You never see the people again, but the lingering sense of their presence in the world is like the glow of an unseen city at night—makes you feel the teemingness of it all.

Then we went on to Marseille where we stopped a few days to repair cars. There, in the glittering comic opera atmosphere of a city full of a scent of voyages to distant places, full of exotic vistas through the ages, I nearly fell in love with a girl I saw in the promenoir of a Variety, the very temporary love of a friend of mine—again one of those fervid people from whom life glows in a sort of halo. Probably fortunately the section was leaving the next morning, so she remains a dazzling memory. Then we passed through the post card colored Côte d'Azur, Nice and Cannes and the rest of them—meaningless places after the crude jingling color of Marseille. The Italian Riviera was a different story; a wonderfully dangerous road winding among brown cliffs and through steep olive gardens and terraced gardens where white pergolas held up the vines arching paths that led to the doors of preposterous pink and mauve and ochre-colored villas with pea green shutters,—a road that dove into villages through ancient machicolated gates and gave you glimpses of court yards and dark doorways where old women sat and shelled beans and where corn hung to dry in bright orange clusters of ears——a road that lasted for two solid days, during which we wound with the sea at our feet and the hills at our left hand and the sky at our right hand.

The convoy turned north outside of Genoa and stopped in a cold and miserable village—Pontedesimo. That night I escaped with another fellow and took a car into Genoa. The glimpse we had of Genoa by night is one of the most fascinating things I've ever done. An oilship was burning in the harbor and lit up the tips of towers and the broad facades of the houses on the citadel with a pearly pink glow. The dark streets near the harbor were the very middle ages made manifest, full of shrines and oaths and meaningful whistles and women leaning seductively from high balconies, and footsteps lost about sudden dark turns. There were drunken sailors there bawling bawdy songs in all sorts of languages, pursuing savage looking women with frowsy hair. We found a café where the orchestra was playing wonderfully noisy Offenbach, where we drank strega and ate ices. Then we wandered about on the smooth mosaic pavements of the main streets of the city, which are very wide and edged with sumptuous colonades. We looked for a long while at the two great marble lions in front of the Cathedral and then came away through harbor streets now dark and sinister and round the point where the great square lighthouse is. From there we got a last view of the city—dark moulded hills holding pools of lights, like stones in the palms of a negro's hands, and the bay still glowing with the burning oil ship. Then we walked back to the place where the cars were parked—fifteen very weary miles. We got past the Italian sentry who was guarding the cars from the natives and then found Gouverneur Morris, our correspondent, a little drunk & reeling about in the moonlight. It was nearly dawn and he couldnt get into the hotel and nor could we—so we all camped in a doorway at the foot of a flight of stone steps in a great mass of army blankets and were stepped on in the morning by the people in the house——altogether an awfully funny affair.

Hah—another break in your letter during which I took a bath & now I am going to bed—I also read some Rabelais and yawned over an Italian grammar——

Love

Jack

By the way what are you reading nowadays? For the Lord's sake don't get the idea that your school work is educating you—'taint—All the education one gets comes from ones own reading or ones own living and you really have to have the reading to have a standard to test the living by——

School & college interfere with ones education most horribly anyway

Addio

1917

Diary: December 9, 1917

Dec 9

Still Milano—

By the way—

An oil ship was burning in the harbor the night we were in Genoa; a pearly rose glow lit up the pedimented facades of the houses on the hill and the square pointed church tower that rose above them, etching them curiously against the dark hills behind the town where the lights along streets dotted out new constellations to match those in the brilliant night sky—

This sentence has haunted me for days, I used to think it was good; now I know it's bad—It is now Dec 10. I am in Milan at the Hotel Cavour—sitting beside Van, who in a bearish mood is trying to compress himself into letters & send himself off to America. The most amiable thing about that curious person is his love for his friends in America.

Have I the faculty for making friends? I wonder—I seem in my life to have made exactly two—which is little for one so greedy as I.

I've just been dining with Fairbanks & his whore, Nita at Compari's—a curious rather sad meal in elaborate surroundings that constantly made me think of *La Dame aux Camélias*—The poor girl had a bad cold and a cough and could eat nothing and was as miserable as only a lady of pleasure can be. We heard the usual story—How universal it is, and, stranger still, how universally true. She was a dancer—balleto classico—before the war took away her trade—did the oriental dance in Aida as première danseuse at the Della Verona Theatre. Then she lived with an American for three years, who finally left her in a furnished apartment with a child, he going off ostensibly to the front but really with a cocotte from Covu's. She had never heard from him since; the child had died.

Her tale of keeping up appearances, from one who knew her lover had deserted her—was pathetic. And now she was in the streets with a certain Nida, a boisterous friend.

After the war she would take a dancing contract for vaudeville & tour America. The high comedy of their hiding from the waiter & chambermaid and director of the Hotel Diana. Jack's sudden leaving of Nida was worthy of a cleverer Congreve, was actually Shakespearian

What marvellously brutal people are the clever & radical young like Jack & Van! I suppose I'm as bad in my supercilious way—Youth is a hideous period—from some aspects—C'est un horrible gâchis, la vie des hommes.

To Rebecca Cummings

Milan
My dear Mrs Cummings,   Dec 16th 1917
    Can you tell me anything new about Estlin? Ever since his arrest last Fall I've been trying to find out about him—but have been unable to get at anything definite, either through Mr Norton, or members of section XXI, or French army people I've talked to about it. Everyone agrees, however, that nothing serious could happen to him—They think he'll be held for sometime at a concentration camp and then sent back to America. If that has happened—everything is probably over by this time.
    I sympathized with him so thoroughly, and my letters being anything but prudent, that I expected I'd be in the same boat but the censor evidently didn't notice me—so I'm still "at large", as the blood and thunder militarists would say of us. I'm in the Italian Ambulance Service of the American Red Cross (address c/o American Consul, Milan)
    I hope it won't be too much trouble to drop me a line—as I'm awfully anxious to get in touch with him again.
    Please remember me to Dr Cummings and to your sister—
                                        Very sincerely yours
                                        John R. Dos Passos
By the way, Mr. Gannett is also trying to find out about Estlin—I got a letter from him on the subject sometime ago from the American Red Cross, Paris.

Diary: December 31, 1917–February 10, 1918

Dec 31st

The Italians are hopeless. They trouble me vastly—because I fear that my reluctance to be American & Anglo Saxon and unsympathetic (not that anyone else is sympathetic with foreigners, God knows) is a hopeless bar to any real estimate, as if anyone could form a real estimate on any country living in it for three weeks in the peculiar parasitic way we do.

I'm fed up with the whole business anyway—now the thing is to retire into that famous shell of mine & open the door ajar, and gird on butterfly wings in the large lands behind it—absolute fantasy is the only escape—the drunkenness of the imagination. . . . .

Meanwhile—as I write—Jack and I are discussing America in a vague way—Its the motto "Be good & you'll have money"—or "have money & you'll be good"—

I wonder—

I'm at the moment terrifically taken with *Julian and Maddalo*—& shall probably write huge amounts in imitation of it.

11:30 The last minutes of the seventeenth abortion of an abortive century are flying and the obstetrics of the New Year are at hand. Funny—Last New Year I was in Cartagena—dark Phoenician streets with latticed bays & big bird cages and shrill whistling of birds—and the ruined castle on the hill where the Gypsies lived—. Since then rather a lot has happened—Didi—those beastly months in New York—and the Rabelaisian roister of the summer on the fringes of death's dull carmagnole.

12:30—Why wont they let a year die without bringing in a new one on the instant, cant they use birth control on time? I want an interregnum. The stupid years patter on with unrelenting feet, never stopping—rising to little monotonous peaks in our imaginations at festivals like New Year's and Easter and Christmas—But, goodness, why need they do it?

Damn it—I shall read Shelley

I've lost the key to my famous door—

Yes the coming of the new year is certainly a gloom—New Years always are—but never so much as this one—I am filled at the moment with a mad desire for poetry—to write it. As a poor substitute I can read it—As an illustration of my pitiful state,—I feel like copying down the entire of Shelley's West-wind, part to feel my fingers forming poetic lines—

Jan 1–1918
> The future has become the present
> A fact for love to resent

as Blake would have written.—Anyway the constant pour of futurity is a bally bore—The present's all right in its way—if only it weren't formed out of the dust of the future's rain-bowings.

To call the war a carmagnole is an unpardonable preciosity. Stupidity has more of the exhilaration of madness.

The New Year—celebration—oh God I hate to write about it: Two majors—the Guy Lowell man who built Emerson Hall and a certain effeminate Wilkins-creature—also a major—came in rather drunk to wish us, out of the real kindness of their hearts—a Happy New York— God! the things they said. We are here for propaganda it seems—more than for ambulance work—we will be used in the most conspicuous way possible—We must show Italy that America is behind them. That is to say—America has entered—with England & France into the publicity contest as to who shall save Italy—

The soldiers, they said, were so stupid and ignorant that if you gave them two packages at once they would look from one to another stupidly like an ass between two bundles of hay or a bally Figian—but, that, with cajoling, he thought they'd be induced to remain in the trenches they had tenacity and fought with the courage of devils when fully aroused—and properly manipulated—God, it made you want to vomit to hear it. So we are here to help cajole the poor devils of Italians into fighting—they dont know why, they dont care why——

Probably—from a coldly intellectual viewpoint—the most interesting feature of the Italian situation will be that here, owing to the simple mindedness and ignorance of the Italians all the issues are vastly simplified. The machinery of how governments are run and controlled into war is more obvious—to a citizen of fairly sophisticated countries the wires will seem plain as day

How damnable is the vast complacency of people about the world.

A wonderfully Rabelaisian luncheon & breakfast combined is worthy of preservation in the scrolls—
1. Caffe latto—uova al olio 2 at café
2. Confiture—toast
2 fried eggs
coffee
Lamb chops
Onions
Honey
Oranges
Nuts—Is that not a meal radical enough to set before Old King Cole?——

Jan 2nd

Thoroughly hors de combat—I have a cold—bronchitis—etc—& have run a thorn into hand which has bitched the mechanism thereof so that I can hardly write.

Great scene in Covas—Either in America Conquers the World or the novel

Sinbad was in bad
In Tokio & Rome
In bad in Trinidad
And twice as bad at home

Dutch girls with golden curls
Standing by the Zuider Zee
And big brunettes with stelelets
On the shores of Italy
Hulas & hulas would pucker up their lips
He fell for their ball-bearing hips
And they were pips

Oh wild women loved that child
He could drive the women wild
Oh Sinbad was in bad
All around——

Tonight we'll wander through the streets and note the qualities
of people . . .   A. & C. Act 1

Jan 2

a cold day of blank fog—read, amid much suffering from ail-
ments, Antony & Cleopatra & Measure for Measure——
    Great enthusiasm thereat
    Drank much tea with figs & lemon in it——
    Van & Jack & I sat all day amid the Russian novel atmo-
sphere of our disorderly room.
    On account of my thorn in the hand I cant write

Jan 3rd

    To write or not to write—fafreddo e umido e oscuro—I shall
write Mickey—inspiration——
    I am sitting in the upper room of our cheerless villa at the
table that has the pink lace skirt-thing on it, a table at which
the lady of the house once sat to do up her hair—now, alas,
fallen & stained with tea and ink and candle grease—In the
center of the table is the peacock blue flame of the famous &
trusty gasoline stove—"Hope-Deferred-Maketh-the-Heart-
Sick". Around it are Van & Jack & me; Van in a dirty tea shirt
with a blanket round him so that he looks like lo the poor
Indian, Jack scrawling large on foolscap, and meeself, cold &
minished.
    We live in a sort of Russian novel atmosphere—cold, dingi-
ness, dirty nails, untidy beds, lack of washing appliances—
idleness punctuated by tempestuous arguments & bitches
personal squabbles over small irrelevancies. All day long we sit
about and drink tea with figs in it, glancing out now and then
at the dreary winter of the Venetian Plain, where rows of pollarded trees make dreary processions of hunchbacks, black &
gnarled in the mist, and where Italian soldiers tramp mean-
inglessly back & forth through the cold.
    On some days the Euganean Hills and the mountains behind
lie in dazzling white and rose above the plains to the North,
then there are airraids at night, and in the day the sun shines
and we walk through the mud and go to look at the campaniles
of Venice across the lagoons, rising commonplacely above the

railway track and freight-yards, and smoking factory chimneys of the landward side—a denial of Romance.

Afternoon—walked with Van & Bragg—They seem to be making a line of defense from Padua to the sea along the canal— Barbed wire stretches in long blue strips across the wheatfields and vineyards looking like some obscure crop sprung up in a nights growth—behind the road this side of the canal trenches are being dug and machine gun emplacements made. The whole defenses show a completeness that seems to mean business rather than insurance against emergency.

I suppose that if the Germans break through at Asiago— the Italians will thus fall back from the line of the Piave to the line of the Brenta Canals & Padua—abandoning Venice & this entire strip of land.

Lets hope they retreat before we leave.

Jan 4th

Breakfasted this morning off huova all'burro at the little trattoria—Sat watching the grey warmish half light of the dark wooden tables coming out from the two walls, regularly, like pews, and the brilliant white light on the wall across the street against which anyone coming in was silhouetted, as he opened the glass door—All the time a string of soldiers marched down the road outside—helmets and guns and blanket rolls showing out strongly against the brilliant light—Exactly that arrangement would make a wonderful stage set——

Note:

At college Fibbie's finding of Suzanne's letter written him a couple of years before about his Uncle James' death— telling about the long summer after his illness when he lay languidly, dying, pouring out all his life into her—Thus Suzanne in future will be the result of those two summers spent with James Clough. They will be the gold by which she tests the tinniness of the world's standards.

Night of Jan 4th

Coles Seeley's room at the hospital in Mestre—watching to keep him from getting out of bed in his delirium.

A cold uncomfortable vigil whiled away by reading Flaubert— Un Coeur Simple, St. Julien l'Hospitalier, & Herodias

At four two big snorting explosions shook the windows and the glasses on the table—air bombs. Then the electric light snapped off and the fun commenced. I stood on the balcony of Seeley's room & watched the searchlights ineffectual in the glare of the moon & the red flashes of guns & the spit of machineguns as everything let loose at the sky. Once I imagined I saw a shadow like a plane across the beam of the searchlight—but it is unlikely—The main effect of the rough-house was the whimpering sound and the menacing rattle as they hit, of pieces of shrapnel falling.

It's quieted down now, so I suppose the Austriaci have done their damnedest & left.

Jan 5th

Flaubert was the most wonderful company in the world last night, and read in their strange context the flaming warmth of the three stories stamped itself strongly on my mind—I feel as if I had lived them.

After the air raid things quieted down and at about five Coles fell into a heavy sleep. I slept too till half after eight—then thankfully drank some coffee & a mouth full of wine & feel awfully chipper.

God, how beastly it is when our bodies go back on us and betray us to a nest of microbes. Yet there is a certain romance about illness in the Mediaeval manner that makes you almost desire it; Arthur, faint unto death, carried away by the queens on a barge to Avilion . . .

Jan 6

Again in Seeley's room in the hospital. He is vastly better this time & I merely sit about & wish I were a chatty conversationalist. It is villainously cold in this room & the light is barely good enough to write by: I try to display my inchoate Italian for the benefit of the very pleasant orderlies—but it is hardly a success—Reading Villon—but I feel too dopy & cold to concentrate on anything except the hope of food. And people say that cold is stimulating, bosh—

The section left today for Bassano—under Monto Grappa—said to be a villainously cold town—but lively with what

liveliness the Italian front can produce——As usual S. F. & I
are left behind on account of the repairs to our blessed bus—
We are to rejoin the section in three days.

I still sit rigid writing cold—waiting for pranzo.

Jan 8th

Women & the war—The new feminism—And the more
women who get mixed up in it the better. Its an education
in gall & wormwood and flesh and hate and the varied
hideousnesses and beauties of life. The idea that a woman is
a high fallutin' uncarnal creature, that, if she has any mind
she must keep it resolutely fixed on the Ideal, whatever that
is, refusing to look at things as they are. Out of things as
they are are ideals made, worthwhile ones, not out of the
waxwork figures that stand about on clouds of pinky sentimentality in the woman's world. The sad part of it is that its
from the women of a generation that the next generation
gets its all-important things—life, attitudes, sensibilities &
revulsions—The men make a great jabber, but they are awfully incidental parts of the machine of reproduction. Its on
the women, that the men to come, as well as the women to
come, depend. That's why it seems to me so infernally necessary for women to be mixed up in the holocaust. American women, especially, for in America lies the future, the
menace & the hope—At present more of menace than of
hope. Our whole life is a childish failure—our inane attitudes towards the war, our ignorance & stupidity, our wom-
anish sentimentality stored up like a vat of dye, ready to be
poured over whatever those who pull the strings of our ideas
& emotions want disguised.

And on this question of wars & nations the future depends—
Whether it shall be the old round of greedy miseries—of
sacrifices to ancient blood tainted tribal gods—or something
new—with hope in it.

Jan 10th

Sitting in the "palatial Villa" occupied by Section III beside
a man who looks the image—God save him—of the typical
Schubert Chorus man in a Broadway show—in the next room,

the billiard room—the Section is playing craps—wonderful
ejaculations & a primeval clink of the bones—come in to me,
mixed with the crinkle of notes—A phonograph plays sentimental pieces fed to it by the Schubert-man.

Yesterday—was the great offensive on Venice—F & I started
out suddenlike on the car & came—following the canal, deep
puttey-green through plains covered with snow, to Fusina,
where the little steamer leaves for Venice. It was a grey day
with a faint rosiness of sunlight that brought out most wonderfully the colors of the houses along the canal—pink with
pale blue shutters—greenish ochre, peeling to pink of old
bricks, magenta covered with black and green lichen. ("My
dice") (He-ow, ten")—and all the roof tiles snow-covered—a
little like some of the brilliantly colored snowy Christmases
imagined by early painters—who felt they must have orient
color & winteriness as well—There was something about the
grey light & the greenish reflecting canal—that raised all the
little houses above the commonplace picturesque—into an
amazing patchwork of beauty. Then came the blank marshes
& flocks of sea birds & the utter classic borediness of a gull
poising over a black stake—& on the boat a little man was in-
forming us—between salutes—that really we could not get
into Venice without the written permit of someone—he didn't
care whom—As a favor, he said we could go over with the
boat so long as we remained on board until she came back—

So there we were standing, ruefully enough, in the bows,
with the feeling of people under taboo in a fairy tale—The boat
slithered through the cold lagoon water & we watched the
factory chimneys & commonplace greyness of the city on
the horizon become Venice. We passed an island with brick
fortalice walls against which were moored black barges &
where the houses stood over the water on black vaults—with
watergates—Then the Hoboken grey became touched with
red—Venetian red—and we were sailing up a wide road with a
row of torpedo boats to the left & an island to the right covered with long houses, off which the stucco peeled in green &
orange leprosy. Then the little boat was coming up to the shore
just beyond a bridge spanning a canal—up which we peeped
into the intricacy & charm of Venice—For some reason one
was impressed—One thought Byronically, de Mussetly—one

hung out of balconies & threw roses to imperious gondolas—
the threadbare garment of a century's romanticizing was for a
moment whole cloth—nay it was the embroidered garment of
an ancient courtesan of Venice, a mistress of Spinello, whom
Titian painted—and who went on a spring day to wander with
Giorgione along the hedgerows of the Euganean Hills——One
joined the vast company whom Venice had for a moment
dragged out of the sordidness of life——little German schoolteachers, fat Jewish bankers, elderly Englishmen full of gout &
decorum——all the imitators of the Shelleys & the Byrons——
——Venice makes one feel a little like a person impressed by
a Coney Island side show—there's a vast & beautiful & varied
vulgarity about it—and yet in Venice there is the Byzantine the
concentrated Oriental that thrills one immeasurably——

Julian & Maddalo—with its color, its touches of pomposity,
& its sentimental psychology—is the soul of Venice.

Then the barges alongside, black—held to the wharf by
ropes of brilliant ochre, and then on their decks what a comic
opera crew—But, damn it, man genuine—the woman in blue
with a great apron & a magenta rose shawl crossed on her
breast—she was genuine——And the lion of St. Mark up on
his column & the St. George standing on his column astride
his dragon that looks like a tunny-fish. And the lace front of
the Ducal Palace with its frillings & flutings bricked up for
fear of aero-bombs—and the string grooved Campanile——

> Doges coming down to the sea
> To inspect wharves & cargoes
> To sniff with the noses of merchant princes
> The quality of pepper and spicebales
> That negro slaves are unloading
> Marmosets pulling at their velvet gowns
>
> Parrots shrieking on chrome yellow bales
> Heat and a smell of ships
> And the sweat of galley slaves
> And the rinds of fruits of the orient
> That drift in the greentide towards the Lido
>
> Venice rises like a dream
> Sharpening dull brains to the brilliance

Of the varied color of earth
Out of the sluggish lagoon
Of the popular imagination

Jan 10
A foot sore walk over slippery kilometers—twenty three of
them or twenty seven of them to Padua—there the severe
coldness of one of its restaurants & a little excitement over a
German plane that calmly sailed to & fro in the azure above
the city. Cold.

Venice achieved Jan 11—Color—Cold—rosy sunlight across
a pale blue lagoon—faintly covered with purple "purpurato
haze"—and the little steamboat crunching through the ice
that skidded ahead & swirled in white chunks astern—
St. Marks—a gilded parchment of the middle ages—St. Mark's.
The usual gondola ride between the beautiful facades of the
palaces of families with old sounding names—Then the ducal
palace—the huge halls full of the romance of dead pompos-
ities, of past injustices—from which the canvases that told
with such gaudy braggadocio the wealth & the arms of
Venice have been moved to Firenze for fear of the Tedeschi
aeroplanes.
Venice is totally dead—swathed in sandbags—shops & shutters closed, windows boarded up—inhabited by soldiers on
permission & by sailors & a few scared civilians—yet there
was enough life left in it to excite me considerable—

The doge goes down in state to the sea
To inspect with beady traders eyes
New cargoes from Crete, Mytilene,
Cyprus and Joppa, galleys piled
With bales off which in all the days
Of sailing, the seawind has not blown
The dust of Arabian caravans.

In velvet the doge goes down to the sea
And sniffs the dusty bales of spice:
Pepper from Cathay, nard and musk,
Strange marbles from ruined cities, packed
In unfamiliar-scented straw.

Black slaves sweat and grin in the sun
Marmosets pull at the pompous gowns
Of burgesses—scuttle in sudden fear
To hide in crimson sails or climb
In gibbering on the naked back
Of lash scarred galley slave. Parrots scream
And swaying clinging to ochre bales—

Dazzle of the rising dust of trade—
Smell of pitch & straining slaves
And out on the green tide towards
Drifts the rinds of orient fruits the sea
Strange to the lips, and bitter, and sweet . . .

Venice, a drugged summer dream
A waking drum, a bewildered momentary life
Rises, thrilling with color sheen
Of the sluggish lagoon
Of popular imagination

O I must go out alone

In velvet state the doge goes down to the sea,
To inspect with sharp beady eyes of a trader the three
Laden galleys from Mytilene, Crete
And Joppa

My verse is no upholstered chariot,
Gliding oil-smooth on oiled wheels,
No swift and shining limousine
But a pushcart, rather . . .

A crazy creaking pushcart, hard to push
Round corners, slung on shaky patchwork wheels,
That jolts & jumbles over the cobblestones
Its very various lading:

A lading of Spanish oranges, Smyrnian figs
Flyspecked apples—perhaps of the Hesperides,

Curious fruits of the Indies, pepper-sweet——
Stranger—choose & taste

Jan 11—1918

Jan 14

Solitary birthday dole-feast in Venice—where I went to buy condensed milk for section 1—I'd describe the marvellous beauty of the lagoon at sunset, the Alps to the north the domes & campaniles and flat intricate facades of Venice—but I've already done so in letters to Dudley & Auk—& my thin ingenuity is completely worked out—
Dolo We are still here—piano—domani—I'd gladly skin alive to a slow fire those bastardly dastards of mechanics at the auto park—

I'm sleepy & have a contented sponge feeling—What's the use though? Sopping up color-impressions is as meaningless as sopping up alcohol if you dont follow it up by any reactive process—I fear I'm a mere sponge.—Sometimes I show stains on the outside—but thats not creation—When one's spirit wants to plunge head down into the abyss & with huge arms measure off——like Blake's drawing——Damn—I'll go to bed!——

Jan 15th

Went up to the garage: the car will be ready domani—as usual. While there I somehow tumbled into a discussion of the war & the world in general . . . Everybody joined in; it was great fun—the corporal and the sergeant and the bystanders. I made my usual little speechifications, thinly spreading the butter with words like militarismo—capitalismo—socialismo—and though now & then I got out of my depth & nearly choked in a flood of Italian—The sergeant was disgusted with all civiltá; he wanted to get away from war and government—and hide in Asia or Africa somewhere, where he could live off the fruits of his toil & till the ground in peace. "Life's a short & painful process at the best—let us for God's sake, live it out untroubled by your greeds & wars and sanctimonious laws—you people who govern—if not we'll eventually show our teeth—à la lanterne!"

God! If people were not so damnably adaptable to any form of misery——

But it gave a glow of delight & comfort to feel that they were not entirely dupes. Universal disbelief in anything is what the dear bourgeoisie are bringing on us with their wars & creeds & cants——

O for a revolution of laughter—couldn't all the world at once see the gigantic humor of the situation—and laughter shall untune the sky.

Midnight Jan 15th

Reading Butler. Someone is playing the *Seraphina* on the phonograph—There's a festival brass in it that makes me think of health resorts—a continental watering place on a warm summer's night with lights & crowds walking about & sharing cafés and a ship—a long string of lights—coming into the harbor from the sea.

Jan 18th

Bassano at last—Day before yesterday—after much desperate waiting about at the garage—we finally dragged the famous Fiat 4, odds curse it, out of the clutches of the automobile park and late in a foggy afternoon—set out for Bassano, giving farewell to Dolo & Mira very joyfully. At Padova we picked up a young English officer who wanted to go to Cittadella. It got very dark and very foggy, and our acetylene headlight wouldn't work. The Englishman got politely nervous and we ended, after fruitless efforts at lighting the acetylene which only made a bad smell—by sticking two candles in our headlight. Even that was unsatisfactory as it was raining & the road was muddy—a notto louta—as Touda, our Sardinian mechanic, said. The Englishman was good enough to have us to dinner—an Italian farmhouse room with four Englishmen, one the Padre & F & I, & an English soldier who waited on us like a butler—and English food & all the appurtenances of a truly British dinnertime. . . How wonderfully true to type the British are! fantastically so. We ended by spending the night there with them—awfully nice young fellows they were, the officers of a trench mortar battery, most courteous & amiably simpleminded, disliking the war yet seeing nothing to do but keep on. Their greatest passion was the fear of being unEnglish. With them we went in the evening to a wonderfully futile cinema entertainment given by the padre to the men of the battery—also a marvelously English affair.

Then we had a very English breakfast—porridge—bacon & eggs & tea & toast—How marvellously they manage to take their isle with them wherever they go!

Run up along the main road to Cittadella, a fortress with huge red brick walls in ponderous decay—a wonderfully fine place, and thence by the muddly main road, since so familiar, in its crowdidness & general excitement & badness, to Bassano.

Bassano's an awfully fine place completely empty—with frescoed house faces & arcades & beautiful towers. There is, too, a wooden bridge across the Brenta—a red covered bridge—that is a braw thing to see—The town stands about on an irregular hill & there are fine views of the gap through which the Brenta breaks through the mountains & of the high hills in front of Grappa.

There are batteries not very far away that make a great racket every day at about dawn. We have evacuation work at present & have so far done considerable. We sit about in a room that smells vilely of gasoline vapor from Fafner & Hope-Differed-Maketh-the-Heart-Sick—and we overeat God! how we overeat!

I am reading with great amusement Don Juan—a pleasant but it seems to me a marvellously unimportant poem—cheap cynicism, cheap sensuality, cheap romantic claptrap—all suffused by a warmth of color & at the same time by a colloquial smartness that is vastly annoying. Its the sincere fervor of coloring that saves it though; and one can't deny moments of acid cynicism that bring up the end of certain stanzas with the snap of a whip.

Jan 20th
Walk with Van up the Brenta Valley—How great the mountains are!

Jan 21st

Last night read my chapters to Jack & Van—their sum of criticism was that things are too jerky, not elaborated enough and that too much is left unsaid, so that the unfortunate reader wallows desperately in a slough of constant misunderstandings. My retort was that happenings meant nothing in themselves, anyway—& that I tried to give that impression—by the recurrence of words & phrases etc—but I rather agree with them that it isn't done successful—still. . . .

I'm sitting in the window feeling a bit chilled—looking at the slender campanile whose dome is shaped like a hare bell— Then there's the wide bed of the Brenta silvery green though sheenless in this light—In the center is the fine covered bridge that crosses the narrow part of the river further down—and to the left the dark green hill of Bassano with towers coming up out of the foliage. One can hear just a little sh-sh from the river and now and then a gun shot reverberates in the mountains behind us. I'm as usual hoping for lunch—Belly is a tiresome god—unapt to any purpose—but he does pass the time particularly as worship at his shrine is sublimely easy, compared to the toiling needed by other divinities—

Jan 24th

Sitting up in bed with a belly ache due to the hellbrew of rum punch last night—a fair grey morning tipped with rose & faint salmon color—I am still struggling to find chapter to write about what ??—in beginning of Book II—

and evening & morning were another day——Zabaglione is a genuinely champagne-tinted drink, thick & velvety, scented of rum & vanilla, oversweet, oversoft, overstrong—but full of a fascination—To be drunk by fat Isoldes on deep champagne colored couches while Tristans with rosy round cheeks & fair flowing hair let their great slow tears plash in the huge cold cup—A vision of a—what's the name of the sad baritone in whose arms Tristan dies? (Jack shouts 'call him James')——beating the posset behind the scenes with his sleeves rolled up——

Red-nosed gnomes roll & tumble in the rosy firelight—roll on their backs and drink out of earthen pots, wriggling their huge round bellies—and the air of the cave is heavy with a smell of crushed vanilla and of hot punches cooking.

One lies in a velvetiness of yellow moths stirring faintly tickling wings—One is heavy & full of sleep and tingling langor—until later one goes and pukes beautifully under the moon.

Jan 25th
Asolo—at the end of a long road—

Bragg to Jack—"You can talk about your soul all you want and all that, but—when I've gone to bed you might moderate your voice"——

Asolo appears in the hills, a squarehold, gray against the sky, and lower hills covered with houses, with towers and tiled roofs—then one climbs and sees no more of Asolo, toiling up a most painful road—and at last you find yourself in a street climbing up much like a street in Dunsany's town at the edge of the world.—O it's a splendid town and after walking through it you come to the Scuola Meletti Browning on the Via Roberto Browning and things are made manifest in the flesh.

Tonight is bright moonlight & a cold keen wind and a sound of a German avion overhead—

> Oh get away from that window
> My light & My life
> Get away from that window
> Wont you please?
> For there's going to be a fe-ight
> In the middle of the ne-ight
> An' the razors come flying through the air.

Sitting on the edge of my bunk—above my watch's ticking, people talking in the next room, Jack & Van snoring—I can hear the tease of an avion overhead—

An the razors come flying through the air

Book II of the novelthing is underway—or is it? It wants— 1. To give a number of pictures of Harvard—*only such* however as lead up to the point—the merry mountain of lies— 2. There must be swagger and rattle and the chorus of the Marvells every four chapters. . . .

(By the way—Suzanne is going on the stage—and there is going to be a rousing echo of her success in the distance—)

3. the People are Fibbie, & John Andrews, new friend—& Weston Nichols & James L. Bridge, & Joseph di Castello, musician, & Weber the wealthy one & a great swarm at Mem. from the Middle West. Then there's Suzanne & the young manager, Epstein, the man who made her. . . .

4. then there's the occasional chorus of the servants at the Marvell's Lizzie, Newman & Bertha.

5. Through it all interwoven—more consciously than ever—in a merry confident—swaggering tune the merry mountain of lies motif & the little & growing tune of the personality of James Clough—

Damn. What on earth is the use of making lists of things—it's like making lists of things you want to do or be in life—You just chug along without regarding them at all anyway:—so you might just as well not tabulate them. All they do is give you a vaguely satisfied feeling—in itself of canker badness.

Jan 25th

Reading Lorenzo de Medici's Apologia—& conceiving wonderful scene in play or story Ecco! Someone has killed the Tyrant and no one will believe that he is dead—He goes about the dark street with the dripping head under his arm—& even to the eye & feel people think it's a tete de veau, vinaigrette—And so are slaves slaves unto the last day—

Jan 28th

Yesterday went Again to Asolo—Van & I took a call early in the morning—at 4 AM, to be exact & after a wild ride to Cittadella in which he ran into some horses and I blew out all the electric lights & the exhaust became red hot & parted in the middle, leaving tongues of blue & red flame squirting about at our feet, getting vastly near the gasoline line—anyway we deposited our blessés & fled away—under a very wonderful moon—Then we started walking along paths & across the fields ghostly with hoarfrost under the moon. We struggled much with barbed wire entanglements prepared for the inevitable retreat—why anyone should retreat God knows, but they are preparing as if it were inevitable——At dawn we were coming down a steep wide avenue that dipped from a high hill into the blue valley. The red sunrise & the yellow trunks of the planes—& then to turn around suddenly & see the mountains, coming out in procession beside us as we went down the hill, rose with violet shadows—and the sky clear green above them. Then over hills & valleys with the changing colors of the mountains on our left, and in front of us the sunrise brightening into obvious light—Then Asolo— and there a breakfast of eggs and red wine & a climbing up to the square bold on the hill from which one can see everything— Mountains—strange regular knobs & welts of foothills—& the mist covered plain——

Every glimpse of Asolo composes into a view of full de- light—through every arch—the whole world seems to open up—lost in the mist of conjecture.

And there is a tavern in the town—Where in a fantastic room which you reach by stairs from the street is a stove—a stove as fine as the kitchen stove in Jack's play—At the head of the stairs stands stuffed the last specimen of the Dodo— On the stove are many pans & pots steaming mingled & fra- grant steams—

One sits down and asks for food—and then the strange thing strikes one—all the peoples of the world, are walking about the room, craning their necks at the food & stirring it with large copper ladles. But when one wonders what is in the pots & pans, when one asks for risolto, one is told niente. When one asks for salata, one is told niente, when one asks for potate, one is told niente, when one asks for verdura, one is told niente. And all the while old old men, and youths with the o fortunate adolescens expression, and all the seventeen little girls carefully gradated in size, all looking exactly the same and with faces like fishes & stringy yellow hair, go back and forth into the rooms beyond—stand over the stove and stir— but when one asks what is in them, the chorus thunders niente.

At last, after much waiting & moaning they very grudgingly dole out of the smallest saucepan the soup the demiurges eat when they are about to create worlds and one eats & is glad and there come throngs bearing big copperpails of water which they pour into the pots and steam rises and the seven- teen with fishy faces & yellow hair go back and forth doing miracles & feeding all the people in the rooms beyond with loaves & minestra—But when one asks for more or for any other thing, they answer in their self-possessed way—Niente.

And all the while there bends over the stove, chuckling, an old woman with a face like Clytemnestra or Clotho. But the patrons of the place go and wrest their food from her in person & peer boldly into the pots and pans and carry away bowls piled with salad & many other things, fragrant to the smell and taste——

The soup being the soup of the Demiurge is filling—and having paid ones tithe one goes forth refreshed—

The name of the Tavern is the Trattoria dell'Paraiso & it is on the little streets that lead towards where the mist cuts off the plains from view

Teatime—Trying to write—God! I have a brain like a peanut. . . . "Found a peanut, found a peanut"—echoes in my head the insane song the section sings at meals—& I am trying madly (Idea! Let Asolo—be the first letter of the Letters of an Embusqué) to be on the shore of the Charles River, marching along with John Andrews & Martin Howe & talking about the horror of existence—The Abbatoir "Thronging generations tread me down"—Yet I must not be there too much, as I am now—I must be there as I was in my Sophomore year at college—In the first throes of elaborating my own particular sort of pantheism, a mushy sort, rather sentimental about the oneness of the protoplasm etc—Just beginning to be sure that the ingrained taboos were taboos & not fast in the core of things—suspicious of the decalogue, etc—over-full, however of morbidities & fastidious barriers, with that infantile feeling of being cut off from all the world—not being en rapport——Now I feel much stodgier & sturdier—I realize there is no all the world to be en rapport with. I suppose I must thank the war for some of it—In fact I'm a much heartier son of a bitch than I used to be much readier to slap my cock against the rocks of fact. But the play's the thing, as is writ in the heart of theatrical managers and on the proscenium of cheap theatres in the provinces—

After dinner At dinner people talked war & Y.M.C.A. two topics that always give me the deepest dyed darkblues——

One thing comes out clear the one thing that enslaves people more than any other to the servitude of war is nationalism—the patriotic cant—Religious cant is feeble; its on a down slope fighting to hold territory—but the patriotism——all the noxious influences of the world seem to have thrown their tentacles about it—Its the mark of all the trade-greed & the glory-breed—and the asininity that makes people insist on sacrificing themselves on the nearest altar—no matter how brazen the God above it.

I got a sort of hallucination while the people were talking—Appleyard & Kohn & Walderspirel & Fairbanks a hallucination whether for good or bad I know not—of all the fanaticism and cant & sacrifice & sincere endeavor suddenly turned against the nations. The Y.M.C.A. becoming a Revolutionary society——and for a minute I felt in me a little of the hard fanatic fire . . . God—someone must come with a single mind and a single purpose and the hard fire of fanaticism in him and batter his life away against it . . . hundreds must batter their lives away . . . and to what good?—to have the baaing sheep fly to worship some other false god. Oh the hopelessness of it. Yet one is dragged helpless to join in the silly processes of time.

We make a funny ménage—I must write it up someday—a rather matrimonial sort of one—as we are thrown too constantly together forwards with the result that personalities clash & wrangle—not so much as Fairbanks thinks—but a good deal. At this moment I am sitting at the table—on the other side of two candles is Van, looking picturesque in his Russiany blouse, typewriting as noisily as possible because he knows it annoys me. Jack is reading Jean Christophe moodily on the bed—Bragg has just gone out but was annoying the company mightily making unusual & unnecessary noises etc. The trouble with me is that I've been trying all day to write—without the least success—which is frazzling to the nerves of the best of men—What smithering idiocy.

Jan 29th

The Heyne Affair—a young fellow of German parentage had to leave the section today because the Italian censorship had intercepted a letter speaking slightingly of the Italians. The

Red Cross was asked to have him arrested and court mar-
tialed; but it was finally smoothed over to the point of allowing him to resign. His resignation was asked for on three
counts—Because he had divulged military information (the
nature of which the Italian officials refused to divulge) 2. unfavorable criticism. 3. for what Lowell called low language—
low moral tone of his letters.

I've never known the man at all personally, but the affair
seems all put up on account of his parentage—God! how
filthy—And the final ungentlemanliness & utter indecency of
Major Lowell's adding the third charge . . . It's maddening.
And how much of just this sort of sheer meanness & small
mindedness is going on everywhere! It makes you long for a
desert island or an ivory tower—somewhere you'd never see
anything so small as a man again.

And there's nothing one can do about it—no more than
one slave can protest when another slave is whipped.

Jan. 31st
The section held high festival. Partly to propagand among the
Italians, partly to express a perfectly sincere fondness for the
French. The chasseurs' band came down to play to us—also
officers & miscellaneous Italians, colonels, majors, captains a
great horde—

The fanfare played and one talked & the French expressed
in different way subtle & unsubtle, their dislike for the Italians—As Jack remarked, when the Italians showed a liking for
the punch, the French called loudly for beer . . . It was all a
great success.

Feb 2nd
Perched on the wall of the Campo Santo—being gazed at
with wonder by an Italian who his chin rested on the world—
in every sense of the world—admires us—perched on the wall
as I said—with the sun wonderful on my right cheek and Bassano piling up its towers against the sky in front. It's a very
bright day—given an unbalanced mournfulness by the fact
that it's winter and that the trees and vines are bare and the
grass olive-grey—("the fact that" cut it out for God's sake—
man alive—you have the beastliest phrases in the wide world.)

Yesterday Van & I did a splendid walk up the valley of the Brenta, that wound up between great drab deep shadowed hills, with rosy rock faces & then snow shoulders towering behind them. There was no one in the towns, that, although whole for the most part, had a bleak air with their big bare houses and dispirited churches. We passed many batteries, variously disguised, and endless amounts of barbed wire strung across the narrowing valley. The road became more and more camouflaged—and we kept thinking we were getting near the front lines. At last we turned across a bridge in a rather smashed up town and went up a road on the left side of the valley that had an uncomfortably shelled look, full of holes and covered with splinters of rock, until, passing numerous machinegun batteries & various sorts of entrenchments, we were motioned by a sentry into a boyau. All the time we were expecting to be arrested; still we pushed forward and at last found ourselves in a narrow trench skirting a steep hill above the valley, where there once had been a railroad track, well made & protected by sandbags & with a tunnel gouged out of the rock along side it, in case of bombardment. That abutted in some machine gun batteries and a tunnel, the old railway tunnel blocked up and made into a huge abri where the people live—The further end was defended by several walls of sand bags and a great lighted fire gun & generator. The gun looked absurdly like a large blunderbuss & the tanks of the generator had a very peaceful air. We stood in front of the vedette for sometime looking at the rockpiles and little white houses that marked the Austrian outpost. Meanwhile we talked to a tragic face man with good natured gorilla face, who spoke very bad English.

There's no real fighting in the valley. In that post they just lie round and shoot off machine guns now and then: the Italians and Austrians play tattoos to each other on them. The men are badly fed and no one seems to take any interest in them. The man we talked to was a Calabrian: he wouldnt be there if he could help it, bet yer goddamn life he wouldnt, his home was in Calabria, and the Germans'ld never get that far; anyway—He had not had a permission for eighteen months and so he hadn't been with his wife and had had to screw other women, which pained him.

Then he led us back through the smoking tunnel, full of people sleeping and lying about listlessly, lighting us with a little oil lamp made from an old hand grenade.

At a machine gun battery some good looking young fellows were amusing themselves throwing hand grenades into the Brenta.

Van took many unhindered photographs, one particularly of a dirty pleasant man with a black beard who appeared suddenly, speaking excellent English, out of a small hole in the ground.

We didn't see an officer all the time we were near the front. 40 kilometers pulled off.

Last night and night before we had rip-roaring airraids over Bassano, three or four a night—one stands shivering in the window and watches the *searchlights* & the electric sparkle of machine guns and the great red flare of bombs that explode with a thunderous snarl that rips the horizon—and the shrapnel bullets and cases simply rain about our heads.

The joke is that you get up in the morning and go about Bassano, just nose in the air for horrors, and try eagerly to find where the bombs exploded, where the widows were made & the orphans bereaved and, nothing,—streets placidly empty—the famous bridge that they are aiming at—arid and untroubled as ever . . . Of course you do find things smashed up a bit here & there, a couple of roofs mashed in or a room turned inside out, or somebody's garden given a new conformation, but it's nothing at all to compare with the wild brilliance of the airraid the night before that makes you expect smoking ruins & entrails smeared about the paving stones.

Finished *Bouvard & Pécuchet*—a rather desperate book which so exposes people's idiocies & the cult of the great gods that it ceases to be funny—It leaves you with a feeling of miserable futility, partly because it's unfinished and partly because it is so brutally bitter—so utterly illusionless . . . of course that's the fault of my own cowardly soul not of Flaubert. Nothing ever more effectual took the wind out of the sails of the fine ship of ones thoughts than Bouvard & Pécuchet.

Dont forget the type of man that must at all costs hold the center of the stage—one could write a wonderful high comedy

performance of some sort—with three or four of that unpleasant sort of beast all brought together. There'd be a wonderful battle royal.

———

A most excellent day of walking with Van. Started up the Brenta
Valley with Jack & Bragg—let them go up to the tunnel that
was our last objective & turned off to the left at Valstagna up a
cañon road. In the bed of the stream, as the road climbed, were
lots and lots of small alpine guns, sitting on their tails and pointing their muzzles up like dogs howling. A few miles up we came
to a road that spiralled straight up, a road literally plastered onto
the face of the mountain that rose almost sheer, with frequent
slides, from the cañon. We walked up the road for pretty nearly
ten miles, finding it surprisingly littered with shrapnel bullets
and éclats from Austrian shells. Van went rhapsodic over the
beautiful workmanship of the fragments of round polished steel.
The valley disappeared below us as we climbed—and at last we
reached a group of soldiers working, boys of seventeen and
eighteen most of them who looked like Sicilians. They produced for our examination a great paper manifesto dropped
from an aeroplane, written in Slovack on the one side and in
Czechish—ungodly language that they in their simplicity expected us to read off. Then we climbed on up a road obstructed
by piles of sand bags & lots of stone fragments & splinters
where shells had exploded until we came to a soft voiced man,
very dirty, a cook I suppose, who spoke excellent English. He
had been in West Australia. Then we kept on up and were produced by a sentry before a bunch of officers. Everybody was
very pleasant and wondered who we were. American Red Cross
had an exotic flavor to them that was quite entrancing. Among
them was a Roumanian, a lieutenant in the medical corps, who
spoke very good English which he had learned, it came out, in
Bucharest. He fed us Marsala and water in the tunnel where his
quarters were—which was to us like a drop of water on the
tongue of the rich man burning in hell, for we'd walked all
morning unfed & un-wetted. In the conversation it came out
that the road we had come on was right under the nose of the
Austrians, who held the ridge to the left and could pick anyone
off on it they wanted. As we had been climbing the road calmly
& puffily for about two hours, the fact was amusing.

The Roumanian was an awfully pleasant man with a beautiful Roman nose and those vaguely liberal ideas always held by travelled Europeans. One thing interesting he did say, sincerely too—'An educated man cannot hate'—Anyway, his conversation gave that balm to the soul that perfect manners only can give.

He piloted us up the steep path, introducing us to all manner of officers, tenantes, capitanos, Majores, that popped out of holes in the ground, as numerous in the mountains, as they'd been scarce in the valley. After much labor & panting, we reached the abode of the commandante, who inside of a little shack in a crevice in the cliff, sat like Old King Cole with his capitanos & tenantes about him, drinking amid a great array of bottles—. We drank white wine with him in solempne splendour; He out of a special glass—a sort of curved beaker—while one stood by who continually wiped glasses. On the table was the apparatus of a dictaphone with which they listened to what the Austriacos were doing.

Then we climbed on up until we came to a cliff-ledge that bulged out overhead, leaving a sort of cave underneath. Until three days ago this was the position the Italians held—The Austrians being on the slope right on top of them. Then one afternoon, the Italians put ladders up in a cleft in the rock-wall, hoisted up a machine gun, popped it over the edge and let fly. They took about eighty prisoners and remained masters of about four feet of the slopes above the cliff. There a company hangs on by its eyelashes, with a row of sandbags in front of them, dangling their feet near the mountains and valleys, and getting their supplies up by means of a pulley.

Then we climbed down the ladders again, and stopped to drink Vermouth with the Commandante and to have tea with our Roumanian friend—tea with real milk in it——and then down by a mulepath to the Valley at Valstagna through the twilight purpling the mountains that had already faded to dim in the smoke of brushfires.

Then home by road with long loose strides and that feeling of being euzooné that comes from great exercise. Followed by a most delicious dinner of rice & cauliflower and by a reading of poetry in bed afterwards and a sleep of marvellous comfort, punctuated by the usual airraid.

Feb 6th

Dragged by S.F. to be a social luminary—funny & marvellously delicious dinner with officers—colonel, major, captains & lieuts.—funny jolly easily amused people. Much food & much drink—

The phallic method of drinking toasts.

Then a funny walk up a hill to view the pan-ora-a-a-m-a, as they called it & much photography & jokosifying & divers cordial asininity—a *solempne processioun* back, colonel in the lead. The colonel deplores the growth of socialism in the north of Italy—tells how when the Principe of something his brother in law visits his estates in the south the peasants kiss his hand. He's a walrusey & jovial man with a broad waistband & he's fond of animals——

A springy day—with catkins out on a beech tree—or something of the sort (elm probably) & the hill where the great searchlight & the great dog were & the pleasant unshaven man who tended it & who, when he patted the dog had the soft look of a faun.

Now the novelthing Bk II Chap V

Nicholas Murray Butler's address to students of Columbia

At this Christmas season when the good cheer & good will that should mark it are so sadly absent from the lives & hearts of millions of human beings, Alma Mater has a special word of greeting and encouragement for those of her brave and stalwart sons who have given themselves to the service of the nation, even though their lives be the sacrifice. No contest in which you could possibly engage can equal this one in moral significance. Everything which distinguishes right from wrong in public conduct, everything which marks off principle from expediency in national life, everything which draws a line between liberty and despotism, everything which removes human opportunity from the grasping hand of cruel privilege, waits for its safety, and perhaps, for its very existence upon your success and that of the noble men of allied nations who are fighting by your side on land and sea.

When this war shall have been righteously won there will be peace on earth for all men of good will.

Feb 7th

An absurd ride on Fiat 4, to Cittadella, Jack Lawson accompanying. Coming back at least fifteen chasseurs piled into the back of the car and a stoutish Italian lieutenant, from Naples, sat in front with us. The Chasseurs kept passing about wine in bidons and the lieut. enlivened matters by passing about hideous pictures of naked women and making one invariable joke asking in very bad French, if one could buy at the coöperative these same pictures of Parisiennes. Each time it caused a riot and the Chasseurs piled three deep inside slapped each other on the back and produced new bidons, which they poked out through the front window. It was a wild ride.

Read Bk. II, chap I to Chap V to assembled quinquumvirate—seems to go fairly well with less jerkiness than before.

Feb 8th

I wonder what day it is—Maybe its the eighth—Anyway it is signalized by the arrival of Dudley & Fred Bird.

We went into Bassano to buy vast amounts of food & drink to celebrate. While paying for some condensed milk I noticed the clerk begin to get flustered. He even refused to put paper round the cans—the shutters came down with a bang & Bragg said "they're shelling the town." Whereupon we went out and found the streets full of scurrying people and bang of shutters being pulled down by nervous storekeepers.

Sh-sh-Sh-Sh-ssss——broom!—overhead and off in the corner of town where the big cement bridge is! We went, laden with bottles & packages to the big piazza—passing the spot where someone had just dropped a Chianti bottle in their flight. In the middle of the square a big staff car was being hurriedly piled with French generals, who were still pulling their caps down on their heads as it scooted into a side street. There was a great scuttle of civilians up arcades and away—as more shells squealed overhead & snorted in among the houses——

The old women who have the fruit stand at one end of the piazza started packing their goods into a cart, and spilt a great lot of oranges, that rolled one by one, out from under the arcade and down the steps and solemnly out over the flag stones—people pursuing them the while—

And we, waving our bottles, shrieked with laughter.

Other shells

A big French camion full of soldiers passing hurriedly through, stalled in front of us, the driver calling out wildly 'vite—vite'—

Another shell

A man jumping out from the back to crank the car slipped on the flagstones and took the most wonderful cropper ever seen of mortal man—Laughter drowned out the next shell—

The camion got started at last & scuttled away and the square was empty—except for four foolish ambulance drivers waving bottles & laughing, with their mouths full of chocolate

But by that time the shelling had stopped.

Today we heard of the first case—in America—of a man sentenced to death by court martial for refusing to undertake military duty, when drafted and assigned. This is probably rather important. Won't it be strange if it comes to that in my case? Might happen pretty soon too—It'll just be luck if it doesn't, as I see it. God! they'll probably even do their best to take the dignity out of death for a conscientious objector.

Feb 10th

Long walk with Dudley over little intimate hills that rise to a great crest that breaks into rock like a wave breaking into foam at the foot of the mountains. Wonderful villages perched among high terraced valleys full of vineyards whose grapes must grow right on the floor of heaven. We climbed along a great ridge, and down the end of it, a valley opening out on either side and a view of Monte Grappa and the great cliffs that stand above the Brenta Valley on the right. Coming down we found heaths blooming on the sunny slopes & on one bank bright purple blue hepaticas, one white violet and yellow primroses . . . Then later, down in the valley, snow drops in the hedgerows and one plant of hellebore in flower.

I wish I could sing spring songs innumerable—feel the sap rising fragrant in the branches and everything droning with life. . . . Perhaps I could if I could be alone enough—I used to feel myself full of rhythms and cadences of words—so many that I could not express them—Now I feel none—except things as banal as The minstrel boy to the War has gone. For

poetry one needs a certain resiliency of soul. I have none—
only hatred and disgust—How can one sing in slavery?

To José Giner Pantoja

Mon cher ami:

   Pardonnez moi une autre lettre mal et hativement ecrite. Encore j'aurais voulu ecrire en espagnole, mais l'idee me donne
une peur bleu, car j'aime tant votre belle langue, que ca me
ferait bien de peine de l'ecrire a l'italienne. Lisant et parlant
l'italian tout le temps que je suis ici, je crois que si j'avais ecrit
en espagnole, je ne reussirais a faire qu'un melange funeste.

   Ici, sur ce point calme, ou l'on a tant de temps, en attendant dans la pluie, dans les cours des hopitaux, ou dans les
ambulances sentant de carbolique, je pense tres souvent a
vous et aux belles plaines de Castille. Deloin, ca doit appa-
raitre un peu theorique la guerre, mais ici, ou n'importe ou
sur le front, je vous assure que c'est tout autre chose. C'est
l'ennui, l'esclavege a toutes les stupidites militaires, la misere
la plus interessante, le besoin de chaleur, de pain, de proprete.
Il n'y a rien de beau dans la guerre moderne, je vous assure.
J'y ai vecu pour un an maintenant, et bien des illusions se sont
alles vers le fleuve du Styx. Ce n'est plus qu'un digression
enorme, tragique dans la vie des peuples.

   C'est plutot a vous autres, dans les pays qui sont au dessus
de la melee, c'est a vous qui rests l'oeuvredu progres de cette
pauvre civilization tourmentee de nos jours. Pour toutes les
choses d'intelligence pour l'art et pour tout ce qu'il faut dans
le monde, la guerre—une guerre moderne je veux dire—c'est
la mort. Et au dela de ces choses la, qu'est ce qu'il y a qui vaut
dans le monde? Non, c'est a vous, qui faites tranquillement et
tumultueusement des revolutions, qui essayez, vainement
peutetre, d'envolververs un but la vie de nos jours, c'est a vous
qui rest de saufguarder toutes les belles choses de l'humanite,
pendant que nous autres, nous luttons brutalement, avec un
acharnement de suicide. Pourquoi? Pour des mensonges,

meme pour des verites, pour les nations lites avares d'un monde
ivre de commerce

J'ai bien peur que vous autre Espagnoles idealisent un peu ce
vilain monde de l'Europe et de l'Amerique-monde en . . . . . .
peutetre, mais, Grand Dieu, vers quel but? Partout il me pariat,
on ne trouve que l'esclavage, a l'industrie, a l'argent, au mom-
mon de business, le grand dieu de nos jours—chez les riches et
les pauvres. Et ou dans tout cela, se trovent les bells choses? les
choses qui font de la vie quelque chose de plus qui transcendent
la lutte pour le ventre, pour l'existance.

C'est seulement chez vous en Espagne et en Russie, il me
parait, que la conquete n'est pas tous a fait accomplie—c'est
un peu pour cela que j'adore tant l'Espagne.

Et mon pauvre pays . . . il me parait qu'avec la guerre, et
avec le passage de la loi de service militaire, la liberte y est
eteinte pour longtemps, et le jour de triomphe de la plutacratie
est venu.

A propos il y a maintenant a Madris un de mes meilleurs
amis—Arthur McComb—qui etant antimilitariste im . . able, a
fallu quitter les Etats Unis, et qui restera, je pense, longtemps
en Espagne. C'est un garcon tres intelligent et tres aimable, et
j'ai pris la liberte de lui dire d'aller vous voir, parce que je savais
qu'il n'y avait personne en Espagne qui pouvait lui donner tant
de renseignments que vous. Pardonnez masans-facon, qu'on
peut attribuer a l'impolitesse americains, d'ailleurs je n'ai jamais
pu m'habituer aux convenances, meme en Amerique.

Je serai enormement content de recevoir une de vos lettres
si charmantes. Mon address est soins Consolato Americano,
C.R.A. Sezione 1. Au revoir, votre tres bon ami.

Bassano, c. February–March 1918

To Rumsey Marvin

Albergo del Sole-Pompeii

Dear Rummy—— March 21

What do you think of that? And of Vesuvius outside the
window, steaming hugely through a rain cloud——

I'm on leave—and am crowding as much galivanting about Italy as possible into fourteen days.

We came out from Naples yesterday—and after wandering about the ruins a little more—we are going to walk to Castellammare—there take the train for Sorrento and then walk again to Amalfi. At present matters are held up by a slight rain storm—

Rummy you ought to be here

Positano—night after dinner Oh Rummy—one of the most glorious days I've ever spent—Morning in Pompeii—Then we walked to Castellammare for lunch—from there to Sorrento by trolley then walked to Positano on the way to Amalfi, along a road that hung on the cliffs above the sea— Almond blossoms, anemones—oh I can't describe things— They were too marvellously beautiful

I dont think—except Denia that I must have told you about—that I've ever been in a town so beautiful as Positano. I'm overwhelmed and smothered in beauty—sight and smell and the soft wind off the sea in your ears—Also I have had one of the best dinners ever invented—risotto, omelet, cheese & such oranges as I think the "apples" of the Hesperides must have been—and wine—a light red wine—a wine full of the brisk hills and the great exhilarating spaces of the sea, and the smell of thyme and gorse and almond blossom and rosemary and basil and lavender from the fields that make little ribbons of velvet among the shaggy rocks.

Cetara

Rummy—

Waiting for a dinner to cook itself after a huge day's walking— We walked from Positano to Amalfi—Then up to Ravello— then from Ravello round Capo d'brio to Cetara and Vietri. Then we took the train next morning for Paestum—where there are the remains of three very early Greek temples from the ancient Poseidonia, a colony of Sybaris—The huge doric temple of Poseidon, a glorious burnt orange—with all the cinnamon richness of thousands of suns——The temples lie in the middle of a solitary plain near the sea—(where we bathed on a wonderful beach) with the mountains behind them. We spent the whole day there—I in the state of prostrate worship

Greek things always put me into. Then we went back to Naples and now I am writing in the Hotel Continental in Rome.

Love
Jack
1918

Diary: April 7–20, 1918

April 7th
Ecco! Here am I, bored at Borso—Have finished my books, got disgusted with my novel—

April 8th
At Gherla—we were told to appear there early this morning & did—result—we wait in boredom for something to turn up—a rainy-blue grey & green day—The mountains are splendidly dark with ragged steamy clouds over them. There's a rather chilly wind in which the engine of the teleferica puffs and chugs amid a sound of steel cables. Have been talking to a poor devil of a Genoese—who seems to have had a lot of brothers killed in the war, and whose mother died while he was on licenza— (The Italians do hold by family affection like the devil)—He had the usual sad story—the war—the officers were all bought— everything came by graft—camossa—He seemed quite borne down by the injustice of everything; he was a little drunk too, which helped. He'd deserted once but had been dragged back to the front—The army wasn't an army, it was a scandalo— Italy was a casino—a whore house—everything was bought and sold and the poor devils of soldiers died.

The war would only end when they'd killed everybody— everybody—he swayed drunkenly and waved his head towards the wide plain in which the green darkened into blue and blue grey on the horizon—quando tutti saranno morti, finirà la guerra—

Serable meglio un terremoto an earthquake, to kill us all outright—

He was going to get an English uniform & get into the English army—anywhere out of this misery—and the humiliation of being kicked and beaten by the officers—They didn't dare kick him though. He was dangerous.

In Genoa he'd seen lots of English they'd drunk together—He'd sold boots and clothes for them—stolen money—he said, opening his pocket book all stolen—from the govreno inglese—Then he showed me the usual little array of cards and photographs of dead brothers and scraps of ordini de movimento—

God it was pitiful.

Some day—soon—he said—I shall shoot an officer—Then it'll be all over—It'll be finished—he said rather in the tone of the end of Pagliacci—

A band's marching and playing along the road below and you can hear the sounds of camions bubbling along—and near at hand the cling-clang of the engine of the teleferica—

Gloire & Servitude Militaire

This is a rather suitable place to have read that curious little book—telling of the hollowness of old wars—O what a different word—de Vigny speaks of the military as a race apart—a race of gladiators hated and feared by the people of the country—And now the people are their own executioners, their own gladiators. The spectacle of the whole world lashed to war in dirty greyish uniforms——ordered about by the middle classes—the shape of petty officers, by the high financier spheres in the shape of generals & such canaille—would have nearly killed de Vigny—with his quaintly stiff ideas of the honor and shame of arms, with his ancient dragoons uniforms, so carefully brushed—and his monastic conception of the army—And where are gone his poor hopes of a warless future? The future is full of wars—of brutalizing slavery for all the young men in the world—and brutalizing dominance for the rich and the cunning and the well-connected—

The strange little sentimental stories in de Vigny's book—with their curiously exciting frames of the retreat from Paris of Louis XVIII and the 1830 Revolution—really cover all of the Napoleonic sort of wars, where people fought for kudos and for personal devotion and for strange outworn stupidities, but stupidities that had a charm and a halo of belief about them. The modern war for butchers and bakers and candlestick makers in which the trader has dressed himself up in the old outworn armor would be to the men of those days inconceivable.

At the bottom of all our nationalities—under the royal robes and the polished imperial helmets and the abstract talk of domination—are hidden the murky factory chimneys that are our world's God—

Boccaccio—I've just finished the fifth day—It is wonderful what a picture he gives you of his time, of the life of the merchants riding forth from the walled towns of Italy, of sea travel with its amusing interludes of Barbary pirates—of the cultured, Saracen-leaning courts of Frederick, and the Rogers in South Italy—heat and gardens and flowers, and lovely women in Kiosks—escaping through shuttered windows into the silk clad arms of their lovers while the shutter creaks in the scented night breeze and there comes on the wind a sound of breakers—a swift galley is waiting on the shore and the lovers lie naked in each others arms on piles of carpets in the stern, cooled by the faint spray borne on the hot breathing night wind—and the rowers row towards a dark orient city where they will land in pomp and all magnificence, and wander and lose themselves in strange streets, full of throat gripping odors, pale scents of flowers, cloying incense smoke and smell of secret lives behind latticed balconies—There they will have stranger adventures with robbers and princes—and return in the end to silken ease on some distant islands where they pass their last contented years to the sound of flutes and fountains, or else, come to violent gorgeous deaths, by flames or stabbing with an emerald handled dagger—

Of course people have always called out against the servitude of their lives, but we, today, do seem particularly enslaved.

Anything you read of or think of—seems to have had some escape in it, some escape from the humdrumness those in charge of the world would infect life with. There has never been a time when a person who despised & detested the world's phrases and turpitudes and heroisms was so utterly bound—for the slaves it's not a bad age; they live fast, have much kudos, and die in the miserable mud of the table lines. But for those who had thought to weave out of their lives something more delicate. . . .

4 PM at Gherla—bored, mon ami, bored to tears—Oh God I want to go to sea, or to Greece or to Spain, or to glory— anywhere away from the Italian rear—I've been trying to draw—I cant draw—I want to novelize—I cant novelize—

I want exotic ultrathings—freedom—Home life—the right spirit

Search for the phrases of Americanism triumphant.

April 9th

Stuck in the damn mud hole of Borso—again the noise of wailing goeth up to heaven—I have no books and I'm—bored and I have no books—was ever a creature more dependent on literature for life & stimulus—I can't live passively—God—I must be either on the move externally or internally via literature— I'm like a dope-fiend about it.

And here am I in Borso without a book—and we seem stuck here for an indefinite period. The lack of reading matter has induced me to peep inside the covers of magazines— always a bad thing to do—for it leaves you with a miserable mental nausea—Even for purposes of satire & collection of phrases—such utter mediocrity, such asinine revamping of conventional phrases—is absolutely sickening——I shall climb up the Campanile to write—

In Muselente, waiting for our captain to finish his business with the corpo d'armata, in a courtyard made delightful & noisy by a big millwheel—I am reading an asinine pamphlet by some mouthy Frenchman—on the great words of Napoleon.

La religion chrétienne sera toujours l'appui le plus solide de tout gouvernement assez habile pour savoir s'en servir. The old whited sepulchre God Bonaparte must have smiled when he said that—

In fact many of N's sayings resemble strikingly those of Barnum—the other great showman of a philosophic trend.

Apropos—in the de Vigny book—Napoleon's interview with Pope Benedict VII is marvellously well done—I think it was Benedict VII—

Afternoon

Seated at the top of my campanile at Borso with the clouds, grey marbled clouds of spring rain—and the silver thread of the Brenta flowing through the distance among blue grey hills——There's the plain green with purple gashes, then purple, then silver grey and far away opposite the Euganean Hills, the Hills that Shelley looked at from Venice—. All of which for some reason makes me think of the Auk—I shall write him—

Sacré mille cochons—in the middle of my letter a soldier's head appeared above the trap door in the floor and informed me that one wasn't allowed to climb up the campanile without a permesso—Damn their asinine rules—So I, cursing the military with a new curse with every rung of the ladder, climbed down—and finished the letter in our cantonment amid the noise of soldiers and soup kettles and the smell of the greasy soldier's food cooking outside and of their poor filthy bodies——

God the nastiness of the petty tyranny the war has plunged the world in—Everywhere in Europe—America—little bumptious sergeants are chasing poor devils off the steeples that afford them the only spots in a crowded world where they can think and look at their poor stock of dreams, the way a soldier pulls out and looks over lovingly the few grimy cards and passes and state papers he carries in his pocket book——

I wonder whether shooting an officer and finishing it as the man told me the other day he was going to do—isn't about the only Solution. It's humiliating to be alive . . . Nous sommes tous des poires, and God! What pitifully taken in, cowardly dupes we are. We half know we're being fooled, yet we haven't the courage to admit it to ourselves—so we follow the merry parade that is stifling in brutishness all the fair things of the world.

This is the feast of death
When we worship the drawn out agony
And the blood and pain of our god's
       last breath

Good Friday 1918

> This is the feast of death
> When we make agony God
> And pain's last choking breath
> When we worship the nails and the rod
> And the bleeding rack of the cross

Good Friday—in Florence
                    at hearing of the death of Claude Debussy

> This is the feast of death.
> We make of our pain God.
> We worship the nails and the rod,
> and pain's last choking breath,
> and the bleeding rack of the cross.
> The women have wept away their tears;
> With red eyes turned on death, and loss
> of friends and kindred, have left the biers
> flowerless, and bound their heads in their
>   blank veils,
> and climbed the steep slope of Golgotha; fails
> at last the wail of their bereavement,
> and all the jagged world of rocks and desert places
> stands before their racked sightless faces
> as any ice-sea silent.

> This is the feast of conquering Death.
> The beaten flesh worships the swishing rod.
> The lacerated body bows to its God,
> adores the last agonies of breath,
> And one more has joined the unnumbered
> death-struck multitudes,
> who with the loved of old have slumbered
> ages long where broods
> the ultimate queen of quietness,
> Earth the beneficient Goddess,
> Taking all tired souls and bodies
> back into her womb of the first nothingness.
> But ours who in the iron night remain
> Ours the need, the pain
> Of your departing.

You had lived on out of a happier age
Into our strident torture cage
You still could sing
Of quiet gardens under rain
And clouds and the huge sky
And pale deliciousness that is nearly pain.
Yours was a new minstrelsy
Strange plaints brought home out of the rich east
Twanging songs from Tartar caravans
Hints of the sounds that ceased
With the casual dawn—wailings of the night
Echoes of the web of mystery that joins
The world between the failing of the hot day and the
    rising of the night
Of the sea and of a womans hair
Hanging gorgeous down a dungeon wall
love in the mist of old despair . . .

They were so few and one by one they go
leave us to our ongoing captivity
To our blank age of shame and agony
Death is a river in flood carrying all in its flow

But ours, who in the iron night remain,
Ours the loss, the pain
of his departing.
He had lived on out of a happier age
into our strident torture cage.
He still could sing
of quiet gardens under rain
and clouds and the huge sky,
and pale deliciousness that is nearly pain.
All to the tune of a new minstrelsy,
Strange plaints brought home out of the rich East,
Twanging songs from Tartar caravans;
hints of the sounds that ceased
with the stilling dawn, wailings of the night
Echoes of the web of mystery that spans
the world between the failing and rising of daylight;
of the sea and of a woman's hair
hanging gorgeous down a dungeon wall,

evening falling on Tintagel,
love lost in the mist of old despair . . .

Against the bars of our torture cage
We beat out our poor lives in vain
We live on cramped in an iron age
Like prisoners of old
High on the world's battlements
Exposed until we die to the chilling rain,
crowded and chattering from cold
For all men to stare at—
And we watch one by one the great,
Those who have spread some splendor round their lives
Stroll leisurely out of the western gate
And without a backward look at the strident city
Drink down the stirrup cup of fate
without solemnity
And ride the road of nothingness,
We worship the nails and the rod,
And pain's last choking breath
We make of our pain God
This is the feast of death

April 10

April 16th

Have been reading Crime and Punishment. It is curious how reading it extinguishes ones proper life and makes one live only in the novel—I am trying to decide to start Part III of my affair. Virtually I only have three weeks to do it in—I must hurry—as yet I don't know how to start—I should like to gabble endlessly about my usual asininities . . .

The passage about the tiny black dots of the nomads' tents in the steppe in the end of Crime and Punishment . . .

Svidrigailov's talk with *Rodya Raskolnikov* about eternity

Part III

The agony of suffering of Crime & Punishment & The sudden whiff of the miseries of the world—Fibbie reads in the place where Rodya kisses the feet of Sonia—

The red haired girl at the cakeshop—what is her name by the way—He reads the passage to her, translating as he goes along—

The Lusitania

The slow realization of the oppression of government—

Begin Chap I with a talk with someone on the subject. The third way of looking at the world. Marx—the battle of the classes—The laughter Weston Nichols comes in quite a lot at first—goes home to England—Letter from him

Chap   I   The oppression
   ″   II   The War
   ″   III   Crime & Punishment & the Red haired girl at the cakeshop
   ″   IV   The War—Conscription in England—
   ″   V   The Last Boredom of College
      VI   New York
                 Fifth Avenue with flags on it—the glorious April Conscription

     VII   The realization of slavery
     VIII   the slave drivers—the Riot in the Bronx etc.
     IX   Suzanne—her friend Revolt revolt & still revolt.

The Laughter Police raid

The Vita nova feeling—on the boat—the dock with uniform and a band playing and people dancing about among the luggage and everyone getting drunk—

         Second Avenue

The idolization of action

Then on through growing cloud of depression—broken by boisterous joyous excitement—

         Pictures of the war front

         Opposing all the strident ugliness of life glimpses of Paris—talks with soldiers—the man from Bordeaux with the long whiskers.

The old woman who had lived for a year on potatoes

Man's description of running a bayonet into somebody— The drunken party in the cart—Revolution

Pinard—cigarettes

                         La ginolle

The man who sang at Givry—

Night under gas—

The shelled roads

The incident of the drunken drivers . . . He has come to die with us.

The talk at the little village near Givry—over champagne.

Atrocities—the mountain of lies—

Part III

Beginning with the first realizings of human slavery—via Crime & Punishment & the red haired woman—

Works up gradually to an overwhelming sense of the slavery of our time—2nd Avenue—Conscription Riots—Salvation Army— a man talking in a whining voice of the wrongs of India.

Then the war—enters with Weston Nichol's death.

joins the slavery-motif—becomes the great experiment of the mountain of lies.

The depression culminates in it—and in the little glimpses through the overwhelming darkness of his world as it might be—even of other's world—were they just a little less slaves

Suzanne in New York—has 'gone red'—is working in a milliners—Aretino's motto was Veritas odium parit.

April 17th

Finished a nasty little life of Pietro Aretino—written by some prudish French flubdub of a professorial prig.

Aretino seems to have been a truly wonderful sort of a person—blackmailer of the first order, satirist with a blunt fury, a sort of literary pirate who loved his friends but had few, played his game supremely without hypocrisy, took the world by the throat and lived free—But the little curs bark and snarl, and every prude that sees fit to handle with gloved prurient hands the shocking life of the cynic, the voluptuary

The maligner of kings and princes thinks himself required to soil his memory, turning his every good action into filth, persecuting every sincerity of clearseeing intellect, putting his image in the pillory of their outraged conventions to appease the furies of the moral gods——

Now—as Jack says I'm about to take up Leopardi—in a serious way

Van says the Colorado Springs High Schools are much troubled by an epidemic of German measles. They were undecided what to call the ailment, but at last decided that liberty measles would be a patriotic name——

The authorizations to wear red white & green service ribbons have just come—what a wonderful joke—They denote us by the title *Il Gentleman*—so the gentlemen volunteers—are still in the running—How does one indicate shrieks of laughter on paper?

Captain Pietra at Borso shot himself in the head today. He was a curious man—the sort of person who crosses the back of the stage in a Dostoevski novel now and then. He was the only embusqué in his family, he would tell you. 'Today I shall go within thirty meters of the Austrians' he would say, *sono il solo emboscato de mia famiglia*. He must have been a coward for he had a sort of nervous mania for taking risks—a hectic anxiety to show you he was not afraid. He had a certain nerve though—he must have had to shoot himself so cleanly. I can imagine him looking down the barrel of the revolver and saying to himself "I am the only embusqué in my family—I'm not a coward

But maybe he did it out of spite—He always used to get into frightful tempers.

All the Americans hated him.

April 20th
Last night I had an awfully interesting talk with Charley A. and Rieser and Torn Wharton about the war and pacifism. C.A. it came out is a believer in the individual, put himself down as a conscientious objector on the draft—He's going—he says—to refuse to serve.

Talk with Tom Wharton & Carolt and even Rieser, who although a violent anti German and in favor of the war in every way and in suppressing antiwar opinion during the war—is sincerely down on militarism——for some reason I suddenly became tremendously hopeful—Here were three people—Americans out of totally different environments all absolutely determinedly against the machine that has been crushing us all—Even if we are slaves we are unwilling ones. When you think of these people and our friends—and of Baldwin and that sort of man, who believes but who is carried along in the swirl out of our natural American easygoingness. Oh I cant write straight this morning, but I am anxious to get this down—

God if I could see clearly what to do—

I suppose one should do something conspicuous if possible— I hate conspicuousness—We have so much to do—it will take generations to leaven the great stupid mass of America—we are in the position of the first Russian revolutionists who struggled and died in despair and sordidness—we have no chance of success, but we must struggle—live—I dont know why—I hardly believe in it—yet

The world as it is at present hardening into organization seems to be a worse place for humanity than it has almost ever been before—too—it has possibilities—It is better to be dead than living

Now is the time when the effort has got to come—perhaps out of the great stupid mass of America—from under the crushing weight of industry—there must be so many of us— yet so few—

Perhaps being in France will teach some of the people

That quotation from Aeschylus about the evil that slunk down the rope that moored the ship to the shore——

> Place in the shrine a last offering
> Of huge red poppies from the field
> Below the vineyard where this spring
> The yokes of old white oxen feed.
> And stand in the gloaming a little time
> Clinking the smoothe age-fingered heads,
> To madonna at our own old shrine
> A few last prayers, tear soaked seeds
> To spring before her throne and gods

To Rumsey Marvin

April 26

Rummy—Just back from Milan, where I had 48 hour leave— delighted by a letter from you——

Lis Flaubert mon vieux, lis Flaubert, lis Flaubert si tu veux le style, lis donc Flaubert, si tu veux la vie, lis Flaubert—— Absolutely I beat my forehead on the ground before him——

But Name of God, the idea of mentioning Carry On in the same breath with Le Feu: What the devil does it mean to call a book *unpleasant?* Of course it does not conform with the hallelujah-breathing standards of the Y.M.C.A. Life according to those standards, according to the Anglo-American Grundy ruling an expurgated earth in behalf of a Heaven too dull to need expurgating, is a pretty poor business.

About style—I think that reading people in order to get 'style' from them is rather soft-headed. Your style is like the color of your hair or the cut of your pants—half accident, half act of God—to take thought to change or improve it results usually in rank affectation.

Of course I dont mean that you should not read and read and reread all the well written things you ever laid your paws upon. Reading Pater "for his style" is like going to a restaurant and ordering a dinner in order to admire the crockery it is served up on.

You don't want to write for style—you want to write—and god knows you will have a hard enough time cudgelling the British language into saying what you want it to—without needing to waste any hours on the trimmin's—The only way of getting the command of English needed to express ideas is by reading & reading a damn lot. English instructors have an idea that 'style' is a subtle art to be practiced for its own sake—a sort of parlor gymnastics of literature that makes people "cultured." O they are a benighted lot.

Paradise Lost is wonderful stuff to read aloud. It says absolutely nothing, but its sound is a symphony—and O the gorgeous jewel-work of names——I think the names in Paradise Lost are almost the most wonderful in English.

I'm awfully interested to hear about your "little group of serious thinkers"—God save the mark. My prep-school was the aridest place on God's earth in that way.

Do tell me more about them.

Poor old America needs so people of brains and courage and art—for the revolt that must come against the stupid moloch we all immolate our lives before——

By the way—on your French Revolution affair—Carlyle's book is wonderfully exciting.

I'm awfully glad you didn't debate—it may be an evil memory of debating at college—but for some reason the very name of debating shocks & grieves me beyond words.

Really I dont think you ought to worry about writing. If you want to do it badly enough—nothing on earth except want of conviction can stop you. Honestly I really think that a person of your lively imagination & general awakeness and gusto for things can do about anything he wants in literature. But he must *want* and damn hard too. He must give up his father and his mother and take no thought for the morrow, or for what he shall wear or what shoes shall be on his feet. Of course one must do all that to do anything worth while— Anyway taking up letters as a career isnt committing oneself for ever & ever amen—It's merely the most convenient way of saving oneself from the chaingang of offices & from the petty thievery of a business career—That we must all do at all costs—If one wants to stop writing one can always become a blacksmith or a cobbler or a peanut vendor or a tramp—all honorable occupations.

O Rummy—I wonder when we will pull off one of our famous plans—We must manage it——But god knows when I'll be in America again—or under what conditions——But manage it we will—if the spheres split——

Love Jack

A cold rainy day in the mountains in a little dirty village full of a smell of wet troops and latrines and soup cooking. It'll be awful when we do meet again—We'll have to talk for 40 days and 40 nights and will probably be found swooning from exhaustion, feebly moving our jaws, after the fourteenth day of solid conversation.

I've been reading Boccaccio a lot and Leopardi in Italian— Then I have got hold of Swinburne's Poems & Ballads & the Rossetti poems—all of which give me great solace & joy—

As you love me—Read in *Poems & Ballads* Swinburne's Song in Time of Order & Song in Time of Revolution

Do you read Walt Whitman?

Bassano, 1918

Diary: May 14–28, 1918

May 14th

Another nastily typical affair of officers—Dudley tells the story from Rova—a cousine of the farmhouse where the officers are quartered appears—causes violent rumpus of sex & smut in the conversation. Is led into the mess room for lunch & tickled and poked and made jokes at . . . she is obdurate and behaves in a quiet rather dignified manner. The stewards look as if they wanted to shoot the officers—wish they had—At dinner the affair is repeated—the girl is forced to drink Strega and wine and is kissed and Ellsworth much annoyed and not knowing what to do is made to put his arm round her—The girl finally gets away, by one of the men of the farm appearing and raising hell Dudley thought she was going to be raped before his eyes. The light comedy kidding is worth remembering. The next day at lunch the officers are in a storm of indignation at hearing the rumor that the girl slept that night with a corporal.

But it does illustrate the swinish uppishness of the Italian officers—God they are a nasty crew . . . When some spoons were not well washed they threw them at the steward's head.

Even the rather decent ones have the same disease—their overbearing nastiness to anyone they dont lick the boots of is disgusting.

May 17

at Rova with Dudley—we each of us have a broken down Ford that won't run; fortunately there is no work to do.

We have an enormously pleasant little room, whitewashed with blue woodwork in the windows and a pale red tiled floor. There is a stove of which the pipe goes up into the wall with the poise of the neck of a startled ostrich—outside is a pleasant jumbled little farmyard with roosters cockadoodledoing and soldiers, rather clean comfortable orderlies of the sanitary section—people who never have anything to do except screw the neighboring women and grumble about their food

The officers here are a nasty illbred arrogant set—the food, however is very good.

The fields round about are simply packed with flowers . . . But to the novel—noteably wonderful great single dandelions of a fine clouded yellow—to the novel—

Chap V
Lizzie's account of the *flucht*

At lunch the tall Sardinian lieutenant gave us an exhibition— There was some talk of a bella ragazza with a very servile red faced sergeant—after a moment the Sardinian jumped up from his chair half seriously and half in earnest and started kicking the sergeant, chased him round the room kicking him in the tail with a long thin leg and finally out of the mess-room, slamming the door behind him——

Dudley & I walked to Possagno to the Tempio di Canova— a rather pleasant round pseudo-classic place whose porch has a superb view of the valleys sloping down to the Piave and the hills opposite. It is one of the best German atrocities in Italy. The Austrians bombarded it and the town and a great hue and cry was raised. The place wasn't improved in the slightest, as a matter of fact, though Italian soldiers have very thoroughly rifled the drawer & cupboards of the sacristy. As it happens a very large battery is concealed behind the Tempio and on its steps we saw a row of Torpedoes—

All of Possagno is full of batteries so it is a little absurd, as usual, to talk of atrocities.

From the roof of the Tempio one gets an excellent view of both banks of the Piave and a bit of mount Tomba and the Austrian mountain overlooking all from across the river.

Chap VI
John Andrews and Fibbie meet in New York—tea—Styvu Stuyvysant Styvesant Styveysant Square Styvesant

The dirty forced labor is the main aspect of the war in Italy— Thousands of poor devils who might be laboring fairly happily at double the wages—brutalized at no wages at all—the army and made to labor most miserably.

Talk of the lies through history.
New construction of a cosmos.

Before I forget it, here's the plan for the rest of Book III mixed up with the main motif of the oppression—the servitude——

Affair with Suzanne—the old Suzanne who ate the jam—who does everything but understand why one must resist and not be enslaved.

John Andrew's jealousy of her—all that makes a jolly fine mess and ends in his total disgust with everything that precedes exit for the war boy's house and asked him to prophecy to them the end of the war, for assuredly he had the gift of second sight.

The boy refused—If he were to tell them that, he said, he would go dumb.

They urged him and bribed him in all sorts of ways.

He told them the war would end in June.

Now he is dumb.

(Folk, pure folk, says Fairbanks)

May 22

At last I am sul Grappa—

At G 1—an awfully pleasant post in the wide grassy valley up which the road to the summit goes—Opposite fir-trees climb up solemnly to the rim—the Monte d'Oro where trenches are—

Yesterday after Fairbanks & I walked up to G 2, then collected T Wharton and walked up to the chapel on top of Grappa—from there is one of the superbest views imaginable—a wonderful confusion of range on range with valleys purple between ending in the great snowy Trentine Alps to the west and to the north and East the mountains leading towards the Julian Alps—Then when you turn round—There is the plain with the Brenta—greenish and the tawny Piave, stretching in huge loops towards the sea. The mist lay thick over the plain and the rivers rose up to it, like the milky way in the Chinese legend—We watched it grow rosy with the late afternoon and the clouds pile up rose colored and pale El Greco green over the mountains——

At dinner—our pleasant Bourgeois captain with his air of bonhommie—the little lieutenant a woosy looking young fellow with a clever aquiline nose—the flaccid red lieutenant and

the curious ecclesiastic, Dom Pietro—who is the image of
Velasquez's first portrait of Philip IV—all talked about the
Madonnina de Grappa—the little shrine of Madonna on
Grappa summit—

—After the war, said the captain—there would be a restaurant
there

After the war, said the chaplain—the broken bronze
Madonna would be mended and set up again and a tumulus
made of all the bones of the dead per la patria on Grappa and
a chapel with a crypt built there to commemorate—

After the war, said I timidly, perhaps people would not
want to remember——

In the evening we went down to see the canteen man—a
flabby pink goodnatured object.

We fortunately tumbled into the general's mess hall and
found ourselves, all of a sudden being introduced to a fair
youngish general, with fair—Kronprinz moustaches and a
conceited boyish air that made him rather attractive. We were
sat and fed coffee and cognac and felt lost and embarrassed
and the gramophone covered our gêne.

I talked to a pleasant Italian from Tunis, who said that the
only good thing the war had brought had been—that people in
the allied countries had travelled about and got to know and
like each other—That is probably true—for though as a mass
the allies hate each other worse than poison—individually—
countless bonds have been struck up—between people of different nations. They've learnt to a certain degree that everything
and everybody's human, 'cept the government.

Fairbanks indulged his base passions in an endless game of
chess—with a young Italian lieutenant who had an enormously pleasant & intelligent face—

Then we went home & I for one vowed never again to
commit the politeness of calling on someone—One always
tumbles into embarrassing situations and one barely escapes
death by boredom—Never again.

This morning is wonderfully fine—the bluest of blue skies,
a brilliant white sunshine—and many aeroplanes; flashing in
the dark sky like mica in a piece of granite—Sparano un po—
Shrapnel has exploded quite near and there's a good deal of
artillery activity on both sides.

May 25
Period of loafing about The Walls of Jericho—I wonder if that's a good title
  at Rova—
  Yesterday day of great excitement—In the morning an English aeroplane fell into Brenta right outside our windows and in the excitement two poor Italians were drowned, Bayard Wharton did the hero & saved the drowning aviator just in the nick of time. And there were all sorts of complications——

Rova May 27
A rainy day—Ellsworth has gone up the mountain to see a captain of his acquaintance I am absolutely crevé de faim waiting for lunch, as I have had nothing except a tiny cup of coffee very early this morning—hunger is not suitable to literature either, alas, at least this stage isnt—
  A wonderful scandal is going on at the Mensa at Rova now—a squabble between the white worm captain—who looks like a wood louse I think more than a white worm—but Dudley insists on the white worm—and the tall Sardinian lieutenant. The captain ordered the lieutenant to go about the yard and quarters of the 67 Ambulanza and pick up the rubbish—the lieutenant refused. (It was hardly an officer's job). The captain put him under arrest—He retorted by sending in a complaint to headquarters on various counts. Yesterday depositions were made against him—large quantities—And at night it was awfully funny—because he sits in his room drawing and playing the mandolin—He has composed a pleasant laughing little march—to show the captain, he says, that he is still allegre—and all through dinner the sound of it came drifting down from his room—which annoyed the worm woodlouse captain like hell.

May 28
Have been talking literature with Randaccio—and music. He's a futurista—an awfully interesting chap—rather instructive as I think he is more or less typical of new Italy—How sublimely self satisfied is their attitude—Italy is, has been, and ever shall be the home of art, literature music—Yet it may be only the Latin bragadoccio—A great hullabaloo of the new and explosive and not awfully much fire—but I may wrong

them—Still as a figure with his handsome rather spanish face and his small beard on the chin and his tall springy stature Randaccio is a pretty fine fellow.

Smoke: talk, talk, talk, & never anything coming of it.

Conversation with the Young Spanish Anarchist
The Russian Jew

Diary: July 21, 1918

July 21st

Finished for the second time James Joyce's Portrait of the Artist—pray God I shant start imitating it off the face of the earth, Cuthbert-like—I admire it hugely—It is so wonderfully succinct and follows such curious by ways of expression—old abandoned roads that are overgrown but where the air is cleaner than in the modern dusty thoroughfares—constantly churned by people's footsteps.

note—How about the parallel between modern industrial overorganization—crushing the soul and mind and ancient savage overorganization, crushing the savage clan and tribe—and getting away from any chance of progress.

In these terms—might not civilization be the crowding of order by the critical intelligence of man.

To Rumsey Marvin

Paris
July 27
in a nasty fancy little patisserie
drinking cold chocolate.

O mirabile puer—insigne homo!

Nothing but bad latin can express the fervor of my admiration. You've pulled off something that I've never had the guts to do more than theorize about. I've all my life wanted to work in a shipyard—They are the most wonderful places in the world, and doing 'unskilled' labor must make one lay hold on the elementary facts of existence in a wonderful way. I've always found it so when I've done work on our erstwhile farm in Virginia—I've found it so very recently working as a volunteer stretcher bearer in one of the hospitals here.

You see I have to marshal my little puny stock of labor to be able even to write to a horny handed son of toil like yourself.

For de lord's sake chile, write me all about it. Your letter make me hugely anxious to hear more. I'm still hanging about in Paris trying to clear myself of the charges I wrote you about. The complete lack of human decency people exhibit at times staggers you—I'll tell you all about it when I can.

I live on the Ile St Louis, in the Seine, a beautifully old seedy part of Paris that I love—I spend my spare time writing and sketching up and down the river. For the first time my drawing is emerging from primal chaos a little and a few of the crayon things I've done seem to exhibit a faint hope—faint as unheard ditties!—of improvement. Après la guerre . . . I shall take a whack at the graphic arts—poor dears—I wander about and go to little restaurants and outlandish little cafés and frequent the few café dansants that are still open, and manage to have an awfully good time in a quiet mournful sort of way.

There is a chance that I can get into an expedition going to Palestine—or maybe I can get into the American or French army as a stretcher bearer—My eyes and my rep are a nuisance wherever I go.

I'll write you as soon as things materialize one way or the other—For God's Sake write as often as you can—as I assure you I need cheering often—studying the Spanish Inquisition from the underside must have been amusing to look back on—like hanging—

> In a jolly little restaurant,
> at a table on the pavement, peeping
> at the world through a fence of bay-
> bushes. Drinking Dubonnet—a not
> unpleasant mahogany colored apéritif.

Someday I want to teach you Paris. The Butte de Montmartre, where I often go to have dinner is I believe firmly the most exciting place in the city in the world. (Apropos—see Louise) The gayest and shabbiest and the most unalloyed people in the world stroll about the little treeshaded squares and the steep streets that become steps every now and then . . . and the views of Paris darkening in the sunset—One reason the people up there are so nice is that it takes so much climbing to get up there that none except the jolliest people ever seem to succeed, the others roll back and eat greasy dinners on the Boulevard de Clichy.

Look—some day very soon after the war has finished, if I'm still above ground and you—let's start out from anywhere in Europe and wander towards no where in particular, on foot, working at grape harvests, and wheat thrashings and pig killings and other rustic joys for our bread and bacon—I shall never have enough of walking down country roads away from places and towards places till the feet wear off my legs. I shall take fat notebooks and make weird sketches of things on the road and you must take a mouth organ or other musical instrument so that if all else fails we can tootle and sing in taverns on the roadside. Look will you do it? . . I'll guarantee to drop anything I'm doing, be it novel or marriage or a sentence in jail and do it too, when you give the word. Among other places—Id like to go to Algiers and Budapest.

But à plus tard—

love
Jack
1918

To John Howard Lawson

Bordeaux
Aug 11
In a most gorgeous cafe with large painted ladies in green and gold and the sunlight scrumptiously hot and white outside . . . Not so hot and white as the sunlight in Rome, though.

Jack—My bitching, my twilight, my soucis proceed. Nothing was of avail and followed by a cortège of curses I am going to

America. I'm not trying Antonio Spagoni or Lope de la Vega, perhaps asininely perhaps wisely, and am in hopes that having thrown myself at the feet of Washington, I shall arise whiter and more patriotic than the lily and with the same attributes as to toiling and spinning.

It will be interesting, though nasty, in God's country and I shall at once undertake démarches not to remain there.

I tried to enlist in the U.S. Ambulance Service, but they fainted at the sight of my eyes; you see I couldn't even see the top letter.

The full tale of my procés would take four volumes of fine print—it will probably appear in a new J'Accuse in the great by and by.

Glorious—Dudley and Van are, I think for six months, or maybe forever, enrolled in the Quaker reconstruction.

C'est moi l'agneau noir.

Write me to 214 Riverside Drive—New York City—how is the Lake of Nemi?

I shall signify my misfortunes, one by one, as they occur— and remember the tryst thirty days after the millennium.

Bobby's a lieut and joy rides with a colonel round about Tours.

Love
Dos

Imagine me in the stern of the S.S. Espagne in a Napoleon in the Bellephon attitude . . . Dirges where dismal will rhyme with abysmal, and howl with Lowell and hates with Bates and fetter with letter.

1918

Diary: August 24–October 1, 1918

Bay Head—Aug 24

Could anything be stranger than the contrast between Bay Head—the little square houses in rows, the drugstores, the board walks, the gawky angular smiling existence of an American summerresort—and my life for the last year. Hurrah for contrast. Americans honestly carry innocence to a vice!

The strange innocuousness of a place like Bay Head. And the dollars—Nom de dieu—the dollars—I am already drowned in dollars—

Still I love America—
O but the Hun-gabbling.

on the beach—Bay Head
Have found a refuge in an old boat in the shade of the board-walk—There by God's grace I shall make much literature—

But with the sound of the waves and the wind and the scent of the sea—and a box of chocolates to nibble on, and wish later I hadn't eaten, how in God's name can one write.

I keep thinking of that poor little Swiss on the boat, his funny little face with its sparse grey hair and his little eyes so close together, as pitiful as a monkey's. His wife was so charm-ing with her pop eyes and her brown skin and her Zut alors! and he doted on her so foolishly—It was as unnecessary to have her die, to extinguish so wantonly such a harmless exis-tence. Poor little man landing in New York with his wife's body—What a hell——

There is something almost beautiful in the harmlessness of a place like Bay Head—It is so completely innocuous—and therefore dead in every sense of the world—and that is one aspect of American life—the external.

Innocence—hiding what?

Aug 25
Still Bay Head
Notes from The Family
    The grotesque, the farce—quality of American life.
    A woman wrestling with the stairs to climb
    The Turn of the cycle from Prosperous—Cousin Sally Car-roll to legendary prosperity and misery and back to prosperity again.

It is not until the last cycle that the *grotesque* comes in—

Cannot we let the old gods die?
Cannot we naked shining strong in
Hugh striding mass untrammeled with loud voice cry

And where are the songs that should slay the old lies
Where is the dawn that should burn through hid skies?
New York
Aug 27

Aug 30th
Washington—
   The idea of individual liberty does not exist any where—
There are inklings of it in the conversations of Englishmen
and Frenchmen—but in all my long talk with Major Scott—
an unusually intelligent man—a man of unusually deep sympathies—but a governor through and through—not a ripple
of it broke the calm of his oligarchic way of looking at things.
That is what must be developed in the new Contract Social.
The balance sheet between the power over the individual of a
national government and the good to the individual of a national government must be drawn.
   Something must come out explaining in terms that the simplest person will understand that all the rights so many centuries
have bled or struggled for, the rights of the governed against
the governors—at the present day are so non-existent as to leave
no inkling in the mind of anyone—and yet they have existed
and they shall exist—The incubus the old man of the sea of national government must be thrown off, as the incubus of feudalism and the incubus of religion have been thrown off—But
God, have they? Haven't they merely appeared in new form? O
it is an unended and unending battle that of man to free himself from the monsters of his own creation——Now and then—
for a second he stands free and then with a rush he is downed
again and is struggling for breath in coils of the Bogg—

Sept 2nd Labor Day
The reason people of the stomach of my uncles so hate the
Bolsheviki is not because they are traitors to Russia but because
they're social revolutionists. Socialist with them is a vague term
of horror. For a socialist no punishment can be too great, no
death too painful—Socialist, Pacifist, Anarchist, these three are
the horror and terror—words that make the mouths of my
uncles curdle with loathing The funny thing is that they never
seem interested in the object of their righteous hatred enough

to ever try to conceive what the words mean—Oh what series and generations of words there must be in the Family
Connection——Changing every ten years—I must show how
the horror of one generation is the joy of the next and how the
same people proudly accept with a sense of ownership even of
I told you so—the things that terrified them not long before.

On the central thread of the Money—from the French Spo-
liation claims must be woven the changing ideology of the
family the phrases and the terrors and the revolts—all marching
time when necessity arises to money—money money. Aristoc-
racy, seedy gentility, plutocracy with occasional revolters.

Sept 15

9
The great discussion
    Jean Chénier jesuit
    André Dubois revolutionist
        Sully anarchist
    Tom Randolph
        Fibbie
    Merrier socialist

The first part was Fibbie's getting of freedom—from the
family—its religion—its way of looking at things its success—
worship—its sex ideas
    The New York and freedom and the gradual feeling of
being caught up in the net of the nations. Flags—The world
—Governments must go in There must be only the church
triumph revolutionary—taking all the men the all mother—
the great civilizer that will rescue men forever from savagery—All the church's faults come from the need to struggle
with Governments. What other Government does man need
but his mind? and his soul?
    You're right there says Sully—but why for a multiform
tyranny substitute a single one—Though that is better let us
raise God and we will find that we've been raising our own image all the while—God is man's shadow in the clouds. Give us
liberty—think of the cost of governments through the ages——
are they worth it? Give man a chance for once. Government

does not accomplish what it sets out to do even if what it sets out to do is necessary——It results in the strong having overwhelming power over the weak. Abolish the idea of property—the great central evil in the world—the cancer that has made life a hell until now civilization has been spurred on by it to suicide. Then what use would there be in fighting, what use in anything but life and love and creation of beauty—People dont commit crimes for the sake of committing them—Abolish property and you'll need no Government to protect it. Disorganization not organization is the aim of life——*Merrier*

It is partial organization that is bad——a partial organization abused by a piratical few. I have not faith enough in human nature to be an anarchist what we must have is by sensible organization organization from the bottom not from the top—democratic organization—a state of affairs in which things are more evenly distributed so that economic war can gradually be supplanted—That will be the first step in civilizing man—individual war economically of every man against his neighbor will be supplanted by cooperation in the great war against nature. The tyranny of the feudal money lords is driving lower classes together into a cooperative fraternal existence—The lower classes are therefore what the new society must be founded on—There is nothing for the rich but extinction. There exists no possible reconciliation, no point of agreement between a rich man and a poor man.

Yes said Andre Dubois, but why talk—we are slaves—we are blind we are deaf—First we must burst our bonds, open our eyes, clear our ears We know nothing but what we are told by interested parties everything is distorted to us—oh the lies the lies—the lies We must make another strike for freedom—O how many times have we men tried and failed—once more, blind, we must strike at our oppressors—hopelessly cynically—ruthlessly. We must indicate the dignity of man——O the lies—the lies they kill us with—all society all is a structure of lies—of lies for self interest by those in power who work on the cowardice of men. O if men were not cowards—If men trusted themselves instead of their lying governors there would be none of this supreme asininity of war. We are all cowards and God we believe what we're told—*Nous sommes tous despoirs.*

Cease: drain not to its dregs the urn
Of bitter prophecy
The world is weary of its past
O might it die or
rest at last.

Camp Crane—Allentown
Sept 27th

The little man who made out my papers at the local board
spoke feelingly, lyrically even, of the excitements of war and the
thrill of thinking you might be potted at any minute and wrang
my hand with considerable effusion as I left to go to Allentown.
The next morning I went early to the camp, a converted fair
ground with a race course and a lovely grove of trees where the
grackles made a pleasant cheering racket last evening. There I
spent the day with a sergeant and his assistant in a large bare
gymnasium-like room, drowsy and over heated. The sergeant
sat at a desk and arranged little stacks of papers in piles, then
pursed up his lips, cleared his throat, took up the papers and
glanced over them with hurried care and rearranged them. His
assistant with great difficulty copied the account of the case of
a man who had been discharged for imbecility. He could not
typewrite and he could not read the writing of the doctor who
had made the diagnosis so he went tick tap click, damn, tick tap
click damn and erased every other word. In the course of
proceedings numerous papers were made out about me, I was
examined physically and my eyes were found wanting. I
telegraphed the miraculous Major to get me a waiver. Now
there is nothing to do but wait to see what forthcomes. A
waiver or a return to my local board with thanks.

Come ennui——

Sunday 30th Sept—

The band plays in the pale blue stand under the tall oak grove
of the fair ground . . . The instruments glitter—silver facets
of sun—in the mottled varying shadow of the tall oak-trees
men and women walk to and fro—and soldiers—mostly soldiers—changing patterns like the bits of a picture puzzle cut
into scraps by the alternation of sun and shade—shifting and
forming into pictures—purple and blue, drab yellow and lilac
against a background of khaki—mostly khaki—Questing faces

of homely young women—questing faces of brown reddish healthy youth—glances meeting comprehending—and behind the glances the invariable picture of skirts lifted and clothes undone—of white legs and hair between them and the necessity of junction of body strain to body. The band plays.

Monday—Oct 1
I might have known it would be like this.
   This is the fourth day:
   I just looked at my watch, expecting it to be say five o'clock—It is just ten past two!
   I might have known I should get like this—
   It drives me mad to think of losing any of my precious hours—hovering this way in an agony of boredom.
   It's so stupidly unintelligent—so emptyheaded—If I took the trouble I could get into conversation with any number of men—I could sit on this bench and think—I could make up verses I could plan novels—I could draw. Why let this beastly paling fence frighten you out of your wits into this strangulation of boredom?
   At least I can sit and meditate upon the great excellence of Queen Ennui

   I've read a terruful lot in the thrice blessed Y.M.C.A.
        Tamburlane
        The Red Badge of Courage
        Vachel Lindsay's Congo Volume
        A book by an ambulance driver that made me terribly
            homesick for the front.
   O Ennui dangle your squirming jumping jacks in front of my eyes——

   There is something enormously nice about southern and western American voices.
   You wanted to be in America—well here you are—drowned in it.

   Marlowe has a wonderful trick of repeating a line at regular intervals—The Second Part of Tamburlane is really a superb piece of bombast——The lament for Zenocrate The diction of Tamburlane

O the railing and the three strands of barbed wire—o the closed in dullness of army life—I'm drinking to the dregs that dusty ennui I've always felt hung round garrisons and garrison towns.

Organization kills.

To John Howard Lawson

Camp Crane
Allentown Pa

The Greeks and Romans with their glorious sense of the necessity for platitude spent all their lives making up suitable mottos for just this sort of thing; so you can pick one out for yourself—But know my dear Jack that I'm in it—in a condition known as Casuals—in it—and done of my own accord. The moth will fly into the candle flame, so why worry—

By the aid of my Aunt of course I got specially inducted into the Ambulance Service and here I am. I hope before long to be packed on a transport and unloaded in France—but who knows, who cares—I have given myself wholly up into the keeping of a grey symbolical paramour Boredom. The depth and the height of my boredom is an inspiration. Its a state that approaches Nirvana.

I might have struggled and squirmed into the Red Cross and perhaps to Palestine—but my lady Ennui had already her arm around my neck—

The after accounts of my scandal are funny. It seems that my aunt mobilized battalions of senators, armies of congressmen who marched with banners and countermarched, who sent telegrams and made promises—but the telegrams didn't get to the telegramees and the thing fell rather flat. If there ever was a funnier tempest in a teapot—and the result is that I am persona non grata in a variety of quarters—As I say and sing

Sinbad was in bad all around

But now I am lost—buried in Khaki.

I should not have imagined that demon Detweiler would have lasted so long. Great and wonderful are the works of Allah—and notably the Red Cross.

There's a green paling fence and three strands of barbed wire all round the camp. One can't go out without a pass and we are under quarantine for Spanish Influenza—

Bulgaria has seen the light—Hurray! When the vultures and the buzzards start wheeling round in the sky there's a hope of an end.

How well the high collar fits American necks! O no we will never unsheathe until the purposes for which it was drawn are accomplished.

You can't imagine the good nature and blundering willingness to be human of the American privates. It gives an idyllic low comedy quality to things—

We have movies every night—on Sundays gentlemen in black hold prayer meetings in the YMCA and preach the Huns to Hell.

I am glad I'm here. I have always been curious about America—now my curiosity is being rapidly—o so rapidly satisfied—

But I am safe in such a mantle of Ennui as the world never saw; it's warm and comfy though and conducive to sleep and dreams—

As to the Schmelkes—I shall certainly go to see them if I get into New York before I am shipped over. I should have gone before but I knew neither their names or their addresses—

As I write—at the other end of the YM.C.A. room a gentleman is lecturing a great many young lieutenants on the subject of court martial—to make the punishment fit the crime, the punishment fit the crime—

Love
Dos

My address later—its
  214 Riverside Drive
  New York City

October 1918

Diary: October 2, 1918

Oct 2nd
And here am I waiting waiting—the length of the days is simply phenomenal—I am beginning to enjoy them just for them-

selves—and then once one has embraced Queen Ennui boldly, kissed her square on the mouth—she's not a bad mistress and she lulls you to waking sleep with her strange nostalgic songs.

Durance Vile—I have been finishing The Confessions of Jean-Jacques—poor Jean Jacques—Like him I long for an Island Avalon where I may go and sleep and dream and build my soul a garlanded altar; white, implacable, where I may place as sacrifices all my past and all my future O to get away from all troubling things from war and governments and the entrenched stupidity of people—to get away and breathe and find myself and then come back to strive and love and hate and blow my little trumpets and unfurl my little flags until I can slip away on my last exile to Avalon or St Helena or Ellis Island—who cares—so long as it is an island where one can be alone with the dawn and the sunset.

I want to write a poem about the coming of The Queen of Cypris and Jerusalem to Asolo—
It is I, the Cyprian—might be a sort of refrain to it.

The Sixth Day of my captivity—Swept 6:30 to 9:30—The Gospel of the army is cunning, as of all other human activities. The wisdom of the snake under the meekness of the sheep is what wins out.

The first Commandment is—never let them get anything on you—
The second: Graft—get privileges others haven't got—worm yourself into confidence
The Third—seem neat and prosperous—as if you had money in the bank——

To Rumsey Marvin

Oct 4

Dear Rummy
Hast ever washed windows? It's a merry sport
It has a philosophic aloofness from the world: ie one is perched on an incredibly high and rickety stepladder. It has

the philosophic concept of eternity: for to the washing of
windows there is no end. I calculate that in the course of the
day I've washed 7,898,976,342,148,264,312,800 windows and
a few more. First one daubs them disdainfully with soap:
"dreams breathed by the everliving on the polished mirror of
the world"—"a dome of many-colored glass stains the white
radiance of Eternity." Then one comes with a cloth and rubs
them clear and shiny—Nirvana burning through the mist of
Karma—"and there was a great ironic god, above all gods,
who gave unto each of the souls a life to polish"——

Now I feel like the unfortunate Huguenots in the Wars of
Religion in France that the followers of the Duke de Guise
made dig up Catholics they had killed out of the ground where
they had buried them—and with their bare fingers—Then I
think they popped the Huguenots in and buried them alive——

Above all things humans love torturing one another—or
seem to——

But I meant to say that my fingers were too tired to write.
We are under quarantine on account of the 'flu.
Write when you can——

Love
Jack

I look most baroque in a high collar—Notice the Pershing
chin——Ecris mon vieux même si tu n'a pas le temps.

Camp Crane, Allentown, 1918

Diary: October 4–7, 1918

The Seventh Day of Captivity

Noon—The camp is Quarantined—we shall never get
out—The world outside the green paling fence and the three
strands of barbed wire may have come to an end entirely for
all I know—Last night I met a man named Johnson who had
been in Section 7—

Evening—Have in the course of the day cleaned a million
windows—with each window I scrubbed my mind got murkier

so now I have no mind at all though the windows shine resplendently—Why number the days of my Ennui?—This is *Oct. 5*

I am still in Casuals, have been, as usual sweeping floors—as usual I wait frustrate in Casuals.

My first encounter today with unpleasantness in high places—I hate to get to that blood-boiling state—it takes so long to get over it. That furious foiled anger drives everything out of one's head—O bitter is the fruit of slavery——

There's comradeship in it though—and one learns—o may it all some day sprout into green shoots of vengeance—my sort of vengeance——

A green picket fence and three strands of barbed wire—does the world outside still exist——

People tell one confidentially the most amusing things about how to get on—Be nice to corporal so and so . . . Smile at sergeant so and so—he has charge of the transfers—Sergeant so and so likes to talk about the weather—He might get you into the garage—He likes Melachrinos

Luck or Cunning—which is the evolutionary factor in the army?

The Grove—Camp Crane Sunday—the band is playing tinnily but with brio—

For the *Sack of Corinth*—just told me this afternoon by a little raucous-voiced Californian named Fuselli. Family went over on the ferry to Oakland—much weeping—In a shop window he spied a service flag with a gilt stripe round it and one star embroidered with the caduceus—the emblem of the Medical Corps—"I didn't give a shit how much it cost"—bought it and as was going into the station gave it to his girl—"Here don't you forget me"—The girl produced with great promptness a large box of candy—"How the devil she got hold of it I dont know"—

Other sexual adventures of the same youngster—Girl named Mabel he got to write love-letters to but real girl found out about it and he stopped—Portugie girl, but she was a toughee—Wants to marry the girl who gave the box of candy when he goes back. Tough street corner lounging crap shooting past——

But why should I make a pseudo-medical diagnosis of the poor kid?

O for a bumper full of the warm south——

The poem about the Lady of Asolo wont come.
The watcher sleeps in Asolo gate
The watcher snores in Asolo gate
But I have a project to start the Letters of an
    Embusqué—to start with the Inn at Asolo where
      every one stirred the soup.
At the top of the stairs stood the dodo-bird.

Monday Oct 7

Last night a particularly inept movie was presented for the edification of young America seated in the grandstand. Yet as German soldiers marched by and were very clumsily atrocious—I could feel a wave of hatred go through the men. Muttered oaths and shouted imprecations—God-damned bastards—cocksuckers every one of them—were sincere. The men were furious with war—kill kill kill. For the fellow beside me I gathered that he had a notion that in The War he would be engaged in constantly snatching halfraped Belgian women from the bloody claws of Huns; that all the Germans spent their time in atrocities and that the American soldiery marching on—actually would step in every few minutes and cry, 'Shoot not this old grey head' etc.

What he saw was a village in an over picturesque country with local color plastered on very thick, donkey carts, dog carts, milk carts with much shell fire and Germans rushing about with cans of kerosene setting things on fire—Germans whom the brave Americans chase out of towns, thereby saving crowds of young girls in peasant costume a la musical comedy—and battalions of dear old ladies in lace caps from being raped and ruined and cut up into small pieces, or toasted in fires by the Horrible Huns.

A cold rainy day—no news as yet—oh the infinite boredom of army camps. This is the eleventh day now since I came inside of the green picket fence with its three strands of barbed

wire. What matter? You are safe in the arms of Ennui, your
paramour—nothing can break you from her embrace.

I can see the room now that I had in the upper school—
with mustard colored burlap on the walls—The bed was under a slant in the roof so that the ceiling rose over it like the
side of a tent. There only did I feel secure from teasing and
harassing and from games. How loath I was to leave its warm
protection in the morning. When I think back at the misery
of those years at school—I rejoice that I have at least got hold
of *things* a little better in the six years that have gone by—But
I'm much the same, by golly——

'I dont fuck women but I'm going to—God—I'd give anything to rape some of those German women. I hate them—
men women children and unborn children—They're either
Jackasses or full of the lust for power just like their rulers are—
to let themselves be ruled by a bunch of warlords like that'—
This after saying that he realized that after this peace move the
Germans would legitimately feel that they were fighting for
their homes and to protect themselves against foreign aggression.—Oct 7 1918—This I should say is the typical American
spirit with regards to the war.

Indeed indeed the country is warmad——

Damn that sense of expectation—it drives you stark crazy—
Hope deferred—The name brings up memory of much boredom—Italy in company of the famous Fairbanks—

O if it were only mess time—Then after it, one thinks o if
it were only mess time—not that there is anything particularly
pleasant about mess—but it is an *event*. This morning I found
myself hoping prayerfully that a slight squabble between
Mirabella and the tall man who gives out the mail would end
in a fight. I pictured the little Italian drawing a dagger and
great pistol-shooting.

The other Event is the movies—every night out in the open
air in the grand stand—they show most excellent ones. The
great indicator of the pathetic state into which I am fallen is
that I gurgle and chortle with delight over them.

As usual people's cowardice surprises me. The attitude of
the papers over the German peace proposal and the speeches

in the Senate all seem to me to show the most abject terror of saying the wrong thing. There's in America no inkling of the conception that a man has a right to his opinion no matter what it is—Therefore there is no honesty in America.

One could make a very decent volume out of the frustrated people in such a limbo as casuals. The war from the point of view of those who merely pace in time with the military machine, but never get to the front.

Girls, letter writing, fortune telling (murder of brother by sister-in-law)—oh the thousands of photos of smirking young women that go through the mails! Of young men too—It's a comfort to be somewhere where sex performances are frank. In the army everyone wears a phallus on his sleeve.

oh what dullness What rot! O Bored, bored bored—lets go and read

Incidentally one is constantly making the mistake of confusing liberty with democracy—They have nothing in common at all—In America the one means "every man as good as his neighbor—liberty means nothing, except possibly political autonomy. I mean that the idea of liberty being the expression of the right of the individual to the freedom of thought and expression and to "the pursuit of happiness" in his own way—does not exist. In England liberty calls to mind successive charters of the rights of man contested by various uprisings of various classes from oppressive privilege.

To Arthur McComb

Camp Crane
Allentown
Oct 5

A green paling fence and three strands of barbed wire—was Lucretius' phrase fulgentia moenia mundi?—anyway three strands of barbed wire and a green paling fence is the rampart of my world—

Therein—are long unpainted buildings here and there including what were once the mirthful edifices of a country fair ground. Signs like *Poultry And Pigeons—Long Horned Cattle Exhibit—Soft Drinks—Bar* Still stick out among the multitudinous uniformity of barrack windows.

A strange Inferno—of enforced labor—and many degrees, from where the prisoners under guard shovel coal in dirt and ignimony to where the chosen lounge in Headquarters—making out to tap typewriters, to copy orders—drowsed into bliss in the coils of red tape—

In this Inferno is a Limbo—by name Casuals—where, as my luck is always with the unclassified,—I languish, waiting a certain paper from Washington and a chance for *Over there*: Overseas service—as we say in the army—.

Organization is death. Organization is death—as I sweep acres of floor space and wash windows many as the grains of sand in the Lybian Syrtes—I repeat the words over and over in anagrams, in French, in Latin, in Greek, in Italian, in all the distortions that language can be put to. Like a mumbled Ave Maria, they give me comfort.

O for a beaker full of the warm South.

O Arthur—write me a letter full of Spain. Go into some corner centuries deep in Spain—into a tavern on the edge of some small white town in Castile, at the door of which one can stand and look long at russet hills and ochre, and a white winding road going towards a mesa that stands up suddenly—purple in the distance against an olive green sunset. Drink the air and tingling wine from the earthen pot, exchange long courtesies in excellent Castillian with the inn keeper—order a dinner of huevos revueltos, con tomate and riz con carne—and while the black raftered room's wine-scented air thickens with the drowsy weight of olive oil and garlic write—write—write

Did I tell you that the novel-thing had ceased. It is finished. Half of it lies in Paris—half in New York—When the Millennium comes—half baked as the worm is, I shall try to join head and tail and publish—

Arthur—are you writing?

I hope to goodness you are—you have far too good a mind to waste on polite incredulity. And, God, there is strife to come—there must be much sharpening of pens—the Dark has conquered and will conquer eternally until the little round world crumbles to dust.—In the scornful trumpets of the light that dies—in the lunge of the beautiful drowning swimmer amid the muddy waters—in the fires of the starving host within the city that burns itself on a great pyre rather than fall slave—is all the beauty that we can have in this shaggy world— The lamp that flickers and goes out is greater and more beautiful in the moment's intensity of flare than all the eternity of dark that follows. Let us flare high in our small hour.

I'm glad I'm here even if I seem to grumble. I've always wanted to divest myself of class and the monied background—the army seemed the best way—From the bottom— thought I, one can see clear—So, though I might have escaped behind my sacred eyes I walked with the other cattle into the branding pen—

Van—God bless him—is C.O.ing—I'll write you details— nothing has happened thus far—He has just received his questionaire and has not yet descended into the flaming fiery furnace.

Write me—I hope to get over very soon to France as an Ambulance Driver or Stretcher Bearer—But ¿quien sabe? Until I let you know you had better write me at 214 Riverside Drive Care Mʳˢ J R Gordon New York—

Love
Dos

Go, a misty autumn day for me to Aranjuez and give my love to the Tajo and its rustling wiers.

1918

Diary: October 14–17, 1918

Oct 14

Have just been talking to a man who has been in camp here for eighteen months. Was going across as sergeant, but went on a joy ride; goggle eyed drunk, up Fifth Avenue and was found out. From every hand as usual in these beastly army camps rises the moan of the leftovers. Oh the incalculable waste of energy—the waste of years and months of young manhood in these armies.

God! how can one write in captivity in quarantine?

The man who loved Service—I must see more of him. Service, with all his rather colorless diction, his banal imitation of Kipling Masefield and Co—must have things to be said for him. He is genuine I think and he expresses things in terms that are exactly those of the untrained who love him. He is expressive, I swear, he's a good example of the sort of poetry that lasts its generation and dies—perhaps this is the background, the loam from which real poetry draws its power to grow into eternity. In music—probably in all art we have the same thing it is no use sneering at it. Jack London, Zane Grey and such people are other examples of the same school.

Here's an idea for the plaything that has thrust itself so obtrusively into my consciousness—

The scene in the garden in Greenwich Village with skyscrapers in the background and garbage cans in the foreground—

Enter the *Garbage Man*—

How about this?

Act I—the first act of James Clough's play—Death in a respectable family

Act II The garbage man in the Greenwich Village garden—gets the fruit and things—the girl who escaped in Act I escapes again in Act II by climbing to the top of the highest building and striking the gong of the moon—at least her lover does it.

Act III Success—The lover has succeeded—the girl has succeeded—a very scantily furnished but beautiful room with a landscape with cedar trees outside Death strolls in at the door—They are middle aged—they talk faintly dismally—Success is death.

In Act I Death is a lousy little man rather like a doctor, with a black bag.

In Act II he is the garbage man

In Act III he is a very gorgeous person—a Wall Street broker's idea of a King

The Cyprian
The air is drenched to the stars
With fragrance of flowering grape

Where the hills hunch up from the plain
Till they blot out half the golden grain
Of stars scattered on the threshing floor
The road winds faint up the hills
So full of the tinkle of bells
Of the climbing trails of mules

Oct 17

Yesterday I was tremendously excited by the prospect of the end of the war—Today all seems cucumber-calm. The allied press talks bigger and bigger as time goes by and the prospect of a democratic Germany fighting for life against the oligarchic allies becomes more and more likely. O Lord how wild it makes me to be stuck in this damn camp—I lay awake last night thinking up complicated swearing to express the situation. I could find nothing strong enough. O for a Jew's wailing place.

The end of the third week of waiting—Jehosophat.

It took me a harf hour in doping out how to spell scissors—In yer medical pouch you've got stuff to bring yer to and bandages and scissors—now how the divil do you spell scissors

O mutter take in yer service flag yer boy's in the medical corps
All this saith the marvellous Kipling O. Flarrety—
I'll open a Irish house in Berlin, I will—and there'll be O Casey and O Brien and Flannagan or Flinnigan, and begad the King of England'll be there.

To Rumsey Marvin

Rummy—   Oct 20

Still stationary—foaming at the mouth, gnashing my teeth, swearing, squirming, raging, pacing up and down in the cadenced monotony of utter boredom—bored as a polar bear in a cage—Golly!

They seem to be keeping you busy—at least they give you the illusion of activity—I wish I had it. I wonder that the U.S.

army hasn't yet found a way of polishing the moon—they will soon, don't worry.

They are sane about sex in the army, aren't they? It is a comfort not to have the sacred phallus surrounded by an aura of mystery and cant, but one sometimes wonders if man is a selective animal at all in matters of sex. Yet I think he is. The fact remains though that the majority of men—allowing for the fact that they talk bigger than they act—, think rather of a piece of tail than of a woman. It means to them the frequent stimulation of a certain part of the anatomy and nothing else. Perhaps I overrate the mating instinct, but I think it is susceptible of slightly higher development. Maybe it isn't. Still I think that the piece of tail attitude is partly caused by the stupid conventional morality that makes copulation wrong in itself, and only licenses it grudgingly through a marriage ceremony. The result is that people degrade their everyday habits to a sexual stupidity hardly shared by animals.

I *almost* think that Europeans have a higher—less promiscuous view of sex than Anglo Saxons. The Frenchmen goes out pour faire l'amour instead of to have a piece of tail. Maybe the difference is mainly in superior phraseology, but I think not. Amour postulates reciprocity, a human relation. A piece of tail might be got off the bunghole of a cider barrel—And the American hates with a righteous hatred born only of outraged morality the goddam' whore who gives him his piece of tail—or rather sells it.

Excuse me for inflicting this ethical disquisition, but it is a subject that interests me hugely—almost in a scientific way. One has no data to go on, as the moralizers have falsified everything; so one has to find out for oneself—and it is so shrouded in the mists of conflicting conventions that research is fascinatingly difficult.

One peels off layers of conventions like skins off an onion.

First there is the family convention that man is a monogamous animal swiving few times a year for the production of offspring.

Then there is the sporty young man convention that a man should want to swive everything in skirts.

Then there is the convention of the god dam' whore as opposed to the real nice girl who'll go just so far but no further—and how many others?

It does seem to me that we of the present day have managed to bring sex to a pitch of ugliness never before reached. We have so muddied the waters that it is hardly possible to see clearly even with the greatest effort.

(To be continued)

The departing of a section for Hoboken and the front is nearly killing me. I had counted on getting into it, but Headquarters refuses to hurry itself in deciding my status. I'd like to dynamite them from Colonels to office boys——

And we are still under quarantine for the floo——

Write lots to the Prisoner of Camp Crane

Talk about the Bastille!

love
Jack

Allentown, 1918

Diary: October 29–November 1, 1918

Oct 29th

now Acting Q.M. Sergeant sect 541 Rumor that we leave tonight for France. The above is a joke——

Nov 1st —Camp Merritt

Am in charge of a barracks full of men with the dull job of keeping anyone from going out. Yesterday after two days and nights of inspections and waiting round without any particular food or sleep—we marched out of Camp Crane—Section 541 USAAS—with much laboring and people falling out of ranks on account of ill arranged packs—entrained and jolted about and waited on sidings for the rest of the day with very little food except for half an apple no an apricot pie—But this existence wipes ideas off ones mind as a damp rag wipes pictures off the blackboard before class——What's the use of writing?

To Rumsey Marvin

Camp Merritt N.J.

Rummy—

Its a great life. Three times we have been ready to pile on a transport and be desperately seasick and louseaten for two weeks of convoy travel. Three times we have been held up. Great is the hand of Allah. Now I wonder if I shall ever see the A.E.F. at all.

A pack is great fun, a regular Noah's Ark on your back. I'm still "acting" sergeant, a nasty, neither flesh, fowl, or good red herring position; but things amuse me much. People are very pleasant and reveal new amusing features daily. Our top sergeant is a delight: a regular New York Irish politician always ready to do a friend a good turn and play a mean trick on an enemy, a darn nice fellow. One of the corporals is an ex-taxi driver, another used to drive a motor hearse. Then there are cowpunchers and railroad men and farmers and bakers and butchers and candlestick makers.

I may leave for France anytime and I may never leave——

love
Jack
November 1918

Diary:November 4–December 18, 1918

Nov 4th

Still Camp Merritt & still about to sail for France; nearly crazy with waiting and with the fear that we wont go. O the maddening uncertainty of the damned army.

Four coons singing in and dancing in a barrack—black shiny coons amid the pinkish faces and khaki of the soldiers crowded round One coon sings with a guitar

> O dis is de song ob the Titanic
> Sailin' on de sea

How de Titanic ran into dat cold iceberg
How de etc.

O de Titanic's a sinking in the deep blue
She's sinking in de deep blue
Sinking in de deep blue
Sinking in de deep blue sea
O de women an de children a floatin in de sea
Round dat cold ice-berg
Sung near-er ma gawd to thee
Nearer ma gawd to thee
  Nearer to thee
O de women an de children
a floating and a sinkin in de cold blue sea

Nov 11

or is it 12th anyway its two AM and we are leaving Camp Merritt at once presumably for the boat—the transport which will take us to France or Siberia or somewhere else.

Rumors float back and forth. Everytime anyone comes back from that great council chamber the can, a new flock appears. Talk is mainly of seasickness and the possibility of French jazz—The married men are sore as they expected to be mustered out and dont want to go overseas to 'clean up shit,' as the war's over they say. Single men on the whole rather excited at the prospect of new lands.

Everything——

Nov 15

A convoy day—Our ship, the Cedric; the Adriatic; the Empress of Britain; the US warship Nebraska, three anonymous cargo-carriers, a converted German liner and a big destroyer make up the convoy, and roll along lazily with a stiff Northwest wind in the quarter. The convoy is greatly delayed by a zebra-striped cargoboat that keeps lagging behind so that the battleship has constantly to go back and pick it up. Imagine: the war has been over for three days. Nov 12, the morning we left Camp Merritt the Armistice was signed. It takes sometime to realize it. The years of that particular sort of darkness are over.

How about collecting my verse and calling it Sketches of the Dark Years Letters of an Embusqué might be called that, but God, with so much on hand how shall I ever get started—The Sack of Corinth isn't started yet and that will take months and months Golly!

I am in charge of the mess hall in the bowels of the ship, where I have to coerce unwilling and half seasick soldiers to sling the hash in an atmosphere unbelievably sordid. How I keep from puking at the thought I dont know—It is fantastic how much more one can stand than one thinks one can——

A troopship is a remarkable place—miserable seasick unwashed with officers stalking about looking for trouble as hens look for worms in a barnyard—eyes steely necks outstretched—Yet that is not absolutely true in my experience—of course always in the medical corps the officers are kindly and gentlemanly and really interested in the welfare of the men. The sergeants etc are pretty blustery and enjoy inordinately showing their authority—but the army, the army, the democratic army—is about as much so as the French army.

As the men troop in and out of the messhall I notice the sheeplike look army life gives them—a dumb submissive look about the eyes. They usually submit cowedly to my shoutings to move on with the hurt look of dogs that have been illtreated. Yet some are quizzical some stupidly truculent—I have more hopes of the U.S.A. since I've been in their damned army than I ever had before—

Nov 17
Ordering people about—habitually—as a daily occupation—is the most remarkable experience I ever had. It is so curious bawling people out—

Nov 18
Oh the sordidness. They call the garbage cans Rosies—that's the only redeeming feature of my frightful K.P. sergeancy—

Nov 19
Free at last from the abominations of K.P.
A sergeant's is a comical sort of existence—sick call— Qualification cards—record boxes—and much amiable rot—

I carry about boxes of CC pills for constipated members of my gang. I get them books and writing papers from the Y.M.C.A. room. I advise them to eat a lot to cure their sea-sickness—I bandage their vaccination scars—It's a curious existence. That is not so bad but being a mess sergeant—was a sordid hell—stuffy stinking of grease and dishwater—enough to keep you from ever eating anything again—

The poking of fingers into the corners of dishpans to see if they were clean and dry—the shouting with the sweat—sweat! I sweat enough in the week in that mess hall to fill the sources of the Nile—shouting at the steward with the sweat rolling off my face, quarrelling about sugar and jam and numbers of oranges and when the K.P.s shall be fed—I shall never forget the stench and the squabble and the gluttonous seasick sordidness of it—But one thing: I can never be seasick again after having lasted out in that mess hall for—let's see—for seven days—Nine meals a day most of the time. It is remarkable what the human organism can stand.

But a troop ship is no place to try to write or read or think——
O if I could have painted the sea as it was yesterday with a great steaming of coppery saffron clouds over it. Or the peacock brilliance of the rainbow the other day over a hazel green sea—one of the few rainbows—by the way that have not seemed to me sentimental—

The Sack of Corinth

Camp & lives
On emerging there
  stories
  Backgrounds
  Tail
  Food

    Transport
    Foreigners
    Petulency   l'esprit
    Conceit   National

    Prologue

Nov 22

Still chugging along in convoy—a seasick homesick rather blue bunch of troops except a few who assert the educational value of foreign travel—

The conversation with a man in the dark—a pitch black moonless rainy night—and the terror of submarines and loneliness and strange unaccustomed things—Can be the climax of a series—The feeling of the frightfulness of the unknown—sea cold, sea dark—the little comfortable soul born out of its groove and shivering in the great shaggy world.

In a dream in Verdun as I looked the sun was filmed over like a bloodshot eye and began to sway and wabble in the sky as a spent top sways and wabbles and whirling rolled into the seas vermillion ways so that pitblackness covered me.

Nov. 27

After four days of miscellaneous and most grievous disease I feel well enough to start to scribble notes again I think I've had symptoms of all known diseases: pneumonia; T.B., diphtheria, diarrhea, dispepsia, sore throat, whooping cough, scarlet fever and beri-beri, whatever that is.

Americans crab so—I wonder if all people do when you get them in unusual positions. Hell I can write with every body singing crabbing mainly crabbing.

Nov. 29

Le Havre This is the most miserable existence imaginable—From camp to camp one wanders weighed down by that beastly heavy pack that gets one into a state of sullen rage so that one can't even talk to new found people for amusement.

This is the beginning of the third month of my servitude. In all that time I haven't once been outside of fences and barbed wire—oh why talk about it all. I have never sunk into such complete sordid misery.

And it's hardly any use marking down names of towns.

Nov. 30 Never mind—

O' Reilly's Travelling Circus is rather amusing when those two old Teutons Schultz and Wiendieck get drunk on beer at the canteen and when Yort has to be carried in to bed—The Beer Canteen is a great improvement over the YMCA as a hanging-out place.

A sergeant is really rather a cheese in a British Camp—the B.E.F. seems a strangely ineffective affair, as I had always thought. Spends all of its time polishing brass buttons and kowtowing to rank.

At this moment the King of England is having Hallelujah festivals in Paris—who the hell wants to see him?

It must infuriate the socialists

Dec 2

At Ferrières—a charming little town in Loire et something at the USAAS base camp. The monotonous army routine drums on round me. I have really nothing to do. An occasional job to attend to as Q.M. Sgt. helps to pass a small part of the interminable days. I have an utterly desperate feeling of helplessness. If we had work to keep us busy it would be different—but this way it is a sullen black dullness all the time, bitter, bitter, bitter.

Dec. 12

The days succeed one another sordid, without a jot of variety. O the unexpressible sordidness of army life—the filth and greasiness of it.

The only interest is getting money. I have not had a cent since I landed in France and neither has that remarkable Irishman Sergeant O Reilly and yet we manage by hook or by crook to get a meal at the Cheval Blanc every night and much drink at different cafés scattered about town

The unforgettable scene with the whore in the back room of the Cheval Blanc—a page out of Artzibasheff. That must go in the Sack of Corinth word for word.

Also the partie Madeleine, at the other café. . . .

Dec 18

The days drag by.

Madeleine and the girl with the red cheeks when the boys cluster like flies on a wet day, loitering hungrily like dogs round a back door where they half expect to be fed, and the whores and the man who is going to marry the French girl.

The artist who left yesterday for Belfast, a funny rather maudlin little man.

I am sitting in the little inner room at the cafe de Madeleine, while they talk about death at the table. The sergeant says what a little thing it is to die—in the generations a man is nothing. Tout est bien fait dans la nature. Dans la mort il n'y a rien de terrible.

Quant on va mourir on pense à tout—mais vite

To Rumsey Marvin

Pvt. J.R. Dos Passos
SSU 541
Convoy Auto
par B.C.M. France
December 29, 1918

Rummy!

A letter from you has turned up with a wonderful project—cocoa-beans and Spanish and poetry and wandering—but mon cher I have no granpère to come across with the dough! And I have a frightful lot of work to do as soon as I can wriggle my neck from out of the collar. Look at this.

1. Rewrite Seven Times Round the Walls of Jericho and get it published, if that is possible.

2. Write a certain Sack of Corinth—a monumental work on America Militant.

3. Write a certain play of which the scenario has been gradually cooking for the longest time.

4. Write a certain The Family Connection an opus a novel of the exegi monumentum aere perennius type

5. Collect numerous fragments into a series of essays.

6. Study the Anthropology of religions or religious anthropology, possibly in some university

7. Learn to paint

8. Paint

9. Visit Abyssinia
and so on ad infinitum.

Now what is one to do with such a program? And here I am wasting days and weeks and months in the state of servitude you so admire. I'll make their ears tingle though, by God, if I die in the attempt. I'll dust their coats with a clanking of printing presses. O things are not what they seem. I wish you had got a larger dose of what you love so. You would have come to know it better, I warrant you.

Don't worry about not having an aim. I felt the same way when I first went to college. It took me a good three years to get rid of family bred inhibitions before I realized exactly what I wanted to do. When I think how far I am from doing it I become terrified. Then too I suffer from a multiplicity of desires. I want to swallow the oyster of the world. I want to peel the rind of the orange. I want to drink the cup to the dregs—no—I want to swallow it and still have it to look at. I want to peel off the rind in patterns of my own making. I want to paint with the dregs pictures of gods and demons on the great white curtains of eternity.

And I do nothing. I blame the army, the weather, the food—O if I could wrench myself out of the blankness of inertia.

Like you I believe in frugal living, unwasteful—Like you I abhor the puppyish lying about of college life, the basking in the sun with a full belly. Life is too gorgeous to waste a second of it in drabness or open-mouthed stupidity. One must work and riot and throw oneself into the whirl. Boredom and denseness are the two unforgivable sins. We'll have plenty of time to be bored when the little white worms crawl about our bones in the crescent putrifying earth. While we live we must make the torch burn ever brighter until it flares out in the socket. Let's have no smelly smouldering.

I wish I could get to South America with you Rummy. Maybe it can be worked. Or couldn't you let cocoa wait a year and come to Spain. That would be cheaper for me and I vow you'll gain as much.

But who knows? Spain, or Peru, Abyssinia or the Yalu River we must go somewhere together very soon—

There's a chance that I'll be able to get a furlough to try for an A.M. in an European University—so a couple of months may find me at Cambridge or the Sorbonne. Then work! work! Gods how the dust'll fly.

I have been bitterly disappointed by the defeat of the British Labor Party—The world has not yet seen an end of its backsliding. Old Bogey is Lord God. Mumbo Jumbo reigns supreme—Hurrah for the dark ages!

Love
Jack
Write Morgan Harjes

To Rumsey Marvin

Paris—March 17/19
A little estaminet—rue St. Honoré

Rummy—

I have been dreadfully mum in the last months—forgive and prepare to receive penitent avalanches.

I am free—at least provisionally

Libertad libertad! As Walt would have cried, tearing another button off his undershirt.

I loll in the groves of Academe. I am at the Sorbonne—a large monumental place that has up to the writing given me no other impression but that of massy dullness—but I live in a pleasant little room on the Montagne St. Geneviève, near the Pantheon, where I typewrite from morning till night with intervals for food—delicious sizzly Paris food and concerts, preparing the M.S. of Seven Times Round the Walls of Jericho for a journey to London and a promenade in publishers' wastebaskets. Furthermore another novel and a play are clamouring for a hearing and I hope that the dear things will be able to see the light before long. There is alas, so remarkably little time in twenty four hours. Why don't days have forty eight?

I am enclosing a couple of poems in case the magazine scheme comes through. Do write me more about it—I'm tremendously interested. Why go out for the business end of the Record? You'ld much better get in by writing comic verses about the Peace Conference or the American Public or God or Joan of Arc, or serious sonnets about the sadness of a beerless Hofbrau.

I saw last night at the Adevil de Musset's most exquisite play On ne Badine pas avec l'Amour—one of the loveliest things I've ever seen on the stage—though it was acted in a heavy classic manner—It shows you what really happens to a romance of syrup and mintleaves and moonlight if you leave it alone—written in a superb futuristic casual style.

Then the other day I heard a whole Debussy concert—— delight of delights—though I was so crowded in with other people that I had to stand for four hours on one leg with the elbow of a very Katisha in my tummy and a gentleman's beard tickling the back of my neck—the whole bunch of us hanging precariously from a brass rail in the highest balcony the while   That is the way to hear music.

Later: I seem to have strayed away from my usual paths into a nasty little restaurant into which I was lured by a pleasant odor of fried fish—it turns out to be full of RedCrossworkers whose conversations are very annoying. They say such madly asinine things about France and always the same things.

Here are more: Y.M.C.A. workers this time; much worse than Red Crossworkers—mealymouthed. They talk about how expensive food is, and about Y.M.C.A. prizefights and how immoral Paris is——

What about coming to Europe next summer? I rather hope to be in Spain—if I can get out of the Army as soon as the University closes at the end of June. Though everything depends on the possibilities of publishing the novel. Why cant you come and galivant about Spain? You could learn Spanish and increase your leg-muscles walking over stony mountain paths and if you want to be "practical" study treatises on quadruple entry bookkeeping under the shade of olivetrees while I sketch the antiquities. Wont you try the project on the family?

I may be trying to collect material for a treatise on Spanish Folklore or something of the sort for a Doctorat or a Licenciat at the Sorbonne

But, as I said, everything depends on the possibility of getting a publisher. I expect to go back to America in the fall to write for my bread and butter, or something of the sort—though there is a vague chance that I may teach out in Roberts College—Constantinople—I've been recommended by a friend of mine. It would be rather fun to be out there for a year I think. One would have a chance to travel all over everywhere in the vacations. But I doubt very much if anything materializes.

If I go utterly broke I shall try to get a job with the Red Cross.

Do write me all about Yale—I suppose it's gradually changing back into an institution of learning—getting out of its degraded state of last year.

A bientôt
Jack—

Spain—Spain—garlic and roses and mountains tawny as panthers.

To Rumsey Marvin

Rummy—

For some reason your letter made me angry as the devil—Why can't you come to Spain? You profess to be ready for anything, yet you refuse even to entertain the hope that you may be whizzed off to Spain in a whirlwind, like a minor prophet. I vow that you need Spain and Spain needs you, and I need you, and you need me.

Have you read Marius the Epicurean? It may be all sheer rot, but its a sort of rot that is at times beneficial. As you love me read at once, furthermore, Anatole France's La Revolte des Anges, L'Ile des Penguins and La Rotisserie de la Reine Pédauque. Also read all the Elizabethan lyrics you can find lying round. Add thereto Shakespeare's Sonnets, Tom Jones, Rabelais and even, possibly the Satyricon. Then cap the whole by Renan's Vie de Jesus and George Moore's The Brook Kerith. All of which means that I feel that you need to be confronted with the eternal verities

This sort of statement is indefensible even on the grounds that your typewriter ran away with you: . . . *as we certainly seem to have come out on top in this war, and we undoubtedly live saner, happier lives than better educated and underdeveloped people with nervous and mental troubles which vigorous bodies etc* Because it very simply isn't so. Any fair minded person will admit that the average Frenchman at the front showed greater powers of endurance than the average American, and that life in Europe is saner, healthier, and happier than in America. I admit that America is more dear to me than Europe—probably its colossal hideousness, its febrile insanity are evolving towards a better life for man. But none of that's to the point. The thing I object to is the mental attitude involved—And at this moment I cant quite explain why I object to it.

O but Rummy will you—for me—plant a little grain of the mustard seed of doubt before your great steel idol of success.

But I'm talking even worse rot than you are. In fact I'm not at all sure that you are wrong. Still something in your letter got my bile up.

By this time you will have received bunches of letters from me all imploring you to try to get to Spain—Constant wearing will—O I'm crazy this afternoon—What I mean is—little drops of water, little grains of sand, make the mighty etc——

I'm in a horrid mood today—and I feel like lecturing so you are getting the brunt of it—But Rummy my love, I hope you read something else in Freshman English than Shakespeare Ruskin Carlyle and Tennyson—Carlyle I'll admit as a good old brute of a minor prophet, and of course Shakespeare is enough to counteract all ills—but why in Gods name Tennyson and Ruskin?—Why is a mouse when it spins?

While I'm still in the pnyx or the pynx or the pyx or the xyp or whatever the thing was that Athenian orators stood in when they talked—and I must be quick for the pallium is falling fast from my shoulders, let me beg you to read a lot of classical stuff.

You know that I hate Nothing worse than old fogyism and looking backward out of the sordid present into the glories of the past sort of bombast, but still I solemnly aver, that the only education in the world that is worth calling an education comes from the stimulation of the spirit that contact with the two great flowerings of our race brings: The Renaissance and the Age of Athens. The Renaissance for us, who speak English is best expressed by the plays and poems and prose of Elizabeth's time. And Greece . . . Do you know G. Lowes Dickinson's *Greek Civilization* (that's not the title, but you can easily find it in the library catalogue)? Then Pater's *Greek Studies* open certain doors—Then there is Andrew Lang's Odyssey and the Gilbert Murray translations of Euripides.

Why don't you—even if you do go to a summer resort—shut yourself up like a hermit and do oodles of reading this summer? You almost make me want to go back to America to do it too.

Forgive this rotten illtempered carping letter, Rummy. It's a boresome irritating sort of afternoon and the vast stupidity of man—my own—my own too—seems to rise in a drowning wave about me.

O we must up and at 'em: we are too lively, we have too much curiosity, too many desperate desires for unimaginable things to let ourselves be driven down into the mud of common life. You and I and a few others and thousands of others we do not know—O it is so much harder than it has ever been before to lead a good life, to dominate life instead of being driven in the herd. Intellect, vigor have more to struggle against than ever before, except perhaps in the darkest of feudal times, when religion held the world crouched in gibbering fear. This all pervading spirit of commerce—this new religion of steel and stamped paper! O it is time for Roland to blow his horn that the last fight may start. To think clearly and piteously, to love without stint, to feel in ones veins the throbbing of all the life of all the world——is that not better than to succeed and to be tapped on tap day and to make ΦBK and grow a paunch on the income from slave-labor?

Forgive much rot, Rummy out of which you may be able to sift a little sense—

Love
Jack

Paris, June 1919

To Germaine Lucas-Championnière

Credit Lyonnais
Alcalá 8
Madrid

Mademoiselle—   1-IX-19

La manière d'une corrida de toros est la suivante.

Il y a des moments dans la vie d'une ville espagnole où on remarque que tout le monde suit une certaine rue, que tout le monde se presse et se bouscule, que tous les landaus, les berlines, les coupets, les voitures de place, les taxis, les limousines, les voitures à bras, les vielles femmes qui vendent l'eau de cruches merveilleusement grecs, les vendeurs de melons, de raisins, de fritures, les chats, les chiens et les pigeons, que toute la population va dans une seule direction. C'est l'heure de la corrida. On entre, comme dans le dernier acte de Carmen, on s'assoie, et on pense aux luttes des gladiateurs romains. On regarde avec dégout et mépris le sable rougâtre des arènes, les barricades en bois peint en rouge et jaune qui protègent les spectateurs, la porte grillé de laquelle vont entrer les chrétiens, non, le taureau.

On hausse les épaules. On est accoutumé a tout ça. Qu'on commence.

Son de trompette. Deux messieurs en noir, se tenant avec grande difficulté sur de beaux chevaux qui santillent dans la lumière écrasante de cirque, entrent, font le tour, et saluent, avec une magnificence un peu gaté par la difficulté qu'ils éprouvent de se tenir sur leur cheveaux, devant la loge royale. Puis les picadores et les matadores, les equippes de mulets qui vont emporter les cadavres, entrent en procession et saluent le loge vide des grandes personnages. Ils sont habillés en toutes couleurs, rouge, orange, violet, et la dentelle d'or scintille au féroce soleil. Encore des trompettes, et le taureau entre, noir, immense, bondissant comme les taureaux que les troglodytes ont peint dans la jeunesse du monde dans la caverne à Altamira. Ce n'est pas une lutte, c'est une rite, un sacrifice qui s'accomplit. On immole un cheval ou deux au cornes du taureau, et les chevaux eventrés se tordent en attitudes grotesques sur le sable rougatre dans la lumière feroce. Puis, avec un geste superbe on applique les banderillas au dos du taureau deja fatigué. Puis il y un crie de joie féroce des trompettes, le matadore se met dans la position préscrite et enfonce la longeur du sabre dans le cou épais et saignant du taureau. Le taureau traine sa langue d'où dégoutte du sang écumeux, et tourne sa tête d'un cote á l'autre d'une manière bête et seduisante comme un petit chien que demande du sucre. Le matadores avec leurs manteaux rouges, et verts et violet font un cercle autour de lui. Il tombe et roule par terre, et deviens petit et sale sur le sable de l'arène. Les equippes de mulets entrent joyeusement et entrainent les cadavres aux sons de grelots et de claquement de fouets. Une autre trompette. Les manteaux rouges et verts et violets prennent leur places, et ça recommence.

Il a du être un peu comme cela qu'on sacrifiaient des centaines de taureaux aux grands dieux, à Cnossos ou à Mycène, ou devants les hautes murailles d' Ilion.

C'est bête, c'est laid, c'est splendide. C'est comme une bonderie ou comme le ballet russe—Mais les nerfs du vingtième siècle, accoutumés comme ils sont à flots de sang repandu sur la terre, font de tout ça une sensation interessante mais disagréable.

Je suis en route pour Málaga.

L'adresse en tête de cette letter est permanente—

Au revoir
John R. Dos Passos

To Rumsey Marvin

Dear Rummy;   Aug 24
I have just come down from some mountains very justly called Los Picos de Europa, where I have been walking about. We got into wonderful lost valleys where no one ever seemed to have seen a foreigner before, and managed to get right through the range down the wildest and most superb gorge I have ever seen. We ended by scrambling over a pass that

nearly did for us, and eventually got to Oviedo, a Rembrandt brown city full of convents that look like palaces and palaces that look like convents. Today I am going on to Leon, on the way to Madrid, where, among other things, I hope to find mail from you.

Avilés is a windy dusty glary little market town, one of those places one gets to by mistake and goes away from on the first train.

However, I saw some excellently red and mammoth lobsters in the kitchen of the place where I expect to have lunch, So it may hold good things to eat.

To lose the habit of writing is the worst thing on earth that can befall one. It is exactly a year since I really wrote anything—though I have worked over lots of stuff—and I am finding it intensely difficult to get into the creative way of thinking. I am trying to finish up a novel I began ages ago in Alsace last winter. At present it calls itself The Sack of Corinth, though I fear the title will have to be changed. I want to express somehow my utter . . . Its not exactly that though. The feeling of revolt against army affairs has long crystalized itself into the stories of three people, a clerk in an optician's in San Francisco, a farmer's son from Indiana and a musical person who appears in S.T.R.W.J.—so much so that I cant get a word down on paper. The story's all ready to be written—but it wont come. A maddening state of affairs.

The first part is at training camp in America, the second part at the front, the third in that strange underground world of deserters and AWOL's, the underside of the pomp of war. There is going to be rather a lot of murder and sudden death in it, I fear. I am rather excited about it, and it is just agony being unable to put it on paper.

> on the train St. Malo to Mt. St. Michel
> My desires have a-hunting gone.
> They circle through the fields and sniff along the ridges,
> Like hounds that have lost the scent.
> Outside, behind the white swirling patterns of coal smoke
> Hunched fruit-trees slide by
> Slowly pirouetting,

And poplars and aspens on tiptoe
Peer over each others' shoulders
At the long black rattling train;
Colts sniff and fling their heels in air
Across the rusty meadows;
And the sun; now and then,
Looks with vague interest through the clouds
At the blonde harvest mottled with poppies,
At the Joseph's cloak of fields, neatly sewn together with
    hedges
That hides the grim skeleton
Of the earth.
My desires have taken ship.
In rain-drenched velvets and brocades
They huddle on the lurching deck
Of a lost galleon.

Out of the mist and the galloping waves
Into the infinite stillness of the bay
Where the pale sea's streaked grey and green
And there lie long reaches of violet sands
like the long clouds in the violet sky.

                                To be continued in our next

Dear Rummy,   Granada Sept 20.
    As you see nearly a month has gone by since I started this
letter to you. At present I am living in a charming little
domed summer house in a garden that overlooks Granada. I
write all the morning and most of the afternoon and then
sally forth and wander in the frivolous courts and halls of the
pastry palace the moors built among the superb red towers of
their fortress on the hill. I've got the first part of my new
novel done, thank heaven. So I feel quite come to life again
after a long sojourn in the blue infernal regions.
    I never seem to be able to get this letter finished. I don't
know why. I had another wonderful walk, along the coast of
the province of Malaga, between the Sierra Nevada and the
sea. Superb burnt hills and irrigated valleys full of banana
trees and sugar cane and of the sound of water running
through irrigation ditches. A wonderful part of the world.

The people in the towns hire a fig tree for the summer and go out under it with their pigs and goats and cats and chickens and eat the figs and enjoy the shade. Life has no problems under those conditions.

I am awfully glad that you enjoyed Tom Jones. To me it is one of the rocks upon which English literature is built. And James Stephens, along with broiled live lobster, is one of the reasons why I shall never commit suicide.

About Joyce. I'm not sure that you're not right. Yet I think its a very expressive book and the hero doesn't seem to me remarkable particularly—a hypersensitive person the like of which abound in our asinine modern society.

One might write a very pretty psychopathic essay entitled "The age of seduction". But I think that you'll find that in America the age of seduction is later among our class than in any other and that in most other countries fifteen or sixteen is a perfectly good average date.

Isn't it curious how completely ignorant we all are of the most important part of our bodily mechanism. It is really criminal. Yet there is no nation in the world that doesnt surround sex with fantastic walls. Of course ours are sillier than any—but not much.

The army's the only place I know where people are frank about it—and there their point of view is strictly limited and offers neither variety nor interest.

A bientôt—

Jack

1919

To Rumsey Marvin

Granada

Dear Rummy: Oct 15

It's raining; from my window I can look over a garden wall at a big clump of pink and white cosmos and at an orange tree where the green of the oranges is just beginning to fade into gold. It is a soft autumnal rain. Through a gap in the trees beside a big funeral cypress I can see the Sierra Nevada and a bit of the tawny foot hills. Il Pleure dans mon coeur.

Comme il pleut sur la ville—I am thinking of how quickly the days slip by and thinking of all the roses I have left un-gathered. Verlaine's language monotone!——Silly.

I've been getting letters from America—a darn good one from you too——and it makes me blue to think of the strange lack of energy that young Americans of attainments and sensibilities seem to have. I know so many who are really brilliant people who seem to be drifting into meaningless boredom. I cant understand it. It would be better if they took to drink or religion or patience. Anything taken up hard is better than that vague dissent from the inelegance of life to-day which is the main quality of the people who ought for good or bad to be getting into the turmoil. You must know lots of them too, fellows who are too intelligent and too alive and have too much poetry in them to take to the regular balderdash of the average sheep, but who just hang about in the world. If they didn't have enough money to be comfort-ably off, their bellies would push them to something—but as it is, there they are, sheer waste.

I'm not thinking of you, Rummy. You've got too much gumption for that. Though why you should want to expend that gumption on "business" is beyond me, I admit. Of course everyone has to do a certain amount of business to keep alive—but its a means not an end. That's the tragic funda-mental fallacy in the minds of Americans—not Americans only, god knows—Everywhere they—take the means for the end. It's inconceivable to me—Just look at their faces, those business men. Talk to them. Can't you see that their sense of values is pathetically wrong?—That they dont know why they're working, that they get to be mules in the tread mill in order that their wives may spend thousands boring themselves elaborately in "society".

A man can't live without a trade. That sounds dogmatic, but I swear that its true. A man to give and enjoy any sort of happiness in this shaggy old world has got to have something that preoccupies him supremely above anything else. You cer-tainly don't want extracting money from other people to be your supreme preoccupation. A man's mind is moulded by his occupation, willy nilly. The ideas of a shoemaker are those which are useful in shoemaking, the ideas of a banker those useful in banking. Think what your mind will be like after forty years of exploiting other people.

If you want to take up manufacturing, for gods sake take up the scientific end of it. You want to be a brain that creates; not a parasite living off other peoples brains, off other people's work. And there's enough work to be done. There are endless possibilities in almost anything anyone takes up; but ones got to sell one's soul for them. To save ones life one must lose it, and lose it hard.

My father who had the best brain I've ever known was a tragic example. He was poor and energetic and lively, and in his day the only thing for a poor boy to do was to make a fortune. He did. But he got so entangled in that famous "business" that interests you so that when he wanted to start being a person instead of a business man he couldn't disentangle himself, and all through his life he could only really live—use his brain (not his wits) creatively in odd moments. He never had time. That was the tragedy of his generation. But the problem of being wealthy is already out of date; what was rather splendid in 1860 becomes mesquine and sordid in 1920——Dont be an anachronism. But Rummy, think of the endless trades from bootcleaning to mathematics. There must be something in all that gamut that suits you better than making a trade of exploitation. Just in science alone think of all there is to do. Why throw in your lot with the old regime, at the last minute. You may think you can keep your mind clean of your occupation—but I swear you cant—a shoemaker has the mind of a shoemaker, a college professor of a college professor, a painter of a painter, a businessman of a bandit—within the law.

Theoretically you are perfectly right about Marxian socialism, of which I am intensely suspicious. [   ] There is an interesting account of the Kansas jails going about which is illuminating—It's a question of *existence-not-of-theories.*

I've just come back from Portugal—and I am thinking of walking from here to Cadiz—if I can get some articles finished I've got to write. If I can scrape up the money I am going to

Tetuan in Morocco—I am curious to see the process of spreading civilization at the hands of the Spanish army.

love
Jack

I may turn up in America during the winter.

1919

To Rumsey Marvin

Granada—Nov 17
Credit Lyonnais—Alcala 8, Madrid

Dear Rummy—

I have just finished wasting a month in a very foolish business. On my way back from Portugal, just at the moment when I had about fifty articles to write, I had the bad taste to go to bed with a damn fool rheumatic fever. Just the day too that I was to start out from Granada to walk to Cadiz! And here I've been ever since, within four walls till yesterday when I first got out to sniff the crisp autumnal air. A most miserable waste of time. And even now I toddle about more or less like a scare crow.

But it was almost worth it for the keenness with which I breathed the tang of drying leaves and overripe fruits, the wonderful fullness and richness that is in the air in autumn. It was as if I'd just been born. The poplars in the valley are all bright yellow like candle flames, and the Sierra Nevada is blue white with snow, and one eats huge squashy Japanese persimmons, that burst with sweetness when you bite into them and drip in orange juice over your fingers. And the custard-apples, full of a flavor of resin, are like a bite taken out of the sparkling cold air itself and the streets of Granada are full of a smell of roasting chestnuts and in the evenings a faint blue haze goes up where the people are lighting their charcoal brasiros in front of the houses, and the little ruddy pile of embers at each doorstep glows through the purpling dusk.

This wretched disease has muddled up everything and all my affairs are bubbling gleefully in the soup. M'en fous!

While in bed I read stories out of a splended unexpurgated Spanish edition of the Arabian Nights—so different from that sickly Lane-Poole affair doled out to Anglo-Saxons—packed with life and color and giving one a splendid idea of that second flowering of Rome that was Arab civilization. Burton's translation must be as good.

As soon as I dare I shall trek for Madrid, as this absurd illness caught me in a dreadful English pension into which I had been inveigled by a friend.

And in the midst of jolly preposterous Spain to be caught in an atmosphere of moral malignancy and Scotch parsimony is too awful for words. My friend and I have our meals with three old hags who sit and hate the Huns and make moral judgements on the Spaniards. I swear it takes many a Byron, many a Marlowe and many a Shelley to expiate the sins of the Anglo Saxon race. They have been able to conquer the world, but they have never been able to understand, which means I suppose to love—probably thats why they were able to conquer it—Brrr—Dont generalize—

Do write me more often—Your letters are as rare as good deeds—again the moral note! I abdicate—

love
Jack
1919

To Rumsey Marvin

Madrid
Dec 6–19

Rummy—you wretch; one never gets letters from you any more. I hope you aren't plying the oar so hard that you've forgotten how to ply the pen—or perhaps your tail is so sore that you cant sit down to write . . . Odd's fish! lad, write standing up.

I'm in the nasty period of convalescence—when one has to be careful. There's nothing in God's earth more annoying than being careful. It takes all the poetry out of existence.

News from America is rather two edged. At the same time as we seem to be shutting ourselves out for ever from the esteem of civilized peoples—if there are any—by the recrudescence of the Inquisition and by acts of the filthiest barbarity, there seems to be growing a realization, among honest people who aren't fools or cowards, of what is going on. At least the period of tame acquiescence seems to be coming to an end. Yet liberty—civilization—have in all ages hung on such a tenuous thread—that one can not but fear for the outcome of the struggle. The trick has been played before—many times— in the gory tortured history of peoples (I can hear the cymbals of your optimism clanging objections even from here) I dont deny that you can never quite trample out the things worth while—but you can crush out the spark in ten generations— and the poor little individual objects to being under the heel— to feel it slowly crushing the life out of him—One doesnt want to belong to one of the submerged generations, does one? If this keeps up you and I will be damn near it, that's all.

Madrid is a chilly jolly town—I have a rather good time here always, although I wish I could be walking across the tawny plains of Castile

Love
Jack

To George Allen & Unwin, Ltd.

c/o Credit Lyonnais
Barcelona

Dear Sir,   March 13, 1920

I am not quite sure what you mean by a descriptive paragraph. I suppose it is the little puff that is used in advertizing. You probably know much better than I what would be suitable. However, it might be useful to say that the volume is made up out of notes written while I was an ambulance driver attached to the French army in the summer of 1917 and that I have tried to picture the state of mind of an American in his first contact with the war as well as the general moral atmosphere of the war at that moment. The notes were scratched down in dugouts and hospitals and were put in their present shape in the autumn of 1918, thinly disguised under a novelistic form.

If there is anything more I can give you in that direction, please let me know at once—c/o Credit Lyonnais Barcelona—

Very sincerely yours
John R. Dos Passos

To George Allen & Unwin, Ltd.

Marseilles
Dear Sir,   April 29

I'm awfully sorry to have held up proceedings in this way. I had forgotten that the British public was so touchy about blasphemy.

Unfortunately I have not the M.S. with me so I cant be quite sure how the sentences read. Please omit entirely the three sentences. I think this can be done without adding anything, but if a sentence of bridging seems needed, put in anything brief and terse that seems suitable. The incident of the soldiers kicking the prop out from under the Cross will carry the idea. If you do not want to print that, please omit the entire scene. I am willing to have almost anything omitted, but I cannot consent to paraphrases.

Very sincerely yours
John R. Dos Passos

1920

To Thomas P. Cope

Tom—

I've been hoping to have news of you—without much result. Are you halfway to Singapore aboard a fullrigged ship, or handling hawsers on a tugboat on the Susquehanna?

I am in London squabbling with my publishers. Verily of the making of books there is no end. The printers refuse to print *One Man's Initiation*—they say it's indecent! So more expurgations and changes must be made. The poor thing will be gelded for fair by the time it comes out. However, I am slightly consoled by the chance of an American edition, which seems to be solidifying. Literature's a silly business.

At present I have not the slightest reason for writing—its ages since I thought or experienced anything amusing or interesting. I have been suffering from an illusion of flatness for some time. Comes from lack of exercise I imagine—almost everything does. America has an unhallowed attraction for me—unless I can find something of unusual interest to do—to *do*—not to feel, see, think, hear; times come when one needs the illusion of action. Its only an illusion—a damn thin one—but I think you feel see think hear more sharply when you have it than when you are floating about swathed in the cottonwool of middle-class existence

To get rid of the cottonwool at all costs is the thing.

All these reflections are possibly due to the curious mental state one gets in when one finishes a work—*Three Soldiers* is irredeemably finished. I wish you were here to tell me what you thought of it.

Tom, when you get to be the Captain of the *Whinnying Wallaboo* you'll give me the job of crew of the captain's gig, wont you?

I must get out of the Doldrums of society,

Love—

Dos

In case you're hard up, cash this. I have about $600 or more in that bank so let me know at once if you need more—

June 1920

To Germaine Lucas-Championnière

Vendredi—Londres—Jour de pluie—ciel de plomb.

C'est aujour d'hui que vous quittez Paris. Bon Voyage. J'aimerais bien aussi m'enforcer dans la campagne quelque part. Je vis trop dans les villes. J'oublie les chants des oiseaux dans l'aube et les grandes nuits solitaires quand on se promène dans les bois, dans cette silence murmurante des choses vertes qui poussent, de petits animaux qui suivent leurs buts trottinant sans peur sous le grand châle protecteur de la nuit—où la vie est serrée comme les petits gens sous le manteau de la Virgen de la Caritad.

Et Londres est un peu comme le beefsteak froid, solide mais inattrayant. Je deteste ces longs crepuscules blêmes et blanchâtres des faubourgs de Londres, où chaque jour finit dans une petite eternité d'ennuie, sans couleur—rues desertes sans vie, petites maisonettes de la drille rouge qui, decoupent le ciel gris aussi loin qu'on peut voir avec leur petits toits d'un similarité accablante. Non, l'Angleterre est ennuieuse, faite à la machine, sans avoir cette atmosphere fantastique et macabre de mon pays.

J'ecris dans une petite chambre grise ou un feu de charbon dur fait des petits bruits comme la sire froussée. Devant le feu un petit chien gras et maledif dort en rouflant. Une petite pendule souffle les demi-heures avec une petite voix douce et frêle. Un petite vielle dame se repose sur un sofa . . . Et la vie est un rituel tres compliqué, arrangé par des petites vielles dames mortes dans des siècles petits et vieux. Je sens, cette après midi, un peu de l'ennuie desespèré de mon enfance—J'ai passé quatre ans quand j'etais très petit dans ce coin de Londres—de ces longues après midis pâles ou il fallait rester à la maison quand mes jambes se tordaient d'envie de courir, quand j'etais trop accablé par les desires fous qui fourmillaient dans mon sang pour lire où jouer, et je pensais de la vie que je vivrais un jour.

Et maintenant que je me trouve dans la terre promis, est-ce que ça vaut les fous desires d'antan?

Des fois je pense que j'ai dedans moi une de ces petites chambers grises, meublée du meilleur gout, d'où les vraies choses de la vie, le soleil et l'amour et la sueur et le bon travail accablant des bras—d'où tout est exclu en cru et ou tout peut entrer en literature, reglé, taillé,—La vie doit se mettre en chapeau de forme et bien s'essuyer les pieds avant qu'il puisse s'assoir dans le petit salon gris de la bourgeoisie.

Et que des fois l'ai je detruit, ce petit salon gris, mais toujours—au grand moment, je m'y trouve enfermé, et je regarde par les fenêtres les grandes processions pondreuses passer et disparaitre sur la grand route. Dieu, si l'on pouvait tuer ses grandpères.

Ecrivez moi—soins Morgan, Harjes—15 Place Vendome Paris.

J'espere que votre mère va mieux—Saluez la pour moi

Mon malheureux livre, quoique tout prêt n'a pas vu la lumière encore.

Bien à vous
JRDP.
June 17, 1920

To Germaine Lucas-Championnière

Dans un café en face du theatre de Cluny. Nuit suave, pleine de voix et de cette premonition desespèrante d'automne. Une lune qui se voile et se dévoile constamment dans de petits nuages de moussiline. Un ragtime monotone viens d'un orchestre grinçant. Connaissez-vous l'histoire que Herodotus conte du Roi Mycerinus d'Egypt? Il consultat un oracle qui lui dit qu'il n'avait que cinq ans à vivre. Avec des torches et des banquets il se moquait des dieux en tournant nuit en jour. Il ne dormait plus et quand il mourait il avait vecu dix ans. C'est une des histories qui m'ont le plus touché. Vos cartes de St. Jean de Luz sont pleines de merveilles. Au moment il me manque de merveilles. Hier quand je me couchait un gros chat brun, à l'aspect tordu et chinois est entré par ma fenêtre. Il m'a regardé avec des yeux de flammes jaune d'un malice effroyable. Puis il a ouvert sa bouche et laissé echapper un miaulement feroce. Ces yeux de topaz sont devenues rouges comme des rubis, et avec un autre cri d'amour ou de haine il c'est enfuit dans la nuit. Peut être c'est une merveille. Esperons.

J'ai retenu une place sur un bateau qui part de St. Nazaire pour le Mexique ou le Cuba le 7 aout. Peut être il me ménera vers des merveilles. Comme le roi Mycerinus d'Egypte je veux redoubler ma vie.

C'est que votre France que j'aime tant est trop civilizée pour moi au moment. I'imprevu n'existe pas. Peut être il n'existe nul part. La vie française est une belle cérèmonie dont toutes les actions s'accomplissent selon un rituel etablis par les anciennes génèrations. Tout—pour nous autres barbares homes d'une rite inachevée—est d'une douceur indicible,— ou est comme les mangeurs du lotus. La bas la vie s'acharne, brutale, cruelle, vers de combinaisons nouvelles. Notre generation à mis la chemise brulante de Nessus. C'est une lutte à mort contre les vaste mechanisms qui sont l'esclavage de demain. La lutte ne terminera jamais. On a beau s'attarder sous les fruitiers, s'enivrer des grands rhythmes tranquilles des vieilles villes le moment arrive toujours où on ne peut plus resister le sang brulant qui pousse toujours vers la lutte, vers de chemins nouveaux.

Matin—tout ça parait bien bête. On ne devrait jamais relire les lettres.

Encore des merveilles et du son du vent remuant les asphodeles au haut des falaises—tout à vous

JRDP

Paris, July 27, 1920

To John Howard Lawson

214 Riverside Drive
Sept. 12-20

Jack—forgive me not having sent the 5000 sooner. I'll send it tomorrow by cable. It has taken time to disentangle pennies.

Floated up from Cuba on the Gulf Stream on a very delapidated boat—trip given over to the study and culture of the gin fizz. When the old thing docked at Brooklyn (with great difficulty as its engines were aweary of this great world) the moment a gang plank was thrown down a great crowd of square jawed men with clubs piled aboard—prohibition officers— There was a marvellous amount of snooping about the dock—little men with sachels and hungry eyes called plaintively to those on the boat—have you any mail? and other cryptic phrases.

New York is rather funny—like a badly drawn cartoon—everybody looks and dresses like the Arrow-collarman. I've been amused, though glutted with relatives, eversince I've been here.

Plays I have not yet investigated, having seen only "The Bat" a bag of all the current melodrama tricks—very entertaining, to be sure, by Avery Hopkins and Rinehart, and an extraordinarily dull and ancient David Warfield play in Boston of which I've forgotten, thank God, the name. Everyone urges you to go to Lincoln & a certain play called The Bad Man.

Have seen the vague and shadowy Brandts and chatted with Mary Kirkpatrick who says she thinks your play will have to be bought back as she sees no chance of a production. The Brandts have carried on a long and rather obscure intrigue with both novels and the Knopf gang, which, to my relief, collapsed with the spewing forth of both MSS by Knopf. Rumor hath it that Monday there will be a signing of contracts for Jericho with Boney lieberwurst. But I think all will relapse into the mists again Mr. Brandt claims to have sat up until three in the morning reading 3 Soldiers and says it "ought" to be published.

But they are very vague, foggy misty, mysterious, mum.

I'm a goddam loafer. On the boat, instead of writing the play I wrote absurdities for the Dionysus novel which may be called Quest of the Core. However I feel murderously energetic, slit'em up and slash'em and blow'em up with T.N.T. so I—if I ever can find a place to lay my weary hind quarters—have hopes.

The Dial has a charming house with paradise bushes in the back yard on 13th Street, a lovely dark stenog named Sophia and some beautiful tall ice-tea glasses. They speak only French during office hours and are genteel, though I admit, delightful.

Griffin's in Provincetown, so I haven't seen him yet. John Mosher is about to retire to Albany to write a novel. He lives wonderfully from hand to mouth and gurgles and giggles and jerks himself about as delightfully as ever.

Everybody I meet is unspeakably unchanged.

Labor's belly up completely—The only hope is in the I.W.W. (which no one mentions even in a whisper) and in the Non

Partisan league which has just captured the Dem. primaries in N. Dakota and I think in Montana, too

I'm going to make a sentimental journey to Virginia to weep over weed grown stamping-grounds. It's ghoulish the hatred of people who do work of any use and the interest in diseases. Everybody's running about having X rays taken of their teeth for fear of abcesses.

Love to Kate After all N.Y.'s damn jolly to look at. Babylon gone mad.

Dos

What about your troubles? Will you have to take another lining of quicksilver? Rotten luck—If you need moneys let me know. I'm either rather wealthy or penniless, I'm not sure which—

To Germaine Lucas-Championnière

23-9-20

Je n'ai jamais bien demandé pardon à Mlle. Profit pour avoir laissé tombe le chou à la crème sur son pied. J'en souffre des remords. Vous me diraz si je suis pardonné. Je suis un ours bien maladroit.

A propos des sirènes de bateau—je vous assure que le plus vous les entendz, le plus d'empire ils auront sur vous. Le son de sirènes lointaines, entendu entre les vastes aridités pierreuses des villes, est le son qui m'emouve le plus. Je me demande pourquoi à New York on n'entends jamais la plainte vibrante des sirènes.

J'y habite, ce New York, dans un chamber garnie très grande et tres laide, qui a un ancien papier verdâtre sur le mur et un affreux tapis rouge, un grand sofa boufie de velours d'un éclarate horrifique et une grande table ronde delicieusement couverte de portefeuilles et de cahiers. C'était tres amusant rencontres tous mes amis après tant d'années. Ce qui est remarquable c'est que personne n'a changé. Tout le monde parle, mange, chante, ecrit, se promène, critique absolument comme il y a trios ans.—Il n'y a que moimême—je me parait plus desoriente, plus hors du chemin, plus errant dans les sentiers poudreux du vallée des indecisions qu'ily a trois ans. Je me sent un peu comme je me sentais dans mes cauchemars d'enfant, ou je rêvais souvent qu'on etaient trés loin dans la campagne et que tout le monde montait en voiture et que je courrais d'un côté à l'autre sans trouver la plus petite place et que les voitures partaient aux sons des grelots et qu'on me laissait seul. C'est comme, ça maintenant. J'ai l'illusion que tous mes anciens compagnons montent dans l'une ou l'autre des voitures qui suivent les grandes processions de la vie—qu'on me laisse seul pietinant au hazard les chemins perdus.

New York—après tout—est magnifique—une ville de troglodytes d'une laideur affreuse et brutale, pleins de bruits foudroyants, de grincements de fer sur fer, plein d'un son eternelle de roues qui tournent tournent sur les pierres durs. Les gens grouillent comme de formis, humblement dans les chemins indiqués, ecrasés par la matière arrogante et impitoyable. Je pense de Ninevah et Babylon, d'Ur des Chaldées, de ces immense villes qui pesent comme des basilisques derrière l'horizon dans les anciens contes des juifs, où les temples se hissaient haut comment les montagnes, et les hommes courraient tremblottant par les petites ruelles sales au bruit constant des fouets au poignées d'or. O pour la voix d'airain qui chantera, comme la voix du Baptiste au desert, encore une fois l'immensité de l'homme dans ce néant de fer et d'acier et de marbre et de pierre. La nuit surtout c'est marveilleux et effrayant, du haut d'un Roof Garden, où dansent des femmes au voix rauques dans une lumière ambrée, l'immensité blueâtre grisâtre de la ville, decompées par les enormes arabesques des enseignes electriques, quand les rues où les autos courrent comme des cafards sont perdu dans une poussière d'or, et quand une pauvre petite lune pale et eblouie vous regarde à travers d'un ciel de plomb.

Si je me rapelle du clocher d'Esconblac—j'ai bien souvent regretté que je n'ai pas dormi sur les dunes en haut de la ville ensevlie. Peut être les pauvres âmes dépossedées des anciens habitants m'auraient soufflé des rêves profetiques, où j'aurais eu des cauchemars bizarres et esoteriques. La prochaine fois je dormirais au pied du clocher d'Esconblac. Mais je suis toujours si eblouie quand on m'offre des richesses au plateaux de

la vie que je ne peux jamais me decider de les prendre jusque
le moment où c'est trop tard. J'aurais bien aimé voir avec
vous les chefs Normands prisonnieres du preu Saint de la ville
de Guirande.

Une autre fois je vous conterais le grande melodrame des
fourberies des editeurs et des machinations des agencies lit-
eraires avec des reflections melancolo-comico-historico-
philosophiques sur le G. A. B. (Great American Bluff).

Tout à vous
D.P.

Bien des choses à votre mère si charmante—Boujour a votre
frère et au petits neveus

To John Howard Lawson

Jack

Everything's belly-up. The acclamations with which Three
Soldiers was first received by the Brandtine world freeze gradually. Leiberwurst, who promised to publish Jericho swearing
by the Torah and the Talmud, has dropped it like a hot
potato, and now, in a last passionate interlude over the telephone in Adelaide's studio Mrs Brandt—says that she thinks
there's the making of a novel in the character of James
Clough—but otherwise. . . . O ye Gods and mermaids and
little puking fishes of the sea!

Last night I went to "Mecca" a dull pompous spectacle
which interested me because of the fornicational goings on
that were allowed on the stairs in a rather delightful badly
costumed ballet by Fokine. People bellowed their lines like
rundown phonographs and there were vast quantities of skinny
undressed chorus men who were shriekingly funny. Also two
camels, a donkey, goats, monkeys, and a comedy chinaman
and his wife who just missed being very funny. General effect
much like Scheherazade—in fact I thought several times it
was Scheherazade.

Good performance of the Treasure—you know the Pinski
play I've always chattered about—very good fun at the
Theatre Guild.

Follies (Greenwich Village) mildly well costumed arty but relieved by a shriekingly funny and very raw man named Larry who dresses as a woman.

Have seen Berenice who gave me an impression of being off duty at the time. She Billy Adelaide & I dined at that dismal Greenwich Village Inn. She is very beautiful and on duty I imagine would quite overpower one.

The general impression one gets of the New York stage is dismal—the only hopeful sign I can see is its undressedness—and in the raw jokes that get by. Shall read the brass check.

The Freeman is a good paper. The Dial and I have little communication so there is no danger of their good manners being corrupted.

Dudley Field Malone is conducting a faint hearted Farmer Labor campaign. Harding will be elected by a large majority. One keeps meeting extraordinary people in all walks of life—mild little people who say with a worm will turn expression I'm going to vote for Debs—like little boys that say damn just because they're scared of the sound of it—

> Write voluminously
> If you get broke—cable—

Dos

Belly up   Belly up   Belly up
NEW YORK CONTINUES TO AMUSE!
  Play's nearly finished—first draft—sounds to me like Percy Mackaye at his worst——!
Belly up   Belly up   Belly up

New York, October 11, 1920

To Robert Hillyer

Bobby—

You are probably going to hate me. Please don't because I am very fond of you. The reverse of this is the result on me of Alchemy. Alas for the poor—penis-bereft, balls-bereft gentlemen of the illustrations

I'll explain. Two gentlemen a certain Levinson & a certain Malcolm Cowley waited on me in deputation one day saying I must review Alchemy for the Freeman. I was not anxious to do it—but I thought I would knock it more understandingly, and more sweetly perhaps than would a harsh outsider.

Anyway our definitions of poetry never did agree—so de gustibus non disputandum.

Thanks for the delightful letter

Who is Fru Christensen?

Tell me about the drama. Do you remember—I have been very enthusiastic over each of your dramatic essays. What eventually happened to the wonderful "Man Without a Visiting Card"?

The G.N. still travels dolefully from publishing house to publishing house. Its younger brother "Three Soldiers" temporarily abodes with Mr. Huebsch. Rumor hath it that *perhaps* he will publish it. "One Man's Initiation" came out in the early fall in London. A lady wrote a long review in which abounded such phrases as "jaundiced pacifist", "crabbed internationalist"—making out that I was an enemy of England.

New York is silly and rather stupendous—I mean skies— buildings garbage cans. One drinks red ink in Italian dives and whiskey for tea. Its all rather like a badly drawn cartoon in the self-style funny section of a Sunday paper.

Plans! I have none, I wish you'ld take a house in the country and let me come to visit you. I have a hope of going towards the east in the middle of winter. Write me still 214 Riverside Drive c/o (My aunt) Mrs J. R. Gordon—as I am likely to move suddenly in almost any direction. Or we might get a yawl and sail the South Seas.

Why don't you take a vacation to Rome or some such sunny place? Dudley Poore & Jack Lawson are both there now. Perhaps I'll go through there on my way to Persia or Armenia or Abyssinia.

Did you see your mug in the Boston Transcript and a slobbery article by the fulsome negroid? I hope you duly vomited on reading it.

Write me about your play and about Copenhagen (scenery) and write me a fine polemic defense of Alchemy in heroic couplets.

What happened about the untying of Hymen's knot?

Love—You're a dear, Bobby and a poet in spite of all my venom—   Dos

New York, November 1920

To Thomas P. Cope

213 E. 15th Street
New York

I wonder where you are Tom. I've been in New York two months and I cant say I have accomplished anything. A few articles in the Freeman. The first draft of what I fear is an utterly futile play—and a certain amount of squabbling about Three Soldiers. The great Bogg.

Still New York is amusing. It has its hanging gardens of Babylon aspect. One talks to starving people on Park Benches. One eats eggplants squashed in oil of sesame in Syrian restaurants and drinks overmuch California chianti in the backs of Italian cafés. There are ferries and the Hudson and the palisades and in Stuyvesant Square the dry leaves murmur their deathrattle as softly as in the Luxembourg.

I see Canby Chambers and Esther Andrews occasionally.

One Man's Initiation is out in London—a measley little business.

Tomorrow Warren Harding is going to be elected president of these United States.

O for a bumper full of the warm south—for that I count on you Lofty—do they still call you that?

Really you cant imagine the old-maid-whose-grandnephew-has-gone-to-the-war-eagerness with which I read your letters.

I'm going to stick for three or four months more to the triste besogne of getting oneself published. Then? La vita commencia domani, domani, domani?

Best love
Dos

In a day or two I'm going to Cambridge for a week. I'll look up Oliver

November 1, 1920

To John Howard Lawson

Jack, Grey purple heavy evening googles over the town like those thick sauces they pour over rice pudding. Little boys are tootling horns for Harding on 15th Street. Notwithstanding the horrible suspicion that that gentleman has 1/100000000 of negro blood—he is in process of being elected by a vast majority, at least so I suppose. Exercized my civic duty for the first time this morning by standing in line for a long while behind a number of overdressed ladies who would not give their ages—said they were over thirty, as if that werent obvious. Debs.

Last night went with Adelaide to what came near being a good production of what came near being a good play by O'Neill at the Provincetown players. "The Emperor Jones" about the negro emperor of a West India island who has to run for his life from his subjects and in diving through a dark wood sinks deeper and deeper into the slave-blackness of his race. Sees a man playing dice he has killed back in the States when he was a pullman porter, convicts, people buying and selling him, the hold of a slaveship and at last the Japanese dancer Itoro as a medicine man who feeds him to a crocodile and he's killed by his subjects. Its nearly all a monologue of the Emperor Brutus Jones—really superb—and played to perfection by a wonderful coon named Gilpin. The only trouble was they were so anxious to show off their in itself beautiful scenery that they let the audience lapse for fifteen minutes between each of the little scenes that made up the play and so lost the entire thing.

My other dramatic adventures (except the National Winter Garden Burlesque foot of Second Ave) have been unbelievable dreary.

But Jesus the alcohol. Prohibition will send the entire population of New York into D.T.'s if it continues. You go into a restaurant and innocently order clam bouillon and before you know it you are guzzling vitriolic cocktails out of a soup tureen. You order coffee and find yourself drinking red ink. You order tea and find its gin. There's no escaping drinks. The smallest wayside inns to which one wanders in New

Jersey become before you've sat down, fountains and cataracts and niagaras of Canadian whiskey

Your Yugoslav epistle nearly gave me convulsions. No literary news. I'll get Gribble's play and send it.—Read your Indian Love. So good it deserves doing—dont you think so—

Love
Dos

November 2, 1920

CHRONOLOGY

NOTE ON THE TEXTS

NOTES

INDEX

Chronology

1896   Born John Roderigo Madison on January 14 in a Chicago
        hotel, the natural son of Lucy Addison Sprigg Madison of
        Petersburg, Virginia, and John Randolph Dos Passos, a
        prominent New York corporation lawyer. (Father, known
        as "John R." or "The Commodore," was born John Ro-
        drigues Dos Passos in Philadelphia in 1844, the son of an
        immigrant Portuguese cobbler; he worked as office boy in
        a law firm and briefly served as a drummer in a Pennsyl-
        vania regiment in the Civil War before opening his own
        law firm in New York City in 1867. He achieved promi-
        nence in 1873 by successfully appealing the murder con-
        viction of Edward S. Stokes, who had shot financier Jim
        Fisk. Later that year he married socialite Mary Dyckman
        Hays; they had a son, Louis Hays Dos Passos. Dos Passos
        moved into brokerage and corporation law, became
        known for his success in establishing several large com-
        mercial trusts, and wrote several books on law. Mother
        Lucy Sprigg was born in 1854 in Cumberland, Maryland;
        her family moved to Petersburg, Virginia, before the Civil
        War. In 1872 she married Ryland Randolph Madison with
        whom she had a son, James Madison, the following year;
        the couple never lived together for any length of time and
        soon separated; James was left in the care of Lucy's
        mother when Lucy went to Washington, D.C., to work in
        her father's surveying office. Lucy may have met John
        Randolph, a business associate of her father, as early as
        1883, and their liaison had begun by the early 1890s.)

1897–1900 Travels through Europe with his mother, staying in Brus-
        sels, Wiesbaden, Paris, and London (will later remember
        having had a "hotel childhood"). Learns French as his
        first spoken language. Father visits Europe frequently on
        business and travels openly with mother; during his fa-
        ther's visits, is often left in the care of friends of his
        mother. In 1899 mother's health begins to fail when she
        suffers the first of a series of strokes and is diagnosed with
        Bright's disease.

1901 Returns with mother to America and enrolls in the Sidwell Friends School in Washington.

1902 Returns to Brussels with his mother, who had felt isolated in America. Father continues to visit three or four times a year.

1903 Suffers an attack of what is probably rheumatic fever (illness will recur throughout his life); after spending a month in bed, accompanies his parents to Madeira to recuperate. Mother's husband, Ryland Randolph Madison, dies. Father publishes a political treatise, *The Anglo-Saxon Century and the Unification of the English Speaking People.*

1904–06 Attends boarding school at Peterborough Lodge in Hampstead, England. Returns to the U.S. with his mother in the summer of 1906.

1907–09 Enters Choate School in Wallingford, Connecticut, in January 1907. Does well academically but is hazed by other students because of his foreign accent and lack of athletic ability. Edits school newspaper, to which he contributes fiction and articles. Visits father during summers at his farmhouse at Sandy Point, Westmoreland County, Virginia (part of extensive Virginia land holdings) and on board his yacht, *Gaivota.*

1910 Father's wife, Mary Hays Dos Passos, dies March 10. Parents marry on June 21.

1911 Begins using name John Roderigo Dos Passos, Jr. Having enough credits to graduate, does not return to Choate for senior year. Passes Harvard entrance examination, then sails to Europe in November with tutor Virgil Jones. Travels in France and Italy.

1912–14 Visits Egypt, Turkey, and Greece. Returns to the U.S. in May 1912 and enters Harvard in September. Studies European languages and literature under teachers including Bliss Perry, Charles T. Copeland, and George Lyman Kittredge. Forms friendships with fellow students E. E. Cummings, Robert Nathan, Gilbert Seldes, and Dudley Poore, and contributes fiction, poetry, and reviews to the *Harvard Advocate* and *Harvard Monthly.* Keeps diaries in which he makes critical comments on books he reads (entries for September 1914, for example, include remarks on Fielding, Stendhal, Goldsmith, de Quincey, Chekhov, O. Henry, Lafcadio Hearn, Henry James, Stevenson, George Sand, Turgenev, and William Morris); major literary influences include *Vanity Fair* and *Don Quixote*. Attends opera and ballet and is interested in modern art; exhilarated by the Armory Show.

1915   Joins editorial board of *Harvard Monthly*. Mother dies on May 15; Dos Passos is devastated and does not want to go back to school, but father insists that he return. Travels across country during summer to visit World's Fair in San Francisco; in San Diego meets Walter Rumsey Marvin, who becomes lifelong friend and correspondent. At Harvard, becomes member of newly formed Poetry Society along with Cummings, Robert Hillyer, S. Foster Damon, R. Stewart Mitchell, and John Wheelwright.

1916   Begins autobiographical novel (later published as *Streets of Night*). After taking final examinations, visits Cape Cod for first time and is enthralled by Provincetown. Graduates cum laude from Harvard in June. Attempts to join Herbert Hoover's Commission for Relief in Belgium, but is rejected as being too young. Publishes essay "Against American Literature" in *The New Republic*: "We find ourselves floundering without rudder or compass, in the sea of modern life, vaguely lit by the phosphorescent gleam of our traditional optimism." Sails to Bordeaux in October and travels to Madrid to study Spanish and architecture. Meets poet Juan Ramon Jimenez and university student Jose Robles, who becomes a close friend. Travels extensively in Spain during his stay.

1917   Stunned by news of father's sudden death from pneumonia on January 27, Dos Passos returns to the U.S. in February and becomes involved in disposition of father's estate, which is encumbered with debt. Authorizes his maternal aunt, Mary Lamar Gordon, to collect his share of interest on Virginia property of which he is now co-owner (over the next two decades, she and her family receive but do not pass on to Dos Passos income totaling approximately $100,000). Settles temporarily in New York City in an apartment on East 33rd Street. Observes rallies against

American participation in World War I; is almost arrested when police raid a party in Greenwich Village. Expresses radical sentiments to a friend: "Every day I become more red." Takes lessons in driving, automobile maintenance, and medical techniques as preparation for volunteer service with Norton-Harjes volunteer ambulance unit, made up of Harvard graduates and serving under the auspices of the Red Cross. Contributes seven poems to anthology *Eight Harvard Poets*, published by Laurence J. Gomme; publishes article "Young Spain" in August issue of *Seven Arts*. Sails to France June 20 on the *Chicago*. Aboard ship forms friendship with playwright and left-wing activist John Howard Lawson. In Paris, reunites with college friends Robert Hillyer, Frederic van den Arend, and Dudley Poore. After several weeks of training at Sandricourt north of Paris, serves at Verdun front during French offensive in late August, where he undergoes German shelling with high explosives and poison gas. Writes to friend Rumsey Marvin: "The war is utter damn nonsense—a vast cancer fed by lies and self seeking malignity on the part of those who don't do the fighting . . . none of the poor devils whose mangled dirty bodies I take to the hospital in my ambulance really give a damn about any of the aims of this ridiculous affair." Collaborates with Hillyer on unpublished novel "Seven Times Round the Walls of Jericho." Returns to Paris and in November drives into northern Italy; remains in Milan for most of December before going to Dolo.

1918   Arrives January 17 in Bassano, headquarters for ambulance unit; town undergoes frequent bombings and shellings. On leave in March, travels to Bologna, Rome, Naples, and Florence. Meets Ernest Hemingway. Accused of disloyalty by Red Cross authorities who disapprove of his rowdy and insubordinate attitude, and of criticism of "stupidities" of modern war expressed in an intercepted letter. Returns to Paris in June after his enlistment ends and is forced by Red Cross authorities to return to the U.S. Sails home in August and enlists in the U.S. Army Medical Corps. On November 12, the day after the armistice, sails with his unit for England, and on arrival is assigned to an American base at Fèrrieres-en-Gatinais, south of Paris.

1919   Reassigned in January to a camp in Alsace, where his light duties enable him to explore the region; in March is re-

leased from active service with Medical Corps. Returns to
Paris to attend classes in anthropology at the Sorbonne.
Sent for several weeks in June to Gièvres for further military service; goes absent without leave to Tours and per-
suades a top sergeant to issue delayed discharge orders.
Returns to Paris in July, then travels to London to arrange
publication by Allen and Unwin of *One Man's Initiation—
1917*, a novel derived from "Seven Times Round the Walls
of Jericho." Goes to Spain with Dudley Poore; travels in
Basque country; arrives in Madrid at end of August and remains there for most of September. Rents house in
Granada; travels briefly to Lisbon to report on a rumored
revolution which does not take place, then returns to
Granada, where he becomes ill for a month with rheumatic
fever. Returns to Madrid at the end of November and
works on novel *Three Soldiers*, also based on World War I
experiences.

1920   Moves to Barcelona in March. Returns to Paris by first of
May and completes manuscript of *Three Soldiers* in June.
Novel is rejected by Allen and Unwin. Sails for America in
August and settles in New York City, on East 15th Street
off Stuyvesant Square; writes to a French friend, "New
York—after all—is magnificent—a city of cavedwellers,
with a frightful, brutal ugliness about it, full of thunderous
voices of metal grinding on metal and of an eternal sound
of wheels which turn, turn on heavy stones." Takes art
classes with Adelaide Lawson, sister of John Howard Lawson. Sees E. E. Cummings frequently, and takes long walks
with him through the city. Publishes essays, poems, and reviews in *The Dial*, *The Nation*, and *The Freeman*, to which
he contributes a series of articles about Spain. *One Man's
Initiation—1917* is published in England in October by
Allen and Unwin, after Dos Passos agrees to make cuts in
allegedly offensive passages.

1921   *Three Soldiers* is accepted for publication by George H.
Doran (after being rejected, according to Dos Passos, by
14 other publishers). Sails with Cummings in March from
New Bedford, Massachusetts, to Lisbon; they travel together in Spain and France, visiting Seville and hiking in
the Pyrenees before moving on to Paris. With the help of
Paxton Hibben, an American friend working in Paris for
the Red Cross's Near East Relief organization, Dos Passos

is able to travel in July to Constantinople and to sail aboard an American destroyer in the Sea of Marmara, observing the devastation of the Turkish-Greek War. Sails on Italian steamer to Batum and then travels through Georgia, Armenia, and Azerbaijan, which had recently come under Soviet rule. Later writes of journey: "Where starving people weren't dying of typhus they were dying of cholera. The flatcars and boxcars that made up our train were packed with refugees escaping from what? Where bound? Nobody seemed to know. In one station corpses were stacked like cordwood behind the stove." After crossing the Persian border, goes by horse-drawn carriage to Teheran, where he suffers from malaria for several weeks before traveling by car and train to Baghdad in October. During three weeks in Baghdad makes arrangements with help of British intelligence officer Gertrude Bell to travel by camel caravan across desert to Damascus.

1922   Arrives in Damascus shortly after New Year's after 39-day journey, then goes to Beirut. Gratified by letters congratulating him on the success of *Three Soldiers*, published September 1921. Travels to Paris, where he meets up again with Cummings before returning to America in February. Publishes three books with George H. Doran: *Rosinante to the Road Again*, a collection of essays on Spain (March), an American edition of *One Man's Initiation* (June), and *A Pushcart at the Curb*, a poetry collection (October). Works seriously at painting as well as writing. Begins close friendship with Edmund Wilson and associates with many writers, including F. Scott and Zelda Fitzgerald, Dawn Powell, John Peale Bishop, Elinor Wylie, Donald Ogden Stewart, and Sherwood Anderson. At funeral in August of Wright McCormic, a Harvard friend killed in an accident, meets Crystal Ross and forms close friendship with her.

1923   Exhibits paintings at Whitney Studio Club in January. Completes first play, *The Moon Is a Gong*, and writes an introduction to John Howard Lawson's play *Roger Bloomer*. Travels to Paris in March, remaining in Europe until August and making a trip to Spain; in Paris becomes close friends with wealthy expatriates Gerald and Sara Murphy, whom he helps paint sets for the Ballet Russe. Through the Murphys meets painter Fernand Léger, poet Blaise

Cendrars, and other leading figures of the modernist movement; is impressed by backdrop of newspaper headlines designed by Gerald Murphy for Cole Porter ballet *Within the Quota*. Returns to the U.S. in the fall and stays in a boarding house in Far Rockaway, Long Island, to work on new novel *Manhattan Transfer*, which he describes to a friend as "utterly fantastic and New Yorkish." *Streets of Night*, autobiographical novel begun at Harvard, is published in November by George H. Doran.

1924   During the winter lives at Columbia Heights in Brooklyn, in building overlooking the Brooklyn Bridge. Travels in February to New Orleans where he stays until early March, and then travels through Florida to Key West. Becomes friends with Hart Crane after he moves into Columbia Heights building in the spring. Goes in June to France, where he meets again with Crystal Ross, now studying at the University of Strasbourg, and forms close friendship with Ernest Hemingway. Travels to Pamplona in July with Crystal and becomes engaged to her. Attends Fiesta of San Fermin with Hemingway and other friends including Donald Ogden Stewart and Robert McAlmon; afterward takes two-week walking trip across the Pyrenees to Andorra before rejoining the Murphys in Antibes. Sees Crystal several more times in Strasbourg, Bruges, and London, but she resists his wish to marry quickly. Returns to New York in September and devotes the fall to working on *Manhattan Transfer*.

1925   Joins executive board of left-wing journal *New Masses*. *The Moon Is a Gong* is performed by the Harvard Dramatic Club in May. After completing *Manhattan Transfer*, suffers bout of rheumatic fever and is hospitalized several times, May–July. Visited by Crystal Ross, who is still reluctant to marry him. Returns to France in late summer, spending time with Hemingway in Paris and cruising on a yacht in the Mediterranean with the Murphys. *Manhattan Transfer* is published in November by Harper & Brothers, receiving mixed reviews; Dos Passos is pleased by praise in *The Saturday Review of Literature* from Sinclair Lewis, who calls the book "a novel of the very first importance . . . the foundation of a whole new school of novel-writing." Sails to Morocco in December.

1926   Travels in Morocco, January–February. Receives cable
        from John Howard Lawson asking him to become a direc-
        tor of the New Playwrights Theatre; accepts and returns to
        New York in March, in time to see a production of his play
        The Garbage Man, revised version of *The Moon Is a Gong*
        (published in July by Harper & Brothers). Receives letter
        from Crystal Ross in the spring announcing her engage-
        ment to another man. First issue of *New Masses* appears in
        May. Becomes increasingly involved with radical causes, in-
        cluding the textile strike in Passaic, New Jersey, but ex-
        presses concern about the influence of the Communist
        Party. Travels to Boston in June to gather information
        about the case of Italian anarchists Nicola Sacco and Bar-
        tolomeo Vanzetti, who were sentenced to death in 1921 for
        robbery and murder. Interviews Sacco and Vanzetti and
        becomes convinced of their innocence; publishes prelimi-
        nary report on case in August *New Masses* and returns to
        Boston for further investigation. Later in the year travels in
        the South and West, spending time in Louisville, St. Louis,
        and Dallas, and arriving in Mexico City in mid-December.

1927   Travels extensively in Mexico, where he meets young
        Mexican artists whose work interests him; also spends time
        with journalist Carleton Beals and former IWW member
        Gladwin Bland (on whom he models character of Mac in
        The 42nd Parallel). Returns to New York in March to con-
        tinue work with New Playwrights Theatre. *Orient Express*,
        an account of his 1921–22 travels in the Near East, is pub-
        lished in March by Harper & Brothers (with a number of
        Dos Passos' paintings as illustrations). Continues to work
        on efforts to procure a new trial for Sacco and Vanzetti;
        his pamphlet *Facing the Chair: Story of the Americaniza-
        tion of Two Foreignborn Workmen* is published in the
        spring by the Sacco-Vanzetti Defense Committee. Ar-
        rested and briefly jailed after protest march in Boston on
        August 21; Sacco and Vanzetti are electrocuted August 23.
        Writes "They Are Dead Now," prose poem which is pub-
        lished in *New Masses* (it is later incorporated in altered
        form in *The Big Money*). Begins work on *The 42nd Paral-
        lel*, the first novel in what will become the *U.S.A.* trilogy.

1928   Goes to Key West in April to visit Hemingway; meets
        Katharine (Katy) Smith, a childhood friend of Heming-
        way's from Michigan. Sails to Europe in May. Visits friends

in London, Paris, Antibes, and Berlin before going to Helsinki in July. Travels to Leningrad where he meets Dr. Horsley Gantt, an American scientist working with Pavlov. Meets theater director Vsevolod Meyerhold and filmmakers Sergei Eisenstein and Vsevolod Pudovkin in Moscow, as well as American publicist Ivy Lee (on whom Dos Passos models character of J. Ward Moorehouse in *U.S.A.*); impressed by "Living Newspapers," improvisational plays performed in workers' clubs and unions. Takes a steamer down the Volga to Astrakhan, then travels through the Caucasus region, visiting Grozny and Tiflis. Spends two months in Moscow before returning to New York at year's end, taking an apartment on Washington Square South.

1929   Dos Passos' second play, *Airways, Inc.*, opens in February at New Playwrights Theatre for unsuccessful four-week run; he resigns from theater group in March, troubled by ineffective organization and internal dissension. Travels in March to Key West, where he sees Katy Smith again, then visits her in June at her home in Provincetown. They marry on August 19 in Ellsworth, Maine, and spend September in Wiscasset, Maine, before moving to her house in Provincetown. In early December they sail to France; they see Hemingway, the Fitzgeralds, Léger, and Cendrars, and spend Christmas skiing in Switzerland with Gerald and Sara Murphy.

1930   Travels with Katy in Austria, France, England, and Spain, before sailing across the Atlantic, arriving in Havana in April. Visits Hemingway in Key West before returning to Provincetown to work on *1919*; is pleased to learn of many good reviews of *The 42nd Parallel*, published in February by Harper & Brothers. Travels in Mexico, May–June. Buys small farm in Truro, near Provincetown (he and Katy will live partly on income from renting out this and two other properties they own). Declares to Edmund Wilson that he is becoming "a middle-class liberal" but continues to support some left-wing causes. Visits Hemingway in Montana in October; escapes unharmed from an automobile accident in which Hemingway breaks an arm.

1931   Dos Passos' translation of *Panama, or The Adventures of My Seven Uncles*, a poem by Blaise Cendrars, is published in January, illustrated with his paintings. Travels with Katy in Mexico, February–March, before returning to

Provincetown to complete *1919*. Harper's balks at publishing satirical profile of J. P. Morgan included in the novel, and Dos Passos arranges for Harcourt, Brace to publish it. Travels to Harlan County, Kentucky, with Theodore Dreiser and others on behalf of National Committee for the Defense of Political Prisoners to investigate situation of striking miners; appalled by conditions there, contributes to *Harlan Miners Speak* (published in March 1932). Refuses to return to Kentucky to stand trial after being indicted for "criminal syndicalism" despite urgings of Communist leader Earl Browder.

1932   Travels with Katy in Mexico and southwestern United States, February–April, visiting Hemingway in Key West en route. *1919* is published in March and receives excellent reviews. Reports on public events, including the "Bonus Army" of protesting veterans camped in Washington, D.C., and the Republican and Democratic national conventions, for *The New Republic*; works on *The Big Money*. Votes for Communist candidate William Z. Foster in November presidential election.

1933   Suffers serious recurrence of rheumatic fever in April. Sails to Europe in May with Katy, a trip financed in part by Hemingway and the Murphys, at whose Antibes home they stay through June. Travels through Spain and, although still convalescing from rheumatic fever, conducts interviews which will form part of travel book *In All Countries*; returns to Provincetown in October.

1934   Signs open letter protesting Communist disruption of a Socialist Party meeting in Madison Square Garden in February. Responds to criticism in *New Masses* by stating that he signed the letter to oppose "the growth of unintelligent fanaticism." Spends much of the spring with Katy in Key West, where they are visited by Dawn Powell. Writes to Edmund Wilson in March that "the whole Marxian radical movement is in a moment of intense disintegration." *In All Countries* and *Three Plays: The Garbage Man, Airways, Inc., and Fortune Heights* are published in the spring by Harcourt, Brace. Flies to Hollywood in July to work on screenplay for Josef von Sternberg's film *The Devil Is a Woman*, starring Marlene Dietrich (little of his work is used). Has another attack of rheumatic fever and is bedridden until Katy's arrival in mid-August. They remain in Hollywood until October, then sail for Havana; while Katy returns to Massachusetts for medical tests (she had suffered several miscarriages), Dos Passos goes to Key West where Katy joins him at Christmas. Criticizes the Soviet Union in letters to Edmund Wilson ("From now on events in Russia have no more interest—except as a terrible example—for world socialism. . . . The thing has gone into its Napoleonic stage") and remarks: "It would be funny if I ended up an Anglo Saxon chauvinist—Did you ever read my father's Anglo Saxon Century? We are now getting to the age when papa's shoes yawn wide."

1935   Visits Jamaica and New York in January, then stays in Key West, with occasional trips to Bimini and Havana, before returning to Provincetown in June. Continues to correspond with Edmund Wilson about his disillusionment with Stalinist Communism: "I'm now at last convinced that means cant be disassociated from ends and that massacre only creates more massacre and oppression more oppression and means become ends." Works steadily on *The Big Money*, the third volume of the *U.S.A.* trilogy, whose completion has been delayed by lingering health problems.

1936   Completes *The Big Money* by March. With Katy and their guest Sara Murphy, visits Hemingway in Havana; returns to Provincetown in May. Embarks on a course of reading in American history. *The Big Money* is published in August and receives major attention; Dos Passos is pictured on the cover of *Time* on August 10, and the book is widely praised despite complaints by some left-wing reviewers about its pessimism. Seeks way to participate in a news service reporting the Spanish civil war. Writes to Malcolm Cowley in December: "A fascist Spain will mean a fascist France and more violent reaction here & in England."

1937   Learns in early January that he has been elected to the National Institute of Arts and Letters. Works with Archibald MacLeish, Lillian Hellman, Hemingway, and others in organizing Contemporary Historians, a group formed to produce a documentary film about Spain (later released as *The Spanish Earth*, directed by Joris Ivens and with commentary by Hemingway). Disagrees with Hemingway about the film's content, seeking to concentrate on the

Spanish land and people while Hemingway wishes to emphasize the war. Sails with Katy to Europe in early March, and after several weeks in France arrives by early April in Valencia, now the capital of the Spanish Republic. Becomes aware of internecine struggles among political factions fighting for the Republic; learns that his friend Jose Robles, an official in the Republican government, has been arrested by Republican security forces, and seeks information about him. Goes to Madrid and stays at Hotel Florida with Hemingway, who berates him for not bringing in food, and accuses him of cowardly behavior. Learns that Robles has been secretly shot by Communists for alleged spying. Rift with Hemingway worsens when Hemingway argues that Robles would not have been executed without justification. Leaves Madrid in April and visits Fuenteduena, a village to be filmed for *The Spanish Earth*. In Barcelona and Valencia others, including English writer George Orwell, further convince him of Communist duplicity and brutality. Returns in May to Paris, where he again argues with Hemingway about Spain. After his return with Katy to the U.S., writes article "Farewell to Europe!" for *Common Sense*, in which he praises the American spirit of individual liberty in contrast to the "stifling cellar" of Europe; criticized by leftist friends such as John Howard Lawson, he responds that "Anglo-Saxon democracy is the best political method of which we have any . . . I have come to believe that the CP is fundamentally opposed to our democracy." Revises and adds a prologue to *The 42nd Parallel* for a Modern Library edition published in November.

1938   *U.S.A.*, uniting *The 42nd Parallel, 1919*, and *The Big Money* in one volume, is published in January by Harcourt, Brace; sales are indifferent, exacerbating chronic financial difficulties. *Journeys Between Wars*, a compilation of excerpts from earlier travel books along with new material about Spain, is published in April by Harcourt, Brace. Goes to New Orleans in the spring; works on a new novel, *Adventures of a Young Man* until he and Katy depart for Europe in June. They cruise the Mediterranean with the Murphys, visit Rome, Pisa, Florence, and Paris, before returning to Provincetown.

1939   *Adventures of a Young Man* is published in June and receives generally weak reviews, particularly from critics sympathetic to the Communist Party (*New Masses* calls it "a crude piece of Trotskyist agitprop"); sales are poor. Travels with Katy in the Southwest during the spring. Despite receipt of Guggenheim grant for book on American history (later published as *The Ground We Stand On*), continues to suffer from financial difficulties. Begins to help care for two boys whose mother, a neighbor, had died suddenly (the boys will sometimes live with Dos Passos and his wife during the early 1940s).

1940 Contributes lengthy introduction to *The Living Thoughts of Tom Paine*, an anthology published in February. Lives in Alexandria, Virginia, from February to April while conducting research at the Library of Congress. Investigates Virginia property held in trust for him by his aunt's family, and discovers that they have withheld income from the land (initiates civil suit in 1941 which is not resolved until 1944). On behalf of New World Resettlement Fund, visits Ecuador and Haiti to help with resettlement of Spanish Republican refugees.

1941 Agrees during summer to serve with Italian anarchist Carlo Tresca as a vice-chairman of Civil Rights Defense Committee in the case of 29 truckers and union members (some of them members of the Trotskyist Socialist Workers' Party) accused of conspiracy by the Justice Department. *The Ground We Stand On*, historical study celebrating the American heritage of "selfgovernment," is published in August. Travels to England in September for a P.E.N. Club conference at which he meets H. G. Wells. Writes articles for *Harper's Magazine* praising the British war effort and emphasizing need for American industrial strength.

1942–43 In late 1942 and throughout 1943 makes a series of trips around the U.S. gathering information for series of *Harper's* articles titled "People at War." *Number One*, a novel based on the career of Huey Long, is published by Houghton Mifflin, his new publisher, in March 1943. Sells house in Truro; despite literary fame, finances continue to be shaky.

1944 Receives favorable judgment in April in lawsuit over Virginia property. *State of the Nation*, book version of the "People at War" articles, is published in July. Works on a

biography of Thomas Jefferson, which will occupy him
for the next decade. Leaves in December for the West
Coast and the Pacific to begin research for series of articles on the war; spends Christmas on Kwajalein in the
Marshall Islands.

1945   Continues Pacific tour, visiting Eniwetok, Saipan, and
Ulithi, and witnesses preliminary bombardment of Iwo
Jima in January; enters Manila on February 5, shortly after
arrival of American troops; interviews General Douglas
MacArthur. Rests from trip in Australia in March; survives,
without major injury, a freak accident in which he is struck
on head by wing-tip of low-flying airplane; returns to U.S.
in April. Travels in Europe, October–December, to report on postwar conditions for *Life*; attends Nuremberg tri-
als, and is depressed by conditions in Europe and what he
views as Russian threat: "Never felt so much sadder and
wiser in my life as after this trip to Europe. . . ."

1946   Expresses political fears in January *Life* article, "Americans Are Losing the Victory in Europe." Travels with
Katy in March and April, visiting Florida and Mexico;
they also make periodic visits to Virginia property to
supervise restoration of colonial home at Spence's Point
where they intend to live. *Tour of Duty*, collecting his war
articles, is published in August. *U.S.A.* is reissued by
Houghton Mifflin in a deluxe three-volume edition with
illustrations by Reginald Marsh.

1947   Travels with Katy to Key West, February–March. In England, July–August, researches articles on British politics
for *Life*. Collides with rear of parked truck near Wareham,
Massachusetts, on September 12; Katy is killed instantly
and Dos Passos loses his right eye. While recovering from
injuries, tells friends of his intention to move to Virginia:
"If I tried to avoid all the places I'd been happy with Katy
I'd have to get off the earth because there's nothing
lovely in life that doesn't make me think of her, but I find
it perhaps a little less painful to be down here than in P'-
town." Travels to Iowa in mid-October for a month's stay
to research another *Life* article; on his return stays with
friends Lloyd and Marion Lowndes in Snedens Landing,
New York, with whom he spends much time over next

several years. Learns in November that he has been elected to American Academy of Arts and Letters.

1948   Article "The Failure of Marxism" published in *Life* in January. Travels, February–March, to Bermuda and Haiti, spending time with friends including writers John P. Marquand and Dawn Powell. Settles ownership of the Virginia property with his half-brother Louis, taking 2,100 acres which he hopes to develop as a farm. Travels in September to South America to report on social and political conditions; visits briefly with Hemingway in Cuba before going to Colombia, Brazil, Argentina, Uruguay, Chile, and Peru; returns to U.S. in December.

1949   *The Grand Design* is published in January. Travels extensively through the U.S. in April and May to research series of articles for *Modern Millwheels*, publication of the General Mills Corporation. Meets Elizabeth (Betty) Holdridge when she visits the Lowndes in Snedens Landing in May (Holdridge, b. 1909, had lost her husband in an automobile accident in 1946). Marries Betty Holdridge on August 6 in Maryland and moves with her and her seven-year-old son Christopher to the restored house at Spence's Point. Travels in September to Italy for a P.E.N. conference.

1950   Daughter Lucy Hamlin Dos Passos is born May 15. *The Prospect Before Us*, a collection of political essay incorporating material on England, South America, and American business and agriculture, is published in October to generally poor reviews. Contributes text to *Life's Picture History of World War II*, also published in October.

1951   *Chosen Country* is published in the fall; the novel, which features a character modeled on Katy, receives positive response from reviewers including Edmund Wilson and Archibald MacLeish, but provokes an enraged reaction from Ernest Hemingway at his own fictionalized portrait. Visits Cape Cod briefly during summer.

1952   *District of Columbia*, one-volume edition of the trilogy consisting of *Adventures of a Young Man*, *Number One*, and *The Grand Design*, is published.

1953   Despite his support for anti-Communist hearings led by Senator Joseph McCarthy, comes to the defense of old friend Horsley Gantt, whose loyalty has been questioned by government investigators. Works to complete biography of Thomas Jefferson which has occupied him for many years.

1954   Travels to New York in January for publication of *The Head and Heart of Thomas Jefferson*. *Most Likely to Succeed*, whose central character is in part a satirical portrait of John Howard Lawson, is published in September by Prentice-Hall. Experiences renewed financial difficulties due to weak sales of recent books and insufficient returns from farming; undertakes a lecture tour, traveling through the Midwest and Pacific Northwest in October and November.

1955–56   *The Theme Is Freedom*, another collection of political essays, is published in March 1956. Devotes much time to farming, and writes to Edmund Wilson that he has "almost ceased to think of myself as a literary gent." Visits Mexico in the fall to attend a meeting of the Congress for Cultural Freedom. Corresponds with William Faulkner about Faulkner's proposal for a writers' conference designed to encourage support for the U.S. among foreign intellectuals.

1957   *The Men Who Made the Nation*, a historical study of America from the Revolution to the second Jefferson administration, is published in February. Travels to New York in May to accept Gold Medal for Fiction from National Institute of Arts and Letters, and comments on his own work: "Satirical writing is by definition unpopular writing. Its aim is to prod people into thinking. Thinking hurts." Travels to Japan for two weeks in September to attend P.E.N. conference; visits Mexico with his family in November.

1958   Spends much time researching article on labor unions for *Reader's Digest* (published in September as "What Union Members Have Been Writing Senator McClellan"). *The Great Days*, an autobiographical novel dealing with the period before and during World War II, is rejected by Prentice-Hall and Doubleday; after considerable revision, it is published in March by Sagamore Press, receiving generally poor reviews. In July and August travels in Brazil; visits Brasilia, then under construction, and meets its architect, Oscar Niemeyer, and Brazilian president Juscelino Kubitschek.

1959   *Prospect of a Golden Age*, another study of early American history, is published by Prentice-Hall. With family and friends, cruises on chartered boat in the Bahamas for two weeks during the summer. In collaboration with Paul Shyre, adapts *U.S.A.* for stage; it opens in October at the Hotel Martinique in New York City and has a successful run.

1960   Works on a new novel, *Midcentury*, which applies the same narrative techniques as *U.S.A.* to the postwar period. Vacations in Europe during August, traveling in Italy, Switzerland, France, and Portugal.

1961   *Midcentury* is published in the spring by Houghton Mifflin and becomes a bestseller; the reviews are the best he has received since *U.S.A.* Travels in Spain in August and September.

1962   Receives award in Madison Square Garden in March from conservative group Young Americans for Freedom, sharing podium with Senator Strom Thurmond and actor John Wayne. Visits Peru, Brazil, and Argentina, August–September; lectures at Brazilian-American Institute in Rio de Janeiro and addresses P.E.N. conference in Buenos Aires. *Mr. Wilson's War*, a historical survey covering the period 1901–21, is published in November.

1963   Serves as writer in residence at the University of Virginia for three weeks in February. Travels in Canada and the American West in August, and in September flies briefly to Rome at the invitation of Centro di Vita Italiana, an anti-Communist organization. *Brazil on the Move* is published in September.

1964   Attends Republican convention in San Francisco in July, and writes enthusiastically of Barry Goldwater's nomination for *The National Review*; travels in Alaska in August. *Occasions and Protests*, a collection of political essays, and *Thomas Jefferson: The Making of a President*, a biography for children, are published.

1965 Receives Alumni Seal Prize from Choate School in May. Suffers mild heart seizure (possibly related to earlier bouts of rheumatic fever) in June.

1966 *Shackles of Power: Three Jeffersonian Decades* is published in March. Travels in Yucatan in March, and in Brazil, July–August. In November publishes *World in a Glass: A View of Our Century* and *The Best Times*, a memoir.

1967 Travels in Portugal, July–August, to research a study of Portuguese history. Flies to Rome in November to receive $32,000 Antonio Feltrinelli Prize for fiction.

1968 Visits old friend Dudley Poore in Florida in February, then goes to California in March. Travels in the Midwest during the summer.

1969 Visits Easter Island in January, continuing on to Chile and Argentina. *The Portugal Story* is published in April; works on *Easter Island: Island of Enigmas*, which is published posthumously in 1971. Travels to Florida in May to watch the launching of Apollo 10 from Cape Kennedy. Suffers minor heart attack while visiting friends in Maine during the summer. Works on final novel, *Century's Ebb* (published posthumously in 1975).

1970 Hospitalized briefly at Johns Hopkins in January for heart problems. Travels with Betty to Tucson, Arizona, in March. Returns to Johns Hopkins in July and August. Dies of congestive heart failure in Baltimore on September 28. Buried at Yeocomico Church near Spence's Point on October 7.

Note on the Texts

This volume contains John Dos Passos' travel books *Rosinante to the Road Again* (1922), *Orient Express* (1927), and *In All Countries* (1934), as well as five essays first collected in *Journeys Between Wars* (1938); the poetry collection *A Pushcart at the Curb* (1922); nine essays published between 1916 and 1941; and a selection of letters and diary entries written between 1916 and 1920.

Dos Passos arrived in Spain for the first time in October 1916 and spent a little more than three months there. Based in Madrid, he visited several towns in the surrounding countryside, and shortly after Christmas he made a trip that included stops in Cartagena, Tarragona, Alicante, and numerous villages. After returning to the United States upon receiving news of his father's death in January 1917, he wrote the essay "Young Spain" (later entitled "The Baker of Almorox"), which was published in *Seven Arts* in August 1917. Dos Passos returned to Spain for a longer stay in August 1919, living and traveling there for eight months. Much of his essay "Antonio Machado: Poet of Castile," based in part on his meetings with Machado in Segovia, was published in *The Dial*, June 1920. Shortly afterward George H. Doran, the publisher who had agreed to bring out Dos Passos' novel *Three Soldiers*, also arranged to publish a collection of his writings about Spain. The following selections from the resulting book, *Rosinante to the Road Again*, appeared in periodicals between October 1920 and its publication in March 1922: "Farmer Strikers in Spain" (here "Cordova No Longer of the Caliphs"), *Liberator*, October 1920; "An Inverted Midas," *Freeman*, November 10, 1920; "America and the Pursuit of Happiness" (here part of "The Donkey Boy"), *The Nation*, December 29, 1920; "A Catalan Poet," *Freeman*, February 2, 1921; "A Gesture of Castile" (here "A Gesture and a Quest"), *Freeman*, March 2, 1921; "Benavente's Madrid," *Bookman*, May 1921; "The Gesture of Castile," printed in eight installments (here the six "Talk by the Road" chapters and "Toledo"), *Freeman*, December 21 and 28, 1921, January 4 and 11, 1922; "Andalusian Ethics" (here "The Donkey Boy," which incorporated the earlier "America and the Pursuit of Happiness"), February 1 and 8, 1922. The final chapters of *Rosinante to the Road Again* were written in Paris during the spring of 1921, and the book was published by George H. Doran on March 18, 1922. There was no subsequent edition. Revised excerpts were included in Dos Passos' 1938 collection

Journeys Between Wars. The 1922 George H. Doran edition of *Rosinante to the Road Again* is the text printed here.

Dos Passos' next travel book, *Orient Express*, is based on his trip to the Balkans, Turkey, the Caucasus, and the Middle East during the latter half of 1921. "Out of Turkish Coffee Cups," the first six sections of "Constant' July 1921," appeared in the *New York Tribune*, October 2, 1921; "In a New Republic," the first five sections of "Red Caucasus," was published in *Freeman*, October 5, 1921. In 1922 *Asia* published "One Hundred Views of Ararat" (April) and "Of Phaetons" (June, entitled "Opinions of the Sayyid"). The poem at the beginning of "Table D'Hôte" was printed in *Poetry*, July 1926, under the title "Crimson Tent," and Dos Passos' essay on Blaise Cendrars, "Homer of the Transsiberian," was published in *Saturday Review of Literature*, October 16, 1926. *Orient Express* was published by Harper & Brothers in March 1927; the first edition contained eight paintings by Dos Passos that are reproduced in the insert of the present volume. An edition brought out by Jonathan Cape and Harrison Smith that appeared in England in 1928 and was distributed in the United States as part of their "Traveller's Library" series followed English conventions of spelling and usage but did not contain any revisions by Dos Passos. A lightly revised version of *Orient Express* was included in *Journeys Between Wars* (1938). This volume prints the text of the 1927 Harper & Brothers edition of *Orient Express.* Copyright 1927 by John Dos Passos; copyright renewed © 1955 by John Dos Passos. Reprinted by permission of Lucy Dos Passos Coggin.

Just before sailing for Europe in May 1933, Dos Passos signed a contract with Harcourt, Brace and Company to write a book about the Second Republic in Spain. His travels in Spain were limited, however, by a continuing case of rheumatic fever, and after returning to the United States he wrote his editor at Harcourt, Brace in October 1933 that the fever had "hampered" his work; he also felt that "things in Spain politically are not as interesting as I'd thought." He proposed that the book (with the working title "The Republic of Honest Men") include essays on events in Mexico, the Soviet Union, and the United States, as well as what he had written about Spain. Harcourt, Brace agreed and published the collection under the title *In All Countries* in April 1934. The following essays had appeared in periodicals: "300 N.Y. Agitators Reach Passaic" (here "300 Red Agitators Reach Passaic"), *New Masses*, June 1926; "The Pit and the Pendulum" (here "The Wrong Set of Words"), *New Masses*, August 1926; "Relief Map of Mexico," *New Masses*, April 1927; "Zapata's Ghost Walks," *New Masses*, September 1927; the first six sections of "Rainy Days in Leningrad," *New Masses*, February 1929; "The New

Theater in Russia" (here the second section of "Some Sleepy Nights Round Moscow"), *The New Republic*, April 16, 1930; "Harlan: Working Under the Gun" (here "Harlan County Sunset"), *The New Republic*, December 2, 1931; "Red Day on Capitol Hill" (here sections I–III of "Views of Washington"), *The New Republic*, December 23, 1931; "Washington and Chicago" (here the fourth section of "Views of Washington" and the opening section of "On the National Hookup"), *The New Republic*, July 13, 1932; "Out of the Red with Roosevelt" (here the second section of "On the National Hookup"), *The New Republic*, July 13, 1932; "Detroit, City of Leisure," *The New Republic*, July 27, 1932; "Doves in the Bullring," *New Masses*, January 2, 1934; "Brooklyn to Helingsfor," *Esquire*, February 1934; "The Radio Voice" (here the seventh section of "On the National Hookup"), *Common Sense*, February 1934; "Notes on the Back of a Passport" (here the seventh section of "Rainy Days in Leningrad" and "Passport Photo"), *American Spectator*, February 1934; "Between Two Roads," *Saturday Review of the Brooklyn Daily Eagle*, February 4, 1934; "The Unemployment Report" (here the opening of "More Views of Washington"), *New Masses*, February 13, 1934; "Another Redskin Bites the Dust" (here "Emiliano Zapata"), *Esquire*, March 1934; "Spain Gets Her New Deal" (here "Topdog Politics" and "Underdog Politics"), *American Mercury*, March 1934; "Washington: The Big Tent" (here the third section of "More Views of Washington"), *The New Republic*, March 18, 1934; "Another Plea for Recognition" (here "The Malaria Man"), *The New Republic*, March 28, 1934; "Mr. Green Meets His Constituents" (here the second section of "More Views of Washington"), *Common Sense*, April 1934. An English edition of *In All Countries*, adopting English spelling and usage and omitting the section "The Caciques" from "Underdog Politics," was published by Constable in 1934; it did not contain any revisions by Dos Passos. Revised excerpts from *In All Countries* were incorporated into Dos Passos' *Journeys Between Wars* (1938). The 1934 Harcourt, Brace and Company edition of *In All Countries* is the text printed here. Copyright 1934 by John Dos Passos; copyright renewed © 1962 by John Dos Passos. Reprinted by permission of Lucy Dos Passos Coggin.

For *Journeys Between Wars*, first published by Harcourt, Brace and Company in April 1938, Dos Passos included a revised version of *Orient Express*, revised excerpts from *Rosinante to the Road Again* and *In All Countries*, and five previously uncollected essays published in *Esquire*: "The Villages are the Heart of Spain" (February 1937); "Introduction to Civil War" (here "A Spring Month in Paris"), October 1937; "Spanish Diary," November 1937; "Road to

Madrid," December 1937 (here divided between the essays "Coast Road South" and "Valencia—Madrid"); "Room and Bath at the Hotel Florida" (here "Madrid Under Siege"), January 1938. *Journeys Between Wars* was published on April 7, 1938, by Harcourt, Brace and Company. An English edition was issued by Constable the same year that did not contain any authorial revisions. The texts of the five previously uncollected essays in *Journeys Between Wars* are taken from the 1938 Harcourt, Brace and Company edition. Copyright 1922, 1927, 1934, 1938 by John Dos Passos; copyright renewed © 1950, 1955, 1962, 1966 by John Dos Passos. Reprinted by permission of Lucy Dos Passos Coggin.

Many of the poems in Dos Passos' only collection of poetry, *A Pushcart at the Curb*, were published in periodicals in 1921 and 1922, though some were composed as early as 1916. "Quai de la Tournelle," IV, was published as "Jardin des Tuileries" in *The Dial*, June 1921, as was "On Foreign Travel" (under the title "On Poetic Composition"). "Embarquement Pour Cythere" ("Quai de la Tournelle," VIII) appeared in *Vanity Fair*, October 1921. "Vagones de Tercera," IV, appeared under the title "Vermilion Towers" in *Bookman*, November 1921. "Tivoli" and "Venice" ("Nights at Bassano," III and IV) were published in *Vanity Fair*, December 1921 and February 1922, respectively. Sections III and IV of "Quai de la Tournelle" were published as "Quais de la Tournelle" in *Bookman*, March 1922. The first section of "Quai de la Tournelle" was published as "Quais: Rive Gauche," in *The Measure*, July 1922. The first half of "Winter in Castile," XVII, appeared in "The Spirit of Spain" in *Mentor*, August 1922. "Winter in Castile," XVIII, and "Phases of the Moon," II, appeared in *Vanity Fair*, November 1922, as "In Denia" and "The Moon's Waning," respectively. George H. Doran published *A Pushcart at the Curb* on October 11, 1922. There was no subsequent edition. This volume prints the text of the 1922 George H. Doran edition of *A Pushcart at the Curb*.

The nine essays in the "Uncollected Essays 1916–1941" section of this volume were not included in any of Dos Passos' books. Their texts are taken from the periodical publications listed below:

"Against American Literature." *New Republic*, October 14, 1916.

"Is the 'Realistic' Theatre Obsolete?" *Vanity Fair*, May 1925. Copyright © 1925 *Vanity Fair* / Conde Nast Publications Inc. Reprinted by permission of Lucy Dos Passos Coggin.

"Paint the Revolution!" *New Masses*, March 1927. Reprinted by permission of Lucy Dos Passos Coggin.

"A City That Died by Heartfailure." *The Lantern*, February 1928. Reprinted by permission of Lucy Dos Passos Coggin.

"Edison and Steinmetz: Medicine Men." *The New Republic*, December 18, 1929. Reprinted by permission of Lucy Dos Passos Coggin.
"Grosz Comes to America." *Esquire*, September 1936. By permission of Esquire magazine. © Hearst Communications, Inc. Esquire is a trademark of Hearst Magazines Property, Inc. All rights reserved.
"Farewell to Europe!" *Common Sense*, July 1937. Reprinted by permission of Lucy Dos Passos Coggin.
"The Death of José Robles." *The New Republic*, July 19, 1939. Reprinted by permission of Lucy Dos Passos Coggin.
"To a Liberal in Office." *The Nation*, September 6, 1941. Reprinted by permission of Lucy Dos Passos Coggin.

The final section of this volume collects 51 letters and 15 diary excerpts written by Dos Passos between May 29, 1916, and November 2, 1920. The texts of the four letters to Arthur McComb, dated c. May–June 1917; June 28, 1917; August 27, 1918; and October 5, 1918, are printed from *John Dos Passos' Correspondence with Arthur K. McComb, or "Learn to Sing the Carmagnole,"* narrated and edited by Melvin Landsberg (Niwot, Colo.: University Press of Colorado, 1991). Copyright © 1991 by University Press of Colorado; reprinted by permission of Lucy Dos Passos Coggin. The four letters written in French to Germaine Lucas-Championnière, dated September 1, 1919; June 17, 1920; July 27, 1920; and September 23, 1920, are printed from manuscripts in the collection of Townsend Ludington, the editor of this volume, by permission of Lucy Dos Passos Coggin. (Translations of these letters appear in the notes.) The texts of the remaining 43 letters and of all 15 diary excerpts are taken from *The Fourteenth Chronicle: Letters and Diaries of John Dos Passos*, edited with a biographical narrative by Townsend Ludington (Boston: Gambit Incorporated, 1973). Copyright © 1973 by Elizabeth H. Dos Passos and Townsend Ludington. Excerpts from *The Fourteenth Chronicle* are reprinted with the permission of The Harvard Common Press.

While preparing the letters and diary excerpts taken from *The Fourteenth Chronicle* for inclusion in the present volume, Ludington checked them against the original manuscripts and discovered that some transcription errors had appeared in *The Fourteenth Chronicle*; these errors have been corrected in the present volume. This volume also prints six passages from Dos Passos' diaries that did not appear in *The Fourteenth Chronicle*. These passages are taken from the original manuscript diaries, now in the Alderman Library at the University of Virginia, and appear at p. 683.6–35 (ending with "Una citta maledita—"), p. 684.19–23, pp. 692.1–693.2, pp. 736.13–737.35, pp. 744.34–745.4, and p. 755.6–12 in this volume. The bracketed editorial insertions used in *John Dos Passos' Correspondence with Arthur K. McComb* and *The Fourteenth Chronicle* to clarify meaning and to supply identifications, place names, and dates have been omitted in the present volume.

This volume presents the texts of the original printings chosen for inclusion here, but it does not attempt to reproduce nontextual features of their typographic design. The texts are presented without change, except for the changes previously discussed and the correction of typographical errors. Spelling, punctuation, and capitalization are often expressive features and are not altered, even when inconsistent or irregular. The following is a list of typographical errors corrected, cited by page and line number: 15.28, mailbag; 39.32, Bilboa; 45.40, Vergniau; 59.2, susration; 72.12, *and*; 85.9, storms; 96.28, antesocial; 97.7, groups the; 99.5, silhouettte; 110.24, Bardo; 121.13, *!Carai!*; 131.5, wet; 177.14, Ervian; 190.11–12, Hassan Hussein; 198.29, Saar; 246.24, kholblackened; 255.7, or out; 284.14, Kirghiz;; 317.5–6, millions; 340.27, worker,; 343.26–27, dyedinthewood; 378.27, *Bartolomco*; 392.28, said.; 393.15–16, fathommeter; 398.3, yell"; 427.6, makes."; 428.21, farmorlaborite; 441.5, that was; 502.29, insistant; 503.28, years'; 525.9, torches; 531.9, inextinguishible; 533.12, dytheramb; 550.13, *Jasdin*; 593.5, frustrate; 600.7, colonades; 600.14, baloon; 601.3, deserted the; 602.13, thinest; 604.3, revolver,; 604.6, said; 614.6, know; 616.23, Appolinaire; 659.1, The're; 660.27–28, ofter; 681.13, halocaust; 698.8, Germans; 747.29, use; 752.11, them

Notes

In the notes below, the reference numbers denote page and line of this volume (the line count includes headings). No note is made for material included in standard desk-reference books. Biblical quotations are keyed to the King James Version. Quotations from Shakespeare are keyed to *The Riverside Shakespeare*, ed. G. Blakemore Evans (Boston: Houghton Mifflin, 1974). For references to other studies, and further biographical background than is contained in the Chronology, see John Dos Passos, *The Fourteenth Chronicle: Letters and Diaries of John Dos Passos* (Boston: Gambit, 1973), edited by Townsend Ludington; John Dos Passos, *The Best Times: An Informal Memoir* (New York: New American Library, 1966); John Dos Passos, *The Major Nonfictional Prose* (Detroit: Wayne State University Press, 1988), edited by Donald Pizer; Townsend Ludington, *John Dos Passos: A Twentieth Century Odyssey* (New York: E. P. Dutton, 1980); Virginia Spencer Carr, *Dos Passos: A Life* (New York: Doubleday & Co., 1984).

ROSINANTE TO THE ROAD AGAIN

3.13   Lyaeus]   A name for the Greek god Dionysus.

3.20   *Tannhauser*]   Opera (1845, revised 1861) by Richard Wagner.

3.21   Jorge Manrique]   Manrique (1440–79) was a Spanish poet.

3.26–37   'Recuerde el alma . . . mejor.']   The sleeping soul remembers / Stirs the brain and wakes / Contemplating / How life passes / How death comes / So silently / When I give myself to pleasure / How afterwards this remembered / Gives pain / How to our thoughts / Whatever time before / Was better.

4.37–39   Nuestras vidas . . . morir.]   Our lives are like rivers / That flow to the sea / That is death.

5.26   Pastora Imperio]   Stage name of flamenco dancer Pastora Rojas Monje (1888–1979).

6.3–8   Decidme: la . . . para?]   Decide: beauty, / The graceful cheek and complexion / Of the face / The color and fairness, / Old age will come / Which way do you want to end?

6.23–28   ¿Qué se . . . amadores?]   What did the women do to themselves, / Their touches, their dresses, / Their scents? / What happened to the flames / Of the burnt out fires / Of lovers?

7.7   Belmonte]   Juan Belmonte (1892–1962), influential Spanish matador.

11.19   *arriero*]   Muleteer.

11.32   *Alemanes*]   Germans.

11.35   Qué burro la guerra,]   How stupid war is.

12.29   *En América no se divierte,*]   In America they don't have fun.

13.8–9   *Ca, en América . . . de'cansar*]   Sure, in America they don't do anything but work and then sleep so they can work again.

13.21–22   Meredith's . . . *Daughter of Hades*]   The poem appeared in *Poems and Lyrics of the Joy of Earth* (1883).

15.27   *la juventud*]   The young.

15.34–39   ¿Qué se . . . truxeron?]   What did King Don Juan do? / The princes of Aragon / What did they do? / What did they do with such gallantry, / What did they do with such invention, / How did they bring it?

16.3–4   the *Mermaid*]   Tavern on Bread Street in Cheapside, London, frequented in the early 17th century by Shakespeare, Sir Walter Raleigh, Ben Jonson, Francis Beaumont, John Fletcher, and John Donne.

16.26–27   ¡Qué incultura! . . . *indecente!*]   How uncultured, how indecent.

25.22   Juan de la Cruz]   Also known as St. John of the Cross, de la Cruz (1542–91), a priest and mystic poet, co-founded the order of Discalced Carmelites with Theresa of Avila in 1568.

25.24–25   Archpriest of Hita]   Juan Ruiz (1283?–?1351), a priest and poet, was the author of *El Libro de buen amor* (*The Book of Good Love*, c. 1330).

25.26   Don Juan Tenorio]   Hero of play (1844) of the same name by José Zorrilla y Moral (1817–93).

39.2   G.B.S. . . . Englishman]   George Bernard Shaw (1856–1950) was born in Ireland and lived there until he moved to London in 1876.

39.9   the Zubiaurre]   The Basque painters and brothers Valentín de Zubiaurre (1879–1963) and Ramon de Zubiaurre (1882–1969).

39.25   the Carlist wars]   Civil wars fought in 1834–39 and 1872–76.

42.13   *Novelas Ejemplares*]   Volume of short stories by Miguel de Cervantes, published in 1613

42.14   Lazarillo de Tormes . . . *Gil Blas*]   *Lazarillo de Tormes* (1553), a Spanish picaresque romance of undetermined authorship; French picaresque narrative (1715–35) by Alain-René Lesage (1668–1747).

53.8   Mausers]   Military rifles designed by the Mauser company in Germany.

59.37   The very pattern . . . major-general.]   Cf. "Song of the Major General" by W. S. Gilbert and Arthur Sullivan, from *The Pirates of Penzance* (1879).

62.15   Amphitrite]   A Greek sea goddess.

62.16   Theda Bara]   Born Theodosia Goodman, Theda Bara (1890–1955) was a silent film actress.

62.30   the movies will profit.]   *The Four Horsemen of the Apocalypse* was made into a successful film in 1921, directed by Rex Ingram and starring Rudolph Valentino.

62.36   Tartarin of Tarascon]   Comic hero of the novel *Les Aventures Prodigieuses de Tartarin de Tarascon* (1872) by Alphonse Daudet (1840–97) and its sequels *Tartarin sur les Alpes* (1886) and *Port-Tarascon* (1890).

66.11–17   'Aquí . . . en amores.']   Here is Don Juan Tenorio; / there's no man like him . . . / Look for those on bad terms with him, / round up the challengers, / who think so well of themselves that they think they can cut him down, / to see if there is anyone who can best him / in games, in a fight, in love.

68.31   Maragall]   Catalan poet Joan (Juan) Maragall (1860–1911).

70.19   Rubén Darío]   Pseudonym of Félix Rubén García Sarmiento (1867–1916).

72.9   gai scavoir]   Joyful knowledge.

80.7   *Leonidas in the Greek Anthology*]   Leonidas of Tarentum, a poet of the 3rd century B.C. whose work was included in the anthology of about 4,500 Greek poems prepared by Constantine Cephalas in the 10th century A.D.

81.15   Ferrer]   Francisco Ferrer (1859–1919), an anarchist and proponent of progressive education free from church and state control, founded the "Modern School" in Barcelona in 1901. He was executed on October 13, 1909, for his alleged involvement in the July 1909 insurrection in Barcelona.

87.18–21   Canta esposa, . . . en pau.]   Sing, my wife, dance and sing / so that the ground becomes smooth / When the wife sings and dances / the land falls asleep in peace.

88.22–23   Patmore and Ella Wheeler Wilcox]   English poet Coventry Patmore (1823–96); American poet and novelist Ella Wheeler Wilcox (1850–1919).

89.9   Pierre Vidal]   Vidal (c. 1175–1206) was a troubadour from Toulouse.

90.27   *Zarzuela*]   Light opera.

93.23   Felipe Cuarto]   Philip IV (1605–65), king of Spain from 1621 to 1665.

93.32   *majas*]   Flirtatious women.

93.36   *dos de Mayo*]   The unsuccessful uprising against Napoleonic rule that began in Madrid on May 2, 1808.

94.1   Burial of the Sardine]   The burial of a sardine, representing winter, at the end of the pre-Lenten carnival.

94.4   Larra, Becquer, Espronceda]   Mariano José de Larra (1809–37), a novelist and playwright; Gustavo Adolfo Bécquer (1836–70), a poet and writer of tales and essays; José de Espronceda (1808–42), a poet and novelist.

94.12   *Tiene el sentido de lo castizo.*]   He has the soul of a *castizo*.

95.30   *tertulia*]   Gathering for conversation.

96.9–13   Yo a las . . . de mí.]   I went down to the hovels, / I went up to the palaces, / and scaled the cloisters, / and everywhere I left / bitter memories of me.

98.14   *Gente Conocida*]   High society, people of importance.

102.17–22 'Sigue la vana . . . hurtando.']   The vain shadow continues, the sham / The man is surrendered / to the dream, of his uncaring luck, / and with a silent step / the sky revolves / stealing the hours of his life.

103.2–10 *Doce días . . . lo ataban.*]   Twelve days have passed / since the Cid finished / preparing his troops / to leave for the battle / with Búcar the Moorish king / and against his rabble. / When it was midnight / they put his body as it was / upon Babieca / and the horse led them.

105.8–9   Cortes of Cadiz . . . Fernando Septimo.]   In 1808 the French occupied Madrid and forced Ferdinand VII to abdicate. When Ferdinand was restored to the throne in 1814 he repudiated the liberal constitution adopted in 1812 by the Cortes (parliament) that had convened in Cádiz in 1810. After the revolution of 1820 Ferdinand was forced to accept the 1812 constitution, but in 1823 French military intervention restored his absolute rule.

109.19   the Digest]   A compilation of writings by Roman jurists that was prepared by order of the Byzantine emperor Justinian and published in A.D. 533.

110.6   *alpargatas*]   Hemp sandals.

110.16   *¡Cáspita!*]   Heavens.

111.18–23 Cara tiene . . . vivo semejaba.]   He has a beautiful face / very beautiful and full of color; / both eyes are open / his beard is elegant / He doesn't appear dead / He looks like he did when alive.

120.28   *fonda*]   Inn.

124.3   "*Ven, flor de mi corazón,*"]   Come, flower of my heart.

ORIENT EXPRESS

130.9 Pico] An island in the Azores.

131.3 Michel Strogoff] *Michel Strogoff* (1876), novel by Jules Verne about a Russian courier crossing Siberia.

131.16 En voiture] Take your seats.

131.21–22 categoria de lusso] Luxury class.

133.3 Kingdom . . . Slovenes] The official name for Yugoslavia from 1918 to 1931.

133.21 Diehl] Probably Charles Diehl (1859–1944), French historian of the Byzantine Empire.

133.31–32 Aller dans . . . le luxe.] Travel in luxury . . . One must always travel in luxury.

135.7 French, Greek, and Italian gendarmes] Constantinople was occupied by the Allied powers from March 16, 1920, to October 2, 1923.

136.22–23 Greek officers . . . Eski Chehir.] The Greeks captured Eskishehr in western Anatolia on July 21, 1921. It was recaptured by the Turks in September 1922.

137.17 Wrangel's army] The southern White army during the Russian Civil War was commanded by General Petr N. Wrangel from April 1920 until its evacuation from the Crimea in November 1920.

138.6 *civilisation mondiale*] World civilization.

140.2 "Moussavat" party] Muslim political party that dominated the government of the independent Azerbaijan republic from 1918 until the Bolshevik takeover in 1920.

141.3 fall of Adrianople] The Greeks occupied Adrianople (Edirne) on July 25, 1920, and evacuated it in the fall of 1922.

142.20 yakmaks] Yashmaks, veils worn by Muslim women.

143.32–33 Manchester goods] Cotton goods.

146.6 khud] A deep ravine.

150.15 Umberto Primo] Umberto I (1844–1900), king of Italy 1878–1900.

151.6 Angora] Ankara.

157.36 N.E.R.] Near East Relief.

158.1 Cheka] The Soviet security police, 1917–22, from *Chrezvychaynaya Kommissiya* (Extraordinary Commission for Combatting Counter-Revolution and Sabotage).

158.2   Republic of Adjaria] An autonomous region in Soviet Georgia.

158.31   green army] "Greens" were peasant partisan movements that opposed both the Reds and Whites during the Russian Civil War.

160.24   Denikin] Anton I. Denikin commanded the southern White
army from April 1918 until April 1920, when he resigned his command to Petr
Wrangel.

161.8–9   Princess Anastasia] Anastastia Nikolayevna (1901–18), youngest
daughter of Czar Nicholas II, was murdered by the Bolsheviks, although
claims that she had survived the mass shooting of her family circulated for
decades.

166.19   *Isvestia* and the *Pravda*] *Isvestia* ("News") was the official newspaper of the Soviet government, and *Pravda* ("Truth") was the official Soviet
Communist party newspaper.

168.36   *Alexandropol*] Gyumri. The city was renamed Leninabad in 1924;
its Armenian name was restored after the collapse of the Soviet Union.

170.9   divs] Evil spirits in Persian mythology.

172.5   Il me fait la cour] He's wooing me.

176.17   *I' fallait pas, . . . pa-as y-aller.*] It wasn't necessary, it wasn't
necessary, it wasn't necessary to go there.

180.31   Miss Bell] Gertrude Bell (1868–1926), an English traveler and
archeologist who served as an influential adviser to the British government
on Middle Eastern affairs during and after World War I. In 1897 she published
Poems from the Divan of Hafiz.

188.16   Saadi's] Persian poet Mosharref ud-din Sa'di of Shiraz (c. 1213–92).

189.34–35 Morris Gest] Gest (1881–1942) was a New York theatrical
producer.

195.30–31 Ah mon ami, . . . très dangereux.] Ah my friend, I have
found a pox. With the typhus he has it's very dangerous.

196.6   Republic of Ghilan] A Soviet republic in northern Persia that was
proclaimed in May 1920. It was suppressed in October 1921 after the Red
Army withdrew from the region.

197.6   time of El Bab] Sayyid Ali Muhammad, a Shia religious leader in
Persia, was proclaimed as a prophet by his followers in 1844 and given the title
of Bab (Gate). He was executed in 1850.

197.19   anderun] Women's quarters.

199.13–14 Isa ben Miriam] The Islamic name for Jesus.

202.26   kahwe] Coffee house.

203.15   Jake and Lee Shubert's] Jacob J. Shubert (1878?–1963) and Lee Shubert (1873?–1953), American theater owners and producers.

205.27   Monsieur en Iraq . . . pastèques] Monsieur, in Iraq one must not abuse the watermelons.

207.21   mazout] Fuel oil.

210.21   Cokus] Sir Percy Cox (1864–1937), the British high commissioner in Iraq from 1920 to 1923.

211.24   King of the Hedjaz] Hussein (ca. 1854–1931), the sharif of Mecca from 1908 to 1916, became king of the Hejaz in 1916 at the beginning of the Arab revolt against the Ottoman empire and ruled until his defeat in 1924 by Ibn Saud. In 1921 the British made his sons Faisal (1885–1933) king of Iraq and Abdullah (1882–1951) emir of Transjordan.

211.30   The last revolt] The revolt against British rule in Mesopotamia in the summer and fall of 1920.

211.33   the plebiscite] The vote was held to ratify the choice of Faisal as king of Iraq under the League of Nations mandate that gave Britain trusteeship over the new state. On August 18, 1921, it was announced that Faisal had been approved by a 96 percent majority, and he was crowned on August 23.

212.13   kaimakom] A deputy administrator.

212.34–36   Go, ye swift . . . have spoiled.] Isaiah 18:2.

214.9   bidon] Metal bottle.

215.2   a prairie oyster] The testicle of a bull or sheep.

221.15   Mudir] The governor of a village or district.

222.33   *Enteuthen exelauni*] "Thence he marched," a repeated phrase in the *Anabasis* of Xenophon.

225.37–38   death of the Prince Napoleon] The son of Napoleon III was speared to death on June 1, 1879, while accompanying the British army in Natal during the Zulu War.

228.29   *And the stars . . . Sisera.*] Judges 5:20.

233.20   L'Amant Magnifique] *Les Amants magnifiques* (1670) by Molière.

245.15   Bilkis] An Arabic name for the Queen of Sheba.

245.21   *comme on s'ennuie*] How boring it gets.

245.24–25   *dans ce sale pays*] In this dirty country.

248.40   kaffir] Infidel.

249.9   Blaise Cendrars] Pseudonym of the Swiss poet and novelist Frédéric Sauser (1887–1961).

251.23–24   de Lesseps attempt]   In 1879 Ferdinand de Lesseps, the builder of the Suez Canal, organized an attempt to construct a canal across Panama. The project failed and in 1889 the French Panama company collapsed.

252.4   Ahasuerus]   The Hebrew form of Xerxes.

258.6   Black Diamond]   Express train that ran between New York and Buffalo.

264.3   tirailleur]   Infantry soldier in the French colonial army.

264.10   ksar]   Palace.

266.23   Fundador]   A Spanish brandy.

IN ALL COUNTRIES

273.3   Peesatyel]   Traveler.

283.27   Boris Godunov]   Opera (1873) by Modest Mussorgsky.

284.27–28   Gaypayoo]   The G.P.U. (State Political Administration), the Soviet security police, 1922–23, and its successor, the O.P.G.U. (Unified State Political Administration), 1923–34.

285.1   comsomols]   Members of *Komsomol*, the Soviet Communist party youth organization.

286.2   Narkompros]   People's Commissariat for Enlightenment.

288.9   Taylor plan]   The principles of industrial management developed by the American engineer Frederick Winslow Taylor (1856–1915).

291.12–13   Trauberg . . . Paris Commune]   *New Babylon* (1929), directed by Leonid Trauberg (1902–90) and Grigori Kozintsev (1905–73).

292.14   Jack Reed's . . . Ransome's despatches]   *Ten Days That Shook the World* (1919) by the American journalist John Reed (1887–1920) and *Russia in 1919* (1919) by British correspondent Arthur Ransome (1884–1967).

293.25   Redhook]   Waterfront neighborhood in Brooklyn.

297.24–25   *The villainy . . . execute.*]   Cf. *The Merchant of Venice*, III.i. 71–72.

302.30   Khovanchina]   *Khovanshchina*, unfinished opera by Modest Moussorgsky that was completed by Nikolai Rimsky-Korsakov and first performed in 1886.

302.32   Ostrovsky's]   Russian dramatist Alexander Ostrovsky (1823–86).

304.13–14   Ivy Lee . . . Tsik]   Lee (1877–1934) was a leading American public relations consultant who became a prominent advocate of U.S. recognition of the Soviet Union during the 1920s. The Tsik was the Central Executive Committee of the Soviets.

308.9   *The Cricket on the Hearth*]   An adaptation of the 1846 Christmas tale by Charles Dickens.

308.11   Vakhtangoff's . . . *Turandot*]   The 1762 commedia dell'arte play by Carlo Gozzi (1720–1806) was staged by Yevgeny Vakhtangov (1883–1922) in 1921.

308.16–17   *The Yellow Jacket* . . . Hoyt]   *The Yellow Jacket* (1912) by George C. Hazelton and J. Harry Benrimo; *The Girl with the Green Eyes* (1902) by Clyde Fitch; *In Old Kentucky* (1893), by Charles Turner Dazey; Charles Hale Hoyt (1860–1900) was a successful playwright in the 1880s and 1890s.

310.12   revolted at Kronstadt]   The naval garrison at Kronstadt mutinied against Bolshevik rule on March 2, 1921. The revolt was suppressed on March 17.

310.13   *Aurora*]   Cruiser that fired on the Winter Palace during the Bolshevik seizure of power on November 7, 1917.

310.15   S.R.'s]   Members of the Socialist Revolutionary party, founded in 1905 and suppressed by the Bolsheviks in 1922.

310.24   the old Okhrana]   The Czarist secret police.

310.28   *Le Jardin des Supplices*]   *The Torture Garden*, novel (1898) by Octave Mirbeau (1848–1917).

315.26   Andrew Mellon]   Mellon (1855–1937), a wealthy financier, served as secretary of the treasury, 1921–32.

316.6   Calles]   Plutarco Calles (1877–1945) was president of Mexico, 1924–28.

316.10   C.R.O.M.]   Confederación Regional Obrera Mexicana, at the time the largest Mexican labor federation.

316.32   Huerta, president in Los Angeles]   Huerta (1883?–1955), a leader of the revolution of 1920, lived in exile in the United States from 1924 to 1935.

319.28–29   *sinverguenza*]   Scoundrel.

335.3–4   "Pobrecito"]   Poor little fellow.

339.14–15   *Internationale*]   Socialist anthem, with words (1871) by Eugène Pottier and music (1888) by Adolphe Degeyter.

341.30   the Sun King]   Louis XIV, king of France 1643–1715.

342.33–34   Ramon Franco's . . . palace]   On December 15, 1930, Ramon Franco (1896–1938), a well-known Spanish aviator and brother of Francisco Franco, flew over the palace as part of a failed military uprising. Though carrying bombs, he decided to drop only leaflets calling for a general strike, and then he fled to Portugal.

342.40   last of the Bourbons left Madrid] On April 14, 1931.

344.31   the first republic] From 1873 to 1874.

349.6   Primo de Rivera] Miguel Primo de Rivera (1870–1930) was dictator of Spain from 1923 to 1930.

353.22   La Cierva or Romanones] Juan de la Cierva (1864–1938), a leading
Conservative, was minister of government (the interior), 1907–9, and minister
of war, 1917–18 and 1921–22. The Count of Romanones (1863–1950), a Liberal,
was president of the council (prime minister), 1912–13, 1915–17, and 1918–19.

355.6   U.G.T.] Unión General de Trabajadores.

356.12   time of the exposition] The Ibero-American Exposition of 1929.

356.19   Third International] The Communist International, founded by
Lenin in 1919 to provide revolutionary leadership to the worldwide socialist
movement.

356.23   General Sanjurjo's uprising] In August 1932.

357.39   C.N.T.] Confederación Nacional del Trabajo.

360.5   el reparto] The sharing, the distribution.

364.33   ley de fuga] Law of flight, i.e. "shot while trying to escape."

370.17   A. Mitchell Palmer] Palmer (1872–1936) was attorney general
from 1919 to 1921.

370.30   Galeani] Luigi Galleani (1861–1931), an Italian anarchist who
lived in the United States from 1901 until his deportation in 1919, was an advocate of revolutionary violence.

379.34   De Amicis] Italian writer Edmondo De Amicis (1846–1908).

379.35   Malatesta] Italian anarchist Errico Malatesta (1853–1932).

384.1   Writers' Committee] See Chronology, 1931.

384.11   N.M.U.] National Miners Union.

387.29   a blind pig] A speakeasy.

388.20   Ford's service men] Members of the security division (Service
Department) of the Ford Motor Company.

390.29   Lahave bank] Fishing ground in the Atlantic Ocean off Nova
Scotia.

391.4–5   Bay of Islands] Bay on the west coast of Newfoundland.

397.32–33   two contested seats . . . Heflin] The results of the 1930 Senate elections in North Carolina and Alabama were contested when the Senate met in December 1931. J. Thomas Heflin (1869–1951) was elected from

Alabama as a Democrat in 1918 but was defeated in 1930 when he ran as an independent. The Senate rejected his election challenge in April 1932.

399.18   Brigadier-General Glassford] Pelham D. Glassford, a retired army officer, was chief of police in Washington, D.C., from November 1931 to October 1932.

401.1–2   moratorium . . . R.F.C.] In the early summer of 1931 President Herbert Hoover arranged a one-year moratorium on the payment of international debts and reparations. The Reconstruction Finance Corporation was established by Congress in January 1932 and authorized to make loans to financial institutions and railroads.

401.16   B.E.F.] Bonus Expeditionary Force.

402.3   CC pills] Compound cathartic pills.

404.7   Mr. Snell] Bertrand Snell (1870–1958), a congressman from New York state, 1915–39, was the chairman of the 1932 Republican National Convention.

405.2   Mr. Scott] Joseph Scott (1867–1958), a prominent Los Angeles attorney and civic leader who had also nominated Hoover at the 1928 convention.

406.32   Senator from Kentucky] Alben W. Barkley (1877–1956) was a senator, 1927–49 and 1955–56, and vice-president, 1949–53.

407.4–6   Byrd's . . . Alfalfa Bill] Governor Harry Flood Byrd of Virginia, Governor Albert Ritchie of Maryland, and Governor William Henry (Alfalfa Bill) Murray of Oklahoma were all "favorite son" candidates at the 1932 convention.

410.35   Judge Panken] Jacob Panken, a New York City municipal judge.

410.38   Mr. Broun] Heywood Broun (1888–1939), a novelist, newspaper columnist, and critic, had run for Congress and for the New York City council as a Socialist candidate.

411.16   Mr. Hillquit] Morris Hillquit (1869–1933) helped found the American Socialist party in 1901.

411.34–35   John F. Curry] Curry was the leader of the Democratic party organization in Manhattan (Tammany Hall) from 1929 to 1934.

411.36–39   O'Brien . . . Walker] A corruption investigation led by Samuel Seabury resulted in the resignation on September 1, 1932, of James J. Walker, the mayor of New York since 1926. Surrogate John O'Brien won the special mayoral election held in 1932, but was defeated in 1933 by Fiorello La Guardia.

412.2   Colonel Lehman] Herbert H. Lehman (1878–1963), lieutenant governor of New York, 1929–1933, and then governor, 1933–42.

413.11   Foster] William Z. Foster (1881–1961), the Communist party candidate for president in 1932.

413.17   Hathaway]   Clarence H. Hathaway, editor of the *Daily Worker*
and a Communist party candidate for Congress in 1932.

413.31   Earl Browder]   Browder (1891–1973) was general secretary of the
American Communist party from 1930 to 1945.

422.5–6   Senator Gore]   Thomas P. Gore (1870–1949) was a Democratic
Senator from Oklahoma, 1907–21 and 1931–37.

422.19   Mr. Pecora]   Ferdinand Pecora, chief counsel to the Senate Banking and Currency Committee, 1933–34.

426.24   General Johnson]   Hugh Samuel Johnson (1882–1942), director
of the National Recovery Administration, 1933–34.

428.9   Farley]   James A. Farley (1888–1976), chairman of the Democratic
national committee, 1932–40, and postmaster general, 1933–40.

428.20   Cosmos Club]   An elite men's club in Washington, D.C.

FROM JOURNEYS BETWEEN WARS

433.16   *Louise*]   Opera by Gustave Charpentier (1860–1956), first performed in Paris in 1900.

435.19   Léon Blum]   Premier of France from June 1936 to June 1937, and
from March to April 1938.

441.17   In Vienna they shelled]   During the violent suppression of the
Austrian Social Democratic party by the right-wing government of Chancel-
lor Engelbert Dollfus in February 1934.

443.31   Ramsay MacDonald]   MacDonald (1866–1937), one of the
founders of the British Labour party, became prime minister of a Labour government in 1929. When the majority of his cabinet refused to support a cut
in unemployment benefits in August 1931, MacDonald resigned, then formed
a National government with Conservative and Liberal support and continued
to serve as prime minister until 1935.

444.37   the Exposition]   The international exposition held in Paris from
May to November 1937.

446.22   *boinas*]   Berets.

449.29–30   Valencia Ministry of War]   The Republican government
moved from Madrid to Valencia in November 1936.

451.35   *Generalitat*]   The semi-autonomous government of Catalonia.

457.40   *Casa de los Sabios*]   House of the Sages.

474.22   Guadalajara]   The battle, fought March 8–18, 1937, ended in a
Loyalist victory.

486.13   P.O.U.M.]   Partido Obrero de Unificacion Marxista, an anti-Stalinist revolutionary socialist party.

487.11–12   Nin . . . suppressed.]   The leadership of the P.O.U.M. was arrested and the party suppressed in June 1937 by the Republican government after the Communists falsely accused it of engaging in espionage for the Nationalists. Nin was tortured and killed by Soviet intelligence agents shortly after his arrest.

A PUSHCART AT THE CURB

498.17   Iacchos]   A Greek god identified with Dionysus.

509.20–21   *Esta noche . . . a dormir*]   This night is a good night [Christmas Eve] / no one thinks about sleeping.

513.7   To J. G. P.]   José Giner Pantoja, Spanish friend of Dos Passos

519.13   Dudloysha]   Dudley Poore, a close friend of Dos Passos from Harvard and a fellow ambulance driver in World War I.

537.24   TO R. H.]   Robert Hillyer, a close friend from Harvard and a fellow ambulance driver during the summer of 1917.

543.32   TO R. J.]   Roland Jackson, Harvard friend killed in World War I.

552.20   TO A. K. MC C.]   Arthur K. McComb, a close friend from Harvard.

555.30–31   *O douce Sainte Geneviève . . . Paris*]   O sweet Sainte Geneviève/ lead me to your city, Paris.

557.15   A L'OMBRE . . . FLEURS]   "In the shadow of young girls in blossom," the title of the second volume (1918) of *À la recherche du temps perdu* by Marcel Proust.

579.28   *Lua cheia esta noit*]   The full moon last night.

UNCOLLECTED ESSAYS 1916–1941

588.31   *erdgeist*]   Earth spirit.

593.7–8   *The Crime in the Whistler Room*]   Play (1924) by Edmund Wilson.

593.26   *Rain*]   Play (1922) by John Colton and Clemence Randolph, adapted from the Somerset Maugham story.

611.13–18   Armory Show . . . Stairs]   Exhibition of modern art held in New York, Chicago, and Boston in 1913 that included the cubist painting *Nude Descending a Staircase* by Marcel Duchamp.

611.30   Count of Orgaz]   *The Burial of the Count of Orgaz*, painting (1586–88) by El Greco.

615.15   Teapot Dome] Corruption scandal involving the leasing of government oil reserves during the Harding administration.

616.25   *les bourgeois à la lanterne*] Hang the bourgeoisie from the lamp posts.

623.8–9   reference to him . . . my last book] In his review of Dos Passos' novel *Adventures of a Young Man*, Cowley wrote that Robles had been "arrested as a Fascist spy" and that "people who ought to know" had told him the evidence against Robles "was absolutely damning."

625.23   he died or was killed] Francisco Robles survived his captivity.

630.8   Coughlinites] Followers of the right-wing "radio priest" Father Charles Coughlin.

LETTERS AND DIARIES 1916–1920

635.1   *Rumsey Marvin*] Dos Passos had met Marvin, a student at St. Paul's School in Concord, New Hampshire, during a trip to California in 1915.

635.22   'Dauber'] Poem (1912) by John Masefield.

636.1   Poor Kitchener!] Field Marshal Lord Horatio Kitchener (1850–1916), the British Secretary for War, drowned on June 5, 1916, after the cruiser on which he was traveling to Russia struck a mine.

636.4   the great sea battle] The Battle of Jutland, fought between the British and German fleets in the North Sea on May 31, 1916.

636.9–10   *Travels with a Donkey*] *Travels with a Donkey in the Cevennes* (1879) by Robert Louis Stevenson.

636.21   poem of Francis Thompson] "The Hound of Heaven" (1893).

636.36–637.3   I heard a partridge . . . red earth stirred] From "The Everlasting Mercy" (1911) by John Masefield.

638.3   videre mundum] To see the world.

646.5–6   almuerzoed] Lunched.

646.28–29   naranjas and manzanas] Oranges and apples.

647.20   Walter L's book] A book of poetry by Walter Savage Landor (1775–1864).

650.9   "Die schöne Tage . . . Ende"] The beautiful day in Aranjuez never ends.

653.9   Le Cid] Tragedy (1637) by Pierre Corneille.

654.35   closing down of the blockade] On February 1, 1917, the German government declared that its submarines would begin attacking all ships trading with Allied ports without warning.

656.10–11 secret treaty . . . Mexico and Germany] Arthur Zimmerman, the German foreign minister, sent a telegram to the German minister in Mexico on January 19, 1917, proposing that, in the event of war between Germany and the United States, Mexico and Germany should fight as allies with the aim of restoring Texas, New Mexico, and Arizona to Mexico. The British intercepted and decoded the telegram, then presented it to the Wilson administration, which made it public on March 1, 1917.

658.26 Roger Sessions] American composer Roger Sessions (1896–1985).

660.22 Tap Day] The day Yale undergraduates are recruited by student senior societies.

661.5 "The Light that Failed"] Novel (1890) by Rudyard Kipling.

661.17–18 the Call . . . Masses] *The New York Call*, a newspaper allied with the Socialist party that was published from 1908 to 1923; *The Masses*, a weekly journal of social criticism published from 1911 until 1918, when it was suppressed by the U.S. government.

663.6 Archie Roosevelt] Archibald Roosevelt (1894–1979), third son of President Theodore Roosevelt.

663.22–23 *jeunes gens . . . le torpiller*] Young people of the best American families; and the Germans, monsieur, would very much like to torpedo them.

663.39 Major R.] Theodore Roosevelt Jr. (1887–1944), the eldest son of Theodore Roosevelt.

673.20 C'etait rigolo, mon vieux!] It was comical, my man.

673.21 brancardiers] Stretcher bearers.

675.9–10 mais il y . . . grandes] But there are somes little beasts inside—come look at the little beasts—how big they are.

675.12–14 abris . . . aumonier] Dugout; chaplain.

676.26 the Sacred Way] The road between Bar-le-Duc and Verdun.

677.35–36 "Mais que voulez . . . la mort] But what do you want? The poor young men, they know that they are going to their deaths.

678.16–17 "ghoul haunted woodland"] From "Ulalume" (1847), poem by Edgar Allan Poe.

680.21–22 ravitaillement] Provisioning.

687.19 Gouverneur Morris] American author and World War I correspondent (1876–1953).

688.22–23 *La Dame . . . Camélias*] Novel (1848) by the younger Alexander Dumas.

689.7–8   C'est un horrible . . . hommes]   It's a horrible mess, men's lives.

689.12–13   his arrest]   The French authorities arrested E. E. Cummings on September 23, 1917, for writing allegedly subversive letters while he was serving with a volunteer ambulance company (section XXI). He was released on December 19, 1917.

690.18–19   *Julian and Maddalo*]   Poem (1818) by Percy Bysshe Shelley.

690.25   Didi]   Dos Passos' nickname for his father, who had died on January 27, 1917.

691.15–16   Guy Lowell . . . Emerson Hall]   Guy Lowell (1870–1927), a Boston architect and the brother of Harvard president A. Lawrence Lowell, had designed the president's house built in 1912 next to Emerson Hall at Harvard.

694.17   huova all'burro]   Eggs cooked in butter.

696.1   S. F.]   Sidney Fairbanks, a Harvard classmate of Dos Passos.

699.20   Tedeschi]   German.

701.11   piano—domani]   Slowly—tomorrow.

702.11   *Seraphina*]   Waltz by Johann Strauss.

703.28   Don Juan]   Long poem (1819–24) by Lord Byron.

705.16   Dunsany's]   Lord Edward Dunsany (1878–1957), Irish writer of fantastic tales.

706.20   Lorenzo de Medici's Apologia]   Written by Lorenzino de Medici (1514–48) to justify his murder of his cousin Alessandro, duke of Florence, in 1537.

708.5   Clotho]   One of the three Fates in Greek mythology.

709.30   Jean Christophe]   A *roman–fleuve* in ten volumes (1906–12) by Romain Rolland.

713.14   éclats]   Splinters.

718.3   *To José Giner Pantoja*]   This letter was intercepted by the postal censors and led to Dos Passos being accused of disloyalty (see Chronology, 1918). In translation, it reads:

My Dear Friend,

   Forgive me for another badly and hastily written letter. Again I would rather have written in Spanish, but the idea puts me in a blue funk because I love your beautiful language so much it would be very painful to make it read like Italian. Having been reading and speaking Italian all the time I've been here, I know that if I had written in Spanish I would have succeeded only in producing a miserable mélange.

Here, in this quiet place, where one has so much time, while waiting in the rain, in the yards of hospitals, or in ambulances smelling of carbolic, I think often of you and the lovely plains of Castile. From a distance the war must seem a little theoretical, but here, or anywhere at the front, I assure you it is a wholly different matter. It is boredom, slavery to all the military stupidities, the most fascinating misery, the need for warmth, bread, and cleanliness. I assure you there is nothing beautiful about modern war. I have lived in it for a year now, and many illusions have crossed the river Styx. It is nothing but an enormous, tragic digression in the lives of these people.

Rather it is for you people, you who inhabit those countries that are above the battle, to assume the struggle for progress on behalf of this wretched and tormented civilization of ours. For all the things of the mind, for art, and for everything that is needed in the world, war—I mean modern war—is death. And beyond those things, what is there on earth that is worth anything? No, it's up to you, who can make revolutions either quietly or violently, who are trying vainly, perhaps, to evolve a purpose for the life of our times, it is up to you to safeguard all the finest human things, while the rest of us struggle on brutally with suicidal madness. Why? For lies, even for some truths, for greedy nations in a world drunk on commercialism.

I am very much afraid that you Spaniards are a little idealistic about this evil European world and about America, in . . . perhaps, but Great God, to what end? Everywhere it seems to me there is nothing, either for the rich or the poor, but slavery; to industry, to money, to the mammon of business, the great God of our times. And where in all that are the good things to be found? The things that give life an added dimension, that go beyond the struggle to fill the belly, for mere existence.

It seems to me that only in your Spain and in Russia is the conquest not complete—it is in part because of that I love Spain so much.

And in my own poor country—it seems to me that with the war, with the military service law, liberty there is extinguished for a long time to come, and the day of triumph for plutocracy has arrived.

In this connection, one of my best friends is now in Madrid—Arthur Mc-Comb—who, being an unshakable anti-militarist, has had to leave the United States and will stay in Spain, I think, for a long time. He is an intelligent fellow and very likable, and I have taken the liberty of telling him to go to see you, because I knew that there was no one in Spain who could give him as much information as you. Excuse my informality, which you may credit to American rudeness. Besides, I have never been able to get used to convention, even in America.

I would be extremely pleased to get one of your charming letters. My address is care of Consolato Americano, C.R.A. Sezione I. Au revoir, your very good friend.

722.14   Pagliacci]   Opera (1892) by Ruggero Leoncavallo (1857–1919).

722.18   Gloire & Servitude Militaire]   *Servitude et grandeur militaires* (1835), three tales by Alfred de Vigny (1797–1863).

724.30–31   *La religion . . . servir.*]   The Christian religion will always be the solidest support for any government clever enough to make use of it

730.18   Veritas odium parit]   The truth seems hateful.

731.13   *emboscato*]   Shirker.

732.20   quotation from Aeschylus]   Cf. *Agamemmon*, lines 192–98.

733.1–2   Lis Flaubert . . . la vie]   Read Flaubert, my man, read Flaubert, read Flaubert if you wish style, just read Flaubert, if you wish life.

733.4–5   Carry On . . . Le Feu]   *Carry On* (1917), a collection of letters written by Coningsby Dawson, a Canadian artillery officer; *Le Feu* (1916), war novel by French soldier Henri Barbusse.

736.22   Torpedoes]   Mortar shells.

740.11   Cuthbert-like]   Cuthbert Wright, a Harvard acquaintance.

743.25–26   Napoleon in the Bellephon attitude]   After his defeat at Waterloo Napoleon surrendered to the captain of H.M.S. *Bellerophon* on July 15, 1815. The ship took him to England, where he was transferred to the *Northumberland* for his voyage into exile on St. Helena.

743.27   Bates]   A Red Cross officer who had sought Dos Passos' dismissal.

751.4   Bulgaria has seen the light]   Bulgaria surrendered to the Allies on September 29, 1918.

752.5   Jean Jacques]   Rousseau.

753.6–7   "a dome . . . Eternity."]   From *Adonais* (1821) by Percy Bysshe Shelley.

756.17   this peace move]   On October 4, 1918, the German government asked President Wilson to arrange an armistice on the basis of his Fourteen Points.

757.31   fulgentia moenia mundi]   Shining walls of the world.

758.14–15   many as the grains . . . Lybian Syrtes]   Cf. Catullus, *Carmina*.

758.19   O for a beaker . . . South]   John Keats, "Ode to a Nightingale" (1820).

758.28   huevos . . . con carne]   Scrambled eggs with tomato and rice with meat.

769.30   Artzibasheff]   Mikhail Artzybashev (1878–1927), Russian novelist, playwright, and essayist.

770.30   exegi . . . perennius]   I have raised a monument more enduring than bronze.

773.13   Katisha]   Female character in *The Mikado* (1885) by W. S. Gilbert and Arthur Sullivan.

774.33–34   George Moore's The Brook Kerith]   Novel (1916) about Jesus by the Irish writer George Moore (1852–1933).

777.1   *Germaine Lucas-Championnière*]   A young woman Dos Passos met in Paris in June 1919 who shared his interest in music. The letter reads in translation:

The manner of bullfighting is the following.

There are moments in the life of a Spanish city when one notices that everybody follows a particular street, when everybody press and jostles, that all the *landaus*, the *berlines*, the *coupets*, the *voitures de place*, the taxis, the limousines, the handcarts, the old women who sell the marvelously Greek jugs of water, the vendors of melons, of grapes, of fruit, the cats, the dogs and the pigeons, that the entire population goes in one direction. It is the hour for the bullfight. One enters, as in the last act of Carmen, sits down, and thinks about the struggles of the Roman gladiators, with disgust and scorn one looks at the reddish sand of the arenas, the wooden barricades painted red and yellow which protect the spectators, the barred gate through which the Christians will enter, no, the bull.

One shrugs his shoulders. He is accustomed to all that. Then things begin.

Sound of a trumpet. Two men in black, holding themselves with great difficulty on handsome horses which prance in the crushing light of the amphitheater, enter, circle, and salute before the royal box, with a magnificence spoiled only a little by the difficulty they have in holding themselves on their horses. Then the picadors and the matadors, the teams of mules that are going to pull off the corpses, enter in procession and salute the box empty of grand people. They are dressed in all colors, red, orange, purple, and the gold lace glimmers in the ferocious sun. Again some trumpets, and the bull enters, black, immense, leaping like the bulls that the cavemen painted when the world was young in the caves of Altamira. This is not a fight that is carried out, it is a ritual, a sacrifice. One sacrifices a horse or two on the horns of the bull, and the disemboweled horses twist in grotesque attitudes on the sand reddened by the fierce light. Then, with a superb gesture a man thrusts the banderillas into the back of the already exhausted bull. Then there is a fierce cry of joy from the trumpets, the matador sets himself in the prescribed position and plunges the length of the sword into the thick and bloody neck of the bull. The bull hangs out his tongue from which frothy blood drips, and he turns his head from one side to the other in a bestial and appealing way like a small dog begging for sugar. The matadors with their capes of red, green, and purple make a circle around him. He falls and rolls on the ground and becomes small and dirty on the sand of the arena. Teams of mules enter spiritedly and drag away the corpses to the sound of bells and the snapping of whips. Another trumpet. The red, and green and purple cloaks assume their positions, and it all begins again.

It must have been a little like that when hundreds of bulls were sacrificed to the great gods at Knossos or at Mycenae, or before the high walls of Ilion.

It's stupid, it's ugly, it's splendid—it's like a jumping contest or like the Russian ballet—But the nerves of the twentieth century, accustomed as they are to bloody floods spreading over the earth, find all that an interesting but disagreeable sensation.

I am in route to Malaga.

The address at the beginning of this letter is permanent.

781.7　　James Stephens]　Irish poet, novelist, and story writer (1882–1950).

782.3–4　　Il pleure . . . la ville]　"There is weeping in my heart / like the rain falling on the town," from the poem "Il pleure dans mon coeur" (1874) by Paul Verlaine.

788.33　　*To Germaine Lucas-Championnière*]　In translation:

Friday—London—Rainy day—leaden sky

It's today that you are leaving Paris. Bon Voyage. I would love to disappear into the countryside somewhere. I live too much in cities. I forget the songs of the birds at dawn and the great solitary nights when one walks in the woods, in that murmuring silence of green things growing, of small animals who pursue their needs trotting along without fear under the huge protective shawl of the night—where life is held tight as are the little people under the cloak of the Virgin of Charity.

And London is a bit like cold beefsteak, solid but unattractive. I detest these long pale and bleached dusks of London, where each day ends in a small eternity of boredom, without color,—deserted streets without life, little houses of red twill which cut up the gray sky as far as one can see with their little roofs of a crushing sameness. No, England is boring, made by machines, without having the fantastic and macabre atmosphere of my country.

I am writing in a small gray room where a fire of hard coal makes little noises like a frightened person. In front of the fire a small fat and malevolent dog is snoring. A little clock sounds the half hours with a small voice that is sweet and frail. An old lady rests on a sofa . . . And life is a very complicated ritual, arranged by little old ladies who died in little old times. I feel, this afternoon, a little of the desperate boredom of my childhood—I spent four years when I was very little in this corner of London—during these long pale afternoons where I had to stay in the house when my legs twitched with the desire to run, when I was overwhelmed with mad desires which swarmed in my blood to read or play, and I thought of the life I would live one day.

And now that I find myself in the promised land, is it worth yesterday's mad desires?

Sometimes I think that I have in me one of those little gray rooms, furnished in the best taste, from which the real things of life—the sun and love and sweat and good, hard work which overwhelms one's arms—from which these things, undigested, are excluded and can only enter ordered and shaped through literature. Life has to put on its formal hat and wipe its feet well before it can sit down in the little gray salon of the bourgeoisie.

And sometimes this small gray room seems destroyed, but always—at the big moment, I find myself shut in there, and I look out through its windows at the large ponderous processions which pass by and disappear down the highway. God, if only one could kill off his ghosts.

Write me—care of Morgan, Harjes—15 Place Vendome Paris.

I hope that your mother is well—give her my best.

My miserable book, although all ready still has not seen the light.

Best to you.

790.12   *To Germaine Lucas-Championnière*]   In translation:

In a café in front of the theater of Cluny. Balmy night, full of voices and of that dispiriting premonition of autumn. A moon which appears and disappears constantly behind little muslin clouds. A ragtime monotone comes from a grinding orchestra. Do you know the story that Herodotus tells about King Mycerinus of Egypt? He consulted an oracle which told him that he had only five years to live. With some torches and banquets he made fun of the gods by turning night into day. He no longer slept and when he died he had lived ten years. That is one of the stories that touched me the most. Your cards from St. Jean de Luz are full of marvels just at the moment when I am lacking any marvels. Yesterday when I went to bed a big brown cat, with a crazy Chinese look about him entered through my window. He looked at me with a frightful malice through flaming yellow eyes. Then he opened his mouth and made a fierce meow. Those topaz eyes became as red as rubies, and with another cry of love or hate he fled into the night. Perhaps it's a marvel. Let us hope.

I have reserved a place on a ship leaving St. Nazaire for Mexico or Cuba on August seven. Perhaps that will lead me toward some marvels. Like King Mycerinus of Egypt I want to double my life.

The problem is that your France which I love so much is too civilized for me at the moment. The unforeseen doesn't exist. Maybe it doesn't exist anywhere. French life is a beautiful ceremony in which every movement is made according to a ritual established by many generations. Everything—for us other barbarians, men of unfinished rituals—is indescribably gentle,—a person is like the lotus eaters. Elsewhere life plunges brutally and cruelly toward new forms of organization. Our generation has donned the burning shirt of Nessus. It is a struggle to the death against the vast mechanisms which are the slavery of tomorrow. The struggle will never stop. A person would do well to pause under the fruit trees, to get drunk from the great tranquil rhythms of old cities for the moment always comes where one can no longer resist the hot blood which pushes him toward the battle, toward new roads.

Morning—all this seems very stupid. One should never reread his letters.

Some more marvels and the sound of the wind stirring some daffodils along the top of some cliffs—All the best to you

792.7   Avery Hopkins and Rinehart]   Avery Hapgood and Mary Roberts
Rinehart.

792.10   The Bad Man]   A comedy by Porter Emerson Browne.

792.18   Boney lieberwurst]   Boni and Liveright.

793.15   *To Germaine Lucas-Championnière*]   In translation:

I have never politely begged Mademoiselle Profit's pardon for having
dropped the creamy bun on her foot. I am remorseful about it. Tell me if I
am pardoned. I am a very maladroit bear.

About the sirens on the ship, I assure you that the more you hear them,
the more effect they will have on you. The sound of far away sirens, heard
among the vast stony aridness of cities, is the sound that moves me most. I
wonder why in New York one never hears the stirring call of the sirens.

I am living in New York in a room furnished very grandly and heavily,
which has ancient greenish wallpaper and a frightful red rug, a large puffed
up sofa covered with a horrible scarlet velour and a big round table deliciously covered with portfolios and notebooks. It's very amusing to meet all
my friends after so many years. What is remarkable is that no one has
changed. Everyone talks, eats, sings, writes, walks, criticizes exactly as they
did three years ago.—There was only myself—I was more disoriented, more
off the road, more wandering along the ponderous paths of the valley of indecisions than three years ago. I feel a little like I felt in my childish nightmares, where I often dreamed that I was very far away in the country and
that everyone was climbing into a carriage and that I was running from one
side to the other without finding a very small place and that the carriages
were leaving to the sounds of bells and that I was left all alone. It is like that
now. I have the illusion that my old friends are climbing into one or another
of the carriages which are following the great processions of life—that I am
being left alone on foot to risk lost roads.

New York—after all—is magnificent—a city of cave dwellers, with a frightful, brutal ugliness about it, full of thunderous voices of metal grinding on
metal, full of an eternal sound of wheels turning, turning on heavy stones.
People swarm meekly like ants along the designated routes, crushed by arrogant, pitiless matter. I am reminded of Nineveh and Babylon, or Ur of the
Chaldees, of the immense cities looming like basilisks behind the horizon in
ancient Jewish tales, where the temples rose as high as mountains and people
ran trembling through dirty little alleys to the constant noise of whips with
golden hilts. Oh for the sound of a brazen trumpet which, like the voice of
the Baptist in the desert, will sing once again about the immensity of man in
which this emptiness of iron, steel, marble, and rock. Night time especially is
both marvelous and appalling, seen from the height of a Roof Garden, where
women with raucous voices dance in amber light, the huge blue gray form of
the city cut up by the enormous arabesques of electric billboards, when the
streets where automobiles scurry about like cockroaches are lost in a gold

powder, and when a pathetic little moon pale and bewildered looks at you across a leaden sky.

If I remember the clock at Esconblac—I have often regretted that I didn't sleep on the dunes above the shrouded town. Perhaps the poor dispossessed souls of ancient inhabitants would have blown some prophetic dreams to me, or I would have had some bizarre and esoteric nightmares. The next time I shall sleep at the foot of the clock in Esonblac. But I am always so dazed when I am offered some of the riches on the plate of life that I am never able to decide to take them until it is too late. I would very much have liked to see you with the Norman chiefs as prisoners of the gallant saint of the city of Guirande.

Another time I shall tell you the great melodrama of the deceits of editors and the machinations of literary agencies with some melancholy-comic-historical-philosophical reflections on the G.A.B. (Great American Bluff).

All my best to you

D.P.

Good things to your charming mother—Hello to your brother and to the little nephews

795.24   "Mecca"] The production had music by Percy E. Fletcher, dances and choreography by Michel Fokine, and a book by Oscar Asche.

795.34–35   Treasure . . . the Pinski play] *The Treasure*, a comedy by David Pinski.

796.4   Berenice] Berenice Dewey, a friend of Dos Passos, Dudley Poore, and John Howard Lawson.

796.33   Alchemy] *Alchemy—A Symphonic Poem* (1920), a long poem by Hillyer.

798.30   triste besogne] Sad need.

799.24   Gilpin] American actor Charles Sidney Gilpin (1878–1930).

800.14   Gribble's play] *The Outrageous Mrs. Palmer*, a comedy by Harry Wagstaff Gribble.

Index

850

Library of Congress Cataloging-in-Publication Data

Dos Passos, John, 1896–1970
    [Prose works. Selections]
    Travel books and other writings / John Dos Passos.
        p. cm.—(The Library of America; 143)
    Includes index.
    Contents: Rosinante to the road again—Orient Express—In all
countries—From Journeys between wars—A pushcart at the curb—
Uncollected essays 1916–1941—Letters and diaries 1916–1920.
    ISBN 1–931082–40–5 (alk. paper)
    I. Library of America (Firm) II. Title: Rosinante to the road again.
III. Title: Orient Express. IV. Title: In all countries. V. Journeys between
wars. Selections. VI. Title: Pushcart at the curb. VII. Title: VIII. Series.

PS3507.O743A6   2003
813'.54—dc21   2003040143

THE LIBRARY OF AMERICA SERIES

The Library of America fosters appreciation and pride in America's literary heritage by publishing, and keeping permanently in print, authoritative editions of America's best and most significant writing. An independent nonprofit organization, it was founded in 1979 with seed money from the National Endowment for the Humanities and the Ford Foundation.

This book is set in 10 point Linotron Galliard,
a face designed for photocomposition by Matthew Carter
and based on the sixteenth-century face Granjon. The paper
is acid-free Domtar Literary Opaque and meets the requirements
for permanence of the American National Standards Institute. The
binding material is Brillianta, a woven rayon cloth made by
Van Heek-Scholco Textielfabrieken, Holland. The compo-
sition is by The Clarinda Company. Printing and
binding by R.R.Donnelley & Sons Company.
Designed by Bruce Campbell.